CONSTRUCTIVIST METHODS FOR THE SECONDARY CLASSROOM

Engaged Minds[SM]

Ina Claire Gabler, Ph.D. and **Michael Schroeder, Ph.D.**

Educational Consultant and Writer

Professor, Augustana College

Contributing Writer

David H. Curtis, Ph.D.

Science and Technology Writer

	DATE

Boston | New York | San Francisco
Mexico City | Montreal | Toronto | London | Madrid | Munich | Paris
Hong Kong | Singapore | Tokyo | Cape Town | Sydney

Series Editor: *Traci Mueller*
Series Editorial Assistant: *Erica Tromblay*
Marketing Manager: *Elizabeth Fogarty*
Production Editor: *Michael Granger*
Editorial Production Service: *Modern Graphics, Inc.*
Composition Buyer: *Linda Cox*
Manufacturing Buyer: *JoAnne Sweeney*
Cover Administrator: *Linda Knowles*
Electronic Composition: *Modern Graphics, Inc.*
Text design: *Carol Somberg*

For related titles and support materials, visit our online catalog at www.ablongman.com.

Between the time Website information is gathered and then published, it is not unusual for some sites to have closed. Also, the transcription of URLs can result in unintended typographical errors. The publisher would appreciate notification where these errors occur so that they may be corrected in subsequent editions.

Library of Congress Cataloging-in-Publication Data

Gabler, Ina Claire
    Constructivist methods for the secondary classroom: engaged minds /
Ina Claire Gabler and Michael Schroeder ; contributing author, David
Curtis.
        p. cm.
    Includes bibliographical references and index.
    ISBN 0-205-36057-2
        1. Education, Secondary—Curricula.   2. Constructivism (Education)   3.
Lesson planning.   I. Schroeder, Michael   II. Curtis, David
III. Title.

LB1628 .G23 2003
373.1102—dc21

2002071739

Printed in the United States of America

10 9 8 7 6 5 4   07 06 05

To Dave, for his devotion
ICG

To Sue, Nick, and Andy, with love
MS

■ CONTENTS ■

Section D Putting It All Together 361

Module Fourteen:
Assessment in a Constructivist Classroom   400

Module Fifteen:
Resocializing   432

■ PREFACE ■

Human beings have always longed for magic. From the mythologies of ancient Greece to snake oil in America, people all through time have looked to powers larger than their own to help them cope with life's endless challenges. Yet, magicians know better than anyone else that magic is a human construct.

Seasoned teachers know that magic in the classroom is the moment when a resistant student risks trying for the first time; when a frustrated student suddenly gains clarity; when a group of students, once passive learners, take initiative and work fruitfully on a problem-solving project. How does a teacher facilitate such breakthroughs?

Constructivist Methods for the Secondary Classroom: Engaged Minds attempts to answer that question. Broadly speaking, we believe that two arenas need to be integrated to shift students from the familiar role of listener to that of active learner: affect and constructivist methods. By *affect* we mean state of mind and state of being, the student's belief in self-empowerment. By *constructivist methods* we mean instructional templates for lessons and units that encourage students to be critical thinkers and independent learners, with the teacher acting as a mentor and facilitator.

We discuss and demonstrate affect in terms of Abraham Maslow's Needs Hierarchy. Our constructivist methods turn to Bloom's Taxonomy as a guide for cognitive growth. By integrating these two arenas, we're carrying out the belief that affect is the gateway and critical thinking is the pathway to meaningful learning.

Constructivist Methods for the Secondary Classroom: Engaged Minds is an all-inclusive professional training program. You'll find a continuum from the components of planning lessons and units to a wide range of techniques that can be used in countless ways to carry out the seven constructivist methods. For standards, we refer to the Interstate New Teacher Assessment and Support Consortium (INTASC), defined in the Appendix. The INTASC Standards govern preservice training and as such are appropriate for this textbook. The INTASC Standards also have influenced standards in specific subject areas that consist of content foci and social learning goals. Both the INTASC Standards and subject area standards emphasize a constructivist, affective approach to learning. In addition, an Instructor's Manual includes, among other things, sample demonstration lessons for each method, suggestions for guiding class analysis of each demonstration, and self-evaluation templates for the preservice learner. As a stylistic feature, we employ alternating gender pronouns (he, she) throughout the text.

As standardized testing increasingly becomes a national measure of achievement, educators may question whether a constructivist approach, which emphasizes the process of learning, can result in enough "right answers" on national multiple-choice exams. The answer is yes. A constructivist classroom encourages quality learning rather than rote repetition. Memorization has an important place in learning definitions, numerical operations, important dates, and so on. However, this retention serves as the foundation for higher cognitive levels. Research has shown that constructivist teaching, which emphasizes critical thinking in authentic contexts, results in at least equal results on standardized tests as traditional teaching (Wiggins & McTighe, 1998). In addition, other assessments that examine conceptual understanding and critical-thinking skills show superior results for constructivist-taught students versus traditionally taught students (Newmann, 1996). Two of our methods are specifically designed to meet the demands of a syllabus with information overload: the Directed Discussion method and the Interactive Presentation method. We discuss and define quality learning in more depth in Module 1 and throughout the book. Also, assessment and evaluation, that is, what constitutes meaningful assessment instruments of learning, are addressed in depth.

The text is organized into fifteen modules. Each module is autonomous yet progressive, permitting flexibility according to preservice training needs and professorial teaching styles. For example, the basics of unit planning appears in Module 13, Part 1, but it may be introduced early in the semester for those who prefer to begin with a global approach rather than with the up-close focus on lesson planning in Module 3. Modules 2 through 5 delve into various aspects of lesson planning, including numerous techniques, and are intended for ongoing reference throughout the semester as the preservice teacher plans several mini-lessons in different methods for a mini-unit. Similarly, any method from Modules 7 through 12 may be introduced before or in conjunction with lesson planning. The methods may also be taught out of sequence. Module 6 looks at integrating technology and constructivist methods.

Scenarios and vignettes, or "glimpses," demonstrate ways to employ various methods in the same unit using the Internet and stand-alone software. Similarly, in each method module we provide a section called *Tip for Integrating Technology.*

Our planning components for lessons and units are not etched in stone. Instead, they are suggestions and provide uniformity for integrating each method into the larger planning framework. We encourage new teachers to adapt or design their own planning components to provide in-depth learning within a constructivist learning environment according to their evolving needs.

In this spirit of experimentation, each method is designed to be used either as the cohesive template for a single lesson or combined into a "combo" lesson, that is, mini-segments of two or more methods can be integrated into one lesson to meet your instructional intentions most effectively.

This book does not attempt to be an all-inclusive survey of pedagogical theories and practice. We assume that preservice teachers have taken or will take courses in educational and learning theories. For this reason, although we discuss the ideology of constructivism, we briefly define all other educational terms and concepts used in the text as well as in the glossary, but we do not discuss these at length. Instead, it provides a roll-up-your-sleeves approach. Our goal is that this book will become the backbone of a professional practicum.

We believe that resocializing students from being passive listeners to being active learners is an important part of the practicum. We also believe that resocializing is important for preservice teachers as well as their future students for a student-centered classroom to succeed. From our own experience, we found that early on, resocializing is more abstract than meaningful to preservice teachers. Therefore, we recommend that you explore Module 15, *Resocializing,* after the preservice teachers have come to value the constructivist approach.

Looking beyond the university context, a college supervisor working with the text may want to consider conducting training workshops in these constructivist methods for the inservice teachers who supervise the college's student teachers. (For convenience, we have also written an inservice version, *Seven Constructivist Methods for the Secondary Classroom: A Planning Guide for Invisible Teaching,* published by Allyn & Bacon.) This commonality enriches the student teacher's apprenticeship, especially because student teachers are often influenced by their supervising teachers in the field regardless of preservice university training.

From our experience as college supervisors, we found that many of the supervising teachers expressed interest in learning the constructivist methods that our preservice teachers implemented. One reason was that many inservice teachers were already implementing a constructivist approach and wanted to enhance their repertoire. Other more traditional inservice teachers were impressed with their students' response to the preservice teacher's constructivist methods and wanted to explore that approach further.

*Constructivist Methods for the Secondary Classroom: Engaged Mind*s slowly emerged from our earlier years as secondary classroom teachers experimenting with what is now known as constructivism and from our more recent times as Teacher Education professors. During the latter years, we adapted and codified the constructivist methods and techniques in this program, often with feedback from our preservice teachers and from our experience as college supervisors.

During our earlier years as secondary teachers of inner-city and mainstream students, when we evolved student-centered methods, our students often worked on projects tailored to their interests. They researched and created products (magazines, videos, and more) for real audiences, not just for the teacher. The higher our expectations, the harder our students worked. Engaged in their original projects, they sometimes pleaded to remain behind when the bell rang. This kind of student reaction is every teacher's dream come true.

So, if we catch ourselves blaming our students for their apathy or supposed "inability to learn," we may need to plan with a more, not less, challenging approach that relates to our students' interests. The results may amaze you as well as the students.

Which brings us back to magic. When you combine positive affect, namely, the students' belief in their ability to learn, with constructivist methods that foster independent learning and awaken love of learning, be prepared for breakthroughs. A resistant student takes his first plunge. A confused student discovers an elusive principle on her own. Groups of once-bored students apply themselves with newfound motivation.

A rabbit may not appear out of either, but the challenges and motivation in a constructivist learning environment can further your classroom as a place of engaged minds and spirit beyond what you may now think is possible.

Ina Claire Gabler and Michael Schroeder

REFERENCES

Newmann, F. N. & Associates (1996). *Authentic achievement: Restructuring schools for intellectual quality*. San Francisco: Jossey-Bass.

Wiggins, G., & McTighe, J. (1998). *Understanding by design*. Alexandria, VA: Association for Supervision and Curriculum Development.

■ ACKNOWLEDGMENTS ■

It's said that it takes a village to raise a child. In a similar vein, we have learned that it takes a community of sorts to produce a book. We could not have written and published *Constructivist Methods for the Secondary Classroom: Engaged Minds* without the help of other professionals from the beginning to the end of the process.

We therefore wish to extend our sincere appreciation to all those who gave their best efforts on our behalf. Our editor, Traci Mueller, has extended her support and enthusiasm right from the start. Her sound advice helped us make important decisions throughout the revision process. Ms. Mueller's assistant, Erica Tromblay, was efficient, sincere, and always helpful.

We also are indebted to our colleagues. Our sincere thanks to all those who provided incisive professional advice, particularly Lisa Bievenue, Bertrum Bruce, and Edee Wiziecki, University of Illinois at Urbana-Champaign; Randy Hengst, Chuck Hyser, Jack Garrett, and Melissa McBain, Augustana College, Rock Island, Illinois; and Mary Ellen Verona, Maryland Virtual High School, Silver Spring, Maryland.

We wish to recognize Robert Gryder, Arizona State University; David Byrd, University of Rhode Island and Thomas Worley, Armstrong Atlantic State University for their excellent feedback on our early drafts.

Mike Schroeder would like to extend his thanks to Charles Weller, Orrin Gould, and George Kieffer, University of Illinois at Urbana-Champaign, for their impact on his professional development, an influence that can be found among these pages.

Thanks also to Deb Nelson and Angel Duncombe for their technical assistance.

We would like to express a special word of appreciation to David Curtis for his invaluable technical assistance and his other expertise.

We are grateful to all these people for their time, effort, and support.

■ ABOUT THE AUTHORS ■

Photo by Judy Gordon

Ina Claire Gabler is an educational consultant and writer specializing in teacher education and language arts. She was codirector of the preservice preparation program at the University of Illinois at Urbana-Champaign. As an Assistant Professor, she was Director of Secondary Methods in Teacher Education at Millikin University, Decatar, Illinois, training preservice teachers and supervising them in the field. Her teaching experience of more than twenty-five years includes conducting inservice teacher training workshops at national and regional conferences. In addition, she has taught writing at the college level and has taught language arts at the junior high school level in East Harlem and the South Bronx. As chair of the junior high English department in East Harlem, she implemented peer-group constructivist learning instruction years before the paradigm shift from teacher-centered to student-centered learning. Dr. Gabler also writes fiction for which she has won several awards. She earned her Ph.D. in Curriculum and Instruction at the University of Illinois in 1996.

Mike Schroeder is currently serving as Director of Secondary Education at Augustana College in Rock Island, Illinois. Dr. Schroeder began his career as an educator as a high school science teacher in the Chicago suburbs. His professional focus turned to teacher education as he completed his Ph.D. at the University of Illinois in the early 1990s. During that time, he was director of the preservice preparation program at the University of Illinois where he introduced constructivist methods. In his twelve years of work at the college level, Dr. Schroeder has taught courses in general methods as well as in science and math methods, and he is heavily involved in the supervision of student teachers. He has conducted a wide range of workshops and presentations for inservice teachers and for colleagues in teacher education. Professional interests include science concept development in learners, the development of critical-thinking abilities, the use of educational technologies, and the history of science.

Photo by Judy Gordon

David Curtis is an independent science writer concentrating on environmental science, biomedicine, astronomy, and learning technologies. With a Ph.D. in biochemistry from the University of Sussex, England, he moved to New York City where he produced science television programming for PBS, and then to the National Center for Supercomputing Applications (NCSA) in Urbana-Champaign. At NCSA he directed production of scientific videos, developed Web-based education and outreach materials, and conducted K-12 professional development workshops on applications of Web-based digital video and geographic mapping technologies. Dr. Curtis is a visiting scholar at the University of Illinois, and a founding Co-Principal Investigator of the Mississppi RiverWeb[SM] Museum Consortium, a multi-institutional collaborative that is pioneering highly interactive, computer-based exhibits on the interplay of human activity with large river systems.

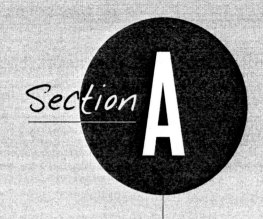

Section A

Constructivist Ideology

Introduction

Constructivism. Educators nationwide talk and write about it, striving for its dynamism in their classrooms. Yet, even professionals sometimes have misconceptions about what constructivism means as an ideology and a practice. Often, the constructivist approach to teaching and learning is oversimplified as a student-centered process that accepts all student ideas as valid. This view ignores the rich layers of constructivism as well as the intellectual rigor it should embody.

In Section A, we discuss the key elements of constructivism. These elements range from the global concept that students "construct" meaning from information by beginning with their own frames of reference to authentic learning, which is the rigorous process of developing critical-thinking skills and creating products, that is, material creations (projects, Websites, publications, enactments, and so on) with value in the real world.

First and foremost, we discuss the nature of learning. We also include a range of related concerns to give you a larger context: national assessment findings, instructional materials, research perspectives, technological innovations, teacher and student roles, and the classroom atmosphere, to name a few. This background provides a framework for the heart of *Engaged Minds,* namely, the seven methods that help you create a constructivist learning experience for your students that goes beyond the classroom.

SUGGESTED READINGS

Airasian, P. W., & Walsh, M. E. (1997). Constructivist cautions. *Kappan, 78*(6), 444–449.

Phillips, D. C. (1995). The good, the bad, and the ugly: The many faces of constructivism. *Educational Researcher, 24*(7), 5–12.

Module One:

The Nature of Teaching and Learning

■ OVERVIEW

Constructivist Methods for the Secondary Classroom: Engaged Minds provides you, the preservice teacher, with a set of guiding ideas and suggestions that will allow you to plan and conduct meaningful lessons in a range of classroom settings. Beyond this, we hope to both challenge and inspire you as you enter a rewarding new profession. The message contained in these pages will help you broaden your own perspective on what it means to teach and to learn. As part of this process, we're also confident that you and your peers will raise a host of important new questions regarding teaching and learning.

■ GOALS

In this module, we outline, in broad terms, some of the challenges and opportunities facing teachers and schools today. In doing so, we address four guiding questions:

- Why won't traditional (i.e., teacher-centered) approaches prepare students for life in the twenty-first century?
- What does research and experience tell us about the nature of learning?
- Why do new research perspectives and technological innovations present teachers and students with exciting new opportunities?
- What can teachers do to help students develop their critical-thinking abilities?

As we investigate each of these questions, we provide evidence for our position that widely held beliefs about the nature of effective teaching and meaningful learning are evolving and will change substantially in the future. We believe that this text will help to prepare you for these opportunities and challenges.

A Scenario

As we begin to study the nature of teaching and learning and teaching as a profession, let's first take a brief look at the past. Imagine for a moment that you wake up somewhere in the United States in 1925. You are a high school sophomore who is about to begin a new school day. After washing your face and putting on your school clothes, you run downstairs to breakfast, where your mother is cooking oatmeal on the cast-iron stove. New jazz music is playing softly (through the static) on the kitchen radio. Dad finishes his breakfast, puts down his morning paper, kisses everyone good-bye, and starts his walk to the local hardware store, which he owns and operates. He's training a new clerk today and has to arrive early. After breakfast, you grab your books, meet your friends in front of the house, and walk three blocks to the neighborhood high school.

And what does the school day hold for you? This year you're taking math, U.S. history, biology, American literature, and Latin. Your classes are forty-five minutes long, with a loud bell marking the end of each period. Your teachers do most of the talking in class, at times stopping to ask factual questions. Your Latin teacher likes to have the whole class pronounce new terms together ("Now, repeat after me . . ."). Lit class is one of your favorites. As you read *Huckleberry Finn* and *Moby Dick*, you try to imagine what it would be like to be Huck or Captain Ahab. In almost every class, you take plenty of notes and try to listen carefully to what your teachers say; that's important at test time. Occasionally, you welcome the opportunity to get up from your wooden desk to do a math problem on the board or to look at a specimen in biology. You actually dissected a frog and had a chance to see and feel some of the things that the teacher had told you about. Those desk seats are hard on the rump, but that's one of the prices you pay to get through school, or so Dad tells you.

After school, you quickly do your chores around the house and then join your friends for some games in the park down the street. Mom made beef stew for dinner, and while eating you listen to Dad as he talks about the latest news from uptown (*The Gold Rush*, starring Charlie Chaplin, just opened at the Virginia Theater). You spend about an hour doing math problems (wondering, again, when you will ever use this stuff outside of school). Then there's a real treat: homemade peach ice cream that you savor as you listen to the *Little Orphan Annie* show on the new radio. Later, it's off to bed to rest for another school day.

Discussion

Now, back to the twenty-first century. Think about this brief nostalgic interlude. This is the kind of day that your grandparents might have lived; it wasn't really all that long ago. What has changed and what has remained the same as far as life in the United States is concerned? You could probably list two dozen major changes in just the next few minutes. Try it.

Think about the changes that technology alone has forged on every level. Today, we can step onto an airplane and be anywhere in the world in a matter of hours. Automobiles have become a major part of everyone's life. How many people do you know who can get to work, shop, or visit friends and relatives without jumping into a car? Modes of communication have changed dramatically, too. How many televisions, cellular telephones, e-mail–sending computers, and answering and fax machines does the average home have today? The Internet has allowed us to access almost unlimited information in seconds. Entertainment options are many and varied. How would your life change if, suddenly, cable TV, VCRs, stereo systems, and computer and videogames disappeared? Then there's the workplace. Do today's factories, offices, stores, restaurants, and other places of business even vaguely resemble those of the past? What kinds of career opportunities are available today that didn't exist in 1925?

Technological development has provided new opportunities, convenience, and comfort, but it has also helped cause a range of new problems. Lifestyles are dramatically different today for a variety of reasons. How different, for example, is the community described in the 1925 flashback from the one in which you grew up? Do people relate to each other differently in today's world of isolated subdivisions, overflowing expressways, multiplex theaters, and home shopping networks? How is the family structure different, and what are the social and economic implications of these differences?

As a people living at the dawn of a new century, we are caught up in a virtual cyclone of change. The challenges we face, many of which have been brewing since the

Industrial Revolution, are increasing in complexity. For example, what are we, as a society, to do about issues related to social injustice, global terrorism, depletion of the ozone layer, energy shortages, overpopulation, drug addiction, clogged transportation systems, and a decaying urban/suburban infrastructure? The challenges associated with preparing citizens for a changing workplace also seem daunting. Today's teenagers are expected to make six or seven career changes in their lifetimes. Even if we could predict and help provide the kinds of background information and associated skills that citizens might need to be successful in these careers, consider the fact that information in many fields doubles every six years, with much of what we know today soon becoming obsolete.

Now, let's turn our attention specifically to you, a student considering a career as an educator, and to the part of life in 1925 that hasn't changed all that dramatically: our schools and the nature of schooling. Despite the implementation of a range of exciting reforms and changes in some schools, from block scheduling to the increased use of cooperative learning techniques, our basic approach to schooling, which involves teachers presenting information while students listen passively and later take tests to show what they have learned, remains the same. One question seems obvious: How can we, as educators, help our students, from the advantaged to the disadvantaged, meet the demands of an increasingly complex world without making dramatic changes in what happens in schools and in individual classrooms? The short answer is that we can't. Traditionally, schools and classrooms have been designed around routines and linear procedures to prepare students for workplaces that offered much of the same. Clearly, the emphasis in many future workplaces will be on employees using good judgment and making well-reasoned decisions, and we argue that traditional schooling has not emphasized the development of these kinds of abilities. Rapidly accelerating change in all facets of our lives will challenge us to think through new situations in new ways.

At this point, let's pose a question that we'll address throughout this book: How can you, as a future educator, help prepare each of your students to deal with the changing world of the twenty-first century? As we begin to address this question, let's first take a realistic look at what school systems are doing today and what accepted modes of classroom interaction tell us about how we view the nature of teaching and learning.

Focal Point 1: The Impact of Didactic Teaching on Students

At this point, you might agree that individual teachers and school systems as a whole must overcome obstacles and make changes if they are to achieve the goal of preparing our young people for life and citizenship in a democratic society in the twenty-first century. In too many instances, and for a number of different reasons, schools and many individual teachers have fallen back on the failed procedures of the past. Educators at the elementary level, for example, must find alternatives to placing students in low, medium, and high groups for math and reading instruction, a practice that is as common today as it was fifty years ago (Goodlad, 1995). Researchers have shown that these practices exacerbate deleterious individual differences and cause the disadvantaged to fall further and further behind (Goodlad, 1990). Another major problem at every level is that curricula tend to be overflowing with disconnected, encapsulated information, compelling teachers to cover vast amounts of material at a frantic pace. Largely because of this, in-depth understanding of important ideas is seldom achieved by even the most gifted students. If we as educators fail to change many of our practices, schools will continue to perpetuate a self-fulfilling prophesy: disadvantaged children will tend to fill the ranks of the lower-level classes in high school and will eventually leave school, with limited employment and postsecondary educational opportunities.

Discussion 1. The Impact of Didactic Teaching on Students

Just what have educational researchers, and our own experiences, shown us about prevalent practices and the associated outcomes in our school system? In reviewing research findings from dozens of studies, Kennedy (1991) noted that American students compare poorly with students from other industrialized nations when it comes to higher-level thinking processes, including collecting and analyzing data, making predictions, estimating, and making well-reasoned decisions in complex, problem-solving situations. How can we explain this dire situation? Among other things, Kennedy and other educators (Sizer, 1984; Goodlad, 1990) noted that although teachers do most of the talking in most classrooms, textbooks have traditionally been the ultimate source of knowledge and authority. What assessment can we make of the quality of these books? Investigating texts from a range of subjects, Kennedy (1991) noted that they "pay scant attention to big ideas, offer no analysis, and pose no challenging questions" (p. 664). Some time in the near future, make a point of examining some middle or high school texts from your subject area, and make your own judgment of Kennedy's assessment. The problem is that such texts, which focus on a superficial presentation of facts, drive instruction in too many classrooms.

What is the nature of interaction in most secondary classrooms? This may represent the greatest problem of all. Sizer and his fellow researchers visited dozens of high schools in the 1980s and observed that "dialogue (between teachers and students) is strikingly absent, and as a result, the opportunity of teachers to challenge student's ideas is limited" (Sizer, 1984, p. 82). His conclusion was that "careful probing of students' thinking is not a high priority" in most schools. In her review of studies, Kennedy (1991) noted that a variety of researchers have found that many teachers at the secondary level "teach content only for exposure, not for understanding" and that our school system on the whole "provides very little intellectually stimulating work for students, and that it tends to produce students who are not capable of intellectual work" (p. 665). What seems to be missing in today's classrooms is "coherence, connection, and depth of understanding" (Paul, 1995, p. 273).

A major theme of this book is that our basic beliefs about the nature of teaching and learning need to change if we are to break the mold and transform the current situation. The last thing we want to do is blame dedicated teachers for problems that are largely the result of the ways in which schools are structured. Certainly, every educator aspires to teach in a way that might help students gain higher-order understanding and depth of knowledge. The problem is that the secondary school experience often leaves students with a fragmented, superficial level of understanding in most subjects. Primary sources of these problems include the nature of school curricula, the overuse of mandated tests, and the hectic, frenetic nature of the school day.

As educators, we have come to believe that many of our current problems are rooted in an overemphasis on what might be called *didactic teaching* (i.e., lecturing/teacher talk) and the often unspoken beliefs about learning that go along with this approach. Richard Paul, author of several thought-provoking books and essays on critical thinking, refers to this prevalent approach as "mother robin" teaching, characterized by teachers "mentally chewing up everything for our students so that we can put it into their intellectual beaks to swallow" (Paul, 1995, p. 304). Researchers have consistently shown that most time spent in typical secondary school classrooms still involves lecturing (Putnam, 1997).

For confirmation of this, walk down a hallway in a typical secondary school and look into the classrooms. Chances are that you will see a teacher in front of the class doing most of the talking, while students sit in desks arranged in straight rows, "physically and mentally slouching" (Sizer, 1996). As a newly graduated and idealistic high school teacher in the mid-1980s, one of the authors clearly remembers being shocked at the lack of student engagement he saw when walking past classroom after classroom. This theme was echoed in journal comments made by a student teacher at Augustana College after watching his cooperating teacher lecture to students in the fall of 2000:

> I had a sort of an 'aha!' moment this week. . . . Our discussion of constructivist teaching in class started my moment, and then watching [my co-op] teach a government class confirmed it. He was lecturing about the judicial branch of the government, and he was doing all of the talking. I looked around, and I am not kidding, there was *not one* student looking at him! I bet at least four students were sleeping, and nobody was taking notes. It was at this point that constructivist teaching took on some meaning for me. . . . The lessons that we teach should be real. They should apply to something the students can relate to. For example, now I know I'm not going to just TALK about the Stock Market Crash, I'm going to [simulate] a Stock Market, and let the students feel some of the ups and downs that people of that time experienced.[1]

True to his word, this student teacher later successfully created a stock market simulation that actively engaged his students. We'll discuss dozens of ideas like this later in this book. Unfortunately, classroom experiences such as these, which demand student initiative and creativity, are rare. Teacher–student interaction in most classrooms consists of fact-oriented questions delivered by the teacher, while meaningful student–student interaction is almost nonexistent. In fact, some studies have shown that students in secondary school classrooms ask, on the average, fewer than one meaningful question per classroom per period (Johnson & Johnson, 1990).

Largely because of our reliance on didactic teaching, what students learn is often very different from what teachers believe they have taught. Research findings have shown us that this seems to be true in virtually every subject at every level of instruction (see, e.g., Osborne & Freyburg, 1985; Schoenfeld, 1982). Students in teacher-centered classrooms in a range of subjects have been found to become proficient at regurgitating vocabulary words, names, dates, and memorized phrases to pass tests, with most of this information soon forgotten. Can you think of occasions in your own career as a student when this was the case? Later in this book, we will describe approaches to teaching that will challenge students to think critically, approaches that don't separate knowing from finding out.

The cumulative effect of years of experience in teacher-centered classrooms is dramatic. By the time students reach high school, most are typically docile in nature, and many seem to resist teacher efforts to disturb this docility (Sizer, 1984; Goodlad, 1990). Students seem to learn early on what it takes to survive in schools, and usually this amounts to conforming to what the school system and teachers demand. As Paul (1995) observed, students respond to years of "mother robin" teaching by becoming "polly parrot" learners, insisting that "I can't understand anything unless you tell me exactly how and what to say and think. . . . I shouldn't have to do any more than repeat what you and the textbook say" (p. 304).

After spending time in dozens of secondary schools and hundreds of classrooms, Sizer (1984) concluded that schools are "anesthetizing" students. Many of the schools that he visited were quiet, orderly, and often cheerful, but "intellectually dull." After reviewing the results of studies completed in the 1980s, Sizer (1992) noted, as did Kennedy, that students' abilities in rote-level, concrete learning had improved to some extent, while their ability to reason, to analyze and synthesize, and "to think critically and resourcefully is lamentably weak and is continuing to weaken" (p. 133).

State and national school-reform efforts, which intensified with the publication of *A Nation at Risk* in 1983 and continue today, have imposed a new series of tests and other mandates on schools and teachers that seem to reinforce the cycle of lecturing, textbooks, and worksheets, the diet that, according to Goodlad (1990), "made the patient sick in the first place" (p. 27). The belief held by many elected officials, and even some educators, is that raising standards and requirements drives change at the classroom level. Other educators derisively term this a carrot-and-stick approach, and we argue that desirable change in classroom practice has actually been hampered by such state-imposed mandates. As educators, we believe that other school-centered, site-based reform efforts currently under way, such as those undertaken as part of the Coalition of Essential Schools, provide greater hope for change at the classroom level (see Sizer, 1996).

Despite these findings, many teachers have broken out of the traditional mold. These professionals experiment with and regularly implement innovative, student-centered methods of teaching. Some of these teachers carry out active learning despite skepticism and often in the absence of collegial support. Others are able to interest colleagues in trying the same approach, even carrying out dynamic interdisciplinary projects or combo units (see Module 13). Still other innovative teachers take part in cutting-edge educational research that investigates various student-centered strategies and authentic-learning practices that can be applied to the real world. So, there is a cadre of professionals dedicated to challenging themselves and their students with a more constructivist approach to teaching and learning. Research shows that these unconventional teachers are in the minority.

One of the most important goals in this text is to provide you with alternatives to the lecture as a method of teaching. It's true that the minilecture can be effective as a summary of a lesson or project; conversely, a creative minilecture can effectively launch a lesson or unit; it can be incorporated into a student-centered approach (see Interactive Presentation, Module 12). However, based on research cited herein and our own experience, we consider lengthy, straight lecture to be an ineffective method of instruction for developing critical-thinking skills and for taking an active role in learning as a process. So, as you read this text and consider the issues raised, reflect on your own experiences as a student. Why will it be important for you as a teacher to use new approaches that actively engage students in the learning process?

The sections that follow present an overview of educational research that supports the use of interactive teaching methods. Although this overview is not exhaustive, it will interest individuals considering a career in education, and it supports our contention that there is a need to move toward the use of more student-centered teaching methods.

Focal Point 2: The Potential Impact of Educational Research

Teachers face many challenges in the classroom today. But here's some good news: as a result of research conducted during the past several decades, we now know much more about the way people think and learn. As a future teacher, you'll have an opportunity to use these new insights to understand learning from the perspective of the learner, which is essential to effective teaching. New research perspectives on learning, along with the development of new educational technologies, have the potential to transform classrooms in exciting new ways.

Discussion 2: The Potential Impact of Educational Research

In What Ways Are Students Unique?: Preferred Learning Styles

Based on classroom experiences, many educators over the years have intuitively sensed that there are significant differences in the ways that students come to understand experiences. In fact, as human beings, there's no doubt that each of us tends to look at the world in our own unique way. Some of the most intriguing research conducted in educational psychology during the past twenty years has focused on differences in student learning styles. Although each individual learner is unique in many respects, research conducted as far back as the 1940s has shown that people may be placed in two general categories based on the ways in which they tend to perceive events. Field-dependent students tend to be more global in perceiving whole patterns rather than their parts. In contrast, field-independent students are much more inclined to analyze, breaking problems down into their component parts. These findings have potentially enormous significance for classroom teachers. Field-dependent students tend to be more people oriented, to work well in groups, and to have some difficulty with analysis-oriented problems, whereas field-independent students are more task oriented, enjoy working with unstructured material, and often prefer to work on their own (Ulrich-Tobias, 1994).

Researchers have developed systems designed to help us describe and understand differences in individual preferred learning styles. We define *preferred learning styles* as *different ways in which people perceive, process, understand, and remember experiences.* Put simply, individual learners vary dramatically in how they make sense of their experiences. For example, after years of observing and interviewing learners in varying situations, Gregorc (1982) described four distinctly different learning styles based on how individuals perceive and subsequently order, or process, information. In terms of perception, concrete-oriented students prefer direct contact through the physical senses, whereas abstract-oriented students prefer more unstructured, inductive learning experiences (Gregorc, 1982). Once an experience is perceived, the information taken in is ordered, or processed, either sequentially or randomly. Considering preferences related to perception and ordering, Gregorc found that individuals displayed concrete-sequential, concrete-random, abstract-sequential, or abstract-random learning styles to varying degrees:

- Concrete-sequential learners prefer highly structured, linear instructional approaches that include direct, hands-on experiences. People with strong concrete-sequential learning preferences tend to see problems in terms of black and white, with no middle ground. They also tend to be organized and patient, to work well within set time limits, and to work alone, and they aren't tolerant of distractions.

- Abstract-sequential students prefer a linear pattern but gain more from stimulating instructor presentations and demonstrations rather than hands-on experiences. People with strong abstract-sequential preferences like to work independently and don't like distractions; they like to thoroughly research topics and tend to perform well on paper-and-pencil tests, but they are often so thorough that they struggle with time limits.

- Abstract-random learners thrive in highly interactive, unstructured learning environments and appreciate group learning approaches. People with abstract-random preferences are generally perceptive, intuitive, creative, spontaneous, and idealistic. In the classroom, they appreciate open-ended discussions and inductive teaching approaches.

- Concrete-random students prefer a stimulus-rich, problem-solving approach that also features abundant interaction. CR learners tend to be most inquisitive and open to new ideas; they thrive on group projects, appreciate options, and *like* to debate (even argue) over meaningful issues (Gregorc, 1982; Ulrich-Tobias, 1994).

Now consider that each group of your future students will display a wide range of learning-style preferences. Some learners tend strongly toward one style, while others are a true blend of preferences. How can classroom teachers use an understanding of learning-style differences to reach individual students more effectively? The educational implications are clear: sticking with any one instructional approach will allow you to reach only a portion of your students effectively. Consistently asking abstract-random and concrete-random students, for instance, to work alone in competitive situations, as is common in many classrooms, may result in these students failing to reach their full learning potential. These studies may help explain why so much of what occurs in classrooms seems to miss certain students; they are perceiving and understanding experiences in different, even unique, ways.

Because learners are unique in how they perceive and understand experiences, varying instructional approaches and methods of assessment, and building some degree of student choice into the learning environment, will result in more students connecting to classroom experiences. Using a range of teaching methods will also help students to stretch and flex in a cognitive and affective sense, as each student is challenged to move out of a comfort zone to both learn and apply knowledge in a range of settings. A knowledge of learning styles will help you understand individual differences in your classroom. Systems for understanding learning styles, such as the one designed by Gregorc, can provide you with valuable tools for reaching individual students. These findings also lend support to our belief that all students can learn, given the right environment and instructional approach. As Sizer (1996) noted, buying into this belief implies an important shift in responsibility for educators: "[I]f a kid does not get it in the usual way, the school should try to help him get it in another way. Everybody has to get it. No one can be sorted out" (p. 35). In later modules, we use Gregorc's system for describing preferred learning styles in advocating the use of a range of teaching methods.

How Do We Think?: The Implications of Cognitive Psychology

Research into learning styles implies that there are significant differences in how students perceive events, process information, commit experiences to memory, and use the resulting cognitive structures to interpret later experiences. During the past thirty years, research in cognitive psychology has had an increasingly significant impact on how educators view the learning process. Those working from a cognitive perspective are interested in investigating how the mind works and, specifically, how human beings perceive, remember, and reason—in general, how we think. The findings of researchers working in the fields of cognitive psychology and education have the potential to influence classroom practice in exciting new ways.

In previous course work, you may have been introduced to the idea that learners commit elements of experience to memory within an individual schema (pl. schemata). Each *schema* may be thought of as a scaffold in which elements of experience are connected in certain patterns. Consider schemata as the wiring of the mind; the patterns and connections associated with this wiring are largely the result of the previous experiences of the learner. These patterns and connections are fairly well established in all of us, and they help us to understand day-to-day experiences. The right kinds of experiences can challenge learners to change these patterns. Essentially, this is what happens in a meaningful learning situation. A number of educational implications are associated with a cognitive perspective on the workings of the mind. For example, research into the thinking of individual learners has also shown that students are liable to interpret the same verbal message in vastly different ways, depending on preferred learning styles and previous experiences (Osborne & Freyburg, 1985; Glynn et al., 1991).

To some extent, the cognitive perspective on thinking originated more than seventy years ago with the memory studies of Bartlett (1932). In his best-known investigations, Bartlett asked participants to read short stories, often folktales from other cultures, and then to write summaries from memory, first after fifteen minutes, then after several weeks. Although participants had similar backgrounds and read the same text under the same conditions, there were major differences in the ways that they recalled the stories. Ironically, participants who were the most confident in their abilities to recall the text were the least accurate in their recollections. The significant differences between subjects in the nature of recall was surprising given the memory-as-a-photograph perspective prevalent among psychologists at the time. It became apparent to Bartlett that study participants had not memorized the stories by taking mental snapshots or by storing the information in imaginary files.

After conducting many such studies, Bartlett concluded that participants were "engaged in more than the passive recall of fixed, lifeless traces" (p. 66). Bartlett (1932) found that in summarizing one unusual story, participants were "especially prone to rationalize, reconcile, omit, or distort" (p. 67) the most bizarre aspects of the story. They were likely to eliminate detail, and they seemed to be actively restructuring the stories presented, based on their own past experiences. The restructuring of their memories continued as they recalled these stories weeks and months later. Bartlett hypothesized that participants were relying on "cognitive schema" to actively interpret the stories. The experience of reading the story was encoded (i.e., understood and remembered) in unique ways and later reconstructed in countless ways, based on the existing wiring of the participant. Clearly, those reading the stories were trying to relate the new material to their existing and unique cognitive structures.

Have you ever played the game "Telephone," in which one person tells a secret to another, who then relays the message to a third person? By the time the message has been relayed around an entire circle of players, it is usually much different than the original secret, as each person has interpreted the words based on a unique set of cognitive structures. The same effect has been seen in studies of eyewitness testimony in court cases, where memory has been found to be fluid, with those involved encoding and recalling events in unique ways. This is the same effect that Bartlett saw when asking his participants to recall stories.

Since the time of Bartlett, psychologists and educators in many fields have investigated cognitive schemata. Cognitive psychologists have put forth the notion that there are a variety of ways to view schemata, including schemata as mental data structures; representations of our knowledge about objects, self, and sequences of events; personal theories; and processes (West et al., 1991). The most useful way to view schemata, according to West et al., is as "packets or bundles in which the mind stores knowledge: they are patterns, structures, scaffolds." It is useful to distinguish between state and process schemata, and West et al. used the analogy between the mind and the computer: "state schemata are to data files as process schemata are to programs which are in execution" (p. 7).

This perspective leads us to two ideas that have been confirmed by a large body of research. First, preexisting cognitive structures (schemata) interact with the immediate situation to determine what gets into memory initially and, second, the identity and accuracy of information is lost in memory as new information is continually assimilated into existing structures. Take a few minutes to think about how this perspective on thinking and remembering should influence your approach to teaching.

What Message Will a Learner Take Away from an Experience?

The grandfather had visited the Sistine Chapel and was showing pictures of the ceiling to his grandson. After explaining each picture of the masterpiece depicted, he went on to describe the problems that Michelangelo had faced and overcome in painting such a lofty ceiling: "It took him a very long time. He spent four years painting the Sistine Chapel on his back." The boy recounted the story to his sister, who came running to ask incredulously: "Did you really say that Michelangelo spent four years painting the Sistine Chapel on his back?" (Hewson, 1981, p. 4)

There is no doubt that miscommunication is common in all of our lives. At times, our words, which seem to make perfect sense to us, confuse others, who seem to take away a completely different meaning from the one we intended. Instances of confusion and miscommunication are common in the classroom, especially when teachers rely mainly on a one-way stream of words to communicate ideas, and many learners are not as willing as the girl in the story was to check on the intended message.

The implications of research in cognitive psychology and other fields are potentially far reaching for educators. Student perception, processing, reasoning, and memory must be seen as active, selective, and constructive. Each of us has constructed a unique set of cognitive frameworks (i.e., schemata) that serve as our frame of reference. Within any complex situation, such as a classroom learning event, each student selectively perceives and interprets experiences based on a personal frame of reference. Meaningful learning involves some change in the learner's frame of reference or schemata, the wiring within each of us). As a result, it will be important for you as a teacher to view learning as "an organic process of invention rather than [as] a mechanical process of accumulation" (Fosnot, 1989, p. 20). The bottom line is that meaningful learning will come only from the active mental engagement of the learner and the sharing of ideas between learners.

Some of the most thought-provoking research into student construction of knowledge has taken place in science classrooms. Interviews with science students confirm what we might predict: individuals perceive instruction in a number of different, even unique, ways. In fact, students often bring surprisingly sophisticated personal theories, based on their own previous experiences, into the classroom with them.

One of the most well-studied areas regarding student conceptions deals with the motion of objects. By the time they reach the science classroom, even young children have had considerable experience with moving objects; researchers have shown that most children have fairly sophisticated ideas about the nature of motion. For instance, most high school students believe that when a ball is thrown, there is something within the ball that continues to propel it through the air (Osborne & Freyburg, 1985). The accepted scientific (Newtonian) perspective is that a force (e.g., someone's arm) has acted on the ball but is no longer acting on it. Students, even at the college level, tend to stick to their original belief tenaciously, despite being told by the teacher and the textbook that their interpretation is not scientifically accurate (Osborne & Freyburg, 1985; Glynn et al., 1991).

In another series of studies, researchers analyzed student beliefs about the shape of the earth. Of course, even young students have considerable experience living on what seems to be a flat earth, despite being told that the earth is round. (Think about it. Why should a young child believe that the earth is round?) A large percentage of children in elementary school who were interviewed constructed a theory that reconciled their experience with the new information: they drew the earth as flat and round, like a paper plate (Glynn et al., 1991).

Dozens of similar studies have been conducted in science classrooms at varying grade levels, with students expressing their beliefs on topics ranging from the nature of living things to electricity. Each researcher found that, in some way, learners of every age perceive and explain objects and events based largely on past experiences. These interpretations are generally personal (again, based on the personal experiences and the resultant frame of reference of the learner), although students of varying ages may hold similar conceptions and misconceptions. Studies across subject areas have also shown that the existing ideas that learners hold are stable and resistant to change, especially through direct instruction. Students tend to stick to their deep-seated, intuitive beliefs regardless of what teachers tell them. (Think about the educational implications of that!)

Researchers have shown that learners' previous ideas must be challenged through *cognitive dissonance* (discomfort from new information clashing with present beliefs) for meaningful learning to take place. New ideas must be seen by the learner as intelligible (i.e., understandable), plausible, and useful in explaining an action or event better than the student's original idea or the student will tend to stick to the original explanation (Osborne & Freyburg, 1985; Glynn et al., 1991). This suggests that an active struggle with new ideas, and a degree of confusion and dissatisfaction with current ideas, may challenge students of any age to learn. Although most research about the nature of student conceptions has been done in the field of science education, it is likely that similar misconceptions have the same profound impact on the learning of new ideas in other disciplines.

Here's the important take-home message from the studies in science classrooms: perception and learning are the construction of meaning via the interaction between the event taking place and our previous experiences, that is, the interaction of the message with the frame of reference of the learner. Have you ever attended a lecture on a complex topic that you found to be exciting and thought provoking? Chances are, the message that you were perceiving had found a certain match with well-developed schemata present in your mind to make the event interesting, and perhaps it challenged your current beliefs. The person in the next row who looked bored and restless may have lacked the necessary frame of reference to make the experience meaningful. The most important application for this research is in the classroom. The message that a student takes away from any classroom experience is not within the experience itself but within the meaning that the student attaches to that experience.

Throughout the teaching process, we, as educators, must keep in mind that we can transmit words but not understanding. Ultimately, it is up to the learner to make sense of the experience. Didactic teaching is ineffective when used exclusively because the students involved are interpreting the teacher's verbal message in unique ways. This implies that teaching effectively is more complex than standing in front of a classroom and presenting information. The use of certain methods in certain situations in the classroom makes it more likely that students with varying learning styles and unique frames of reference will leave the classroom with meaningful messages and some degree of shared understanding.

Focal Point 3. **Toward a Constructivist Learning Perspective**

The constructivist perspective on learning holds particular relevance for teachers at all levels and is the central focus of this text. In some respects, the origins of constructivism may be traced to the perspectives on the learner portrayed by John Dewey during the first half of the twentieth century. Dewey (1934) placed great emphasis on connecting to students' "capacities, interests, and habits" through the establishment of interactive, student-centered "learning communities" within the classroom. Jean Piaget articulated a developmental perspective on constructivism as he investigated the influence of experience on the actions of children in various settings. Piaget's later research and writing (1965–1980) focused especially on learning as a dynamic, multidimensional, nonlinear process involving stages of disequilibrium, consideration of existing ideas in light of new information, and subsequent construction of new cognitive structures (Fosnot, 1996). Lev Vygotsky placed even greater emphasis on the importance of a social context as learners actively construct knowledge. Vygotsky (1931/1978) asserted that knowledge cannot be imposed by adults and that the creation of productive new cognitive structures in learners is best facilitated in an interactive setting in which learners have some degree of control over the nature and direction of discussions and activities.

Discussion 3: Toward a Constructivist Learning Perspective

Learning, from the constructivist perspective, is best promoted through an active process that emphasizes purposeful interaction and the use of knowledge in real situations. We believe that much about the constructivist perspective can be conveyed through an ancient Chinese proverb: "I hear and I forget; I see and I remember; I do and I understand." If we operate from this mindset, the important question for teachers should no longer be "How shall I best present this information to students for maximum recall?" but rather "What is the student doing mentally during instruction, and how can I provide opportunities for active mental processing?" (West et al., 1991). Truly effective teaching must go far beyond presentation. It is interesting to note how different this perspective is from the former ideas that memory is like photography and that students are passive blank slates or empty vessels.

The implications of a constructivist perspective are revolutionary, and we hope that this perspective challenges you to think about the processes of teaching and learning in new ways. A constructivist teacher recognizes the following:

- Learners of any age make sense of new experiences by relating them to their own previous experiences. Making ideas understandable from the learner's point of view is not merely a motivational ploy or nice when possible, but essential.

- Memorizing facts and reproducing information on tests is not the path to developing a deep, flexible understanding of any subject. Although it may be necessary to memorize certain facts as part of a learning experience, deeper learning involves active cognitive restructuring on the part of the student.

- Learning is something that the learner does, not something that is done to the learner. Because meaningful learning involves active cognitive restructuring, students must be involved in the learning process, making their own inferences and experiencing and resolving cognitive dissonance (i.e., struggling with ideas). The teacher is the stage setter and facilitator of this active learning process.

- Effective teaching involves continual probing of the nature of student understanding, that is, getting into students' heads to the greatest extent possible.

- Deeper understanding includes gaining insights into the connections between disciplines and knowledge of the ways of thinking within them.
- Superficial, encapsulated information is the result of teaching and curricula that emphasize the coverage of content. This implies that learning must be a continuous process that involves building connections from lesson to lesson and from the classroom to the outside world.
- Continual reflection on practice (i.e., thinking carefully about what we're doing and why) is a vital part of teaching effectively, an activity that promotes the learning of students and the empowerment of teachers as professionals.

We return to these elements of the constructivist learning perspective throughout this book. Each technique and method that we suggest will reflect these central beliefs. As a preservice teacher, the challenge for you is to begin to think in these terms in your methods courses, as you participate in your clinical experiences, and as you move into the classroom as a student teacher and then as a professional. A constructivist classroom must be an ACTIVE environment that features the following dimensions:

- **A**ssessment through performance, using a wide range of assessment methods.
- **C**urricula that emphasize big ideas, depth over breadth, and interdisciplinarity.
- **T**eacher as guide/facilitator/coach and student as worker/independent thinker.
- **I**nteraction, with value placed on teacher- and student-generated questions, and consistent use of methods that promote student–student interaction.
- **V**ariety in teaching methods, even within a single class period.
- **E**ngagement of students in the subject matter, with students *becoming* historians, writers, scientists, mathematicians, etc.[2]

Helping you, as a future teacher, learn how to establish this ACTIVE setting is the focus of this book.

The constructivist learning perspective also has a direct connection to you as a graduate of the current educational system. Each individual in a teacher education program is cognitively constructing his or her own beliefs about effective teaching. Because of our past experiences as students, we all arrive at this point in time with a very well-developed set of teaching schemata, and these may or may not change as a result of experiences in education courses (Lortie, 1975). This text will help you recognize and potentially reconsider some of your existing beliefs regarding teaching.

In these opening sections, we have touched on just some of the fascinating research findings regarding teaching and learning that should have a profound impact on classroom practice in the future. It is an exciting time to be starting a career as an educator, as we now know much more than ever before about how people think and learn. This knowledge will have a major positive impact on what happens in individual classrooms (and hopefully in your classroom) in the future. Another reason for optimism regarding the future of education is the incredible array of new educational technologies that teachers will have at their disposal. In the following section, you will get a tantalizing glimpse at some of the possibilities presented by these new technologies.

Focal Point 4: The Potentially Transformative Role of Technology in a Constructivist Classroom

The Internet, the Web, virtual reality, mobile computing. These are some of the technologies emerging from the Digital Age that we live and work in. These and other technologies are already transforming the workplace, as well as the ways many of us live our lives. Think about it. When was the last time you watched a TV program and were directed to the station's or network's Website for further information? Have you recently booked a flight, hotel, rental car, or entire vacation via the Web? Did you also happen to locate your destination on the Web, then print a map and driving directions to your destination? Do you read your favorite newspaper online? How about quickly peeking at the *London Times* or China's *People's Daily* (http://english.peopledaily.com.cn/) and seeing what the people of other countries are thinking? Or have you used instant messaging with friends and colleagues time zones or oceans away? If this sounds foreign to you, take note. Many of the students you'll be teaching view using the Internet to talk to friends, play videogames, and surf "cool stuff" as commonplace. They don't even think twice about it. That's life in the Digital Age.

That's all well and good, you might say, but what has this got to do with education? A whole lot. We're already seeing that even if new digital technologies are left out of the equation, there are compelling reasons to take a fresh look at the fundamentals of what it means to learn and teach. In particular, new insights into the nature of learning and what they imply for the active stance that learners can and need to take toward their learning. Now introduce technologies that can connect you (and your students) to the Vatican Library or the Library of Congress, enable you to explore the surface of Mars, permit you to control distant telescopes or microscopes and see their images, or construct sophisticated video programs that embed what you've learned using low-cost software that can run on any modern personal computer. And that's barely the tip of the iceberg.

Such capabilities enormously extend the range of experiences and information that today's learners can access and the breadth and depth of interesting questions that can be asked to motivate and guide learning. Plus, in using new digital technologies, students can learn both procedural and process skills, especially critical-thinking and problem-solving skills, that will serve them well throughout their lifetime. However, the benefits are realized only if the technologies are chosen and applied wisely. Knowing how takes more than keeping up with the latest technology. It requires understanding how different types of technologies mediate distinct aspects of learning, how they cater to different learning styles, and how their potentially transformative effects on learning are vitally determined by the classroom context in which they are deployed.

These and other important—and exciting—ideas about making technology an integral part of your teaching are addressed in Module 6

Focal Point 5: A Primary Goal of Constructivist Teaching: Challenging Students to Think Critically

SELECTION A

In 1875, the U.S. government had promised the Sioux permanent control of the Black Hills area in South Dakota and Montana, a region that they considered sacred. Months later, gold was discovered in the area. One morning in June, 1876, the sound of gunfire cracked through the air as an encampment of Sioux and Cheyenne men, women, and children was attacked by a mounted cavalry force under the command of General George Custer. Despite the surprise nature of the attack, warriors led by Sitting Bull and Crazy Horse were able to drive the invaders from the village. As fighting continued on the other side of the Little Bighorn River, the warriors were able to defeat their enemy and later flee with the other villagers to the north.

SELECTION B

In May 1876, General Custer was ordered by the War Department to remove Sioux and Cheyenne inhabitants from the Black Hills region. As part of this operation, he and his 264 men attacked an encampment of Sioux and Cheyenne warriors along the Little Bighorn River in Montana. Custer and his men fought valiantly against overwhelming odds. The battle raged for hours on both sides of the river. Outnumbered more than 10 to 1, every man in Custer's detachment was massacred. The victorious warriors mutilated many of the bodies after the battle was over.

Imagine asking a ninth-grade history class to read these two interpretations of an actual event and then inviting them to ask questions. They might generate any number of questions. Why did this happen? Who wrote these descriptions? How are the two accounts different? When were they written? What should I believe? Who was General Custer and what else had he done in the West? What do we know about Sitting Bull and Crazy Horse and their people? What finally became of them? What really happened? Imagine further that you challenge the students to find ways to answer their own questions, and others that may arise, including questions that you may pose as the teacher, all in the ACTIVE classroom setting that we've described. Your role as the teacher will be to help them find the resources that they need and to ask the kinds of questions that might push their investigation of this event further. In planning a sequence of experiences such as this, you'd be challenging your students to think critically about not only this historical event but also about the processes associated with thinking historically.

Discussion 5: A Primary Goal of Constructivist Teaching: Challenging Students to Think Critically

A frequently stated goal of educators at every level is to challenge students to think critically. Critical thinking has become a major curricular focus at the middle school, high school, and college levels. In fact, critical-thinking skills are tested at the state level in California and New York (Kurfiss, 1988). Life in the twenty-first century will place greater emphasis on critical-thinking abilities, as individuals are challenged to think creatively in the workplace and to consider and make decisions on issues vital to those living in a democratic society.

As noted earlier in this module, the need for individuals to think critically comes at a time when researchers have noted the limited influence of high school and college experiences on the thinking abilities of students. Although educators at every level value critical-thinking abilities, the skills associated with critical thinking are seldom taught overtly. Teachers at every level frequently focus on presenting products (information) associated with a discipline without challenging students to experience the processes by which ideas are generated, including the analysis of information; the conflicting interpretations of pieces of literature, bodies of data, or works of art; or the collection of evidence and the finding of patterns in complex and ill-defined situations. As Kurfiss (1988) noted, "Students are often assigned tasks that require (critical-thinking) skills, but the problem of acquiring the requisite skills is left to the ingenuity, good fortune, or native ability" (p. 4) of the individual student. In other words, there are often mismatches between the teaching methods used and what educators expect students to be able to do as a result of learning experiences. But there are ways in which teachers can challenge students not only to think critically but to develop abilities associated with critical thinking that they might apply to a range of contexts.

We've all heard the term *critical thinking.* There's a good chance that teachers have exhorted us to think critically about a topic that they (and perhaps we as students) felt was important. Just what do educators mean by critical thinking? How can we challenge our students to think critically? In the following sections, we investigate both of these guiding questions and, in doing so, lay the groundwork for the introduction of innovative teaching techniques and methods, each designed to challenge students to think critically and to develop skills and abilities that one could associate with critical thinking.

What Does It Mean to Think Critically?

Educators have generated a number of definitions for critical thinking that can help you to get your mind around these thinking processes. Ennis (1987) described critical thinking as *reasonable, reflective thinking focused on deciding what to believe or what to do,* placing a clear emphasis on informed decision making. He also articulated a number of abilities and dispositions associated with critical thinking. Consider these questions for a moment: What abilities and dispositions would you associate with critical thinking? What should a critical thinker be able to do?

Several educators have characterized critical thinking by addressing these questions, that is, by looking closely at the attributes or dispositions associated with quality thinking (Ennis, 1987; Kurfiss, 1988; Paul, 1995; Beyer, 1997). The most important attributes associated with critical thinking include the following:

- A desire to stay well informed.
- A driving curiosity, manifested by the willingness and ability to ask insightful questions.
- Open-mindedness and a willingness to suspend judgment until evidence can be carefully considered.
- Persistence, focusing on a problem situation that may be ill defined.
- A willingness to gather and consider evidence from a variety of sources, and the ability to assess the credibility (and possible biases) of these sources.
- Creativity in generating alternative perspectives and in viewing situations through the frames of reference of others.
- The ability to think about one's own thinking (metacognition), as well as the willingness to change one's ways of thinking as situations warrant.

As educators, we think that a definition of critical thinking developed by Kurfiss (1988) that connects to these attributes will provide preservice teachers with another useful perspective. Kurfiss (1988) describes critical thinking as an *investigation whose purpose is to explore a situation, phenomenon, question, or problem to arrive at a hypothesis or conclusion that integrates all available information and can therefore be convincingly justified*. In describing critical thinking as a process of inquiry, Kurfiss emphasizes that "all assumptions are open to question, divergent views are aggressively sought, and the inquiry is not biased in favor of a particular outcome." The result of such a critical inquiry is a conclusion (or hypothesis). The justification offered to support a conclusion is generally stated as an argument, which may be defined as "the sequence of inter-linked claims and reasons that, between them, establish the content and force of the position" that a particular person is taking (Kurfiss, 1988, p. 2).

This is not to say that the process of critical thinking is a dispassionate, Spock-like series of steps aimed at uncovering ultimate truth. A constructivist perspective on learning would, in fact, lead us to believe that each person necessarily brings certain ways of thinking and personal biases to any situation, given the fact that we have each had unique experiences and operate through different frames of reference. The process of critical thinking should involve creativity, intuition, and a thinking-outside-of-the-box spirit that should touch everything that you and your students do in the classroom. In later modules we'll see that the process of critical thinking could result in a decision communicated in the context of a discussion, a speech or position paper, a short story or poem, a dramatization, a debate, a painting or sculpture, or myriad other forms of expression.

This implies that there is no lockstep procedure to critical thinking or foolproof method or quick fix to help students become critical thinkers. But here's some good news: students, even young children, are capable of engaging in complex reasoning. Certain teaching methods can both challenge your students to think critically in the classroom and develop abilities that one might associate with critical thinking. In the following sections, we begin to explore a set of practical suggestions for doing these things.

A Closer Look at Critical-Thinking Processes

Educators and researchers in a range of disciplines frequently make a distinction between critical thinking and problem solving. Many see critical thinking as reasoning about ill-structured or open-ended problems, issues, or situations, whereas problem solving involves working through a more well-defined situation using established procedures. Problem-solving processes investigated in cognitive research frequently involve situations (problems) that, although complex, usually have one right answer, and perhaps one right way (process or procedure) to arrive at the right answer (Kurfiss, 1988). As a result, problem solving is often associated with deductive reasoning, with the learner assessing the situation, gathering information, and forming and testing hypotheses until the desired goal (answer) is reached.

In the minds of many educators, critical thinking may be more closely associated with inductive reasoning (Kurfiss, 1988), with learners looking for patterns in complex bodies of evidence. As a result, the goal in critical thinking is "not to find and execute a solution but to construct a plausible representation of the situation or issue that could be presented in a convincing argument" (Kurfiss, 1988, p. 2).Critical-thinking processes can take place in a variety of contexts and situations. In fact, many educators feel that critical-thinking processes could look different depending on the discipline. (Would the processes of critical thinking look different when applied in chemistry versus literature?) Nonetheless, it is useful to think of critical thinking as a recursive, two-phase process involving discovery and justification.

THE CONTEXT OF DISCOVERY. When faced with a problem, issue, or puzzling or perplexing situation, a critical thinker (learner) enters into the context of discovery (Kurfiss, 1988). A student engaged in the context of discovery may be asking initial questions, searching for evidence, questioning/arguing with a text, making and interpreting observations, or devising methods for testing initial ideas. As Kurfiss (1988) notes, the context of discovery is "the inventive, creative phase of critical thinking," (p. 2) the phase in which the learner not only asks questions but also finds ways to test initial ideas.

Let's return briefly to the vignettes describing the incidents at Little Bighorn River. Because of the unusual nature of the event described, and the conflicting descriptions in each paragraph, chances are that most students will be curious and at least somewhat interested in investigating the event further. This will be especially true if your students feel that their present frames of reference will not allow them to understand the situation and the disagreements involved (Beyer, 1997). To challenge students to enter into the context of discovery, you, as a teacher, should encourage your students early in the process to brainstorm questions via a brief Exploratory Discussion (see Module 10). In an Exploratory Discussion, the teacher asks a broad opening question and allows students the opportunity to generate responses. In this example you might ask, "What do you wonder most about after reading these two paragraphs?" In facilitating this discussion, you might contribute questions of your own, especially if students struggle initially; this allows you as the teacher to model the asking of critical-thinking questions ("When I read conflicting accounts like this, I ask myself . . ."). You might then allow students to choose what they believe are the five most important questions and assign groups to research the questions after discussing possible print and Web-based resources and the kinds of evidence that might further the investigation.

At this point, your students will be fully engaged in the context of discovery, finding ways to address interesting questions and generating and considering new questions along the way. Once students have begun to address questions and search for resources, you will want to provide them with frequent opportunities to critique information, evaluate the soundness of arguments made by authorities, and develop preliminary arguments of their own. These activities can be done within peer groups, as part of individual writing assignments, or in the context of full class discussions.

A constructivist perspective on learning would lead us to believe that teachers must carefully promote/nurture the context of discovery to promote critical thinking and the development of critical-thinking skills and abilities. We've already introduced evidence that indicates that students of any age impose meaning on events through active mental processing. Students use frames of reference (i.e., their personal set of schemata) to make sense of experiences. Researchers in a range of subject areas have shown that these cognitive structures provide a powerful set of lenses that allow learners to make sense of experiences. However, these lenses can sometimes inhibit learning of ideas that don't match previous experiences and associated expectations (recall Bartlett's findings showing that learners change details when trying to remember the elements of an unusual story).

Does this imply that encouraging students to learn, and to think critically, is much more complex than we had previously believed? Certainly, but use of a variety of methods that challenge students to actively process information will make it much more likely that critical thinking (and true learning) will occur.

THE CONTEXT OF JUSTIFICATION. Once learners have considered the situation, articulated questions, and gathered and considered evidence, they enter into what Kurfiss (1988) calls the context of justification. In this critical-thinking phase, the learner comes to tentative conclusions (hypotheses or arguments) and articulates reasons to support the decision that has been made. This part of the critical-thinking process should include sharing of ideas, active testing of one's own ideas and the ideas of others, and the search for disconfirming evidence that Kurfiss emphasized in her definition of critical thinking.

What teaching techniques and methods will promote critical thinking as students struggle through the contexts of discovery and justification? After your students have had an opportunity to investigate initial questions and gather information relevant to a topic, for example, the Battle of Little Bighorn, you might use a variety of methods to help students make decisions. Inductive lessons (see Module 8) challenge students to articulate concepts associated with the event (e.g., freedom and self-determination). Lessons using peer-group learning techniques (see Module 5) would allow students to discuss and debate their interpretations of different references, a process that should also occur during the context of discovery. Finally, Reflective Discussions (see Module 11) could be conducted to challenge students to make decisions and defend arguments regarding questions central to this event and related episodes (e.g., given the situation, were Custer's men justified in firing on the Sioux and Cheyenne?). Remember, it will be useful for you as the teacher to engage in the contexts of discovery and justification as you challenge students to think critically and to articulate, present, and defend products of their critical thinking. We will discuss this and other recommendations in modules describing specific teaching methods.

What Can You Do During the Contexts of Discovery and Justification to Promote Critical Thinking?

Researchers in education and cognitive psychology have suggested that teachers must do four things to challenge their students to think critically during the contexts of discovery and justification and to develop abilities associated with critical thinking (Ennis, 1987; Paul, 1995; Beyer, 1997).

1. Establish a thinker-friendly environment (Beyer, 1997; Wiggins, 1998) in which students are regularly challenged to engage in higher-order thinking in an encouraging atmosphere. Students must feel safe enough to take risks, to share ideas that are sometimes incomplete, and to make and learn from mistakes.

2. Make explicit the thinking of others skilled in the process and encourage students to share their own thinking processes. Teachers should also model their own thinking. Students can benefit by becoming aware that there are multiple ways to think about complex situations and by comparing their own ways of thinking with the thought processes of others.

3. Provide guidance and support (coaching) for students who are being challenged to think critically about complex issues or problems. Coaching may include helping students raise actions to a conscious level and continually make adjustments in their performance, a facilitative role that certainly applies to the development of critical-thinking abilities.

4. Provide students with something worthwhile and meaningful to think about. Students must perceive learning experiences to be generative, allowing them to explain something important or worthwhile within their own experiences. As a teacher, continually challenge yourself to ask the question, "Why would my students need to know this?" It's a question that is often left unanswered by educators at all levels.

Making Your Classroom Thinker Friendly

In suggesting that you use the teaching methods described in later modules, we're really encouraging you to make your classroom not only student centered but also thinker friendly (Beyer, 1997). This can be done in classrooms at a range of grade levels, from kindergarten through college.

As a teacher, you will find that it takes time to help students develop critical-thinking abilities. Research and experience have shown that students have difficulty developing such abilities in a hostile atmosphere or in classrooms where superficial coverage of subject matter is emphasized over depth and higher-level understanding. The obvious question becomes: How can I, as a teacher, establish a safe, thinker-friendly environment?

In considering how to make your classroom thinker friendly, let's focus on two important questions investigated in research on thinking. First, what are students and teachers doing in the classroom? Second, what is the focus of the class in terms of subject matter? Five major classroom studies conducted during the 1990s and reported by Beyer (1997) provide us with snapshots of what tends to happen in thinker-friendly classrooms. These characteristics of thoughtful classrooms may also be taken as suggestions for promoting a thinking community. In summary, the following elements characterize thinker-friendly classrooms:

- Teachers provide frequent (i.e., almost daily) opportunities for student-centered discussions that feature students raising substantive questions, debating ideas, and offering creative explanations and reasons to support them.
- Students "demonstrate understanding by explaining, analyzing, and generalizing about topics studied in depth" (Beyer, 1997, p. 21).
- Teachers provide structure by raising challenging initial questions for consideration, using questions raised by students, establishing (and helping students to establish) learning goals, and providing (and encouraging students to provide) summaries of points made.

- Teachers encourage and facilitate brainstorming and risk taking and provide students with frequent choices about what to study and how to study it, as well as choices about how to demonstrate their understanding (think about why this might appeal to students with a range of learning-style preferences).
- Teachers help students make connections with ideas in other disciplines (i.e., there is an interdisciplinary emphasis).
- Students and teachers engage in polite interactions, active listening, and recognition and acceptance of conflicting points of view.
- Teachers consistently play a facilitative role by asking initial, higher-order questions and probing questions that encourage students to clarify and expand on their ideas.
- Teachers and students accept the fact that mistakes will be made and recognize that mistakes can provide useful learning opportunities (so-called teachable moments).
- Teachers explicitly discuss and model thoughtfulness and join students in learning rather than standing above students as an authority figure.

Note that the elements associated with thinker-friendly classrooms closely parallel our portrait of constructivist classrooms. In general, thinker-friendly, constructivist classrooms can be characterized by the active engagement of students in collecting, analyzing, and using knowledge, generating and testing ideas, and constructing meaningful solutions to complex problems and issues.

A Thoughtful Curriculum: Providing Students with Something Meaningful to Think About

Providing students with something meaningful to think about is closely related to challenging them to think critically. As a classroom teacher, you may find yourself fortunate enough to be in a position to develop and enact a curriculum that consistently challenges students to think at higher cognitive levels. Based on our experiences as educators, and on research conducted in a broad range of fields (Kurfiss, 1988; Paul, 1995; Beyer, 1997), the following initial suggestions can provide students with a curriculum that consistently challenges them to think at higher cognitive levels. First, make it a practice in your classroom to promote *cognitive dissonance,* which is the sustained struggle with thought-provoking questions, issues, or situations. Challenging history students to consider the two vignettes provided earlier in this section is an example of cognitive dissonance. The same approach could be taken in English, science, math, or any other subject area. Such situations can provide the cognitive jolt (Wiggins, 1998) that will motivate students to investigate a situation. Jolts can be provided by introducing uncertainty or ambiguity or by investigating conflicting interpretations or points of view, puzzling problems, unusual quotes, or mysterious and open-ended situations. A math teacher might introduce a genuine problem situation requiring the application of math principles. A science teacher could do a puzzling demonstration (a so-called discrepant event) and ask students to speculate about it. An English teacher might invite students to read a short story except for the conclusion and then challenge them to write, present, and defend what they feel is the best ending.

Cognitive jolting of students may seem contradictory when you consider our advice to promote a thinker-friendly classroom community, but this is not the case. Jolts are actually highly motivational in challenging students to tackle perplexing problems in a setting that emphasizes collaboration and the sharing of ideas. Promoting cognitive dissonance can actually help create a thinking community, with students working together in a supportive environment.

Structuring Learning Experiences with Guiding Questions

Providing cognitive jolts will encourage the framing of critical-thinking investigations through guiding questions. In a constructivist classroom, both you and your students can provide these questions. In fact, you will find as an educator that you can often predict which questions your students might generate when you introduce a perplexing issue, situation, problem, etc. Guiding questions will be an important component of each teaching method that we introduce and will play an especially crucial role in classroom discussions.

What educational advantages may be gained through the use of guiding questions? Thoughtful questions can serve to encourage students of any age to think beyond the levels of knowledge and comprehension. Such questions can both stimulate and structure the thinking of students. In a cognitive sense, guiding questions can challenge students to process both familiar and new information in new ways to arrive at new levels of understanding. It is has been our experience as educators that the use of guiding questions can help students develop critical-thinking abilities that can be transferred beyond the classroom and applied in real-world contexts.

Guiding questions can be used to structure individual lessons, units of study, or entire courses and curricula. In fact, we urge you to develop guiding questions for each of these purposes. At Central Park East High School in New York, for example, an entire interdisciplinary language arts/social studies course is structured around the question "Whose country is it, anyway?" (Chion-Kenney, 1987). A high school English teacher might frame an entire course in literature with the question "What and who make great works of literature 'great'?" A ninth-grade course in biology might focus on the guiding questions "What is science?" and "What methods can and should be used to investigate the nature of life?"

Guiding questions can and should be used to structure units of study as well as individual lessons. To use a familiar example, almost every course in U.S. history includes a focus on World War II. A teacher of such a course might frame a World War II unit with any number of possible questions (e.g., What were the main causes of World War II? and What advantages allowed the allies to prevail?). A guiding question such as "To what extent was World War II a 'just' war?" could prove to be much more thought provoking, as it challenges students to seek out and analyze information, evaluate data, develop and test hypotheses, and articulate, share, and defend arguments, all important critical-thinking abilities.

In Modules 9, 10, and 11, we introduce a series of discussion methods and suggest that classroom discussions are essentially the investigation of thought-provoking questions by a group of people. Articulating a central, guiding question (a structuring device) is an important part of planning such discussions.

Creating a Critical-Thinking Classroom Community

Meaningful interaction is a hallmark of the constructivist classroom, and for good reason. In promoting what we would now call a social constructivist perspective on learning, Vygotsky (1931/1978) noted that most meaningful human learning takes place in interactive social settings. The clear implication is that teacher–student and student–student interaction is absolutely necessary, as teachers must challenge students to collaboratively investigate, research, articulate arguments, consider/debate new ideas, and gain insights into the thinking of the teacher and classmates. Brain-based research, as well as studies in cognitive psychology, suggests that interactive settings are much more likely to promote active mental processing (i.e., thinking). In addition, an interactive setting provides the teacher with invaluable insights (windows) into student thinking and opportunities to think out loud, modeling effective thinking practices. In discussing questioning techniques (see Module 4), we will go into some depth in making suggestions regarding questioning and active listening techniques that will promote meaningful interaction.

A commonsense but often overlooked necessity in promoting critical thinking is to arrange students physically in settings that encourage interaction (Beyer, 1997). Even if your space is limited, seating arrangements other than straight rows will make it much more likely that interaction will occur. In using some methods, circular or semicircular seating patterns allow students to face and respond to each other. Arranging students in groups or pods is more appropriate for group-oriented approaches. Creating short rows with an open center in the room can be effective for more teacher-directed lessons. It is difficult for students to remain anonymous in an interactive setting.

In short, we suggest varying your room settings frequently, depending on the predominant approach that you'll be using. You'll also want to consider the placement of thinking-inducing posters, photographs, maps, prints, props, and resource materials, depending on your intended focus. Examples of student work should also play a prominent role in enhancing your physical setting.

Remember that in-depth thinking takes time. Unfortunately, many teachers, often because of genuine or imagined pressure to cover material, rush through their curricula. Based on what we know about learning, a rush to cover material is completely unjustifiable. In fact, recent research (Peak, 1996; Newman et al., 1997) has shown that an approach that emphasizes quick, superficial coverage of subject matter results in lower scores on standardized tests (i.e., the I-need-to-cover-this-for-the-test rationale doesn't make much sense). It is important to allow students time to think critically on a daily and weekly basis throughout the year.

Constructivist classrooms, in which critical thinking is a major emphasis, are characterized by action and interaction. Use two or three different methods during each class period to keep students engaged cognitively. This does not mean that time spent in your classroom should feel rushed or hurried. Depth should be emphasized over breadth to the greatest extent possible.

Time is also a major long-term consideration. The emphasis on covering material has had a profoundly negative impact on our school system in general. We suggest using the guiding metaphor *less is more* (Sizer, 1984) when making decisions on subject matter.

Challenging Students to Think about Their Thinking

In a thinker-friendly, constructivist classroom, sharing ideas and talking about thinking processes is the norm. Take opportunities to explain your own thinking to your students (When I see a situation like this, I usually . . . When I thought about this, the first thing that I did was . . .). Encourage your students to be open about their thinking, to share their own ways of looking at things with their peers. Ask them questions that promote this inquiry (What did you do first? Why did you do ___? What evidence did you consider when making this claim?). These questions should also be asked in writing. You can include metacognitive reflection questions on assignments of any kind; they can also be part of a testing process. Some teachers find it useful to ask students to keep a reflective journal in which they provide insights into their own thinking processes and beliefs. Regardless of which subject you are teaching, journals can be immensely valuable in challenging students to share their ideas and to consider the strengths and weaknesses of their own thinking (see Module 14 for an expanded discussion of journaling).

■ ROUNDUP ■

The dawn of a new century represents an exciting time to embark on a career in education for a number of important reasons. From our brief review of educational research, it is apparent that we now know more than ever before about how people think and learn. As a classroom teacher, you can use this knowledge to your advantage by utilizing teaching methods that promote the active processing of ideas in a thinker-friendly setting. Finally, use of newly developed educational technologies can have a profound impact on students' learning.

In concluding this first module, we pose a final question: What professional responsibilities will be placed before tomorrow's teachers given both the challenges and the opportunities previously outlined? Many of the responsibilities of teachers will remain relatively unchanged. As a teacher, among other things, you will be asked to plan thoroughly and to form appropriate goals and objectives, to use (and frequently develop) curriculum materials, to motivate students, to manage (i.e., operate) your classroom, and to assess student progress and present feedback in a constructive way, responsibilities that teachers have long shared. It is our belief that your responsibilities as a teacher will change as schools change in light of new challenges and emerging research on learning. Based on the research discussed in this module, and on our own experiences in the classroom, the following abilities and dispositions will also be vital for those entering the teaching profession.

First, teachers must conduct themselves as resourceful, enthusiastic, critical-thinking role models. To help students develop their own thinking skills, teachers must not only model but help students develop their own thinking abilities. Modeling is a powerful teaching technique, and making constructive critical-thinking processes a personal habit is one key to developing these habits in our students. In this way, teachers may put themselves into a position to genuinely excite students not only about knowing but also about discovering, inventing, and imagining.

In a closely related theme, tomorrow's teachers must inquire into "the nature of teaching and schooling and assume that they will do so as a natural aspect of their careers" (Goodlad, 1990, p. 290). Early on, teachers must assume an inquiry-oriented, problem-solving approach when confronted with dilemmas related to teaching and learning. As educators, we must learn to cast a critical eye on practices and procedures in schools and classrooms and to distinguish between what works and what may best lead to maximum learning for all students. It is, frankly, unconscionable for teachers to fall into practices that they do not believe to be right simply to avoid offending colleagues or to maintain things as they've always been. As Goodlad (1990) pointed out, if we believe that schools truly need restructuring and renewal, then teachers must be "committed to and capable of effecting change" (p. 294). One of the most dramatic changes impacting teachers is the integration of computer-based technology into learning situations and the use of computers in the classroom. Using and critically evaluating Internet resources and computer-based programs, as well as communicating with other students and classrooms via the Internet, provide students with exciting new learning opportunities that add a new dimension to classroom experiences.

Teacher collaboration will also be a key component to effecting true change in our schools. Teachers must be willing and able to collaborate with students, colleagues, parents, and the community at large if we are to make our schools as good as they can be. Site-based reforms place a premium on teacher collaboration and leadership, and educators must be prepared to take responsibility for restructuring schools.

We agree with Goodlad (1990) and others that it is the "moral obligation" of all teachers "to ensure equitable access to and engagement in the best possible education for all children" (p. 23). If large numbers of students continue to be shut out of the right to a quality education, the results for the nation will be disastrous. Goodlad (1990) and his fellow researchers have found that "belief in the incapability of many children and youths abounds. Horrifyingly large numbers of teachers share this belief; indeed, they use it to excuse their own failures" (p. 23). Teachers must enter this profession committed to the ideal and convinced that they have the ability to teach all students to the best of their ability; we cannot simply manage and control students as many of them intellectually disengage in the classroom. The future demands this attitude and commitment.

Finally, teachers must use a broad range of approaches in reaching students with varying interests and talents. The use of innovative, student-centered approaches to teaching provide such opportunities for all students who wish to take part and result in greater understanding and the ability to use knowledge outside of the classroom. Research in teaching and learning has provided solid evidence that enhancing and improving classroom interactions allow more students to reach their highest educational potential. Teachers entering the field in this new century must have the ability to use innovative teaching methods and must see the educational value in doing so.

ENDNOTES

1. Thanks to Brian Miller, B.A. Augustana College Class of 2001, for this journal excerpt.
2. Thanks to Chuck Hyser, Ph.D., Education Department, Augustana College, for his help in articulating the ACTIVE acronym.

REFERENCES

Bartlett, F. C. (1932). *Remembering.* Cambridge: Cambridge University Press.

Beyer, B. K. (1997). *Improving student thinking: A comprehensive approach.* Boston: Allyn & Bacon.

Chion-Kenney, L. (1987). A report from the field: The Coalition of Essential Schools. *American Educator,* Winter, 11–21.

Dewey, J. (1934). *Art as experience.* New York: Minton, Balch.

Ennis, R. H. (1987). *Critical thinking.* Pacific Grove, CA: Midwest Publications.

Fosnot, C. T. (1989). Enquiring teachers, enquiring learners: A constructivist approach for teaching. New York: Teachers College Press.

Fosnot, C. T. (Ed.). (1996). *Constructivism: Theory, perspectives and practice.* New York: Teachers College Press.

Glynn, S. M., Yeany, R. H., & Britton, B. K. (Eds.). (1991). *The psychology of learning science.* Mahwah, NJ: Lawrence Erlbaum Associates.

Goodlad, J. I. (1990). *Teachers for our nation's schools.* San Francisco: Jossey-Bass.

Goodlad, J. I. (1995). *Educational renewal: Better teachers, better schools.* San Francisco: Jossey-Bass.

Gregorc, A. F. (1982). *The style delineator.* Cambridge, MA: Gabriel Systems.

Hewson, P. W. (1981). The role of conceptual conflict in conceptual change and the design of science instruction. *Instructional Science, 13,* 1–13.

Johnson, D. W., & Johnson, R. (1990). *Learning together and alone.* Englewood Cliffs, NJ: Prentice-Hall.

Kennedy, M. (1991). Policy issues in teaching education. *Phi Delta Kappan, 73*(5), 661–666.

Kurfiss, J. G. (1988). *Critical thinking: Theory, research, practice, and possibilities.* AHSE-ERIC Higher Education No. 2. Washington, DC: Association for the Study of Higher Education.

Lortie, D. C. (1975). *Schoolteacher: A sociological study.* Chicago: University of Chicago Press.

Newman, F. N., Secado, W. G., & Wehlage, G. G. (1997). *Authentic achievement: Restructuring schools for intellectual quality.* San Francisco: Jossey-Bass.

Osborne, R., & Freyburg, P. (1985). *Learning in science: The implications of children's science.* Oxford, England: Heinemann.

Paul, R. W. (1995). *Critical thinking: How to prepare students for a rapidly changing world.* Santa Rosa, CA: Foundation for Critical Thinking.

Peak, L. (1996). *Pursuing excellence: A study of U.S. eighth grade and science teaching: learning, curriculum, and achievement in international context.* Washington, DC: U.S. Department of Education.

Putnam, J. (1997). *Cooperative learning in diverse classrooms.* Upper Saddle River, NJ: Merrill.

Schoenfeld, A. (1982). *Mathematics problem solving: Issues in research.* Philadelphia: The Franklin Institute Press.

Sizer, T. R. (1984). *Horace's compromise: The dilemma of the American high school.* Boston: Houghton-Mifflin.

Sizer, T. R. (1992). *Horace's school: Redesigning the American high school.* Boston: Houghton-Mifflin.

Sizer, T. R. (1996). *Horace's hope: What works for the American high school.* Boston: Houghton-Mifflin.

Ulrich-Tobias, C. (1994). *The way they learn: How to discover and teach to your child's strengths.* Wheaton, IL: Tyndale House Publishers.

Vygotsky, L. S. (1931/1978). *The mind and society: The development of higher psychological processes.* Cambridge, MA: Harvard University Press.

West, O. K., Farmer, S. F., & Wolff, P. M. (1991). *Instructional design; Implications from cognitive science.* Englewood Cliffs, NJ: Prentice-Hall.

Wiggins, G. (1998). *Understanding by design.* Alexandria, VA: Association for Supervision and Curriculum Development.

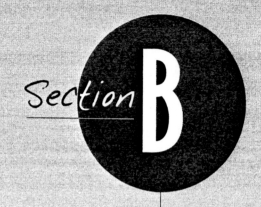

How-To's

Section B includes Module 2 through Module 6. We call this section *How-To's* because each module contains practical procedures in the skills of teaching. Modules 2 and 3 address various aspects of planning professional lessons from elements of the thinking process and deductive and inductive structures to Core Components of a lesson plan along with various techniques and tools. Modules 4 and 5 focus on techniques that deserve in-depth focus: questioning skills and peer-group learning, respectively. Module 6 provides an extensive look at integrating technology with the methods and techniques in this book.

We hope that you use *How-To's* for ongoing reference as you plan each new lesson for your methods practicum and as you student teach. We also encourage you to refer to this section when you plan lessons as an established teacher in the future. The *How-To's* section will help you use a varied repertoire of practices and avoid the trap of growing repetitive and stale.

Module Two:
Prelude to Lesson Planning

PART 1:

The Cognitive Ladder of Facts, Concepts, Principles, and Themes

■ OVERVIEW AND GOALS

Fact. Concept. Principle. Theme. These are the components of the cognitive ladder. Put them all together and you've got the foundation for a lesson that shoots for critical thinking. Most of us have not paused to reflect on the differences among these components because we tend to assume their meaning and to integrate them transparently as we learn and think.

As educators, we must put the brakes on and closely examine the nature of facts, concepts, principles, and themes. As you aspire to be a challenging and inspiring teacher, you need to structure your lessons with this cognitive scaffolding. It's like climbing a mountain: you secure your students' footing as they scale into higher regions.

In Part 1 we (1) describe the differences and the interrelationships among facts, concepts, principles, and themes and (2) demonstrate how facts, concepts, principles, and themes are the building blocks of thought that help you guide your students' critical-thinking skills.

Focal Point 1: Two Broad Views of the Cognitive Ladder

Figures 2.1 and 2.2 provide the overall schema or outline of the cognitive ladder. The template briefly describes the components of the Cognitive Ladder to clarify the hier-

Step 1: Provide *facts*	Instructional materials provide items of information for a knowledge base.
Step 2: Define *concept*	Students interrelate the facts to characterize an abstract concept (*impressionism, stereotype, democracy, probability*).
Step 3. Establish *principles*	Principles are rules that students generate from a concept (*impressionism heightens awareness, a stereotype distorts reality*).
Step 4. Explore *themes*	Students synthesize a concept and principles into a broad, abstract idea (*democracy: economics or ideals?, probability tames chance*).

FIGURE 2.1 Template for the Cognitive Ladder

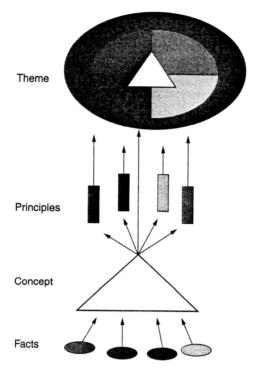

Theme

Principles

Concept

Facts

©2002 Ina Claire Gabler

FIGURE 2.2 Cognitive Ladder

archy; the focal points that follow provide in-depth information about each step in the ladder. For now, try to get a global sense of how you might structure a lesson from lower to higher levels of thinking as you consider both the template and the graphic representation.

Discussion 1: **Two Broad Views of the Cognitive Ladder**

You may be wondering if lesson planning needs to be so structured. After all, didn't all the teachers you had in high school and college just talk?

Yes. Most of your teachers did just talk. But the most effective ones used questions with, quite literally, a method to their madness, being so effective at teacher–student dialogue that you might not have noticed the skillful sequencing of the questions. Perhaps these terrific teachers also fostered learning with projects that required original, critical thinking.

Other teachers may have known a lot and talked at you about their subject, perhaps engagingly, but may not have challenged you to think for yourself. Just reflect: How often had you arrived at your own interpretation? How often were you encouraged to conceive of and justify an assertion? When did you think critically in history, English, science, math, art, foreign language, PE, or health? How often did you generate your own strategy for problem solving?

Talking *at* students—tossing content at them—does *not* equal teaching. To put it another way, stuffing young people's heads like so many sausages, filled with facts, definitions, and events, does not result in meaningful learning that matters to your students beyond test questions.

In addition, many of your students won't have a stake in tests and grades. So why are you up there cramming their heads with facts they don't care about? The art is to get your students to value necessary information, to apply and go beyond facts into concepts, principles, and themes as you guide your class with a rigorous and imaginative approach.

All this brings us to the good news: you are being primed to join the best teachers. A constructivist classroom requires you to be a well-prepared facilitator, a catalyst enabling your students to apply a factual knowledge base to higher-order thinking. Your future students can be among those who exhilarate in conceptualizing, problem solving, and perceiving interrelationships. It's true that your students may arrive at insights similar to yours, but the important measure is how they get there: passively, through mindless repetition of your ideas, or actively, through a stimulating and empowering process that makes the same idea a discovery.

Active, constructivist learning applies to the entire spectrum of teaching and learning styles, from teacher-led Directed Discussions and Interactive Presentations (among the methods described in this book) that prompt students to think critically to self-motivated cooperative learning projects. And it all begins with facts, concepts, principles, and themes inviting your students to become original thinkers.

As we begin with the definition and discussion of facts and move on to concepts, principles, and themes, you will notice an increasing complexity. For clarity's sake, we discuss these cognitive components in a linear sequence, beginning with the most basic.

In the classroom, of course, the learning experience is never so linear and rigid. A student may have sudden insight from a fact to a theme, for example, leapfrogging over the sequence. But as a teacher, you need to be aware of the cognitive ladder to facilitate critical thinking and to provide scaffolding for students who are temporarily left behind in a peer's leap of understanding.

Focal Point 2: **A Fact**

fact Fact fact **fact** *fact*

Fact is
my name.
A knowledge base is
my game.

A bird on the wing.
A bell that won't ring.
A singer who suddenly finds
she can't sing.

Something's wrong beyond our sight:
The singer's got a touch
of fright:
Without the bell to sound the pitch,
she can't sing well and won't get rich.

And that is that.
A *who-what-when-where-how-and why*
am I.
It makes me
sigh.

You see, I dream
I'm the star in a stream
of *a lofty thought*—Ah! supreme
innovation,
the heart's ovation,
cream
of the mind, a find,
a treasure.
But woe is me!
I'm smaller measure.
I'm a
here-you-have-it-truth,
just a bit of proof:
It's candy ruined your tooth.
Just a two-feet-on-the-ground
sound fact.
  —©2002 Ina Claire Gabler

<hr />

Discussion 2: A Fact

As the verse conveys, a *fact* is *an item of information considered to be true*: World War I created the conditions for World War II. Calcium must be absorbed for it to build sturdy bones. We depend on oxygen for life. Interrelated facts combine to form a knowledge base that your students can use to justify their interpretations. Similarly, your students can cite facts to arrive at a concept that is universally accepted. Keep in mind that facts and concepts that are considered true today can be disproven tomorrow by new compelling evidence to the contrary; for example, a flat earth and the spontaneous generation of life were once considered indisputable "facts." However, the relationship of facts to a concept is constant. It's similar to the way you play Scrabble, arranging the letters (facts) to form a word (a concept).

Examples of Facts

Let's take an extended look at the three examples of facts or truths given in the previous paragraph.

EXAMPLE #1/THE CONDITIONS OF SURRENDER IN WORLD WAR I CREATED THE CONDITIONS FOR WORLD WAR II

This item of information states a cause-and-effect relationship between the two world wars, combining the events from the end of World War I, including conflicts, the Great Depression, weak national leaders, and the Treaty of Versailles, which stripped Germany of its dignity as well as its army. Interrelating items of information from the intervening years between the two wars enables an interpretation, namely, that one war bore the seeds of another.

EXAMPLE #2/CALCIUM MUST BE ABSORBED FOR IT TO BUILD STURDY BONES

It took a lot of facts to realize that the ingestion of calcium in and of itself does not guarantee strong bones. Calcium absorption is essential for bone building. Absorption depends on the presence of specific hormones, vitamin D, and/or magnesium as well as a person's individual metabolism. Efficient absorption also depends on the type and source of calcium and food combinations. Researchers inferred from these facts that calcium must be absorbed for it to build sturdy bones.

EXAMPLE #3/WE DEPEND ON OXYGEN FOR LIFE

When oxygen was discovered, its significance to life on earth was not immediately understood. Only by observing particular occurrences (items of information), for example, various animals dying in an environment without oxygen, did scientists recognize the truth of oxygen's role for life.

Now let's turn to the *Fact* verse you read earlier. Even though it's playful, it conveys the relationship between facts and larger ideas. In the second verse, you're given a list of facts: *A bird on the wing./A bell that won't ring./A singer who suddenly finds she can't sing.* Each of these items is isolated without significance.

Now try combining the facts into a possible cause-and-effect relationship. Using imagination, we could say that "a bird on the wing" flies through a garden party at which a singer is about to perform for strangers. The bird knocks down the bell "that won't ring," the bell being the singer's. She depends on the tone of the bell for the starting note, and when it fails to sound, the singer panics from stage fright and "suddenly finds she can't sing."

The third verse conveys this interpretation. It begins with the line, *Something's wrong beyond our sight*, suggesting that we need to interpret the facts into an apparent—or possible—truth.

This scenario may stretch credibility a bit, but the exaggeration sticks and helps to make our point: Interrelated facts supply evidence for larger ideas. In other words, learning facts is not the end point for your students. Knowing facts is just the beginning, even when facts are important to memorize and understand.

Using Facts as Stepping Stones

How are facts meaningful to you as a teacher of history, English, art, Spanish, science, math, PE, or health?

Consider this. You're a science whiz struggling with an English lesson. The teacher begins the lesson with high-level questions about the poetry you read for homework. He may think he's challenging the class, but you're lost because poetry isn't your thing and you don't know where to begin figuring things out.

Across the hall, your friend's English teacher, Ms. Dynamite, is also teaching poetry. However, your friend tells you that Ms. Dynamite begins with far more basic questions than the ones your teacher immediately poses. Ms. Dynamite asks her students to cite the details they notice. Which images strike them first? Which are interesting? Confusing? In this way, Ms. Dynamite establishes the facts in the poetry, the raw information. Then she invites her students to see which images work together. Some of the questions she now asks are, "How might some images relate to each other? What might they symbolize or represent to you? Can you come up with more than one interpretation? How could you apply these ideas to your everyday life?" In this way, Ms. Dynamite encourages her students to interpret the facts into concepts, principles, and themes.

Using this approach, you as the teacher can guide or facilitate your students' understanding of your subject, even students who believe that they just can't get it. With Ms. Dynamite, students build their understanding from facts to original insights and feel less intimidated. Who knows. They might find the subject intriguing—for the first time.

<hr>

Focal Point 3: **A Concept**

concept Concept concept **concept** *concept*

liberté, fraternité, equalité:
I dare say
that's me.
A *concept,*
you see:
common as care,
important as *fair.*
I'm
an abstract notion,
a metaphoric ocean.
Ubiquitous realities
No one hears,
touches,
smells,
or
sees.
Yet examples abound

when facts are found.
I'm marked
by signs
both naughty and nice.
I'm full
of spice:
Theocracy, Courage & Paradise.
I'm sound as meat:
Democracy, Genocide, Defeat.
Dynamic as trumpets
that stir your feet.
And more replete
than you thought
I ought
to be.
I'm laughing, weeping,
high, deep and sweeping
—expanding your spirit, engaging your mind—
a sometimes surprising
find.
    —©2001 Ina Claire Gabler

Discussion 3: **A Concept**

A *concept integrates facts into a larger, cohesive idea.* As the verse states, a concept is an "abstract notion." Often, we don't stop to think deeply about many concepts that we use frequently in conversation or even in our private thoughts. For example, *justice, freedom,* and *change* are concepts whose meanings we assume in our everyday lives. Yet, how often have you stopped to ponder exactly what *justice, freedom,* and *change* encompass as defined concepts? How often have you paused to identify the characteristics of these and other concepts? How often have you tried to identify examples and nonexamples to fully grasp the scope and implications of these concepts?

Exploring a concept fully is so important that we included two methods in Module 8 for developing a concept: one deductively, the other inductively (see "Focal Point 2: Cognitive Frameworks" in Part 2 of this module for the difference between deduction and induction). The reason? When your students define a concept, when they establish and analyze concrete examples and nonexamples of that abstract idea, they develop critical and original thinking skills. They may even enjoy learning. (Note: After Focal Point 5, we ask you to supply some facts that support our examples of *justice, freedom,* and *change* throughout Part 1 of this module. You may want to keep this upcoming challenge in mind as you read on.)

Examples of Concepts

A concept's definition requires a host of facts as examples and nonexamples of the concept's manifestation to convey various implications. Consider these examples.

EXAMPLE #1/JUSTICE

To generate a definition of justice, some examples of the manifestations of justice might span from the personal to the societal. A personal sense of justice could take the form of an individual's revenge. Let's say that the conduct of a well-known figure is misrepresented to the point of slander by a powerful rival quoted in the newspaper. The victim seeks revenge by slandering the rival in turn. On the other hand, an example of justice could be the disinterested weighing of evidence by governmental bodies, for example, a jury trial, to arrive at a fair outcome. Yet a third example of justice could be a hardworking and devoted teacher teaching for many years without recognition finally receiving official acknowledgment from her principal or district superintendent. This example concerns *fairness*, a different order from the previous dramatic examples.

A possible nonexample of the manifestation of justice is corruption, say, of lawyers dropping the slandered victim's case because of threats from the powerful rival. Another nonexample of justice is imprisonment of an innocent person. In the case of the teacher, a nonexample of justice might be giving official recognition to a new although talented teacher with few notable accomplishments while overlooking the veteran teacher's outstanding professional work over many years.

These and additional examples and nonexamples might generate a definition of justice as the act of exercising appropriate and equitable treatment for legal and moral violations or the act of executing fairness.

EXAMPLE #2/FREEDOM

Examples of the manifestation of freedom might be behaviors protected by the Bill of Rights in human society, such as the right of free speech and the right to public assembly. In the animal kingdom, examples of freedom might be wild animals living unencumbered in their natural habitats.

Nonexamples of the manifestation of freedom might be censorship of the press; people being imprisoned because they voiced protest against their government's policies; human slavery; or imprisonment of someone, whether guilty or innocent of a crime. Other nonexamples of freedom are caged animals in a zoo or ants enslaved by other ants.

These and other examples and nonexamples might point to one concept definition of freedom as the state of unencumbered behavior in both private and social and political contexts.

EXAMPLE #3/CHANGE

At first glance this concept seems so obvious that you may think it's a waste of time to read this example. But bear with us. You most likely agree that the most common belief about change is that it denotes a transformation. A monarchy is toppled and a republic is installed. An illiterate young person learns to read at the age of 40. A person replaces aggressiveness with kindness. Someone overcomes an addiction.

Various factors alter one condition into another. For example, political revolution and newfound self-confidence might account for the first two changes, respectively. All domains evidence transformation, from personal to political. From this perspective, your students might define change as an alteration between an earlier state and a later state.

If we reflect beneath the surface, we could say that the potential for the altered condition is always present. If this aspect of potentiality is elicited from your students, then the definition of change becomes more subtle: Change is a process of developing a dormant perception or possible state contrasting with a previous perception or state of the same thing.

Application of Concepts

Concepts often serve as the underpinning for in-depth inquiry. For example, your students can explore their definition of justice applied to Hamlet's avenging of his father's death, or the prosecution of national leaders and army officers for war crimes, or the benching of an unruly athlete. Freedom might be discussed in terms of scientists in historic times who risked their lives when their theories challenged the Church; or in terms of the creation of "acceptable" versus "unacceptable" art forms in different epochs; or the role of mathematics in the invention of the airplane, flight being the ultimate symbol of freedom. Change is a useful concept with which to examine the paradox of history as both the story of altered conditions and the demonstration that conflicts and motives keep repeating; or to explore the outcome of mixing primary colors when you paint; or to learn and highly regard the language and other cultural practices of a foreign country you once considered inferior.

Remember, for your students to articulate a competent and workable definition of a concept, they must first analyze, that is, compare and contrast, pertinent facts. Your students draw inferences from this knowledge base that enable them to define and apply a given concept.

Importance of Facts

Concept definitions lead to further questions. Consider the definition of justice we offered (the act of exercising appropriate and equitable treatment for legal and moral violations or the act of executing fairness). What is the standard of "appropriate" and "equitable"? What constitutes "legal and moral violations"? What is meant by "fairness"?

Similarly, our proposed definition of freedom (the state of unencumbered behavior in both private and social and political contexts) can lead to the following questions: What is the difference between "unencumbered behavior" and criminal behavior? Is behavioral freedom always the ultimate aspiration of Western democracy? Is it ever appropriate to limit freedom according to this definition? When and why? Should we modify or adapt this definition of freedom to reflect the conditions inherent in the previous questions?

Reflecting more in depth on our definition of change (a process of developing a dormant perception or possible state contrasting with a previous perception or state of the same thing), we could ask, What are the causes that govern the apparent reasons for change? For example, what were the underlying social, economic, and other conditions that brought about the French Revolution? What were the experiences that led a 40-year-old to learn how to read? What is the difference between growth and change? In what way(s) do they overlap?

Exploring these and similar questions calls on facts for concrete evidence of a given explanation. In this way, facts enrich the learning and thinking process from two directions: leading *toward* the definition and plunging *into* the definition. In other words, facts supply the grounding with which to conceive of a concept definition. The definition in turn implies questions whose possible answers rely on more facts with which to delve more deeply into the scope of the definition. In addition, a concept definition that leads to further inquiry, that is, to more facts, can result in more concepts (e.g., the concept of freedom can lead to the concepts of change and justice). You can see the possibility for a terrific cross-fertilization of facts and concepts. A lesson that incorporates this process sparkles with intellectual rigor.

As accomplished learners, we engage in this mental play spontaneously, without thinking to define the elements of thought as facts, concepts, and so on. But as teachers, if you have meta-awareness[1] of these elements, you can plan a more richly developed lesson than if you rely on intuition only—or on the textbook only.

Focal Point 4: A Principle

principle principle principle ***principle*** Principle

I'm a cut-to-the-heart-of-it
principle.
A rule or law that's firm,
not slippery like
a worm.
A light
in the night that
opens
your sight.

I'm glorious,
brazen,
uproarious,
amazin'.
Flying up there in the sky,
Leaves a shinin' in your eye.
Shootin' stars,
Stompin' mars.

I strain
your brain.

Heck, you're sayin', *anything goes!*
With an upturned pose, an eye's a nose.

Now, if that's a principle
you'll believe,
you need to search
beneath my sleeve
and pluck out a fact,
or two or three,
and find some concepts
spawning me,
to ground your thinkin',
yesiree!
Yeah, I'm a principle,
aimin' high.
But don't forget:
Sight
needs
an eye.
                —©2001 Ina Claire Gabler

Discussion 4: **A Principle**

A *principle defines a rule that expresses a relationship between facts and concepts.* Whereas a concept defines a general abstract idea, *a principle is a single rule or law of that concept.* One concept can generate many rules or laws as various facts or examples and nonexamples are considered.

Examples of Principles

Now we're going to build on the concepts of justice, freedom, and change by generating some corresponding principles.

EXAMPLE #1/JUSTICE

An infamous nonexample of justice is the practice of intentionally framing an innocent person who cannot afford a private attorney so that he is convicted of a crime that he did not commit. If new forensic evidence proves that person's innocence so that he released from prison without a record, that is an example of justice. A possible rule or principle derived from the nonexample is that the application of justice is inequitable according to economic class. A principle of justice derived from the example might be that science plays an increasing role in the execution of courtroom justice.

EXAMPLE #2/FREEDOM

An example of freedom might be that people in Western democracies have the right to carry out their political persuasions. This example of freedom in Western democracies could generate the principle or law that everyone has the right to openly express one's views without fear of recrimination. Another principle could be that in Western democracies every adult citizen has the right to cast one vote in any political or governmental election.

EXAMPLE #3/CHANGE

If we consider change as an altered condition that always has the potential to exist, then a general principle of personal change might be that new behavior is always possible and requires self-discipline along with the desire to replace one behavior with another. Or we can adopt a more specific context. Looking at examples of at-risk students suddenly aspiring to earn high grades because an adult they respect encourages them, we could say that new behavior can occur because of outside influences. This expression of a more specific principle embodies the elements of the general principle, that is, self-discipline along with the desire to replace one behavior with another.

Application

The specific content of principles and their examples, as well as a full range of their implications, need to be examined beyond their face value or intuitive appeal.

- *Justice.* Principles raise questions even as they seem to establish justified rules. You may remember that the principles we formulated for justice were that the application of justice is inequitable according to economic class and that science plays an increasing role in the execution of courtroom justice. Citing the example of an innocent person convicted of a crime but eventually released from prison, you could ask your students the following questions: Is justice delayed really justice? Is true justice possible when cruel conditions result from delayed justice?

- *Freedom.* Principles that seem appropriate may contain undesirable implications or subtly encroach on each other. Consider our example of freedom: People in democracies have the right to carry out their political persuasions. This example generated the principle that everyone has the right to openly express their views without fear of recrimination. However, this principle could protect a political group attempting to establish anarchy by violence, such as bombing federal buildings or assassinating government figures. After reflection, your students may therefore generate the modifying principle that legal political activities are limited to those that do not endanger the lives and freedom of others. How does this modified principle calibrate with the principles of freedom in Western democracies?

- *Change.* Let's reconsider our principle of personal change that new behavior is always possible and requires self-discipline along with the desire to replace one behavior with another. Despite the existence of potentiality and the appeal of that idea, there are conditions that may undermine this principle. For example, suppose you want to change your procrastinating ways so that you always—or almost always—do things promptly (writing that dreadful paper, paying the bills, doing the laundry, etc.). You desire to replace your procrastination with promptness. You are known for your self-discipline in how you apply yourself to any task or responsibility. So you should be able to transfer this self-discipline to conquering your procrastination. But here comes Catch-22: you procrastinate applying your self-discipline to your habit of procrastination.

The *Principles* verse you read earlier serves as a warning: a principle is shallow if it's not grounded in documented facts and defined concepts. We hope this discussion has given you a taste of the loopholes within ideas and the need to keep your students on their mental toes. Insist on rigor, that is, objectively supported viewpoints, whoever your students are. It's the stuff of critical thinking (see Module 1). In time, once your students learn to expect more of themselves they may enjoy the challenge of spotting loopholes and may thrive on the stimulation. But this breakthrough won't happen overnight or in a week or even in a month if your students have been socialized to be passive. Our modules on questioning (Module 4) and resocializing (Module 15) give helpful tips for encouraging students to be active learners in this way.

Focal Point 5: A Theme

theme Theme theme **theme** *theme*

I am a *theme.*
The roof above the concept beams
that rest upon a floor
that's packed
with facts.

I sing the tune
that fills the house
in every principle's room.
I keep the house
together
whether
beams are short or tall,
whether
rooms are large or small.

A singing roof? you bray.
Do-ray-me, I say.
I'm a scream,
I'm a dream and rising steam.
I'm a roof with a song
that can't go wrong
as long as I'm solid
on rooms and beams.
Attached to
concepts,
facts and principles

—not lax—
Why, I can be
intriguing.
A screaming, dreaming, steaming
even, yes, a singing
—and while we're at it, why not swinging—
theme.
   —©2001 Ina Claire Gabler

Discussion 5: A Theme

Whereas facts are fixed, and concepts and principles are rooted to those facts, a theme goes further: *a theme integrates facts, concepts, and/or principles into a unifying idea with broad application.* As a result, a theme may apply to the past as well as the present. It invites varied interpretations, rather than establishing a fixed notion. For these reasons, a theme may serve as the title for a unit. For example, a theme that arises from a unit on Victorian novels, such as Society's Role in Victorian Lives: Protection or Dominance?, can be meaningfully applied to society's role today as well.

Individual students may perceive different themes from the same knowledge base, concepts, and principles. Your job as a constructivist teacher is to facilitate your students' critical thinking, enabling them to generate original themes or to explore and evaluate prepared themes. Either way, themes must be justified with facts, concepts, and principles.

Examples of Themes

Conceiving of themes isn't easy, but it's fun. It's creative mental play. At the same time, formulating themes sharpens the mind. See what you think of the examples below. As you read, try to come up with your own themes that may work better with the facts you may have already thought of.

EXAMPLE #1/JUSTICE

Theme #1: The feasibility of justice in a society with populations that lack political power. This theme combines the principles that the application of justice is inequitable according to economic class and that science plays an increasing role in the execution of courtroom justice; each principle provides a different viewpoint of the theme.

Theme #2: Revenge as justice: just or unjust? This theme explores the dual aspect of revenge as an example of justice.

EXAMPLE #2/FREEDOM

Theme #1: The dangers of freedom. This theme expands on the concept of freedom as the state of unencumbered behavior in both private and social and political contexts; it also embodies the principle that legal political activities are limited to those that do not endanger the lives and freedom of others.

Theme #2: Are personal and political freedoms the only conditions for an equitable society? This theme relates to nonexamples of freedom such as censorship of the press, people imprisoned because they voiced protest against their government's policies, and human slavery; it also calls on the definition of freedom as the state of unencumbered behavior in both private and social and political contexts implying possible excesses and exploitation.

EXAMPLE #3/CHANGE

Theme #1: Personal change: transformation or growth? This theme relates to a principle of personal change that new behavior is always possible and requires self-discipline along with the desire to replace one behavior with another; it also relates to the following concept-related questions: What is the difference between growth and change? In what way(s) do they overlap?

Theme #2: Similarities and differences between individual and political change. This theme calls on the principle that new behavior can occur because of outside influences and on the examples of the French Revolution and the 40-year-old man learning to read; it also relates to the principle that new behavior is always possible and requires self-discipline along with the desire to replace one behavior with another.

Your Own Application

If you haven't already jotted down some facts related to our examples of justice, freedom, and change, pause now to do this. The point is to identify series of facts that can be processed (combined and interpreted) as the foundation of the concepts, principles, and themes offered in this module. Review the examples you've just read to come up with meaningful facts rather than relying on your memory.

● Stop now to carry out this challenge, then continue with the following paragraph.

Once you have a list of facts that support the concepts, principles, and themes we've just discussed, fill in Figure 2.3. This table asks you to formulate your own con-

Concepts	Facts	Concept Definition	Two Principles	Two Themes
1. Justice				
2. Freedom				
3. Change				

FIGURE 2.3 Cognitive Ladder Fill-In

cept definitions, principles, and themes based on the facts you developed for our concepts, principles, and themes. (Your concept definitions may not significantly differ from ours, but your principles and themes can be very different from those here.) Our intention is for you to experience the variety of credible interpretations based on the same facts. This variety is one reason that a constructivist approach encourages students to arrive at their own justified interpretations, which may differ from yours as the teacher but may be just as worthy.

We suggest that you duplicate Figure 2.3 and then fill in the columns according to the headings. We also recommend that you swap ideas with a peer for feedback and to see the large range of possible interpretations.

Now that you've formulated your own ideas across the cognitive ladder, take a look at Figures 2.4 and 2.5 for examples of facts, concepts, principles, and themes in two subject areas. You can apply what you learn from these tables to another extensive practice for your own subject in the "Hands-On Practice" section.

■ ROUNDUP ■

Facts are specific items of information that describe an apparent truth. Sometimes today's fact is tomorrow's myth or illusion (e.g., the accepted "facts" in earlier times that the sun revolves around the earth and that the earth is flat). For this reason, we're referring to a working concept of facts in a given time, otherwise known as conditional truth. Misinterpreted facts point to the constructivist view of respecting your students' perceptions of reality as a starting point, no matter how misconceived those perceptions may be. Perceptions can be processed and reinterpreted as appropriate facts or conditional truths.

Facts in turn provide the foundation for concepts, principles, and themes. A concept defines a general notion or idea, such as liberty, that embodies the distinguishing characteristics of that idea. One concept can generate many principles, used here to mean rules or laws that are broad interpretations of concepts and related to the facts, examples, and nonexamples. Finally, a theme expresses a unifying idea that incorporates facts, concepts, and principles, synthesizing these elements in depth.

Remember that thinking does not constrain itself to a linear process, as represented in this module. A fact can spark a principle, making it necessary to back up and define the concept(s) inherent in that principle. Similarly, a concept can inspire the formulation of a theme. So, we are not suggesting that your students be encouraged to think according to this step-by-step linear ladder. But if you and your students have meta-awareness of this ladder, then your students can fill in gaps as they work independently. Meanwhile, you've planned a facilitative lesson ahead of time that is thorough and rigorous. Using the Cognitive Ladder in your lesson enables you to guide your students confidently when one student takes a sudden leap and the others are confused, or vice versa. You can also guide students who need to justify a burst of insight in terms of the taxonomic component(s) that they skipped.

Facts: A knowledge base	Concept: Defines an abstract idea; embodies characteristics, examples, and nonexamples	Principle: A rule expressing a relationship between facts and concepts	Corresponding Theme: Interprets knowledge base, concepts, and principles into a unifying idea; can be applied to today's world
Examples of facts (items of information): 1. Southern states established their own union called the Confederacy. 2. Northern industry had only paid labor. 3. Abolitionists formed the Underground Railroad. Many women were abolitionists and demanded the right to vote. 4. Slave labor was cheap for the plantations. 5. Illiterate slaves were more passive about slavery than those who could read. **Examples of interpreted facts:** 1. Slavery created tension between slave and nonslave states before the Civil War. 2. Abolitionists believed slavery was immoral. 3. Female abolitionists related the issue of freed slaves to their own suffrage. 4. Slavery reaped large profits for plantation owners. 5. Freed slaves who could vote could influence elections. 6. Southern states seceded from the Union to maintain the lifestyle that slavery brought. 7. Literacy exposed slaves to concepts of freedom and motivated them to escape.	SLAVERY = the state of forced servitude *Characteristics* a. involuntary b. unremunerated c. usually cruel d. often permanent except by uprising by slaves or sympathetic others *Examples* a. Those conquered in war in ancient times, regardless of race, religion, or culture. b. Those kidnapped or sold and forced into servitude, both in the past and present. c. The biblical Hebrews in ancient Egypt. d. African Americans in the Confederate United States. e. Poor people in parts of the world today. *Nonexamples* a. "masters" or slave owners b. national leaders c. free citizens	1. The practice of slavery was as much a political issue as a moral and economic issue. 2. Abolitionists had various motives, at times drawn across gender lines. Motives affected strategies. 3. Reading enabled the transmission of ideas that countered the practice of slavery.	1. The Civil War: Moral or immoral? Just or hypocritical? 2. The abolitionist movement: Reaching beyond the Civil War. 3. Literacy as empowerment.

FIGURE 2.4 Differences Among Facts, Concepts, Principles, and Themes: History

Facts: A knowledge base	Concept: Defines an abstract idea; embodies characteristics, examples, and nonexamples	Principle: A rule expressing a relationship between facts and concepts	Corresponding Theme: Interprets facts base, concepts, and principles into a unifying idea; can be applied to today's world
Examples of facts (items of information): 1. Romeo and Juliet are children of feuding families. 2. They fall in love despite their families' antipathy. 3. The friar marries them in secret. 4. After their secret marriage, the friar tries to save Juliet from an arranged marriage by giving her a sleeping potion. 5. Romeo finds Juliet asleep and commits suicide because he thinks she is dead. 6. Juliet awakes, sees Romeo dead, and commits suicide. 7. Feuding families make peace after Romeo and Juliet commit suicide. **Examples of interpreted facts** 1. Romeo and Juliet transcend family hostilities by seeing each other as individuals rather than as objects of hatred. 2. The young lovers believe that their lives are unbearable without each other. 3. The friar's well-intentioned interference is risky.	FATE = unavoidable destiny *Characteristics* a. beyond one's control b. attributed to divine influence, karma, etc. c. unforeseen d. may possibly be tempered by free will *Examples* a. those who love us b. success c. personal abilities *(Possible) Nonexamples* a. commission of honest vs. dishonest deeds b. mental attitude; religious vs. atheistic beliefs c. taking responsibility for one's actions and thoughts	1. Romeo and Juliet were victims of fate. 2. Love transcends and changes circumstances. 3. Young people may lack perspective of a larger view. 4. The young can teach their elders.	1. Love: Illusion of forbidden fruit or expression of courage? 2. Death as elixir. 3. Fate: Inescapable destiny vs. rationalization.

FIGURE 2.5 Differences Among Facts, Concepts, Principles, and Themes: English/Language Arts

■ HANDS-ON PRACTICE ■

Directions: Decide on at least two concepts that you might teach in your subject for a given grade level. Then fill in Figure 2.6 according to the headings. Be sure to get feedback from at least one peer, preferably in a different subject area. Peers within your subject domain may share your assumptions, which results in blind spots or gaps. If possible, always ask your instructor for feedback as well. Keep in mind that your well-planned lesson will help you guide your students to arrive at their own facts, concept definitions, principles, and themes. The mantra is "don't tell."

Your Subject: _____		Grade Level: _____		
Concepts	**Pertinent Facts**	**Concept Definition**	**Two Principles**	**One Theme**
1.				
2.				

FIGURE 2.6 Using the Cognitive Ladder

ENDNOTES

1. *Meta-awareness* is the perception of the thing itself, for example, thinking about the act of thinking or learning about the process of learning. *Meta* in this usage means "beyond," so *meta-awareness* literally means "awareness beyond the thing itself." Module 15 on resocialization discusses meta-awareness in more depth.

SUGGESTED READINGS

Bloom, B., Engelhart, M., Furst, E., Hill, W., & Krathwohl, D. (1956). *Taxonomy of educational objectives: Cognitive domain.* New York: Longman.

Paul, R. W. (1995). *Critical thinking: How to prepare students for a rapidly changing world.* Santa Rosa, CA: Foundation for Critical Thinking.

Peters, T., Schubeck, K., & Hopkins, K. (1995, April). A thematic approach: Theory and practice at the Aleknagik School. *Phi Delta Kappan, 76*(8), 633–636.

Tomlinson, C. A. (1995). *How to differentiate instruction in mixed-ability classrooms.* Alexandria, VA: Association for Supervision and Curriculum Development.

PART 2:
Deductive and Inductive Frameworks

Overview

Goals

Focal Points and Discussions

Bloom's Taxonomy

Cognitive Frameworks

ROUNDUP

HANDS-ON PRACTICE

REFERENCES

SUGGESTED READING

■ OVERVIEW

Part 2 of this module introduces you to an abbreviated version of Bloom's Taxonomy in table form and provides examples of taxonomy application. You'll also learn about two patterns of sequencing facts, concepts, principles, and themes: deduction and induction.

■ GOALS

The gallery of facts, concepts, principles, and themes provides the substance of Bloom's Taxonomy, along with the deductive and inductive frameworks described in this section. We familiarize you with their use via the following:

- Acquainting you with the structures of Bloom's Taxonomy and deductive/inductive frameworks.

- Introducing the importance of these structures as the underpinnings of lesson (and unit) planning.

- Providing practice in organizing a cohesive lesson that's more than a collection of facts, concepts, principles, and themes. We'll show you how using Bloom's Taxonomy along with deduction or induction can guide your students' progress from one level of thinking to another.

Focal Point 1: **Bloom's Taxonomy**

How do you facilitate top-notch learning? Part of the answer lies in the cognitive hierarchy of Bloom's Taxonomy. "Cognitive" refers to thought or the process of thinking, and "hierarchy" refers to rank. So, simply put, Bloom's approach orders logical thinking from lower to higher levels.

Bloom's Taxonomy hooks up with facts, concepts, principles, and themes, and it can also be used as an underpinning for both the deductive and the inductive frameworks since the heart of Bloom's approach is to guide the thinking process.

Study the concise representation of Bloom's Taxonomy shown in Figure 2.7. You may be in for a surprise or two. We recommend that you make a copy of Bloom's Taxonomy for ongoing reference as you plan your lessons.

Discussion 1: **Bloom's Taxonomy**

Many preservice teachers are surprised to see that Application is a lower-level category. Another common surprise is that "interpretation" is placed under Comprehension as lower-level cognition as well. Yet, students often are not required to go beyond inter-

Questioning Category	Bloom's Category	Student Activity	Questions (Stem Words for Directions)
Lower Level	Knowledge	Memorizing facts, terms, definitions, concepts, principles	What . . . ?, list . . . , name . . . , define . . . , describe . . . .
Lower Level	Comprehension	Understanding the meaning of material beyond factual recall	Explain, interpret, summarize, give examples, predict, translate
Lower Level	Application	Selecting a concept or skill and using it to solve a problem	Compute, solve, apply, modify, construct
Higher Level	Analysis	Breaking down material into its parts and explaining the hierarchical relations	How does . . . apply? How does . . . work? How does . . . relate to . . . ? What can we infer from/ about . . . ? What distinctions can be made about . . . and . . . ?
Higher Level	Synthesis	Creating/producing something original after having broken down the material into its components	How do the data support . . . ? How would you design an experiment that investigates . . . ? What predictions can you make based on the data?
Higher Level	Evaluation	Making a judgment based on a preestablished set of criteria	What judgments can you make about . . . ? Compare and contrast . . . criteria for . . . .

FIGURE 2.7 Table of Bloom's Taxonomy

pretation and application in the classroom. Mostly, students are expected to do little more than memorize. Memorizing, whether that entails facts, concepts, or principles, is a lower-level cognitive activity—even when it's important to memorize. Working with concepts, however, could be either a lower-level or a higher-level cognitive category. For example, if a concept definition or a principle is given to the students and they are asked to interpret and support or apply the concept or principle, those skills are low level. However, if the students articulate the concept or principle themselves after analyzing and synthesizing information, then they are working on a high cognitive level. The same distinction applies to working with principles and themes, especially when you invite your students to synthesize facts and concepts into principles and themes and then to evaluate them.

Bloom's Taxonomy (Bloom, Engelhart, Furst, Hill, & Krathwohl, 1956) is an eye opener. Most of us don't pause to consider the varying levels of thinking and the different quality of thought among those levels. We just think and hear others think as a transparent experience. However, as a teacher who applies awareness of the thinking process, you will be able to develop lessons that draw your students in with confidence, asking them lower-level questions to steady their feet about the tough stuff, then guiding their thinking with questions that skillfully travel up the taxonomy. As a "Bloomer," you know that asking the high-level questions right off the bat intimidates and discourages learners before they've grasped the basics. Just wait. Posing the same challenging questions when your students are ready for them—now that's a charge.

Questions Are the Heart of It

We emphasize the importance of asking questions in a constructivist classroom because of the tendency for most teachers to talk too much (Cuban, 1996; Johnson & Johnson, 1989; Kyle, Schmitz, & Schmitz, 1996; Putnam, 1997; Slavin, 1995).

Why do questions facilitate learning? If you're weighing a response to that question, then you're experiencing the answer. Questions make us think. Telling takes away the thunder. The skill—the art—of questioning takes some time to cultivate. Bloom's Taxonomy and questioning are discussed in depth later in this module. Let's start by looking at some characteristics of the thinking process and specific ways to guide that process. The last column in Figure 2.8 gives examples of questions and directions that incorporate Bloom's Taxonomy for a lesson on wrestling that uses a demonstration video.

Focal Point 2: **Cognitive Frameworks**

Another process that you can rely on for top-notch teaching is the use of a cognitive framework. *A cognitive framework is an organized progression of facts and ideas that guide thinking to or from a concept or principle.* The *deductive framework* defines a concept or principle then develops it with facts. Simply put, deduction moves from the general to the specific. The *inductive framework* analyzes pertinent facts to generate a concept or principle. In other words, induction moves from specifics to a general idea. A deductive framework may contain inductive minisections, and vice versa.

The following two scenarios depict deductive and inductive frameworks. Try to identify which scenario demonstrates which framework.

Questioning Category	Bloom's Category	Student Activity	Questions (Stem Words for Directions)
Lower Level	Knowledge	Memorizing facts, terms, definitions, concepts, principles	1. *What* are some of the positions in the wrestling video you just saw? 2. *List* three ways in which the opponents tried to overwhelm each other. 3. *Name* one wrestling strategy mentioned in the video. Is it physical or psychological? 4. *Define* and *describe* that strategy.
Lower Level	Comprehension	Understanding the meaning of material beyond factual recall	1. *Explain* the difference between having a strategy and relying only on physical strength. 2. *Interpret* what is meant by "psychological strategy." 3. *Summarize* three major points of the wrestling video. 4. *Give* two *examples* of each of the three major points.
Lower Level	Application	Selecting a concept or skill and using it to solve a problem	*Construct* a wrestling strategy of two different holds and one psychological behavior for someone physically lighter than his or her opponent.

FIGURE 2.8a Bloom in Action: Lower Level/Wrestling

Scenario 1

In a hypnotic trance you are transported back to ancient Egypt. You see yourself among those workers chosen for the honor of building the Pharaoh's pyramid. You heave stones, large and variously sized, each one wrapped with rope. You and your fellow workers drag the stones from your shoulders as the ropes cut into your sun-baked skin. You give thanks that camels are used for the heaviest stones or you would

Questioning Category	Bloom's Category	Student Activity	Questions (Stem Words for Directions)
Higher Level	Analysis	Breaking down material into its parts and explaining the hierarchical relations	1. *How does* sheer strength *apply* in wresting? 2. *How does* psychology *work?* 3. *How does* psychology *relate to* physical strength? 4. *What distinctions can be made about* physical strength *and* psychology in the ring? 5. *What can we infer* about the characteristics of an unsuccessful wrestler?
Higher Level	Synthesis	Creating/producing something original after having broken down the material into its components	1. *How do the details* in the video *support* the importance of combining psychological and physical strategies? 2. If you were a wrestling coach, *how would you design a training program* for a novice like yourself? Justify your decisions.
Higher Level	Evaluation	Making a judgment based on a preestablished set of criteria	1. Based on the video, *what judgments can you make about* wrestling as a legitimate sport? 2. *Compare and contrast* training a novice wrestler and training a professional wrestler. 3. What are the *criteria for* the differences in training a novice vs. a professional wrestler?

FIGURE 2.8b Bloom in Action, Higher Level/Wrestling

surely die from exhaustion. You are too burdened with physical labor to notice the structure that the great stones are building as you work. Only when you briefly rest do you notice that many of the stones have been fitted to form the foundation. Those stones that have not been fashioned to fit well are put aside for other uses.

Weeks, months, years pass. One day when you take stock of the emerging structure, you notice that its distinctive shape is emerging. Broader at the base, it gradually narrows upward from four sides. Finally, it is completed. The pinnacle is the narrowest part, and it points to the sky.

You stand back, amazed that each stone, one at a time, has a place in the magnificent pyramid; just individual stones and yet, a single, three-dimensional shape stands before you. Even more—the great structure will house the Pharaoh's mummy along with charmed artifacts. "A stone at a time!" you keep saying to yourself. "Just one stone at a time!" And even though you are but one worker among many who have lived near the site for years, you feel proud that your individual efforts have helped make the sacred pyramid possible.

Scenario 2

You are brought back to modern times and (here we ask you to suspend disbelief) you possess a film of constructing the pyramid. Curious, you play the film backwards. You discover it's more than fun. The reversed images unravel the completed pyramid from the pinnacle right down to the base. You watch the individual stones being "removed" in reverse motion, one by one. Then you replay the film from start to finish. You watch in awe as the first stone to the last rise up to shape the pyramid anew, with its many chambers and antechambers, and you fully grasp the complexity of building the pyramid as a feat of intellect as much as muscle.

Discussion 2 **Cognitive Frameworks**

Induction

Let's apply the concept of cognitive frameworks to the pyramid scenario. Perhaps you realized that Scenario 1 represents an inductive approach: one stone at a time became part of the larger structure, the pyramid. At first the shape could not be discerned, but as each stone was fitted against the other stones, the pyramid eventually took on its distinctive form.

In a similar way, an inductive framework in a lesson or project uses facts that are related or unrelated to a concept or principle, similar to the individual stones that fit or do not fit well. Your students examine these facts until they can define the concept or principle and grasp, with deepened understanding, the significance of the individual elements that inform the definition, similar to perceiving how individual stones shaped the form of the completed pyramid.

Deduction

Conversely, Scenario 2 illustrates a deductive approach. It begins with the completed pyramid, breaks down the structure into its components, and then returns to the broad picture again.

Whether using an inductive or a deductive approach, facts, concepts, and principles are integrated into a larger theme. A possible theme based on the pyramid scenarios could be that human beings may be dwarfed by their own accomplishments. Depending on how it is planned, any lesson or project will take on an inductive or a deductive organization, or a mixture of the two. Either framework may incorporate traditional materials, stand-alone software, or the Internet.

Example of a Deductive Framework

Deduction is a thinking process in which you as the teacher define a concept or principle, then your students explore pertinent facts that develop the definition. Students obtain examples and facts from instructional materials and their life experiences. Take a look at Figure 2.9 for an example.

Example of an Inductive Framework

Induction is a thinking process by which your students consider various facts and then define a corresponding concept or principle. With induction, it's important to re-

Concept or Principle First	Supporting Facts (Examples and Nonexamples)	Possible Theme(s)
Provide a definition of the concept *democracy*. This is a working, although accurate, definition and need not be absolute. The concept can be increasingly developed, its complexity built in a sequence of lessons for a unit.	In various source materials (textual, visual, auditory, electronic, etc.), students consider examples of democracies, such as the United States, England, and Israel, in a 3-lesson sequence. They also examine nonexamples such as mainland China, Indonesia, and Nepal. Students identify the political characteristics in each government, comparing and contrasting similarities and differences among examples and nonexamples and decide which countries are examples of the definition.	One possible theme could be the contradictions of a democracy's theory and practice. For example, the ideology of communism as the perfect society or democracy vs. the historical implementation; the impact of internal and external influences on democracies; variations in the nature of democracies; comparing the context and impact of a benign despot to those of the president of a given democracy.

FIGURE 2.9 Deductive Approach

member that the students, not you, articulate the definition of the concept or principle in a complete statement. This often is done as a collective effort, with your facilitation. Figure 2.10 gives an example.

Application

Most thinking processes or problem solving is either deductive or inductive or blends of both. As you can see from Figures 2.9 and 2.10, the shapes of deduction and induction are mirror reflections of each other.

However, avoid the mistake of thinking that deduction and induction are nothing more than inversions of each other. For the most part, deduction operates on a lower cognitive level than induction. The reason is that deduction involves the lower cognitive skills of comprehending the definition and applying that comprehension to a knowledge base of examples and nonexamples. A creative teacher can incorporate some higher cognition, such as analyzing the relationship of the examples to each other and to the definition and guiding students to synthesize the facts and examples into a unifying theme. But, overall, deduction provides learners with the toughest part, namely, the definition of a concept or principle.

On the other hand, induction operates on a high cognitive level by asking your students at the outset to analyze the information and decide which items in that knowledge base interrelate. In other words, your students must infer common and disparate characteristics among the facts in the knowledge base. Then your students attempt to synthesize and even evaluate the knowledge base to articulate the definition of the concept or principle.

Supporting Facts	Concept or Principle Last	Possible Theme(s)
In various source materials (textual, visual, auditory, electronic, etc.), students consider examples of democracies, such as the United States, England, and Israel, in a 3-lesson sequence. They also examine nonexamples such as mainland China, Indonesia, and Nepal. Students identify the political characteristics in each government, comparing and contrasting similarities and differences among examples and nonexamples.	Students (not you) articulate a definition of the concept *democracy*. They define the concept based on their analysis (comparing and contrasting) of examples and nonexamples. This is a working, although accurate, definition and need not be absolute. The concept can be increasingly developed, its complexity built in a sequence of lessons for a unit.	One possible theme could be the contradictions of a democracy's theory and practice. For example, the ideology of communism as the perfect society or democracy vs. the historical implementation; the impact of internal and external influences on democracies; variations in the nature of democracies; comparing the context and impact of a benign despot to those of the president of a given democracy.

FIGURE 2.10 Inductive Approach

Deduction versus Induction?

Usually, fledgling teachers prefer to teach complex concepts or principles deductively (the teacher provides the definition) and more accessible concepts inductively (students arrive at the definition themselves). We encourage you to develop your inductive teaching skills by using the methods in Module 8 so that you are comfortable facilitating inductive thinking on high cognitive levels whoever your students may be. Keep in mind that a lesson may combine mini-deductive and mini-inductive segments.

Units

The deductive or inductive cognitive framework provides the overall structure for a sequence of lessons that develop a unit (discussed in Module 13) as well as an individual lesson or project.

Why Not Just Plan Spontaneously?

Deduction and especially induction are two ways to guide critical thinking. An organized process of thinking contrasts with repetition of a list of facts without a unifying concept, principle, or theme that helps your students interpret and analyze the significance of information. A wide assortment of instructional techniques—procedures and practices that carry out methods—are your tools for planning deductively or inductively or for combining both cognitive strategies. Some examples of instructional techniques are questioning, role-playing, using activity sheets, personalizing, brainstorming, creating concept maps, and peer interaction.

If you consciously plan deductively, inductively, or with mini-deductive and mini-inductive combinations, you will design a stronger lesson than the teacher who plans mechanically or haphazardly; such a teacher does not reflect on a given thought process and the corresponding elements that could challenge learners to think critically. A conscious approach strengthens the nature and sequence of your questions and other techniques.

Both cognitive strategies are important in reaching students with a variety of learning styles and in developing stronger teaching styles. Students who have learned to rely on the teacher cramming their minds with facts, concepts, and principles need to develop confidence in thinking for themselves. Induction encourages this higher-level learning. Some students are too insecure to attempt induction at first; these learners benefit from a deductive approach at the outset, while still being encouraged to think for themselves as they analyze the appropriateness of examples or synthesize information into a theme. In time, these same students will be comfortable with the challenge of induction.

As for you, the new teacher struggling just to plan a well-structured and cohesive lesson, you run the risk of getting stuck in the familiar, talking-at-them mode. Challenging yourself to master a facilitative role and encouraging your students to take an active learner role will expand your pedagogical repertoire beyond your wildest dreams as you keep growing as a constructivist teacher.

By all means, start out mostly using the student-centered deductive lessons that we've just described, and then broaden into applying the more challenging inductive framework. As you expand your teaching style to meet your students' various learning styles, you yourself are learning—learning how to probe ideas in more depth and how to teach in new ways.

For a graphic representation of deductive and inductive strategies, see Figure 2.11. As you study the graphic, try to imagine blending deduction and induction in the same lesson or project. These strategies are presented separately here so that you can get a handle on their distinctive "shapes" as clear schemata.

Tying Things Together

Figures 2.12 and 2.13 integrate Bloom's Taxonomy, the cognitive ladder, and deduction and induction.

■ ROUNDUP ■

Facts, concepts, principles, and themes are the ingredients of effective planning and the essence of subject matter within each academic discipline. They need to be sequenced in a way that invites your students to comprehend and think independently. That's when you pull a cognitive framework out of your hat.

A cognitive framework helps direct thinking. Bloom's Taxonomy is an indispensable tool to help you fashion questions, directions, and activities in keeping with the cognitive framework you choose.

A Cognitive Framework Directs Thinking

Deduction = development of a concept or principle with facts.
General to specific.

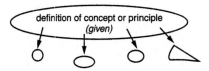

Induction = use of facts to arrive at a concept or principle.
Specific to general.

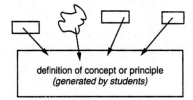

©2001 Ina Claire Gabler

FIGURE 2.11 Cognitive Frameworks: Deduction and Induction

Bloom's Taxonomy	Cognitive Ladder	Deduction
Questions to establish knowledge	Assemble facts	Provide the foundation for the defined concept/principle
Questions to build comprehension	Work toward supporting a concept/principle	Develop the defined concept/principle
Questions for application	Solidify and use the concept/principle	Consider significance of the concept/principle
Questions for analysis	Break down the concept/principle into its aspects	Establish distinctions of the concept/principle
Questions for synthesis	Combine aspects of the concept/principle	Arrive at new insight(s) about the concept/principle
Questions for evaluation	Facilitate a judgment about the concept/principle	Compare and contrast criteria of the concept/principle

FIGURE 2.12 Bloom's Taxonomy, the Cognitive Ladder, and Deduction

You and your students benefit from working within a deductive, inductive, or combination thought process. Deciding on a cognitive framework makes planning a lesson both easier and more rigorous than does planning automatically. It also helps your students participate if they know they're working from a definition of an idea and developing it, or if they're trying to arrive at a definition from various facts culled from instructional materials. In this carefully sequenced approach, your students will be able to grasp and arrive at themes that they might otherwise find threatening, grounded on facts and moving skyward. For these reasons, facts, concepts, principles, and themes together with cognitive frameworks provide the background for a dynamic lesson or project.

Most preservice teachers insist that their subject is not as well disposed to induction or constructivist methods as other subjects. The novice math teacher is convinced that her objectives just can't be carried out by induction or most constructivist methods, but she can see how English could be taught that way. Then, of course, the English teacher asserts that math, not language arts, lends itself to induction or constructivist methods. The truth is, induction and constructivist methods are relevant to every subject, from physical education to science, from math to art. We have been so saturated by the talking-at-students model of teaching that at first we can't envision teaching our own subject differently. It takes imagination to shift your mind-set. You may also need to resocialize yourself and your students to an active student learning model (see Module 15).

■ HANDS-ON PRACTICE ■

Now try your hand at planning within deductive and inductive frameworks in your subject. Refer to your concepts in Figure 2.6 in the "Hands-On Practice" section of Part 1 of this module. Develop one or both of those concepts using Bloom's Taxonomy.

Bloom's Taxonomy	Cognitive Ladder	Induction
Questions to establish knowledge	Assemble facts	Provide factual clues for the definition of the concept/principle
Questions to build comprehension	Work toward building a concept/principle	Establish categories for the clues
Questions for application	Solidify and use the factual clues	Consider significance of the factual clues
Questions for analysis	Compare and contrast the factual clues	Establish distinctions among the clues
Questions for synthesis	Combine aspects of the factual clues	Define the concept/principle
Questions for evaluation	Facilitate a judgment about the concept/principle	Compare and contrast criteria of the concept/principle

FIGURE 2.13 Bloom's Taxonomy, the Cognitive Ladder, and Induction

Then organize one concept definition and the corresponding facts within a deductive framework and the other within an inductive framework. Use the prompts below to guide you.

With this Hands-On Practice you are accomplishing four important things:

- Integrating the focal points in this module with your own original input. If you get stuck, refer back to this module before you move on.
- Initiating thoughtful use of Bloom's Taxonomy.
- Preparing yourself to plan more fully developed deductive and inductive concept lessons later on.
- Getting a head start on planning lessons in general.

Self-Instruct Planner #1: Deductive Framework

Subject _____ Grade level _____

(Work on a separate piece of paper.)

REMINDER: Pause now to look over Figure 2.6 in Part 1 of this module to help you formulate questions (or directions) that you could pose in this practice.

Deductive Framework

1. Decide on a concept or principle (from Figure 2.6).
2. Consider possible instructional materials.
3. Write a working concept or principle definition.
4. Write four to five possible facts manifesting this concept or principle that students can derive from the instructional materials and their life experience.

5. If possible, give two or three facts that contradict the concept definition derived from instructional materials and life experience.
6. Refer to Bloom's Taxonomy in Figure 2.7. Compose six to eight questions moving up the taxonomy to guide your students in relating the facts to the concept definition.
7. Anticipate one possible theme that your students could generate: design questions based on Bloom's Taxonomy to facilitate student formulation of a unifying theme.

Self-Instruct Planner #2: Inductive Framework

Subject _____ Grade level _____

(Work on a separate piece of paper.)

Inductive Framework

1. Write a concept or principle different from that in the deductive framework. (Refer to Figure 2.6 in Part 1.)
2. List possible instructional materials.
3. Write four to five possible facts manifesting this concept or principle that students can derive from the instructional materials and their life experience.
4. If possible, give two or three facts that contradict the concept definition or principle derived from instructional materials and life experience.
5. Refer to Bloom's Taxonomy in Figure 2.7. Compose eight to ten questions moving up the taxonomy. Use the questions to guide your students in first understanding and then analyzing and synthesizing the facts to the concept definition or principle.
6. Write a possible working concept or principle definition that your students could generate.
7. Again referring to Bloom's Taxonomy, compose as many questions as you think necessary to facilitate your students' working concept or principle definition based on the facts.
8. Write one possible theme that your students could generate.
9. Compose three to five questions based on Bloom's taxonomy to facilitate student formulation of a unifying theme.

REFERENCES

Bloom, B., Engelhart, M., Furst, E., Hill, W., & Krathwohl, D. (1956). *Taxonomy of educational objectives: Cognitive domain.* New York: Longman.

Cuban, L. (1996, October 9). Techno-Reformers and classroom teachers. *Education Week on the Web.* Available at: http://www.edweek.org/ew/vol 16/06Cuban.h16.

Johnson, D., & Johnson, R. (1989). *Cooperation and competition: Theory and research.* Edina, MN: Interaction Books.

Kyle, W. Jr., Schmitz, C., & Schmitz, E. (1996). Possible lives or shattered dreams? *Electronic Journal of Science Education.* Available at: http://unr.edu/homepage/jcannon/ejse/kyle.html.

Putnam, J. (1997). *Cooperative learning in diverse classrooms.* Upper Saddle River, NJ: Merrill.

Slavin, R. (1995). *Cooperative learning: Theory, research, and practice.* Boston: Allyn & Bacon.

SUGGESTED READING

Vygotsky, L. (1994). *Thought and language.* Cambridge, MA: The MIT Press.

B

Module Three:

Planning Professional Lessons

PART 1:
Core Components

■ OVERVIEW

You're worried. At first there had been those great discussions in methods class about student-centered learning. But that was before the moment of truth. Now you have to plan your own lesson. Perhaps you're even thinking of a long-term project with various segments that might challenge and motivate students. You've got the ideas, but you don't know where to begin.

This module is devoted to that "not knowing." Planning lessons, at least effective ones that charge your students, is not as easy as merely knowing your stuff and talking about it. Chances are, if that's what you're up to, you may be the only one in the room who's interested. But top-notch teaching isn't a mystery, either. Think of it as a dance routine that someone else just sails through. It's a surprise when you try it yourself for the first time and flop and realize that there's more than meets the eye. But you also realize that it's learnable. Yes. Every dancer needs to learn the steps and practice to raise the craft of dancing to an art.

■ GOALS

Part 1 of this module provides you with a concrete procedure for lesson planning. Here's what's in store:

- A template of the suggested Core Components for professional lesson planning.
- A description of each of the seven Core Components: Rationale, Performance Objective, Materials, Hook, Aim, Development, and Culmination.
- A discussion of the importance of assessment.
- A distinction between form and function regarding the Core Components in a traditional versus a constructivist approach.
- The use of various analogies to accommodate different frames of reference.

■ DISCUSSION

The Core Components of planning that we describe in this module are the underpinnings of a constructivist approach to teaching, or what we call invisible teaching. *Invisible teaching* refers to a facilitative approach in which you guide or enable students to learn. As a facilitator, you'll reflectively plan questions and directions, which we called prompts, that guide the learning process via the cognitive ladder and Bloom's

Taxonomy. You'll also thoughtfully gather various instructional materials that your students can refer to in addition to a textbook. Finally, you'll be crucial as a live resource in the classroom. In this way, you become invisible as the teacher because your students may not be consciously aware of the role you're playing behind the scenes as they learn.

As a constructivist teacher, you learn along with your students, the quintessential mentor. Your students, in turn, learn how to learn. Thomas J. Carruthers captured a constructivist teacher at his best when he said, "A good teacher has been defined as one who makes himself progressively unnecessary" (Atwell, 1987, p. 88). As your students come closer and closer to this ideal, you will never be idle. In pursuit of independent learning on new levels, your students will turn to you as their mentor, the catalyst who gets them thinking about the next step, where and how to fill in the gaps, while you increasingly learn along with them. We have had such experiences with our own secondary students from all backgrounds, suburban and urban.

With didacticism, the teacher is the star. With constructivism, your students are the stars. The constructivist teacher shines too, but you can't tell unless you know what to look for.

A Scenario

You grab a hammer and some wood. You're about to build a chair. You've never done this before. But that doesn't stop you. After all, you've sat in hundreds, thousands, maybe can't-count zillions of chairs since before you could walk. You know all about chairs. They're meant to hold you up while you sit down. A seat, a few legs, a bit of glue. No problem. You borrowed an electric saw to cut the lumber. You bought ready-made legs. You'll have it built by lunchtime. It's a birthday gift for your sweetheart.

Confident, supremely optimistic, with visions of a smile and bright eyes of appreciation on the special day—not to mention admiration for your handiwork—you hum your favorite tune and get to work.

Trouble is, as you hammer, saw, and screw in screws, blisters blooming in your palms, it's not as easy as you thought. First of all, you're beginning to realize that your assortment of tools may be incomplete. And depending on the type of chair you want to build, you'll need different materials as well. Do you want to build a simple desk chair? An upholstered chair? With or without arms? Glue doesn't seem to be enough. But do you need nuts and bolts? Wood dowels or metal joints? And when? Should you dig up your drill?

One thing you do know: it looks lousy. A piece of crooked junk ready for the trash. Well, at least it holds you up—if you hold on tight. You suspect that there may be more to this than you know what to look for. You consider two options:

- Buying a chair that works, or, in other words, giving up and leaving it to the skilled professionals.
- Hanging in there because you've always wanted to be a carpenter. A fantastic carpenter who can transform lumber into serviceable works of art. The blisters alert you to the fact that you may need a mentor, someone who has figured out what you're still blind to.

A chair, even the simplest style, will never look the same to you again. It's the same with planning a lesson. As fledgling teachers, most of us think we know what teaching is all about. After all, we've witnessed teachers for 16 years, more or less, and from this prolonged exposure have evolved a schema of what teachers do. Lortie (1975) refers timelessly to this incidental learning as *apprenticeship of observation.*

So it's like building that chair. You think that because you have had so many teachers, you know what teaching is all about. But even the simplest effective lesson requires enormous thought and skill. You'll need an assortment of techniques, tools, materials, and methods to plan wisely for your students, whose learning styles are as varied as their hair styles. It all begins with Core Components.

Focal Point 1: Lesson Structure with Core Components

We begin with two bird's-eye views of a lesson plan structured with our recommended Core Components. The first, Figure 3.1, is a broad schema that shows the Core Com-

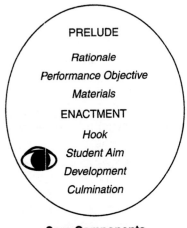

Core Components

Rationale = focused instructional intention that provides cohesion

Performance Objective = activity that generates a physical or digital product in Development (could take twenty-five minutes or two weeks)

Materials = sources of information

Hook = attention grabber; relates to Rationale

Aim = captures the Rationale in catchy language

Development = unfolds the method and carries out the Performance Objective (could take thirty minutes or days/weeks for a project)

Culmination = brings together key concepts with new insights (could take several minutes or two days of project presentations)

©2001 Ina Claire Gabler

FIGURE 3.1 Core Components for Lessons or Projects: Bird's-Eye View of Lesson Planning.

ponents contained in two of three segments of a lesson plan: the Prelude and the Enactment. The Prelude describes the foundation of the lesson, the information for your own reference as a teacher. The Enactment describes the process that engages the students in the learning process.

Now, Figure 3.2 fills in the parts of each Core Component in an outline that serves as a planning template. The third part of a lesson plan, Assessment and Evaluation Plan, is briefly described in this module and is developed in depth in Module 14.

Core Components do not need to be sequenced in a set fashion, although for clarity we introduce them in a linear sequence. Core Components work whether you teach a fifty-minute lesson or a month-long project or whether you teach within a block program.

Discussion 1: Lesson Structure with Core Components

We recommend that for now you approach lesson planning in these four steps:

1. Decide on a focused topic.
2. Outline your complete lesson using the template in Figure 3.2.
3. Fill in the details sequentially from the Rationale to the Culmination.
4. Adjust the content of the Core Components for cohesion and logic as necessary.

With experience, once you outline the complete template you can develop the details in any sequence—wherever the inspiration hits. In time, you might want to experiment with combining components or varying their sequence according to a given lesson or project. In this way, you can eventually develop your own repertoire of lesson formats.

Always check the final product in linear sequence for cohesion and logic so that your department chair, supervisor, or mentor can envision the lesson and even provide helpful feedback. Finally, look over the lesson or project as you plan, fine-tuning the Core Components in conjunction with one another, like tuning a guitar. You may find it helpful to make a copy of Figure 3.2 for reference as you study each Core Component in depth.

Focal Point 2: Rationale

The *Rationale expresses your instructional intention.* In this way, the Rationale is the rudder. We recommend three features to help you focus and plan a strong, meaningful lesson:

1. *What* are you teaching?
2. *Why* are you teaching this?
3. *Justification.*

Discussion 2: Rationale

The *What?* should be a specific and clear topic for you as well as your students. Then ask yourself: Why is this lesson valuable to my students? Having fun or even being interesting is an insufficient reason. Yes, the effort should be engaging, stimulating, chal-

PRELUDE
(for teacher's reference)

1. Rationale
   a. *What* are you teaching?
   b. *Why* are you teaching this?
   c. *Justification* in terms of INTASC Standards (see Appendix)
2. Performance Objective
   a. *Preparation* for creating a product
   b. *Product* that demonstrates learning
   c. *Criteria* that ensure acceptable achievement
3. Materials
   a. *Textbook*
   b. *Primary sources*
   c. *Audio/visual*
   d. *Information technology*
   e. *Etc.*

ENGAGEMENT
(student involvement)

4. Student Aim
   Captures the Rationale in colloquial language
5. Hook
   a. *Grabs interest*
   b. *Relates to Rationale*
6. Development
   a. *Unfolds a given method with the Performance Objective*
   b. *Contains prompts*
7. Culmination
   a. *Wrap-Up summarizes the specific key points*
   b. *Leap elicits a related new concept or application of the topic.*

ASSESSMENT AND EVALUATION PLAN
(what has been learned and how well)

Performance-based examination of
- *Student projects*
- *Presentations*
- *Journals*
- *Portfolios*
- *Group/lab activities*
- *Role-playing*
- *Etc.*

FIGURE 3.2 Template for Lesson Planning with Core Components

lenging, and even enjoyable, all integral to instructional soundness. But you are not in the entertainment business. Also, we suggest that, in the *Why?* segment, you include some of Bloom's cognitive skills (comprehension, application, analysis, synthesis, etc.) that you want your students to cultivate during the lesson. Art and PE teachers should jot down the perceptual and motor skills, respectively.

Part	Purpose
1. *What* are you teaching?	1. Clarifies your instructional intentions
2. *Why* are you teaching this?	2. Establishes the worth of the topic
3. *Justification*	3. Confirms instructional value/INTASC Standards

FIGURE 3.3 The Rationale

As for the *justification,* reflect on the Interstate New Teacher Assessment and Support Consortium (INTASC) Standards embodied in your lesson (see the Appendix at the end of the book). The INTASC Standards for teacher training promote a constructivist-style, student-centered, facilitative approach to teaching and learning; they have also influenced specific subject standards. Checking that your lesson embodies these standards is a way to ensure a constructivist plan.

Examples of Rationale

Below are some examples of the Rationale in various subjects. We provide nonexamples contrasted to examples as a way to clarify the importance of a specific focus. Figure 3.3 encapsulates the parts of the Rationale for quick reference.

Jot down the various wordings that introduce the *What?* and *Why?* segments in the following examples. You'll be asked to use these various wordings in the "Hands-On-Practice" section at the end of Part 1.

EXAMPLE #1A/HISTORY (AMERICAN REVOLUTION)

What?: Students will enlarge their scope of causes of the American Revolution to include economic motives.

Why?: Analyzing and evaluating economic influences provides students a more in-depth understanding of the American Revolution.

Justification: INTASC Standards 2, 5, 6, and 8.

ANALYSIS OF EXAMPLE #1A

The *What?* expresses a specific focus, namely, the inclusion of economic conditions as another cause of the American Revolution.

The *Why?* is also specific and indicates the cognitive or thinking skills.

The *Justification* cites relevant INTASC Standards.

NONEXAMPLE #1B/HISTORY

What?: Students will learn more about the American Revolution.

Why?: Better student understanding of the American Revolution.

Justification: Meets four INTASC Standards.

ANALYSIS OF NONEXAMPLE #1B

The *What?* is too vague. What specifically does "learn more" refer to?

The *Why?* is nonspecific and does not indicate the nature of the topic's value.

The *Justification* must specify which standards.

EXAMPLE #2A/ENGLISH (CHARACTERIZATION)

What?: To explore the behavior of Ichabod Crane and Brom Bones in Washington Irving's *The Legend of Sleepy Hollow.*

Why?: Students will interpret facts about Ichabod Crane to analyze Brom Bones's motives. This lesson introduces the concept of characterization.

Justification: INTASC Standards 2, 3, 5, and 8.

ANALYSIS OF EXAMPLE #2A

The *What?* is well focused.

The *Why?* states the specific values of the lesson—both for content and thinking skills.

Justification: The Rationale makes clear how the INTASC Standards are satisfied.

NONEXAMPLE #2B/ENGLISH

What?: To learn about the characters Ichabod Crane and Brom Bones in *The Legend of Sleepy Hollow* by Washington Irving.

Why?: Student understanding of Bones and Crane.

Justification: Critical-thinking skills.

ANALYSIS OF NONEXAMPLE #2B

Although the *What?* specifies the characters and the work, the instructional intention is not focused. What will the students "learn about" the two characters?

The *Why?* is also vague. What kind of "understanding" does the teacher hope to establish?

Justification: This lacks specific INTASC Standards. In addition, the Rationale is too vague to suggest specific standards.

EXAMPLE #3A/SPANISH (PREPOSITIONS)

What?: Students will learn the pronunciation and meaning of five important Spanish prepositions.

Why?: Prepositions are crucial for conversation and reading. Learners will be encouraged to infer and apply the meanings on their own.

Justification: INTASC Standards 2, 3, and 5.

ANALYSIS OF EXAMPLE #3A

The *What?* is well focused.

The *Why?* cites the practical use as well as thinking skills and also indicates active student learning.

The *Justification* cites specific standards appropriate to the lesson.

NONEXAMPLE #3B/SPANISH

What? and *Why?:* To teach about prepositions so that students can use them effectively.

ANALYSIS OF NONEXAMPLE #3B

The *What?* and *Why?* are too vague.

There is no *Justification.*

Focal Point 3: **Performance Objective**

As the name suggests, the *Performance Objective results in a physical, digital, or enacted product that your students create.* With this in mind, take a look at three features of a Performance Objective:

1. *Preparation:* Develops the knowledge and thinking skills necessary to create the product.
2. *Product:* Demonstrates your students' learning with a concrete outcome.
3. *Criteria:* Include a specific, minimum number of items correctly carried out for satisfactory achievement of the product. In PE, art, or other subjects, criteria may cite a specific time duration for a given task.

Discussion 3: **Performance Objective**

The Performance Objective directly relates to the Rationale. The Performance Objective is described in the Prelude of the lesson to help you focus as you plan.

However, the Performance Objective is carried out in the Development section. Accordingly, the preparation helps your students develop the knowledge and skills they need to generate the product. Think of the preparation as the foundation for creating the product. For a fifty-minute lesson, the preparation may take fifteen to twenty minutes. For a project, the preparation may take eight to ten days of research and discussion.

The product can be anything concrete: a list, a magazine, a computer graphic, an original concept map, a series of questions, an original Website, a debate, an enactment of a scene from a play, a video minidocumentary, etc. The product may take twenty-five minutes or three weeks to complete.

In the process of creating a product, your students keep learning, hands-on. In addition, you'll also learn as you facilitate and discover new ideas from your students.

Doing versus Talking

The activity product is usually not an oral activity such as a student–student discussion or a teacher–student dialogue. There are meaningful exceptions to this, for example, acting scenes from a play or formal debating. The key is to ensure that every student participates. However, in a typical lesson most students will not have the opportunity to orally demonstrate what they've learned because of time constraints (and sometimes shyness). You need evidence that everyone is ready to move on, and you must be able to spot the students who need extra help. For the most part, oral dialogue is part of the preparation. It's a concrete product, however, that demonstrates the quality—and quantity—of learning for an entire class. In addition, the products demonstrate what the students have and have not yet grasped related to the Rationale.

Finally, the criteria cite a minimum number of tasks that must be successfully completed. Criteria may also define a length of time for a task, for example, at least twenty minutes of dribbling a basketball across the court. In this way, criteria establish standards.

Performance Objective versus Tests

The Performance Objective is not a test, quiz, and so on. These are assessment instruments that help to judge the quality of learning. By contrast, a Performance Objective is usually an integral part of the daily learning experience. We say "usually" because sometimes, for example, a two-day lesson devotes the first day to developing concepts and principles; in this case, the Performance Objective may constitute the entire second day.

A Scenario

You're a master pizza chef. Making pizza is the obsession of your life, and you want to pass on your expertise and appreciation of this fantastic food. Disciples surround you in the kitchen. A natural teacher, you use the Socratic method of questioning to open your disciples' eyes to the art of baking incomparable pizza. You direct their attention by questioning their observations as you make the dough and shape it, as you assemble grated cheeses, peppers, mushrooms, sausages, and onions along with anchovies, olives, and other assorted toppings. You probe your disciples for the most delicious blends of various combinations; you ask them to justify their conjectures as they strive to orally describe exquisite pizzas for individual tastes. Yes, you have done a beautiful job of facilitating their creative thinking. Your students even make your masterly mouth water at the mere sound of their original concoctions because you have the powers to envision their gustatory glory.

But until each disciple has baked a pizza of her own, neither you nor the would-be master can be certain that meaningful learning has taken place. Indeed, the first efforts may show promise but may not yet flood the palate. For this to happen, your disciples must practice, guided by recipes, and be encouraged to explore original versions based on what they've learned. Then and only then will each disciple succeed in creating pizza with pizzaz.

Like baking a pizza, a Performance Objective combines the ingredients of a lesson into a product that affirms learning. In this way, like the pizza, the Performance Objective is greater than the sum of its parts.

Part	Purpose
1. *Preparation* develops the ideas that prepare students for the product or activity.	1. Forces you to plan thoughtfully and to relate to the Rationale; enables your students to generate a physical product that demonstrates learning.
2. *Product* results in a physical outcome for a lesson or project. The product must directly relate to the Rationale.	2. Demonstrates to you and the student that he or she has grasped the concept(s). The constructivist product *demands critical thinking and/or problem solving rather than rote repetition.*
3. *Criteria* include a specific, minimum number of items correctly carried out or a specified time duration, especially in PE and art, for satisfactory performance of the product.	3. Criteria establish standards.

FIGURE 3.4 The Performance Objective

Examples of Performance Objectives

Before we give the examples in three subjects, take a look at Figure 3.4 for a summary of the Performance Objective that you can match to each example.

The following examples are based on lessons by preservice teachers in our constructivist training labs or in the field as student teachers. Consider these examples in terms of Figure 3.4 and Bloom's Taxonomy. They include the Rationale so you can see how the Performance Objective relates to it.

We suggest that you jot down the introductory phrases to the three parts of the Performance Objectives. You will need this for the Hands-On Practice to come.

EXAMPLE #1/SCIENCE[1] (WATER PURIFICATION)

RATIONALE

What? and *Why?:* Students will name and comprehend the three steps of water purification and why it is important. Students will analyze facts and then apply that knowledge to categorizing bottles of water at different stages of purification.

Justification: INTASC Standards 1, 2, 3, 5, 6, 8, and 9.

PERFORMANCE OBJECTIVE (RELATED TO THE RATIONALE)

Preparation: Students will discuss the appearance of different bottles of water. Each student will write a description of the water sample, using pH and visual qualities.

A discussion will compare and contrast the various bottles with factual information about water purity and pollution.

Product: In groups of three, learners will be able to compose an overhead transparency that represents the process of water purification either graphically or in writing.

Criteria: Students will be able to establish the three steps of water purification. Students will be able to identify at least two differences and two similarities among all the samples.

EXAMPLE #2/ART² (DRAWING)

RATIONALE

What?: To develop an understanding of line, shape, and proportion.

Why?: Learners will heighten their perceptual awareness of the elements of forms and space.

Justification: INTASC Standards 1, 2, 3, 5, and 6.

PERFORMANCE OBJECTIVE (RELATED TO THE RATIONALE)

Preparation: Students will discuss the various types of lines, shapes, and proportions in the upside down line drawing of Mount Rushmore projected by the overhead projector. The subject matter is not identifiable upside down.

Product: Students will be able to draw the upside down image, imitating the characteristics of line, shape, and proportion.

Criteria: Learners will draw for at least ten minutes or until they complete the task. Then they will turn their work right side up and see if they can identify the subject matter without being told. Students will discuss and analyze at least three relationships of lines, shapes, and proportions and their importance in drawing Mount Rushmore or anything else we see.

EXAMPLE #3/PHYSICAL EDUCATION (THROWING A FOOTBALL)

RATIONALE

What?: To learn how to successfully throw a football within twenty-five feet.

Why?: To develop arm-eye coordination, balance, and timing. To coordinate movements between arms, feet, and the intended distance.

Justification: INTASC Standards 2, 3, 5, and 6.

PERFORMANCE OBJECTIVE (RELATED TO THE RATIONALE)

Preparation: Demonstration of the proper throwing form. Students are asked to identify what they notice first, second, third, and so on. Open the discussion by analyzing the characteristics of each movement.

Product: Students will be able to successfully throw a football according to the Rationale by the end of class.

Criteria: At least twenty minutes of practice with a partner. Each student will be able to throw a football and succeed with all characteristics of a successful throw. Each student must analyze the throw for each characteristic on a chart.

Focal Point 4: Materials

Beware of just air! Materials matter. Your students cannot pluck sufficient information out of the air or from their life experiences to sustain a rigorous dialogue and meaningful Performance Objective. If they already knew what you wanted them to learn, they wouldn't need you as their teacher. This may seem obvious, but many preservice teachers plan lessons without ample instructional materials and pose questions that assume significant knowledge of their topic while their students often have a naive, inappropriate, or incomplete schema. As a result, the lesson hits a dead end before it really begins. You know more about your subject than you realize. The basics to you are news to your students.

Discussion 4: Materials

Instructional materials introduce your students to information from which they obtain facts, concepts, and so on. Then, as your students go beyond the information—when they analyze, synthesize, and evaluate the substance—they can point to the materials to support their assertions. In this constructivist approach, *materials provide both the foundation for critical thinking and the validation of those insights.*

The textbook has long been the kingpin of instructional materials. We encourage you to supplement this mainstay with a variety of other materials: primary sources, your own original materials tailored to a lesson or project, videotapes and audiotapes, graphics of all kinds, objects, the Internet, stand-alone software, and more. Provide your learners with—and encourage them to contribute to—a cornucopia of resources.

Use Bloom's Taxonomy as your right hand. With questions, directions, and activities, you can guide your students through the abundance of information so that they learn to identify the facts, concepts, principles, and themes that serve as the springboard for their own insights. That way, your students and you learn together.

Selecting appropriate materials is an important skill that takes experience and imagination. There are materials that promote rigor, materials that add color, and materials that serve as practical tools, for example, the overhead projector. (Citing the latter reminds you to order them from the supply room in time.) Incorporating materials into a constructivist approach that stimulates interest instead of passive ingestion—that's the art and, yes, the excitement of being a teacher.

Examples of Materials

Figure 3.5 provides an overview of materials organized into categories. The materials described do not compose an exhaustive list, but they can help you experiment with a

Textual	Visual	Audio	Objects	Tools	Teacher-Designed (tailored to learning needs or topic)
Books	Video and film	Songs and music	Models (of forms, scenes, relation-ships, etc.)	Chalkboard or white board	Scenarios
Magazines	Cartoons	Speeches	Physical/visual meta-phors	Overhead and opaque projec-tors	Fact sheets
Lyrics	Graphic rep-resenta-tions	Readings	3-D mock-ups (e.g., DNA, cubes, sentence structure, etc.)	TV, VCRs, tape and CD players	Handouts of various formats (columns, tables, outlines, concept maps, graphs, drawings, activity prompts, etc.)
Primary sources	Websites	Sound effects		Computers (single or net-worked)	Facsimiles for skill building (e.g., simulated refer-ence texts for tailored note-taking and for learning how to organize a bibli-ography for a re-search paper)
Websites and email; stand-alone software	Software simula-tions for learning in all subject areas; stand-alone software				

© 2001, Ina Claire Gabler.

FIGURE 3.5 Materials

variety of materials, some of which you may not think of at first. Soon you will be able to add to the list from your own ideas and experiences.

Focal Point 5: The Hook

The Hook begins the Student Engagement segment of the lesson for good reason. *The Hook is an attention grabber.* When you plan a lesson, it's useful to assume that the only person in the classroom interested in the lesson is you. How do you pique the students' interest? For starters, you can use an effective Hook with two elements:

1. Content based (relates to the Rationale).
2. Personalized (relates to the students in some way).

Discussion 5: The Hook

By content based we mean alluding to facts or concepts in the lesson. But you don't want to be dry. If you tie the Hook to your students' frames of reference, then you'll personalize the Hook and capture interest.

If planned well with a motivating theme, varied materials, and engaging techniques, the entire lesson should "hook" the students. But they will often need something catchy to pull them in at the outset.

Sometimes an idea for a Hook will occur to you in a flash of inspiration. Other times, an effective Hook will occur to you as you plan the Performance Objective or the Culmination. There are also times when you will not be able to think of an effective Hook. In that case, the Aim, described in Focal Point 6, can double-dip as a Hook. Or a description of the upcoming Performance Objective might engage interest.

A Hook should not be merely a gimmick. A meaningful Hook begins the learning process. There is no such thing as disposable time in a lesson. Every Core Component should contribute to the instructional value.

Examples of Hooks

Here are some sample Hooks to get you started:

- A Hook may be a provocative question (not an academic question that only a teacher could love).
- A Hook may find you in costume, role-playing.
- A Hook may invite students to briefly role-play.
- A Hook may be an engaging videoclip or audio segment.
- A Hook may be a positive, nonrivalrous challenge.
- A Hook may be an anecdote that students can relate to, an analogy of the concepts to come.
- A Hook may be a preview of a computer simulation.
- A Hook may be props that represent ideas and concepts in an accessible format.
- A Hook may be anything else you dream up that relates to the lesson and jump-starts your students.

Content Based	Personalized for Students
Anchored to an integral concept in the lesson	1. Poses an analogy to which students can relate; may employ one or more physical props. 2. May challenge students' belief system in a respectful way. 3. May involve some or all students in a brief role-play or a demonstration.

FIGURE 3.6 The Hook

However imaginative the Hook may be, you need to relate it to the heart of the lesson. A question–response dialogue with your students is one way to achieve this. Consider the subject-specific examples against Figure 3.6.

EXAMPLE #1/SCIENCE[3] (WATER PURIFICATION)

HOOK

Content based: Show class four bottles of water in varying stages of purification.

Personalized: Ask students to describe what they observe and to infer possible significance. Which water would they be willing to drink? Not willing to drink? Why? Can they describe various characteristics (odor, color, consistency) of water they have encountered that has not been safe? Of water that has been safe? Are they not sure how to tell if water is safe or not? Have they heard of someone drinking impure water? What happened to that person? Would they be willing to swim or wash in impure water? Why?

EXAMPLE #2/ART[4] (DRAWING)

HOOK

Content based: Project a black ink drawing of Mount Rushmore on a transparency. The image is upside down and unrecognizable.

Personalized: What do you have to notice to copy this faithfully? Do you think drawing this will be more difficult or easier than drawing it right side up? Why? What is the advantage of drawing this upside down? What do you think I want you to focus on? Why?

NOTE: In this example, the Hook becomes the vehicle of the lesson's substance.

EXAMPLE #3/MATH (DISTANCE PROBLEMS)

HOOK

Content-based and Personalized: How long does it take you to get to the pizza parlor at lunch? Do you need to run there and back to return to school in time? Or can you walk? What determines if you walk or run?

Focal Point 6:   The Aim

An effective Aim contains the same two elements as the Hook:

1. Content-based. The Aim points to the heart of the lesson.

2. Personalized. An appealing Aim relates or speaks to your students in some way.

The Aim expresses the Rationale, formally expressed for you as the teacher, into colloquial or catchy language. The Aim is a rudder for your students. It should also whet curiosity. It sometimes includes the cognitive skill with such words as list, interpret, and analyze. The same Aim may be expressed with different language for different classes, tailored to the interests of each student group.

Discussion 6:   The Aim

Because both the Aim and the Hook are content-based and personalized, they can interrelate and build on each other as the heart of the introduction to your lesson.

The Aim may be written clearly on the board, on an overhead transparency, or elsewhere. It can be phrased as a statement or as a question. The Aim may also serve to steer you back on track, away from digressions, as a glance at the Aim on the board or transparency reminds you of your Rationale.

Not every lesson benefits from an Aim at the outset, particularly inductive lessons in which students arrive at the major concepts and principles themselves, with your guidance. For example, the sample lesson plan on a metaphor in Focal Point 11 is an inductive lesson. You will see that the students are guided to define a metaphor themselves at the end of the lesson.

Sometimes a Hook builds up to the Aim, or you can provide no Aim and at the outset challenge the students to infer the Aim of the lesson later on in the Culmination. In other words, sometimes the Aim is explicit, other times it's implied. Ideally, you would vary these approaches.

Aim as Hook

Finally, a compelling Aim can substitute for a Hook or serve as an additional Hook. An academic-style Aim, including a question, will not likely hook your students even if *you* think the question or statement is brimming with significance. For example, we do not consider the Aim (What is a metaphor? How do metaphors affect you?) in the

Elements of the Aim	Purpose
1. Content based 2. Personalized	1. Captures the heart of the Rationale. 2. Relates or speaks to students in some way.

FIGURE 3.7 The Aim

sample lesson in Focal Point 11 to be intriguing enough to serve as a Hook. A compelling Aim is something surprising, mysterious, inventive. In the sample lesson, the Hook is a picture of a magician raising a torch at a dragon. An Aim as a Hook could be, "Can you uncover the magician's metaphors in the time limit of this lesson?"

Examples of an Aim

Use Figure 3.7 as a handy reference for each example of an Aim that follows.

EXAMPLE #1A/SCIENCE (PHOTOSYNTHESIS).

Aim: How does photosynthesis result in a hamburger?

NONEXAMPLE #1B/SCIENCE (PHOTOSYNTHESIS)
Aim: To learn about photosynthesis.

EXAMPLE #2A/MATH (DISTANCE PROBLEMS).

Aim: How long would it take you to get from your seat to the nearest pizza parlor?

NONEXAMPLE #2B/MATH (DISTANCE PROBLEMS)
Aim: Distance problems.

EXAMPLE #3A/SOCIAL STUDIES (POLITICS OF HUNGER).

Aim: There's an overabundance of food in the world. So why are people going hungry?

NONEXAMPLE #4B/SOCIAL STUDIES (POLITICS OF HUNGER)
Aim: To learn about the politics of world hunger.

Focal Point 7. Development with Method and Method Markers

The Development contains your chosen method and includes a Performance Objective. Because each method is different from another, the Development is a variable Core

Component, with specific method features called *method markers*. For this reason, the Development is only indicated, not demonstrated, in the sample lesson plan in Focal Point 11.

In Section C of this book, each method module contains full sample lesson plans with the corresponding Development and method markers. For now, we want you to focus on the Core Components without the method.

Focal Point 8: The Culmination

The Culmination contains the following two elements:

1. Wrap-Up. The Wrap-Up summarizes the key points of the lesson.

2. Leap. As the name suggests, the Leap introduces a related but new concept, principle, or theme, an implication of one or more of the key points developed in the lesson.

The Culmination is otherwise known as a conclusion because the Culmination effects closure. Too often, however, the conclusion is considered a throwaway. Teachers often provide a superficial statement, such as, "Today we've learned about gases," or "Tomorrow we'll learn two more drawing techniques." Sometimes teachers ask for or express a summary of the lesson, a meaningful practice. But a lesson's closure can be thought provoking as well. This is the reason we use the term Culmination.

Discussion 8: The Culmination

You must tie the threads of a lesson together. A strong Culmination, a terrific culmination, serves as a pinnacle of the lesson. The Culmination should bring together specific key points, reaffirming the lesson's Rationale. But the fun comes when, for example, you prompt your students to predict principles or articulate themes beyond those established in the lesson relating the ideas to today's world: What is the significance—beyond the classroom— of World War II, of discovering the atom, of stereotyped characters? How have those events and concepts shaped present-day attitudes? Shaped your students' lives? Could McDonald's exist without photosynthesis? Or without geometric proofs? Why?

Of course the Culmination supplies cohesion, a practical necessity. For example, referring to the Aim is an effective transition into the Culmination, especially if the Aim asks a question. Or the Culmination can establish the Aim inductively, that is, guide the students to retrospectively determine the Aim themselves.

At the same time, the Culmination can inspire your students to leave your classroom still talking about the ideas in the lesson. So think of the end of a lesson not as a mere summary or disposable formality but as a sparkling peak.

Examples of the Culmination

Compare each subject-specific example that follows to Figure 3.8.

The Wrap-Up	The Leap
1. Refer to the Aim as a lead-in. 2. Review key facts and concepts. Be specific.	Probe with thought questions: 1. What is the significance of __? 2. How has __ affected your life, directly or indirectly? 3. What if __? 4. Can you compare __ to __?

FIGURE 3.8 The Culmination

EXAMPLE #1/ENGLISH (WRITING WITH MAIN IDEAS AND DETAILS).

Wrap-Up: What is the difference between a main idea and supporting details?

Leap: Think of a profession besides writing that might interest you. How could it be useful to distinguish between main ideas and supporting details in that profession?

EXAMPLE #2/FRENCH (IRREGULAR VERBS).

Wrap-Up: What are the five irregular verbs you've learned today?

Leap: What are some situations in which you would need to use these verbs to make your needs understood?

EXAMPLE #3/SCIENCE (EXPERIMENTAL METHOD).

Wrap-Up: What are the elements of the experimental method?

Leap: What is a real-life situation that we haven't discussed in which the experimental method is useful? If you wanted to find out how much your friends liked you, would the experimental method be effective? Why?

Focal Point 9. Assessment and Evaluation

To begin, you need to know the difference between evaluation and assessment. *Evaluation* is the process of making a judgment about the quality of student learning. *Assessment* is the means by which you gather information to make these judgments: portfolios, presentations, questionnaires, tests, oral interviews, and so on.

Discussion 9. Assessment and Evaluation

As a constructivist teacher, you need strategies in addition to multiple-choice or fill-in examinations for judging what your students have learned. Students in a constructivist environment are active learners. They create original products. They learn to question and to think critically. In time, they become independent learners, selecting their own topics for projects and constructing their own insights justified with sources. Evaluation and assessment are explored in depth in Module 14. For now, we introduce it as an important part of lesson planning. To assess and evaluate the quality of learning, ask yourself two questions:

- What products will my students generate? (research paper, Website, role-play, enactment or debate, presentations, drawing, portfolio, motor coordination, etc.)
- What are the criteria for acceptable achievement? (create your own rubric or categories for evaluation of organization, thoroughness, appropriate skills for the task, satisfaction of the Aim, originality, critical thinking, motor ability, growth, test results, etc.)

Focal Point 10: Form versus Function

Constructivism highlights the difference between form and function. *Form* refers to the *definition or content* of the Core Component, for example, the Rationale clarifies the teacher's intention and focus for a given lesson, or the Performance Objective includes an interpretation of the fourth chapter in *Huckleberry Finn* by Mark Twain. *Function* refers to the *role* of a Core Component. Function separates passive from active student participation and rote learning from critical thinking.

Discussion 10: Form versus Function

Imagine that two Performance Objectives center around the form or content of an urban design that addresses ecological concerns. The first Performance Objective instructs students to label a diagram, defining and explaining the significance of each feature. This first Performance Objective functions on only low cognitive levels; it merely requires the students to paraphrase what you and the textbook have imparted.

The second Performance Objective requires students to plan the urban design from scratch, not only defining and explaining the various features but also analyzing the interrelationships and predicting outcomes with supported judgments. This Performance Objective carries your students across Bloom's Taxonomy, generating a product that embodies original analysis and solutions. It functions as an original critical-thinking experience.

Consider another example. In a teacher-centered lesson, the Rationale or form is to learn the definition of photosynthesis. For the Performance Objective, students memorize the definition of photosynthesis and explain the stages in the process. These are low-level functions, all conveyed with teacher talk or lecture and a textbook. This knowledge may mean nothing to the students beyond the questions on a multiple-choice test.

Or, in a student-focused[5] lesson with the same Rationale, the Performance Objective may function as student analysis of photosynthesis as part of the ongoing transformation on earth, energy being converted into matter and matter into energy in countless ways. For the concrete product, your students might generate a concept map with examples from their everyday lives and arrive at the relationship between the process of photosynthesis and this larger perspective. For example, how are a burger and french fries related to photosynthesis? Or the clothes your students wear? Or the books they read? How else are your students' lives affected by photosynthesis?[6]

You can see that the didactic Performance Objectives promote prescribed answers and the constructivist Performance Objectives enable discovery. This is not to imply that all didactic lessons lack value. Minilectures are useful to introduce projects or units, to summarize discussions (Atwell, 1987), and to present information for a content-rich syllabus. In fact, one of our methods, the Interactive Presentation in Module 12, incorporates minilectures. However, long lectures or on-going teacher talk tend to promote a passive student role with little if any critical thinking.

Focal Point 11: **Building a Lesson Plan**

Now you're down to the wire. How do you put the Core Components together and write a great lesson plan? At this point, there seems to be a lot to remember. However, once you select a topic, the Core Components will actually help you develop it more easily than if you "wing it."

Discussion 11: **Building a Lesson Plan**

For starters, consider this almost too obvious—yet essential—concept. A lesson unfolds a story. Like a story, your lesson plan needs structure, with a beginning, middle, and end. Instinctively, most preservice teachers grasp the developmental nature of a lesson. Chances are that the following questions have been floating around in your mind:

- How should I open my lesson? (beginning)
- How do I develop the idea(s)? (middle)
- How far should I develop the lesson? (end or closure)

Study the sample lesson that follows. It contains all the Core Components for an eighth-grade lesson on metaphors. We chose this topic because it is accessible to people across all subject areas. Similarly, we chose eighth grade so that the content would not obstruct the Core Components. A rich assortment of sample lessons for various levels and subjects awaits you in Modules 7 through 12.

In keeping with our discussion on the Development, that Core Component is indicated but not filled in for now because it varies according to the method it unfolds. Even without this crucial Core Component, you can gain a strong sense of the progression or "story" of this lesson from the other Core Components. Try to spot the cognitive skills from Bloom's Taxonomy.

Example of Building a Lesson Plan

SAMPLE LESSON PLAN WITH CORE COMPONENTS.
Topic = Metaphors, Eighth Grade

PRELUDE

A. Rationale

1. *What?:* To introduce the concept of a metaphor as a concrete image with various interpretations.

2. *Why?:* Students will comprehend and apply the concept of a metaphor. They will analyze (compare and contrast) symbolic versus literal meanings of various images to develop abstract thinking.

3. *Justification:* INTASC Standards 2, 3, 4, 5, and 6.

B. Performance Objective (carried out in Development)

1. *Preparation:* Project picture of magician and dragon. Students will write one literal interpretation as a caption. Class discussion will explore different interpretations of the same picture.

2. *Product:* Students will be able to write a caption that expresses their own symbolic interpretation of the entire picture. Students will compare and contrast the literal and symbolic captions that they wrote for the same picture.

3. *Criteria:*

   a. Students must write the two captions on their own, without consulting anyone else.

   b. Learners must compare and contrast the literal and symbolic meanings of at least three images they used to write their captions.

   c. Students will work in pairs, comparing and contrasting their captions.

C. Materials

1. Magician costume

2. Overhead transparency graphic as the focal point for developing the concept

3. Chalkboard

ENACTMENT

D. Hook

1. Dress in a cape and pointed hat as a magician, complete with "magic wand." Role play with "magic" words and "spells." Ask students what they would wish for. Wave the wand and tell them their wishes are granted.

2. Say, "I am the magician who grants your wishes. Now I'll show you another magician. See if you can figure out what *this* magician is doing."

3. Project a colorful picture of a magician facing off a huge dragon with a burning torch and amulet.

E. Aim

(On the board or overhead projector): What is a metaphor? Can metaphors affect you?

F. Development (Inductive Concept Method with Method Markers; Carries Out Performance Objective)

G. Culmination

1. *Wrap-Up:* Refer to the first question of the Aim, "What is a metaphor?" Elicit a simple definition from students based on the symbolic interpretations, something like this: A metaphor is a concrete image with a symbolic meaning.

2. How many levels of meaning can a metaphor have? Why?

3. *Leap* (second question of the Aim): "Can metaphors apply to you?" How might the different meanings affect the way you understand what you read, see, and so on?

4. *Leap:* Recount the ending of the film *The Postman* in which the postman asks the poet Neruda, "Is the whole world a metaphor?" Elicit interpretations.

5. "Tomorrow we will expand the definition of a metaphor."

ASSESSMENT AND EVALUATION PLAN

For homework: In their own words, students will write the difference between the literal and symbolic meanings of their own and their partner's captions for the same picture. Also in their own words, students will define a metaphor based on the partial definition developed in the lesson. They will also define two ways in which a metaphoric meaning differs from the literal meaning in general. Finally, students will describe an object in their home (e.g., a lamp) from both a literal and a metaphoric perspective. To be collected.

■ ROUNDUP ■

Remember: everyone wants to learn. Really learn. There is nothing more stimulating and motivating than a learning challenge that students consider meaningful.

The Core Components supply a foundation for just such a learning environment. They are your prompts for direction and focus. Every teaching style can succeed with the Core Components: the Rationale, Performance Objective, Materials, Hook, Aim, Development, and Culmination.

The Development unfolds the method between the Hook and Culmination. As the name implies, the Development builds the substance of the lesson, employing a method (a cohesive template) with method markers (features of a method). Therefore, the format of the Development is different for each method.

Form refers to the definition or procedure of the component, for example, the Rationale clarifies the teacher's intention and focus for a given lesson. But it's function that separates passive from active student participation and that separates rote learning from the challenge and stimulation of critical thinking. These Core Components have traditionally functioned as a lecture and/or teacher-dictated practices that emphasize right answers rather than a process of discovery. Both extensive lecture and the right-answer approach assume a passive student role.

Instead, we encourage you to employ the form of Core Components to function in a student-as-active-learner approach. Rather than tell your students what they should think, try to foster their critical-thinking skills; emphasize the process of learning so that student-generated products embody original insights and solutions, products that build their thinking skills.

With this approach, student products become milestones in formulating ideas—far beyond filling in blanks on worksheets.

■ HANDS-ON PRACTICE ■

Get ready to roll up your sleeves and plunge in. We are about to take you through the steps of planning six of seven Core Components.

Alone or with a partner, choose a topic from your subject area and develop it sequentially from the Rationale to the Culmination, omitting the Development for now. You do not have to complete this in one sitting.

Self-Instruct Planner: Core Components

Subject _____ Topic _____

(Work on a separate piece of paper.)

Refer to Bloom's Taxonomy as you work with the Self-Instruct Planner.

PRELUDE: Rationale, Performance Objective, Materials

A. *Rationale* (Refer to Figure 3.3)

1. *What?* (incorporate italicized words): *To introduce . . . , Students will learn . . . , To increase students' mastery of . . . , To develop . . . , Learners will enlarge their understanding of . . . , To develop students' perception of . . . , etc.*

2. *Why?* (Be specific. Cite what the students will learn, physically coordinate, visually perceive, etc.)

3. *Justification:* Refer to INTASC Standards in the Appendix.

Self-Check
Does your Rationale have a clear and specific focus? Or does it try to do too much? Have the cognitive, perceptual, or motor skills specified their application? We encourage you to get peer feedback from a peer in a different subject area from your own. Same-subject peers may not see conceptual or scope problems as clearly as someone not familiar with your subject—like your students.

B. *The Performance Objective* (Refer to Figure 3.4)

1. *Preparation*

2. *Product* (*"Students will be able to . . ."*)

3. *Criteria*

Self-Check

Does the product relate to the Rationale? Does the product call on students to bring together and interpret, analyze, and/or synthesize the significant concepts and principles? Are there clear and specific criteria? Did you fall into the frequent trap of making a discussion the product (except for oral "products" such as debates or enactments)? Get feedback from a peer.

C. *Materials* (Refer to Figure 3.5)

Listing the materials is not busywork. Your materials suggest the variety and scope of your lessons to the department chair, supervisor, mentor, and so on. Most important, thinking through the materials you'll need ensures that you'll be fully prepared to teach the lesson. In addition, a materials list serves as a check for yourself that you are not falling prey to routinized habits or not using enough substantive sources.

The materials you select for a lesson or project should work integrally with and enrich the learning experience.

Remember: Beware of just air between you and your students!

Materials (three or more)

ENACTMENT: Hook, Aim, Development, Culmination

D. *Hook* (Refer to Figure 3.6)

1. *Content-based*

2. *Personalized*

3. (Winging it) Write a transition from the Hook to the Development of the lesson

Self-Check

Does your Hook relate to the lesson's substance? Does your Hook connect to students' frame of reference? Get feedback from a peer.

E. *Aim* (Refer to Figure 3.7)

1. Heart of your Rationale

2. Aim/Version #1 (Question)

3. Alternate Aim/Version #2 (Statement)

Self-Check

Does each Aim capture the heart of the Rationale? Or does it indulge in an engaging feature that is not the essential aspect? Is the wording in each version significantly different? Swap with a peer for mutual feedback.

F. *Development* (Method with Method Markers)

G. *Culmination* (Refer to Figure 3.8)

1. *Wrap-Up*

    a. Possibly refer to Aim (may serve as entree for the Culmination)

    b. Establish key points of the lesson

  2. *Leap*

    a. Two or three possible interpretations related to students' frames of reference

    b. One or two challenge questions related to students' frames of reference

Self-Check

Does your Wrap-Up reestablish key points? Does the Leap ask students to arrive at new insights with justification? Does at least one challenge question relate to students' frames of reference? Get feedback from a peer.

ASSESSMENT AND EVALUATION

Describe what student materials you will use to assess and evaluate the success of the lesson in terms of the Rationale. What would be the important criteria for acceptable achievement?

ENDNOTES

1. Based on a lesson written by Sarah Holtschlag when she was a preservice teacher at Millikin University in Decatur, IL.
2. Based on a lesson written by Marianne Stanton when she was a preservice teacher at Millikin University in Decatur, IL.
3. Based on a lesson written by Sarah Holtschlag when she was a preservice teacher at Millikin University in Decatur, IL.
4. Based on a lesson written by Marianne Stanton when she was a preservice teacher at Millikin University in Decatur, IL.
5. For the difference between student-focused and student-centered lessons, see the table on pedagogical settings in Module 15.
6. Thanks to Dr. Bertram Chip Bruce for this example of meaningful learning.

REFERENCES

Atwell, N. (1987). *In the middle: Writing, reading and learning with adolescents.* Upper Montclair, NH: Boynton/Cook Publishers.

Lortie, D. C. (1975). *Schoolteacher: A sociological study.* Chicago: University of Chicago Press.

SUGGESTED READINGS

Arenson, K. W. (2001, October 3). One philosopher's alchemy: Teaching as romance. *New York Times.*

Bonwell, C. C., & Eison, J. A. (1991). *Active learning: Creating excitement in the classroom.* Washington, DC: Washington University, School of Education and Human Development.

Brooks, G., & Brooks, M. G. (1993). *In search of understanding: The case for constructivist classrooms.* Alexandria, VA: ASCD.

Hunter, M. (1982). *Mastery teaching.* El Segundo, CA: TIP.

Perkins, D. (1992). *Smart schools: From training memories to educating minds.* New York: Free Press.

PART 2:
Techniques versus Tools

■ OVERVIEW

A Scenario

You're about to audition at the Village Gate in New York, down in Greenwich Village. It's the first time you'll play the guitar in public, far from the ears of rooting friends and family who think you'll be the blues star of the new millennium. And, man, you sure do play a mean tune. Pickin' up strums here and there, imitating the blues singers you admire, just chompin' at the bit, yeah, to take your place among 'em. *Man.* You'll knock those Village Gate gatekeepers off their odd shod feet.

Ahead of you in the auditions is Mame the Dame. Big and brassy. She sings just one number and you deflate down to a punctured balloon. Her guitar astonishes: she runs a real glass bottleneck along the frets (talk about authentic), changes keys like a janitor, dazzles with finger picking that leaves you breathless. As for her voice, she sings alto real smooth to a clear falsetto that shakes the glasses on the gatekeepers' table. And being a real pro, Mame the Dame with inimitable style suits her techniques to each song, sometimes uses the same pick but in different rhythm or volume, or uses a technique just once, hitting the mark and knowing when to move on, man, to another effect.

Your turn comes, but man, you're gone, dashing home, determined to learn those techniques yourself.

Hey. You know a mean dose of blues when you see it.

Get you some.

—©2001 Ina Claire Gabler

A lesson needs dynamite techniques just like the *real* blues singer in the scenario you just read. After all, the same song has been sung by countless singers. Likewise, the same topic has been taught by many a pedagogical predecessor. It's easy to fool ourselves. A creative idea isn't enough for a lesson or project to have substance. As a budding blues singer in Mame the Dame's wake, you got the idea pretty quick!

As a budding teacher, you also need effective techniques. Lots of them. Just what are instructional techniques? You've probably heard the term often but weren't clear about it. In fact, many experienced teachers confuse techniques for methods. For now, we limit the discussion to techniques; methods are covered in Modules 7–12.

■ GOALS

In this section we discuss the following:

- The difference between techniques and tools with examples.
- The interrelationship between techniques and tools.
- The difference between techniques and methods.

■ DISCUSSION

Think of an assortment of techniques and tools as your collection of instruments that work together. *Techniques* are practices that can engage your students in critical thinking and active involvement instead of passive repetitions. Techniques provide procedures for independent learning for both individuals and peer groups. Techniques lend spice and imagination to the learning experience.

Tools are materials and devices such as activity sheets and instructional machines. Each tool has its advantages and disadvantages for implementing various techniques.

Focal Point 1: **Techniques**

A *technique is the use of a task or procedure that helps carry out a method.* A *method*, in turn, is a cohesive template or blueprint. For example, a series of techniques like modeling and role-playing can develop the Exploratory Discussion or Interactive Presentation Methods. Expanding a bit, we can say that techniques are practices occurring in a sequence that develops the Rationale within a method template.

Discussion 1: **Techniques**

All techniques can be used in all methods. To choose the techniques that will be most effective for a given method with a particular group of students requires experience. Like the Core Components, techniques have been around a long time. It takes clear focus and imagination to design the use of a technique so that it cultivates original thinking instead of lurking around those low cognitive levels too long. The difference between using techniques for passive or active student learning is another example of form (a specific technique, such as questioning) versus function (the role of questions as yes-no vehicles or prompts for critical thinking).

Examples of Techniques

There are countless techniques and countless adaptations of every technique. As you gain teaching experience, you will undoubtedly invent your own techniques tailored to your teaching styles and your various students' needs. The only limit is your imagination. Module 4 provides an in-depth look at questioning.

EXAMPLE #1/QUESTIONS

Questions generate teacher–student or student–student dialogue. Questions are the underpinnings for many other techniques. There are three types of questions:

- *Trigger question.* As the name suggests, a Trigger question opens a discussion. It gets things going. A Trigger generates a broad-based beginning.

- *Probe question.* This type of question asks a respondent to explain an answer further. In other words, a Probe follows a Trigger question and focuses on the same student, probing for more ideas, but in a nonthreatening way.

- *Redirected question.* When you pose the same or related questions to various students or the entire class, inviting them to add their ideas to the same issue, you're asking a Redirected question.

Figure 3.9 outlines the differences among these three question types.

Trigger **Opens the discussion with a broad question**	Probe **Asks the respondent to explain further; guides the respondent to insight that benefits the student and the class**	Redirected **Poses a question on the same issue to other students or the entire class; invites various angles on the same issue**
Why did the United States drop an atomic bomb on Japan in World War II?	1. In addition to wanting to win the war, what other reason might have motivated dropping the A-bomb on Japan? 2. That's an interesting idea. Could you explain a bit more how national pride could have been a factor, citing some facts? 3. Can you justify national pride in this situation or not? Why?	1. Could someone put that in your own words? 2. Does anyone agree? Disagree? 3. Can anyone think of yet another motive for dropping the A-bomb?

FIGURE 3.9 The Differences Among Trigger, Probes, and Redirected Questions

EXAMPLE #2/HEURISTICS

A *heuristic* is a codified procedure or a formulaic series of steps for carrying out an activity. Perhaps the most famous heuristic is the journalist's *who, what, when, where, why, and how.* You can invent your own heuristics. Heuristics enable students to work independently and/or to interact fruitfully.

English: For peer-group feedback on freshman papers, an English professor invented the following heuristic[1]:

1. I think your essay (or paper) is about . . .
2. The major points in your essay (or paper) seem to be . . .
3. What I like most about your essay (or paper) is . . .
4. I think your essay (or paper) could be strengthened by . . .

Math: Here's a formulaic process for solving word problems:

1. Work backwards.
2. Define the end product.
3. List the ingredients of the end product.
4. List the sequence for solving the ingredients.

EXAMPLE #3/ROLE-PLAYING

Role-playing is the act of adopting another identity. Taking on various identities in role-play enriches discussions, debates, or individual exploration of a concept. Your students play the part of real or imaginary figures. You may supply background information for each role, or students may write their own background information if the role-play serves as a review or the application of research. Students argue according to their roles regardless of their own point of view. Later, students break role and express their own perspectives with documented justifications. Or, students may argue from their own perspective within the assigned role or the context of a simulation. The continuum of role-play arguments is as follows:

- Students argue from their own perspective.
- Students argue from another perspective and break role.
- Students argue completely from another's perspective.

The configurations may vary. For example, students may role-play in groups of three to four members, each group playing out the same roles simultaneously. Or the entire class may sit in a circle in which all students role-play, with several taking on the same role so that all viewpoints are argued by various people. Using another format, several students role-play in front of the class while the class in turn poses questions to the role-players. The class itself may role-play a group, for example, Southern plantation owners during the American Civil war. Here are some other examples:

- Students role-play animals foraging for a limited food supply, "surviving," "breeding," and "perishing" according to their success, before a class discussion on ecology.
- Students enact a school board meeting about a controversy.
- Students debate issues related to the Vietnam War, role-playing various figures.

The possibilities are endless. If planned well with in-depth materials for background information, role-playing forces students to think critically as they expand on the background information and consider their own viewpoints with justification when they break role.

EXAMPLE #4/PERSONALIZING

Personalizing is the practice of connecting your topic to the students' frames of reference. Personalizing provides a familiar frame of reference, related to the students' own life experience, that connects to a new context. It bridges the familiar to the foreign. When you relate your students' experiences of school, family, friendship, TV shows, popular movies, sports, favorite music, and so on, to the knowledge base or concepts in a lesson, you hook student interest and clarify ideas that may be foreign at first. The reason? Personalizing provides analogies or metaphors in students' own terms that further understanding. Role-playing is another way to personalize: by pretending to be someone else, a student feels "ownership" of that person and related situation. Here are some examples:

- For a social studies mini-unit comparing and contrasting the differences and similarities of the American and Russian judicial systems, play a song of a murdered rap singer. Distribute a brief newspaper article or write a brief summary of the news story, with a transparency image if possible, about a record producer accused of murdering the singer. Ask pairs of students to role-play the producer's lawyer and the state prosecutor. Russian and American "lawyers" and "prosecutors" cite their cases and evidence, including the assumption of guilt or innocence. Break roles. Discuss circumstantial versus documented evidence and possible motives for the murder and motives, if any, to frame the suspect.

- For a unit on characterization in literature, ask students to write a list of three to five characteristics of the opposite sex. Discuss the responses. Compare and contrast the stereotypes with real boys and girls the students know. Discuss the hallmarks of a stereotype and possible reasons for stereotyping. What role do stereotypes play in society? How might stereotypes weaken or strengthen literature that depicts human life?

- For an art lesson on Cezanne, ask students to draw three objects in the room as corresponding geometric shapes. Share and compare. Discuss the nature of underlying shapes. Invite your students to discover the underlying geometric shapes in a Cezanne print.

EXAMPLE #5/BRAINSTORMING

Brainstorming is the practice of encouraging students to free associate responses to a question, word, idea, and so on. In a brainstorming session, students call out their ideas, which are written on the board or overhead transparency as an expanding reference. From the potpourri of ideas, students can infer and supply corresponding categories and headings.

You enhance the value of this activity when you pose guiding questions every so often that help your students perceive connections among the ideas, thereby generating a network of interrelated concepts, headings, themes, and so on. Consider Figures 3.10 and 3.11, which build on free association, generating categories and concepts.

Explanation of Brainstorming Examples

Students supply the specific items and ideas in Figure 3.10, responses which are written on the board or transparency for ongoing reference. You facilitate a discussion, developing the larger concepts related to the Aim. In the discussion, students inductively supply the headings or organizers in Figure 3.11 in their own words similar to our examples.

Memory is not always a robust or reliable source for meaningful discussion grounded in facts and a variety of concepts. You and the students therefore benefit when the knowledge base and concepts are visible on the board or overhead transparency for supporting evidence and intellectual rigor.

EXAMPLE #6/CONCEPT MAPPING

Concert mapping is the process of organizing ideas into categories and subcategories represented in a graphic depiction. Often an extension of brainstorming, a *concept map* is a pictorial representation of the interrelationships of concepts and their facts and examples. Concept maps may use circles and lines, boxes, a tree effect, and more. The process is an effective technique for visual thinkers.

Figure 3.12 employs the brainstorming categorized in Figure 3.11. Notice how the same information is organized differently, delving a bit deeper into categories within

---

Aim: How has the evolution of transportation changed the world?

airplanes   horses   walking   cars   boats
rowboats   canoes   rafts   steamboat   horse and buggy
helium balloons   helicopters   walking   running   donkeys
camels   dog teams   trains   chariots   swinging from tree to
tree   space missiles   jets

FIGURE 3.10 Brainstorming Examples of Transportation/
Free Association

Aim: How has the evolution of transportation changed the world?

Kinds of transportation

airplanes   horses   walking   cars   boats
rowboats   canoes   rafts   steamboat   horse and buggy
helium balloons   helicopters   walking   running   donkeys
camels   dog teams   trains   chariots   swinging from tree to
tree   space missiles   jets

Categories of transportation

Land   Air   Mechanical   Animal   Water

World changes because of transportation
types of war   national power   scope of living   societal changes
personal power and self-perception

FIGURE 3.11 Brainstorming Examples of Transportation: Generating Categories and Concepts

categories. Here too, your students infer and supply the concepts from the variety of examples that they provided during brainstorming. Your job is to guide their thinking with questions—another technique—without spilling the beans.

Obviously, a lesson on transportation may not reach high cognitive levels if only because of familiarity. But getting learners to identify categories within categories, and then to reorganize the examples according to even different categories is the beginning of higher cognitive-thinking skills.

In constructivism, the thinking process takes priority over memorizing categories and examples given to the students. It's stimulating when your students think their way to the categories based on their own examples and then reassign the examples according to a different organizing concept—realizing that an example can fall under more than one category. From the perspective of how trees grow, "swinging from tree to tree" can be considered a land modality. From the perspective of the nature of travel—through the air—"swinging from tree to tree" can be considered a form of air travel. See if you can find "swinging from tree to tree" in other categories as well!

Compare the concept map in Figure 3.12 to the original items in the brainstorming activity, represented in Figures 3.10 and 3.11. Note the development of complexity from the brainstorming to the concept map.

EXAMPLE #7/MODELING

Modeling is a demonstration of a task before your students attempt to do the task themselves. Whenever possible, modeling includes teacher direction along with student participation in a kind of dress rehearsal. Your materials should therefore include a brief sample of the task you want your students to do. For example, Figure 3.13 demonstrates a modeling activity for identifying categories and related details. Modeling an activity is especially important for projects and peer-group work so that learners will know exactly how they should carry out a given assignment on their own. Think of modeling as a run-through before the cameras roll.

EXAMPLE #8/TRANSITIONS

Transitions are statements that logically connect segments in the lesson into a seamless flow. Transitions bridge what just took place in the lesson with what is about to happen. They are particularly important when moving from the introduction (i.e., after the Aim and Hook or other opening) to the Development. Transitions are also essential within the Development, providing logical connections from one stage of thinking to another, or from one activity, such as discussion, to another activity, such as the Performance Objective. Here are some examples:

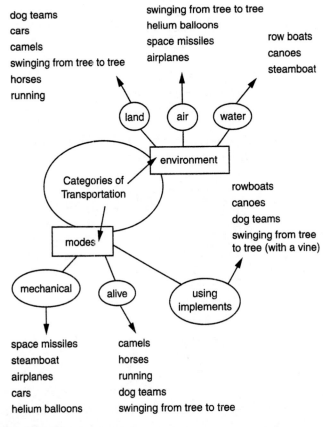

dog teams
cars
camels
swinging from tree to tree
horses
running

swinging from tree to tree
helium balloons
space missiles
airplanes

row boats
canoes
steamboat

land   air   water

environment

Categories of
Transportation

rowboats
canoes
dog teams
swinging from tree
to tree (with a vine)

modes

mechanical   alive   using
implements

space missiles   camels
steamboat   horses
airplanes   running
cars   dog teams
helium balloons   swinging from tree to tree

©2001 Ina Claire Gabler

FIGURE 3.12 Concept Map

Directions: Organize this shopping list according to categories. Provide headings for the categories.

milk

bananas

potatoes

cheese

cereal

bread

eggs

grapes

chopped beef

chocolate chip cookies

ice cream

carrots

lettuce

doughnuts

chicken

bagels

soap

frozen juice

shampoo

vitamins

FIGURE 3.13 Organizing a Shopping List

- "Now that we have established X, let's see how Y is affected."
- "We've looked at how Huck Finn seems to have matured on the river trip with Jim. Next we're going to see ways in which Huck was not so mature."
- "Let's quickly review the steps of photosynthesis before you represent its various impacts on plants—and on humans."

EXAMPLE #9/ADVANCE ORGANIZERS

Advance organizers alert students to an upcoming task to orient the students' attention. Advance organizers do as their name suggests: they organize students' focus in advance of a task. They can even activate relevant schemata and can begin to create cognitive dissonance (the clash of new information with one's beliefs) within students—a guaranteed Hook! This forward-looking directive improves your students' attention as they watch, read, or listen and in that way creates the foundation for a fruitful discussion after the video, reading, or presentations. Otherwise, discussions rely on recall and may not reach the same rigor as discussions founded on notes and focused attention. An advance organizer may also be an anticipatory alert of an upcoming task or a guiding question. Here are some examples:

- "When you read the article, underline at least five causes and effects of obesity."

- "As you listen to your classmates present their conclusions, jot down as many ways as possible in which their views differ from or agree with yours."

- "You're about to watch a video clip from *Frankenstein*. Can you find at least two reasons to sympathize with the monster?"

- "After designing the concept map, you'll have to write a justification for each of the interrelationships you've depicted."

EXAMPLE #10/PEER-GROUP LEARNING (PGL)

Peer-group learning is a category of various types of peer interaction in dyads or groups. In PGL, your students can be paired in dyads or grouped together, comparing their ideas, solving problems, carrying out an extensive activity, and so on. To be successful, this interactive exchange needs thorough teacher planning of prompts and activities, including activity sheets with defined social roles that enable the students to function independently.

We consider PGL to be a technique because the practice can be used in every method as appropriate. There is an in-depth description of PGL and activity sheets in Module 5.

Focal Point 2: **Tools**

Tools are materials and various devices, such as activity sheets and instructional machines, respectively. Tools can also generate materials that contain techniques. For example, a computer (tool) may have a program that helps your students categorize (material) and that may contain questions and role-play (techniques). Each device and material has its advantages and disadvantages for implementing various techniques.

Discussion 2: **Tools**

In this age of dazzling technology, the temptation is to confuse the tool (e.g., computers, VCRs and videotapes, and closed-circuit TV) with the substance of a technique or even a method. This confusion is another example of the difference between form and function.

The truth is that tools and their materials are just that. Nothing more. How you decide to implement the tools as conveyers of techniques is the issue. The simple, conventional-looking overhead transparency can be the vehicle of teacher–student and even student–student dialogue that gets your students thinking. A jazzy stand-alone software program or simulation may look great, but if you're working mostly with low-level cognitive skills, bring out the transparency.

Examples of Tools

If tools are used flexibly and imaginatively, they can incorporate all the techniques described in the previous focal point. For example, an activity sheet can include role-playing, questions, modeling, personalizing, concept mapping, and so on. Similarly, a computer-based project can also use those same techniques. So it's important to keep the techniques in mind when you contemplate using instructional tools.

EXAMPLE #1/ACTIVITY SHEET

This time-honored material has been largely overused and misused. It has also been an indispensable vehicle for independent student learning. Why the difference? Form versus function, or the role and content reflecting the teacher's concept of the activity sheet. When thoughtfully prepared, the activity sheet works across a range of contexts: class discussion, individual student input, and peer exchange. Effective activity sheets help organize ideas in discussions or for individual reflection. These may be charts, tables, diagrams, or questions that require student response. The pitfall: designing short-answer, right-wrong, or fill-in-the-blank worksheets. Try to think of an activity sheet as a compass pointing the way to discovery rather than as an exercise that calls for repetition of what you and the textbook have said. Sample activity sheets are provided in Module 5, Part 2.

EXAMPLE #2/OVERHEAD PROJECTOR AND TRANSPARENCIES

Even in the computer age with electronic slides, well-planned overhead transparencies remain an effective facilitator for discussions and critical thinking. *Linguistic prompts* may take any written form: questions, quotations, heuristic guides, fill-in or filled-in tables, fill-in or filled-in concept maps, and so on. Fill-in materials may be useful in the thinking process as prompts (questions and directions) for discussions or a reference for more in-depth analysis, for example, comparing and contrasting differences and similarities. For the most part, however, keep in mind that fill-in materials should not be used as end products in and of themselves.

Visual grabbers may be colorful or black-and-white pictures, charts, graphs, cartoons, and so on that hook your learners' attention. Ideally, visual grabbers are accompanied by a thinking task, either oral or written.

Both linguistic prompts and visual grabbers help focus your students' thinking, generating ideas for discussion. Transparencies may be used as a Hook to introduce a lesson, as a midpoint or final summary, or as an ongoing reference during activities.

LINGUISTIC PROMPTS FOR TRANSPARENCIES

Transparency #1 (Figure 3.14) for Class Discussion: Science

1. A real, dying plant as a Hook and as a vehicle for introducing elements of a controlled experiment. Students must analyze the symptoms of the plant's distress and infer possible hypotheses for the plant's failure to thrive.[2]

Signs of Pathology	Possible Reasons
A. List three to six signs of pathology for the sample plant. 1. 2. 3. 4. 5. 6.	B. List two possible reasons for each pathology. 1. 2. 3. 4. 5. 6.
Variables to Isolate	**Method of Control**
C. List three to six variables that could contribute to the plant's health. 1. 2. 3. 4. 5. 6.	D. List one or more methods to control for each variable. 1. 2. 3. 4. 5. 6.

FIGURE 3.14 Designing a Controlled Experiment

2. A transparency, Figure 3.14, that serves as a prompt for focused observations and analysis in class discussion.

Transparency #2 (Figure 3.15) for Class Discussion: History

1. History readings about the dire effects on Germany resulting from the Versailles Treaty and about the relationship to Nazi anti-Semitism.
2. Excerpts from *Mein Kampf* by Adolf Hitler.
3. Photographs of *Kristallnacht*.
4. A transparency, Figure 3.15, that serves as a prompt for concept analysis in class discussion.

VISUAL GRABBERS FOR TRANSPARENCIES

Transparency #3 (Figure 3.16) for Class Discussion: Math

1. Textbook chapter on probability.
2. Probability problem solving in dyads with activity sheet.
3. A transparency, Figure 3.16, that serves as a prompt for probability analysis in class activity as a Performance Objective.

ORAL DIRECTIONS:

- Draw a chart any way you choose that interprets the information in this graph in a different format from that of the graph.

If there were no Jews, the anti-Semite would make them.

—Anti-Semite and Jew by Jean-Paul Sartre

- Explain Sartre's statement.
- Describe and justify at least two reasons why the statement might be true.
- Compare and contrast anti-Semitism with racism.

FIGURE 3.15 Concept Lesson: Bigotry

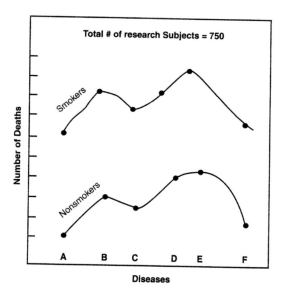

FIGURE 3.16 Concept Lesson: Probability

- Based on your chart, write an argument that tries to persuade a smoker you know to stop smoking, citing the probability of that person getting lung cancer.
- One rule: use percentages in your argument.

Using overhead transparencies as facilitators for dialogue and critical thinking transforms this simple, traditional material into the vehicle for an interactive technique. The value lies in your implementation as well as in the content: the difference between form and function.

EXAMPLE #3/COMPUTER TECHNOLOGIES

Computers are many tools in one. They utilize many applications in addition to accessing the Internet and the Web. Computers are one resource among several. In some ways they serve as additional information sources to books and other traditional printed materials. In other ways, the computer is a tool that can facilitate a technique, for example, as a tool for asynchronous discussions with students around the globe or across the country. The computer can also serve as a vehicle for writing with guiding software, etc. Finally, sophisticated stand-alone software in all subject areas embed various methods and techniques for critical thinking in their operations. Module 6 provides an extensive look at embedding computer-based software and information into methods and ways in which they incorporate techniques.

■ ROUNDUP ■

The techniques described in this module have been around for a long time. So, to repeat what we said before: try to remember the difference between form and function.

For example, the form of questioning can function either as a technique of right-wrong answers in a teacher–student exchange or as a technique that prompts critical thinking. Similarly, activity sheets and overhead transparencies are forms that are being used nationwide as you read these words. In the hands of some teachers, activity sheets and transparencies function merely as fill-in-the-blank rote repetition exercises; in the hands of other teachers, the same materials serve as prompts for higher-level thinking either in class discussions or among students in peer groups. Even role-playing can end up being nothing more than fun, merely lending some color to a lesson that fosters passive student learning. Conversely, role-playing can be the vehicle for student interaction and interpretation of a unit's facts, principles, and themes.

So, you must give a lot of thoughtful planning to the function of the techniques you employ. Sometimes you will decide that an entire lesson will be devoted to the establishment of a factual knowledge base, preparing for a second lesson that encourages students to interpret and evaluate the facts and to infer principles and larger themes based on those facts or serving as the foundation for an extensive project. Even a knowledge-based lesson should engage your students in some interpretation or in organizing the facts according to principles or categories.

Other times you will prepare a lesson with high-level cognition, with your students synthesizing and evaluating, reaching for the moon with feet well grounded in a knowledge base. Most often, you will want to combine establishing a knowledge base of facts with critical thinking (see Figure 3.17). All techniques lend themselves to this variety of instruction.

● Always remember: You yourself must use critical thinking to facilitate your students' critical thinking.

■ HANDS-ON PRACTICE ■

Refer to Figure 3.17 as a visual summary, then try hands-on practice using the following techniques.

A Cognitive Framework Directs Thinking

Deduction = development of a concept or principle with facts. General to specific.

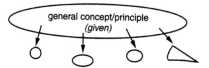

Induction = use of facts to arrive at a concept or principle. Specific to general.

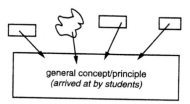

A Technique is a Specific Practice or Procedure

questions   *personalizing*

role-playing

brainstorming   *concept mapping*

peer groups   **modeling**

Techniques Develop Deduction or Induction

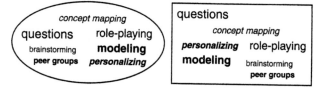

©2001 Ina Claire Gabler

FIGURE 3.17 Cognitive Framework versus Techniques

Self-Instruct Planner: Techniques and Tools

Subject _____ Topic _____

(Work on a separate piece of paper.)

Directions:

1. Decide on a Core Component that you will develop using each technique and tool below.
2. Try your hand with some of the techniques and tools that interest you.
3. Whether you work with the topic you developed in the Core Components "Hands-On Practice" section in Part 1 or whether you work with a different topic, write down the complete Rationale as the rudder for selecting techniques and tools.

RATIONALE

TECHNIQUES:

1. Questions (Refer to Bloom's Taxonomy)
   Trigger (1):
   Probes (3):
   Redirected (3):
2. Role-playing
   Describe the context:
   Describe three roles and the purpose of each:
3. Heuristic
   Invent a pattern or codified steps for carrying out an activity:
4. Brainstorm (work with a partner for this and brainstorm together)
   Concept to be developed:
   Responses:
   Categories of responses:
5. Concept mapping
   Interpret your brainstorming responses and categories from at least two different perspectives and draw a concept map that represents those perspectives.
6. Personalizing
   Try inventing a Hook or Aim that includes personalizing.
7. Modeling
   Design a brief activity that models the activity in the Performance Objective. Modeling should include student participation via questions, directions, and performing a minitask.

TOOLS:

1. Overhead projector with transparencies. Design a transparency that will supply prompts to guide student analysis of a concept or principle or theme integral to the Rationale. Describe any visual grabber you may use.
2. Activity sheet (see Module 5, Part 2).
3. Computer technology (see Module 6 and Technology Tips in Modules 7 through 12 if you're unsure of how to work with this one).

ENDNOTES

1. Based on a heuristic written by Allan Brick at Hunter College in New York City.
2. Based on a lesson by Cyndie Morain when she was a preservice teacher at the University of Illinois in Urbana-Champaign.

SUGGESTED READINGS

Ausubel, D. P. (1960). The use of advance organizers in the learning and retention of meaningful verbal material. *Journal of Educational Psychology, 51*, 267–272.

Bruner, J. S. (1960). *The process of education.* Cambridge, MA: Harvard University Press.

Clark, J. H. (1991). *Patterns of teaching.* Boston: Allyn & Bacon.

Dunn, R., & Dunn, K. (1992). *Teaching secondary students through their individual learning styles: Practical approaches for grades 7-12.* Boston: Allyn & Bacon.

Michaels, S. (1987). Text and context: A new approach to the study of classroom writing. *Discourse Processes, 10,* 321–346.

Novak, J. D. (1990). Concept maps and Vee diagrams: Two metacognitive tools to facilitate meaningful learning. *Instructional Science, 19*(1), 29–52.

Richardson, L. (1994, January 31). More schools are trying to write textbooks out of the curriculum. *New York Times.*

Module Four:
Questioning Skills

PART I:
Promoting Effective Questioning

■ OVERVIEW

questions Questions questions *questions*

Ask questions.
Why?
Questions tackle
you
(wrestlin' with askin')
and your students
(wrestlin' with answerin').
Yeah, questions
make you think
about thinking,
make you think, yeah,
about your students'
thinking. About how to make their
brains buzz.
It's tough
stuff. Students,
they ain't
use-ta it.
You may not be
use-ta it. But
once you both get
use-ta it,
the classroom you gave
up for dead
starts a-shakin' with the wind
of wings.
This takes time.
But you've got
that, yeah.
Try again. And again. And—
Hey, you guys. Study
turtles.
You know, you
ain't goin' nowhere with-
out ploddin'
power.
Yeah.
　　—©2001 Ina Claire Gabler

■ GOALS

So just how do you promote that struggle with new ideas that's so vital in a constructivist classroom? What can you do to challenge your students to immerse themselves in your subject matter? How do you energize those passive students and challenge them to truly think? That's where effective questioning comes in.

Fortunately, there have been a great number of studies completed regarding effective classroom questioning and interaction. This body of research and our own classroom experiences enable us to make a number of suggestions regarding effective teacher questioning techniques in any classroom setting. Effective questioning is the essence of effective teaching and one of the most useful ways to promote critical thinking. As educator Eleanor Duckworth (1987) so aptly noted, "The right question at the right time can move (students) to peaks in their thinking that result in significant steps forward and real intellectual excitement" (p. 5). Because of the central importance of questioning in all constructivist teaching methods, we present a fairly extensive discussion of effective (and ineffective) questioning techniques and then build on these ideas as we introduce a set of innovative teaching methods in Modules 7–12.

In Part 1 of this module, we begin to investigate classroom interaction more specifically. In doing so, we focus on several dimensions of effective questioning, including the following:

- The importance of varying the cognitive level of questions.
- The powerful impact of Wait Time I and II.
- What you should do as you students answer questions.
- Asking effective follow-up questions.
- Other things that you should or should not do when interacting with students.

Focal Point 1: The Importance of Varying Question Cognitive Level

In any setting, it will be important for you to use different kinds of questions, both to help students make cognitive connections and to gain insights into the nature of their thinking. To accomplish this, we suggest that you use Bloom's Taxonomy of Educational Objectives (Bloom, 1956), which is a useful tool for making decisions regarding what to teach and how to go about teaching it. Perhaps the most practical use for the taxonomy is in planning questions that you might ask in the classroom. We call these initial, planned questions *trigger questions*.

Discussion 1: The Importance of Varying Question Cognitive Level

What Is Bloom's Taxonomy?

Bloom's Taxonomy describes six levels of cognitive activity, with each level presumed to require different kinds of thinking processes. Questions formed at the first two levels of the taxonomy are used to elicit facts or information from students. At these levels, information is recognized and recalled. Student ability to perform these tasks reflects a basic understanding of the ideas involved. The next four levels of the taxonomy represent higher-order cognitive thought processes. Individuals who can function at these levels have a much richer understanding of the facts, concepts, and principles involved; we can often infer that the relevant learner schemata (conceptual "bundles" or "parcels" of perceptions or beliefs) are well structured and connected to ideas from other domains.

Before discussing the use of Bloom's Taxonomy in more detail, note that the contexts in which questions are asked can affect not only students' answers but also the way we classify or interpret them. For example, the question "What factors determine an economic recession?" could be used as a knowledge question, a comprehension question, or an analysis question. If students' answers were based on memorized factors listed in a textbook, then the question falls at the knowledge level. However, if the answer was based on speculative trends perceived by a student, the question falls at the analysis level, requiring a much more complex cognitive process. Only by knowing the context for questions can you determine with any certainty if students are working at lower or higher cognitive levels. We have seen teachers fooled into believing that students had developed in-depth understanding of important ideas because they could answer higher-order questions when in fact they were merely repeating words provided earlier by the teacher.

The First Level in Bloom's Taxonomy Is Knowledge

At this level, students are asked questions that require recall or recognition of facts, definitions, and observations. In other words, these questions test your students' basic memory. You must use questions at this level to some extent, since facts, definitions, and so on can provide a foundation for higher-level thinking. Overuse of these basic questions, however, can result in a student memorizing information that is largely disconnected from her frame of reference. Such knowledge is not only meaningless to the student but is also quickly lost (or never really connected) to elements of long-term memory.

EXAMPLES

The following words are often used when asking knowledge-level questions: define, recall, recognize, remember, who, what, when, where, repeat, name, list, record, underline.

In most contexts, the following examples could be classified as knowledge questions: In what year did the Civil War begin? How is a thesis statement defined? What is an independent clause? Who developed the first rabies vaccine? What is the Spanish word for groundhog?

The Second Taxonomic Level Is Comprehension

Questions posed at the comprehension level challenge students to phrase information in ways that make sense to them. Students demonstrate that they understand subject matter by being able to rephrase it, to give a description in their own words, and to use information in describing similarities and making comparisons.

EXAMPLES

There are four types of comprehension questions: those in which students are asked to interpret, translate, provide examples, or define in their own words. Interpretation questions require that students understand the major ideas in a verbal or written statement and how the ideas are related to each other. These relationships are characterized by how and why questions: How do the two poems use a bird metaphor? How do anthropology and sociology differ in respect to what they study? Why would you use this equation to solve this problem?

In translating ideas for themselves, students change ideas from one form of communication to another while retaining the meaning. Data in a graph may be cast as summarizing statements in a paragraph, for example.

The categories of example and definition consist of asking students to give examples of something and to define concepts or principles in their own words. A teacher might ask, for instance, "Who can draw an example of a polygon?" or "Can you tell me in your own words what irony means?" The following words are often used in comprehension questions: describe, compare, contrast, rephrase, explain, translate, restate, discuss, express, identify, locate, review, tell, and summarize.

The Third Taxonomic Level Is Application

At this level, students are given a problem of some kind and are asked to solve it. In doing so, they are able to use what they've learned to do something. They must know when and how to use a particular method of solution. It is important to remember that application is a two-step process. First, students are presented with the problem, requiring that they recognize what kind of problem it is. Second, they must select a solution and solve the problem. It should be noted that some problems may have only one solution. For other problems, there may be several solutions, and those provided will depend on students' individual knowledge and perception. In a science class, for example, students could be asked to write an essay in which an environmental problem, such as overuse of pesticides, is described and a solution is offered. In a history class, students could be asked to state a problem connected to an event and to offer solutions.

EXAMPLES

The following verbs are often used in application-level questions: interpret, apply, employ, use, demonstrate, practice, compute, solve, modify, construct, prove, and illustrate.

The Fourth Taxonomic Level Is Analysis

Questions at this level require students to look at something as a whole and to break it down into component parts. Analysis questions are especially important in helping students develop the critical-thinking skills and abilities described in Module 1.

EXAMPLES

Analysis questions encourage students to use three kinds of cognitive processes:

1. Identifying motives, reasons, and/or causes for a specific occurrence. Examples: What factors caused the economic recession of 1893? What motivated citizens to riot in Los Angeles after the Rodney King verdict? Why haven't the Cubs won a World Series since 1908?

2. Considering available information to reach a conclusion, inference, or generalization based on this information. Examples: What happens at the molecular level if you combine this type of acid with this type of base? Why did state department officials believe that the elimination of the al Qaeda network in Afghanistan would decrease the likelihood of future terrorist attacks in the United States?

3. Analyzing a conclusion, inference, or generalization to find evidence to support or refute it. In this case, students are being asked to present an argument. Examples: How do local recycling programs preserve the quality of the environment? What evidence can you give that supports this interpretation of the poem?

It is important to remember that analysis questions challenge students to learn and understand events and/or concepts and to search for reasons behind those events or concepts. The following words are often used in analysis questions: examine, relate, draw conclusion, provide evidence, support, analyze, why, distinguish, appraise, test, compare/contrast, and criticize.

The Fifth Taxonomic Level Is Synthesis

Questions at this level promote creativity in students because the teacher is asking them to rely on their individual personalities, experiences, and cultural background to produce something original. In constructing knowledge at the synthesis level, students are adding new information and/or developing original products in completing products such as artwork, short stories, orally presented arguments, projects/presentations, and research papers. The key words related to this cognitive level are *original* and *creativity*.

EXAMPLES

Synthesis questions can challenge students to produce original communications, such as poems, plays, and collages; to make predictions (what would happen if . . .); to solve problems; to develop a plan; or to create a set of abstract relations. The following verbs are often used in writing synthesis questions: predict, produce, write, design, develop, compose, create/construct, organize, prepare, and propose. The following phrases are often used within synthesis questions:

How can we improve ___?

What would happen if ___?

Can you devise ___?

How can we solve ___?

The Sixth Taxonomic Level Is Evaluation

In asking questions at this level, you'll be challenging your students to combine the cognitive processes used in answering application, analysis, and synthesis questions. In effect, students are being asked to establish a set of appropriate values or standards and then to determine how closely the idea or concept meets these standards or values. In other words, students must make value judgments that should be reasonable and rational and then defend those judgments in a logical way. These judgments should be based primarily on logic rather than on emotion, and the processes used include many of those associated with critical thinking. In promoting the development of critical-thinking abilities, evaluation questions allow students to recognize and take a stand on issues and to reevaluate their own positions as they consider the ideas of others. In providing feedback to evaluation questions as a teacher, you should remember that there are no right and wrong answers but that some viewpoints may seem to be more defensible and reasonable than others. We investigate these important considerations in more detail in Module 11.

EXAMPLES

Evaluation questions will be especially important in conducting reflective discussions, but they can and should be used in many types of lessons. Examples: Should patients be allowed to choose euthanasia as an option in extreme medical cases? Is Communism really "dead" as a viable form of government? What is more important: preserving old growth forests or providing lumber-related jobs in the northwest? What is the best way to complete this geometric proof? Were the actions of Friar Lawrence justified? The following verbs are used in writing evaluation questions: judge, argue, decide, appraise, evaluate, choose, rate, compare, evaluate, select, assess, and select. The following phrases can also be used in writing and asking evaluation questions:

What is your opinion of___?

Do you agree with this position? Why/why not?

Which is better (more effective, more beautiful, etc.)?

As we introduce a variety of constructivist methods in Modules 7 through 12, you'll see that questions at some cognitive levels are closely associated with certain methods (e.g., Inductive Concept lessons feature an abundance of analysis questions). But remember that almost any kind of lesson should include a mix of questions from these cognitive levels. Varying your trigger, probing, and redirecting questions will make your lessons challenging for your students and more intellectually stimulating for you as the teacher. We also invite you to teach the taxonomy to your students directly; they can use it to generate their own intriguing questions for you and each other. Urging students to ask insightful questions should be a major part of the constructivist classroom experience. As you compose questions for future lessons, keep our earlier admonition in mind: the cognitive level, and the cognitive processes initiated, by any question depends on the context in which the question is asked. Remember that teachers sometimes fool themselves into believing that they are asking higher order questions when in fact students are relying on lower order (i.e., memorized) responses.

Focal Point 2: **The Powerful Impact of Wait Time I and II**

Imagine that you've stepped into your own classroom with an exciting lesson plan in hand. You've prepared a series of challenging trigger questions. You begin the lesson, and ask the first of these thought-provoking questions. What should you do immediately after asking each of those important questions? The answer is simple: wait! Actually give your students enough time to think about the question that you've just posed.

This brief period of silence is known as *wait time*, and it is one of the most important teacher behaviors associated with effective questioning. There are actually two different types of wait time. *Wait Time I* is the pause between the end of a teacher's question and the teacher saying or doing something else (e.g., calling on another student or rephrasing the question). *Wait Time II* is the pause between the end of a student's response and the teacher doing something else (e.g., asking another question or giving feedback).

Subtle though they may seem, a number of studies on classroom interaction have shown that the use of Wait Time I and II are the most important variables in effective teacher questioning (Rowe, 1974; Tobin, 1987; Dillon, 1988). In cognitive terms, it is easy to see why wait time is important: learners of all ages need time to perceive the question, process its meaning, formulate an answer, and begin to respond. It also makes sense that complex, higher-order questions would require extra wait time.

An important question becomes, "How long should a teacher wait after asking a question or receiving a student response?" Research has shown that teachers should wait a minimum of three seconds before replying, asking another question, or saying or doing something else (Tobin, 1987). Again, wait time should be considerably longer when associated with more complex questions. These same studies (and our own classroom experiences) have shown us that the benefits of wait time diminish after twenty seconds because students tend to stop thinking about the question at this point and begin to feel uneasy about the silence. Unfortunately, research also shows that the average teacher wait time is less than one second (Tobin, 1987), which doesn't leave students much time to come up with thoughtful replies. As a vivid example of lack of wait time, have you ever seen the comedic movie and television teacher who asks students questions and then drones "Anyone, anyone?" before answering the questions himself? Many teachers feel uneasy in allowing even brief periods of silence. It is important to become comfortable with allowing brief periods of silence as vital thinking time in your classroom.

Research Findings

Why are these brief periods of silence so important? Researchers have shown that the use of sufficient wait time has a profound effect on the learning of students. For example, the following changes have been noted in classrooms where teachers have been taught to extend wait time:

- Student learning, as reflected in the number of correct oral responses and in scores on written tests, increased significantly.
- The number of students who failed to answer when called on decreased.
- The number of unsolicited but appropriate responses increased.

- The length of student responses increased.
- The number of student statements where evidence was used to make inferences increased.
- The number of responses from students identified by teachers as less able increased.
- The number of student–student interactions increased (i.e., students were more likely to listen and respond to each others' ideas).
- The number of student questions increased (Dillon, 1988; Rowe, 1974; Tobin, 1987).

In addition, teachers who extended wait time were perceived by students to be more caring and patient. Students interviewed seemed to feel that these patient teachers were truly interested in their ideas. In extending wait time, it was also found that teachers made fewer errors characterized by responding illogically or inappropriately to student comments; a little silence also provides teachers with important thinking time (Tobin, 1987).

The educational benefits of using extended Wait Time I and II are obviously dramatic. This makes sense when you stop to consider that everyone needs time to think! This is especially true of students with particular learning-style preferences (Module 1). Many learners (e.g., those with strong abstract-sequential preferences) are particularly deliberate and thorough thinkers and perhaps are more cautious when it comes to volunteering ideas. It has been our sad observation that these are the students who don't actively participate in classrooms where teachers fail to extend wait time.

Specific Recommendations

Based on the extensive research conducted, and on our own classroom experiences, we can make the following recommendations related to wait time.

- Extend Wait Time I to at least three seconds for lower-order, factual questions and to at least five seconds for higher-order questions.
- For particularly complex questions, extend initial wait time and allow students to spend two to three minutes considering the question and noting their initial ideas on paper.
- For complex questions, allow five to ten seconds of thinking time and then ask students what processes they are using to answer the question. This reinforces the critical-thinking notion that the process is as important as the answer and that there may be many ways to solve problems or consider issues.
- After fifteen to twenty seconds of wait time, rephrase or simplify your initial question if you feel that students are unsure of how to begin.
- Extend Wait Time II to promote student–student interaction. It is vital for teachers to challenge students to listen to and build on each others ideas, and extending Wait Time II is a subtle way to do this.
- Explain your reasons for extending wait time to students. Tell the class that you are allowing them a few seconds of thinking time after you ask a question.

Some students, like some teachers, are initially uncomfortable with periods of silence.

Focal Point 3. **While Your Students Answer Questions**

As we have discussed the importance of varying question cognitive level and extending Wait Time I and II, an important question may have occurred to you: What should I, as the teacher, do while a student is actually answering a question? You can promote a thinker-friendly classroom atmosphere by consciously considering these attending behaviors. In general, it will be vital for you send the message that you're listening closely to what your students are saying. You'll want to encourage them to continue and focus the attention of the entire class on the student who is responding. You can promote a thinker-friendly classroom atmosphere by consciously considering the following attending behaviors:

1. Maintain eye contact with the student who is speaking. Glance around the room from time to time to be sure that everyone is listening. If necessary, ask the student to repeat the response, and remind classmates to listen.

2. Use nonverbal gestures to indicate your support and understanding. Our experiences have shown that subtle head nodding, encouraging facial expressions, hand gestures, and assuming an open physical stance that shows that you are thinking about what the student is saying all make a difference.

3. Demonstrate to students that you're listening. Do not interrupt, even if you believe the student is headed in the wrong direction; this will discourage students from participating and taking intellectual risks in your classroom. At times, students will realize their mistakes and correct them. On other occasions, you may simply have misunderstood where the student was headed with the response. Even when students provide partially incorrect or even far-out responses, remember that both you and your students can learn much from mistakes. This is characteristic of thinker-friendly communities. Listening is the best way to encourage further participation and to alert you to the nature of students' understanding.

4. Remember your Wait Time II. Pause for two to three seconds; the student may add to the initial response, or a classmate might jump in with an insightful comment. You might find that using Wait Time II is even more challenging than using Wait Time I, especially when a student makes a truly insightful statement. Be patient.

5. Reply on some occasions with a reflective comment. Paraphrase all or part of the student response as a statement or a question ("It sounds like you feel that . . ."). In most cases, we have found that the student will add more detail to the original answer. Again, this technique, when judiciously applied, makes students aware that you are listening and challenges them to expand on their ideas and to explain what they've said. Don't overdo it.

We've now taken a close look at that critical few seconds as and after you ask your students a question. Let's now suppose that they've given you a response. What might you do next?

Asking Effective Follow-Up Questions

Using student responses to ask effective follow-up questions will be one of the biggest keys to promoting thought-provoking discourse (i.e., intelligent, purposeful conversation) in your classroom. In this section, we discuss two important types of follow-up questions that we refer to throughout the text: the probe and the redirect.

Probing Questions

It is vitally important to ask probing questions during any type of lesson. Probing questions challenge students to think in more depth and to add detail or otherwise build on what they've said. More than anything, asking these questions challenge students to think at higher cognitive levels. Probing questions are essential if you are to help students move beyond a superficial understanding of ideas.

EXAMPLES

Probing questions can take on a variety of forms. When used effectively, they can challenge students to do the following:

1. Clarify and add detail to what they have said.
   - What do you mean by _____?
   - Could you say that in another way?
   - Can you give us an example?
   - Would you tell us more about _____?
   - *Why* would you say that?
   - When you say that, do you mean ____ or ____?

2. Think about assumptions that they or others might be making.
   - What are you assuming in saying this?
   - What assumption is John making here?
   - Why would/could anyone assume that _____?
   - Is this always the case?

3. Provide support for what they are saying.
   - Why do you think this is true?
   - How do we know that ____?
   - What evidence do you have for saying that?
   - What other information do we need?
   - Do these reasons provide enough support for your statement?
   - How could we find out whether this is true?

4. Consider the frames of reference of other people.
   - How would someone who believes _____ feel about this?
   - What other alternatives are there?
   - What would someone who disagrees say?

- How would somebody like _____ respond to what you said?
5. Consider implications of a statement.
   - What impact would _____ have?
   - Would this always happen in a case like this?
   - Why is this question important/difficult?

As we introduce a series of methods in Modules 7 through 12, we'll discuss the use of probing questions. You'll see that different kinds of probes are often emphasized when you use certain methods, but that asking probing questions (and encouraging your students to ask them) should be a major part of any constructivist classroom experience.

Redirect Questions

The second type of follow-up question is the redirect. In its simplest form, redirecting refers to repeating the question, not necessarily verbatim, to another student. This technique is useful for determining the degree of consensus in the group regarding any statement.

EXAMPLES

Regardless of which student responded to the question "How would you define surface area?" a math teacher might redirect the question by merely asking, "Does the definition express the concept as you understand it, Vince?" or "How would you define surface area, Sara?" Another option would be to ask for a quick show of hands to gauge how other students feel about a statement made by a classmate (How many would agree that _____?). You can also combine elements of the probe and redirect by asking something like "How are Sara's and Vince's ideas different?" Using redirecting questions frequently will encourage your students to listen to each other and to think about what their peers have said.

Focal Point 5: **What Else Should Teachers Do (or Not Do) to Question Students Effectively?**

Engaging each of your students through questioning will be a key to your success as a teacher. This will be true regardless of the teaching method you use. As we introduce a variety of methods in Modules 7 through 12, we will place great emphasis on promoting effective classroom interaction. In this way, we hope to help you develop skills and abilities that will transfer to any teaching situation. When conducting any type of lesson, we recommend that you maximize student participation by doing the following:

1. Encourage students to participate in all of your lessons, especially when using highly student-centered methods. In general, speak in a friendly tone of voice; use positive nonverbal cues (e.g., smiling and eye contact) and provide positive feedback

judiciously to establish a thinker-friendly environment. When students provide truly insightful comments, get specific with your praise ("Cindy's comment is interesting because _____").

2. Ask questions of the entire class frequently as a way of encouraging all students to participate. One advantage of calling only on volunteers is that this may be less threatening to those who are not used to active participation. One obvious disadvantage is that the same small group of students may answer all of your questions unless you direct some questions to specific students.

3. Call on specific students frequently as a way of gaining insights into the nature of their understanding and to encourage participation. Be sure to ask the question first, pause, and then call a student's name. This helps ensure that each student will listen to your question. Calling on a range of students early in a lesson can break the ice and encourage even shy students to take part in the lesson. Use a student's name first in cases where student attention may be lacking. You can deliver an effective wake-up call by doing this.

4. Randomly select students as you ask questions. If you follow a predictable pattern students may relax if they are sure that they will not be called on. Be sure to call on students in the back corners of the room. Researchers have shown that students in the front and center of the room are far more likely to become involved in classroom discussions (Dillon, 1988). In your classroom, you may want to experiment with index cards or Popsicle sticks with students' names on them, pulling a stick or card randomly to determine who should answer the question. These methods can be effective if they are not used too often.

5. At all costs, avoid repeating student responses. Teacher repetition will result in students listening to you, not each other. If necessary, ask students to repeat or rephrase softly stated or vague responses; this will be challenging at first, since many students will not be used to active, thoughtful participation. By not repeating responses, you send the message that teachers and textbooks are not the ultimate sources of knowledge in the classroom. In any case, insist that students listen to and respect one other's statements.

6. Don't allow certain students to dominate a lesson. Call on other volunteers and nonvolunteers, and remind outspoken students that everyone needs to have a chance to speak as necessary. It is vital to emphasize careful listening in your classroom and to model positive listening behaviors yourself.

7. Avoid asking all of your questions at the end of a lesson. When using any teaching method, ask questions throughout your lessons. In this way, you are in a position to challenge your students to process new ideas and to continually assess the nature of student understanding. As a general rule, never talk for more than three minutes without asking a question, even when you are presenting new ideas.

8. Encourage students to ask questions of you and each other. Meaningful student questions are surprisingly rare in most classrooms. Again, openly praise students who

ask thoughtful questions, and tell them why the question is worthwhile ("That's a good question because _____"). Make the most of opportunities to explore points that students may find interesting and relevant by redirecting student questions ("Would anyone care to reply to Sue's question?").

9. Don't rely on the use of "Any questions?" as a check on student understanding. Some students may be so confused or disinterested that they won't say a word. Never assume that students understand new ideas simply because they don't ask you questions. We have witnessed situations in which students seemed so bored or hopelessly confused that they didn't know what to ask.

■ ROUNDUP ■

Effectively questioning students in the classroom is no easy task. However, you can't become an effective teacher without being an effective questioner. We hope that the practical advice provided in Part 1 of this module will help you begin the process of becoming an effective questioner.

In Part 1, we introduced a number of important ideas that we'll expand on throughout the text. The first of these is the importance of varying cognitive level in the questions that you ask. Use Bloom's Taxonomy as a tool for planning effective trigger questions (more on this in Parts 2 and 3 of this module). You'll find that varying question cognitive level will help your students do more than simply recall information; higher-order questions will challenge them to think deeply about your subject matter and to use what they've learned.

We also explained Wait Time I and II, and provided a rationale for extending wait time. It has been our experience that providing this thinking time is critical. This can also convey to your students that you really do care about what they think, which is an especially important factor in creating a thinker-friendly environment for your students. They'll be much more likely to take desired intellectual risks if they feel that you're a thoughtful and sympathetic listener.

We also introduced probing and redirecting questions. Asking these follow-up questions will be a major part of every teaching method that we'll introduce in this text. Remember that your ultimate goals in asking these questions are to engage more of your students in classroom dialogue and to challenge everyone to think more deeply about the topic at hand. We also invite you to consider the other practical advice regarding questioning as you plan and teach your initial lessons. Effective teaching can't take place without effective questioning.

REFERENCES

Bloom, B. (1956). *Taxonomy of educational objectives.* New York: David McKay.
Dillon, J. T. (1988). *Questioning and discussion: A multidisciplinary study.* Norwood, NJ: Ablex Publishing.

Duckworth, E. (1987). *The having of wonderful ideas and other essays on teaching and learning.* New York: Teachers College Press.

Rowe, M. (1974). Wait time and rewards as instructional variables, their influence on language, logic, and fate control. *Journal of Research in Science Teaching, 11,* 81–94.

Tobin, K. (1987). The role of wait time in higher cognitive learning. *Review of Educational Research, 57,* 69–95.

PART 2:
Questions: Do's, Don'ts, and Tips

Overview

Goals

Focal Points and Discussions

Designing Individual Questions

Trigger, Probe, and Redirected Questions

Question Patterns

Designing Question Clusters

Wait Time

ROUNDUP

REFERENCES

SUGGESTED READINGS

■ OVERVIEW

Questions. Questions. A mind feels dead without them. The challenge is this: How do you as a teacher pose questions that your students want to answer?

Designing questions is a honed skill before it becomes an art. It all begins with learning how to write a single, well-pitched question. The question itself may actually be very simple—even just a single word, "Why?" or "How?" It's the context and the timing as well as the question itself that combine to make a question sing with just the right pitch. For this reason, writing questions is not as easy as it may seem. Pitfalls await the unsuspecting: embedded answers, obvious answers, yes-no answers, and plain old boring answers not worth the efforts of your student's raising their hands.

■ GOALS

This section is devoted to techniques for writing effective questions. Using a roll-up-your-sleeves approach, we convey the following:

- Do's and Don'ts for all question types.
- Effective Trigger, Probe, and Redirected questions described in Part 1 of this module.
- Principles of designing question clusters.
- Suggestions for question patterns.
- A two-part formula for writing any type of individual question.

■ DISCUSSION

As you've seen in Part 1 of this module, planning is essential for effective question writing. The engaging constructivist teacher poses a thought-provoking individual question as well an effective question cluster, that is, a thought-out sequence or "package" of several questions, each one building on the previous one. Imagine a series of question clusters that facilitate higher and higher levels of thinking. This engaging teacher could be you.

We are not advocating prescripting every question. Talented teachers ask pertinent, electric, and challenging questions spontaneously as the discussion or peer exchange requires. Instead, we are promoting the practice of planning individual questions and question clusters that help move the thought process along, guiding your students to their own interpretations and analysis of the information at hand; that jump-start the discussion when it stalls; and that motivate your students to research a new angle on a familiar concept.

Beware! If you do not thoughtfully plan key questions in advance, then you risk not being able to effectively depart from your planned lesson, to be able to pluck questions out of your pocket and guide the discussion meaningfully if your students take a different route from the one you had anticipated. In fact, we guarantee that your students will explore unexpected terrain—if you engage their interest. So you need preplanned questions to complement spontaneous ones. This way, you'll be prepared to travel the back roads along with your students while you guide them meaningfully.

Focal Point 1: Designing Individual Questions

There is no magic formula to ensure that you compose terrific questions. After all, it's your intelligence and imagination, your grasp of your subject matter, and context and timing in the moment—not to mention experience—that combine to generate effective questions.

EXAMPLES OF DO'S AND DON'TS

DO'S

1. Include both a question word (who, what, when, where, why, how) and a precise term (a concrete concept, detail, or idea).

   a. (Vague) "What can we say about the main character?"

   b. (Includes precise term) "What was a strength of the main character?"

   c. (Vague) "How did we approach this experiment?"

   d. (Includes precise term) "Why was the first step important in this experiment?"

   e. (Includes precise terms) "What do you think was one of the three most important variables in this experiment?" (then follow up with: "What was another important variable?" and so on).

DON'TS

1. Don't embed the answer in the question.

a. (Embedded answer) "So can we say that slavery was a major cause of the Civil War?" (This question states that slavery was a major cause.)

b. (Nonembedded answer) "What was a major cause of the Civil War? Please explain." (Note the question word and the precise term.)

c. (Nonembedded answer) "Why was slavery a major cause of the Civil War?"

d. (Embedded answer) "Do you see that line and shape affect proportion?" (This question tells the students that line and shape affect proportion.)

e. (Nonembedded answer) "How do line and shape affect proportion?" or "What are two elements that affect proportion?"

2. Don't ask a run-on question (two or three questions in a row). Students don't know which question to answer. In addition, effective questions get lost in the shuffle. Ask one question, then wait.

a. (Run-on) "Why did the United States drop the first atomic bomb on Japan? Was it to win the war? Or to demonstrate our military superiority? Do you think the Japanese would have surrendered if we hadn't dropped the bomb?"

b. (Run-on question organized as a question cluster with individual questions posed between responses.)

"Why did the United States drop the first atomic bomb on Japan?"

Student response.

"Who gained from this?" (This is a possible question appropriate for the second part of the run-on that asked, "Or to demonstrate our military superiority?" The latter contains an embedded answer.)

Student response.

"Do you think the Japanese would have surrendered if we hadn't dropped the bomb? When?"

Student response.

"Why?"

Run-ons often result from insufficient planning. The question cluster is far more effective and requires advanced teacher reflection.

3. Don't ask the most challenging questions before a knowledge base has been established. Without low-level warm-up questions that bring your students into the discussion, guiding their insights, the students won't be prepared to answer the high-level question(s) and will likely be intimidated.

a. (High-level cognitive question at the outset of discussion) "What does the headless horseman symbolize?"

b. (Building knowledge base first according to Bloom's Taxonomy.)

"What is the conflict between Brom Bones and Ichabod Crane?"

"How does Brom Bones try to frighten Ichabod Crane?"

"How does Brom Bones succeed or fail in scaring Ichabod Crane? What happens?"

"Who or what is the headless horseman?"

"What do you think the headless horseman symbolizes?"

4. Don't ask yes-no questions without a tag such as "Why?" or "Please explain."

    a. (Yes-No questions)

    "Did the United States drop the first atomic bomb on Japan?"

    "Did the bomb demonstrate U.S. military superiority?"

    "Was there a conflict between Brom Bones and Ichabod Crane?"

    "Does the headless horseman symbolize our (ignorance, fear, desire for power, evil)?"

    b. (With tag)

    "Did the United States drop the first atomic bomb on Japan? Why?"

    "Did the bomb demonstrate U.S. military superiority? Please explain."

    "Was there a conflict between Brom Bones and Ichabod Crane? Please describe it in your own words."

    "Does the headless horseman symbolize our (ignorance, fear, desire for power, evil)? In what way?"

5. Don't ask "what about" questions. They always need clarification. Use a precise term.

    a. What about slavery?

    b. (Instead): Why did the North oppose slavery?

    c. What about X and Y?

    d. (Instead): How does X relate to Y in this word problem?

Focal Point 2: Trigger, Probe, and Redirected Questions

An effective question cluster consists of Trigger, Probe, and Redirected questions (see Module 3, Part 2, and Module 4, Part 1). Naturally, specific Probes and Redirects are often improvised, relating to the students' responses. But you can preplan approximations according to your instructional intentions.

Discussion 2: Trigger, Probe, and Redirected Questions

Different types of questions yield different results. As you will soon see, the question sequence also matters. It's like building a house from the bottom up. Without a foundation, everything sinks. Trigger, Probe, and Redirected questions work together in a kind of choreography, creating a step-by-step sequence that helps process information beneath the surface.

A *Trigger question opens a topic on any level.* You may decide that a principle, for example, may embody three features necessary for your students to grasp for them to formulate the principle. You will need at least one Trigger question to introduce each feature. A Trigger question can also spark exploration of a concept or theme. So think of a Trigger question as a launching pad.

OK. You've launched the idea. What's next? The *Probe* question does what its name suggests: it digs a bit for substance. *Probes elicit examples and further explanations of the response to the Trigger question.* "Can you build on that idea?" you say to a student's unfounded assertion, directing her to the article or video notes or computations in a software application. Be careful that your Probe questions coax rather than intimidate your students. It helps a lot if you make them aware of what Probe questions are and why you pose them.

You want to bring everyone into the discussion. That's when you pose a *Redirected* question. *Quite literally, you redirect the intention of a Trigger or Probe question to another student or to the class at large.* Redirects can be broad: "Who has a different point of view about X?" or "Can anyone else think of another example?" or "Who can compare and contrast what Jose and Lucretia have said about Z?" In this way, you can sequence Trigger, Probe, and Redirected questions to facilitate your students' thinking process.

Remember to select pertinent materials. Insist that your students justify their viewpoints by referring to specific content in the materials. Assertions made from life experience must also be supported with specific examples.

EXAMPLES OF TRIGGER, PROBE, AND REDIRECTED QUESTIONS

Take a look at the examples of interrelated Trigger, Probe, and Redirected questions in Figure 4.1 for an overview. More examples appear in context in Focal Point 4.

Trigger Opens the discussion with a broad question	Probe Asks the respondent to explain further; guides the respondent to insight that benefits the student and class	Redirected Poses a question on the same issue to the entire class; invites various angles on the same issue
Why did the United States drop an atomic bomb on Japan in World War II?	1. In addition to wanting to win the war, what other reason might have motivated dropping the atomic bomb on Japan? Why? 2. That's an interesting idea. Could you explain a bit more how national pride could have been a factor, citing some facts? 3. Can you justify national pride in this situation or not? Why?	1. Could someone put that in your own words? 2. Does anyone agree? Disagree? 3. Can anyone think of yet another motive for dropping the atomic bomb?

FIGURE 4.1 Trigger, Probe and Redirected Questions

Question Patterns

Both deductive and inductive frameworks (see Module 2, Part 2, and Module 8) are most successful when you interrelate questions progressively. Our examples of question clusters in Focal Point 4 demonstrate this kind of interrelated progression. But first, take a look at some techniques used for posing questions, what we call *question patterns* that can be repeated for a specific outcome. Consider the examples below like training wheels on a bicycle. See if you like our examples, and try to come up with your own after you've had some experience. Refer to Figure 4.1 for these question patterns.

EXAMPLES OF QUESTION PATTERNS

EXAMPLE #1/QUESTION SEQUENCE TO GUIDE INTERPRETATION

Question 1 asks for a reaction to the text, visual, etc.

Question 2 asks for textual or visual examples.

Question 3 asks for an explanation, that is, "How/why is this description an example of ___?," and/or asks any one of the questions that follow.

EXAMPLE #2/SAMPLE PROBES

1. Explain the reason for _____.
2. How does _____ apply?
3. Can you predict what would happen if _____?
4. Predict the outcome if _____.
5. Why?
6. Compare and contrast _____ and _____? What do you think is significant here?

EXAMPLE #3/SAMPLE REDIRECTS

1. Does anyone agree? Why?
2. Does someone have a different way of seeing things? Please explain.
3. What could be another interpretation of _____?
4. Could someone find another example that's evidence for _____?
5. What do you think the relationship is between _____?

EXAMPLE #4/SAMPLE MINI-SUMMARY CLARIFICATIONS DURING DISCUSSIONS

1. Based on what Ella, David, and Sue have said about _____, we can say that _____.
2. So are you saying that _____?
3. How could you combine these ideas into a single statement?

EXAMPLE #5/SAMPLE PERSONAL INTERPRETATIONS

1. How would you feel about _____? Why?

2. How might the appearance of things be (e.g., misleading/convincing/the opposite of what was expected)? Why?

3. What do you think is significant about _____ and _____? Why?

Focal Point 4: Designing Question Clusters

A *question cluster is a series of three or more interrelated Trigger questions (along with corresponding Probe and Redirected questions) that are sequenced to guide students' interpretation of a targeted concept, principle, or theme* (see Module 2, Part 1). Effective question clusters take thought: it's a tricky balance of establishing a knowledge base en route to higher-level analysis and synthesis without being too obvious (boring) or intimidating (scaring students away from taking risks).

One approach is to organize your questions into two broad categories that elicit two strands of understanding. Strand One questions elicit the literal information or facts, what we refer to as the *knowledge base*. Strand Two questions elicit analysis, synthesis, and evaluation, the original insights founded on the facts. Such insights can be thought of as hidden stories. Each strand of interrelated questions consists of a question cluster.

Both question strands and question clusters are most effective when designed according to Bloom's Taxonomy. Strand One questions correspond to Bloom's low-level cognitive questions. Strand Two questions correspond to Bloom's high-level cognitive questions.

Discussion 4: Designing Question Clusters

To the teacher, Strand Two questions are the most exciting to pose. Typically, new teachers ask these difficult questions first as a way to motivate their students. This often backfires. The reason is that you know far more than your students do in your subject area. What is mental fun for you may be beyond the grasp of your students. At first.

Sequence Matters

In your effort to stimulate your students with challenging questions early in the lesson, you may only intimidate your learners. They may not be able to answer an evaluation question posed at the beginning of the lesson, before they are grounded. This inability fosters insecurity and reluctance to answer. But they will be able to answer the very same question toward the middle or end of the lesson, after they grow familiar with related facts and concepts.

The Takeoff Factor

Think of an airplane. Before it takes flight, it needs to run along the ground to gain momentum. In the same way, your students need to ground themselves with factual information and basic concepts before they venture into higher thinking. Your thought-out question sequence facilitates the takeoff factor.

Technique for Designing Question Clusters

Try out these steps for writing question clusters.

1. CONCEPTUALIZE: Reflect on your ideas. Plan backwards, from the insights to the facts. What are the concepts, principles, or themes you want your students to name, interpret, and analyze? What are the facts that build these insights? Reflect on how you can facilitate a thought process to get there. With this approach in mind, consider A and B below.

 A. Strand Two/Insights (concepts, principles, themes)
 - Decide what concepts, principles, and themes(s) and/or hidden stories are implied between the lines. There may be several possibilities.
 - Jot down the concepts, principles, and themes and hidden stories you deem significant for the lesson Rationale.

 B. Strand One/Salient Facts
 - Decide on key facts in the learning materials that are integral to the target concepts, principles, and/or theme.
 - Jot down these key facts as a reference.

2. COMPOSE: Write your questions, referring to your facts and Bloom's Taxonomy (see the full version in Module 4, Part 1). Think through the sequence. Order the questions so that they facilitate increasing insight for your students.

 A. Strand One/Fact Questions
 - Write questions that elicit the important facts you wrote down for Strand One.
 - Start with low-level questions that interpret and apply the facts.

 B. Strand Two/Insight Questions (concepts, principles, themes)
 - Write Strand Two questions that guide analysis, synthesis, and/or evaluation of the facts from Strand One questions. These questions elicit the concepts, principles, or themes, the hidden stories you identified, or others you may have missed but which the students perceive.
 - Move up the cognitive levels.

 C. Question Formula: Remember that effective questions contain a question word plus a precise term. Question words are who, what, when, where, why, and how. A precise, concrete term directs your students' focus.

3. Keep this in mind: you must employ critical thinking as a facilitator of your students' critical thinking.

EXAMPLE OF QUESTION CLUSTERS

EXAMPLE/SOCIAL STUDIES

Principle: The application of justice is inequitable according to economic class and race. (Induction)

1. CONCEPTUALIZE

   A. Strand Two/Insights (concepts, principles, and themes based on sources and life experience.)

      - Our society does not value poor racial minorities as much as it does affluent people.

      - Despite advances in social practices and professed egalitarian attitudes concerning racial minorities, racism may still pervade on an unspoken level.

      - Racism today may have insidious consequences, especially for poor minorities. Although racism may not be considered a socially acceptable attitude, it seems to exist, sometimes with pernicious consequences.

   B. Strand One/List Pertinent Facts

      - Poor minorities are convicted of and executed for committing homicide more frequently than are their white counterparts.

      - Poor minority defendants are often assigned a court-appointed lawyer who is significantly underpaid and overworked. Such an attorney will not devote enough time to his client's case.

      - Affluent defendants hire clever lawyers equipped with researchers to prepare a strong defense.

      - In 2000, Governor George Ryan of Illinois ordered a temporary halt to executions because of the large proportion of prisoners on death row discovered to be innocent based on genetic testing. The majority of those on death row were minorities.

2. COMPOSE QUESTIONS

   A. Strand One/Fact Questions:

   Cluster 1

      - According to the *New York Times* article, what change did Governor George Ryan order in Illinois prisons in 2000? (Trigger)

      - Why did Governor Ryan issue this order? (Probe)

      - Are there any other reasons? (Redirect)

      - What racial or economic groups of prisoners were affected by this order? (Trigger)

   Cluster 2

      - Based on the video clip, explain how the racial population on death row compares proportionately with that of the general population. (Trigger; implied question)

- Based on the article, what is one reason for this disparity? (Probe = inferior legal defense versus strong legal defense of the more affluent)
- What is another reason? (Redirect = possible racism)
- Support your answer. (Probe)

B. Strand Two/Insight Questions (concepts, principles, themes)

Cluster 1

- In what ways can racism be obvious? (Trigger)
- Can you think of another way? Explain. (Probe)
- Can anyone think of yet another? (Redirect)
- Give us an example. (Probe)

Cluster 2

- What distinction can be made about open racism and concealed racism? (Trigger)
- Can you give an example? (Probe)
- What could be another example? (Redirect)
- What other differences could be made between open and concealed racism? (Redirect)
- What are some examples of this second distinction? (Probe)

Cluster 3

- In the *Newsweek* article, how do the data support the relationship between poverty and race? Explain. (Trigger)
- How do the data support the relationship between poverty and crime? (Probe or Redirect)
- Support your answer. Be specific.
- How might all this apply to prisoners on death row? (Trigger)
- Explain. (Probe)

Cluster 4

- How could concealed racism affect our society in general? (Trigger)
- Please give an example. (Probe)
- Any other examples? (Redirect)
- What is a possible definition of justice? (Trigger)

Cluster 5

- According to your definition and based on the topic of our discussion, what limited judgments can you make about the application of justice in our society and why? (Trigger)
- How could the application of justice be more equitable? (Probe)
- Who can add to that? (Redirect)

Remember: you must employ critical thinking as a facilitator of your students' critical thinking.

<u>Focal Point 5:</u> **Wait Time**

We'll repeat some points about wait time, ideas that we mentioned earlier in Module 4, Part 1, because they're so important: First use Wait Time I, that is, wait after you ask a question. Let ten to thirty seconds go by and smile as you look around the room. Students need time to think. An effective Strand Two question should require students to think.

Next, use Wait Time II, meaning, wait after a student answers. Such a pause invites other students to add their own thoughts. It also invites the original responder to expand on his response.

<u>Discussion 5:</u> **Wait Time**

Wait time is difficult for teachers because we have a particular answer in mind and expect the students to arrive at the same answer immediately: it seems so obvious to us! The silence after a question also makes us nervous that our students aren't "getting it." Not to mention that many teachers are accustomed to doing most of the talking in class (Johnson & Johnson, 1989; Putnam, 1997; Slavin, 1995).

Just imagine yourself as a student in a subject not your specialty. How long does it take you to dare to answer a question whose answer you may not be certain of? It takes time to digest new or unfamiliar information. Machine gun questions, referred to earlier as run-on questions, overwhelm and confuse students. Which one do they answer? Let your students think. Their answers may be different from the one you have in mind, but they may also be fertile ground for more questions and more thinking.

Imagine wait time as a fertilized egg (Figure 4.2), hanging in the air, the silence being the sound of gestation. Try envisioning this image a few times, and after you grow accustomed to the sound of thinking, wait time will become fun because you will learn that it invites response.

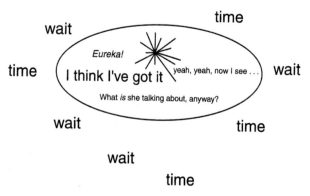

©2001 Ina Claire Gabler

FIGURE 4.2 Wait Time

■ ROUNDUP ■

Who gains from questions?
What are the gains?
Where are the gains found?
When?
Why?
How do you keep the gains coming?

Effective questioning is essential for the constructivist teacher, the technique that wears the crown in all methods. A lesson or project planned without effective questions, whether written on an activity sheet or posed orally, is like a house built without a strong framework. It all tumbles down, despite the best of ideas.

Relying predominantly on questions-in-action (the inspiration of the moment) to articulate questions is risky. The result may likely be run-on questions as you think aloud, or vague questions, or questions with embedded answers—or all of the above.

We urge you to preplan, meaning, prethink your Trigger, Probe, and Redirected questions and question clusters, those inquiries that keep the lesson on target, even as your students take you down unexpected roads. The masterful teacher can improvise effective questions amidst the unexpected because she or he has preplanned and thought out the essential questions, thereby keeping a mental compass. Become that master teacher.

NOTE: Part 3 of this module serves as an in-class minipracticum Hands-On Practice for questioning skills.

REFERENCES

Johnson, D., & Johnson, R. (1989). *Cooperation and competition: Theory and research.* Edina, MN: Interaction Books.

Putnam, J. (1997). *Cooperative learning in diverse classrooms.* Upper Saddle River, NJ: Merrill.

Slavin, R. (1995). *Cooperative learning: Theory, research, and practice.* Boston: Allyn & Bacon.

SUGGESTED READINGS

Armstrong, T. (1994). *Multiple intelligences in the classroom.* Alexandria, VA: Association for Supervision and Curriculum Development.

Bloom, B. (Ed.). (1956). *A taxonomy of educational objectives: Handbook I. Cognitive domain.* New York: McKay.

Gardner, H. (1983). *Frames of mind.* New York: Basic Books.

Nickerson, R., Perkins, D., & Smith, E. (1985). *The teaching of thinking.* Hillsdale, NJ: Lawrence Erlbaum.

Rowe, M. (1974). Wait time and reward as instructional variables, their influence on language, logic and fate control. Part 1: Wait time. *Journal of Research on Science Teaching, 11,* 81–94.

PART 3:
Designing Questions: In-Class Hands-On Practice

Overview	**Designing Questions**
Goals	Activity Sheet: *John Henry*
	Self-Instruct Planner: *John Henry*
Sample Text: *John Henry*,	
Traditional American Folk Song	**ROUNDUP**

■ OVERVIEW

Try your hand at composing two question clusters for the song below. Then try out your questions on your peers, perhaps sitting in small circles, taking turns posing questions—Trigger, Probe, and Redirected—to one another.

■ GOALS

This section guides live practice with formulating individual questions and designing question clusters, as well as posing your questions to your peers in class.

The advantage of practicing with your peers is that you're all in the same boat, so you can help each other out by giving feedback about what questions worked and how to improve others.

■ SAMPLE TEXT: *JOHN HENRY,* TRADITIONAL AMERICAN FOLK SONG

John Henry is a song about a nineteenth century African American folk hero. He's known for hammering many of the first railroad tracks across the country at astonishing speed. Many people had claimed to know him. He has become a legend, both for his tremendous strength and for what he represented.

JOHN HENRY

When John Henry was a little baby,
Sitting on his mama's knee.
Well, he picked up a hammer and a little piece of steel.
He said, "This hammer's gonna be the death of me."
He said, "This hammer's gonna be the death of me."

The Captain says to John Henry,
"I believe this mountain's cavin' in."

John Henry said to the Captain,
"'Tain't nothin' but my hammer suckin' wind,
'Tain't nothin' but my hammer suckin' wind."

The captain said to John Henry,
"I'm gonna bring that steam drill around.
I'm gonna bring that steam drill out on the job,
I'm gonna whack that steel on down,
I'm gonna whack that steel on down."

And John Henry said to the Captain,
"A man ain't nothin' but a man.
And before I let that steam drill beat me down,
I'm gonna die with a hammer in my hand,
I'm gonna die with a hammer in my hand."

And John Henry said to the Shaker,
"Shaker, why don't you sing?
You know I'm throwing thirty pounds from my hips on down,
Just listen to that cold steel ring,
Just listen to that cold steel ring."

The man that invented the steam drill,
He thought that he was mighty fine;
John Henry made his fourteen feet,
The steam drill only made nine,
The steam drill only made nine.

John Henry went down to the railroad
With a twelve-pound hammer at his side,
He walked down the track but he didn't come back,
'Cause he laid down his hammer and he died,
'Cause he laid down his hammer and he died.

They took John Henry to the graveyard,
And they buried him in the sand.
And every locomotive come roarin' round
Says, "There lies a steel-drivin' man."
Says, "There lies a steel-drivin' man."

John Henry had him a woman,
Her name was Polly Ann.
On the day John Henry he dropped down dead
Polly Ann hammered steel like a man.
Polly Ann hammered steel like a man.

There's a widow that comes to the graveyard.
Her name is Polly Ann.

And every time that church bell tolls,
Says, "There lies my steel-drivin' man."
Says, "There lies my steel-drivin' man."

■ DESIGNING QUESTIONS

Activity Sheet: *John Henry*

(Note: If you prefer, use a different lyric of your choice. Check that the literal story contains elements for a larger theme. You might also want to use lyrics in addition to those here so that members in each peer group practice with a different text on one another.)

Overarching Question

Can you write two question clusters? One that elicits the literal story and one that inductively elicits a hidden story or theme in *John Henry*?

Materials

Song lyrics

Bloom's Taxonomy

Examples of questions, question clusters, and question patterns in Module 4, Part 2.

Examples of deductive and inductive frameworks in Module 2, Part 2.

Reminder

Effective questions contain a question word plus a precise term. All Trigger questions need Probing and Redirected questions for development of an idea.

Time for the Task

About 45 minutes, depending on the number of participants.

Your Job Description

1. Read the lyrics twice: once to establish the literal story in your mind and then again to infer at least one other story or theme between the lines.

2. CONCEPTUALIZE your ideas. Work backwards from Strand Two, the large picture.

- Briefly jot down the literal story.

- Jot down one possible hidden story or one theme. Justify your own interpretation to yourself with facts from the literal story. Jot down your own justification based on details in the lyrics. Your written ideas serve as a reference for designing questions.

3. COMPOSE your questions.

- Write a question cluster of at least three Strand One Trigger questions that elicit the complete literal story first. This establishes the knowledge base.
- Write a second question cluster of at least three Strand Two Trigger questions that attempt to inductively elicit from your peers the hidden story or theme that you have perceived.

4. When the time comes, pose your inductive story questions to your peers and see what happens. Prepare yourself for unexpected responses. As you probe, ask your peers to justify their own interpretations and analyses by citing specific details in the song. Insist on this justification whether or not a peer's story or theme agrees with your own. It's the thought process that matters, the logic and critical thinking, more than a particular answer.

Self-Instruct Planner: *John Henry*

(Work on a separate piece of paper. Refer to the complete Bloom's Taxonomy in Module 4, Part 1.)

Question Cluster for the Literal Story

1. CONCEPTUALIZE: What are the distinctive details that compose the literal story?

2. COMPOSE: Refer to the details in #1 (conceptualize). Sequence a question cluster of at least three Strand One Trigger questions along with corresponding Probing and Redirected questions designed to facilitate your students' comprehension of the literal story. Avoid chronology questions, that is, asking what happened first, second, and so on. Instead, use the question formula (question word + a precise term) to briefly elicit the setting and events in an interesting way.

   a. Strand One, Trigger:
- Probe
- Redirect

   b. Strand One, Trigger:
- Probe
- Redirect

   c. Strand One, Trigger:
- Probe
- Redirect

   d. Strand One, Trigger:
- Probe
- Redirect

Question Cluster for the Hidden Story or Larger Theme (Inductive)

1. CONCEPTUALIZE: What is the hidden story or theme that you perceive? What details or facts in the lyrics lead you to this perception?

2. COMPOSE: Refer to the details or facts in #1 (conceptualization). Sequence a question cluster of at least three Strand Two Trigger questions along with corresponding Probe and Redirect questions designed to facilitate your students' perception of the hidden story or theme.

   a. Strand Two, Trigger:
      - Probe
      - Redirect

   b. Strand Two, Trigger:
      - Probe
      - Redirect

   c. Strand Two, Trigger:
      - Probe
      - Redirect

   d. Strand Two, Trigger:
      - Probe
      - Redirect

■ ROUNDUP ■

Focus on posing questions that guide your peers to support their assertions. Encourage logic by your questioning. Try to facilitate your peers' higher cognitive skills of analysis (comparing and contrasting the elements), synthesis, and evaluation once the knowledge base has been established. If you achieve all this, even if your peers arrive at different hidden stories and themes than you had intended, you will have been successful.

Remember that you are not aiming for agreement with your own perceptions. A constructivist approach fosters the process of critical thinking. This means that insights must be justified by a knowledge base and concepts. Critical thinking matters more than a desired answer without sound logic.

Module Five:

Peer-Group Learning

PART 1:
Peer-Group Learning Techniques

■ OVERVIEW

groups *peer groups* peer groups ***peer groups*** Peer Groups peer

Peer groups?
Plain and simple
I'll tell you how
it's gonna go.
They won't have a clue,
that's what.
Go tell your theory types—
Peer groups are a hype.
I've been in the real world and I
know that
kids in groups don't hack
it. Why, I tell 'em
what to do and they
don't do it. I give'em
worksheets, fill up
the blanks, I say,
copy
from the board or the textbook,
tank up
real
easy.
I tried it once, all
day. But
their lives are so messy.
They can't get it
on their own,
you see.
I've got to be the one that
tells 'em. Then they
know the scoop.
That's the way to get 'em to write
the right words in groups.
Now, that's the way it
really
is.

And I still have to
tell 'em what
to write on
my test.
I've got to be the whiz.
I fill up their tanks.
They don't even say
thanks.
Go back and tell your prof
that.
—©2001 Ina Claire Gabler

■ GOALS

We talked about it in Module 1. As the opening verse hints, there's a long tradition of whole-group, teacher-led instruction in our schools, and change is difficult when it comes to breaking the traditional way of doing things in classrooms. Some teachers resist it; many still see the instructor's role as one of filling students' tanks with information. At times, even students resist being shaken out of their comfort zones when it comes to new or different classroom approaches. However, during the past ten to fifteen years, we have witnessed an increasing acceptance of peer-group learning techniques (PGL), approaches that allow students to work together in at least semi-autonomous groups of two to eight to accomplish an academic task. Cooperative learning techniques are considered to be a special subset of peer-group learning techniques; they feature heterogeneous groups of students working together for common academic and social purposes, with an emphasis on group and individual accountability (based on Johnson & Johnson, 1989). Remember that a constructivist classroom is an ACTIVE classroom and, as we'll see in this module, peer-group learning techniques are an essential ingredient to the mix of techniques and methods in a constructivist learning experience. Not only do they allow learners enhanced opportunities for collaboration, student–student interaction, and direct involvement with materials, but they also create a feeling of positive interdependence that affects the entire group.

In the sections that follow, we address the following important guiding questions:

- Why should teachers use peer-group learning techniques?
- What should teachers do to make peer-group learning experiences worthwhile?
- What peer-group and cooperative learning techniques have been shown to be effective in the classroom?

Focal Point 1: Why Should Teachers Use Peer-Group Learning Techniques?

Peer-group learning techniques, especially cooperative learning techniques, are among the most widely researched instructional approaches. More than 300 studies focused on the effectiveness of group work have been conducted during the past twenty-five years (Johnson & Johnson, 1993). This body of research represents a compelling case for making peer-group learning techniques a major focus in your classroom.

Just what does this research show? That peer-group, and especially cooperative, learning techniques, when properly implemented, offer a number of advantages compared with approaches that emphasize individualized, competitive learning situations. Cooperative learning techniques have been shown to have the following impacts when properly implemented:

- They enhance how much and how deeply students learn material, how long they remember it, and how effectively they can use higher-level cognitive reasoning strategies. In reviewing and analyzing data from hundreds of studies (using a process known as meta-analysis), Johnson and Johnson (1993) and Slavin (1995) found that fifty to seventy-two percent of the studies completed showed enhanced student learning when teachers emphasized cooperative learning techniques in the classroom. Only ten to twelve percent of such studies found learning advantages in classrooms featuring individualized, competitive, whole-group instruction. Moreover, studies that found an advantage to a more competitive approach tended to emphasize rote learning skills (i.e., memorizing information at the knowledge level) as opposed to higher-order understanding of material (Putnam, 1997). Most encouragingly, researchers have shown that these advantages hold for students considered low achieving as well as for those considered gifted.

- A number of researchers have shown that the use of peer-group and cooperative learning techniques also has wide-ranging affective benefits. Some of these studies show that the use of peer-group learning techniques enhances student self-esteem (Johnson & Johnson, 1989; Slavin, 1995). Happily, we have experienced this positive trend indirectly while teaching in middle school, high school, and college classrooms. Students working in peer-group settings often come to feel that they have something meaningful to contribute to the group, and this seems to have a powerful impact on their feeling of self-worth (more on this when we discuss re-socializing in Module 15).

- In addition, the use of peer-group learning techniques seems to have a highly positive impact on the degree of acceptance and understanding between students of different racial and ethnic groups (Sharan, 1990; Slavin, 1990, 1995) and between students with and without disabilities (Johnson & Johnson, 1989). As David Johnson (1989) summarized, the use of peer groups promoted positive interactions between individual students and allowed them to move beyond stereotypes in coming to know and understand classmates.

- Many students seem to make impressive gains in developing their own written and especially verbal communications skills as a result of peer-group experiences (Putnam, 1997). We have noted this trend in a wide range of classrooms, and the reason seems clear to us: Students who are regularly challenged to express opinions and to listen and respond to others, rather than sit passively listening to teachers, will become better communicators.

- Finally, students working in classrooms in which cooperative learning techniques are a central feature tend to show more positive attitudes toward school in general, less disruptive behavior, a greater feeling of autonomy in the classroom, and enhanced conflict resolution skills (Johnson et al., 1990).

These findings are significant for two reasons. First, they should dispel the fear that many teachers have that giving up a degree of control will result in increased discipline problems; in fact, just the opposite effect has been shown. This leads to a second point that we will expand on in Module 15. Second, the best way to prevent discipline problems in the classroom is to keep students engaged in meaningful learning experiences.

Again, space allows but a brief review of the many interesting studies done regarding the impacts of peer-group learning experiences on students. The reference list for this module lists a number of terrific resource materials focused on these studies if you're interested. Certainly, this body of research, and our own classroom experiences, have clearly demonstrated to us that peer-group techniques are incredibly beneficial to students.

Focal Point 2: What Should Teachers Do to Make Peer-Group Learning Experiences Worthwhile?

The next two sections will clarify the somewhat mysterious caveat used earlier in this module: when properly implemented. Let's start first with some practical advice that cuts across each technique, and then get specific about different techniques that you might use in conjunction with constructivist methods.

First, keep in mind that a peer-group learning technique is any technique that features inviting students to work together autonomously in small groups. This would include such informal arrangements as asking randomly chosen partners to work together for a few minutes on a single task. It would also include cooperative learning arrangements that might feature groups of students working together in specialized ways for several days or longer. The general advice provided in this section cuts across this range of peer-group possibilities.

How Often Should You Challenge Your Students to Work Together in Peer Groups?

We recommend that you try to spend one quarter to one third of your total classroom time with students working in peer groups. This doesn't mean that you should earmark fifteen to twenty minutes per day for peer-group work; we're referring to more of a long-term guideline in this case. Some class periods will include no peer-group work at all; others will feature students working in groups for almost entire periods. It all depends on your objectives (instructional intentions) for that session and the methods you'll use to carry out these objectives.

Remember that before they reach your classroom, students have probably had a huge range of experiences working in groups. They've been in classrooms where they never worked in groups. They may have worked in groups in which they had to do most of the work or in which they could get away with doing almost nothing. Some will have had very enjoyable and academically worthwhile experiences in group settings. Our advice is to tell your students early on that working in peer groups will be an important part of their experience in your classroom. Then tell them why. Invite your students to share any positive or negative experiences they've had working in groups, and describe how you will attempt to address any of their concerns. Taking this approach helps students understand what you're doing and will result in them taking peer-group learning opportunities more seriously.

Should You Assign Students to Groups in Advance, Allow Them to Choose Groups, or Arrange Them Randomly?

You've made the commitment to make peer-group work an integral part of your students' experience. Now, one of your first considerations is how to arrange the groups. We suggest that, for the most part, you assign students to heterogeneous groups based on academic (and other) talents, gender, ethnicity, and personality. Make your groups diverse. Research on cooperative learning has shown that heterogeneous groups have academic and social benefits. Invite students who would not normally socialize to work together; this will allow you to break down some of the cliques that you'll find in middle schools and high schools. We have seen this approach produce dramatic effects in the classroom. Students who would normally never associate with each another will come to know and better understand each other. On most occasions, especially if you're forming groups that are going to work together for days or weeks, we suggest assigning groups intentionally. Here's a suggestion: when you have extended peer-group work planned for a class period, arrange your desks in pods (i.e., groups of three to six) in advance, and place name cards on the pods before the class enters the room. It's a real time saver.

Randomly chosen groups can accomplish many of these same objectives. If you're transitioning from a full class setting to peer groups (as often is the case with constructivist experiences), and your students are seated in a large circle, ask them to count off in 4's, 5's, or 6's or to pick numbers written on slips of paper out of a hat. Then have each group meet in some predetermined part of the room. This is usually quick and efficient, and chances are you'll end up with diversity built into your groups.

For the most part, we don't recommend letting students choose their own groups. What happens when you do this? The same circles of friends tend to sit together, and students who are typically left out will be left out of the peer groups. You might make occasional exceptions to this in the case of projects or presentations. If you're going to ask students to spend time working together outside of class, let them pick partners who might make this more convenient, but make sure that everybody gets a partner.

What Group Size Is Optimal?

It takes time for students to develop small-group communications skills, so we recommend starting with smaller peer groups and shorter, more structured tasks or assignments. Early in the school year, experiment with groups of two, three, or four, and ask students to work together for five to ten minutes. It has been our experience that asking students to work in groups larger than four, especially early in the school year, will lessen the positive impact of the peer-group experience. With larger groups, some students will likely feel left out of the conversation. Easing into peer-group experiences like this will tend to smooth over any transitions that your students will need to make. Over time, you'll find that they'll be able to work productively together for extended periods.

What Should You Do to Make Your Expectations Clear?

Experience has shown us the importance of explaining specifically what you'd like students to accomplish when they work together in peer groups. Of course, in a constructivist classroom, you'll be allowing students greater freedom and responsibility than they've likely experienced before. When it comes to peer-group work, you still need to talk to your students specifically about what can and should happen in their groups. What are they going to produce as a result of their work together? If you're going to allow them options in this regard, what will they be? How much time will they have? Significantly, how will you build group and individual accountability into the activity? This last point is important; you've got to convey to your students that there's a good reason for them to work together, and that each person in the group will be responsible in some way for learning something as a result of the experience. Ask each group to produce something that shows critical thought, creativity, and a degree of teamwork. Let each student know that he or she will need to understand the important ideas that were part of the group experience when you ask them to write a reflective essay, take a quiz or test, or complete some other kind of assignment (more on this when we discuss assessment in Module 14).

You can assign two grades: individual grades for individual tasks and a group grade. That way, each student can weigh his or her impact on the overall performance, and assiduous students won't be penalized for the lesser effort of others if there's only a collective grade.

How Can You Help Groups Develop Communication Skills?

Whether you're teaching art, PE, math, or any other subject, this is an important question. It's vital to help your students develop their abilities to work together in peer groups. We have found that it helps to develop, with input from your students, guidelines that will help them become better communicators. Early in the school year, ask your students what might help them to work together productively in groups; give them your suggestions on this. Consider some of the suggestions that we've made regarding critical thinking when you do this. For example, adopting the following guidelines will help students work together effectively:

- Criticize ideas, not people.
- Listen to other ideas, even if you don't agree.
- Ask each other clarifying questions when you don't understand something.
- Change your mind when evidence suggests you should do so.
- Encourage everyone in your group to participate.

There's an important, implicit message that you send students when you help them develop guidelines like this: peer-group work is important; it's an opportunity for you to think about something important and to share your thoughts and opinions. (See Module 15 for more ideas on modeling peer-group interaction.)

Is It Helpful to Have Students Play Certain Roles Within Their Groups?

Has a teacher ever asked you to play a role within a group? We have found that this will help your peer groups be more productive and that it can help students develop the communication skills that we just mentioned. Consider just a few of the possible roles for group members:

- Leader/moderator
- Recorder
- Presenter
- Spokesperson
- Challenger (specializes in asking probing questions of other group members)
- Timekeeper
- Reference person (has sole responsibility for finding necessary information in the available materials or on the Internet)
- Gatekeeper (ensures respectful exchanges and prevents domination by a few)

Most often, we suggest allowing students to choose roles. Occasionally, it is appropriate to assign roles and then to ask students to rotate periodically ("Sue, I'd like you to act as group leader today"). This last option is especially effective when students are working in peer groups for extended periods. See Part 2 of this module for the difference between social and task roles.

As the Teacher, What Should You Do While Students Are Working in Groups?

This is a major consideration. There are some important (and often very subtle) things that you can do to help make peer-group work effective. Our suggestion is to become an active facilitator whenever your students are working in peer groups. Move around the room. When you approach a group, sit down with the students; towering over the students usually disrupts the interaction. Listen for at least thirty seconds before saying anything; this will allow you to pick up the gist of the conversation without disrupting. At that point, you might interject with appropriate trigger or probing questions; model effective questioning for the students. If a student raises an important point, let the group know, it's a great way to encourage them to think in more depth. Finally, you might make suggestions on points that the group could consider next. If the group interaction is productive and on target, you might even move on to the next group without saying anything.

When you sit with individual groups, try to put yourself in a place where you can see the entire room. Over time, you'll find that you'll be able to listen to and watch multiple groups at the same time and to pick up a lot about the progress of other groups just by noticing subtle visual clues.

Any Other Suggestions?

When reconvening the full class after a peer-group activity, allow students to share ideas generated in the groups. This is crucial, and again reinforces the notion that what happens in the peer groups is important. For extended peer-group experiences, we also suggest allowing group members to monitor the progress of the group in writing. Ask students to respond to a questionnaire that challenges them to reflect on what they've learned and to describe which students contributed what to the group's progress. An effective final question on such a questionnaire is "Our group could have accomplished more if _____."

So much for the general advice on making peer-group work productive. At this point, let's take a look at some specific peer-group/cooperative-learning techniques that have been shown to be effective across subjects and grade levels.

Focal Point 3: What Peer-Group and Cooperative Learning Techniques Have Been Shown to Be Effective in the Classroom?

Jigsaw I and II

One of the most frequently used cooperative learning techniques is called *jigsaw*. Developed by Aronson (1978), jigsaw has been shown to be highly successful across subject areas and grade levels. We highly recommend the technique to both middle school and high school teachers.

Jigsaw is based on the belief that you can learn a lot about important facts, concepts, and principles by trying to teach them to another person. Jigsaw events usually focus on a unit of study that can be broken up into four to six component pieces or sections. For example, let's say that Mr. Nathan, an eighth-grade geography teacher, is preparing to teach a unit on India and he wishes to make the jigsaw technique a major focus. He could break the material into five essential geographical themes: location, place, human–environment interactions, movement, and regions. The teacher would then arrange his students in heterogeneous groups of five; each student would then choose (or be assigned) to become an expert with regard to one of the chosen themes as it relates to India. The jigsaw groups are then broken up; each student who has chosen to investigate one of the themes then meets together in what are known as expert groups (e.g., each student investigating location as it relates to India meets in one group). Students in each expert group then research their part of the unit, learning as much as they can about it, and make decisions about how they might teach their theme effectively to the members of their jigsaw group. The teacher facilitates this research process (note the terrific opportunities for using the Internet and investigating relevant Websites as part of this research).

After some period of time, the jigsaw groups reconvene, and each expert has a chance to teach his or her subject to the rest of the group. To ensure some level of group and individual accountability, all students are tested or complete some other assignment on the entire unit and also receive a group grade based on the cumulative grades received by all members. We have found that the jigsaw approach allows for other forms of assessment as well; there are wonderful opportunities for students to complete individual or group projects as part of this process.

Again, research has shown that the jigsaw method is highly effective in a wide range of settings. As for using the technique in a constructivist classroom, we encourage you to connect projects with the process and to allow groups of students options in choosing how they show what they have learned.

The Structured Controversy Approach

One of our favorite techniques, known as the *structured controversy approach* (Johnson & Johnson, 1988), features structured debate and an emphasis on development of critical-thinking abilities within a peer-group setting. The process starts with students working together in heterogeneous groups of four. At that point, the entire class is introduced to a controversial issue; within each group of four, pairs of students are asked to argue for one side of the issue. Students in each group are given time to research their side of the issue and to prepare arguments (again, note the opportunities for emphasizing in-depth research and the use of outside resources). The groups then meet for a discussion, with each group presenting its arguments on both sides of the issue. As an interesting twist, toward the end of the session, challenge the pairs to switch sides and to argue for the other position. We suggest asking each group to try to reach consensus on a solution. Although this isn't always possible, or desirable, it is often a worthwhile goal for the groups to strive for.

You can tie a range of assessment approaches to this technique. The students can write group or individual reports, prepare presentations, or develop HyperStudio or PowerPoint presentations that convey their position on the issues. As a variation, you can ask different groups in your class to research and debate related but different issues and then to report their findings to the rest of the class through presentations.

We have had a great deal of success with this technique in a wide range of classroom settings and in different subjects, and we highly recommend the approach. All subjects *do* lend themselves to this technique. For example, a student teacher working with one of the authors recently included a structured controversy debate on the possible repeal of legalized gambling in the state of Illinois as part of a high school probability and statistics course. The students found the experience tremendously effective because it challenged them to apply statistical concepts at the highest levels as they researched an issue that is real and highly relevant.

Teams-Games-Tournaments

This approach (Slavin, 1990) combines elements of cooperative learning and individual and team competition. In a constructivist classroom, we advise you not to overuse this technique, but we have found that it can provide an interesting change of pace if used infrequently.

To start, arrange your students in heterogeneous peer groups of four to six. Ask the members of each group to study (and possibly research) assigned material together and to help one another understand the main ideas as deeply as possible; this interaction is one of the best features of this approach. After this researching/studying period, assign your students to sit in groups of three with members from other groups. This provides the tournament setting. As the tournament leader, you now direct questions to the entire class, with each student answering the questions on paper; one, two, or three points are awarded to the original teams based on how well team members do compared with students from other teams seated at the same table. Individual scores on the tournament test are also recorded, again emphasizing group and individual accountability. The process is later repeated with different material and new tournament groups. Keep track of the points earned by the teams over time, and make these team points part of each student's overall course grade.

Group Retellings

This relatively simple peer-group technique can be used in the context of many of the methods introduced later in the text. You'll divide your class into heterogeneous groups of two to four. Ask each person in each group to read a different piece of material on the same subject. A biology teacher conducting a unit on immunology might ask students to read different articles focused on the AIDS epidemic. For example, one student in each group might read an article on the latest research findings on treatment of the disease; another might read about the scope of the epidemic in Africa; a third might read a position paper calling for increased funding for research. After the students read the articles (possibly as homework), convene the groups and ask students to take turns telling others in the group about their article in detail (again we use the knowing-through-teaching approach). Then, encourage others in the group to add to the retelling with a related point from their article or from their own experience (here's where facilitating/asking of follow-up questions by the teacher can help). After completion of the small-group discussions, you can challenge the groups to process the discussions by summarizing the main points emphasized for the rest of the class or through some kind of group or individual writing assignment.

Again, this is a very versatile technique suited to any subject or grade level. We have found it to be particularly useful when the discussion focuses on recent articles that reflect differing viewpoints on important issues.

Response Groups

In groups of three or four, each member reads or presents a piece of original work he or she has done for the course, for example, an essay, a brief experiment, or an original drawing. The other group members respond to the presenter according to a heuristic (a coded pattern of responses; see Module 3, Part 2) that ensures that the other members are both supportive as well as critically helpful. Response groups can be motivating when the presentations consist of products that will be evaluated by the teacher, peers, or professionals as part of authentic learning.

Cybernetic Sessions

This final peer-group learning technique is a great way to review ideas in any subject and at any grade level. The basic idea is to help students through a process of analysis, synthesis, and problem solving by discussing thought-provoking questions. Prepare for a cybernetic session by writing six to ten challenging new questions regarding important concepts or principles introduced earlier. For example, an English teacher conducting a unit on Shakespearean tragedy might prepare questions based on the way that different players are characterized during the first act of *Hamlet*. A science teacher might write questions that would be included in a lab practical and assemble materials that might allow students to determine or discover the answers.

The next step is to prepare your classroom for the session. We suggest writing your questions on poster board and fastening them to the walls in different parts of your room, placing any accompanying materials nearby. Arrange your class in groups of three to five for the start of the session; begin with each group placed at a different station. Start the session by asking the groups to consider and discuss the question at their station, with a recorder in each group jotting down a group response. After a set time period, ask the group to rotate to the next station, until each group has completed the entire circuit. After the session, you might include any number of assessment approaches. We also suggest asking the groups to process the experience by sharing ideas in a wrap-up discussion.

■ ROUNDUP ■

In Part 1 of this module, we addressed some of the initial questions regarding peer-group work in the classroom. We noted that the impact of group work, and especially of cooperative learning techniques, has been studied in some depth during the past twenty years. These findings, and our own classroom experiences, provide convincing evidence that peer-group learning techniques can have a dramatic, positive impact on the learning of students across subjects and grade levels. Not only do these techniques enhance students' understanding of new ideas and their abilities to utilize higher cognitive reasoning strategies, but they also provide a wide range of positive affective benefits. We have seen first-hand the impact that well-planned peer-group experiences can have on students who are discouraged, alienated, and/or struggling to understand material.

In addressing our second guiding question, we provided some important practical advice for implementing peer-group events in your classroom. We discuss peer-group learning in more detail throughout the rest of the text. As we do so, keep some of these general suggestions in mind. Remember that peer-group events take a lot of thought and careful planning. We've also seen first-hand the impact that negative group experiences can have on young people, so remember to be thoughtful and intentional when implementing group events.

Finally, we took a look at some of the many possible techniques available to teachers. In Modules 7–12, we provide additional examples and discuss in more detail what it takes to embed peer-group learning techniques into larger teaching methods. Remember that peer-group learning events are quintessential components of the constructivist classroom; they provide students with thought-provoking and truly empowering learning experiences. Figure 5.1 gives you a look at the generic features of peer-group learning.

■ HANDS-ON PRACTICE ■

1. Start by writing a Rationale for your peer-group learning event. What will you challenge students to do? How will you accomplish this?

2. Will you utilize a specific peer-group or cooperative learning technique? If so, which one?

1 = justify activity *Eat this, kids!*
It's good for you!

2 = distribute activity sheet
directions include social roles as well as task roles
think through the roles and steps for the task

> moderator
> gatekeeper
> Step #1 =
> Step #2 =

3 = model activity with mini version of task
refer to activity sheet with t-s exchange
model task with the activity sheet

4 = circulate and eavesdrop
ask questions to aid individual students and groups
try not to spill the beans

? *Have you asked why it's ...?* ?
How might ...?
If you did ..., what might happen?

?

5 = group share
presentations
intergroup dialogue

6 = culmination: review groups' outcomes + implications
Cows can't fly.
The difference between a genus and a species is ...
It seems that the abolitionist movement led
to the woman's movement because ...

Hey, I didn't think
of that before!

©2001 Ina Claire Gabler

FIGURE 5.1 Peer Group Learning Technique Flow Chart

3. How will you arrange students for the peer-group event (e.g., randomly or in assigned groups)? What is the optimum group size?
4. What will you ask students to do in their groups? Try phrasing your instructions as you would provide them for your students. Consider roles for group members.
5. How much time will you allow for this event?
6. What questions might you ask group members as they work?
7. How will you process the group learning event (e.g., through a summarizing discussion)?

REFERENCES

Aronson, E. (1978). *The jigsaw classroom.* Beverly Hills, CA: Sage Publications.
Johnson, D., Johnson, R., & Holubec, E. (1990). *Circles of learning: Cooperation in the classroom.* Edina, MN: Interaction Books.

Johnson, D., & Johnson, R. (1993). *Cooperation in the classroom.* Edina, MN: Interaction Books.

Johnson, R., & Johnson, D. (1988). Critical thinking through structured controversy. *Educational Leadership,* May, 58–64.

Johnson, R., & Johnson, D. (1989). *Cooperation and competition: Theory and research.* Edina, MN: Interaction Books.

Putnam, J. (1997). *Cooperative learning in diverse classrooms.* Upper Saddle River, NJ: Merrill.

Sharan, S. (1990). *Handbook of cooperative learning methods.* Westport, CT: Greenwood Press.

Slavin, R. (1990). *Cooperative learning: Theory, research, and practice.* Englewood Cliffs, NJ: Prentice-Hall.

Slavin, R. (1995). *Cooperative learning.* Boston: Allyn and Bacon.

PART 2:
Activity Sheets

Overview

Goals

Focal Points and Discussion

Varied Quality of Handouts

ROUNDUP

HANDS-ON PRACTICE

SUGGESTED READINGS

■ OVERVIEW

You're feeling your oats. Your students, heads bowed close to the desk, scratching their answers on paper, are industriously at work. The principal glimpses your class through the door window, and she smiles with approval. And it's only your first year! But the story isn't over. Not until we look at those papers and the nature of your students' responses.

Aye, here's the rub: What kinds of questions are your students answering? Neat blanks that fit into statements like pieces into a jigsaw puzzle? A collection of "right" answers? Multiple choices? Responses that repeat what you and the textbook said?

Reflect on what your students have learned. What will they retain in a week? A month? A year? Will they remember just a handful of facts, or will they be contemplating interrelated concepts that give meaning to facts? To check this out, reflect on what you have learned after spending years of filling in blanks in ready-made statements and circling multiple-choice answers.

■ GOALS

Our intention is to convey the difference between effective activity sheets and busy-work sheets. With this in mind, we discuss the following topics:

- Activity sheets versus worksheets
- Activity sheets and techniques
- Activity sheets as versatile learning guides
- Effective and ineffective handouts
- Activity sheets for peer-group learning

■ DISCUSSION

Broadly speaking, we categorize handouts as worksheets and activity sheets. *Worksheets,* which we call busywork sheets, are about inserting and circling discrete answers.

They tend to operate at low cognitive levels, rarely challenging students to think; they imply low expectations. In addition, for the most part, they're boring. Why should your students care? If they don't care, they won't retain much. That's when you and they think that they're not "good learners." Or, just as undesirable, because your students may be able to temporarily rattle off a string of dates, events, and details, or briefly complete a sentence, they think they're learning a lot.

Activity sheets, by contrast, serve as prompts (questions, directions, and tasks that generate original interpretation) for critical thinking and problem solving. Your students are writing original, justified interpretations; drawing original diagrams or graphics such as concept maps; exploring both sides of an event, issue, or hypothesis; and then providing the answers to conceptual and thematic questions.

The more students are challenged with high expectations, the higher their performance level. This applies especially to students whose abilities are often underestimated because conventional teaching methods fail to relate to their frames of reference and, as a result, fail to motivate. This phenomenon is no surprise. Boredom deadens the mind and will.

Activity sheets need a careful balance between the familiar and the new, between Bloom's low and high cognitive prompts, so that learners gain firm footing before they take leaps with critical thinking. Writing an effective activity sheet should be a creative process for you. If writing it feels mechanical or formulaic, then working on it will merely be busywork for your students, so start over!

Focal Point 1: **Varied Quality of Handouts**

Form versus Function

Handouts vary greatly in their role, that is, their function, whereas the form (e.g., questions and fill-in tables) may be identical (see Module 3, Part 1). Even when two handouts both contain open-ended questions that invite students to respond in their own words, there may be tremendous differences between those handouts regarding cohesion and cognitive demands.

Our aim is to help you discern mediocre handouts such as busywork sheets or worksheets from activity sheets. We suspect that, as a student, you worked mostly on worksheets, especially fill-in-the-blanks and open-ended statements that required repetition of what the teacher or textbook had said. This apprenticeship by observation (Lortie, 1975) can foil you as a budding constructivist teacher.

Examples of Handouts

Let's start by comparing and contrasting Figures 5.2 through 5.4. They all attempt to promote original thinking for the same lesson Rationale. However, they all need improvement. For each example, jot down what you think are the strengths and weaknesses. Then compare your analysis to ours after each figure. Try to identify the handout that best facilitates original thinking with the least chance for student frustration. How could you make it even better? Notice that there are two sets of roles. *Social roles* help your students interact productively and carry out the task well. *Task roles* describe the steps that carry out the learning activity.

What's This?

Within a moon that has no face,
A curtain shields a silent place
In which a sea both still and clear
Contains a sun that doesn't sear.

The moon is cracked; the sun goes free—
Until it's part of you or me.

© 2001 Ina Claire Gabler

FIGURE 5.2 A Riddle

Answer (backwards): gge na.

The three sample handouts in Figures 5.2 through 5.4 apply to the same lesson. We provide the lesson Rationale to orient you.

EXAMPLE #1/ENGLISH LESSON, SEVENTH GRADE. *Class arranged in groups of four.*

RATIONALE

What?: To solve the riddle, *What's This?,* by Ina Claire Gabler.

Why?: To build further understanding of how metaphors work. To develop high-level cognitive skills, especially analysis and synthesis applied to the clues and solution of this riddle. (Inductive process with Bloom's Taxonomy.)

Justification: Interstate New Teacher Assessment and Support Consortium (INTASC) Standards 2, 3, 4, 5, and 6.

Jot down what you think the strengths are in Figures *5.2a* and *5.2b* from a student's point of view. Consider these features:

- Sequence of questions and tasks
- Clarity
- Cohesion
- Cognitive levels

Also consider possible strengths in terms of how the peer-group learning technique has been organized. From the same student perspective, what do you experience as weaknesses or omissions? What other features might help learners succeed with the task of deciphering clues that are charged with cognitive dissonance (contradictions with commonly held associations)?

After you analyze Figure 5.2a and 5.2b, see if you agree with our analysis.

"What's This?"

1. Assign social roles
   a. Moderator—makes sure that everyone participates at least twice. Moderator starts off the activity by responding first.
   b. Prompter—probes and encourages others when responses need more explanation.
   c. Gatekeeper—makes sure everyone is respectful of others' ideas.
   d. Timekeeper—watches the time indicated below and announces when there are two minutes left.
2. Guidelines for task
   a. (Twenty minutes) Write down each clue in the riddle on the accompanying chart and describe your usual association with that clue.
   b. When you finish with task "a," discuss possible metaphoric meanings or associations with each clue and jot them down alongside the literal associations.
   c. Decide if the answer is animal, mineral, or vegetable. Explain why.
   d. (Ten minutes) Try to guess the answer to the riddle.
3. Can you explain how every clue fits the answer?

(Continued in Figure 5.2b.)

FIGURE 5.2a Active or Passive Thinking?

Clues	Associations for Each Clue (literal and metaphoric)
1. "A moon without a face . . ." (Model this example with student input.)	1. (student responses to the model) Literal = unlit moon, a moon of another planet. Metaphoric = something not fully formed, something sad, something resembling a moon without markings.
2.	2.
3.	3.
4.	4.
5.	5.
6.	6.
7.	7.
8.	8.
Is the answer animal, mineral, or vegetable and why? What do you think the answer is?	

FIGURE 5.2b Active or Passive Thinking?

Our Analysis of Figure 5.2 (a and b)

Strengths

- Clear social roles that facilitate productive student exchange.
- Clear and well-sequenced task guidelines.
- Rigor: every clue must be matched to a possible solution.
- Table includes a model example for which students must provide responses as a rehearsal for the task, perhaps in a teacher-led mini-discussion.
- The "animal, mineral, vegetable" question helps to synthesize students' thinking about the metaphoric value of the clues.
- Cohesion carries out the Rationale by guiding the thinking process from literal to metaphoric meanings of the riddle's clues according to Bloom's Taxonomy. Metaphoric thinking is integrated into the task that's structured by the table, yet the table is open ended for original input.
- Prompts and criteria are clear and provide appropriate focus.

Weaknesses and Omissions

- No overarching question for direction.
- The table needs a "proof" column to demonstrate how each clue fits a possible solution to the riddle.

Now take a look at another handout, Figure 5.3 (a and b), designed for the same lesson. Jot down your analysis on Figure 5.3, then see what we think.

Our Analysis of Figure 5.3 (a and b)

Strengths

- Clear social roles that facilitate productive student exchange.
- Question at the top of the handout gives direction.
- Attempts to challenge students to think on higher cognitive levels.

"What's This?"

1. Assign social roles
   a. Moderator—makes sure that everyone participates at least twice. Moderator starts off the activity by responding first.
   b. Prompter—probes and encourages others when responses need more explanation.
   c. Gatekeeper—makes sure everyone is respectful of others' ideas.
   d. Timekeeper—watches the time indicated below and announces when there are two minutes left.
2. Guidelines for task. Follow directions on the handout below.
<div align="center">(Continued in Figure 5.3b.)</div>

FIGURE 5.3a Active or Passive Thinking?

Directions: Answer the questions thoughtfully. Always explain.

BIG QUESTION: What is the answer to the riddle, "What's This?"
1. Name at least three clues in the riddle that you think are most important. Why?
2. Try to integrate these clues to guess the riddle's answer. Defend your
   answer.
3. Why are metaphors important to solve the riddle?

FIGURE 5.3b Active or Passive Thinking?

- Clear criteria for the product (combining at least three clues to write a possible solution).

Weaknesses and Omissions

- Allotted time for the task not specified, thereby making the role of timekeeper superfluous. Also, students need to learn to gauge their time.

- Similarly, there are not enough prompts (guiding questions and tasks) for more than two students for the moderator's and prompter's roles to apply. Therefore, while the form of social roles is included, the function is rendered meaningless in a peer group (as opposed to a dyad).

- The "Big Question" does not give insight into the value of the task beyond "getting the answer" to the riddle. An improved overarching question might be, "What metaphors in the clues help you solve this riddle?" This is another example of the difference between the form (the definition or intention of an "overarching question") and its function (the role or instructional value).

- No model item. Even open-ended questions like the ones in Figure 5.3b can be modeled to demonstrate how the answer must be thorough. Modeling can also address the criteria in the questions, for example, whether the answers must be written in complete sentences or whether phrases will do.

- Metaphoric meaning is not integrated into the task. It is brought in only as a sudden and separate concept in question #3 in Figure 5.3b. Compare this approach with that in Figure 5.2b. Thinking metaphorically is the only way to solve the riddle.

- Because thinking metaphorically all along is essential to succeeding in the task, the prompts as questions #1 and #2 might frustrate rather than assist the students in thinking through a solution.

- Compromised rigor. The criteria call for only three clues. Not only is this too easy, but it also, ironically, makes the task more difficult. The demands are insufficient for students to succeed with the task.

- The Rationale may fail because of the flaws in the handout.

Now examine the handout in Figure 5.4 (a and b) and see how it compares with the others. What strengths and weaknesses did you spot? Think it through before you look at our analysis.

Our Analysis of Figure 5.4 (a and b)

Strengths

- Overarching goal is clearly stated on the handout.
- Attempt to apply metaphoric thinking.
- Enough items for a group of four.
- Open-ended response required for the riddle's answer.

Weaknesses and Omissions

- There are no social roles to guide student interaction.
- Allotted time for the task not specified, thereby making the role of timekeeper superfluous. Also, students need to learn to gauge their time.
- Overarching goal does not give insight into the value of the task beyond the answer itself. An improved overarching goal might be, "Solve the riddle with metaphors." This is yet another example of the difference between form (a goal) and function (instructional value).
- No model item. The cognitive level is low so that a model item might not even be useful.
- The definition of a metaphor is too constrained by fill-in blanks embedded in a fixed expression.
- Metaphoric meaning is not effectively integrated into the task despite an effort to do so. The provided clues along with multiple-choice answers reduce this task to a mechanical exercise. Teacher expectations are low since there is too much spoon-feeding. Again, compare this approach with that in Figure 5.2b, whose prompts encourage student interpretation.
- Compromised rigor. There are only four clues that are teacher selected. In addition, students are restricted to three possible interpretations, all teacher supplied, rather than encouraged to think freely on their own.
- The Rationale may fail because of the flaws in the handout.

"And the Winner Is. . ."

Figure 5.2 a and b contains an activity sheet rather than a busywork sheet because it encourages students to work independently and to think creatively. Remember that the social roles are clear. The task is also clear and well sequenced, integrating

---

Solving "What's This?"
1. Everyone is to work together respectfully. Swap ideas and use your imagination!
2. Follow directions on the handout below.
(Continued in Figure 5.4b.)

FIGURE 5.4a Active or Passive Thinking?

Directions: Answer the questions thoughtfully.

Your Goal: Solving the Riddle!

A. A metaphor is a(n) _____ that has a _____ meaning.

B. Tell how each clue is a metaphor. Choose the best answer for each clue.

#1 ". . . moon without a face . . ."
(a) a monster (b) dark moon (c) something smooth and white

#2 "A curtain shields a silent place"
(a) something protective (b) a cover (c) a kind of flimsy wall

#3 ". . . a sea both still and clear"
(a) a large crossing (b) calmness (c) a pool of liquid

#4 ". . . a sun that doesn't sear"
(a) a picture of a sun (b) something round and yellow (c) a happy event

C. What is the answer to the riddle? Put your heads together to figure it out!

FIGURE 5.4b Active or Passive Thinking?

metaphoric thinking, which is crucial for success in solving the riddle. The prompts (items in the table) guide students to focus their thinking process, keeping their eye on the metaphoric values. The "animal, mineral, or vegetable" question helps students zero in on the answer. Overall, this activity sheet unfolds a cohesive process, designed for peer groups to use social roles to full advantage. That means that the activity has a high chance of satisfying the Rationale. Even if the students don't solve the riddle, this activity sheet promotes a successful lesson because the prompts and criteria keep learners thinking and guided so that their frustration level is minimized.

Contrast Figures 5.2 and 5.4, which are at opposite extremes. The latter is too teacher controlled. Like Figure 5.3b, Figure 5.4b employs too few clues. This approach may seem to be less overwhelming to the students, but it also uses insufficient information. In Figure 5.4b, the teacher's attempt to be helpful results in spoon-feeding and shuts the door to critical thinking before it opens. For these reasons, Figures 5.3 and 5.4b contain busywork sheets.

Now take a look at Figure 5.5, the improved version of Figure 5.2b. It contains an overarching question and a column to justify interpretations. Compare this improved version with Figures 5.3 and 5.4.

EXAMPLE #2/SOCIAL STUDIES, TWELFTH GRADE

Now that you have an idea of the difference between a busywork sheet and an activity sheet, see what you think of the example that follows. We're not asking you to compare and contrast different versions for the same lesson this time. Instead, try to spot the strengths and weaknesses in each example that follows, applying what you've learned from the handouts in Example #1. For starters, we think you'll have fun with Figure 5.6. Jot down your own analysis before you look at ours.

Clues	Associations for Each Clue (literal and metaphoric)	How Each Clue Fits the Same Possible Solution
1. "A moon without a face . . ." (Model this example with student input.)	1. (student responses to the model) Literal = unlit moon, a moon of another planet. Metaphoric = something not fully formed, something sad, something resembling a moon without markings.	1. An egg resembles a moon and has no markings.
2.	2.	2.
3.	3.	3.
4.	4	4.
5.	5.	5.
6.	6.	6.
7.	7.	7.
8.	8.	8.
Is the answer animal, mineral, or vegetable and why? What do you think the answer is? Prove it in the last column!		

FIGURE 5.5 BIG QUESTION: What Metaphors in the Clues Help Solve the Riddle?

Our Analysis of Figure 5.6

Analyze Figure 5.6 before you read our analysis here. Figure 5.6 is designed for students socialized for peer-group or cooperative learning in which each member contributes individually. Did you catch that students are even instructed to define and assign their own social roles within the group? The role-play technique is applied to a research assignment, thereby personalizing the application of the research findings. The debate as a Performance Objective demands high-level cognitive skills of analyzing, synthesizing, and evaluation. The activity sheet governs this self-directed project so that the teacher becomes a facilitator or mentor. Finally, this project is an example of what constructivist teaching aspires toward. If you resocialize even middle-school students from all backgrounds to shift from passive to active learners, they will be able to carry out this project with just such an activity sheet and amaze themselves (see Module 15).

EXAMPLE #3/SCIENCE, TENTH GRADE

You might want to steal the idea in Figure 5.7a-c even if you're not a science teacher. The idea in Figure 5.7b is to model two different ways of organizing the same data.

The dare: Prepare a case that argues (for/against) flying the Confederate flag in public today

Your Job:

1. Dig up as much information about the Confederate flag as you can from various sources (books, journals, newspapers, the Internet, documentaries, etc.).
2. Employ this information to write a persuasive argument that either (a) supports the right to fly the Confederate flag in public or (b) denies the right to fly the Confederate flag anywhere in the United States.

The Challenge:

1. You will be assigned to a group that argues for a given position (for or against flying the Confederate flag in public), regardless of your personal view on the matter. Your group will establish its own social roles and delegate appropriate tasks.
2. You will assume the identity of a historical figure of your choice who would support your assigned viewpoint. This may be a famous person of your choice (American president, military general, writer, abolitionist) or a typical private citizen of your choice (Northern industrialist, plantation owner, freed slave, religious person, racial or religious minority child). Each person in the group must assume a different identity.
3. You must argue from the historical perspective to people in the twenty-first century. This means that your research must focus on the individual perspective you select.

Prompts:

1. Is flying the Confederate Flag today in the twenty-first century an act of treason or an expression of First Amendment rights of free speech?
2. Is the Civil War really over?
3. What does the Confederate flag symbolize? To whom?

Criteria:

1. Refer to a minimum of six substantive sources, including:
   (a) at least two books (no textbooks);
   (b) at least one Website with documented sources;
   (c) at least one reputable journal or newspaper with documented sources (may include historical publications from past centuries on microfiche).
2. The written argument must adhere to the form of a persuasive essay learned in English class, complete with bibliography.
   (a) Include at least six paragraphs: introduction, conclusion, and at least four paragraphs in the body. Each body paragraph should have at least three details to support its main idea.
   (b) Cite and counter at least one opposing argument to your position.
   (c) Include historical background as well as cultural factors. Include at least one authentic anecdote to support your position or to undermine your opposition.
3. The oral debate must employ your research findings from the individual perspective you assume. Be prepared to debate one other group for fifteen minutes. There will be three rounds with different groups.

FIGURE 5.6 Social Studies/Twelfth Grade: Role-Play

Big Question: Can you design two concept maps that depict two valid taxonomies for fruits and vegetables?

Social roles:
1. Approach this brainstorm as a fully cooperative team.
2. Take turns being prompters who ask something like: "What are the distinguishing characteristics in this (tomato, avocado, potato, etc.)?" "How does this (tomato, avocado, potato) compare with the (banana, coconut, etc.)?" The person with the earliest birthday begins.
3. Select a scribe who draws the concept maps.
4. Select a presenter who will share your concept maps with the class.
5. Assign a timekeeper who alerts the group when only 5 minutes is left.

Your job:
1. Problem solve in groups of four. You have forty minutes.
2. Cut open and examine the fruits and vegetables given you. (Each group has different specimens.) Observe textures, inner contents, shape, manner of growth, etc.
3. Infer what characteristics fruits have in common and what characteristics vegetables have in common.
4. Design concept map #1 that demonstrates the interrelationship between larger categories and subcategories.
   (a) Decide on at least three broad categories for the taxonomy.
   (b) Identify at least two characteristics for each category.
   (c) Compare and contrast your specimens to sharpen your observations.
5. Then reconsider the categories represented by concept map #1 and use different characteristics to establish different categories. Represent this second taxonomy in concept map #2. Repeat the criteria in instruction #4 above.

(Continued on next page)

FIGURE 5.7a Science: Designing Concept Maps

In Figure 5.7c, the same principle is applied to designing two different concept maps for fruits and vegetables.

Pause to consider what you think the strengths and weaknesses are of Figure 5.7c. Then compare your analysis with ours.

Our Analysis of Figure 5.7a, b, c
This lesson is another example of what constructivist teaching aims for. The task of reorganizing the same data under different characteristics or criteria requires moving through Bloom's Taxonomy from definition, comprehension, and application to the high cognitive levels of analysis and synthesis, all as independent learners, guided by the activity sheet. It also demonstrates the enormous flexibility and potential of the activity sheet as a tool that uses a wide variety of techniques. Figures 5.7b and 5.7c could also be used for individuals without peer exchange.

Big Question: Can you organize data for a concept map that depicts a valid taxonomy for animals?	Big Question: Can you organize data for a concept map that depicts a valid but different taxonomy for animals?

Sample Concept Map #1/Data:
[Filled in with student responses for modeling purposes. *Italics represents student input]*
Broad category: Animals
Characteristics:
1. self-reproduce (given)
2. *respire*
3. *eliminate bodily wastes, etc.*
Subcategories and characteristics #1:
1. fish (given)
   a. *have gills*
   b. *live in water*
   c. *carnivorous and herbivorous*
2. *mammals*
   a. *warm-blooded*
   b. *live births (etc.)*
3. *reptiles*
   a. *cold-blooded*
   b. *external birth (eggs), etc.*
	Sample Concept Map #2/Data:
	[Filled in with student responses for modeling purposes. *Italics represents student input]*
	Broad category: Animals
	Characteristics:
	1. self-reproduce (given)
	2. *respire*
	3. *eliminate bodily wastes, etc.*
	Subcategories and characteristics #2:
	1. land animals (given)
	   a. *human beings*
	      walk on 2 legs, warm-blooded, mammals, have live births, different racial groups
	   b. *reptiles*
	      cold-blooded, lay eggs
	2. *sea animals*
	   a. *fish*
	      have gills, swim, lay eggs
	   b. *whales*
	      mammals, live births
	3. *amphibians*
	   a. *frogs*
	      develop as tadpoles in water, adults live on land and in water, lay eggs
	   b. *newts, etc.*

FIGURE 5.7b Science: Designing Concept Maps (continued)

Putting It All Together

We designed this part of Module 5 as an inductive learning experience for you. In other words, we displayed and analyzed several examples of the concept of an activity sheet and invited you to analyze along the way. Now we invite you to identify or define the salient elements of an effective activity sheet. You may want to review the examples to refresh your memory and even to catch new details you may have missed.

● Stop here to do this task, then read on and compare your key elements with ours. If you caught some elements that are not on our list, please let us know via the editor for Curriculum and Instruction.

Big Question: Can you design two concept
maps that depict different taxonomies for
fruits and vegetables?

Directions: Fill in and enlarge this concept map for fruits and vegetables
similar to how you organized the data in the "animal" sample.

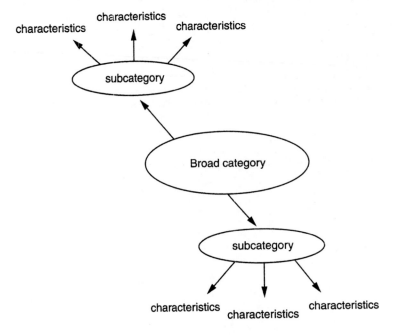

FIGURE 5.7c Science: Designing Concept Maps

Elements of an Activity Sheet

1. Provides an overarching question that relates to the Rationale, not to the task itself.
2. Unfolds the Performance Objective.
3. Embeds the parts of the Performance Objective into the directions of the activity sheet.
4. Incorporates various techniques, including but not limited to the traditional use of questions and fill-ins that carry out the Performance Objective.
5. The Performance Objective contains clear prompts.
6. Fill-ins on a constructivist activity sheet serve as stepping stones to critical thinking and are not the terminal task.

7. Applies to peer-group or solo activity. Write directions accordingly. For a peer-group activity, remember to specify social roles (see Module 5, Part 1).
8. Includes or describes any necessary materials.

■ ROUNDUP ■

An activity sheet can function as a compass for your students, guiding them independently through a lesson or project that involves traditional sources and/or technology. Substance is revealed and critical thinking is achieved through effective instructional methods, such as those in this textbook. Techniques are practices and procedures that carry out a method or a combination of methods. So your students need techniques that enable them to meaningfully learn with and without a computer. One effective material that maximizes learning with any resource and numerous techniques is the activity sheet.

We recommend that you don't limit your handouts to fill-in questions, even those that facilitate critical thinking. Use your imagination to incorporate other techniques into the activity sheet, similar to those in this module and in Module 3, Part 2. For example, you can include Hooks that personalize a frame of reference; write prompts for role-playing animate or inanimate figures; require original concept maps; employ heuristics, brainstorming, or guidelines for question writing for peers; and so on. The list is as endless as your imagination.

■ HANDS-ON PRACTICE ■

Writing terrific activity sheets combines intellectual rigor with creativity and clear focus, with an understanding of how your students learn at a given point in time. We supply some prompts here to get you going and to remind you to draw on a full repertoire of techniques. But you'll soon be coming up with your own prompts and designs.

Self-Instruct Planner: Designing Activity Sheets
(Work on a separate piece of paper.)

NOTE: If you want, keep building on the same topic you used in other self-instruct planners. Or choose another topic. Remember to refer to Bloom's Taxonomy as you plan.

Subject _____ Topic _____

PROMPTS TO HELP YOU FOCUS

1. Formulate your Rationale.
2. Decide on an overarching question that relates to the Rationale, not to the task itself.
3. Decide on an appropriate Performance Objective.
4. Embed the Performance Objective into the directions of the activity sheet.

5. Review the various techniques you have learned, including those you used in the Hands-On Practice in Module 3, Part 2.
6. Decide which technique(s) will carry out the Performance Objective.
7. Write several clear step-by-step prompts, like the ones here.
8. Decide if you want this to be a peer-group activity or a solo activity. Write directions accordingly. For a peer-group activity, remember to specify social roles.
9. Include or describe any necessary materials.

SUGGESTED READINGS

Bonwell, C. C., & Eison, J. A. (1991). *Active learning: Creating excitement in the classroom.* Washington, DC: Washington University, School of Education and Human Development.

Dale, H. (1994). Collaborative writing interactions in one ninth-grade classroom. *Journal of Educational Research, 87*(6), 334–344.

Fenton, C. (1992). Cooperative learning: A view from the inside. *Contemporary Education, 63*(3), 207–209.

Hill, M. (1992). Strategies for encouraging collaborative learning with a traditional classroom. *Contemporary Education, 63*(3), 213–215.

Jacobs, G. (1988). Co-operative goal structure: A way to improve group activities. *ELT Journal, 42*(2), 97–101.

Johnson, D. W., & Johnson, R. (1990). *Learning together and alone.* Englewood Cliffs, NJ: Prentice-Hall.

Kahn, E. A., Walter, C. C., & Johannessen, L. R. (1984). Making small groups work: Controversy is the key. *English Journal,* February, 63–65.

Lortie, D. C. (1975). *Schoolteacher: A sociological study.* Chicago: University of Chicago Press.

Putnam, J. (1997). *Cooperative learning in diverse classrooms.* Columbus, OH: Prentice-Hall.

Sharan, S. (1980). Cooperative learning in small groups: Recent methods and effects on achievement, attitudes and ethnic relations. *Review of Educational Research, 2,* 241–271.

Wood, K. D. (1987). Fostering cooperative learning in middle and secondary level classrooms. *Journal of Reading,* October, 10–19.

Module Six:

Technology in Your Practice
by David Curtis

■ OVERVIEW

Seven methods and a bevy of techniques, new terms, and new ways of thinking about teaching and learning. That's a lot to absorb and apply. Then there's the Big IT: information technology. Virtual reality, chat rooms, the Net, the Web, palmtops, wireless devices, you name it. Hardly a day goes by without news about the latest technological innovations. Feeling overwhelmed? You're not alone. The good news is that the latest digital technologies have potential not merely to enhance learning and teaching but also to transform them, but only if applied with insight and wisdom. In this module, we provide a framework with which to integrate new digital technologies with constructivist methods, as illustrated by the following scenario.

A Scenario: Fishy Mystery

Katie and Daryl, aspiring tenth- to twelfth-grade earth science and social studies teachers, respectively, are being mentored by cooperating teachers, Ms. Hernandez and Mr. Cole. Both these teachers team-teach in the same two subject areas at a nearby high school. After consulting with them about possible themes and topics, Katie and Daryl jointly develop a unit that they will teach together as part of their practicum. They decide to organize the unit's theme around an authentic student inquiry into a local water-quality problem, emphasizing students' problem-solving and critical-thinking skills. The unit is entitled "What's Killing the Fish Downstream?" and comprises five block lessons (each made up of two lessons back to back, lasting one-and-a-half hours). It will adopt a teacher-directed/student-focused setting (see Module 15, Part 1). The unit will also integrate Internet-accessible and stand-alone software tools with selected constructivist methods and techniques.

Katie will use a decidedly "low-tech" hook, a dead fish on ice, to kick off the unit, which will be held in one of the school's computer labs. After holding up the fish, smelling it, and grimacing with disgust, Katie will present a short, local digital TV news clip about summer fish kills in a nearby lake. She and Daryl will then investigate students' previous exposure to and knowledge of key concepts and information technology (see Module 7) while laying the groundwork for a guided student investigation. Their insights into the students' understanding will be applied during the ensuing lesson, which will integrate the Inductive Concept (Module 8, Part 2) and Exploratory Discussion (Module 10) methods. Twice during the Exploratory Discussion section, the students will break away in pairs to their assigned computers.

Guided by activity sheets (Module 5, Part 2) embedded into their digital notebook, students will use digital geographic mapping software accessible via the Web to investigate spatial relationships between the lake and nearby features. Such features might include streams, drainage basins, roads, land cover, farm fields, a sewage treatment plant, a large shopping mall, and outlying subdivisions. Through a simple-to-use Web interface, the mapping software tool enables the students to zoom, overlay, and identify distinct features. In doing so, Katie will introduce the students to Geographic Information Systems, a powerful computer-based technology with which to integrate data collection, visualization, and analysis.

During the discussion, Katie, assisted by Daryl, will moderate student–student dialogues about possible factors linked to weather, climate, and land use that could affect the water quality of the downstream lake. The class will collectively articulate a list of closely related questions to guide the investigation. Is runoff from the farm fields along streams that feed into the lake causing the fish to die, and if so how? Might all those fertilizers have something to do with it? What about runoff from the shopping mall alongside the lake—could it be the cause of the fish dying? Or might that sewage plant further north be the culprit? What is happening to the nitrogen and oxygen levels in the lake? Is there a connection with broiling summer temperatures that coincided with the fish kill? How were other lake creatures faring during this time? Were they also suffering ill effects, even dying? Using software for concept mapping (Module 3, Part 2), the class will also develop an initial schema of factors thought to affect water quality and related social issues.

The initial schema file will be saved and placed on the unit Website, specially created to document the students' investigations for later assessment and presentation to peers. For homework, students will be required to access the Web from home, the public library, or the community technology center. They will read and evaluate information on water quality at an authoritative educational Website, and then individually propose a tentative hypothesis as to what could be causing the fish kills, together with supporting arguments and ways to test it. They will write and upload their conjectures in their individually assigned digital notebook spaces for referral in upcoming class discussions.

During the next one-and-a-half block lessons, Exploratory Discussions will be combined with peer-group learning techniques (Module 5, Part 1) to sift through the varying hypotheses and pursue the most promising ones. Katie will guide the students as they develop strategies to gather and analyze data to test their theories. To accomplish this, they will utilize a variety of tool and data sets, including the Web-based mapping tool, which is linked to environmental data sets accessible via a statewide natural resources information Website; a graphing tool to investigate quantitative relationships between putative water quality factors; and an educational, Web-based computer simulator to invoke and examine various "what if" scenarios. In one scenario, for instance, selected factors such as land use are changed while others (such as the amount of rainfall) are held constant, and the impacts on third factors, such as nitrogen levels, are viewed graphically.

The students' simulation experiments will be structured via carefully layered, open-ended question prompts that Katie is developing via email correspondence with the cooperating teachers. By the middle of the third lesson, through class and group work and individual homework assignments, the students will have refined their earlier schema or concept map to include causal interrelationships thought to account for the fish kill. Their theory is that farm field runoff containing excessive fertilizer is the leading suspect. In stimulating overgrowth of algae whose subsequent dying and decay depletes dissolved lake oxygen, the nutrient-enriched runoff is thought to bring about a precipitous decline in oxygen, aided by the high summer temperatures. As a result the fish can't breathe, and they die off in droves.

Now comes the tougher part; figuring out how to prevent, reduce or eliminate the problem. Working in small groups, students will run the Web simulator again and test alternative mitigation strategies that are most likely to prevent or decrease algae overgrowth, as judged by how well each strategy would diminish or remove the mediating causes leading to the fish kill. Again, the students will be guided by teacher prompts embedded in the students' digital notebooks. Students will then write up their findings and recommendations with justifications in their notebooks. The scene is now set for the final lesson.

Daryl will begin by using the Inductive Concept Method. Students will generate a concept map of the social costs and issues with which to evaluate the alternative strategies, drawing on their digital notebook entries from the previous lesson and incorporating the concept map refined in the third lesson. Employing peer-group learning techniques, Daryl will then moderate a Reflective Discussion (Module 11) of potential solutions to the runoff problem. Pairs of students will take on distinct roles—farmer, land-use planner, wildlife manager, suburban developer, citizen group, and so forth, to evaluate the candidate solutions and weigh their social costs and impacts. In a summative assessment (Module 14) to be carried out during an extended period, individual students, using multimedia-authoring software, will create a final Web report. They will be required to propose and justify, with evidence (charts, graphs, and maps "captured" into their digital notebook during the unit) and reasoning, a cost-conscious plan that addresses the fish-kill problem while balancing different stakeholders' interests and concerns.

In the final block lesson, students will present their reports to the class and receive peer and teacher feedback, after which they will be able to fine-tune and edit their reports. Their reports will be compiled into a class Web project that will be posted on the school's Website. Parents, the local media, stakeholder groups, city and regional planning authorities, and other interested parties will be notified of the address and invited to comment via an electronic discussion board linked to the site.

© 2002 David Curtis

Katie and Daryl's unit is ambitious, requiring that students draw on impressive technology skills gained from their previous education. The purpose of the scenario was not to focus so much on the technology itself but to demonstrate its potential to mediate engaged learning. The scenario illustrates an optimal classroom setting in which considerable technical resources are applied to support an active, student-centered pedagogy rather than simply reinforcing old ways of teaching and learning. Its core ideas are equally applicable to less optimal settings in which you might find yourself teaching. While this scenario emphasizes science and social studies, the incorporation of technology it illustrates is applicable to other subject areas, including language arts and the humanites.

■ GOALS

The Fishy Mystery scenario provides a glimpse of how technology can support the constructivist classroom when integrated with methods. The overriding goals for this module are twofold:

- To provide a framework through which you as an aspiring teacher can grasp the range, scope, and potential of digital technologies to enhance and transform learning and teaching.

- To impart principles and motifs by which you can evaluate, choose, and integrate emerging technologies with constructivist teaching methods presented in this book.

Note that in this module, unless stated otherwise, *technology*, also termed information technology, means digital computing and communications technology.

■ DISCUSSION

The pace of innovation in digital information and communications technologies is accelerating, promising to revolutionize how we work, live, and learn (Brown, 2000; PITAC, 1997, 2000). Many of the students you will be teaching are already surrounded by technology. For better or worse, they live with it, by it, and through it each and every day. They do not think that they are "doing technology" when they surf the Web to download tunes or view digital clips of their favorite rock or rap groups, play Internet videogames with friends near and far, trade instant messages or just plain email with family, or, if conscientious, do their homework with a word processor. It's just *stuff that you use to get stuff done, be cool, and maybe have fun.*

Then there is school. Some teachers are on the leading edge, engaging their students in active learning. But too many teachers, particularly at the high school level, are talking and talking (Cuban, 1993, 1996; Kyle, Schmitz, & Schmitz, 1996). All too often students are seated in neat rows like they were a hundred years ago, all facing the teacher, some taking notes, some staring, lost in facts upon disembodied facts. Yes, there is a computer lab down the corridor, but typically its layout resembles the traditional classroom. Here "computer literacy"—learning how to use software—is likely taught separately from lesson content, with the expectation that the students will later apply it to their studies. The result is that students' exposure to technology is often split off from the rest of the curriculum and from the world beyond the classroom, where they will be expected to participate as productive citizens after they graduate (Brown, 2000; Maddux, Johnson, & Willis, 1997; PITAC, 1997; Valdez, McNabb, Foertsch, Anderson, Hawkes, & Raack, 2000).

But things are changing, albeit slowly. Ongoing efforts to reform education emphasize hands-on, minds-on learning. Reformers advocate that teachers guide rather than drill their students, tapping into and channeling their intrinsic curiosity and motivation to build things, communicate with peers, and express themselves (Bruce & Levin, 1997; Dewey, 1956). Reformers also stress the importance of students' developing progressive awareness of and taking increasing responsibility for their own learning, both as individuals and with peers (Blumenfeld, Marx, Soloway, & Krajcik, 1996; Bransford, Brown, & Cocking, 2000; Linn, 1998; Means, 1994). Reformers advocate that different types of assessments be adopted (Module 14), assessments that are embedded in the learning process itself and that examine higher-order thinking skills and not the rote memorization that often passes for learning (see Standards, 1992–2000). Appropriate uses of digital technologies can support enactment of such reforms, which in turn would provide an environment in which these same technologies more fully promote and deepen the learning experience. Realizing that promise will ultimately depend on the dedication, skill, and ongoing professional development of tomorrow's teachers (PITAC, 1997, 2000). People like you.

Appropriate use of technology can increase your ability to guide and inspire your students to learn, throughout your and their careers. But this requires a vision. The same constructivist vision embedded in this book. A vision of active learners doing the learning. In this module, we do not seek to describe any particular technology in detail. Instead, we aim to provide a big picture to help you understand an otherwise bewildering array of educational technologies, choose them wisely, and integrate them effectively into your practice.

Focal Point 1: Technology Viewed as Learning Media

What, then, constitutes an educational technology? Books, chalk and blackboard, pen and paper, television, and radio—all of these are just as much educational technologies as the latest laptop computer, or wireless palmtop device, but only potentially. They become educational only when and where they are embedded into activities designed with explicit pedagogical intent.

How and to what extent does a given technology offer ways for students to experience the world, reflect on it, and analyze, extend, and apply that experience? Later in this module (Focal Point 4), we examine this question more closely. First, though, we expand on the role of technology when used with tools, techniques, and methods discussed in Module 3, Part 2, and illustrated in Section C, Introduction to Methods, Figure C.1.

In Module 3, we described a *tool* as a device or material for implementing *techniques*, such as peer-group learning, concept maps, heuristics, role-play, and advance organizers, and selected to enact chosen *methods*. For example, following a segment to Investigate Learners' Previous Experiences (Module 7), a teacher might utilize Web-based software to design, distribute, and assess electronic activity sheets as part of a peer-group learning exercise. Each component, the Investigate Learners' Previous Experiences method and a technology-enabled technique, is likewise embedded in an Inductive Concept lesson. Based on the students' responses and using the electronic activity sheet software, the teacher quickly adjusts the sequence of lesson activities to build more precisely on the students' previous concepts. The digital activity sheets also provide spaces for students to share their observations, conjectures, and evidence with each other and with the teacher. In this way, the tools, incorporated here into Web-based software, support the peer-group learning techniques through which the Investigate Learners' Previous Experiences method assesses the students' learning. A tool such as Web-based electronic activity sheets in turn relies on a whole range of computing and telecommunications technologies that together enable that tool to function as intended.

The major point here is not to get lost in the particulars of this or that technology. Our concern is how the tools support constructivist learning activities and how to organize these activities and tools cohesively around the evolving needs of the learner. To this end, it is helpful to view technologies in terms of the mediative roles that they play and the ways they can alter how and where we think, communicate, and act in the world.

When observed from this perspective, digital technologies have the potential to become new media for learning (Bruce & Levin, 1997). This view contains and extends the traditional view of media as receptacles for storing information to a perspective in which media connect otherwise separate processes of learning and discourse. These processes include our innate curiosity (especially when we are very young) to find things out, express ourselves, use language to interact with others, and, as we grow and mature, to explore relationships between ideas and what they purport to represent in the real world (Dewey, 1956). In adopting this perspective, the learner and learning activities take center stage rather than the tools and underlying technologies. Emphasis shifts from students learning about technology to learning through technology (Bruce & Levin, 1997). In other words, as your students repeatedly use a technology it becomes progressively embedded into the learning process.

For instance, as we write this module, we are unaware that we are word processing. We're simply writing. When you drive down to the store, you're not thinking, *I'm using internal combustion, transmission, and hydraulics technology.* You just drive. This view of technology, in which it becomes progressively transparent through continuing individual and social use, echoes its mediative role. Later in this module (Focal Point 4) we return to this theme when describing a framework for evaluating and applying technology in the classroom, and we will see how this dynamic, learner-centered perspective on technology as media affects the role of you, the teacher.

Focal Point 2: **Technology in the Fast Lane**

Without doubt, the times they are a-changing. To comprehend how emerging technologies are increasing pressure for reforming how we learn and teach, it is necessary to grasp five key motifs in technological innovation.

MOTIF #1/THE PACE OF INNOVATION

The first motif is the sheer pace of technological innovation in computing technology. The only sure thing is change, and exponential change at that. Today's consumer workstations, laptops, and video playstations pack yet greater computer power than even the Big Iron mainframe computers in the 1950s, the 1960s, and the 1970s. That is because microprocessors or microchips (also known as chips), the microscopic workhorses of digital computing, pack ever more parts (transistors) into tinier and tinier spaces. This is a manifestation of Moore's Law, the doubling of chip density every 18–24 months, which has held for the past three decades, a trend that is not only holding firm but may even accelerate in coming decades (Fixmer, 2002). Also, microprocessors are crunching ever faster. Many home PCs today come equipped with chips that are ten times speedier than their counterparts of less than a decade ago.

MOTIF #2/THE GLOBAL VILLAGE

Then there is the telecommunications revolution, starting with the invention of the telegraph in the nineteenth century and, in the past two decades, the invention of fiberoptic cable that can carry billions of bits of information every second. More recently there is the arrival of high-capacity, digital wireless communications, ushering in a new era of mobile computing, where information can be instantly accessed and you can communicate with others almost anywhere on the globe twenty-four hours a day, seven days a week irrespective of where you are. The number of people and places getting hooked up to the Internet continues to mushroom. Global digital networks are ushering in what the visionary Marshall McLuhan termed "The Global Village." Already the Internet links upwards of 200 million people and institutions in more than 180 countries (Hobbes, 2002).

MOTIF #3/CONVERGENCE

The past decade has seen a quickening convergence of the television, telephone, and computer into multifaceted digital information appliances. The key to this convergence is the rise of digital technology (see Figure 6.1). When converted into digital ones and zeros, it doesn't matter if the information conveyed through hardware is video, imagery, text, sounds, or graphics as long as it is represented digitally. As a result, previously separate media—film and video, audio, text, photography, 3-dimensional (3D) graphics, Virtual reality—are becoming increasingly mixed and matched into a multimedia tapestry. When linked together in hypertext, multimedia documents stored in distant computers are woven into a seamless web of information. Convergence, combined with increased availability of inexpensive media tools adapted for personal use (e.g., word processing and Web page authoring programs and digital video and image creation, editing, and processing software) is allowing just about anyone to become a producer, publisher, and broadcaster, including you and your students.

MOTIF #4/INFORMATION EXPLOSION

The first three motifs, the accelerating pace of innovation in both computing and telecommunications, together with quickening convergence, are also feeding another phenomenon: the explosive growth of information. It is estimated that the content of the Web—which already contains tens of millions of pages—has been doubling every one hundred days and has surpassed the total stored in the entire Library of Congress. A significant portion may have educational value, although the quality is highly variable. Added to this stored Web information are the billions of bits of data exchanged every day via email or transmitted between millions of digital pagers and cellular telephones worldwide.

MOTIF #5/WEB IN FAST FORWARD

Many educators refer to the Web as a tool for learning. Depending on the context in which it is used, it can be viewed as a learning tool, material, or both. We believe it is more helpful to view the Web as a multithreaded medium that can support an incredible diversity of tools, materials, and activities.

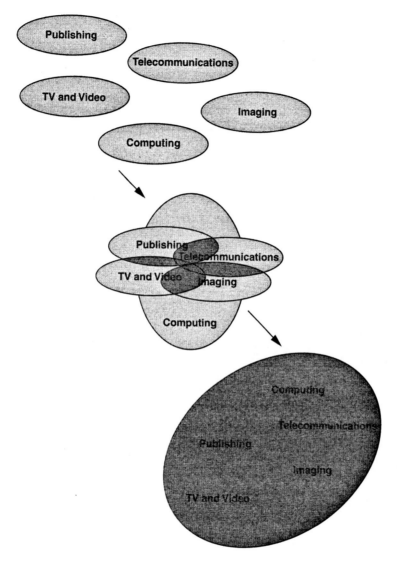

FIGURE 6.1 Media Convergence

WHAT YOU WANT, WHEN YOU WANT IT

In its original form in the early 1990s, the Web supported documents such as text, videos, animations, and sounds precreated for consumers of information. Interactivity was limited to clicking on hyperlinks in a given document, which took you to another Web document stored on local or distant computers. In today's Web, more and more data are generated and displayed to the user on demand, that is dynamically.

WHAT YOU WANT, HOW YOU WANT IT

The Web does more than put vast amounts of information at everyone's fingertips. Thanks to advances in technology, information can also be individualized to match what the user wants and needs here and now. If properly designed and constructed, Web-based learning tools and materials can accommodate a range of individual learning styles, abilities, and disabilities, including physical, visual, and hearing impairments.

FROM CONSUMERS TO PRODUCERS

Besides allowing cheap, fast access to a universe of information, the Web also enables users to produce and share information products with others, anywhere and anytime. You can now create your own personalized vacation maps and itineraries, and peruse online newspaper articles, add your own comments, and send them to others. You can communicate on the Web asynchronously via email and chat services or synchronously through instant messaging and Web conferencing tools that accommodate live video and voice communications.

GOING MOBILE

With digital wireless communications now being added to the mix, teachers and students will be able to tap all these resources instantly from hybrid devices that combine the features of palmtops and cellular phones, precursors to tomorrow's fully integrated, portable information appliances.

The Web continues to evolve at breathtaking pace. Digital media are fast becoming pervasive, ubiquitous, and persistent. The Web is evolving from being the equivalent of a vast library of information to becoming a social medium in which not only information but also understanding about that information can be constructed and shared with any number of others. The same Web technologies that are being driven by the rapid explosive growth of electronic commerce are now being adapted by educators to construct learning experiences that meet the developing needs of individuals or groups of learners. Moreover, as the Web goes mobile, those experiences will no longer have to be limited to a single setting inside the school or any other building. Portable computing has the potential to support greater *persistence* and integration of learning experiences across multiple settings, from the classroom, laboratory, or library to museum or field trip. Back in the classroom or lab, portable, wireless computing devices in the hands of the students imply changes in the traditional set up: from students individually seated in rows, all facing the front, to a more open configuration in which you, the teacher, can better act as coach, guide, and facilitator.

Discussion 2 **Technology in the Fast Lane**

Into what world will today's kindergarten students graduate tomorrow? What skills and knowledge will they require to participate as full, productive citizens? We can glimpse the future (the near future at that) by looking at what's happening today. Rapid advances in technology, particularly digital technologies, are both responding to and propelling important shifts in the socioeconomic structure in which we live and work. More and more, it is vital that students are prepared not to fill a job in a single line of work for a lifetime but for multifaceted careers. They need to be able to learn how to learn throughout their lives and not just in school or college, and they need to be able to apply what they learn in rapidly changing circumstances.

In particular, the accelerating pace of technological innovation is both driving and being driven by a parallel, exponential growth of knowledge, particularly in the sciences but also in social sciences and to a lesser degree in the humanities and allied disciplines. When historians, for example, need to discern population trends over a chosen time period, they might employ digital geographic mapping, database and statistical analysis tools more typically used by scientists (Burton, 2002). These same or similar tools could also be used in high school settings. Propelled by new technologies, knowledge is not only growing at breakneck speed but is also rapidly changing and can become quickly obsolete. What we consider to be hard and fast truths today may be questioned tomorrow. Small wonder there are mounting concerns about the accuracy and lack of depth of many college and secondary-level textbooks, quite apart from the didactic pedagogy they embody (Tyson, 1997; Roseman, Gerald, & Shuttleworth, 2001). Simply put, you and your students cannot rely on textbooks alone to access the latest, most accurate information. However, although the Internet offers a treasure-house of information, this information varies hugely in quality and usefulness. It is important that you and your students evaluate all information sources critically, whether book based or online, as an integral part of the learning experience and as part of their development into productive, informed citizens (Bruce, 2000).

It has been clear for more than a decade that traditional modes of schooling not only fail to take into account the unprecedented educational opportunities afforded by new information technologies but also the societal changes they are helping to bring about. Digital media and telecommunications are still knocking loudly on the walls of the classroom, promising to break artificial boundaries between learning in the home, classroom, workplace, and community; overcoming the separation of teaching and learning in school from the rest of life; and pointing toward the need to view learning new skills and acquiring new knowledge as a lifelong endeavor in multiple settings and not just in the classroom, lecture hall, or lab (PITAC, 2000).

Focal Point 3: How Can Digital Media Transform Learning?

However sophisticated or engaging, new digital media cannot by themselves transform learning. How you teach can enrich your students' learning experiences, enabling them to learn more and to learn what they need to know when and where they need to know it. Successful classroom incorporation of technology depends on a larger context. In addition to access to technical resources, such as adequate Internet connectivity or ongoing hardware and software maintenance, that context includes the pedagogical setting, for example, teacher versus student centered, and the stances of distinct groups of stakeholders, for example, administrators, other teachers, students, parents, and the community at large, with respect to that setting. Do these groups strive for creative uses of digital technologies that promote constructivist approaches to teaching and learning? Or do they view technology as a means merely to streamline and strengthen traditional, didactic modes of teaching or to support lower-level learning processes, for instance, drill and practice?

Here we take a closer look at the roles of both the teacher and the student. Related to this, we look at how effective deployment of learning media requires understanding students' distinct learning styles. We also briefly address two other important pieces of the larger context into which technology is deployed: concerns about student assessment in technology-enabled, constructivist classrooms and the persistent technology access and useage gap between haves and have-nots, otherwise known as the Digital Divide.

Teacher Role

Teachers can and should actively define and shape the overall pedagogical setting in which they apply technology. However, the likelihood and extent to which digital media provide experiences that actually foster active learning among your students will depend on the pedagogical strategies that you employ; these in turn will depend on your ideology of learning. Insights from cognitive research and classroom practice (Means, 1994; Saettler, 1990; and see Module 1) suggest that for media to engage students, help them structure their learning experiences, and apply their understanding, the teacher needs to become less of a sole purveyor of knowledge and more of a facilitator (Jones et al., 1995). In this setting, emerging digital media can help foster authentic classroom environments in which learning becomes situated, "being in part a product of the activity, context, and culture in which it is developed and used (Collins, Brown, & Duguid, 1988, p. 32), rather than decontextualized, concrete rather than abstract, and social rather than relying on individual cognition alone. Web-based multimedia communications in particular can afford you and your students unprecedented opportunities for discourse with outside experts or peers. Through such interactions, your students can gain not only conceptual knowledge but also tacit knowledge and skills; not simply knowing what something is, but how it is known, how it works, how it can be fixed, improved, adapted, and so forth. Such process skills—how to comprehend, generalize, and apply the knowledge gained in one context to another, different situation—are vital for preparing to succeed in a rapidly evolving economy.

Competent use of digital media in your classroom implies a shift from pedagogies that seek to control every aspect of your students' learning to those that embed activities, supported by appropriate media, and that teach them how to learn as they learn. Often this requires that you, the teacher, take on distinct stances: knowledge expert, expert learner, and co-learner.

TEACHER AS KNOWLEDGE EXPERT. This may be an appropriate role to set the stage for teacher-directed/student-focused or, in some instances, student-centered activities (Module 15, Part 1), such as presenting the big picture via a mini-talk at the start of a lesson or unit using the Deductive Concept method (Module 8) or at the beginning of a Directed Discussion (Module 9). In this stance, having framed the structuring question, the teacher might present a Website, for instance, to convey initial concepts to later build on through more student-centered approaches. Students actively engage with the presented material through mini-tasks structured by an advance organizer (Module 12).

TEACHER AS EXPERT LEARNER. Here, you as the teacher shift roles toward that of a facilitator of learning. Our opening scenario, Fishy Mystery, illustrates this stance. The rapid growth and turnover of new knowledge is making it difficult, if not impossible, for the teacher to act solely as knowledge expert. In contrast, the teacher as expert learner demonstrates to students how to utilize different types of media as needed to identify interesting problems to explore and solve. At the same time, the expert learner helps them tap their curiosity and imagination, while supporting or scaffolding them as they evaluate the evidence at hand, draw appropriate inferences, and as they test their conjectures against further data. It is not enough to demonstrate the specific technical steps in using this or that tool. The teacher also needs to model to the students the thinking behind using a tool in support of a defined cognitive task. One thing is certain: students model not only what teachers do in the classroom but also what they do not do. Modeling includes showing your students how they can learn from their mistakes. In gaining meta-awareness—discerning the big picture—of your own classroom practice and explicitly sharing that awareness with your students, you will promote habits of mind that go hand in hand with the more diverse sets of skills they will need to acquire to flourish as lifelong learners and productive citizens. This requires that you, the teacher, reflect on your own previous socialization and that of your students. If, for instance, they have previously been spoon-fed facts upon facts, it will be necessary to apply methods and techniques that help resocialize them toward taking an active role in their learning (see Module 15).

TEACHER AS CO-LEARNER. This stance is bound up with a pedagogical setting that stresses student-centered, open-ended, inquiry-driven learning. Here, students take yet greater charge of their own learning, whether individually or in groups. They frame and then investigate their own questions, selecting the tools with which to pursue their inquiries. Inquiry learning both depends on and promotes higher thinking skills. Often it is combined with *project-based learning*, in which students undertake extended projects that may be organized around a single theme or topic (see Module 13). In this setting you, the teacher, may genuinely take on the role of co-learner insofar as answers to the driving questions at hand typically are not cut and dried and known in advance. Indeed, using communications tools such as email and Web-based discussion or chat spaces, you and your students can support sustained inquiry by tapping into expertise from other quarters beyond the classroom—scientists, historians, and writers, for example.

Student Role

The role of students is often modeled on that of their teachers, and it is also subject to many other influences, for example, parents, peers, and the wider culture (as expressed in the popular media and advertising). The shift from teacher-centered to student-centered pedagogical settings implies that students become active learners, take charge of their own learning, and learn to learn with others (Sandholtz, Ringstaff, & Dwyer, 1997). That shift entails focusing less on what and how much the student knows (or, worse still, remembers but doesn't really understand) and more on the following types of questions:

- *Knowledge:* How do students find out what they need to know and when they need to know it?
- *Resources:* What resources, including tools and media, are available to them for this purpose?

- *Navigation Skills:* What information navigation skills do they require to succeed in this? For example, can they navigate through multiple linked documents on the Web, make productive use of a search engine, and retrieve the pages, images, and other online materials that they need for a given assignment or project?

- *Evaluation:* Are students able to evaluate the information they find? Do they know what to look for, what to ignore, what to question, and how to ascertain the validity of what they find? In addition to weighing evidence individually, students need to cultivate an openness to insights and recommendations from others—peers, teachers, or experts. This social dimension of learning is particularly important in the constructivist classroom.

- *Application:* Can they apply what they find to solving a specific problem, such as constructing a product, physical or digital, that demonstrates the principles and concepts they were supposed to learn?

When taking account of the rich multimedia capabilities of digital media, especially the Web, these questions imply different ways of thinking about what it means to be literate that go beyond traditional text-based notions. Literacy might also include abilities to navigate through information, to understand imagery both static and moving, and to comprehend, represent, and express ideas in various types of media. Certainly it is important that students master the three R's—Reading, 'Rriting, and 'Rithmetic—but the new media also bring attention to the growing importance of fostering other forms of literacy linked to higher-order thinking skills (see Module 1). These skills include applied reasoning, communicating clearly and effectively (both verbally and in writing, which also means the ability to listen actively), and working in groups or teams.

John Seeley Brown (2000) forcefully makes this point in his article "Growing Up Digital," in which he assesses the impacts of the Web on work and education. He reasons that discovery-driven learning that employs the Web requires information navigation skills. These skills are deepened when combined with activities in which students not only find what they need, be it a document, software tool or dataset, but also construct something with it that is important to them. Then, not only can students feel empowered by mastering technology, but in so doing they create digital artifacts—electronic products such as drawings, graphics, images, movies, or multimedia documents—that embody what they learn as they learn it. When appropriate, these products may be shared via the Web with teachers and peers as well as audiences beyond the classrooom, including parents and local communities, providing both motivation and adding authenticity to student activities.

Where Style Meets Technology

In Module 1 you read about students' preferred learning styles and the importance of taking these into account in your classroom rather than adopting a one fits all orientation. We named four distinct learning styles—concrete-sequential, concrete-random, abstract-sequential, and abstract-random—corresponding to current understanding about ways that individuals perceive and process information. Other cognitive research suggests a different although complementary perspective on preferred learning styles that relates to the sensory modalities through which people perceive and acquire information. In probing that age-old question "What is intelligence?" cognitive scientist Howard Gardner (1983) developed a theory that human cognition is bound up not with intelligence viewed as a single entity but with multiple intelligences. Gardner categorized these as follows:

- *Linguisitic:* language abilities, oral and written; musical capacities to listen to, discern meaning in, and express onself in patterns of sound.
- *Logical-Mathematical:* problem-solving and reasoning skills (overlapping with abstract/sequential).
- *Spatial:* understanding how things work in space (and time).
- *Bodily-Kinesthetic:* emphasizing awareness of the body's position and movement in dance, play, and sports and in other activities such as videogames or sky writing sometimes used with young children.
- *Interpersonal:* abilities to communicate, play, and work with and process feedback from others.

Digital learning media have the potential to cater to individual learning needs and styles. Focusing on linguistic intelligence alone, the typewriter, for instance, favored those who expressed themselves best in writing. But it was a bane to many individuals with stonger propensities in music, drawing, painting, dance, athletics, and even mathematics. In contrast to the typewriter, the Web blends many distinct types of media that favor different learning styles. As John Seely Brown (2000) puts it, "[The Web] is the first medium that honors the notion of multiple forms of intelligence . . . [It]affords the match we need between a medium and how a particular person learns" (p. 12).

Successful integration of learning media in the classroom requries becoming sensitized to your students' distinct learning styles. Watch how they learn, what types of activities and tools supporting those activities they take to, which ones they are less inclined toward. Notice their specific strengths and weaknesses in reading and creating imagery and text, abstract reasoning, social communication, and so on. Apply that awareness when designing lessons and selecting and incorporating specific learning media that address individual student's learning styles as well as those of the group. Remember, everyone wants to learn!

Testing Mania

During the past five years, billions of dollars have been and continue to be spent at federal, state, and local levels on wiring up schools and installing hardware and software. What have been the benefits to education? The short answer is that the jury is still out (Cuban, 2001). The drive for national testing has reached fever pitch in response to continuing concern about perceived deficiencies in literacy and levels of achievement in science and math among fourth, eighth, and twelfth graders (Bracey, 2001; NAEP, 2000; PISA 2000; TIMMS, 1995). Many people wonder if the answer lies with more and better technology, and still more dollars to pay for it. But trying to demonstrate that any learning technology actually improves learning inevitably raises the following questions: Who is learning? What is being learned? How are they learning it? The problem is that traditional, standardized, short-answer tests are not well suited to address these questions, as they tend not to take technology into account. In particular, they fail to examine what combinations of cognitive processes are involved when students are actively engaged in learning and how well they can apply what they learn to solve meaningful problems (Baker, 1999; Bransford, Brown, & Cocking 1999; Cuban & Pea, 1998; McNabb, Hawkes, & Rouk, 1999).

In the constructivist classroom, it is important to determine what learning resources—media and materials—facilitate higher-order thinking skills. Short-answer or multiple-choice tests alone simply won't do the job of assessing these skills. Authentic, performance-based assessments are needed that measure not discrete cognitive abilities but rather a wider range of student abilities and products and that also examine the types of skills and knowledge required beyond the walls of the classroom: in the workplace and community (Hawkins, Frederiksen, Collins, Bennet, & Collins, 1993; also see Module 14). Digital media are well suited to supporting such assessments insofar as they enable your students to produce artifacts of their learning as they learn. For instance, electronic portfolios might incorporate objects selected from multimedia resources accessible on the Web and/or CD-ROM. In the Fishy Mystery scenario, we see how the Web may support digital notebooks for student explorations that can be structured through questions posed either by the teacher or, in student-centered inquiry, by the students themselves. The key point is that the students' notebook entries constitute artifacts of their explorations that are embedded in the learning process itself. In another example, concept-mapping software used during an Inductive Concept and Exploratory Discussion lesson can yield intermediate products that open a window into your students' thinking processes. Likewise, Internet-based peer-group discussions can generate a wealth of artifacts that can reveal much about your students' previous understanding, mastery of content, and thinking processes.

Through these insights, you will be better able to adjust content and pedagogy in pace with students' cognitive growth. Moreover, those same artifacts also help your students visualize their own thinking processes. In doing so they are more likely to be able to apply what they learn in different situations and not just in the one in which the learning occured in the first place (Bransford et al., 1999).

Wither the Digital Divide?

The constructivist methods in this book may be implemented with or without the latest digital media. However, their enactment can be enriched through appropriate use of such media. Not using information technology in your classroom could deprive your students of access to a bounty of information, ideas, tools for knowledge construction and sharing, and opportunities to master important information literacy skills. However, the reality is that many classrooms still do not have adequate technology resources and support. Significant gaps remain between different population groups in their access to new digital information and communications technologies.

In education, this Digital Divide includes two key components. One is quantitative—the extent of access to the Internet and to up-to-date hardware and software. The second gap concerns the quality of learning through technology. The good news is that substantial public and private investments during the past decade have steadily narrowed the Digital Divide. According to recent U.S. government statistics (NTIA, 2000), most population groups are rapidly adopting the new technologies "regardless of income, education, race or ethnicity, location, age, or gender." (Disturbingly, people with disabilities remain an exception to that trend.)

Nevertheless, as societal disparities in access to hardware, software, and connectivity are progressively overcome, some educators are questioning not just whether but also how media are being used in the classroom among distinct groups of students (Pea, 2001; Smerdon, Cronen, Lanahan, Anderson, Iannotti, & Angeles, 2000). Does the quality of those media support activities that address higher cognitive skills associated with analysis, problem solving, and critical thinking? Are they being used fully for this purpose? It is important to consider these questions in your own teaching.

Focal Point 4: Taxonomy of Learning Media

Depending on how they are designed and used, digital technologies have the potential to support a large variety of learning activities that address all levels of cognition articulated in Bloom's Taxonomy (see Modules 2 and 4). Drawing on the arguments of Dewey (1956) that the curriculum be structured around children's natural impulses to find things out, communicate, build things, and express themselves, Bruce and Levin (1997) developed a complementary taxonomy of learning media (Figure 6.2).

Bruce and Levin classify information technologies according to their abilities to mediate four related learning processes: inquiry, communication, construction, and expression. By making new kinds of experiences accessible, digital media can tap students' intrinsic motivations to learn. Because they are interactive, the new media favor active or engaged learning. Depending on the pedagogical setting (i.e., teacher directed/student focused or teacher facilitated/student centered—see Module 15, Part 1), students are guided verbally or via an activity sheet, for instance, or can choose for themselves what they see, hear, and do and can use appropriate media to document, apply, or extend what they learn. Note that the boundaries between the taxonomy's categories and subcategories are not rigid. Their overlapping reflects how digital technology can connect and integrate otherwise separate processes of learning and discourse. The taxonomy of learning media offers a coherent framework in which to comprehend and evaluate digital technologies and incorporate them into your practice.

Media for Inquiry

Inquiry consists of several interrelated processes (see Figure 6.2): framing questions, exploring (accessing, observing, and collecting data), analyzing, and sense-making and knowledge integration (concept mapping, theory, or model building). Inquiry usually starts with a question or with definition of a problem. Most very young children are naturally curious, often persisting in asking why this, why that, expressing their curiosity in language. As they master and assimilate more abstract concepts (Piaget, 1970), their questions become more elaborate. The heuristic (see Module 3, Part 2) Who, What, When, Where, Why, How systematizes these questions, which are at the basis of inquiry. However, all too often in the present education system, children are socialized to stop asking questions.

Enacting the constructivist classroom is in part about rekindling that questioning mindset. By making accessible a rich array of experiences, new media can spark that curiosity to discover something, then to check it out. It should be noted that from the standpoint of pedagogy, inquiry learning belongs in both teacher-directed/student-focused and student-centered classroom settings. The difference is the extent to which

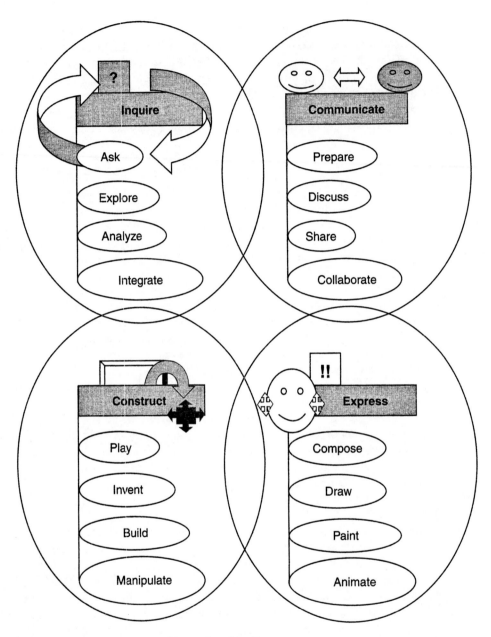

FIGURE 6.2 Taxonomy of Learning Media

the teacher provides an overarching structure to the inquiry. As students learn how to learn, both individually and with each other, the pedagogical setting can become more student centered, where the teacher acts not only as a facilitator but also a co-learner. Digital media can support you and your students in the following aspects of the inquiry process: accessing and collecting data, analyzing data, and synthesizing information, or sense-making.

ACCESSING DATA. A huge range of data spanning the physical, biological, and social sciences and the arts and humanities is readily accessible and can be gathered in various formats via the Web as well as other media such CD-ROMs. Multimedia digital libraries and databases contain music, sounds, voices, imagery, graphics, animations, video, and text as well as scientific data sets. The first step in exploring data is to define the question to be answered or the problem to be solved with that data, such as during Directed and Reflective Discussions. That question or problem in turn must be linked clearly to a lesson's Rationale and Performance Objective (Module 3, Part 1) or a unit's goals and driving questions (Module 13, Parts 1 and 2). Examples of media for accessing and collecting data are provided in Figures 6.3a and b.

COLLECTING DATA. Digital technologies have spawned a wide range of devices with which to gather data from the world around us. Using digital cameras and microphones, students can capture sounds, sights, and movements in the classroom, lab, or field (see Figure 6.3b).

A GLIMPSE

The junior high school's football team, "The Bulldogs," is hard at practice. At the request of the physical science teacher, Ms. Rodriguez, the physical education teacher, Mr. Katz, is showing his students how to use a digital video camera to record the motion of the ball as it is thrown and kicked. Later, Ms. Rodriguez and many of the same students will examine the path of the ball's motion using video analysis software as part of a science unit on Newton's Laws of Motion.

Also available are low-cost sensors to monitor motion, heart rate, pulse, and a variety of environmental factors, from air temperature and barometric pressure to water-quality factors such as acidity, dissolved oxygen, and bacterial count. Low-cost, handheld Global Positioning System (GPS) units, which utilize satellite signals to pinpoint any position on the earth, allow your students to map that same environmental data and discern how it might change over distance. After mapping the data, your students' next step might be to generate conceptual models to account for the spatial variation and to test their conjectures against further data or to use computer simulations as illustrated in the Fishy Mystery scenario.

In addition to using instruments locally, students can conduct observations on faraway instruments or can download and view previously archived data and images gathered with those instruments. It may be possible to secure time for them on remote telescopes and microscopes that can be controlled via friendly Web interfaces designed for learners rather than specialists. Or they can explore striking images of Mars and other planets transmitted from distant space probes.

ANALYZING DATA. Inquiry is as much about finding interesting problems to explore as it is about solving them. Usually there is no absolutely right or wrong answer when interpreting data. Often data are frequently ill structured or incomplete, whether gathered by your students during field trips or via Web pages that they locate and cite as evidence to support an argument. From a cognitive standpoint, the challenge for teachers and their students is to frame questions or define problems whose investigation reveals patterns in otherwise messy data. A variety of software can be brought to bear on this problem by permitting students to view data in mul-

Name	Attributes	Web Links
Search Engines		
Ask Jeeves	Websites are returned in response to student questions. (All)	www.ask.com
Open Directory	Volunteers manage links based on area of interest or expertise. (All)	dmoz.org
Northern Light	Teachers or parents can filter out unwanted content. (All)	www.northernlight.com
VisIT	Search results are displayed as maps that group sites according to relevance to the topic under investigation. (All)	www.visit.uiuc.edu
Archives and Databases		
Alexandria Digital Library	Geographical, biological, and geological data on the continents and oceans. (Sc, SS)	www.alexandria.ucsb.edu/adl
United States Geological Survey	Web mapping, satellite, and aerial imagery. Extensive data on geography, biology, geology, and water resources. (Sc, Ma, SS)	www.usgs.gov
World Watcher	Public domain data on energy, climate, and geography. (Sc, Ma, SS)	www.worldwatcher.nwu.edu
National Atlas	Make your own maps of anywhere in the United States. (Sc, SS, Hi, Hu)	www.nationalatlas.gov
National Weather Service	Current maps on weather, climate, rivers, and soil. (Sc, Ma)	weather.gov
Windows to the Universe	Space and earth imagery. (Sc)	www.windows.ucar.edu
Amazing Space	Activities, images, and links on astronomy and the earth. (Sc)	amazing-space.stsci.edu
Artemis Digital Library	For middle and high school students. Supports searching, tracks students' questions, and organizes and archives past queries. (Sc, SS)	www.goknow.com
Chickscope	Database of magnetic resonance images of developing chick embryos. (Sc, Ma)	chickscope.beckman.uiuc.edu
Virtual Center for Digital History	Texts and images on Afro-American history and culture. (SS, Hi, Hu, A, LA)	www.vcdh.virginia.edu/
Electronic Text Center	Advertising, urban development, Native-American history, Egyptian parpyruses, etc. (Hi, Hu, SS, A, LA)	scriptorium.lib.duke.edu/ scriptorium/projects.html

FIGURE 6.3a Media for Inquiry: Accessing Data
Examples are only illustrative and do not signify endorsement. Web links are current as of August 2002. Subject area key: All = all areas; Sc =sciences; Ma = math; Mu = music; SS = social studies; Hi = history; Hu = humanities; A = the arts; LA = language arts; FL = foreign languages; PE = physical education.

Name	Attributes	Web Links
Remote Instrumentation		
Hands-on Universe	Internet access to telescopes in the United States and overseas; image analysis. (Sc)	hou.lbl.gov
EarthKam	Web-mediated picture taking of Earth as viewed from the orbiting International Space Station; image analysis. (Sc, SS)	www.earthkam.ucsd.edu
Bugscope	Web interface to a scanning electron microscope trained on insects. (Sc)	bugscope.beckman.uiuc.edu
Probes, Sensors, Data Recorders		
GLOBE Program Concord Consortium	Information and links about easy-to-use instrumentation and motion, software relating to weather, water quality and conditions, force, light, sound, temperature, and pressure. (Sc, Ma)	www.globe.gov probesight.concord.org
Image Capture		
Measurement in Motion	Video capture and graphing of form and motion. (Sc, Ma, PE)	www.learn.motion.com

FIGURE 6.3b Media for Inquiry: Data Collection
Examples are only illustrative and do not signify endorsement. Web links are current as of August, 2002. Subject area key: All = all areas; Sc = sciences; Ma = math; Mu = music; SS = social studies; Hi = history; Hu = humanities; A = the arts; LA = language arts; FL = foreign languages; PE = physical education.

tiple representations, including text outlines, flow charts, images, movies, graphs, and tables. Doing so helps students build and refine their mental models of the factors and processes underlying the patterns. Figures 6.3c and d illustrate media that support related aspects of data analysis: visualization, virtual reality, image processing, and spreadsheets and graphing.

- VISUALIZATION. Originally developed by scientists, computer scientists, and artists and adapted for education, visualization technology uses computer graphics to translate numerical data into graphical representations of that data—contours, surfaces, shadings, and colors—that enable learners to discern patterns. Sounds (changes in tone or amplitude) may be added to highlight the patterns still further. When animated, visualizations can reveal dynamics—change over time. Visualization technologies extend our senses, tapping into the incredible powers of our eyes and brains to visually process information. Visualization offers novel, often

Name	Attributes	Web Links
	Visualization	
ArcVoyager	Geographic Information System software. Local and Web-based tools to create and display maps and other graphical representations, query, and analyze spatial data. (Sc, Ma, SS, Hi, Hu)	http://www.esri.com/industries/ k-12/voyager.html
ArcExplorer		http://www.esri.com/software/ arcexplorer
WorldWatcher	Various tools for interpretation and analysis of global environmental data. (Sc, SS)	www.worldwatcher.nwu.edu
GLOBE		www.globe.gov
Biology Student Workbench	Web-based tools for visualization of genetic and biomolecular structures (DNA, RNA, proteins) and their evolutionary relationships. (Sc)	peptide.ncsa.uiuc.edu
Chemviz	Web-based and local tools for visualization and analysis of atomic and molecular structures. (Sc)	chemviz.ncsa.uiuc.edu
e Chem		hice.org/sciencelaboratory/ echem/index.html
Virtual Molecular Dynamics Lab		polymer.bu.edu/vmdl
	Virtual Reality	
Augmented Reality Toolkit and Magic Book	Virtual world-building and storytelling tools that require some programming and computer graphics background. (Sc, Ma, LA, A)	http://www.hitl.washington.edu
QuickTime VR (QTVR)	Tools to create 3-D–like interactive movies and panoramas for viewing and distribution via the Web. (Sc, A)	www.apple.com/quicktime/qtvr
Virtual Toolbox		www.vrtoolbox.com
The Web3D Repository	Information on current software, educational uses, and demos of interactive 3-D objects and worlds. (Sc, Ma, A)	http://www.web3d.org/vrml/ vrml.htm
	Image Processing	
NIH Image	Public domain tool set for acquiring, displaying, editing, enhancing, and analyzing 2-D and 3-D images. (Sc, Ma)	rsb.info.nih.gov/nih-image
LView Pro	Image processing, editing, viewing, and capturing tool suite that works with digital cameras and scanners. (All)	www.lview.com/index1024.htm
Mars Pathfinder	Quicktime Virtual Reality (QTVR) and Virtual Reality Mark Up Language (VMRL) models of the red planet's surface, as imaged by this space probe. (Sc)	http://mars.jpl.nasa.gov/MPF/ vrml/vrml.html

FIGURE 6.3c Media for Inquiry: Data Analysis (1)—Visualization, Virtual Reality, and Image Processing

Examples are only illustrative and do not signify endorsement. Web links are current as of August, 2002. Subject area key: All = all areas; Sc = sciences; Ma = math; Mu = music; SS = social studies; Hi = history; Hu = humanities; A = the arts; LA = language arts; FL = foreign languages; PE = physical education.

Name	Attributes	Web Links
Spreadsheets, Graphing, Math Manipulation		
Microsoft Excel and Works	Multiple representations of quantitative information: tables, line graphs, bar charts, pie charts, etc. (Sc, SS, Ma)	www.microsoft.com
CorelWorks		www3.corel.com
Measurement in Motion	Graphing of motion data captured on video. (Sc, Ma, PE)	www.learn.motion.com
Project Interactivate	Probability, statistics, algebra, and geometry software. (Sc, Ma)	www.shodor.org/interactivate
SimCalc (also for Modeling)	Exploring numeric, graphical, and symbolic representations of the mathematics of change. (Sc, Ma)	www.simcalc.umassd.edu
Virtual Manipulatives	Web-based K-8 mathematics tools for exploring numbers, geometry, algebra, probability, data analysis, and statistics. (Sc, Ma)	matti.usu.edu/nlvm/nav
Mathematica	Advanced tools for mathematical and technical computing. (Sc, Ma)	www.wolfram.com
Knowledge Representation		
Causal Mapping	Web-based causal mapping tool (see also Figure 6.7). (Sc, SS)	cilt.berkeley.edu/synergy/ causalmap
PicoMap	Concept mapping tool and presentation software. (All)	http://palm.hice-dev.org/ picomapAppPage.htm
Inspiration and Kidspiration	Concept mapping and presentation software. (All)	www.inspiration.com
Chemsense Knowledge Building Environment (KBE)	Integrated tools to view, edit, and share chemistry representations (text, images, drawings, animations) and insights. (Sc)	chemsense.org
Sensemaker	Web-based tools to organize evidence and share ideas when using the WISE Website (see Figure 6.7). (Sc)	wise.berkeley.edu
Modeling and Simulation		
Shodor Foundation	Web simulations in physics, astronomy, and environment. (Sc, Ma)	www.shodor.org
Agent Sheets	Builds simple computer models that run locally and on the Web. (Sc, Ma, SS)	www.agentsheets.com
Model-It/ Investigation Station	Middle school software to conceptualize and build simple computer models and observe their behaviors graphically. (Sc, Ma, SS)	investigationstation.org/ sciencelaboratory/modelit/ index.html
StarLogo	Computer modeling tools to explore how dynamic systems (e.g., bird flocks, ant colonies, and traffic jams) evolve. (Sc, Ma, SS)	el.www.media.mit.edu/ groups/el/Projects/starlogo/ ccl.northwestern.edu/cm/
StartLogoT		starlogoT

FIGURE 6.3d Media for Inquiry: Data Analysis (2)—Spreadsheets, Math, and Sense-making Examples are only illustrative and do not signify endorsement. Web links are current as of August, 2002. Subject area key: All = all areas; Sc = sciences; Ma = math; Mu = music; SS = social studies; Hi = history; Hu = humanities; A = the arts; LA = language arts; FL = foreign languages; PE = physical education.

compelling ways through which to bring alive phenomena that are otherwise inaccessible to normal experience. From colliding black holes to the combination of atoms into molecules, such phenomena are too far, too small, too big, too hot, too cold, or too dangerous to witness other than in visualized computer simulations.

Students may also peer beneath visual representations to analyze the numbers underlying them. Some visualization tools are tied to data in one or more specific subject areas, such as astronomy, biology, ecology, physics, chemistry, mathematics, or economics and social sciences. Other types of tools—particularly Geographical Information Systems (GIS), as illustrated in the Fishy Mystery scenario, and spreadsheet and graphing software—permit students to visualize multiple representations of data traversing many different subject areas, including history, environmental science, physical science, and math.

Visualization technologies are useful not only in data analysis but also in sense-making (see below). In using visualization media, students can develop perceptual, cognitive, and technical skills. Visualized images or animations may confirm or conflict with previous intuitions students have about how things work in the natural or designed worlds, thus prompting them to develop or revise their own understanding.

On the negative side, visualizations are only as "truthful" as the underlying data or computer simulations from which they are generated; garbage in, garbage out no matter how good the imagery looks. Teachers and their students need to develop a critical awareness of the strengths and pitfalls of visualization. Students are then less likely to be misled by attractive or compelling imagery that misleads, intentionally or not. Such critical powers will serve them well throughout their lifetimes.

- VIRTUAL REALITY. Closely related to visualization, virtual reality, or, VR employs a variety of computational, interactive, and graphical display technologies to generate artificial worlds in which are represented phenomena, spaces, and even abstract imaginings of our minds, such as mathematical objects otherwise not perceivable. The key difference with visualization itself is that the viewer is no longer outside the visual scene being projected but is immersed in it. Also, the perspective changes in response to his or her movement. VR enables participants to interact with a simulation more naturally than with a standard computer screen, mouse, and keyboard.

  There are many different flavors of VR, each utilizing distinct types and levels of display. The most high-end VR systems totally surround the viewer with projection panels or walls and sound and may occupy a whole room or a theater. Others utilize one big projection wall and may require viewers to don special eyewear to be immersed in the virtual scene. Scaled down VR setups are less immersive but take up less space, require less powerful computation hardware, and therefore cost much less.

  Virtual reality systems now deployed at selected science centers, museums, and planetariums can make for compelling student field trips. You may well ask, "How can I bring VR to my own classroom?" Moderately priced hardware and software technologies now exist with which to generate interactive 3-D worlds that provide a taste of VR but not its full immersivity. Many such worlds can be explored on standard desktop computers, even laptops. If you or your students possess modest technical skills, you and they might be able to create 3-D worlds that can be shared with other students via the Web or CD-ROM and DVD (which are now becoming much easier and cheaper to produce). Otherwise, you and your students can access Web-based collections of 3-D worlds precreated by educators and students elsewhere.

- IMAGE PROCESSING. Behind every image are data. In photographs, that data consist of tiny dots whose density controls the level of detail contained in the image. Once digitized, such images can be analyzed and manipulated to bring out selected features or to deemphasize others, revealing subtleties in the image that might otherwise be missed. In this way, image processing overlaps with visualization. A variety of affordable image-processing tools often packaged with standard image editing and graphics software can be deployed in the classroom. There are many sources from which to obtain image data that can be used with these tools, particularly in astronomy, earth sciences, and biology (see Figure 6.3a).

- SPREADSHEETS AND GRAPHING. Most standard office productivity software packages include spreadsheet tools used to organize and manipulate data and to produce multiple representations of data: bar charts, pie charts, histograms, line graphs, scatterplots, and so on. By offering alternative views into observed or acquired data, these representations can spur ideas into possible underlying causal connections, as illustrated in the Fishy Mystery scenario, or provide insights into key physics principles or the behavior of mathematical functions. Feedback to students is rapid and circumvents the tedium of traditional, manual graphing methods. More sophisticated statistical, graphing, and mathematical programs can support yet more advanced data manipulation and analysis (see Figure 6.3d).

MAKING SENSE OF DATA. Data access, collection, and analysis are key components in inquiry learning, whether guided or open ended. Additional sets of media address higher-order thinking skills, such as those involved in making sense of and integrating information and building models and theories, thereby aiding the creation of personal and group understanding. In supporting more intuitive, sensory engagement with the underlying data, visualization and VR media (see above) may also facilitate sense-making. By viewing technologies as media for thinking, attention is drawn to the importance of making it visible, both to teachers and students themselves. In making their conceptual processes explicit to themselves and peers, students become progressively empowered to take charge of their learning (Collins, Brown, & Holum, 1991; Linn, 1998). Figure 6.3d illustrates digital media that support the related sense-making processes: knowledge representation, in particular concept or causal mapping and modeling and simulation.

- CONCEPT MAPPING. When enacting the Concept and Discussion methods, a major goal is to enable students to generate, develop, and characterize their concepts about a topic at hand. Used inductively, concept-mapping software can readily help students visualize relationships between categories or processes that define a given concept (Novak, 1990). In some subject areas, particularly in the sciences and social studies, causal mapping can promote student understanding of how systems behave by identifying distinct system factors and mapping their possible causal connections. This is demonstrated in the Fishy Mystery scenario at the outset of this module. Alternatively, the teacher might run such software in presentation mode, and the students then further develop the concept map individually or within groups.

A GLIMPSE

At the outset of his lesson on the Great Northward Migration of 1910–1930, ninth-grade history teacher Mr. Hanes frames a main question to structure a Directed Discussion. The question: What propelled two million African Americans to pick up and leave their homes down south and head toward Chicago and the other great northern cities? Based on contributions from his students, he creates a concept map. In this way, he models to them how to examine and refine concepts and their interconnections, as well as providing them with a representation of their thinking. Next, Mr. Hanes distributes electronically the class concept map to pairs of students. Each pair is charged with assembling evidence that suggests alternative perspectives. The students gather relevant information by following an online activity sheet that lists questions designed to scaffold their research using preselected Web links. Mr. Hanes also encourages them to think up their own questions and to pursue their own links. Then, using the concept-mapping software in conjunction with a digital notebook, the students refine the concept map and document their reasoning in preparation for an Exploratory Discussion the next day, and a class research project to explore how African American music changed during the period.

These activities may take place, for example, during a block lesson that utilizes methods such as the Interactive Presentation (Module 12) or the Deductive Concept together with peer-group learning techniques.

In the preceding Glimpse, preparing a structured list of Websites as part of an activity sheet would usually entail drawing from previously bookmarked Websites or conducting a search for new ones. Most current search engines are lacking in that often they return thousands of site listings to sift through, a daunting challenge given teachers' busy schedules. But help is on the way. New Web searching software (for instance, VisIT—see Figure 6.3a) returns a prioritized map of sought-after sites rather than long, long lists. Teachers are provided with a bird's eye view of the links that they can then rearrange to suit their needs and also share with their students or other teachers. In a student-centered classroom (see Module 15, Part 1), for example, when employing the Exploratory Discussion method, students themselves might structure (or restructure) the Web links as part of gathering evidence for an argument. The structures they generate reflect their thinking about a concept and its defining characteristics.

Outlining tools that come with standard word-processing or presentation software provide another way for you, the teacher, and your students to represent conceptual structures and hierarchies. Outlines also help students organize their research, writing projects, and culminating presentations.

- MODELING AND SIMULATION. Like concept maps, interactive, computer-based models represent the dynamic relationships between factors in a system, whether an ecosystem, an economic or political system, a natural process such as photosynthesis, a simple mechanical device, or a cast of characters in a short story or novel. Using low-cost computer-modeling software available on CD-ROM or via the Web, learners can construct their model from scratch, adding (or removing) factors and defining qualitative or quantitative relationships that govern their interactions and behaviors, including effects such as feedback. A graphical interface allows students to state whether adding a given factor causes a big or little change, either negative or positive, and so forth (Spitulnik, Stratford, Krajcik, & Soloway, 1998). More advanced programs represent quantitative relationships between factors mathematically. Once these factors are defined and entered into the model, students can run it and view the output as simple, animated graphs showing change over time. In running the model, students are investigating if and how well it simulates the phenomenon under study. Such computer-modeling software allows students to experiment with and test their conjectures in simulation and to compare the results with actual data gathered in the field or from the Web (Verona, 2001).

In addition to software that supports model building and testing, precreated simulations (whose variables have already been determined) are also useful in a constructivist setting, whether teacher directed/student focused (guided) or student centered (open ended). Such simulations underlie many interactive educational software programs with which players design virtual buildings, run digital cities, construct imaginary creatures or characters, or manage simulated wildlife parks. Players juggle between constraints, then run the simulation and see the consequences of their decisions unfold. For instance, in the Fishy Mystery scenario, the students used a Web-based simulator to examine dynamic relationships between factors affecting water quality.

Behind all computer-modeling and simulation activities lie observation, inference of patterns, hypothesis forming, and testing. In that sense, modeling and simulation software offers rich opportunities for authentic learning not just in the sciences but also in geography, social studies, and, as part of Combo Units (Module 13), in physical education and the arts and humanities, if used with imagination and creativity.

Media for Communication

The constructivist perspective of learning views knowledge building as both an individual and a social process. Learning entails perceiving and interpreting information about the world we live in, building and refining conceptual structures that organize that information, and testing those mental structures in action and through dialogue. There is a whole spectrum of media that supports communication, whether one-way or interactive/two-way and asynchronous or in real-time. In utilizing such media in your classroom, attention should be focused not on the technology mediating the conversation but rather on the substance of what is being communicated and who is talking or writing to whom. As long as you keep this in mind, media for commmunication, examples of which are provided in Figure 6.4, have a place in most if not all subject areas taught in the secondary classroom.

DOCUMENT PREPARATION. To participate effectively in social discourse at any level, in the classroom, or later on in the workplace, students need to learn to express

Name	Attributes	Web Links
Document Preparation and Presentation		
Word and Power-Point (Office); Works	Authoring tools for writing, drawing, out-lining, presenting, and exporting to the Web. (All)	www.microsoft.com
Word Perfect		www3.corel.com
HyperStudio	Multimedia authoring software. (All)	
Kid's Media Magic	CD-ROM multimedia reading and writing tool. (LA)	www.hyperstudio.com www.humanitiessoftware. com
MediaWeaver	Bilingual (English/Spanish) multimedia writing software. (LA)	
Dreamweaver	Website production tools with page cre-ation and multimedia integration ca-pabilities ranging from basic to advanced. (All)	www.macromedia.com
GoLive!		www.adobe.com
Frontpage		www.microsoft.com
Coffee Cup (shareware)		www.coffeecup.com
Internet Notebooks and Portfolios		
Progress Portfolio	Capture and annotation of Web objects. Prompts and templates aid structuring and presentation of ideas. (Sc)	www.progressporfolio. northwestern.edu
WISE (Web-based Inquiry Science Environment)	Features a project notetaker for recording observations, drawing inferences, and proposing explanations. (Sc)	wise.berkeley.edu
Asynchronous Internet Communications		
Eudora	Email programs.	www.eudora.com
Outlook (Micro-soft		www.microsoft.com
CYBERFIBER	There are newsgroup discussions around almost any topic. Caution: the hosting	www.cyberfiber.com
Google		groups.google.com
Blogger	Tool for publishing annotations, links, news, writings, etc. to the Web.	www.blogger.com
Synchronous Internet Communications		
TAPPED-IN	Web-based, synchronous (and asynchro-nous) multi-user electronic discussion spaces supporting teacher profes-sional development. (All)	www.tappedin.org
NetMeeting	Text, audio and video conferencing, and collaborative document authoring software. (All)	www.microsoft.com
CUSeeMe	Internet video messaging and chat tool suite. (All)	support.cuseeme.com/cu5/
AOL Instant Messenger	Text-based messaging tools and services. (All)	www.aim.com/index.adp

FIGURE 6.4 Media for Communication
Examples are only illustrative and do not signify endorsement. Web links are current as of August, 2002. Subject area key: All = all areas; Sc =sciences; Ma = math; Mu = music; SS = social studies; Hi = history; Hu = humanities; A = the arts; LA = language arts; FL = foreign languages; PE = physical education.

their thoughts clearly. Encapsulating thoughts in writing, video, graphics, or any other format should not be seen just as creating finished products but also as an iterative process by which thoughts are formulated, refined, and communicated. By using document creation media, including word processors, Web page editors, graphics, and desktop video and image editing and publishing software, your students can flexibly develop and revise their ideas. Such media can support your students' efforts to concretize their thinking in text (linear and nonlinear, i.e., hypertext), images, sounds, and movies and make their thinking visible to others.

Some document creation programs also support seamless integration of these varied formats into multimedia documents that can be shared with peers, teachers, and others across the Internet or locally. After feedback from peers and you, your students can revise their work and turn the results into finished products for individual or group presentations and/or summative assessments (Module 14). Aside from accommodating images, movies, and animations, current presentation software programs contain outlining capabilities that you and your students can use to help organize individual and group thinking during lessons that employ Concept and Discussion methods, for instance. Although hands-on production of attractive presentations containing the latest "bells and whistles" can motivate your students to express themselves (see the "Media for Expression" section later in this module), it is equally or more important that you and they concentrate on the content to be communicated and the thinking behind it.

SHARING AND COLLABORATION. The past decade has witnessed a remarkable growth and development in communications media. Email is rapidly becoming commonplace. Palmtops and laptops fitted with wireless modems or linked to cellular phones allow rapid communication with anyone, from and to anywhere, at any time. Low-cost software for real-time and asynchronous conversations mediated by text, video, or audio can be installed and run on almost any desktop or laptop computer. Nowadays, the Internet supports shared document spaces, in which participants at different locations can exchange documents and/or view and edit the same document as well as data sets on their screens, in conjunction with voice and video communications. Data might include environmental information downloaded from the Web, as in the Fishy Mystery scenario, or gathered by students in the vicinity of their school, using palmtop devices equipped with low cost probes and sensors (Soloway et al., 1999), or by their peers who may reside on the other side of the globe.

In the constructivist classroom, use of communication and collaboration media such as email, with which students exchange ideas with peers located near or far, can both motivate and give added authenticity to student learning. Digital communications media that support group work can add value to peer-group learning techniques as part of concept- or discussion-driven lessons, for instance, particularly when these lessons are organized into units that accommodate sustained cooperative (peer-group) learning components. In extended, project-based units, email and other asynchronous communications media can facilitate correspondence with primary sources of evidence, such as war veterans, old timers, and other witnesses to past events, thus personalizing history or social studies. Telecommunications can also support mentoring relationships, also known as *teleapprenticeships* (Levin & Waugh, 1998), with scientists, writers, journalists, athletes, artists, composers, or other professionals volunteering in this role.

TEACHING. Digital media can bring students into contact with a wealth of new experiences and people, including peers and mentoring experts beyond the classroom. But what can communications media do for you, the teacher? With a dense curriculum to cover, and specializing in one or two subject areas, you may feel isolated from peers and lack a sense of belonging to a larger community of practice. Email, Internet conferencing, document sharing, and discussion spaces can support peer interactions, mentoring, and ongoing professional development focused on a range of practical issues (Bransford et al., 1999, Chapter 8).

These issues include classroom management; pedagogy and instructional techniques; curriculum materials and media, including useful Websites and tools, with tips on how to integrate them into practice; standards; review and feedback on lesson plans; advice; and mentoring from content specialists in their topic. Aided by such support, teachers are better able to keep up with the accelerating pace and turnover of knowledge and to address the inevitable surprises that arise in constructivist classrooms, where students are being encouraged to take progressive charge of their learning.

Media for Construction

Engaged learning implies a bias toward action, where students learn through hands-on and minds-on activities. According to Piaget's view of cognitive development (Piaget, 1970), before children can develop abstract schemata to structure their world they first need to construct meanings through concrete operations, such as playing with physical objects and discovering or creating patterns among them. This implies that abstract processes represent a later, more advanced level of cognition. Later research has suggested that building things—concrete operations—retain their importance in knowledge formation beyond this early stage (Turkle & Papert, 1990). Not only are such concrete processes significant to the construction of meaning, but they also provide avenues through which ideas about the world can be applied and tested.

New hybrid learning media that embody concrete and abstract cognitive processes are emerging from this research, signifying a convergence of digital and physical worlds. The resulting hybrid devices are termed *Digital Manipulatives* (Resnick et al., 1998). For decades, modular toys such as LEGO® have endlessly entertained and fascinated children, even adults, enabling them to construct their own toys and to populate imagined worlds with them. Now, they can endow their creations with behaviors by embedding cheap, yet sophisticated sensors to detect light, motion, and pressure and actuators linked to gears, wheels, pulleys, and levers under the control of simple computer programs that children can write and run. With LEGO®/Logo software, and its successor LEGO® Mindstorms™, a computer-controlled construction kit developed at the Massachusetts Institute of Technology, children can invent and build playful devices out of so-called programmable bricks, blocks, and balls. While having fun doing so, children are exposed early on to the fundamentals of computer programming and can explore mechanics, motion, feedback, and the emergence of complex behaviors, all of which are usually addressed much later in the curriculum.

A GLIMPSE
To begin a middle school unit on insect behavior, Ms. Green shows a silent video of different species encountering each other, then giant close ups of the insects' moving

heads and body parts. The class reacts with disgust. Next, Ms. Green plays back the last video sequence in slow motion and poses the structuring question: What are the different ways that the bugs appear to get about and react to one another? She then launches a Directed Discussion, listing and grouping the students' observations. Their initial schema is encapsulated in a concept map projected onto a screen for all to see. At the start of the next lesson, a double period, she sets loose onto a table two prebuilt, preprogrammed robotic creatures. "Watch them closely as they move and make contact." This time the students react with "oohs," "ahs," not exclamations of disgust. After a brief discussion to explore how the LEGO® creatures resemble the insects in the video, Ms. Green brings out a box of unassembled LEGO® components. An orientation session follows, in which she models the basics of assembly, and then she lets the students "mess" with the components for a while. Afterward, she divides the students into groups with activity sheets that prompt each group to build an insectlike construction that resembles how insects move and react in at least one respect. After several more computer lab sessions devoted to construction, the resulting "creatures" are finally set loose among each other. Exclamations of "wow" and "that's cool" accompany the LEGO® creatures as they collide into, climb over, or avoid each other. The unit concludes with an Inductive Concept segment in which the teacher encourages the students to look out for unanticipated behaviors and to develop ideas about why their creatures didn't behave as designed.

It is no surprise that hands-on exhibits featuring digital manipulatives are appearing at several museums and science and technology centers. Also making their appearances are computer-based exhibits that employ nontactile, "virtual manipulatives," for example, the *Virtual Fish Tank*. At this exhibit, visitors assemble imaginary fish from a menu of digital parts, then set their creations loose and observe how they make out in the simulated environment. These types of experiences, as well as those gained through modeling and simulation, including some computer games (see the earlier discussion in the "Media for Inquiry" section) can address students' natural propensities to learn by construction. Web links to further information about both digital and virtual manipulatives are provided in Figure 6.5.

Media for Expression

In the constructivist classroom, much attention is focused on designing activity structures that cultivate students' abilities to develop their own understanding from diverse sources of data and to refine that understanding by experiment, analysis, and discussion. However, knowledge construction entails not only logic and reason but also examination of attitudes and values, as might be developed during a Reflective Discussion, for instance. Authentic learning requires that students be able to build tangible artifacts, whether digital or physical, that embody both their ideas and feelings and that demonsrate their understanding of what they learn.

Insofar as communication, expression, and construction are related functionally to each other, the types of media that support them share many common charactistics. Like media for communication, media for expression (Figure 6.6) also include programs for document authoring and presentation as well as for digital composing, recording, and overlaying music and for drawing. Similarly, your students may benefit

Name	Attributes	Web Links
Digital Manipulatives		
LEGO®	Modular bricks for constructing machine-like toys limited only by imagination. (Sc, A)	www.lego.com
LEGO®/Logo	Adds gears, motors, and sensors to LEGO bricks to create dynamic machines that can be controlled via simple computer progams written in a modfied form of the Logo Programming Language. (See also Table 6.3d) (Sc, A)	http://el.www.media.mit.edu/el/projects/legologo/
LEGO® Mind-Storms™ Programmable Bricks	In development are programmable bricks—tiny, portable computers embedded inside a LEGO brick—for assembling autonomous robots or "creatures." (Sc, Ma, A)	http://el.www.media.mit.edu/groups/el/projects/programmable-brick/ http://mindstorms.lego.com
Virtual Manipulatives		
Virtual Fishtank	Digital tools to construct "virtual" fish online and watch them interact in a simulated fish tank at the Boston Museum of Science or on the Web. (Sc)	www.virtualfishtank.com
The Sims: computer-based "edutainment" games	Sim City: players "construct" whole cities and "run" them, observing unfolding consequences. Sim Earth: players set up and manipulate a planet's atmosphere, geology, climate, and life processes, then watch the planet evolve. (Sc, SS)	thesims.ea.com/us
National Library of Virtual Manipulatives	Web-based K-8 mathematics tools for exploring numbers, geometry, algebra, probability, data analysis, and statistics. (Sc, Ma)	matti.usu.edu/nlvm/nav

FIGURE 6.5 Media for Construction
Examples are only illustrative and do not signify endorsement. Web links are current as of August, 2002. Subject area key: All = all areas; Sc =sciences; Ma = math; Mu = music; SS = social studies; Hi = history; Hu = humanities; A = the arts; LA = language arts; FL = foreign languages; PE = physical education.

Name	Attributes	Web Links
Drawing, Image Creation, Editing, and Painting		
Photoshop Illustrator Paintshop Pro Corel Draw and Photo-Paint KidPix	Tools for drawing, producing, and editing 2-D images for print or online viewing. KidPix offers simpler tools for younger users. (Sc, Ma, Hu, LA, A)	www.adobe.com www.jasc.com www3.corel.com www.kidpix.com
3-D Graphics and Animation		
Alice Blender Creator Poser Bryce	Most 3-D software is high priced and requires expertise. Cited here are low-cost tools for constructing 3-D objects and animating them. (Sc, Ma, A)	www.alice.org www.blender3D.com www.curiouslabs.com www3.corel.com
Digital Video		
Premiere i-Movie	Toolsuites for capturing live video and assembling digital video and audio clips or programs for recording to tape and viewing on TV (may require additional hardware) or distribution via the Web. (All)	www.adobe.com www.apple.com
Interactive Multimedia		
Hyperstudio	Toolsuite for creating and integrating text, video, audio, and images into multimedia presentations for viewing locally or via the Web. (All)	www.hyperstudio.com
MediaWeaver and Kid's Media Magic	MediaWeaver supports multimedia writing. Media Magic introduces children to reading, writing, word processing, and multimedia. (All)	www.humanitiessoftware.com
Music-Making		
Homestudio, Plasma, and Pyro	For recording, mixing, composing, and editing audio and outputting to the Web, CD, or sheet music. (Mu, Hu, A)	www.cakewalk.com

FIGURE 6.6 Media for Expression
Examples are only illustrative and do not signify endorsement. Web links are current as of August, 2002. Subject area key: All = all areas; Sc =sciences; Ma = math; Mu = music; SS = social studies; Hi = history; Hu = humanities; A = the arts; LA = language arts; FL = foreign languages; PE = physical education.

Name	Attributes	Web Links
Web-based Inquiry Science Environment (WISE)	Structures and supports online teaching and learning, with tools and electronic spaces for gathering and evaluating evidence, modeling concepts, building and running simulations, and reflecting and sharing insights. (Sc, SS)	wise.berkeley.edu
Symphony	Organizes inquiry-based learning around a driving question. (Sc)	www.investigationstation.org/ sciencelaboratory/ symphony
BGuILE (Biology Guided Inquiry Learning Environments)	Contains learner-centered, scaffolded tools for data gathering, graphing, visualizing, model building, and reflecting. (Sc)	www.letus.org/bguile
WorldWatcher	Supports and integrates inquiry, communication, construction, and expression via Web-based environmental data visualization tools and notebooks. (Sc)	www.worldwatcher.nwu.edu

FIGURE 6.7 Integrated Learning Environments
Examples are only illustrative and do not signify endorsement. Web links are current as of August, 2002. Subject area key: All = all areas; Sc = sciences; Ma = math; Mu = music; SS = social studies; Hi = history; Hu = humanities; A = the arts; LA = language arts; FL = foreign languages; PE = physical education.

from media for construction, through which they can build artifacts that help them visualize, touch, test, and refine their ideas.

Putting It All Together

Remember that the boundaries between the taxonomy of learning media catgeories intentionally overlap. Such crossover echoes the potential of digital technology to integrate different aspects of learning and to promote synergy between them. Recognizing this, educational technologists and researchers, in partnership with educators, are using the latest Internet technologies to develop Web-based integrated learning environments. Focused on science, history, language arts, or other areas of the curriculum, these environments link different areas of content and learning process skills related to inquiry, communication, construction, or expression.

To this end, Web-based learning environments, such as those listed in Figure 6.7, integrate distinct combinations of online tools. These may be used to identify problems; gather, visualize, analyze, weigh, and integrate evidence; make thinking visible; communicate findings and insights; and maintain ongoing discourse with peers and teachers, all as part of a sustained individual or shared learning experience. As such, online environments are also designed to support activities that address different cognitive levels—knowing, comprehension, application, analysis, synthesis, and evaluation—as classified in Bloom's Taxonomy (see Modules 2 and 4). Also, experimental Web learning environments tend not to prescribe fixed pathways for learning. Instead, they allow teachers such as yourself to adapt and customize your own pedagogical strategies. These may include scaffolding and sequencing of activities linked to individual tools, and staging of student access to online materials, in keeping with the evolving needs and learning styles of individual learners or groups.

■ ROUNDUP ■

One thing is certain about technological innovation: relentless, rapid change. That is why, when contemplating how to incorporate technology into your practice, it is important to focus more on the learning activities that a particular tool or set of tools can mediate and on the cognitive processes they facilitate rather than on the technical features of a given tool. Whatever your eventual specialty, strive to be innovative in how you incorporate various media into your teaching rather than seeing technology as something your students need to be taught separately from the actual content they are learning at any time. In any event, that content should be substantial and authentic. Remember, "beware of just air," even if it's hi-tech "air."

By viewing educational technologies in terms of their mediative functions, that is, as media for inquiry, communication, expression, and construction, it becomes possible to construct a flexible schema or taxonomy with which to comprehend and apply fast-changing technologies. The secondary arts (including language arts) curriculum tends to favor media for expression, whereas science and math lean more toward media for inquiry (Bruce, 2000; Bruce and Levin, 2002). However, in a constructivist classroom, where learners actively construct rather than passively absorb knowledge, both types of media, as well as those supporting communication and construction, can benefit students across most subject areas and grade levels while accommodating their distinct learning styles and intelligence.

What do you think of the taxonomy of learning media described in this module? How well does it resonate with your existing notions and experience of technology, both in the classroom and in your everyday life? Might you and your students classify learning technologies differently? We would like you to pause and discuss these questions with your peers and instructor. Later, when you have completed this course, we suggest you revisit the Fishy Mystery scenario and ponder these questions yet again.

As you guide your students to inquire, communicate, express, and construct as they learn, not only will they learn with and think about technology but they will also learn through technology. In doing so, they will acquire higher-level process skills with which to associate specific technical skills and procedures. Once contextualized, such skills will be more durable and flexible and less dependent on individual technologies that are here today, gone tomorrow. As a result, they (and you) will have gained the most important skill of all: learning how to learn and how to support that learning by gathering whatever resources are needed, when they are needed, throughout their professional and personal lives.

REFERENCES

Note: Web addresses are current as of August, 2002. Acrobat Reader, available from http://www.adobe.com, is required to view electronic documents in the PDF format.

Baker, E. (1999). Technology: How do we know it works? In: *The Secretary's conference on educational technology-1999*. Washington, DC: U.S. Department of Education. Available at: www.ed.gov/Technology/TechConf/1999/whitepapers/paper5.html.

Blumenfeld, J., Marx, R., Soloway, E., & Krajcik, J. (1996). Learning with peers: From small group cooperation to collaborative communities. *Educational Researcher, 25*(8), 37–40.

Bracey, G. (2001). The condition of public education. *Phi Delta Kappan, 83*(2), 157–169.

Bransford, J., Brown, A., & Cocking, R. (Eds.). (2000) (Expanded edition). *How people learn: Brain, mind, experience and school*. Washington, DC: National Academy Press. Available at www.nap.edu/books/0309070368/html/.

Brown, J. (2000). Growing up digital: How the Web changes work, education, and the ways people learn. *Change: The Journal of the American Academy of Education*, March/April, 11–20. Available at: www.aahe.org/change/digital.pdf.

Bruce, B. (2000). Credibility of the Web: Why we need dialectical reading. *Journal of the Philosophy of Education, 34*(1), 97–109.

Bruce, B. (2000). Modeling and visualization across learning contexts. In: M. Linn, L. Bievenue, S. Derry, M. E. Verona, & U. Thakkar (Eds.). *Panel papers from workshop to integrate computer-based modeling and scientific visualization into teacher education programs*. Champaign, IL: NCSA/EOT-PACI. Available at: www.lis.uiuc.edu/~chip/pubs/mvxcontexts.shtml.

Bruce, B., & Levin, J. (1997). Educational technology: Media for inquiry, communication, construction, and expression. *Journal of Educational Computing Research, 17*(1), 79–102. Available at: www.lis.uiuc.edu/%7Echip/pubs/taxonomy/index.html.

Bruce, B., & Levin, J. (2002). Roles for new technologies in language arts: Inquiry, communication, construction, and expression. In: J. Flood & D. Lapp (Eds.). *Handbook of research on teaching the English language arts*. Mahwah, NJ: Lawrence Erlbaum Associates.

Burton, O. (Ed.). (2002). *Computing in the social sciences and the humanities*. Urbana: University of Illinois Press.

Collins, A., Brown, J., & Duguid, P. (1988). Situated Cognition and the Culture of Learning. *Education Researcher, 18*(1), 32–42.

Collins, A., Brown, J., & Holum, A. (1991). Cognitive apprenticeship: Making thinking visible. *American Educator, 15*(3), 6–11, 38–46.

Cuban, L. (1993). *How teachers taught: Constancy and change in American classrooms, 1880–1990*. New York: Teachers College Press.

Cuban, L. (1996). Techno-reformers and classroom teachers. *Education Week on the Web*, Oct. 9. Available at: www.edweek.org/ew/ewstory.cfm?slug=06cuban.h168key words=cuban.

Cuban, L. (2001). *Oversold and underused: Computers in the classroom*. Cambridge, MA: Harvard University Press.

Cuban, L., & Pea, R. (1998). The pros and cons of technology in the classroom. Presented at: Bay Area School Reform Collaborative Funders' Learning Community

Meeting, Palo Alto, CA, February 5, 1998. Available at: www.tappedin.org/info/teachers/debate.html.

Dewey, J. (1956). *The child and the curriculum & the school and society.* Chicago: University of Chicago Press. (Originally copyrighted 1902 and 1900.)

Gardner, H. (1983). *Frames of mind: The theory of multiple intelligences.* New York: Basic Books.

Fixmer, R. (2002). Internet insight: Moore's Law and order. *E-Week,* April 15.

Hawkins, J., Frederiksen, J., Collins. A., Bennett, D., & Collins, E. (1993). Assessment and technology. *Communications of the ACM, 35,* 74–76.

Hobbes R. (2002). Hobbes' Internet timeline. Available at: http://www.zakon.org/robert/internet/timeline/#Growth.

Jones, B-F., Valdez, G., Nowakowski, J., & Rasmussen, C. (1995). *Plugging in: Choosing and using education technology.* Oak Brook, IL: North Central Regional Educational Laboratory. Available at: www.ncrel.org/sdrs/edtalk/toc.htm.

Kyle, W., Jr., Schmitz, C., & Schmitz, E. (1996). Possible lives or shattered dreams? *Electronic Journal of Science Education, 1*(2). Available at: unr.edu/homepage/jcannon/ejse/kyle.html.

Levin, J., & Waugh, M. (1998). Teaching teleapprenticeships: Electronic network-based educational frameworks for improving teacher education. *Interactive Learning Environments Journal, 6*(1-2), 39–58. Available at: www.ed.uiuc.edu/TTA/Papers/TTAs.html.

Linn, M. (1998). The impact of technology on science instruction: Historical trends and current opportunities. In: B. Fraser & K. Tobin (Eds.). *International handbook of science education* (pp. 265–294). Dordrecht, The Netherlands: Kluwer Academic Publishers.

Maddux, C., Johnson, D., & Willis, J. (1997). *Educational computing: Learning with tomorrow's technologies.* Boston: Allyn & Bacon.

McNabb, M., Hawkes, M., & Rouk, U. (1999). Critical issues in evaluating the effectiveness of technology. In: *The Secretary's conference on educational technology-1999.* Washington, DC: U.S. Department of Education. Available at: www.ed.gov/Technology/TechConf/1999/confsum.html.

Means, B. (1994). *Technology and education reform: The reality behind the promise.* San Francisco: Jossey-Bass.

NAEP. (2000). *The nation's report card: National assessment of educational progress.* Washington, DC: U.S. Department of Education. Available at: nces.ed.gov/nationsreportcard/.

Novak, J. (1990). Concept mapping: A useful tool for science education. *Journal of Research in Science Teaching, 27*(10), 937–949.

NTIA. (2000). *Falling through the Net: Toward digital inclusion.* Washington, DC: U.S. Department of Commerce, National Telecommunications and Information Administration. Available at: www.ntia.doc.gov/ntiahome/fttn00/contents00.html.

Pea, R. (2001). Technology, equity, and K-12 learning. Presented at: California Public Affairs Forum Bridging the Digital Divide, Stanford University, December 8, 2000. Available at: www.ccst.ucr.edu/cpa/bdd/agenda.html.

Piaget, J. (1970). *Science of education and the psychology of the child.* New York: Orion Press.

PISA (2000). *Outcomes of learning: Results from the 2000 program for international student assessment of 15-year-olds in reading, mathematics, and science literacy.* Washington, DC: U.S. Department of Education, National Center for Education Statistics. Available at: nces.ed.gov/surveys/pisa/.

PITAC (1997). *Report to the president on the use of educational technology to strengthen K-12 education in the United States.* Arlington, VA: National Coordination Office for Information Technology Research and Development. Available at: www.ostp.gov/PCAST/k-12ed.html.

PITAC (2000). *Using information technology to transform the way we learn.* Arlington, VA: National Coordination Office for Information Technology Research and Development. Available at: www.itrd.gov/pubs/pitac/pitac-tl-9feb01.pdf.

Resnick, M., Martin, F., Berg, R., Borovoy, R., Colella, V., Kramer, K., & Silverman, B. (1998). Digital manipulatives: New toys to think with. *Proceedings of the 1998 Conference on Human Factors and Computing Systems (CHI 98), Los Angeles* (pp. 281–287), New York: ACM Press/Addison-Wesley Publishing. Available at: el.www.media.mit.edu/groups/el/papers/mres/chi-98/digital-manip.html.

Roseman, J. E., Gerald, G., & Shuttleworth, S. (2001). Putting textbooks to the test. *ENC Focus, 8*(3), 56–59.

Saettler, P. (1990). Educational technology in the 1980s. New theoretical and research vistas. In *The evolution of American educational technology* (pp. 478–500). Englewood, CO: Libraries Unlimited.

Sandholtz, J., Ringstaff, C., & Dwyer, D. (1997). *Teaching with technology: Creating student-centered classrooms.* New York: Teachers College Press.

Smerdon, B., Cronen, S., Lanahan, L., Anderson, J., Iannotti, N., & Angeles, J. (2000). *Teachers' tools for the 21st century: A report on teacher's use of technology.* Washington, DC: U.S. Department of Education, National Center for Education Statistics. Available at: nces.ed.gov/pubs2001/quarterly/winter/elementary/e_section5.html.

Soloway, E., Grant, W., Tinker, R., Roschelle, J., Mills, M., Resnick, M., Berg, R., & Eisenberg, M. (1999). Science in the palms of their hands. *Communications of the ACM, 42*(8), 21–26.

Spitulnik, M., Stratford, S., Krajcik, J., & Soloway, E. (1998). Using technology to support students' artifact construction in science. In: B. Fraser & K. Tobin (Eds.). *International handbook of science education* (pp. 363–381). Dordrecht, The Netherlands: Kluwer Academic Publishers.

Standards (1992-2000):

Inquiry and the national science education standards: A guide for teaching and learning. (2000). Washington, DC: National Academy Press. Available at: books.nap.edu/books/0309064767/html/index.html.

Benchmarks for science literacy (Project 2061). (1993). New York: Oxford University Press. Available at: www.project2061.org.

National science education standards. (1996). Washington, DC: National Academy Press. Available at: books.nap.edu/books/0309053269/html/index.html.

Standards for the English language arts. (1996). Urbana, IL: National Council for the Teaching of English. Available at: www.ncte.org/standards.

Model standards for beginning teacher licensing and development. A resource for state dialogue. (1992). Washington, DC: Interstate New Teacher Assessment and Support Consortium. Available at: www.ccsso.org/intascst.html.

TIMMS. (1995). *The third international mathematics and science study.* Washington, DC: U.S. Department of Education, National Center for Educational Statistics. Available at: nces.ed.gov/TIMSS/timss95/index.asp.

Turkle, S., & Papert, S. (1990). Epistemological pluralism. *Signs, 16*(1), 128–157.

Tyson, H. (1997). *The teaching gap.* New York: The Free Press.

Valdez, G., McNabb, M., Foertsch, M., Anderson, M., Hawkes, M., & Raack, L. (2000). *Computer based technology and learning: Evolving uses and expectations.* Chicago: North East Regional Educational Laboratory.

Verona, M.E. (2001). WebSims: Creating an online science lab. In: L. Vendervert & L. Shavinina (Eds.). *CyberEducation: The future of long-distance learning* (pp. 237–256). New York: Liebert.

Constructivist Methods

Suppose you want to strengthen a lesson beyond a deductive or inductive framework or even combinations of both of these. Suppose you want the techniques to guide student ideas within a cohesive plan. In other words, suppose you patterned your lesson according to a method. How does a method go beyond a cognitive framework? Take a look at this analogy for starters.

Imagine stepping inside Notre Dame Cathedral in Paris. In some ways, it's like a private dwelling. You enter through a door and walk on a floor. There are windows and places to sit. A roof protects you from the elements, supported by beams both visible and hidden within the walls. You may find rooms designed for distinct uses. Such are the components of most human-made buildings regardless of their functions.

The exterior of the ancient Notre Dame Cathedral may dazzle you with stone figures: gargoyles with fantastically monsterlike features, venerated saints, and biblical figures. Flying buttresses lend support as well as aesthetic power. Inside, the ceiling is arched and high and dwarfs you. There is holy water, and many candles burn as flames of prayer, too many to count, each one lit by a worshipper. There are nooks with ornate statues, larger than life, and nooks behind screens for contemplation. An organ waits to fill the cathedral with resonant chords. The cathedral embraces you within a womb-like design; its intention is to fill you with awe and inspiration, to create an other-worldly atmosphere, yet to provide a feeling of protection within a solid structure.

So a church, synagogue, or mosque has specific features that both include and go beyond characteristics of personal dwellings. For example, the exterior of a religious building will boast a symbol of that faith. Inside, you'll find some kind of altar whose objects differ according to each religion. Often, in addition to clear windows there are stained glass windows that depict religious scenes and/or icons important to each faith. Pews, rather than chairs and couches, may stretch across a chapel, with a bible at each place. Or perhaps there's an open floor where worshippers kneel and pray without any formal seating. Candles or incense or nothing may burn. The decorations may be lavish or austere according to religious dictates and beliefs.

215

Now let's return to a typical private dwelling. You enter through a door. Often there's a vestibule that branches out into a hallway with other rooms. You let air in through plain glass windows. You put on electric lights, cook in a kitchen, shower in a bathroom, sleep in a bedroom. In this way, a personal dwelling provides a plan with rooms within which you can function in defined ways. It is similar to a lesson planned with a deductive or inductive cognitive framework: there's a defined shape that branches out in specific ways but that shares a commonality with many other lessons with the same cognitive framework.

In contrast, a church, synagogue, or mosque corresponds to a method. Though supported by the same type of underpinnings like the everyday dwelling just described, a house of worship contains additional features with prescribed uses beyond the commonplace.

Another way to say it is this. A method is an architectural blueprint, a template with distinctive characteristics. We call these characteristics *method markers*, analogous to the artifacts of a house of worship. In this way, a method brings added focus to the learning experience. Each method in turn is supported by a deductive or inductive cognitive framework with techniques. The same cognitive framework and techniques may be used for different methods similar to the way a generic floor plan supports embellishments for different houses of worship. You'll find a graphic representation of this relationship in Figure C.1.

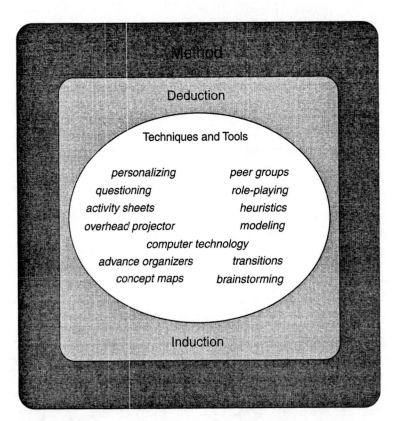

FIGURE C.1 Method with Cognitive Framework, Techniques, and Tools

Section C describes seven constructivist methods, each with a discrete instructional strategy. The intention is that these methods provide clear direction as you plan individual lessons and units. We also believe that the variety of templates will help you develop your imagination as a creative as well as an intellectually rigorous teacher. Please keep in mind that the variety of individual templates is enhanced by possible combo lessons in which you combine two or more methods in mini-segments in a single lesson plan according to your instructional intentions.

■ SUMMARY OF METHODS

Here's a brief description of each method covered in Section C to give you a bird's-eye view, an advance organizer, of what's ahead.

1. ILPE METHOD (Investigating Learners' Previous Experiences): This method has two goals: (1) to introduce the teacher and to begin to know the students and (2) to discover what the students know about a given topic. Mostly the teacher employs selective techniques that elicit students' ideas. This information will be used to plan future lessons, adjusting to student needs.

2. DEDUCTIVE CONCEPT METHOD: In this approach, the teacher defines the concept first and provides specific examples and nonexamples of the concept. Your students arrive at classifications by using feature analysis and comparison/contrast of examples and nonexamples. (General to specific.)

3. INDUCTIVE CONCEPT METHOD: One or more concepts are taught inductively. The format is the reverse of the deductive format. You provide examples and nonexamples of a concept. With questions (not teacher talk), you lead students to a conceptual understanding, which includes student generation of the concept. (Specific to general.)

4. DIRECTED DISCUSSION METHOD: Teacher–student interaction is emphasized here. Your series of questions related to materials facilitate students' grasp of one or more principles. The teacher's role is more dominant in this discussion than in the two subsequent discussion methods.

5. EXPLORATORY DISCUSSION METHOD: Through promotion of student–student interaction, this discussion allows the class to examine different perspectives of one concept or controversial issue. Students do not arrive at a value judgment. Rather, they explore different points of view based on documentation. This is a student-centered method that may include role-play. The teacher's role is to ask broad questions to steer the discussion if necessary. It is a prime example of invisible teaching.

6. REFLECTIVE DISCUSSION METHOD: This is similar to the Exploratory Discussion method. The significant difference is that this method both explores different viewpoints and also requires students to arrive at their individual value judgments with logic based on documented justification. This method may include role-play. The Reflective Discussion is another prime example of invisible teaching.

7. INTERACTIVE PRESENTATION METHOD: This template combines discrete parcels consisting of teacher mini-talks and student mini-tasks. The object is to engage students in active rather than passive listening and in independent thinking in a presentational format.

These methods are more than templates. They hold the potential to create a learning environment, a context, an approach to learning that expands the classroom. The student's role in learning becomes that of critical thinker, initiator of ideas and learning procedures. Your role becomes that of informed catalyst and even co-learner as your students mature as learners (see Module 15).

As you read this section and possibly feel some resistance to implementing a given method, keep in mind that, yes, this method applies to your subject. Once you break through the constraints of your past experiences in teacher-centered classrooms, be prepared for a sense of freedom and endless possibilities that these methods and your own future adaptations can realize.

■ METHOD MARKERS

As you acquaint yourself with each of the methods, you'll notice the distinguishing method markers. These are features of each method that guide you to carry out the template thoroughly and reflectively.

When you write a lesson plan, each of these methods is embedded in the Core Components. The chosen method appears in the Development component of a lesson or project (see Module 3, Part 1). In other words, the method with your chosen techniques develops the Rationale after the Hook or other kind of introduction. This means that the method, with its distinguishing features or markers, constitutes the body of your lesson. Take a look at a sample lesson outline in Figure C.2 to get an idea of what we mean.

The constructivist methods described in this section are designed to give you direction, a cohesive strategy for thorough and reflective planning. They will also help you expand the repertoire of your teaching styles, enabling you to better accommodate your students' varied learning styles. With experience, you will undoubtedly adapt these methods or even invent offshoots to suit a class here or a project there, continually enriching the variety and scope of your craft. The resulting benefit is that as you increasingly meet your students' varied needs, you will sidestep the danger of standing still. As you stay fresh, always growing professionally, teaching will remain new, an ongoing challenge, a labor of love for years to come.

FIGURE C.2 Sample Lesson Outline with Core Components and Method

---

PRELUDE (for teacher reference)

Rationale
What are you teaching?
Why are you teaching this?
Justification with INTASC Standards

Performance Objective
Preparation
Product
Criteria

Materials

ENACTMENT (student engagement)

Aim

Hook

Development
Method Markers with Techniques and Tools
- *ILPE Method*
- *Concept Methods*
- *Discussion Methods*
- *Interactive Presentation Method*

Culmination
Wrap-Up
Leap

ASSESSMENT AND EVALUATION PLAN

Assessment Products
Evaluation Rubric with Point Scale

Module Seven:

Investigating Learners' Previous Experiences (ILPE) Method

■ OVERVIEW: SCENARIO DEPICTING AN ILPE METHOD

It's Monday morning, just before the start of Mr. Newman's third period physical science class. The students had taken a test the previous Friday, and they are about to embark on a new unit. There's an air of anticipation among the ninth- and tenth-grade students in the room. They know that their teacher likes to introduce new topics with open-ended, interactive activities.

The students settle into their seats, which are arranged in a circle today. The bell rings, and Mr. Newman steps out of the stockroom door. The students laugh as they see their teacher. He's wearing a string of blinking Christmas lights!

"Isn't it a little late for the lights, Mr. N.? It's March!" laughs Andy.

"Ha—it's never too late for this kind of excitement," replies Mr. Newman in mock surprise. "We're going to talk about a subject today that's a little shocking. I hope nobody minds." Nobody seems to mind; the students watch Mr. Newman as he trails his string of lights into the circle of seats, dropping carefully into an empty chair. "What do you think of when you hear the word 'electricity'?" Hands fly into the air, and the teacher begins calling on students. The responses vary widely. Students mention things like microwaves, computers, cords, power plants, energy, batteries, and more. After most of the responses, Mr. Newman asks a follow-up question: "Why did you say energy, Nicole?" "How are power plants connected to electricity, Casey?" At one point, Nick volunteers "lightning."

"That's an interesting answer! Can anyone tell us how lightning is connected to electricity?" says Mr. Newman enthusiastically.

"I remember hearing that people a long time ago weren't sure what lightning was," responds Ami. "Didn't Ben Franklin fly a kite during a storm to learn more about lightning? I saw something about that at the museum." Other students add to Ami's answer; Mr. N. encourages this sharing of ideas with further questions. After a brief exchange, he tells the students that the class can investigate what Franklin did if they are interested.

During the next five minutes, Mr. Newman asks more open-ended questions and receives a range of ideas. "How have you used electricity in the past 24 hours?" provokes the most responses. The students seem to recognize that this mysterious "thing" called electricity plays a big part in everyone's life, although they express a lot of wonder about what electricity is really like.

Ten minutes into the class period, Mr. Newman thanks the students for their input and tells them that they'll have a chance to learn more about many of the ideas that they have listed. "Now, I'm going to invite you to investigate electricity! A few minutes ago, Nick told us that batteries can supply electricity to toys and radios and other things. We're going to learn what we can about electricity by trying to get batteries to do some work." Mr. Newman, now without the blinking lights, moves to the projector screen, which had been covering part of the board, and rolls it up with a dramatic flourish, revealing directions for a class activity. He provides pairs of students with a D battery, two wires, and a small light bulb; their challenge is to find as many ways as they can to light the bulb using these materials.

For the next twenty-five minutes, Mr. Newman moves around the room, watching each pair of students work to light the bulbs, asking occasional questions. There is a buzz of excitement in the room as successive pairs of students discover ways to meet this challenge. Some groups make their discoveries quickly, while others struggle; Mr. N. encourages these groups but never directs them toward a solution. He invites those groups that find more than one way to light the bulb to try other configurations and to vary the number of batteries, wires, and bulbs in what they would later call the *circuits*. The teacher also asks each group to diagram any configuration of materials that lights the bulb. He is especially careful to ask probing questions regarding their use of terms ("What do you mean by voltage, Keelan?") and to make careful observations. With a few minutes left in the period, Mr. Newman asks the students to turn in their materials and to share what they had learned, comparing and contrasting their diagrams (again, lots of teacher- and student-generated questions). The period ends with students writing a one-minute essay in response to the question, "What is one important question that you now have regarding electricity?"

Focal Point 1: What Makes the ILPE Method Distinctive?

Welcome back from your short classroom visit. You have just taken part in an ILPE lesson; ILPE is an acronym for "investigating learners' previous experiences." There are two main goals in any ILPE lesson:

- To gain insights into your students' initial understanding of and interest in a topic.
- To introduce a new topic in an engaging way.

Think of ILPE lessons as opportunities for you as the teacher to open windows into your students' minds. Although there are countless ways to conduct an ILPE lesson, these lessons generally include our main Core Components and some distinctive methods markers, as we'll see in the sections that follow. You'll also discover that these lessons may last from a few minutes to an entire class period, depending on a number of factors.

Discussion 1: What Makes the ILPE Method Distinctive?

From a constructivist perspective, it makes sense to purposefully investigate the nature of student understanding frequently, since much of what they will learn depends on their previous experiences and associated frames of reference. In any case, students' varying frames of reference regarding any topic will have a major impact on their understanding of the subject matter (once again, think back to Module 1 and the ways in which participants in Bartlett's studies interpreted and remembered the stories). It follows that one of the most important tasks for teachers is to investigate the nature of knowledge that students have regarding important concepts and principles, how this knowledge is organized, and how learners use the knowledge. Student attitudes regarding topics (and entire subjects), or perhaps how these topics were taught, also have an impact on their subsequent learning, so it makes sense to learn as much as we can about these attitudes as well.

In addition, two of the biggest decisions that we face as teachers are where to begin and how to proceed when embarking on a new instructional unit. These important decisions will depend not only on your curriculum but also on your students and their initial understanding of important ideas related to your topic. It is obvious that a lesson focused on limits in a calculus class will fail if students have little grasp of important algebraic concepts. Similarly, if each of our students had played competitive volleyball for years, a lesson on the general rules of the game would be a waste of their time. You'll find that most individual differences in understanding are much more subtle. As a constructivist teacher, one of your most important goals will be to get into your students' heads to the greatest extent possible when deciding not only what to teach but also how to teach it.

Gaining insights such as these are really what ILPE lessons are all about. Whether these lessons last a few minutes or an entire class period, they can provide teachers with some important perspectives regarding the existing conceptions that students hold and can also offer glimpses into their attitudes, values, and preferred learning styles and modalities. In addition, these lessons provide students with opportunities to generate questions that might serve to structure future lessons, all in a highly interactive, motivational setting.

In Modules 7 through 12, we introduce a series of constructivist methods. Early in each of these modules we share a *lesson planning template*, which is a suggested outline for a lesson or a portion of a lesson featuring that method. Before we describe the features of an ILPE lesson in more detail, take a look at Figure 7.1. This template should help you gain some initial insights into what it takes to plan and conduct a lesson like this.

Focal Point 2: ILPE Method Markers

The following method markers make the ILPE method unique among the constructivist methods that we'll introduce in the next several modules. This list will help you get acquainted with the method before we discuss planning such lessons in more detail.

- The Hook and/or Aim will include some kind of introduction to the topic, and it may also include teacher and student personal introductions if the lesson is planned for early in the school year.
- The Development of an ILPE lesson will include a sequence of broad trigger questions that will serve as an initial inquiry into student experiences related to the topic.
- The Development will also include an open-ended activity that will provide you with further insights regarding students' understanding of important facts, concepts, and principles related to your topic.
- The Culmination will usually feature a look ahead. You'll let your students know what's in store for them in future lessons and why the topic is important.

PRELUDE

_____

- Rationale (with connection to national standards)
- Performance Objective
- Materials and Lesson Aids

ENACTMENT

_____

- HOOK (begin with an attention-grabbing question, demonstration, problem, skit/performance)
  1. Teacher/student introductions (in a start-of-the-year ILPE)
  2. Brief introduction/discussion of the topic, using the Hook as a springboard
- STUDENT AIM—Your statement of purpose for the lesson; remember that it can be effective *not* to be specific about what the students will be doing! You can *keep them wondering.............*
- DEVELOPMENT
  1. INQUIRY
     a. Assess students' initial understanding regarding the topic through questions (open-ended trigger questions are especially useful at this point)
     b. Probe and redirect, based on students' reponses
     c. As an option, list student-generated questions or construct a concept map
  2. OPEN-ENDED ACTIVITY
     a. Conduct a related activity that will allow you to assess students' understanding of important facts, concepts, and principles and their attitudes
     b. Observe students' actions and listen to the interaction; ask Trigger, Probing, and Redirecting questions when appropriate; encourage them to expand on ideas presented by others
- CULMINATION
  1. WRAP-UP—Summary of information gathered. As the teacher, what did you learn about their understanding, interest, etc.?
  2. LEAP—Closing statement, with possible preview of next/future lessons(s). What's in store as the unit proceeds?

ASSESSMENT AND EVALUATION PLAN

_____

  1. Assessment products (What will students produce in this/a later lesson?)
  2. Evaluation (How will you evaluate this product, e.g., with a scoring rubric?)

FIGURE 7.1 ILPE Lesson Planning Template

Focal Point 3: **Up Close: Planning and Conducting an ILPE Lesson**

As we begin our discussion of planning ILPE lessons, think back to the general planning suggestions that were presented in Modules 2 and 3. Your actual planning for any kind of lesson might begin at various points; remember that the starting place might be anyplace. As a teacher, you might find yourself beginning a planning process for a unit by considering a set of district unit objectives and then searching for appropriate materials as you make decisions on possible methods. On occasion, you might read about or participate in an interesting activity during an in-service experience and think about how you might incorporate the activity in your classroom. Or you may become familiar with a new piece of technology (e.g., a Palm Pilot) and instantly brainstorm ways to incorporate the new gizmo into future lessons.

Whatever the source of your inspiration, you'll need to sit down and outline in detail what you might say, do, and ask from the start of a lesson to its completion. As we introduce each in a series of constructivist teaching methods, we'll walk you through this planning process, in a start-to-finish way, in the belief that this will allow you to feel confident in planning lessons in which you'll use each method.

Now to the specific processes involved in planning and teaching an ILPE lesson. Our detailed discussion of the integration of Core Components with ILPE method markers (i.e., specific features) includes suggestions related to both the planning and conducting of lessons utilizing this method.

Discussion 3: Up Close: Planning and Conducting an ILPE Lesson

Rationale

Recall from the planning chapters that a lesson Rationale includes some mention of the content involved, the cognitive skills that students might develop through the experience, and some justification for conducting the lesson as intended (addressing what we call the "So what?" question; why would you ask students to do this?). As noted in Module 1, you'll begin your teaching career in a standards-driven era. Learned societies, such as the National Council of Teachers of Mathematics (NCTM) and the National Council of Teachers of English (NCTE), have established curriculum standards that have heavily influenced state and local standards. In considering your justification for any lesson, we suggest that you consider curriculum standards established for your subject area. To help illustrate this process, we will refer to national standards for beginning teachers in all disciplines developed by the Interstate New Teacher Assessment and Support Consortium (INTASC) as we walk you through the planning process for each method.

Let's consider the electricity lesson conducted by Mr. Newman as we think about writing a Rationale for an ILPE lesson. In this lesson, Mr. N. is most interested in gaining insights into his students' thinking regarding the nature of electricity. In starting the planning process for this lesson, he might have written a Rationale like this: "Students will first reveal some of their conceptions regarding electricity by responding to open-ended questions. They will then be challenged to apply their understanding of this topic by attempting to create (synthesize) as many electrical circuits as possible in a group setting. The experience will enhance individual and group communication and abstract thinking abilities and connects to INTASC Standards 1, 3, 4, 5, 6, 7, and 8." In many cases, your planning for any lesson, including one in which you use the ILPE method, should start with writing such a Rationale. In these three sentences, Mr. Newman has clearly conveyed some powerful reasons for conducting the lesson in this way and has begun to specify what his students might be able to do as a result of this experience. That's where the next Core Component, the Performance Objective, comes into play.

Performance Objective

Keep in mind that when you provide constructivist learning experiences for your students, they will often surprise you by doing the wonderfully unexpected (e.g., asking important new questions or expressing breathtaking new insights that you as the teacher hadn't considered). This is the real beauty of a student-centered classroom. By setting the stage with intellectually challenging lessons, you can provide opportunities for students to make exciting leaps in their thinking. In addition to the wonderfully unexpected, we as teachers also need to get specific as we plan about what our students should be able to do as the result of the experiences that we provide and how they will be able to show us what they've learned. This is where Performance Objectives fall in the planning process.

Recall from Module 3 that a Performance Objective includes statements indicating how you'll help students prepare for the learning experience; what they'll produce; and something about the quality of the product. In planning any lesson, including an ILPE, think specifically about what you'll expect (or at least hope) that your students will be able to do and what they can say, do, or create to show you that they've learned something. For example, our Mr. Newman may have written a Performance Objective like this as he planned his shocking ILPE lesson: "Students will share their conceptions related to electricity during the early phases of the lesson (preparation). Then, using a set of batteries, bulbs, and wires and working with a partner, they will light the bulb in as many ways as possible, diagramming each successful method (product). In a full class setting, each group will then share their diagrams and discover at least three similarities in each circuit (criteria)." Note that Mr. N. is definitely encouraging his students to take risks and experiment. One of your authors has conducted similar lessons in seventh-grade, high school, and college classrooms and has found the experience to be extremely challenging (and often motivationally frustrating) for students at each grade level.

In his Performance Objective, Mr. Newman has specified preparation (setting the stage), what the students will produce, as well as the relevant criteria (how many, for how long, etc.). Writing Performance Objectives for ILPE lessons can be tricky since you can never be sure, in advance, about students' experiences related to the new topic. As you plan your first ILPE lessons, try to predict what your students might be able to do, and specify how they can show you what they know. This is the heart of a Performance Objective, which can then serve as a road map for planning the Enactment of your lesson.

Materials

We strongly urge you to list necessary materials directly on your lesson plan. This is especially important in ILPE lessons, since they almost always include an activity. In considering materials, one of your biggest concerns will be the setting for your activity. Will students do their creating alone? In pairs? In groups of three to six? In general, we suggest a small-group setting for ILPE activities; this setting provides more students with an opportunity to get directly involved, and there is a greater chance for the teacher to observe and listen to the interaction and to ask the right question at the right time. Mr. Newman conducted his activity in pairs. For his class of 24, he would need at least 12 bulbs and batteries and 24 pieces of wire—and certainly plenty of extras in case things get misplaced or students wish to use extra materials to construct more complex circuits. Whatever you choose to do during your ILPE lessons, list your materials. It will help you to clearly envision the activity.

This behind-the-scenes discussion of the lesson Prelude section provides you with a feel for the initial planning that you'll need to do for ILPE lessons. Let's now move on to the Enactment of an ILPE.

Hook

In planning an ILPE Hook, you'll be seeking to establish the mood for the lesson, to share general information about your purposes, to convey something about the nature of the lesson, and to model the kind of interaction desired from your students. When entering any new situation, people tend to form impressions quickly of the norms and expectations involved. For us as teachers, either meeting a new group of students or re-convening a familiar class at the start of a period, the first five to ten minutes of class time provide an opportunity to orient the group to a set of positive expectations that can help establish an open, thinker-friendly environment.

We suggest that you set high expectations in your ILPE lessons, especially those conducted early in the school year. To help do this, hook the group with an attention-grabbing question, picture, statement, cartoon, poem, problem, demonstration, song, skit, film clip, and so on, that will serve to preview the lesson. A chemistry teacher could dress as a wizard and demonstrate a chemical reaction; an English teacher might do a dramatic or comical reading; a history teacher might dress as a historical figure; a math teacher might begin with a puzzling, real-world problem. The possibilities are endless, and a start like this to any lesson can create some excitement and make your students feel more comfortable with you and one another. Mr. Newman certainly grabbed the attention of his students with his string of blinking lights. A little gimmicky, perhaps, but certainly something that would cause students to wonder what's in store.

An effective introductory technique for an early-year ILPE is for you as the teacher to introduce yourself in the manner that you would like the students to introduce themselves. Simply let your students know what you'd like to know about them, and then model that introduction by revealing something about yourself. It is often effective to work an activity, such as a simple game, into your Hook (this is a good option later in the lesson, too). These activities can often serve as effective icebreakers, encouraging your students to be more open with their thoughts than they would be given a more straightforward introduction. Activity options include asking students to interview each other and then to introduce their partner to the class; inviting everyone to grab a handful of candy and, for each piece taken, to reveal something about themselves; having the group fill out a brief questionnaire and then find others with common answers; or playing a bingo game in which players answer questions about themselves and try to match answers with classmates, winning the game when they complete a row. Again, a key to the success of any such activity is for you to model the desired behaviors for the students. They will tend to follow your lead.

Frequently, this introductory process can lead to a general discussion of student experiences and attitudes related to your topic and subject area, especially if there is some topic connection to your initial questions. You can enhance your chances for a natural transition into the rest of the lesson by planning appropriate elements to include in the Hook and asking the right questions. For example, foreign-language teachers might describe their own experiences in traveling abroad in their self-introduction and ask students to discuss places that they'd like to visit. Physical education or dance teachers might choose to discuss preferred leisure-time activities. English teachers might poll students' reading habits or talk about favorite films, plays, novels, or authors ("If you had a free afternoon and could read anything, what would you choose?").

Student Aim

After a brief, general discussion, you can begin to focus the interaction on your specific topic(s). Planning an introductory statement of purpose as a Student Aim can facilitate this transition. Your purpose statement could include (1) a tentative overview of the content to be explored in this lesson and throughout your unit ("For the next two weeks, our lessons are going to focus on cross-cultural interpretations of Romeo and Juliet," "Now I'm going to invite you to investigate electricity") and (2) the Rationale for later discussion and activity. A brief (one- or two-sentence) statement regarding your topic will help orient your students as the unit begins. Remember that a structured, specific Student Aim (i.e., previewing statement) is optional. Another possibility is to keep your students in suspense, initially, about your topic, revealing it late in the lesson. We have found that an approach like this can lead to curiosity within any class ("I wonder why she's asking us these questions.").

Lessons of all kinds should usually include a statement at some point as to why the lesson is important and what purpose it serves (exceptions include lessons in which the teacher wishes students to make these connections on their own). These statements help overcome the recurring (but often appropriate) question from students: "Why are we doing this?" A statement such as "Today, we're going to be talking about the 1980s. I hope to find out how much you know about this period in history to help me plan future lessons," accomplishes this purpose. Again, you can save a statement like this for later in the lesson if you think it's a good idea; this approach is characteristic of more inductive teaching approaches. But do address what we call the "So what?" question in some way during each lesson that you plan.

Development: Using Questions and an Activity to Open Windows into Your Students' Minds

Properly planned, your Hook and Student Aim will lead smoothly into the Development phase of the ILPE. Early in the Development, we recommend asking open-ended, brainstorming-type trigger questions that invite multiple student responses; without a doubt, one of the best ways to assess the nature of students' understanding is to ask them questions. As part of ILPE lessons, questions can be addressed to students in a full class setting, in small groups, or as part of a written assignment. In our introductory scenario, for example, Mr. Newman asked his class, "How have you used electricity in the past 24 hours?" A question like this could offer the teacher a wide range of insights into the students' understanding of what electricity is, how it is generated, and how natural resources must be utilized to produce and distribute it. The question also connects directly to the personal experiences of students (i.e., they have to think about and share something that they have done). In our experience, word association trigger questions are especially effective during this phase of the lesson (e.g., "What do you think of when I say the word ____?"). You may ask questions that relate more directly to the past experiences of students at this point (e.g., "How many of you have ever visited ___? How would you describe it to your classmates?"). We suggest writing important trigger questions like this directly into your lesson plan. This can help you avoid fumbling for words, asking run-on questions (i.e., asking-rephrasing-rephrasing), or doing too much talking yourself.

The questions planned for ILPE lessons should be designed to touch on as many aspects of the topic as possible. For example, suppose a geometry teacher wants to investigate students' initial understanding of the concept *volume*. The teacher could begin with a structuring statement before asking her students a series of questions:

> Teacher: I am going to ask some questions related to the term "volume" because I want to know what that word means to you before we begin the unit. What do you think about when you hear the term "volume," Jake?
>
> Jake: _____
>
> Teacher: Good! You mentioned that containers have volumes. What do you mean by that?
>
> Jake: _____
>
> Teacher: Can you add anything to Jake's definition of volume, Candy?
>
> Candy: _____

Again, in planning the Development of your ILPE lessons, it is important to plan a brief sequence of such open-ended trigger questions. You're not necessarily seeking right answers but inquiring into the current thinking of your students.

As we discussed in Module 4, there are two general types of teacher follow-up questions asked after a student responds: the probe and the redirect. Although probing and redirecting questions aren't planned in advance, since they depend on initial student responses (although you can anticipate some as mental rudder), the use of these follow-up questions is especially important in ILPE lessons. Probing questions acknowledge student responses and encourage them to expand on their ideas, as in the teacher's reply to Jake. In asking students to expand on a response, the teacher may request clarification of something that the student said, justification of an idea expressed, or the adding of information to a previous response. The type of probing question used depends on the nature of the initial answer; asking the right probing question at the right time can allow you to take advantage of the teachable moments that students provide with their initial responses. Remember that in an ILPE lesson your main goal is to gain insights into your students' understanding of and attitude toward your topic, so asking clarifying probes will be vital. We will see that when using other methods, asking other types of probing questions will become equally important (see Module 4 for a description and examples of probing questions).

The second type of follow-up question is the redirect (see Module 4). Recall that in its simplest form, redirecting refers to repeating the question, not necessarily verbatim, to another student. This technique is useful for determining the degree of consensus in the group regarding an expressed idea. Regardless of which student responded to the query, "How would you define the term 'volume'?," the teacher can redirect the question by merely asking, "Does Jake's definition express the concept as you understand it, Candy?" or, "How would you define volume, Candy?" A teacher can combine elements of the probe and redirect as well by asking something like, "How are Pam and Marty's ideas different?" Another useful redirecting technique is to ask for a show of hands to see who agrees/disagrees with a certain statement. Using redirecting questions is crucial: far too often, teachers who receive a detailed, accurate response from one student will assume that everyone else holds a similar level of understanding. This is almost always far from the case .

In the sample questions discussed so far, note that the teacher can invite specific students or anyone in the class to respond. Directing questions to particular students will allow you to sample the understanding that particular individuals hold. In general, we recommend that about half of the questions designed to reveal learners' previous experiences should be addressed to specific students. Remember to state the question and then the name of the student, as in the questions addressed by the teacher in the example to Jake and Candy. In this way, the teacher improves the chance that each student will begin to respond cognitively to the question.

As you conduct ILPE lessons, remember that your main purpose will be to determine what your students know or don't know about the topic and not for the students to be impressed by your knowledge, so these questions should be answered by students, not by you. As they discuss your topic, students will certainly learn something more about it, and it will be worthwhile to expand on ideas that students introduce. Be careful not to turn any ILPE lesson into a lecture on your topic. As in any teaching situation, if students can't answer a question, then you as the teacher have several options. You may wish to rephrase or simplify the question, breaking a complex concept down into its component parts. You could also direct the question to another student, or to the entire group, in a way that minimizes potential embarrassment to the student who couldn't answer the question. Remember that one absolute key to successfully eliciting student responses is to extend wait time before rephrasing or redirecting questions. In any event, it is always more useful for the teacher to identify the reason that students cannot answer questions rather than to answer the question for them. Don't feel that you're not accomplishing anything simply because the students fail to give the correct responses to the questions posed. In ILPE lessons, you can learn a lot by finding out what students don't understand.

You have a wide range of other options available during the development of an ILPE lesson. You can do a demonstration, read a piece of text (e.g., a poem or quote), or show a video clip, photo, or piece of artwork and ask students for a personal response. It is often useful for a teacher to list student-generated ideas on the board or overhead sheet or to arrange these ideas within a concept map so that you and your students have a developing reference point. Whatever you choose to do, try to involve each of your students during this portion of the lesson through directed trigger questions and redirecting questions.

An Open-Ended Activity

We also recommend planning an activity of some kind during the development of ILPE lessons. Engaging your class in activities, especially those that are open ended and provide students with an array of options or choices, can provide you with some terrific insights into their established ideas (and possibly their misconceptions) regarding your topic. Activities also provide you with further opportunities to investigate students' personalities, learning styles, and attitudes toward this and other topics.

Why are more open-ended activities, such as Mr. Newman's batteries and bulbs investigation, especially well suited to ILPE lessons? In these types of activities, students are challenged to rely on their current frames of reference to make sense of the situation, and consider their past experiences as well as elements of the current situation, to decide where to start and how to proceed. Challenging students to participate in such activities in groups of two to four is a terrific option; this allows you as the teacher to make observations, listen to student–student interaction, and ask the right question at the right time to push their thinking deeper or in new directions. In deciding what kind of activity to plan for your ILPE lessons, ask yourself the following three questions:

1. What could I ask my students to do that would provide me with insights into their current ways of thinking about this topic?

    The good news is that your options are almost unlimited in this regard. A science teacher might challenge students to do a hands-on activity in which they investigate a mysterious substance, process, or collection of objects, as Mr. Newman did. A math teacher could ask students to work through a puzzling, mathematics-rich problem or situation, as recommended in current NCTM standards. A speech or theater teacher might have her students write and perform a brief skit or presentation on a topic chosen at random. A history teacher could challenge his students to analyze a set of drawings or photographs and sequence them chronologically, defending their choices on the basis of what they see in the pictures. Again, the actions of your students in any of these activities could provide you with invaluable insights.

2. Is the activity best suited for a large- or small-group setting? What size group might be advisable?

    This is a crucial question. Smaller groups allow for greater observable interaction among students, so consider groups as small as two to four. You'll have to consider the materials and space that you'll need when making this decision; lack of necessary materials and space might dictate larger groups. Management considerations might play a part in this decision as well. It might be difficult for fifteen pairs of students in some classes to maintain their focus and to later share their ideas. As in any activity, you'll also need to decide whether to arrange the groups heterogeneously, in advance, or perhaps randomly.

3. How should I explain/provide directions for the activity?

    In general, you want your directions to be thorough without being overly restrictive (see the sample lesson plans throughout this book for examples of directions). In suggesting that ILPE activities be more open ended or exploratory in nature, we recommend giving students options to the greatest extent possible. What they decide to do and how they decide to do it will reveal a great deal. But even in an open-ended activity, you'll want to explain carefully that the students have options; you may want to suggest possible ways to do the activity. As in planning for any direction-giving situation, we suggest being ready to show directions on the board, an overhead sheet, a computer program slide, or a hand-out and to explain them verbally (you'll tend to catch students with strong visual and auditory modality preferences this way). Question students during and after giving directions to check on their understanding ("To review, what will each group want to do first? Jamal?"). Remember to model any tricky or potentially unsafe procedures for students, and perhaps allow them to practice before going any further.

Note that in an ILPE lesson, the activity usually provides the setting for students to carry out the Performance Objective. Whenever possible, challenge students to produce some physical product that will show you something about the nature of their understanding. In his science lesson, Mr. N. asked his students to diagram every arrangement of batteries, bulbs, and wires that produced a lighted bulb. There are several advantages to doing something like this in an ILPE. Students can share and discuss their product later in the lesson or even the next day, a process that can push their thinking in new directions. The teacher could collect, examine, and use in later classes physical products like this; an interesting product might even serve as a useful Hook for a future lesson. So think carefully about what you might ask your students to create (i.e., synthesize) in your ILPE activities.

As in the Hook and inquiry, teacher questioning during your activity will play a big part in the success of the lesson. Watch and listen carefully as students do the activity; look for clues about their attitudes toward the topic. Are they thoroughly engaged in what they are doing, asking each other questions? (Carry a notepad with you as you move among groups and record meaningful questions or comments to share later with the full class.) Or is their interest level less intense? Remember that the ways in which students interact in any group setting can reveal a great deal not only about their previous experiences but also about their learning-style preferences. These are insights that you can use to your advantage in planning future lessons. As always, put yourself in a position to ask trigger, probing, and redirecting questions to push their thinking in new directions. In completing your ILPE activity, be sure to first plan a sequence of questions that will challenge students to share and think deeply about what they experienced during the activity (again, see sample lesson plans for examples). Whenever possible, use these questions as a springboard into your Culmination.

Culmination: Concluding Your ILPE Lesson

As an ILPE Wrap-Up, we suggest providing your students with a summary of some of the things that you learned, as a teacher, during the lesson. This summary could include mention of the knowledge that some students have demonstrated and may bring up areas on which you will focus during future lessons ("Today, I've learned that we'll need to review mean, median, and mode before we conduct our first class poll"). This can be a very effective way of addressing the "So what?" question. Let the students know what you've learned and how the class will be using the information.

In many instances, planning a closing statement is helpful in wrapping up an ILPE lesson. A closing statement, as used here, simply refers to a final sentence that indicates that the lesson, or this part of the lesson, is over. In the Leap, encourage your students to apply the concepts in new ways. Finally, it's often a good idea to use the closing statement as a transition into the next lesson, what we call the *Look-Ahead* (e.g., "From today's lesson it is apparent that many of you are very familiar with the Great Depression. So tomorrow, we'll begin to look at . . .").

As a constructivist teacher, one of your main goals will be to challenge your students to generate questions that they have regarding a topic. We recommend that you make these student-generated questions a central, curriculum-driving focus as you proceed into each instructional unit. The concluding portion of an ILPE lesson presents a golden opportunity to allow students to voice burning questions that they have regarding the topic at hand. You can challenge your students to do this orally and can cover the chalkboard with relevant student questions, or you can ask students to write questions on index cards and turn these in ("One thing I'm wondering about _____ is _____"). Yet another option is to give students some kind of written questionnaire that they can complete in class or at home.

Assessment and Evaluation

Remember that ILPE lessons won't usually include a formal assessment and evaluation event (see Module 14). As is the case with many ILPE lessons, Mr. N.'s electricity lesson included many opportunities for the teacher to informally assess and evaluate the nature of his students' learning by observing their actions and listening to their comments. As you plan your own ILPE lessons, consider possible assessment products (i.e., something that the students would produce during or immediately after the lesson) that you might evaluate. Examples could include reflective papers, drawings, journal entries, or presentations. We discuss these options and more in Module 14.

Focal Point 4: When Should You Use the ILPE Method In Your Classroom?

Obviously, the ILPE method is very well suited for the opening day of the school year, or whenever you meet with a group for the first time. Plan a brief ILPE lesson every time you introduce major topics or units of instruction. During the school year, a brief ILPE lesson may consist of just a few relevant questions. ILPE lessons can be highly motivating and fun for students and teachers, since they are fast-paced and center on students' ideas. In addition, you, as the teacher, will send the positive message that you truly care about what students think, an important step in creating that thinker-friendly community in your classroom.

Asking your students to answer written questions or to complete other assignments will help in your learning process, as you look for clues as to the nature of your students' understanding. Supplement your classroom ILPE lessons with creative writing assignments, or design questionnaires to gauge students' knowledge and interest. Remember that assigning what we call a *one-minute essay* (e.g., "On your index card, complete the following sentence: When it comes to American culture in the 1960s, I'm most curious about _____") can provide you with a range of valuable insights. Remember that this does not imply that the only time that one would assess student interest and knowledge level is at the outset or conclusion of a lesson or unit. This kind of assessment must be an ongoing process. A conscious, concerted effort at such an assessment is vital when meeting a class for the first time or when introducing a new topic to a familiar group of students.

Challenging students to articulate questions that can be investigated within a unit should be a major emphasis in a constructivist classroom. Concluding lessons with one-minute essays can provide students with opportunities to generate questions. What do they wonder most about when they consider your topic? Starting future lessons by returning to these student-generated questions is not only highly motivating but also truly empowering.

In any case, conduct frequent ILPE lessons in your classroom. All that you learn about your students will prove invaluable as you plan future lessons.

A GLIMPSE INTO A CONSTRUCTIVIST CLASSROOM

Ms. Klein is beginning a theater unit that will focus primarily on playwriting. After learning about her students' theater-going and acting experiences during the inquiry phase of her ILPE, she asks the class, "Has anyone ever heard of improv?" Many of the students were able to explain something about improv to the rest of the class. "At this point, I'd like to challenge each of you to take part in your first improv-type experience!" says Ms. K. enthusiastically. She explains the situation. Each person in the class will choose a partner; each pair of students will have five minutes to write (and later act) a scene involving a waiter and a customer ordering dinner. "To add another twist, I'm going to ask each of you to choose a persona for the character that you'll portray," Ms. Klein continues. "Write and act the scene as you think a person like this would react." There is a buzz of excitement as each student reaches into a bag to choose a slip of paper describing a persona. The students excitedly begin to write scenes involving conflicts between such characters as a knight of the Round Table, a lady of the old South, a 1940s New York detective, a modern-day talk show host, and a range of other characters. The teacher learns a great deal about the initial playwriting and acting abilities of her students, their understanding of history and culture, and their personalities, as the class watches and discusses each performance.[1]

Tips for Technology Integration

- A middle school or high school teacher in any subject could develop a biographical computer program entitled "About Me" and share it with the class as part of an early-year ILPE lesson. Later in this lesson, students might work in small groups to plan and share ideas for personal "About Me" programs as a way to introduce themselves to classmates and then later develop their own program as an introduction to programming.[2]

- In pairs, students can explore relevant Websites as part of ILPE lessons, completing and later sharing responses to questions on a teacher-provided "treasure hunt" activity sheet. Students are provided with an introduction to a new topic and further develop their ability to use the Internet, all in a highly interactive setting.

■ ROUNDUP ■

ILPE lessons are planned with a number of important goals in mind. First and foremost, they are designed to allow you to gain insights into the thinking of your students. What is the nature of their understanding regarding important facts, concepts, and

1 = Overview of Unit
+
Introductions: students'
attitude toward subject

2 = INQUIRY
How many of you have heard of . . . ?
Have you ever thought about . . . ?
What comes to mind when I say . . . ?
If we compare this and that, what do they . . . ?

3 = exploratory activity related to unit topics
What do your students know?   How ready are they for the unit?

4 = culmination: How could this topic relate to your life? Any idea of where it could lead?

©2001 Ina Claire Gabler

FIGURE 7.2 ILPE Flow Chart

principles related to some new topic? What are their beliefs and attitudes regarding these ideas? How have their previous experiences impacted their thinking? Addressing these questions is vital for any teacher working from a constructivist learning perspective, and conducting ILPE lessons will allow you to do this directly.

These lessons also allow you to introduce a new topic in an engaging, motivating way. ILPE lessons tend to be highly interactive and fast paced. They also send the message that you truly care about what your students think. Another unmistakable message is that student questions will influence what subsequently happens in future classes. Make sure that you later address questions raised in the course of ILPEs.

Remember that ILPE lessons can vary in length from a few minutes to an entire class period, depending on a number of factors. In seeking to establish a thinker-friendly, constructivist setting, we recommend conducting such lessons whenever you embark on a new topic. You'll not only gain invaluable insights but you'll also send some powerful messages about the nature of learning within your classroom. See Figure 7.2 for a review of the main components of an ILPE lesson.

■ ILPE SAMPLE LESSON PLAN

Unit Title: Developing Effective Communications Skills (intended for a high school speech class)[3]

Prelude

Rationale

(Combines *What? Why? Justification*): By conducting a lesson that includes both performance components and an exploratory-type discussion, I will have an opportunity to assess students' speaking skills and confidence level with regard to public speaking and to begin to establish an open, relaxed classroom atmosphere conducive to the development of effective communications skills. The experience will enhance verbal communications skills and connects to INTASC Standards 1, 3, 4, 5, 6, 7, and 8.

Performance Objective

(Combines *Preparation, Product,* and *Criteria*): After drawing a personal question at random, students will display and then reflect on their speaking skills by providing a one-minute response to the question chosen. In the final phase of the lesson, students will reveal a possible professional/career aspiration and will state in writing at least three ways in which effective communications skills could be part of the chosen profession.

Materials and Lesson Aids

1. A set of questions designed to encourage student response, written on individual slips of paper.
2. Poster board with "What makes me most nervous?" poll results.

Enactment

Time Estimate	Core Components and Method Markers
Seven to eight minutes	*Hook.* We're going to start today with an important question: • What does it mean to be "nervous"? (probe/redirect)

- The first thing that I'd like to do today is to talk about things that make you nervous!
- What are some things that make you nervous? (survey class; list ideas provided; probe/redirect)
- How many of you like to speak in front of people? To perform/act? To appear on camera?

Twenty minutes

Student Aim.
*Our goal in this lesson will be to begin to ease some of those nervous feelings! The first thing that we're going to do is play a game.

Development. Open-Ended Activity
*What I'd like to do is ask for a volunteer to pull a slip of paper from the hat. Tell us what your question is, and then take thirty seconds to a minute to answer your question in front of the class. Answering some of the questions might require that you do some acting—don't be afraid to do this, everyone is going to have a chance to try it. I'll go first!
**Teacher models procedure; volunteers answer questions; probe/redirect based on responses.
Opening questions addressed include:

- If you had one day to do whatever you like, what would you do and why would you do it?
- In your mind, what is a perfect world?
- If you could be any animal, what animal would you choose to be and why?
- How would you describe your worst date?
- Describe your most embarrassing moment in a classroom.
- If you could choose to give a speech on any topic in front of a group of strangers, what would you talk about and why?
- What is your favorite school subject and why is it your favorite?

Five to six minutes

Transition: In the first part of the lesson, a number of you said that speaking in front of people makes you nervous.

Open-Ended Questions
- Why do you think public speaking frightens people so much? (probe/redirect; possible responses: fear of criticism, self-disclosure, others not paying attention)

- If we were to do a poll to see what situations make people nervous, what do you think we'd find? (probe/redirect based on responses)

**Reveal poll results on poster board, showing public speaking, attending a party with strangers, meeting a date's parents, and going to a job interview as top four "nervous situations"

- Is anyone surprised at these results?
- What do all of these situations have in common? (meeting people for the first time, trying to communicate with strangers in new settings)

Our first unit is going to focus on effective public speaking. One of my major goals will be to help you feel more comfortable doing this! (Provide a brief overview of the unit.)

Six to eight minutes

Culmination-Wrap-Up

I have another important question for you. What do you hope to become once you finish high school and college? (Survey class; probe/redirect, based on responses.)

Think about the answers that you and your classmates gave us. Choose one of these professions, and describe at least three ways in which effective communications would be a part of that profession.

Leap/Share Responses

- What role would effective communication play in any of these professions? (Direct questions based on professions chosen.)
- Would any of these professions involve giving speeches? Or speaking in front of other people?
- What kinds of speeches might be involved?

Notice that in one way or another, every profession that you might choose involves effective communication skills! Provide a summary of student comments.

Three to four minutes

Thanks for participating in the lesson today! I learned a lot about you, including some of your fears and your aspirations. (Review student comments.)

Look Ahead

During the next few weeks, we're going to focus on effective communications skills. We're going to learn about relaxation techniques, speech genres, and how effective communications skills apply to you in general.

For next time, think about at least one topic that you would feel comfortable talking about in front of a group of classmates. See you then!

Note: This individual lesson would not include a formal assessment and evaluation event. As is the case with many ILPE lessons, assessment and evaluation would be of an informal and formative nature and would come mainly through teacher observations of student performance.

■ HANDS-ON PRACTICE ■

Try planning an ILPE lesson by using the lesson template below. Refer to Modules 3 and 7 for suggestions.

Prelude

1. Start your planning process by writing a Rationale for the ILPE. Briefly describe the content that will serve as the focus of the lesson (consider your unit topic).
   - What will you be teaching?
   - Why will you be teaching this? (What cognitive skills might be emphasized in this experience?)
   - What overall justification (e.g., standards) could you provide for doing the lesson this way?
2. Now connect your Performance Objective to your Rationale.
   - First articulate your preparation. What will you do to prepare your students to complete the task that you have in mind?
   - Next, describe the product. What will you ask students to do during the lesson?
   - What criteria will you use to evaluate the quality of this product (e.g., how many, for how long)?
3. What materials and lesson aids will you need for the lesson?

Enactment

4. Next, think about what you'll actually say, do, and ask during the lesson. First, the Hook. What will you do to grab the attention of your students?
   - How can you personalize the content?
5. Consider the Student Aim. What might you say to let the students know where the lesson is going? (Remember: you can be direct with the Aim, or a bit more open and mysterious.)
6. Now plan the Development, the true heart of a lesson.

- We suggest asking open-ended questions to gain initial insights into your students' thinking. What might you ask?
- Include an open-ended activity. This approach can be extremely effective in telling you something about your students' previous experiences and their initial understanding of your topic. Describe an activity that you might do as part of your ILPE lesson.

7. Finally, the lesson Culmination.
   - What might you do/say/ask to provide a lesson Wrap-Up?
   - Now consider the Leap. What might you say/do/ask to preview the rest of the unit? To let them know how you might use the insights you've gained?

(Hint: Remember that planning a specific closing statement is an option. Leaving them with a question to consider for next time is often very effective.)

Assessment and Evaluation

- What could you do to evaluate student products from this lesson? We invite you to develop an evaluation instrument (i.e., rubric) for this assessment product by (1) specifying the key product features and (2) a assigning point scale.

Congratulations. By addressing these questions, you've planned your first ILPE lesson. Now add some detail and a time line, and you'll have a lesson plan that's ready to use.

ENDNOTES

1. Thanks to Sara Marquis, Augustana College Class of 2001, for her contributions to this scenario.
2. Thanks to Dr. Randy Hengst, Augustana College Education Department, for contributing this suggestion.
3. Thanks to Megan Peterson, Augustana College Class of 1998, for her contributions to this lesson plan.

Module Eight:
Teaching Concepts

PART 1:
The Deductive Concept Method

■ OVERVIEW: SCENARIO DEPICTING A DEDUCTIVE CONCEPT LESSON

Students enter Ms. Vargas's Spanish I class one Monday morning to the lively sounds of traditional Spanish music. It's early in the school year, but the class has already become accustomed to hearing music from Spain, Central America, and South America. The rhythm seems to energize the students just a bit as they take their seats, which are arranged in a circle today.

As the bell rings, Ms. Vargas says, "Welcome back! Hope everyone had a terrific weekend. Today, we're going to think about a term that we often hear in our day-to-day lives. What do you think of when you hear the word 'culture'?"

Hands shoot up as the students recognize this invitation to brainstorm. Their contributions vary widely. They quickly mention various kinds of food (Mexican food seems to be popular), including some made by their relatives; music ("People from different parts of the world like really different kinds of music"); Maria mentions the Cinco de Mayo parade that she attended last year.

"That's interesting!" says the teacher enthusiastically. She asks Maria what she saw in the parade and what this tells her about Mexican culture, as the other students listen. After this exchange, Ms. Vargas tells the class, "We're off to a great start. In this class, we're going to define *culture* as *the way of life of a group of people who share similar customs, beliefs, and values.* We're also going to investigate *cultural artifacts*, which are objects that reflect something about the people who made them." Students busily write both definitions, which Ms. Vargas has revealed on the overhead. "Let's talk about what this means and why it's important in Spanish and how it will help us learn the language."

Ms. Vargas first invites the class to expand on the list that they've begun to brainstorm by asking, "What might we mean by 'way of life'?" and then, "What could be a part of the way of life of a group of people?" She lists *food, music/art,* and *holidays* on the board and the students provide a range of new ideas. In the next few minutes, *language, books/literature, clothes, family structure and values, religion,* and *living space* are all added to the list during the conversation. The teacher asks trigger questions that push the students' thinking further. They add *recreation, forms of government,* and *technology* to the list as the teacher subtly introduces some Spanish vocabulary ("Repitan clase, por favor-familia"; ". . . fiesta," ". . . tecnica").

"Outstanding list! Now we're going to expand on some of these dimensions of culture. Investigating Spanish culture is going to be a big part of what we do in this class," emphasizes Ms. Vargas. "Let's take a look at some cultural artifacts produced in Spain during the past fifty years. As we look at these items, tell me what they tell you about Spanish culture." During the next ten minutes, Ms. Vargas pulls a succession of artifacts, or pictures of artifacts, from a large bag. There's a noticeable sense of anticipation as students examine articles of clothing, a movie poster, an intricately carved wooden box, a collection of money, menus, CD covers, pictures of homes and family holiday gatherings (including a recent picture of the royal family), and other items, many of which were collected by the teacher on her recent trip to Spain. For each item, Ms. V. first holds up the object, lets the students know how to say the relevant term in Spanish, and then passes it around the circle of seats as students share observations and impressions of what each artifact might reveal about Spanish culture. Ms. Vargas frequently asks probing and redirecting questions as students excitedly share ideas. After the class examines all of the Spanish artifacts, she asks, "So based on everything that we've seen so far, what words would you use to describe Spanish culture today?" She lists more than twenty words that the students agree on, challenging them to provide support for each contribution.

"We'll expand on many of these ideas during the next few months. We'll talk a lot about culture as we learn the language," concludes the teacher. During the last fifteen minutes of class, Ms. Vargas reminds that students that cultures can be broadly or narrowly defined and that "we actually have a culture here at Carver High School." She quickly arranges the class into groups of four and challenges each group to brainstorm and later share a list of ten cultural artifacts that they would include in a Carver High School time capsule. The resulting lists reveal a lot about the students' understanding of the main concepts and about their initial feelings regarding their new high school.[1]

Focal Point 1: What Makes the Deductive Concept Method Distinctive?

You have just participated in what we (and other educators) call a deductive concept lesson. Based on what we've already said about deductive thinking, and about concepts, ask yourself, "What made this lesson deductive, and what concepts were involved?"

First, recall that *deductive teaching* is defined as a style of teaching in which the instructor presents the class with one or more concepts or principles, challenges students to investigate a set of examples that are related to these main ideas, and then asks the students to test or apply the central ideas. Your main goals in a lesson like this will be to do the following:

- Challenge students to develop a deeper understanding of one or more important concepts (or principles).
- Then apply this new understanding in some way.

Discussion 1: What Makes the Deductive Concept Method Distinctive?

We believe that deductive lessons like the one conducted by Ms. Vargas are refreshing alternatives to lectures because they clearly focus on the big ideas within a subject and because students are actively engaged in the analysis of these main ideas. We'll see that effective deductive lessons are highly interactive, with students challenged to connect important new ideas (e.g., a working definition for 'culture' and a consideration of the dimensions of Spanish/other cultures) with their own previous experiences.

Figure 8.1 displays a suggested planning template for a deductive concept lesson. As you read through this template, think about how each part of Ms. Vargas's lesson on culture/cultural artifacts fits within the different stages.

PRELUDE

- Rationale (with connection to national standards)
- Performance Objective
- Materials and Lesson Aids

ENACTMENT

- HOOK—Begin with an attention-grabbing question, statement, quote, demonstration, or skit. As always, the possibilities are endless!
- STUDENT AIM—Your statement of purpose for a deductive lesson will be fairly direct. Present a definition of the concept(s) or principle(s) involved. Display this definition prominently (e.g., on the board, overhead, computer program slide). Ask questions to check for initial student understanding of the definition; focus especially on key words or phrases.
- DEVELOPMENT
  1. INVESTIGATION OF EXAMPLES/NONEXAMPLES
     a. Share examples (perhaps nonexamples if possible) of the concept with students. This can be done in a full class or peer-group setting.
     b. Challenge students to investigate (especially compare and contrast) examples with a mix of specific and open-ended trigger questions. Be sure to refer to the concept *rule*. Ask students to *test* the rule as they investigate.
     c. If possible, elicit further examples from the students.
  2. APPLICATION
     a. Conduct a brief activity or provide an assignment that challenges students to apply (i.e., actually *use*) the concept, fulfilling your performance objective(s).
     b. Again, elicit further examples from students if possible.
- CULMINATION
  1. WRAP-UP—Review, or challenge *students* to review, the main ideas generated. Be sure to address the "so what?" question: Why is this concept important?
  2. LEAP—What new ideas or insights relate to the concept? What's in store for the class; how will we use the important idea that we've investigated?

ASSESSMENT AND EVALUATION PLAN

  1. Assessment products (What will students produce in this/a later lesson?)
  2. Evaluation (How will you evaluate this product, e.g., with a scoring rubric?)

FIGURE 8.1 Deductive Concept Lesson Planning Template

Focal Point 2. Initial Planning: Choosing and Articulating the Concept

Why Teach Concepts?

We have discussed concepts, and their relationship to facts and principles. Why are concepts well suited as a central focus for lessons like this? In an educational sense, concepts are especially important for a number of reasons. First, they help all of us make sense of the many things that we experience. Second, they represent some of the central, defining ideas in each discipline. Because these ideas are so essential in understanding every subject, it makes sense to occasionally teach lessons in which students are challenged to develop a deep and flexible understanding of important concepts.

We have already introduced just some of the exciting recent findings regarding perception, memory, and thinking. The pioneering research in concept formation and attainment was done in the 1960s, primarily by Jerome Bruner, Jacqueline Goodnow, and George Austin (1967). David Ausubel (1963), Robert Gagne (1965), Hilda Taba (1966), and a host of other educators have contributed much to our understanding of thinking (and teaching) at the conceptual level. To summarize some of these important research findings, we point out that as human beings who actively perceive and process several million bits of information during a normal day, our brains have developed mechanisms to help us sort information so that we are not overwhelmed by the task. One way that each of us deals with this constant flood of sensory input is by placing pieces of information into the ever-changing set of schemata that constitute each person's frame of reference. This processing allows each of us to make sense of sensory input at a much quicker pace.

At this point, concepts come into play as we attempt to understand human thinking from a cognitive (and constructivist) perspective. There are many definitions for the term *concept*, but the most appropriate definition for our purposes is *a word that conveys a set of categories that allow us to classify objects or ideas.* We might also think of a concept as *a word or phrase that activates a schema or a set of schemata.* Many writers have used the words *concept* and *schema* to mean virtually the same thing, but we invite you to remember this important distinction: a concept is a word or phrase that activates a schema. Think of it this way: the concept (word) is like a light switch that turns on a select set of wiring within the mind (a schema or a set of schemata). Also keep in mind that many different types of sensory inputs can activate a schema. For proof of this, think of sights, smells, and sounds that trigger a flood of memories and images in your own mind.

Since our personal set of cognitive structures allows each of us to make sense of the pieces of information that we perceive, it will be important for teachers to consider the nature of concepts when introducing new ideas to students. Since concepts represent some of the big ideas within any subject area, and form the building blocks for principles, clear communication and shared understanding of concepts is essential to effective teaching and learning. In the next few paragraphs, we briefly review the nature of concepts.

Book, inertia, glasnost, truck, reptile, chair, war, poetry, isosceles triangle, characterization, middle class, metaphor, pollination, and *insanity* are all examples of concepts. Each of these words activates a schema that allows us to form a mental image of an object, event, or process without having to reprocess and analyze every piece of sensory input that we experience. We have seen that each individual constructs meanings for objects and events based on previous experiences. As a result, if several people try to define concrete or abstract concepts from *lion* to *love*, you would find that there would be considerable individual differences. In an educational setting, helping students to reach shared understanding of even seemingly simple concepts is vital and can present major challenges.

Our opening scenario hints that within any culture, people have shared certain experiences, and, as a result, may have similar frames of reference that they use to understand certain objects and events. It is not surprising that individuals from the same culture often share meanings for some concepts. This allows them to communicate with each other without giving long, complex explanations. If a person states "I saw a small animal with four legs, a tail, two ears, and brown fur," the creature in question could be a squirrel, a mongoose, a woodchuck, a cat, a dog, or a rabbit. But if the person says, "I saw a brown tiger cat today," most of us would be able to identify and produce an image of the object with more clarity.

Because each of us has had certain unique experiences, no two people will have exactly the same image of the brown tiger cat. One person might associate the cat with a striped kitten that she had as a child. Another person might think of an adult tiger cat that lives in the house next door. While the images may not be exactly the same, the conception of cat allows the two people to focus on the same type of object without a lot of further explanation. When information sharing breaks down, it is often because two or more people taking part in the conversation do not have shared meanings for the same concepts. Many of the communication problems that occur in classrooms can be attributed to this effect, underlining the importance of students sharing common experiences in learning about concepts. This is especially true with concepts that are process oriented or highly abstract.

Discussion 2: Initial Planning: Choosing and Articulating the Concept

Obviously, one of the first major steps in planning a deductive or inductive concept lesson is to choose a concept to serve as the central focus. Within any subject area, there are hundreds if not thousands of important concepts that connect to each other in myriad ways. Your first challenge is to choose concepts that are important enough to serve as a central focus, and then to think carefully about how to define the concept and how to challenge students to investigate this big idea. The following discussion of the nature of concepts should help you to think through this process. Remember that many of these considerations will apply whether you choose to teach the concept deductively or inductively (inductive teaching is the focus of Part 2 of this module).

Concepts have certain *critical attributes,* or essential features, qualities, or characteristics, that establish a certain degree of sameness between two examples of the concept. Mammals, for example, share the ability to control their internal body temperature. A critical attribute of democracies is that citizens are allowed to vote or otherwise express themselves. In probability and statistics, a permutation is a situation in which the order of events matters and a combination is a situation in which the order of events doesn't make a difference. These critical attributes must be present to distinguish an example of a concept from a nonexample. A concept may have only one critical attribute or several that work in conjunction.

Critical attributes (like events in a permutation) often have to be presented in a certain pattern or sequence so that they can be placed into specific conceptual definitions. The order in which these critical attributes are presented create the concept's definition or rule. If we took off in an airplane and observed land, water, and a surrounding body, we may have observed either a lake or an island. The concept rule for a lake would be a body of water surrounded on all sides by a land mass. The concept rule for an island would be a body of land surrounded on all sides by water. If what we observed was a land mass surrounded on three sides by water, we would know that it was not an island, but a peninsula. Of course, we have used a simple concept and concept rules to illustrate a point. If a river enters a body of water, it is no longer surrounded on all sides by a land mass. Is it now a lake? The point of this last question is to remind you that even simple concept rules can be challenged on various points.

Along with critical attributes, many concepts can also have *noncritical attributes*, which are features, characteristics, or qualities that are not essential parts of the concept. In our lake example, whether the lake contained saltwater or freshwater would not affect the concept rule. The same goes for the size of the lake, its depth, or its shape. In the mammal example, the presence of hooves, a tail, or a certain color fur are examples of noncritical attributes. Concepts may have a number of noncritical attributes or none at all.

Types of Concepts

Concepts can be classified in several different ways, and it will useful for you as a teacher to keep these categories in mind. A *concrete concept* refers to that which we can experience through the five senses. An *abstract concept* refers to that which we cannot experience or perceive directly through our senses. Another way to look at concepts is to categorize them as conjunctive, disjunctive, or relational. A *conjunctive concept* has a single set of characteristics or qualities that a person must learn in order to identify it. In contrast, a *disjunctive concept* requires a learner to identify two or more sets of alternative conditions under which the concept can and will occur. It often has an "or" in its definition. For example, a *citizen* could be defined as a native or naturalized member of a state or nation who owes allegiance to its government and who is entitled to its protection. As the definition indicates, there are different conditions under which the concept can be fulfilled.

Although disjunctive concepts may be difficult for students to understand, *relational concepts* are often more challenging to teach. This type of concept requires a student to form a comparison between objects, events, or qualities; you'll often find that it makes sense to introduce two to three relational concepts together so that they can be compared and contrasted. *Waste, pollution,* and *symmetry* are all examples of this type of concept. Waste, for instance, has to be viewed in relation to its source, to the people who produce it, and to whether it has any value after it has been discarded. If you throw away an aluminum can, is it, in fact, a waste product? Although it may be to some people, environmentalists would consider the can a resource because it is a recyclable product that could be used over and over again. If the value of such cans goes down to the point where it is no longer economical to collect and process them, are the cans waste again? In teaching relational concepts, it is obviously crucial to describe relationships between the concepts involved.

Concepts can be classified in many different ways. The examples discussed here are meant to help you think about some of the ways in which you might teach concepts in the classroom and why the teaching of concepts should be a vital part of instruction in any subject. When choosing which concepts to teach and how to teach them, there are several questions that you should consider:

1. Is the concept considered significant enough to serve as the central focus for a lesson? Do subject matter specialists and state/local learning standards suggest that the concept is an important one?

2. Why would your students need to learn about the concept? Does the concept have relevant real-world connections that make it significant for your students?

3. Is there sufficient agreement on the critical attributes and the concept rule to have a basis for designing a lesson plan? Can clear and specific guidelines that reflect the essential characteristics of the concept be obtained from resource materials?

Once you have decided that a concept is important enough to teach, you should then ask yourself a series of questions that can help you plan a concept lesson (remember that these questions should be considered whether the lesson will be taught deductively or inductively). As you plan any concept lesson, consider these questions:

1. What is the name most commonly associated with the concept? (Example: democracy)

2. What is the concept's rule or definition? (Example: government in which political control is shared by all citizens, either directly or through elected representatives)

3. What are the critical attributes of the concept? (Examples: shared political control, participation of citizens)

4. What noncritical attributes are associated with the concept? (Example: elected representatives)

5. What are some interesting, learner-relevant examples or cases of the concept that can be used during the lesson? (Examples: ancient Athens, nineteenth century constitutional monarchies, modern United States)

6. What are some contrasting nonexamples that will help clarify and illustrate the concept? (Examples: Europe in the Middle Ages, Nazi Germany, modern China)

7. What are the most interesting, efficient, and thought-provoking media that can be used to teach the concept? (Examples: speech excerpts, case studies, interviews with local elected officials)

We suggest using these questions as an initial planning template for teaching concept lessons. Once you have answered them, you will have established a rationale and direction in teaching a concept to your students. Teaching at the conceptual level can be very powerful, since learning a concept can provide your students with a useful lens for understanding new ideas and making real-world connections. Developing an un-

pattern energy logic organic/inorganic imperialism citizenship observation
symmetry rhythm integration existentialism migration literacy racism
evolution revolution cycles nonviolent protest isolationism density motion
manifest destiny natural selection genre relationship community tangram
observation unit permutation gene pool compromise fertility frontier
algorithm competition acid/base inference hero/villain surface area

love (pertrarchan/platonic) rebellion responsibility freedom
tendon/ligament/cartilage dispersal mechanism(s) youth catalyst reciprocal
terrorism coalition equation Popular Sovereignty hypothesis research treaty
health exploration diversity environment electric circuits classism blockade
cape joints/sockets plot mass buoyancy patriotism supply/demand
feudalism functions perpendicular zone defense cubism self-determination

FIGURE 8.2 Examples of Concepts from a Range of Disciplines

derstanding of concepts such as democracy, for example, would enable students to better understand a wide range of historical and cultural events.

In short, teaching concepts makes sense because people naturally think in conceptual terms. Just as importantly, understanding concepts can help students to make sense of the major principles within each knowledge domain. Choosing one or more relevant concepts will be the first step in planning such a lesson. The list of potential concepts is almost endless, regardless of which subject you teach. Read through the list of potential concepts in Figure 8.2 and think about the images that each generates. Would there be some educational value in teaching any of these concepts within your subject area?

Focal Point 3: **Deductive Concept Method Markers**

Now let's turn our attention specifically to teaching concepts deductively. The method markers described below will help you understand what makes this approach different from other constructivist methods.

- In conveying the Student Aim, you will clearly define the concept(s) for your students.

- During the Development, you will challenge students to investigate examples and possibly nonexamples of the concept(s) to better understand the critical attributes (i.e., essential characteristics) of the concept.

- Later in the Development, you will invite students to apply the concept in some way, possibly through an activity, to test and deepen their understanding of this important idea.

- The Culmination will include some discussion of the implications of the concept. Why is this idea important, and how will we as a class use it in future lessons?

Up Close: Planning and Conducting a Deductive Concept Lesson

Before taking a closer look at planning deductive lessons, we'd like to remind you that this method, like all of the others that we'll introduce, is incredibly flexible. There are countless ways to effectively conduct a deductive lesson. Our guiding suggestions are meant to help you begin the planning process and think about what you'll need to do to successfully conduct lessons like this.

Up Close: Planning and Conducting a Deductive Concept Lesson

Prelude: Rationale

Let's use the opening scenario as an example of an engaging deductive lesson. Ms. Vargas is most concerned with helping her students gain a deeper understanding of culture as a concept and with helping them learn to apply the concept. Notice that she was also, in a subtle way, trying to gain greater insights into her students' initial understanding of the elements of culture (you'll see that ILPE-type trigger questions can be an important part of any constructivist classroom experience). Our Spanish teacher might have written a Rationale like this: "Students will develop a deeper understanding of culture as a concept first by considering a provided definition, then by comparing and contrasting cultural artifacts from modern-day Spain, and finally by applying the definition to their own school culture. This experience will enhance critical-thinking abilities and help develop group communications skills, and it connects to INTASC Standards 1, 3, 4, 5, 6, 7, and 8." As in any well-conceived rationale, Ms. Vargas has articulated, for herself but also for a substitute teacher or administrator visiting her class, some important reasons to do the lesson this way. In her Performance Objective, she gets more specific about what her students should be able to do as a result of this experience.

Performance Objective

Performance Objectives focus on what students should be able to do to show you what they've learned. Again, the important caveat: we can't always (in fact, usually) predict exactly what students will learn; the process of learning is far too complex (thankfully) to be predictable. But writing Performance Objectives is a vital part of the planning process, since they focus you as the teacher on the importance of student doing and because they connect directly to the assessment of student learning. With this in mind, let's consider a possible Performance Objective for Ms. Vargas's lesson: "Students will be introduced to concept definitions for *culture* and *cultural artifact* early in the lesson and will then be challenged to consider the dimensions of culture by brainstorming examples of the 'ways of life' of groups of people. Later in the lesson, students will apply these concepts by articulating, in a group setting, a list of at least ten defensible cultural artifacts that reflect something about Carver High School culture" (preparation, product, and criteria). Once again, note that Ms. Vargas has articulated an interesting, and potentially highly challenging, way for her students to show what they've learned, the essence of a Performance Objective.

Materials

One of the most challenging aspects of planning concept lessons is to think about what examples and nonexamples might convey the main concept and its attributes; more on this when we move on to the enactment of the lesson. Ms. Vargas had to think carefully about which cultural artifacts would accomplish this, and then she had to actually assemble these props. Listing these materials would certainly help her consider how she might introduce the examples, and in what sequence.

Now that we've taken a closer look at the Prelude, on to the Enactment of a deductive lesson, where the guiding question becomes: How can you challenge your students to *actually experience* your chosen concept?

Enactment: Hook

As in any lesson, an effective Hook can set the tone for what is to come later. Anything is possible. Your Hook can consist of something elaborate (e.g., a skit written by you or the students and performed by volunteers) or something as simple as a truly challenging, open-ended question. We suggest that the Hook for any concept lesson connect in some way to the main concept.

In our opening scenario, Ms. Vargas began her lesson with some music and a related, straightforward question ("What do you think of when you hear the word *culture?*"). In doing this, she subtly established one dimension of culture (music/the arts) that students might focus on later, and she gained some important initial insights into some of the background experiences of her students (the varied "cultural" foods enjoyed by her students; Maria's connection to the Cinco de Mayo parade). In addition, the teacher established an interactive, thinker-friendly tone for the rest of the lesson. Once again, our general advice is to get your students involved in each of your lessons as soon as possible, through either questions or activities. Through years of experience, we have found that breaking the ice in this way helps engage students for the entire class period.

In conducting either deductive or inductive concept lessons, another option is to somehow share interesting examples of the concept as a Hook. In fact, providing a brief inductive introduction to a lesson that is predominantly deductive can be very effective. For example, an English teacher introducing poetry of the Romantic era might read an intriguing example and challenge students to analyze it. An art teacher wishing to introduce Impressionist painting might invite students to examine a set of prints showing examples and nonexamples. A chemistry teacher introducing "indicator" as a concept might conduct a series of eye-catching demonstrations in which solutions dramatically change color on mixing and then invite students to make observations and predictions about what might happen next. In each of these examples, the teacher would be creating some sense of wonder and anticipation and introducing dimensions of the main concept. This engagement is what you should hope to accomplish in the early minutes of any concept lesson.

Student Aim

As constructivist methods go, deductive concept lessons are fairly structured. This is reflected during the Student Aim phase of the lesson. Your most important goal at this point is to clearly share your concept rule (i.e., definition) with the class. Ms. Vargas displayed definitions for *culture* and *cultural artifact*, read these to the students, and asked a clarifying question to make sure that they understood a key phrase. Remember that showing and stating these definitions will help you reach both visual and auditory learners. We also highly recommend a visual display of the concept rule, since students will be referring to this definition throughout the lesson; place the rule on the board, on a computer slide displayed on a TV screen, or on a handout.

In planning a lesson like this, think carefully about how you'll define the concept(s) for your students. Obviously, it's vital to make the definition as understandable as possible. If it is important to use certain terminology in the concept rule, plan questions that would allow you to check for student understanding before moving to the next phase of the lesson. When planning concept lessons, it's useful for you as the teacher to think in terms of concept rules and critical and noncritical attributes, but remember that these terms can sound needlessly complex and intimidating to students. Instead, get used to discussing important features, qualities, or characteristics when investigating concepts with your students.

After introducing your concept rule(s), we suggest planning a transition statement of some kind to let the students know that they will now be applying the rule as they investigate a set of examples. This could be something as simple as Ms. Vargas's statement, "Let's talk about what this means and why it's important in Spanish."

Development: Investigating and Applying the Concept(s)

What really sets a deductive concept lesson apart from teacher presentations is that students are actively involved in the investigation of examples and, later, in the application of the concept. This is the phase of the lessons in which you challenge your students to "become" scientists, historians, mathematicians, and so on, as they think critically about the concept, the examples, and why these are important.

One of your biggest planning considerations will be to choose and collect examples that students will find intriguing. Obviously, the nature of your examples will depend on your concept. Ms. Vargas shared a variety of cultural artifacts with her class. In this case, as could be the case with concepts from just about any discipline, your examples might consist of actual, concrete objects or pictures of objects. In math lessons, examples could include geometric figures or manipulatives, various types of problems, or statistical data. In English or history lessons, pieces of text shown on an overhead screen or distributed on slips of paper could serve as examples. In many of the example lessons that we'll describe, video clips or recordings could be used to illustrate the concept. In physical education lessons, a teacher might demonstrate two to three different techniques for passing a basketball, making a block, or doing a high jump and challenge students to compare and contrast the processes involved. Again, the possibilities vary as widely as concepts do.

Once you decide on the examples that you might share, we suggest planning a series of questions that will challenge students to observe the examples closely ("What do you notice about ____ ?"), compare and contrast them ("How are these alike? Different?"), and connect them to the concept rule ("Are these examples of ____? How can you tell?"). Questions that challenge students to consider the broader meaning/implications of the examples are important at this point as well. For example, Ms. Vargas asked her students what the various artifacts might indicate about Spanish culture;

questions like these can challenge students to think more deeply about the meaning of what they are experiencing.

Remember that the analysis of examples can take place in a full class or small-group setting. If you have enough examples to share, a brief (even five-minute) peer-group event at this point in the lesson can be very effective; this can provide each student with ample opportunities to experience the examples. If you do this, ask each group to compile a list of observations and tentative conclusions about the examples (e.g., "Are they examples of this concept? Why/why not?") which your students can share when the class reconvenes.

Again, planning appropriate questions for this phase of the lesson is a must. Chances are that it will take time and effort to collect the examples that you share. Make sure you get the most bang for the buck by challenging students to investigate them thoroughly.

Following the investigation of examples, we advise you to plan a brief activity or discussion that will challenge your students to apply the concept and meet your Performance Objective. Ms. Vargas subtly showed her students just how generative the concepts could be by challenging them to consider artifacts that might show something about a culture that they are all a part of (side note: this could be revealing on a number of levels, as one of your authors found when conducting this lesson in a college classroom). This application could involve individual or group writing or performing, problem solving (e.g., "Can you use the quadratic equation to find ____?"), or brainstorming (e.g., "Where have you experienced evaporation, condensation, and sublimation, and how did these processes impact you?"). The application phase is important. It serves as another check on student understanding and challenges students to extend the ideas involved beyond the walls of the classroom (see sample lesson plan and *Glimpse* for additional examples of this). Again, questions that challenge students to generate their own additional examples of the concept are very effective at this point.

Culmination

As you plan the Culmination for a deductive concept lesson, think about how you might provide an effective Wrap-up. We recommend some type of review of the concept and the dimensions of the concept that were investigated during the lesson. As in any lesson, you might plan on reviewing the main ideas yourself and/or asking reviewing questions that could challenge the students to provide a recap.

It's especially important in the Leap to ask the students why they think that the concept is important. Then you might ask them to apply the concept in a new way. Finally, let them know how you'll be using the concept in the future (once again addressing the "So what?" question). For example, Ms. Vargas might let her students know that they would be investigating additional cultural artifacts throughout the school year, thereby expanding their understanding of the cultures of Spanish-speaking countries.

As a constructivist teacher, remember that you'll regularly want to challenge your students to generate questions regarding classroom experiences. Another option in the Culmination of a deductive concept lesson is to invite students to complete an ILPE-like one-minute essay ("One thing I'm wondering about Spanish culture is ____").

Always look for opportunities to gain insights into your students' thinking. Working techniques like this into lesson Culminations is an interesting, efficient way to do this.

Assessment and Evaluation

Like lessons featuring any constructivist approach, the deductive concept method includes multiple opportunities for a teacher to informally assess the learning of students through watching their actions and listening to their comments. Formal assessment could come through the collection and evaluation of something that the students produce during the application phase or through a reflective assignment (e.g., a reflective paper, a journal entry, or even a research project) that they might complete after the lesson. As you plan your own deductive concept lessons, consider assessment products that you might evaluate (see Module 14 for examples).

Focal Point 5: When Should You Use the Deductive Concept Method in Your Classroom?

We believe that both deductive and inductive concept lessons can serve as challenging, thought-provoking alternatives to lectures or as complements to interactive presentations. Although constructivist classrooms are far more interactive and student centered than more traditional classrooms, you will still have occasion as a constructivist teacher to introduce new ideas in your subject area. The frequent use of the deductive concept method is an effective, interactive way to do this.

We suggest considering both deductive and inductive methods whenever you have a need to introduce and challenge students to apply important concepts and/or principles. On these occasions, one consistent question will be whether to use a deductive or an inductive approach; this is a question that we'll challenge you to consider throughout this module. We'll see that inductive methods would generally be considered to be more discovery oriented and student centered. But, for a number of reasons, we suggest a mix of deductive and inductive lessons. Consider the variety of learning-style preferences among your students, for example. Random learners find great challenge and appeal in inductive experiences, whereas more sequential learners are most comfortable with deductive lessons. A mix of inductive and deductive lessons will likely allow you to connect to a range of learners while frequently nudging all students out of their learning comfort zones. Deductive lessons are often especially appropriate when concepts or principles are completely novel and especially complex (although we'll see that inductive lessons are certainly useful when you introduce ideas that are likely to be new to your students). When choosing either a deductive or inductive approach, consider the ability of your students to connect their own previous experiences to the central concept.

A GLIMPSE INTO A CONSTRUCTIVIST CLASSROOM

Mr. Kondo and his junior American Lit class are in the early stages of a unit that he has entitled "The Voice(s) of America," which will focus on the investigation of literature written by authors from disenfranchised cultural groups within our country. Mr. K. begins today's lesson with an enthusiastic reading of the Langston Hughes poem *Theme for English B.* He then asks students to respond to the poem by asking open-ended Trigger Questions: "What is the author telling us? How would you describe his life at this point? What words would you use to describe the poem? Does he feel he's an American? How can you tell? Could anyone else have written this poem in the same way? Why?" Students debate their viewpoints vigorously; they spend several minutes debating elements of the poem before Mr. Kondo begins guiding the lesson a bit more directly. The teacher provides students with a definition for what he calls authentic voice: words written in such a distinctive, original way that the reader feels that only that author could have written that particular piece. The writer conveys knowledge, passion, and genuine concern regarding the subject. After a brief discussion of the definition, Mr. Kondo asks students to read three additional poems, and the class discussion focuses on the degree to which each reflects authentic voice. He then asks his students to write (and later share) a poem that reflects their own authentic voice.[2]

Tip for Technology Integration

The Internet can provide students with unique opportunities to experience concept examples as part of deductive or inductive lessons. During the Development stage of a lesson, you as the teacher might direct students to one or more Websites that feature pictures, text excerpts, audio or video segments, and more that students might analyze individually or in peer groups as part of the testing or discovery of a concept.

■ ROUNDUP ■

Deductive concept lessons can serve as engaging alternatives to didactic presentations. Even though most of our educational experiences have been deductive in nature, the format that we suggest here is highly interactive and intellectually engaging. Lessons like this typically focus on a concept(s) that is a big idea within a discipline, an idea that can be used by the class later to understand events, processes, etc. They feature an early presentation of a concept definition by the teacher, followed by the active investigation of a set of examples and the application of the concept to potentially real situations.

Use the Deductive Concept Method as a lecture alternative, especially when you wish to challenge students to learn and apply a central concept or principle that might be utilized in future lessons. There are several keys to effectively planning such a lesson. First, think carefully about how you might define the central concept(s); use the guiding questions posed earlier to help you through this process. Consider how you might share examples (and possibly nonexamples) of the concept(s), and whether you will do this in a full class or small-group setting. As in any lesson, write your main trigger questions into your lesson plans. Our experiences have shown us that this will help any teacher challenge students to carefully investigate the examples and to think deeply about why the concept is important. Finally, challenge students to apply the concept during the final phases of the lesson, and in future lessons.

Take a look at the flow chart in Figure 8.3. Then read the sample lesson plan that follows. It will alert you to just a few more of the many possibilities for deductive concept lessons.

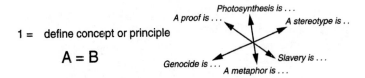

1 = define concept or principle

$$A = B$$

Photosynthesis is . . .
A proof is . . .
A stereotype is . .
Genocide is . . .
Slavery is . . .
A metaphor is . . .

2 = compare and contrast

examples with examples and nonexamples
from instructional materials
Hmmm . . . Nope!
Hey, that one is . . . than the other one.

3 = establish characteristics of concept or principle

It itches!   Sometimes it can result in . . .   It always affects . . .

4 = elicit more examples from students

"I read somewhere that . . ."

5 = culmination: *reestablish definition of concept or principle*

$$A = B + \text{implications}$$

If this happens when that happens, then . . .

©2001 Ina Claire Gabler

FIGURE 8.3 Deductive Concept Method Flow Chart

■ DEDUCTIVE CONCEPT SAMPLE LESSON PLAN

Unit Title: The American Legal System (intended for a middle school social studies class)

Prelude

Rationale

(Combines *What? Why? Justification*): Introducing and deductively analyzing the concept *law* will challenge students to consider both the nature of laws in the United States and the ways in which laws impact our lives and serve to pique student curiosity as to how laws originate at the local, state, and federal levels. The experience will enhance the critical-thinking abilities of the students involved and connects to INTASC standards 1, 3, 4, 5, 7, and 8.

Performance Objective

(Combines *preparation*, *product*, and *criteria*): After being introduced to the main concept, students will decide and state verbally whether they believe each of a set of examples is a law. Then, working with a partner, students will describe in writing at least three examples of laws not previously mentioned in class.

Materials and Lesson Aids

A humorous film clip featuring a bumbling police officer writing a ticket.

Enactment

Time Estimate	Main Ideas/Concepts, Questions, and Teaching Methods Utilized
Five to six minutes	*Hook.* Let's start the lesson by watching a film of something that happened on a street in Rock Island last week. Keep a close eye on the policeman. See if you can figure out what he's doing and why he's doing it (play a movie scene in which a policeman gives a man a ticket while a bank robbery takes place behind him). • Did this really happen on the streets of Rock Island? • What was the policeman trying to do? Why? • What was going on in the background? • What were the bank robbers doing? (Breaking the law!)
One to two minutes	*Student Aim.* This little scene leads us to the main focus of the lesson. What is a law? In the United States, we could define law this way (write on chalkboard): A rule of conduct laid down and enforced by a person or group with official authority and that carries some penalty for being broken.
Five to six minutes	*Development: Investigating Examples.* Teacher presents/discusses initial examples: Let's talk about some examples of that might impact our lives as citizens. • Why are all of you in school today? (allow multiple responses) • What would happen to your parents if they didn't enroll you in school? (list compulsory schooling law: children must attend school until the age of 16) • When you or your mom or dad are driving to the store, can they go as fast as they want to? Why not? What else do they have to do as they drive? (list traffic laws)

	• What do your parents have to do by April 15 every year? Why? (list paying state and federal taxes)
Seven to eight minutes	Challenge students to determine why each example fits the definition of law.
	Now, lets talk about why each of these examples fits our definition of law. (connect to critical attributes by comparing/contrasting examples; ask probes/redirects)
	• What rule(s) is involved?
	• What was this law intended to do?
	• Who was responsible for making this law?
	• What would happen to a person who breaks this law?
	**Discuss noncritical attributes through examples:
	the level at which the law was passed (federal, state, local)
	the body that enforces the law (local/state police, FBI)
	whether the law involves money
Four to five minutes	*Applying the concept.*
	Let's talk for a few minutes about some other situations that may involve laws. For each example, let me know whether you think a law is involved. (ask probes/redirects in discussing examples)
	• Obeying the "No Swimming" signs along the Mississippi River
	• Paying credit card bills on time
	• Giving money to charity at Holiday time
	• Seeking shelter during a tornado
	• Wearing seatbelts/motorcycle helmets
Eight to ten minutes	Place each student with a partner to generate new examples:
	Now I'd like to give you a chance to talk about laws with your partner. In the next five minutes, write down as many examples of laws as you can.
	Be ready to share your ideas with the class. I'll be around to help each group.
	Call on groups to share ideas; ask probes/redirects
Five minutes/as time allows	*Culmination.*
	Wrap-Up: Today, we've introduced laws—what they are and what they're designed to do.
	• Who can tell us what a law is? (review concept rule; use examples generated by students to illustrate each critical attribute; ask probes/redirects)
	Leap: I'm wondering what you would like to know about laws. Let's do a one-minute essay (hand out index cards). Please finish this sentence for me:
	When it comes to laws, I'm still wondering about_____.

Assessment and Evaluation

In a future project assignment, the teacher might ask groups of students to investigate the origins of national, state, or local laws of interest, with a special focus on how the laws originated, how they were enacted, how they are enforced, and how they impact the lives of citizens.

■ HANDS-ON PRACTICE ■

Try your hand at planning a deductive concept lesson, using this self-instruct planning sheet. Answering each of the following questions will help you think through each phase of the process.

Step One: Selecting a Concept

1. What is the name most commonly associated with your concept(s)?
2. What is the concept's rule or definition?
3. What are the critical attributes (i.e., essential characteristics) of the concept?
4. What are some of the noncritical attributes (i.e., nonessential features) associated with the concept?
5. What are some interesting, learner-relevant examples or cases of the concept that can be used during the lesson?
6. What are some contrasting nonexamples (if any) that will help illustrate the concept?
7. What are the most interesting, efficient, and thought-provoking media that might be used to illustrate the concept?

Step Two: Planning the Lesson

Now add the details to complete your lesson plan. Think about what you might say/do/ask during each phase of the lesson. Refer to the following template to remind yourself of the core components and method markers.

PRELUDE (for teacher reference)
- Rationale (with connection to national/state standards)
- Performance Objective
- Materials and Lesson Aids

ENACTMENT (student engagement)
- Hook
- Student Aim
  - Concept definition
- Development
  - Investigation of examples and nonexamples

- Application of the concept to new/problematic situations
- Culmination
  - Wrap-Up: What did the students learn?
  - Leap: How will they use these important ideas?

ASSESSMENT AND EVALUATION

- What will students produce to show you what they've learned?
- How will you evaluate this product?

PART 2:
The Inductive Concept method

Overview: Scenario Depicting an Inductive Concept Lesson

Focal Points and Discussions

What Makes the Inductive Concept Method Distinctive?

Inductive Concept Method Markers

Up Close: Planning and Conducting an Inductive Concept Lesson

When Should You Use the Inductive Concept Method in Your Classroom?

ROUNDUP

INDUCTIVE CONCEPT SAMPLE

LESSON PLAN

HANDS-ON PRACTICE

ENDNOTES

REFERENCES

■ OVERVIEW: SCENARIO DEPICTING AN INDUCTIVE CONCEPT LESSON

As a high school math teacher, Chuck Morgan's philosophy is to challenge his students to become mathematicians. In keeping with the vision put forth by the National Council of Teachers of Mathematics, Mr. Morgan consistently challenges his students to work through math-rich problem situations and to later apply what they've learned.

Today's geometry lesson is no exception. As Mr. Morgan's third period class begins, he flashes a scanned photograph of a modern downtown building on the large monitor in the corner of the room.

"I took this picture on one of my trips downtown last summer," the teacher begins. "What do you notice about this building?"

Students eagerly provide a range of responses. They note the color of the building, its huge size; Mia mentions "some unusual shapes" within the design.

"Great. Let's all take a look at the shapes that Mia pointed out. How would you describe these shapes?" asked the teacher. He receives a flurry of answers; students note straight lines, curves, connections between figures, different-sized figures. They begin to compare some of the angles within the various shapes. After many of these answers, Mr. Morgan asks probing questions that challenge students to expand on what they've said.

"Excellent observations. Keep these in mind as I show a few more pictures," continues the teacher. "Please tell the class what you notice about each." During the next five minutes, he displays several colorful pictures in succession: a close-up of the leaf of a tropical plant that includes some unusual venation; an M. C. Escher print; an intricate ceramic tile mosaic from a European cathedral. Mr. Morgan accepts three to four observations for each picture and asks a few probing and redirecting questions to pull new students into the conversation.

The teacher thanks students for sharing their observations, then he tells them, "Today, we're going to investigate some of the shapes that we've seen here to see what we can learn about them. We're going to work in groups of four. During the next ten minutes, I'd like each group to examine a set of figures that I've drawn on poster board." He holds up a set of 15 drawings, each on a six-inch square sheet, for the students to see. "Your challenge is to make as many observations of these figures as you can and to arrange them in groups based on their similarities and differences: how are they alike, and how are they different?" Mr. Morgan reviews the directions, and the students begin their investigation.

There is a hum of focused conversation in the room as the teacher moves between groups. He pauses to listen to the interaction, and he occasionally asks questions ("How are these two examples different, Carolyn?" "What do you mean when you say the angles are 'wide,' Dave?" "If you had to place these figures into groups based on their characteristics, how would you do it?"). After ten minutes, Mr. Morgan asks the groups to begin sharing their observations. The teacher lists these ideas and frequently asks follow-up questions. He then asks the class, "How did you group the figures, based on their similarities and differences?"

It turns out that some of the student groups had arranged the figures differently. Mr. Morgan asks each group to defend their system for grouping the shapes. One of the groups had categorized the figures based on whether they were open or closed; another used the presence or absence of curved lines as their main criterion. The teacher noted that each of their grouping systems made sense but that "for our purposes today, let's look at the way that groups 1, 3, and 4 arranged the figures. If we were to group the figures like this—" (showing the figures placed in three groups on a scanned slide on the monitor) "—what would you say are the main characteristics of the figures in this group?"

The students volunteer observations as Mr. Morgan lists the similarities provided. His questions become more focused as he challenges the students to closely examine the examples ("What does this figure have that this one doesn't, Emily?" "What makes this figure unique among all of the examples?"). Finally, he notes that the students have "discovered all of the important characteristics. Now, if you had to describe the figures in this group in one sentence, how would you do it?" Brian provides an initial response; Joanna quickly adds something to it. With the help of further guiding questions from the teacher, other volunteers define the figures in the first group as "closed, two-dimensional figures formed by line segments that connect only at their two endpoints, with no indentations inside the outermost boundaries of the figure."

"Does anyone know what a figure like this is called?" asks Mr. Morgan. A couple of students offer possibilities. The teacher lets the class know that such figures are known as *convex polygons*. The class is then able to define the figures in the second group, which Mr. Morgan labels as *concave polygons*. Mr. Morgan then tells them, "I'll keep you in suspense about the figures in this third group. We'll investigate them a little later in the course."

"Now, to learn a little more about convex polygons, I'd like to challenge each group to solve a riddle involving Pattern Blocks," says the teacher enthusiastically (the students had used Pattern Blocks before and were somewhat familiar with them). Each group is given a separate riddle (e.g., "There are eight blocks total. The three smallest blocks exactly cover the largest block. There are three different-colored blocks. Which blocks are in this bag?"). Each group has five minutes to solve its riddle. The class ends with Mr. Morgan asking the groups to describe in writing how they solved their riddle and what they discovered about their set of polygons as they worked.

Focal Point 1: What Makes the Inductive Concept Method Distinctive?

As young children, we learned some of life's most important early lessons by actively investigating the world around us. We all learned to walk, eat, throw a ball, communicate with others, and ride a bike through trial and error, doing something one way, observing the results, thinking about patterns, making adjustments, and trying again. In working through these learning experiences, we were actually using *inductive reasoning*, which we have defined as *the process of observing objects or events, recognizing patterns, and making generalizations based on observations*. In our opening scenario, Mr. Morgan challenged his geometry students to work through just such an active thinking process as they "discovered" convex polygons. Some of the most important lessons in your life have been learned inductively, and inductive reasoning serves as a foundation of all disciplines, particularly science and mathematics. For these and a number of other important reasons, we urge you to make inductive learning experiences regular events in your classroom.

Discussion 1: What Makes the Inductive Concept Method Distinctive?

In an inductive approach, students experience a number of examples and nonexamples and develop a pattern of critical and noncritical attributes (see Part 1 of this module) based on their experiences. Unlike in the deductive approach, teachers do not give students the concept name or rule at the beginning of the lesson. Instead, it is up to the students to generate (in a sense, to discover) the concept rule based on their experiences. For this reason, inductive lessons can be not only very challenging intellectually but also empowering and fun for your students.

At this point, you might be asking yourself, "Why should inductive lessons be regular events in my classroom?" We would argue for the frequent use of inductive methods for a number of reasons. As a teacher, one of your main tasks will be to help your students develop an understanding of important new ideas within your discipline. A constructivist learning perspective would lead us to believe that you can't simply tell students everything that they need to know. There is a mountain of evidence that indicates that students never truly understand much of what teachers tell them and that they forget most of what they are told within a short time. As teachers, we must provide students with every opportunity to grapple with new ideas, constructing meaning through the interaction of their current frames of reference and elements of the new experience. Inductive concept lessons can provide exactly this type of challenging classroom experience. You are pushing your students to think historically, scientifically, mathematically as they try to make sense of complex, problematic situations. Also, keep in mind that the interactive nature of inductive lessons allows us, as teachers, to gain insights into the meanings that our students attach to newly introduced ideas.

Most of us would also agree that teaching students how to think is more important than covering subject matter. Deductive and inductive concept teaching, when done effectively, can promote the development of critical-thinking abilities to a much greater extent than asking students to listen passively to teacher presentations or lectures. Although debate continues over the extent to which students might transfer such thinking abilities from one context to another (e.g., from a classroom situation to the real world, or from one discipline to another), experience has convinced us that students can apply inductive reasoning skills developed in the classroom to new situations. The potential for inductive experiences helping students to develop thinking abilities is perhaps the most important reason for their inclusion in the classroom. As educator Bruce Joyce once put it, "We need to (challenge students to) reinvent the wheel once in a while, not because we need a lot of wheels, but because we need a lot of inventors" (Joyce & Weil, 1980, p. 138).

Inductive methods are especially challenging intellectually because there is so much emphasis on the ideas generated by students themselves. We feel that another reason for providing frequent inductive experiences in the classroom is that they promote students taking ownership of ideas. Helping students to develop and later apply their own working definition for a concept such as *freedom*, for example, might help students not only connect with their personal experiences but also feel a sense of ownership of the ideas produced, a powerful educational and motivational factor in the classroom.

Figure 8.4 displays a planning template for an inductive concept lesson. As you take a look at the various stages, think about how Mr. Morgan followed such a path in his geometry lesson.

Focal Point 2: Inductive Concept Method Markers

You'll find that the features described in this section combine to make the inductive teaching method one of the most thought-provoking approaches that we investigate. As you explore these specific method markers, try to envision how inductive lessons differ from those that are taught deductively and what experiences an inductive lesson in your subject area might include:

- The Student Aim will be fairly open, indicating only the general direction the lesson will take. As the teacher, you will not define or even hint at what the concept(s) is during the early stages of the lesson. In effect, your Aim will challenge the students to discover/articulate the concept(s).

- During the Development, you will invite students to investigate examples and possibly nonexamples of the concept, making observations and looking for patterns. As the teacher, you'll facilitate this process by asking a sequence of broad trigger questions.

- By asking progressively more focused trigger questions, you will challenge students to name, define, and apply the concept later in the development.

- As in the deductive approach, the Culmination will include some discussion of the implications of the concept. Why is it important, and how will we use this "idea" in future lessons?

PRELUDE

- Rationale (with connection to national standards)
- Performance Objective
- Materials and Lesson Aids

ENACTMENT

- HOOK—Start with an attention getter that is somehow related to the concept. One option is to begin with an intriguing example(s) *of* the concept.
- STUDENT AIM—Unlike the Aim for a deductive lesson, your statement of purpose for an inductive lesson will be open, at times almost mysterious ("Lets see what we can learn by investigating these objects/events").
- DEVELOPMENT
  1. INVESTIGATION OF EXAMPLES/NONEXAMPLES
     a. Share examples (and perhaps nonexamples) of the concept with your students in either a full class or peer-group setting. When utilizing a more guided approach, tell the students whether each example is *positive* or *negative.*
     b. Challenge your students to first observe and then to compare and contrast the examples by asking open-ended questions (e.g., "What do you notice about these?" "How are they alike/different?").
     c. As students experience the examples, begin asking progressively more focused questions that deepen their analysis of the examples (e.g., "What do all of the objects/events in this group have that those in this group don't?").
  2. DISCOVERY OF THE CONCEPT
     a. Once your students have grouped the examples based on their critical and noncritical attributes (i.e., characteristics), challenge them to name the concept (optional) and to articulate the concept rule, based on these attributes.
     b. Question students to get them to "test" their concept rule (e.g., "Is this true for each/this example?"). When using a more guided approach, confirm (and possibly adjust) the concept rule generated by the students (e.g., "I would add this to our definition").
- APPLICATION
  a. If possible, elicit further examples of the concept from your students.
  b. To fulfill your Performance Objective, conduct a brief activity or provide an assignment that challenges students to test/use the concept.
- CULMINATION
  1. WRAP-UP—Review, or ask students to review, the main ideas generated. Again, focus on the "So what?" question: Why is this an important concept/principal?
  2. LEAP—How will we use the *big idea* that we've discovered today?

ASSESSMENT AND EVALUATION PLAN

1. Assessment products (What will students produce in this/a later lesson?)
2. Evaluation (How will you evaluate this product, e.g., with a scoring rubric?)

FIGURE 8.4 Inductive Concept Lesson Planning Template

Focal Point 3: ## Up Close: Planning and Conducting an Inductive Concept Lesson

In planning and conducting inductive lessons in our own classrooms during the past several years, we have been heavily influenced by the work of Bruner et al. (1967) and Taba (1966). Our suggestions for planning and conducting such lessons are based in part on their pioneering work.

In suggesting a series of stages in the Enactment section of inductive lessons, we'll make a distinction between guided and unguided approaches. In a guided lesson, the teacher exerts more control over the interaction by asking more focused questions and directs students toward a more precise, predetermined definition of the concept(s). You'll also see that there is no absolute boundary between the two approaches. In fact, we feel that it is more useful to think of inductive lessons as falling on a continuum from guided to unguided, with wide variation between. As we further describe guided and unguided induction, ask yourself which approach Mr. Morgan was taking in his geometry lesson.

Discussion 3: ## Up Close: Planning and Conducting an Inductive Concept Lesson

Prelude: Rationale

At this point, let's transport ourselves back to Mr. Morgan's classroom as we discuss planning and conducting inductive lessons in depth. In this geometry lesson, the teacher challenged his students to carefully analyze a set of examples to articulate a definition for convex polygon, a concept that they would then use extensively in this math course. The Rationale for his lesson could look like this: "Through the peer-group analysis of a set of geometric figures, students will articulate an appropriate concept rule for convex polygons and will later investigate this concept in more depth by solving polygon riddles through the use of Pattern Blocks. These experiences will help students develop abilities related to analytical thinking, critical thinking (as they share and defend their agreed on 'system' for grouping the blocks and consider other grouping arrangements), and group communication skills. This lesson connects directly to INTASC standards 1, 2, 3, 4, 5, 6, and 7." As we'll see in the following section, the Performance Objectives that you write for a lesson like this will be closely linked to your Rationale.

Performance Objective

Performance Objectives for inductive lessons usually link directly to the discovery/articulation or application of the concept. We would urge you to think carefully about what you might ask students to do to show you that they understand and can use the concept/concept rule. In his math lesson, Mr. Morgan challenged his students to investigate convex polygons in more depth by solving complex riddles involving their properties. His Performance Objective might have looked like this: "After comparing and contrasting 15 varied geometric figures, students will articulate an acceptable definition for convex polygons. In a peer-group setting, they will then solve at least one riddle involving Pattern Blocks, recording in writing how they solved the problem and at least five observations of the polygons involved." A Performance Objective like this clearly conveys how the teacher might assess what students have learned. As you plan your own inductive lessons, think carefully along these same lines.

Materials

Just as in deductive lessons, one of your biggest planning challenges in inductive lessons will be to assemble a set of concept examples/nonexamples that students can investigate. As you do this, think carefully about what physical objects, pieces of text, pictures, songs, and so on, exemplify important concept attributes. In conducting his geometry lesson, Mr. Morgan would likely have to create several sets of figures (computer graphics might help here) and assemble enough pattern blocks and write (or find in a resource) accompanying riddles. Again, this might sound like hard work, but the payoff comes when students are provided with an exciting, thought-provoking experience. Consider also that once you assemble a set of examples for a quality inductive lesson, chances are that you can reuse these materials in coming years.

Enactment: Hook

In inductive lessons, an intriguing possibility is to start the lesson by sharing one or more examples of the concept or principle, as noted in Part 1 of this module. If you choose to do this, we suggest being intentionally cagey about what you have in store in the lesson. You're merely inviting students to investigate something interesting and to share their observations or reactions with you and their classmates. Eye-catching science demonstrations are especially effective in this way, as are pictures, songs, poems, written or recorded speech excerpts, and actual objects (props). The possibilities vary as widely as concepts do. As an avid film historian, one of your authors is especially fond of using movie clips as Hooks for concept lessons. We have also enjoyed a great deal of success by asking students to perform and then analyze skits with subtle examples of the concept embedded in the lines (try writing such a skit for an inductive lesson).

In our opening math lesson, Mr. Morgan shared a series of interesting scanned photographs with his class and asked a series of open-ended questions about them. Not only did this introduce the central concept in an engaging way, but it also sent some other subtle but powerful messages to the class (i.e., this concept extends beyond the walls of our math classroom, and it might be worthwhile to investigate it).

Of course, you have a great many options in planning a Hook for an inductive lesson. For example, we have found that open-ended questions that somehow relate to students' experiences are very effective. But whatever you choose to do as part of your Hook, remember not to get too specific about what the examples are and how they relate to your main concept. Leave this open enough for the students to discover later in the lesson.

Student Aim

Your goal in inductive lessons is to challenge your students to analyze examples and in a very real sense discover the main concept/principle(s). It follows that your stated Student Aim for such a lesson should be open and indirect, especially compared with a deductive lesson. For example, Mr. Morgan simply told his class, "Today, we're going to investigate some of the shapes that we've seen here to see what we can learn about them." Such a statement can provide students with a basic feel for what you're going to do without directing their thinking to any great extent.

We have found that it's possible to lend a little mystery to inductive lessons by carefully planning the Hook and Student Aim. Most students seem intrigued by the openness of these lessons, and we have discovered that even learners who feel comfortable with more direct, deductive approaches will buy into inductive methods once they become a familiar part of your teaching repertoire.

A Student Aim like the one that Mr. Morgan used in his geometry lesson can serve as a nice transition to the heart of an inductive lesson: the investigation of concept examples.

Development: Investigation of Examples and Nonexamples

The key to designing an effective inductive lesson is to plan each phase of the lesson so that it builds on the previous phase, with each step gradually guiding students toward an understanding of the concept. A crucial point in any inductive lesson comes with the introduction of examples (and possibly nonexamples) of the concept or principle. Of course, the nature of your examples will depend completely on your main concept or principle, but the possibilities are just about endless. Anything, from sentences (as in an English or foreign language grammar lesson) to demonstrated dance steps to historic photos can serve as examples. When planning how and when to introduce your examples, ask yourself the following questions:

- Will it be most effective to introduce the examples in a peer-group or a full-class setting? If your examples consist of a set of objects or sections of text, and several sets are available (as in our polygon lesson), we suggest that you begin the example investigation in a peer-group setting, even for just a few minutes. This will allow each student to experience the examples and to share observations to the greatest extent possible (and you can circulate around the room, listen, and ask questions, as Mr. Morgan did). If your examples consist of film clips, a series of demonstrations, and so on, you will probably need to conduct your initial investigation as a full class, although you can ask students to share ideas regarding an experienced example in peer groups.

- Will you introduce examples one at a time, inviting students to respond to each, or can they investigate an entire set at once? Many of the same considerations that we mentioned in the previous point apply here. With demonstrations, video clips, or unique props, it's best to ask students to respond to a series of examples, one at a time. In this case, we suggest listing their observations on the board/overhead so that you might compare and contrast them later.

- Perhaps most important, what might you ask students as they investigate the examples? Remember that the inductive method is as interactive as any constructivist approach. This part of the lesson should feature a great deal of student–student interaction, especially if you are using a more unguided approach. You can set the stage for this interaction with the right sequence of questions. During this portion of the lesson, we suggest planning a broad-to-focused sequence. Start as our math teacher did by simply inviting students to share initial impressions (e.g., "What did you notice about ____?"). Move on to questions that focus on specific, important features (e.g., "Take a look at line 3. What do you think she meant when she said ____?").

As you write an inductive lesson plan, we suggest getting specific about the sequence in which you'll introduce your examples and the sequence of questions that you might ask throughout the development. Remember that in doing this you're not trying to script yourself; as you conduct the lesson, you may find yourself veering away from your plans, especially if a student raises an interesting point that's worth pursuing. But, in observing hundreds of student teachers over the years, we've found that planning the main trigger questions in advance has a huge positive impact on the quality of interaction in lessons. As a beginning teacher, you'll ask more questions, and better questions, if you plan in advance (see the sample lesson plans throughout this book for examples of this).

As this part of the Development unfolds, you as the teacher should guide the students (to some degree) with increasingly focused questions. Move the students from making general observations to analyzing specific features to grouping the examples based on similarities and differences. Then comes what we call the aha! moment in an inductive lesson: when your students actually discover the concept.

The Discovery

In a well-planned and well-conducted inductive lesson, your students will eventually reach that aha! moment. They'll connect enough of the pieces in the puzzle to recognize what your concept is and how it might be described in words. Your questioning will help them do this.

By this point in the lesson, your questions are becoming more specific. For example, after investigating the examples in peer groups and sharing and defending the various ways in which they had arranged the figures into categories, Mr. Morgan asked his students to take a closer look at the way that student groups 1, 3, and 4 had done this. He asked them about the main characteristics of the figures in these categories and then how the students "might describe the figures in this category in one sentence." As a class, the students generated the definition, with the help of further questions from their teacher; the key here is that the class arrived at the definition based on their analysis.

Note also that Mr. Morgan asked the students if they knew what figures like this are called; this is the kind of clinching question that you'll want to ask in an inductive lesson, perhaps even before the students articulate the concept rule. They may know the right label or term for the concept, especially if this main idea has some familiarity. The teacher may have to provide the words, as the math teacher did in our example (not many novice geometry students could have come up with convex polygon, to be sure!). Our advice here is to ask students to provide the right word for the concept, but be ready to supply the label, especially if the term is new to the class or especially technical ("We call figures like this _____").

Back to a question that we posed a few pages back: Was Mr. Morgan's lesson guided or unguided induction? In some respects, it's a trick question. We would say that the lesson is fairly guided, since the teacher determined in advance what the concept was, which figures were examples and which were nonexamples, and what important attributes should be included in the definition. But he did offer his class some latitude in deciding how the rule would be phrased; we have found that challenging your class to provide a working definition for a concept, as Mr. Morgan did here, can be very powerful educationally. Their definition can be used and tested in later lessons ("Based on what we know now, is there anything we should change in our definition of ____?").

One more note before moving on. Remember that you have discretion, as a constructivist teacher, over how much to guide any lesson, particularly an inductive one. If students struggle in their analysis of the examples, you can step in and ask more direct guiding questions. If their analysis takes off in exciting, unanticipated directions, you might back off and do less guiding than you had planned.

The development of any inductive lesson ends with some challenge to test and apply the concept/concept rule. In most cases, this is that point at which you challenge students to show you what they've learned, fulfilling the Performance Objective(s). In many cases, you can begin this application process by simply asking the class to brainstorm additional examples of the concept ("What else have you seen that fits our definition?"). Mr. Morgan developed a novel way to do this, inviting the class to solve engaging riddles in order to make additional discoveries related to the polygons. Remember that your challenge to apply the concept could come in the form of an in-class or take-home writing assignment or in something that takes place during future class sessions. One of your authors is particularly fond of ending class sessions with application-type questions for students to consider for the next day. Try this approach as a way to buy into your students' time away from your classroom.

Culmination

As in a deductive lesson, it's important in an inductive lesson to plan a wrap-up that conveys the importance of the concept. It's generally very effective to ask students to review the main ideas generated, at least partially, as a final check on their understanding of the concept(s). We would also advise either asking or telling the students directly why the concept is important and how they'll be using these ideas in future lessons (the leap). As always, inviting your students to generate questions that they have regarding the concept can provide you with insights into their thinking as well as guiding questions for future lessons.

As you can see, inductive lessons tend to be even more student centered than deductive lessons. The challenge is for the students to participate in an in-depth analysis of the examples and to (frequently) name and articulate the concept. As teachers at the middle school, high school, and college level, we have found inductive lessons to be incredibly challenging and empowering for students, and they can be a refreshing change of pace in any classroom. Inductive lessons are often more challenging to plan and conduct than are deductive lessons, but we have found that it is well worth the effort.

Assessment and Evaluation

Just as in a deductive concept lesson, a formal assessment and evaluation event could take place either in the application phase of the inductive lesson or immediately following this experience (see the sample lesson plan at the conclusion of this module for an excellent example of this). In Module 14, we discuss numerous examples of events that might be connected to inductive concept lessons. As you plan your own inductive lessons, we invite you to consider the many possible assessment products that you might challenge students to generate.

Focal Point 4 When Should You Use the Inductive Concept Method in Your Classroom?

It's important to note that, like any lesson, a concept lesson should not stand alone in your classroom. Lessons like these will serve to effectively introduce new concepts and to begin the process of analysis. Follow-up discussions and activities will provide students with additional opportunities to construct meaning for the concept and to connect it with other ideas. These follow-up lessons will be essential in developing a more complete understanding, so consider inductive and deductive lessons to be part of a series of classroom experiences. Use these methods frequently when introducing new ideas in your own classroom. Remember that concepts are the vital building blocks for high-level thinking and are particularly important in understanding the major principles in any discipline. Using these strategies may push you, as the teacher, to consider the most important themes, or big ideas, within your curriculum. This is a vitally important process, lest students become lost in the information provided in the classroom, losing sight of connections to their own world. Once introduced, major concepts can be used to help students make connections between important ideas. Inductive lessons are often challenging to plan, so a mix of deductive and inductive lessons is most realistic when planning time is considered. In thinking about students' preferred learning styles, using a mix of deductive and inductive methods will allow you to reach more students more effectively.

A GLIMPSE INTO A CONSTRUCTIVIST CLASSROOM

Ms. Wagner's sixth period U.S. history class has embarked on a unit focused on race relations and the Civil Rights movement. Students enter the room today to the sound of Bob Dylan's *Blowin' in the Wind*. They had analyzed the lyrics the day before, when they had learned that the song was written about the Civil Rights movement. The teacher starts this lesson by inviting students to listen and respond to video excerpts of speeches by Malcolm X and Martin Luther King Jr.; she asks them to compare and contrast the tone of the speeches and the content, and she lists students' ideas on the board. Minutes later the teacher challenges students to analyze video excerpts that include authentic footage of protests held across the South during the early 1960s. Ms. Wagner asks broad questions at this point in the lesson ("What happened in this scene?" "What were the people involved doing?" "Why do you think they did what they did?" "What is the response of the authorities?"), then asks the group to begin comparing and contrasting the events and to connect to comments made in the speech excerpts. The teacher then challenges the class to put the pieces together by asking, "How would you describe the approach used by the people who wanted to change things in the South?" With the help of further guiding questions from the teacher, the class develops a working definition for *nonviolent protest: an attempt to achieve desired social change through mass, organized, lawful, passive resistance designed to raise public awareness.*[3]

Tip for Technology Integration

Teacher- and student-designed computer programs can provide students with a medium for sharing their understanding of concepts. As a teacher, challenge students to complete such projects on systems that allow them to extend their understanding of central concepts.

■ ROUNDUP ■

Inductive lessons challenge students to investigate examples and nonexamples of a concept or principle, to analyze their similarities and differences, and ultimately to discover the main idea and articulate and test a definition for it. We consider the inductive method to be a quintessential part of a constructivist classroom. In effect, you're challenging your students to "become" historians, linguists, scientists, mathematicians, and so on, as they directly experience concept examples and develop and utilize critical-thinking abilities to make sense of complex situations. Done effectively, inductive lessons provide students with excellent practice in developing reasoning patterns, presenting and defending clear statements of position, and listening to and challenging the ideas of others. Our experiences have shown us that the frequent use of the inductive method can have an intellectually invigorating, empowering effect on students. We urge you to make frequent use of this method in your own classroom as an alternative to didactic teacher presentations.

Remember that there are several keys to conducting effective inductive lessons. Grab the attention of your students early in the lesson. Sharing an intriguing example or two of the concept early on is a good way to do this. Think carefully about what examples of the concept to share, in what sequence, whether the investigation of the concept should take place in a peer-group or whole-class setting, and what questions you might pose along the way. Remember to start with broad questions that will challenge your students to analyze the examples. Again, the real beauty of inductive lessons is that students are doing the thinking and discovering. Your questions should become progressively more focused as you guide students toward the concept; carefully consider how much guiding you'll do and what type of concept rule you'll want the students to articulate. Finally, consider how you might challenge your class to apply the concept during the final phases of the lesson, and in future lessons. Figure 8.5 summarizes the inductive concept method.

1 =   compare and contrast examples and nonexamples
of a concept or principle
from instructional materials

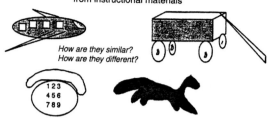

How are they similar?
How are they different?

2 =   establish characteristics of examples and nonexamples

Which attributes are constant?   Which attributes are variable?

mobility   human controlled   *materials   machines or animals*

nonexample

telephone doesn't carry a product or person somewhere else

3 =   guide student expression of the concept or principle

characteristics ⟶ $A = B$ Transportation is . . .

animate or inanimate   moves people and things

4 =   elicit student examples of the concept or principle

spaceships   *submarines*   with characteristics
camels   *elephants*

5 =   culmination: $A = B$ ⟶ ! ?

reestablish the concept definition with implications

transportation has shrunk the world   increases the need for fuels   delivers people and goods
increases peace?   changes the nature of war

©2001 Ina Claire Gabler

FIGURE 8.5 Inductive Concept Method Flow Chart

■ INDUCTIVE CONCEPT SAMPLE LESSON PLAN

Unit Title: Characterization in Novels, Short Stories, and Poems (intended for a high school literature class)

Prelude

Rationale

(Combines *What? Why? Justification*): Using a guided inductive approach focused on an analysis of two characters within the poem *Daddy* will allow me to challenge students to articulate broad, working definitions for flat and round characters that can then be applied to other written works as the unit progresses. This experience will enhance the group communications skills and critical-thinking abilities of my students, and it connects to INTASC standards 1, 3, 4, 5, 6, 7, and 8.

Performance Objective

(Combines *preparation*, *product*, and *criteria*): After completing a visual representation of one of the characters in the poem, students will explain elements within their drawings and support decisions made by citing excerpts from the poem. Then, after articulating definitions for flat and round characters, the learner will provide at least one example of each character type from a written work or film and defend that choice.

Materials and Lesson Aids

1. Copies of the Sylvia Plath poem *Daddy* for the entire class.
2. One piece of construction paper for each pair of students.
3. One set of colored pencils for each set of students.

Enactment

Time Estimate	Main Ideas/Concepts, Questions, and Teaching Techniques Utilized
Five to six minutes	*Hook.* • I'd like everybody to think about one of your favorite books or movies (pause) • Who were your favorite characters in the book or movie that you picked? (survey the class for ideas; ask probes/redirects) • Why did you pick this character? • Did you like/dislike this character? Why? • Does this character remind you of anyone that you know? Yourself? • How is your character like ____? • What did the author/film director do to introduce this character to you?
Three to four minutes	*Student Aim.* Today we're going to learn something about how writers introduce characters to us. I'm going to read a short poem to you. It's called *Daddy* and it was written by Sylvia Plath. The poem involves two characters, the narrator and her father. As I read the poem, try to imagine what each of the characters might be like, based on what the author tells us. ** Read *Daddy* out loud.

Eight to ten minutes

Development: Investigating Examples.
I'd like to challenge you to think about the two characters in the poem! You're going to work with a partner. I'd like you and your partner to talk about what you've learned about one of the characters. I'll tell you which one.

Then, I'm going to give you five minutes to draw a visual representation of your character. You can draw what you think the person might actually look like, or you can use symbols to convey something about the character. Be ready to share your drawing with the rest of the class (assure students that their drawings don't have to be artistically perfect).

**Arrange students in pairs; provide each pair with a piece of construction paper and set of colored pencils.
Potential questions addressed to groups:
- Do you like the poem? Why/why not?
- How did the poem make you feel?
- What's the significance of the title? How does the narrator feel about her father?
- Does she say anything that's confusing? Which line(s)?
- What did the author do to introduce the character to you?
- Why would you draw _____ this way?
- What does _____ in your drawing symbolize?
- How could you explain _____ when you share your drawing?

Six to eight minutes

Discovering/Defining the Concept:
Ask groups to volunteer to share their drawings. Ask questions, including those listed above; probe/redirect as groups share their ideas.

Guide students toward concepts through the following questions:
- How is _____'s drawing similar to _____'s? How are they different? Why might you see these similarities/differences?
- What does Plath tell you about the narrator? Her father? How does she tell you these things? (list student-generated ideas in "father" and "narrator" columns).
- Which character do you feel that you know better? Why?
- Which is better developed? Why/how?
- Which character seems more complex? Why?
- Which do you feel more emotionally attached to? Why?
- What devices does she use to describe the father? Do we ever really get to know him? (What is a stereotype? How are stereotypes used here?)

Five to six minutes

To summarize what we've done, what words could you use to describe the narrator character? (refer to list: complex/developed; know motivations; emotional attachment; less predictable)

- What about the father? (refer to the list: more one dimensional; stereotypical; more predictable)
- Has anyone heard the terms round or flat character before? Which might apply to the father? To the narrator?

***Challenge students to articulate working definitions of round and flat characters.

Five minutes/as time allows

Applying the concept.

Again, think back to a favorite book, short story, or movie. Pick a character from your choice. Is the character flat or round? Why do you think so? (get a range of responses from students; compare contrast examples; probe/redirect).

- Do you think that there might be degrees of flatness and roundness? Why?

Culmination. Wrap-up:

- What are some ways in which authors introduce us to characters?
- What are some purposes for which characters can be used?

Leap: How could you apply the concept of round or flat characters to your own personal experiences?

Look-Ahead: Tomorrow we'll start to explore a favorite short story of mine, and we'll use what we've learned about flat and round characters as we try to find meaning in the story.

Assessment and Evaluation

As a written assignment, ask students to choose a character from a favorite written work or movie. In a three- or four-page reflective essay, challenge them to describe the character based on what the author tells them and to label the degree of flatness or roundness of the character. Remind them to justify their choice by using the class definitions and using supporting evidence from the book or film.

■ HANDS-ON PRACTICE ■

Try your hand at planning an inductive concept lesson using this self-instruct planning sheet. Answering each of the following questions will help you think through each phase of the process.

Step One: Selecting a Concept

1. What is the name most commonly associated with your concept(s)?
2. What is the concept's rule or definition?
3. What are the critical attributes (i.e., essential characteristics) of the concept?
4. What are some of the noncritical attributes (i.e., nonessential features) associated with the concept?
5. What are some interesting, learner-relevant examples or cases of the concept that can be used during the lesson?
6. What are some contrasting nonexamples (if any) that will help illustrate the concept?
7. What are the most interesting, efficient, and thought-provoking media that might be used to illustrate the concept?

Step Two: Planning the Lesson

Now add the details to complete your lesson plan. Think about what you might say/do/ask during each phase of the lesson. Refer to the following template to remind yourself of the core components and method markers.

PRELUDE (for teacher reference)

- Rationale (with connection to national/state standards)
- Performance Objective
- Materials and Lesson Aids

ENACTMENT (student engagement)

- Hook (consider possible introduction of examples)
- Student Aim (open ended)
- Development
  - Investigation of examples and nonexamples
  - Discovery of the concept
  - Application of the concept
- Culmination
  - Wrap-Up: What did the students learn?
  - Leap: How will they use these important ideas?
- Assessment and Evaluation
  - What will students produce to show you what they've learned?
  - How will you evaluate this product?

ASSESSMENT AND EVALUATION

- What assessment products will your students generate?
- What criteria will you use in your evaluation rubric?

ENDNOTES

1. Thanks to Deanna DeBischopp, Augustana College Class of 1998, and Carolyn Carter, Augustana College Class of 2000, for their contributions to this scenario.
2. Thanks to Sarah Knoblauch, Augustana College Class of 2000, for her contributions to this scenario.
3. Thanks to Eric Turley, Augustana College Class of 1998, for his contributions to this scenario.

REFERENCES

Ausebel, D. (1963). *The psychology of meaningful learning.* New York: Grune & Stratton.

Bruner, J., Goodnow, J., & Austin, G. (1967). *A study of thinking.* New York: Science Editions.

Gagne, R. (1965). *Psychological principles in systems development.* New York: Holt, Rinehart, & Winston.

Joyce, B., & Weil, M. (1980). *Models of teaching.* Englewood Cliffs, NJ: Prentice-Hall.

Taba, H. (1966). *Teaching strategies and cognitive functioning in elementary school children.* San Francisco: San Francisco State College Press.

Introduction to Classroom Discussions

■ OVERVIEW

Constructivist classrooms are both ACTIVE and interactive places. As we've seen in describing a number of techniques and methods, constructivist teachers place great emphasis on what we might call *classroom discourse,* which is the respectful and purposeful exchange of ideas between teachers and students and among the students themselves. Such discourse is the focus in classroom discussions.

Focal Point 1 **What Is a Discussion?**

You may have noticed that *discussion* is one of those words that people seem to have vastly different meanings for. For example, there may have been occasions in your life when one of your parents has told you, "We're going to have a discussion about this," and then proceeded to do all of the talking while you sat and listened (this is a vivid childhood memory for one of your authors). Unfortunately, this is also what many teachers mean by discussion: a one-way stream of words from the teacher to the students. Our approach to discussions is much different. In fact, we'll define a *discussion as the verbal investigation or consideration of a question by a group of people.* Another useful way to think of a discussion is that it's *a conversation with a purpose.* In the three modules that follow, we'll introduce three distinctly different types of discussion methods: Directed, Exploratory, and Reflective. You'll see that each method is highly versatile but that each is characterized by specific goals, a specific type of structuring question and resulting pattern of interaction, and a specific conclusion or outcome. In this section, we present a brief overview of these three discussion methods and some of the general characteristics of discussions.

In planning discussions in middle school or high school classrooms, it will be important for you to first reconsider the nature of students' typical classroom experiences. As noted in Module 1, many students typically aren't used to classroom interaction. Most of their classroom experiences have consisted of a teacher talking in front of the classroom, with classmates listening (perhaps appearing to listen) passively. As a result, students are frequently docile, sometimes receptive to teacher statements, but not open to speculation. When using any discussion method, let the class know that you'd like them to participate, that it's a time to express opinions and contribute new ideas. You will see that in some discussions, it will be important to remind students of your critical-thinking ground rules (stay open minded as you listen to others and consider their ideas; support your statements with evidence or examples; criticize ideas, not classmates for having ideas; change your position when the evidence presented suggests that you should, and so on). In any case, it's often a must to let students know what kind of discussion you've planned. Teach them the differences among Directed, Exploratory, and Reflective discussions. This meta-awareness often motivates students because you are including them in the "inside story" (see Module 15).

Two other conditions must be met if discussions are to be effective. First, students should have an appropriate understanding of the topic to allow them to speculate and form opinions (again, beware of only air between you and your students). Quite often, their previous experiences will provide them with enough background information, if you can help them to make the right connections. Second, the classroom atmosphere must be thinker friendly, encouraging an open exchange of ideas. We'll continue to talk about ways in which teachers can establish this kind of environment. Relatively simple moves, such as altering the seating pattern, can often help.

Students can't be expected to discuss issues with which they are completely unfamiliar (one can't think in a vacuum). As a teacher, you will frequently have to furnish some type of prerequisite information, unless students have some experience with the issue/topic in another setting. We have urged teachers to investigate students' previous experiences when venturing into a fresh topic. A brief ILPE-type dialogue (see Module 7), either the day before or the day of the discussion, will provide you with insights regarding student experiences related to your topic and perhaps influence your choice of discussion method. You can also help ensure the success of a discussion by asking students to complete an interesting reading assignment beforehand, by conducting a lesson (e.g., a concept lesson) that will set the stage for the discussion, or by using a short presentation, a skit, a film clip, or an activity during the lesson Hook. Think about yourself as a student. Wouldn't a lesson Hook featuring an interesting video clip or a teacher-planned skit performed by classmates pique your curiosity and possibly make you feel more willing to participate? (See Module 3, Part 2.)

Focal Point 2: Establishing a Thinker-Friendly Classroom Atmosphere

The general atmosphere that you establish in the classroom will depend in part on the types of questions that you pose. As you will see, the nature of your questions will depend on the type of discussion being conducted and on your desired objectives. We discussed effective teacher questioning techniques in detail in Module 4. Effective use of Wait Time I and II, appropriate feedback, and clearly stated and challenging questions will promote meaningful discussions. Your patience will often be the biggest key. It's a challenge, but be sure to extend your wait times to the breaking point, especially when conducting highly student-centered discussions. Make judicious use of directed and redirected questions to get everyone involved. Be careful about asking too many questions or giving too much feedback in cases when student–student interaction is desired, as in Exploratory and Reflective Discussions. If you get too involved, students will continue to look to you for a comment rather than speak to one other.

We have found that the right physical setting can also promote classroom interaction. Arranging desks in a circle, giving students the opportunity to look directly at one another, can facilitate interaction. This often makes an amazing difference. Usually, it's a good idea to seat yourself in the circle of chairs, at eye level with your students, especially when conducting Exploratory and Reflective Discussions. If you stand over the group or position yourself in front of the classroom, students will tend to look to you for a response after every comment that they make. Students in any setting will not speculate on issues if they feel that they will be embarrassed by making an incorrect or half-conceived answer. Remember that your students must feel secure enough to take chances, and this will depend largely on your questioning and the response from you and their classmates (see Module 15). Practice playing the role of moderator when conducting discussions; provide a quick critique of the discussion to let students know how you feel about their progress. You may even consider what has come to be known as a "fishbowl" approach early in the school year to introduce discussions to your students. Ask a small group to take part in a discussion while the rest of the class observes and critiques the effort. Again, with certain groups of students, it may take several weeks of patience on your part before discussions start to click. Your reward comes when you begin to see reluctant students articulate and defend their ideas and ask you and their classmates intelligent questions.

The Nature of Directed, Exploratory, and Reflective Discussions

Let's first define a set of terms that we'll use in describing class discussions. The three discussion methods share five general characteristics. Each has certain distinctive goals, a structuring device, procedures for boundary maintenance, a desired communication pattern, and a culmination. In the section that follows, we compare and contrast the three discussion methods with regard to these characteristics before moving to a more detailed description of each approach in the next three modules. Don't worry too much about specific details at this point. Concentrate instead on understanding the basic terms associated with each of the discussions.

As you might expect, each of the three discussion methods will have different overall goals and a distinctly different feel. In short, you'll utilize different discussion methods at different times to accomplish different things. You'll see that Directed Discussions are appropriate when you wish students to analyze a challenging, focused question that does have a specific answer. You'll want to use the Exploratory Discussion method when you want students to brainstorm in response to a very broad question. The Reflective Discussion method is the choice when you want students to make and defend values-based decisions.

Structuring devices are questions, statements, quotations, situations, and so on, that are used to establish a framework for a discussion. They can be broadly or narrowly focused, depending on your objectives and on the type of interaction desired. Structuring devices are almost always questions; in fact, they are the main question on which the entire discussion is based. In Directed and Reflective Discussions, the structuring device is generally a question that obliges students to take a position and defend it, with the Directed structuring device much more narrowly focused. In Exploratory Discussions, a very broad structuring device challenges students to brainstorm in identifying alternatives, not to reach conclusions or defend positions. We will discuss structuring devices in more detail in each of the discussion modules.

The term *interaction pattern* is fairly self-explanatory. When we speak of interaction patterns, we are referring to the basic structure for verbal discourse that the teacher desires to establish for the discussion. In Directed Discussions, you're heavily involved in questioning and providing feedback, and the lesson will feature, for the most part, a teacher–student–teacher–student interaction pattern. Reflective and Exploratory Discussions include much more student–student interaction, promoted by broad questions and extended wait time. The term *boundary maintenance* refers to the degree to which you wish students to stick to the subject. In Directed Discussions, the focused structuring device and more frequent teacher input imply that students should stick closely to the subject at hand. Peripheral topics are usually not investigated, although they can be, especially when students generate insightful questions (again, we urge you to take advantage of the so-called teachable moments that come when students ask thoughtful questions). Reflective and Exploratory Discussions are more broadly focused, with teacher questions encouraging the investigation of peripheral topics.

The nature of culminations differs in each of the three discussions. In a Directed Discussion, students will reach a conclusion that you predetermine in some way. In essence, your students will be answering the structuring device that you pose. This conclusion is generally not value-laden, and it might involve the solution to a problem or a decision that is beyond debate or disagreement. In Reflective Discussions, individual students use their own knowledge and value system to reach a conclusion on an issue or question; the group may reach consensus, or there may be considerable disagreement. In Exploratory Discussions, students brainstorm to generate a list of pros and cons, implications, alternatives, and emergent questions, many of which you will not anticipate. In effect, the brainstormed list of ideas serves as the culmination. As we will see, brief or extended Exploratory Discussions can be incredibly useful as starting points for future lessons, with the teacher using ideas and questions that the students generate.

Use Figure C.3 to compare and contrast the three discussion types. As you experience and practice each method, remember that there are no absolute boundaries between them; much will depend on questions and ideas that you and your students spontaneously generate. At this point, start to consider ways in which you might use each discussion method in your subject area, and continue to think in these terms as we introduce each discussion method in detail.

Discussion Type	Nature of Discussion	Teacher Preparation	Nature of Structuring Device	Interaction Pattern	Role of Students	Role of Teacher
Directed	Structured investigation analysis of a focused question. Decision somewhat predetermined by teacher.	Lists points to raise and writes questions designed to help students understand each point.	Highly focused, provides a direction for interaction.	S ↔ S / T ↔ S / S ↔ S (arrows connecting)	Reach new levels of understanding by responding to focused questions.	Guide: poses a series of focused questions that help students reach new insights. Asks frequent Probes/ Redirects.
Exploratory	Brainstorming: investigation of 1) alternatives 2) pros and cons 3) Implications Decisions made by students.	Plans open-ended questions by anticipating possible areas of student response.	Extremely broad/ open ended, designed to *include* peripheral topics, alternative explanations.	T ↔ S / S ↔ S (cross arrows)	Free thinkers: generate ideas *and* new questions in an open setting.	Moderator: sets initial direction, asks occasional Trigger, Probe, and Redirected questions.
Reflective	Decision making: Investigation of a value-based question.	Plans potential questions based on implications/ issues connected to main question.	Somewhat focused: challenge students to make/ defend a *best* decision.	T ↔ S / S ↔ S (cross arrows)	Decision makers: struggle with debating a question that has no *right* answer.	Moderator: aids flow of discussion, challenges students to justify/ support decisions.

←——→ interaction strong in both directions
←—→ interaction less emphasized

FIGURE C.3 Classroom Discussion Methods

Module Nine:

The Directed Discussion Method

Overview: Scenario Depicting a Directed Discussion

Focal Points and Discussion

What Makes the Directed Discussion Method Distinctive?

Directed Discussion Method Markers

Up Close: Planning and Conducting a Directed Discussion

When Should You Use the Directed Discussion Method in Your Classroom?

ROUNDUP

DIRECTED DISCUSSION SAMPLE LESSON PLAN

HANDS-ON PRACTICE

ENDNOTES

■ OVERVIEW: SCENARIO DEPICTING A DIRECTED DISCUSSION

For the past two weeks, Ida Jackson's senior American and British literature class has been engaged in a unit on satire. They started by investigating a wide range of more recent examples of satire, from literary works to political cartoons, even excerpts from an episode of *The Simpsons*. As one of the newest teachers in the English department, Ms. Jackson is excited about teaching this topic for the first time. She recently told a colleague how happy she has been with the results of introducing more recent examples of satire first. "They've been a really effective hook for the rest of the unit," she noted cheerfully. One of her most effective lessons so far came early in the unit. Students inductively analyzed a series of text excerpts from satirical pieces and articulated a working definition of satire for the class: "A humorous and/or serious convention, intended for a specific audience, used to ridicule a particular person or situation for purposes of raising awareness or causing social change." The class has been using this definition as they have investigated other examples of satire.

The class is now in the process of investigating works from earlier historical periods. Ms. Jackson is determined to connect works of literature to events taking place at that time. To prepare for today's lesson, her students (most of them, anyway) have read Jonathan Swift's *A Modest Proposal*, as well as a brief overview that the teacher has written describing relations between Ireland and England during the early seventeenth century, as a homework assignment. As the second-period bell rings, Ms. Jackson flashes a recently published political cartoon (focused on school violence and gun control issues) on the large computer monitor in the front corner of the classroom. "What message do you think this cartoonist was trying to send the public when he drew this?" she asks the class.

Hands fly in the air as her students offer comments; school violence seems to be an issue that concerns these soon-to-be graduates. There is some debate among those in the class over exactly where the cartoonist stands on Second Amendment rights. For a few minutes, Ms. Jackson moderates a fairly heated discussion over specific features of the cartoon. A couple of students express some concern over the content of the cartoon. Monica pointedly tells the class, "I'm not sure it's right to publish a cartoon about such a serious issue that's supposed to be funny!"

"Monica raises an outstanding question," says Ms. Jackson to the group. "Should people use humor to express their opinions about serious issues? Is this justified?" Several students offer opinions, both pro and con. Ms. Jackson promises the class, "We'll focus on this issue specifically in tomorrow's lesson; it's an important question. And it certainly connects to the piece that we read for today, *A Modest Proposal*. What general reactions did you have to that piece?" The students' reactions range from "outrageous" to "funny" to "cruel" to "totally gross." "His suggestions don't sound all that bad to me!" says Brian to a chorus of laughs.

Ms. Jackson asks a few questions to check on the students' understanding of the history of the period, based on their reading of the overview. She then asks the class to "Keep these points in mind as we discuss *A Modest Proposal* in depth. It's a piece that most of us agreed is funny, that deals with issues like hunger, poverty, and homelessness, about as serious as issues get. Our main question for the next several minutes is this: *Who or what does Swift seem to be ridiculing here, and how does he accomplish this?*"

During the next 20 minutes, the teacher asks a sequence of focused questions that guide students through an analysis of the text. Ms. Jackson asks questions about specific passages that connect directly to the main question ("Why do you think he opened the piece this way?" "What point do you think he was making when he mentions admirable boots and fine gloves for ladies and gentlemen?" "Who or what was he criticizing in mentioning 'the papacy'?"). Slightly broader questions, such as "What is the significance of the title?" and "What is the intended audience for this piece, and how might they have responded at that time?" also elicit a range of responses from the students. Ms. Jackson asks numerous probing and redirecting questions; the focused nature of the questions results in a largely teacher–student–teacher–student interaction pattern.

Fifteen minutes before the end of class, Ms. Jackson returns to the main question: "So who or what was Swift ridiculing in this piece? And how did he do it?" Several students contribute to a summary of the points raised. "You did a terrific job analyzing the text!" says Ms. Jackson enthusiastically. "I want you to remember these points when we move on to writing our own pieces of satire later this week. Today, we're going to conclude by writing a one-minute essay in response to two questions: How does *A Modest Proposal* compare with other pieces of satire that we've seen? And would you change anything about our definition for satire, based on our discussion today? We'll share our responses when you're done writing."[1]

Focal Point 1: What Makes the Directed Discussion Method Distinctive?

Welcome back from Ms. Jackson's lit class. You have just taken part in what we call a Directed Discussion. Directed Discussions are designed to serve as highly interactive substitutes for more teacher-centered methods (e.g., lecturing). As the facilitator of this type of discussion, your main goal will be to utilize a sequence of focused, thought-provoking questions to guide students through a series of points in addressing a structuring device to arrive at new insights with regard to this main, guiding question.

Discussion 1: What Makes the Directed Discussion Method Distinctive?

Think about Directed Discussions this way: It's almost as if you're guiding your students up a complex, winding, wooded path, with a destination that is too far away to see from the start. You begin the journey with a major initial question. At each important point along the path, you ask a secondary question that will guide the group a bit further along. As you near your destination, students begin to put the pieces together; they come closer and closer to a more complete understanding of that big question. Then, daylight. You emerge at the end of the trail; you return to the structuring question, which the students can now fully address. They have met each of the intellectual challenges that they faced on the path.

Depending on how you plan them, you'll see that Directed Discussions can feel like very interactive concept lessons, especially if students are challenged to compare and contrast objects, events, pieces of writing, types of problems, or other examples. Directed Discussions can be planned to include deductive or inductive elements. There will be much less teacher input of new information in a discussion like this compared with a concept lesson. Again, your main goal will be to challenge your students to arrive at higher and higher levels of understanding through your questions (you'll be asking, not telling).

Remember that in a constructivist classroom, teachers will be challenging students to develop a deep understanding of new ideas almost every day. Using Directed Discussions is a thought-provoking, interactive way to do this. As the discussion leader, you will be guiding your students to new insights by letting them make the connections themselves rather than by spoon-feeding them predigested bits of information. This is a vitally important distinction. We'll see that topics chosen for Directed Discussion are usually focused and well defined, especially since, to a large degree, the conclusions that students reach will be somewhat predetermined by the teacher. For this reason, heavily value-laden topics are not appropriate for Directed Discussions because you as the teacher will play a strong leadership role, and you shouldn't be perceived to be pushing your students toward a certain values position (more on this in the following sections).

Take a few minutes to explore Figure 9.1, a suggested template for Directed Discussions. Remember that there are countless ways to implement each of our constructivist methods; in general, Directed Discussions will follow this path.

Focal Point 2 Directed Discussion Method Markers

Now let's focus on the features that make the Directed Discussion unique among the three discussion methods. We'll see that this is the most highly structured of our three discussion methods, but that the design of such lessons will challenge students to reach new levels of insight as they struggle (in a positive way) to address new ideas and thought-provoking questions.

- As you might expect, the Student Aim will be fairly structured and specific. After establishing the context for the discussion in your Hook, you'll establish the Aim by posing the structuring device as a question. Note that the structuring device is posed almost rhetorically at this point; this question will not be fully answered until you reach the Culmination.

- During the Development, you'll pose a sequence of focused secondary trigger questions that will challenge students to come to new levels of understanding with regard to a series of teacher-determined points.

- As students struggle (in a cognitive sense) with each of the secondary trigger questions, they begin to reach new levels of insight with regard to the main question (i.e., structuring device). The entire development features a teacher–student–teacher–student interaction pattern, with the teacher asking focused trigger questions and frequent probes and redirects.

PRELUDE

- Rationale (with connection to state/national standards)
- Performance Objective
- Materials and Lesson Aids

ENACTMENT

- HOOK—Your attention grabber should connect to the main focus of the discussion and should help establish a context for the lesson.
- STUDENT AIM—Statement of purpose for your discussion is conveyed through the initial posing of the structuring device (optional: display this main question on the board or overhead.)
- DEVELOPMENT
  - Pose a sequenced series of challenging, secondary trigger questions.
  - Students reach enhanced levels of understanding as they discuss each main point introduced by your secondary questions.
  - Probe and redirect to engage each of your students and to push student thinking to higher cognitive levels.
- CULMINATION
  - WRAP-UP—Pose the structuring device once again. Students can now *answer* the structuring question completely.
  - LEAP—How will they use/apply these new insights in the future?

ASSESSMENT AND EVALUATION PLAN

---

1. Assessment products (What will students produce in this/a later lesson?)
2. Evaluation (How will you evaluate this product, e.g., with a scoring rubric?)

FIGURE 9.1 Directed Discussion Lesson Planning Template

- During the Culmination, the students answer the structuring question as the discussion comes full circle.

Focal Point 3. Up Close: Planning and Conducting a Directed Discussion

Remember that Directed Discussions can last from a few minutes to about one-half hour, depending on a number of factors. From our opening scenario, you can see that Directed Discussions are highly interactive and can be among the most engaging of constructivist teaching methods. The teacher–student interaction pattern will allow you as the facilitator to ask literally dozens of challenging questions that can involve each student in the classroom. At this point, let's take a closer look at what it takes to plan and conduct such discussions, focusing closely on composing engaging questions.

Discussion 3: Up Close: Planning and Conducting a Directed Discussion

Prelude: Rationale

Once again, let's consider our opening scenario as we investigate the Directed Discussion method. Ida Jackson's ultimate goal is to challenge her students to carefully analyze the text of Swift's *A Modest Proposal* as a piece of satire and to consider just how this author used satire to criticize both people and institutions of his time. The teacher might have started her planning process by writing a Rationale like this: "Through the guided analysis of *A Modest Proposal*, students will apply much of what they have learned about satire to discover who and what one author was ridiculing during a historical period and how he accomplished this. This experience will enhance a wide range of critical-thinking and verbal communication skills, and it connects to INTASC Standards 1, 3, 4, 5, 6, 7, and 8." In the next section, we'll see how Ms. Jackson could use a Rationale like this to articulate her Performance Objectives.

Performance Objective

Performance Objectives for discussions usually describe how students might show you, as the teacher, that they can address the structuring device. Obviously, the statements that students make during the discussion can show you this. We would also recommend, whenever possible, that you ask them to produce something (e.g., a written statement) that will provide further evidence that they've learned something from the discussion. Ms. Jackson challenged her class to address two questions in writing, and she let them know that they would be creating their own piece of satire soon. One of her Performance Objectives might have looked like this: "After analyzing a recent political cartoon for content and intent, students will analyze and discuss who and what Swift was satirizing in *A Modest Proposal* and how he accomplished this. Students will then individually address two specific questions in writing in appropriate detail." Ms. Jackson has specified what students will do to show what they have learned from the discussion (and note that student responses to these questions could serve as springboards into a lesson tomorrow or later in the unit).

Materials

Although discussions can include activities, they are often less activity oriented than other lessons (e.g., concept lessons). The materials that you utilize for a discussion will often be used during the Hook or for reference as the discussion progresses. Our satire lesson is a case in point. Ms. Jackson used an interesting (and to the students timely) political cartoon, as well as her brief historical background piece and the text of *A Modest Proposal*. When thinking about materials you might use for any discussion, always consider providing something concrete (like a piece of text) that students can talk about.

Enactment: Hook

Our classroom experiences have shown us, time and time again, that an effective discussion Hook can make a world of difference. Intuitively, this makes perfect sense. You'll want your students to be attentive, truly interested in your topic, and willing to share their ideas about it in any discussion. Using a Hook that's unusually visual, funny, or controversial seems to work well for discussions. As you might expect, getting students involved as quickly as possible is a must. Breaking the ice early with some kind of interaction can set the stage for engaging discussions.

Although Ida Jackson's Hook (the political cartoons and accompanying questions) didn't connect directly to Swift's text, it offered a number of advantages. It certainly got the students' heads back into the topic (satire) effectively; it connected satire to a current issue (school violence) that they cared about; and it gave them an opportunity to debate viewpoints and raise questions. Students will raise important, insightful questions like Monica's if given these opportunities (this very question was raised by a student during the actual lesson on which this scenario is based). Our spotlight teacher took advantage of Monica's question to springboard into her planned analysis of the text. Look for opportunities like this when conducting discussions of any kind.

As in any type of lesson, we will also remind you that the sky's the limit when it comes to Hooks. Pictures, demonstrations, poems, quotes, newspaper headlines, intriguing problems, daunting questions, film clips, even jokes or a teacher costume can all accomplish your goals during this part of the lesson (see Module 3, Part 2). It needn't be elaborate or showy, but plan a hook that'll get 'em involved and get 'em thinking.

Student Aim

In each of our three discussion methods, the Student Aim is most clearly expressed by the nature of the structuring device, or main question, that you plan. Recall our definition for discussion: *the verbal investigation or consideration of a question by a group of people.* As this implies, this main question is really the heart of your discussion. We have found that planning for classroom discussions usually begins with the writing of an effective structuring device (as we'll see, the nature of the structuring device will dictate your choice of discussion method). Your structuring device, and what you say immediately before posing it, will convey to students not only the topic for the discussion but also the type of interaction that the discussion will feature. The structuring device will say a lot about what you will ask students to do in the coming minutes.

We'll see in Modules 10 and 11 that Exploratory and Reflective Discussions, which are highly student centered, feature open-ended main questions that allow students to move in any number of directions as they think carefully and share their ideas. The structuring device in a Directed Discussion is designed to begin a focused discussion, to a certain extent excluding peripheral topics and alternative explanations. Ms. Jackson asked her class "Who or what does Swift seem to be ridiculing, and how does he accomplish this?" This is a question that has some definite right answers and that establishes a direction for the discussion. Let's consider another example. The following three questions might be posed to begin a Directed Discussion in a history classroom:

A. What were the main causes of the Civil War?

B. How was the Doctrine of the States Rights a cause of the Civil War?

C. How was the Right of Secession a cause of the Civil War?

Which question would be the best structuring device for a Directed Discussion? Remember that the degree of focus in your structuring question depends on your goals in conducting the discussion. Question C is obviously the most focused. Question B or C might be appropriate for a Directed Discussion. Question A is probably not appropriate, since it is too broad and calls for students to make value-oriented decisions in choosing the main causes for the war. We'll see that such a question would be better suited for a Reflective Discussion, since it allows for greater student freedom to make and defend decisions based on individual beliefs.

The following questions might serve as effective structuring devices for Directed Discussions. The questions indicate the kinds of topics that are appropriate for a discussion like this. See whether they provide you with clues on Directed Discussion topics that might connect to the first units that you might be asked to plan.

1. How is the theme of _____ reflected in this poem/story?
2. Why does this type of collision provide support for Newton's First Law?
3. Given this information, how can we show that _____? (when completing a proof or demonstrating a problem-solving approach)
4. How does the study of logic lead to a better understanding of literacy?
5. Shown are two circles that intersect at R and Q. PQR is a straight line, and PM and PN are tangents to the circles. Prove that PM = PN.
6. How can we use limits/matrices to find _____ (e.g., the optimum price for product X)?
7. Which government policies helped to cause the stock market crash of 1929?
8. What changes in trading patterns should have been expected in the United States and Mexico after the NAFTA treaty was ratified?
9. Now that we know parental genotypes, what are the potential genotypes of any offspring?
10. How does the author use (literary element) in this story?
11. How has the artist used (light/shading/color/shape) to achieve a desired effect?
12. How did this person (e.g., Pythagoras/Britt/Balinsky) derive this theorem?
13. How do bones and muscles work together to allow your body parts to move?
14. How does the author use a _____ metaphor to convey meaning in this passage?
15. How are tenses formed in regular and irregular French verbs?
16. What can we learn by investigating the arrangement of colors on a color wheel?
17. What trash disposal method has been shown to be the safest environmentally?
18. What can the various symbols used in *The Great Gatsby* tell us about Fitzgerald's intended message?
19. What are the main differences between familiar and formal sentence structure in German?
20. What can these sculptures tell us about the artists and about the cultures in which they lived?
21. What can we conclude about the early and late works of Hemmingway by comparing *For Whom the Bell Tolls* with *The Old Man and the Sea*?
22. In Spanish, how are pronouns used to refer to prepositional phrases?

Again, how you phrase your structuring device can have a big impact on your discussions, so think carefully about what you'll ask students to consider. As far as the Student Aim is concerned, we would also recommend alerting students to the importance of this main question with a questioning preface. For example, Ms. Jackson invited students to "Keep these points in mind as we discuss *A Modest Proposal* in depth. Our main question for the next several minutes will be _____." In making this statement, she clearly emphasized the importance of the question, and she reminded the students to consider points they had already raised.

Development: Investigating the Structuring Device

You've planned that enticing structuring question. Now what? Once you have articulated the structuring device, decide what points you need to make to help your students reach an understanding of this guiding question; what will they need to know to answer the structuring device? Then, think carefully about what secondary trigger questions you might ask to enable your students to reach an understanding of your main points. In our satire discussion, Ms. Jackson walked students through a careful analysis of the text with a planned sequence of questions. She called their attention to the title, to the opening paragraph, and to especially interesting lines within various sections. Notice that her trigger questions weren't too leading; she clearly challenged the students to do the analyzing as they put the pieces together in coming to a better understanding of the guiding question.

In planning your secondary questions, it is often effective to relate the known to the unknown. Asking students, for example, to compare and contrast the conveying of tenses in French and English verbs, a familiar science process with a new one, or the elements of ancient and modern cultures can help them come to a greater understanding of the unknown.

Let's consider another planning example. Suppose that a United States history teacher had decided to discuss the Right of Secession as a cause of the Civil War. In planning this lesson as a Directed Discussion, this teacher should sequence focused questions that will lead logically to the idea that the Right of Secession was a cause of the war. Consider the following sequence of points that the teacher would want raised through questions concerning secession:

A. Sovereignty rests with the people, as stated in the Declaration of Independence.
B. The states represent the people.
C. The union represents the states.
D. Hence, the people, acting through their sovereign state government, can dissolve the union.

Each of these propositions could be expressed in question form, put by the teacher and considered by students. Each secondary question would require a significant amount of discussion before it was understood. When actually conducting the planned questions, the students exercise some degree of control over the direction of the discussion because the teacher cannot move to the next point until the answer to the present question is understood.

Ordinarily, you'll need to ask additional questions to help students understand your main points. These questions will include probes and redirects, as you continually check on the understanding of each student regarding each point in the argument. Also note that the questions asked in Directed Discussions involve both lower and higher cognitive processes. Many of the questions asked initially involve knowledge and recall. The entire discussion is directed at analysis and then synthesis in the collective insights offered by the class as a group. Responses to specific questions in the examination of the structuring device involve analysis as students sift through what they know to find justification for the assertions that make up the argument. The entire discussion, if well planned, will challenge students to think critically at each stage, as students move toward a deeper understanding of your main question.

Multiple examples can help illustrate each of your main points and can make your discussion interesting, relevant, and fun. "How is this similar to this?" questions are often a mainstay of Directed Discussions. For example, if Ms. Jackson's students had seemed confused at any point in the discussion, she might have asked them to refer back to a previously analyzed piece to aid their understanding of an important point. Remember that the key to a truly interactive discussion is to plan your main questions in advance. Since these discussions are fairly fast paced, it's difficult to articulate effective questions on the spot; you risk clumsy questioning and too much teacher talk if you don't think carefully about the questions that you'll ask. We also recommend that you direct as many as half of your secondary questions to specific students in the class and that you ask abundant redirects to engage as many students as possible in the discussion. On many occasions, we have observed teachers conduct Directed Discussions in which a few students provide most of the answers to the main questions. Don't fall into this trap.

Again, remember that your students do not answer the structuring question immediately. You will generally state (or ask) the structuring device rhetorically at the start of the discussion, and return to address it toward the end. The real learning in this type of discussion comes in the process of analysis that comes in answering the main and secondary questions. For example, a math teacher might pose the following problem: "Given this diagram and these conditions, prove that segments 'A' and 'B' are equal." The problem itself is entirely novel to students. Solving it will involve a student analysis of the situation, then sorting through knowledge associated with related experiences and a selection of various known definitions and theorems. As such, the overall problem involves analysis and application, yet experience shows that certain students may have the splash of inspiration that allows for a quick solution. If this should happen, you should conduct the discussion in such a way that the inspired student doesn't reveal the answer prematurely, perhaps allowing the student to play a large part in explaining the process (again, direct a large number of your questions to help prevent this). In this way, the rest of the class has the opportunity to engage in high-level thinking.

In addition, there may be more than one way to solve the problem, and the discussion may allow for investigation of alternative solutions. Students do leap ahead and lag behind. It will be important for you to diagnose which students are following your thought processes, and to what degree. When group members do leap ahead, take care to require students to make the logical steps that they have followed clear to others within the class, that is, ask students to justify their responses. Those students lagging behind will often catch up during the descriptive process that comes with the answering of your questions.

When you conduct Directed Discussions, remember that brief digressions from the main questioning sequence are useful at times for further developing your main argument or for providing illustrations or examples. We recommend that you keep these digressions to a minimum, lest the main points become lost in a more open format. As always, it's important to seize a teachable moment if a student raises an insightful question that you hadn't anticipated; discuss the question/point raised, but try to return to your main line of questioning. In addition, you may find that you have to digress to teach or reteach a certain point if students are confused, so your involvement in the discussion will depend largely on how the class responds.

At least two additional topics should be considered when planning Directed Discussions: pacing and teacher feedback. The pace of Directed Discussions should range from deliberate to moderately rapid. The questions asked do not as a rule require an inordinate amount of pondering, yet much more thought is required than in a drill-and-practice–type recitation. Extending your wait time will be important in this type of discussion, as always. If an answer is not forthcoming, redirect to another student, or break the question into smaller parts to simplify it. Occasionally, Directed Discussions break down because none of your students can make the next logical step in the argument. Again, you can help students over these sticky points with mini (two- to three-minute) teacher presentations or a series of simpler questions. Overall, the tempo for a Directed Discussion will usually be quicker than that for an Exploratory or Reflective Discussion.

We briefly discussed teacher feedback to student response in Module 4. To reiterate, one key is to recognize and sometimes complement correct answers without heaping so much praise on students that your replies are meaningless (side note: one of your authors once supervised an incredibly enthusiastic student teacher who gave students a cheery "Super!" after virtually every response. It didn't take long before students began to tune her out completely). Of course, not all responses will be correct. Some will be incorrect, some partially correct. For these answers, let your students know that part of the answer is correct, and tell them that part of the answer is incorrect. It is often advisable to initiate another question to correct the questionable portion of an answer without causing embarrassment or a loss of face to the student who offered the original response.

Truly insightful answers should be praised openly. Let students know why their answers are excellent (or even super). Again, encouraging students to make their thinking process explicit and to discuss these processes is an effective way to help them develop critical-thinking skills. In general, feedback that is explicit and moderately positive will encourage participation and will contribute to the social atmosphere of any classroom.

In conclusion, pacing and teacher feedback are important to the success of Directed Discussions. Keep the tempo fairly quick. Reinforce answers in a positive way, and let students know why certain answers are partially incorrect, correct, or outstanding. Take care that confusion does not occur regarding what aspects of student answers are acceptable.

Again, note that because teachers play a strong leadership role in Directed Discussions, this method is not appropriate for coming to decisions on value-laden issues. In our society, individuals are free to value what they wish. Never put your students into the position of being railroaded into a values position that they find repugnant. Such issues are better saved for a more open (Exploratory or Reflective) Discussion in which students can present and defend a values position of their choice.

Remember that the development of a Directed Discussion features the use of a planned sequence of questions in the consideration of a structuring device, and the utilization of probing and redirecting questions in involving everyone in higher-level cognitive processes. Be careful about the introduction of tangential topics unless they are closely related to the issues at hand. If a student interjects with a truly insightful question, be sure to address it, but attempt to keep this kind of discussion focused.

Culmination

You've conducted your first Directed Discussion. During its development, your students have raised a number of thought-provoking points as they addressed your secondary questions. What do you do to bring the discussion to an effective close? Challenge students to return to and answer your structuring device. Restate your major question and ask your students to put the pieces together as they provide a detailed class response. We recommend involving a number of students in this wrap-up process. Use probes and redirects that will challenge the group to respond fully.

You should also reiterate the importance of the lesson by reviewing how these ideas connect to your main unit focus, to topics or ideas discussed earlier in the course, and/or to important events taking place beyond the walls of the school. This process could include a review of ideas introduced in past lessons and/or a preview of future lessons. As in the leaps that you might plan for any lesson, it is often incredibly effective to leave students with a question to think about for next time. Whenever possible, challenge your students to extend their thinking outside of your classroom. Try to buy into their time away from your classroom.

In meeting your Performance Objective at some point in the Culmination, challenge your students to apply what they've learned during the discussion. Can they write a sentence or paragraph, or participate in a conversation, using their new knowledge of Spanish pronouns, for example? As time allows, or the next day/class session, challenge your students to put their new insights to work.

Assessment and Evaluation

There is a wide range of possibilities for both informal and formal assessment events in connection to Directed Discussions. These discussions provide you with multiple opportunities to listen to student responses, comments that can provide valuable insights on their thinking. For example, think about Ms. Jackson's satire lesson. Throughout the discussion, her students are revealing their thoughts not only regarding *A Modest Proposal* but also about both historical and current events connected to this general topic. It is possible (even desirable) to use discussions as a springboard for research projects and other assignments (we discuss such options in Module 14). As with any constructivist lesson, think about what you might ask students to produce during or after your Directed Discussions to show you what they have learned and how they might apply their new knowledge.

Focal Point 4: When Should You Use the Directed Discussion Method in Your Classroom?

The Directed Discussion is one of the most versatile teaching methods that we will introduce in this book. Since the teacher has an opportunity to introduce and encourage discussion of new ideas, and students interact with both the teacher and each other, this type of lesson is a welcome alternative to a straight teacher lecture in any subject area, from art to calculus. This kind of discussion is valuable when used in conjunction with activities and demonstrations as well, as it allows you to walk students through a process, questioning them at each step. As a result, you'll find that Directed Discussions can be used at any point in a unit, from beginning to middle to end. They also serve well in applying and reviewing previously introduced ideas, as the suggested structuring devices described imply. Discussions of this type are useful in helping students review for an exam or a quiz and in summarizing and connecting the main points generated in a concept lesson, interactive presentation, or activity. As a result, your Directed Discussions might vary in time span from five to thirty minutes, depending on when they are used.

At this point, it is important to start to visualize what your fifty-minute (or longer) class period might look like (we'll expand on this when we discuss unit planning in Module 13). Based on what you've learned about learning, it should be obvious that you, as the teacher, cannot lecture for fifty minutes (or more than ten minutes) without the risk of losing (and probably boring) most of the students in your classroom. All students need the opportunity to process the new ideas that you will introduce, and this is difficult if they are consistently in the role of passive listener. During each class period, allow your students to apply, analyze, and, in general, reflect on what they've learned. As one example, you might begin with a concept lesson, move into a peer-group activity, and end the period with a brief Directed Discussion. In this way, each of your students will be given some opportunity to consider important new ideas. Such variety in methods will be especially important if you are teaching in a setting that features block scheduling and class periods of eighty to ninety minutes. As you might imagine, providing different kinds of settings for cognitive processing will have a number of advantages in terms of reaching students with diverse preferred learning styles and previous experiences. As with every method that we'll introduce, our general advice is not to overuse Directed Discussions, even though the method is so versatile. Give your students frequent opportunities to participate in more open discussions (i.e., Exploratories and Reflectives) and activities that allow them even greater freedom to direct the interaction, express their own views, and generate their own questions. Keep our general advice in mind: use a wide variety of methods to connect with the diverse learners in each class.

A GLIMPSE INSIDE A CONSTRUCTIVIST CLASSROOM

Mr. Nelson's European History class has been investigating life in the Middle Ages. The unit has included a look at the sometimes mythical world of castles, quests, crusades, knights, and ladies of the court and has incorporated multiple connections to literature. But the teacher is also determined to promote an understanding of the actual living conditions of the time. The class enters the room today to the sound of monks chanting; as the bell rings, their teacher appears, dressed in a monk's robe. He reads an authentic (and somewhat terrifying) account of the Black Death, written by a witness in the thirteenth century. Mr. Nelson then poses the structuring device for the discussion: "How did the Black Death spread to kill 25% of Europe's population?" The teacher then asks a series of focused secondary questions, many of which challenge students to apply what they had recently learned: How would you describe living conditions in a typical medieval city at this time? How would you describe the sanitation? What would garbage and rotting food attract? What parasites do rats and other mammals often carry? (Here the teacher shares a microscopic picture of a flea, to multiple "yuks" from the class.) What main foods consumed by people at that time would the rats be attracted to? How else could fleas spread disease to humans? How would the city population respond to the spread of the death? As the students respond to (and sometimes debate) answers to the questions, Mr. Nelson writes agreed on responses on the board. Twenty-five minutes after reading the account of the Black Death, Mr. Nelson once again asks the structuring question, and the students review the sequence of conditions and events that led to the rapid spread of the Black Death.[2]

Tip for Technology Integration

Programs such as HyperStudio and PowerPoint can be used to enhance the visual quality of Directed Discussions. We have integrated (and observed other teachers integrate) these programs by using them to display the structuring device and secondary questions on large monitors visible to the entire class. Then, as points are introduced through the discussion, the teacher can list these below each secondary question. The advantages? The visual display of the questions can include color and motion; the discussion can be further enhanced by the display of pictures, maps, and even video clips.

■ ROUNDUP ■■

Directed Discussions are used to develop an argument or point of view. They are initiated with a focused, convergent structuring question that is posed during the Student Aim. The teacher then asks a series of focused secondary questions that challenge students to come to an enhanced understanding of a number of secondary points. Have your main and secondary questions written into your lesson plan, ready to develop the argument. There may be times when you won't use all of these questions, but have them ready just in case. As with each of the methods we will introduce, we provide you with a sample lesson plan that will illustrate the kind of sequential questioning that is part of planning a directed discussion.

The boundaries of Directed Discussions are largely maintained by sticking to the predetermined set of key questions that form the framework for the argument being developed. The basic communication pattern is teacher–student, but student–student interaction is often fruitful in developing the argument. As always in a constructivist classroom, allow student-initiated digressions if you feel that valuable points are being made. Directed Discussions are concluded by restating the structuring question and reviewing the key points (remember that this reviewing can be done by you or your students). Try to avoid pressing for the resolution of value-laden issues in a discussion like this, since students may feel that they are being pushed into positions that they may find objectionable.

We feel that there are several keys to conducting effective Directed Discussions. Obviously, an interesting topic and an engaging structuring device are vital. Plan your structuring device and secondary questions carefully. Make these questions thought provoking without being leading; as in each of the constructivist methods that we introduce, your ultimate goal will be to challenge your students to do the thinking rather than you as the teacher providing them with bits of information. Also consider each of our earlier recommendations for effectively questioning students; this type of discussion is as interactive as any method you'll ever use, and asking thought-provoking questions and encouraging interaction will be crucial. As we discuss in Module 15, it will take time for your students to warm up to discussions of any kind. Be patient when conducting your first classroom discussions. See Figure 9.2 for an overview of the directed discussion method.

1 = structuring device: question as Aim

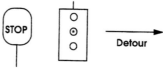

2 = questions elicit predetermined main points in instructional materials

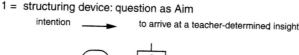

3 = compare and contrast main points

elicit, do not tell, predetermined insight based on compare and contrast of main points

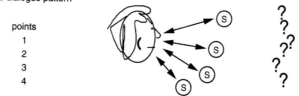

4 = culmination: students answer structuring device question

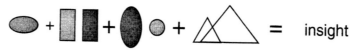

FIGURE 9.2 Directed Discussion Method Flow Chart

■ DIRECTED DISCUSSION SAMPLE LESSON PLAN

Unit Title: Weather and Climate (intended for a high school physical science class)

Prelude

Rationale

(Combines *What? Why? Justification*): By challenging students to analyze and compare and contrast three demonstrated science phenomena, I will create an opportunity to help students to understand air pressure and its impact on living and nonliving things in a challenging, interactive way. This experience will help students develop their ability to reason scientifically, and it connects to INTASC standards 1, 2, 4, 5, 7 and 8.

Performance Objective

(Combines *preparation, product,* and *criteria*): After observing each phenomenon, students will articulate at least five observations related to each event. Then, after comparing and contrasting the events, students will verbally describe the related causes for each phenomenon and will cite at least three additional examples of the effects of air pressure on living and nonliving things.

Materials and Lesson Aids

1. hot plate
2. three or four empty pop cans
3. bowl of ice water
4. candles
5. water tray
6. large and small glass jars/glasses
7. matches
8. two flasks
9. a hard-boiled egg
10. three balloons

Enactment

Time Estimate	Main Ideas/Concepts, Questions, and Teaching Methods Utilized
Eight minutes	*Hook.* • Who can tell us what an observation is? (possible answer: using the senses in perceiving an object or event) • I'm going to start this lesson by asking you to observe something. Watch closely as I place a jar over this burning candle. (candle/tumbler demo)

- What observations can you make? What did you see/smell/hear/feel? (list observations; possibilities include candle went out, smoked; water filled glass; glass felt hot)

Three minutes

Let's watch a second event and compare it with what you just saw!

I've been heating a pinch of water in these cans. (three or four cans placed on a hot plate)

- What do you predict will happen if I pick up a can and turn it upside down in water? (probe; get students to justify predictions)
- Let's try it. Make as many observations as you can. (can demo)
- What did you see/smell/hear/feel? (list observations)
- Anyone surprised?
- Possible observations: can was crushed quickly; can cooled down; water filled can; sound of can crushing

Ten to twelve minutes

Student Aim: Posing Structuring Device as a Question.
I'd like to address an important question in the next few minutes: How can we explain these two events?

Development: Addressing the Structuring Device Through Sequence of Focused Questions.

- First of all, how are these two events similar? How are they different?

Similarities	Differences
* heat involved	* can crushed; glass wasn't
* air heated	* different heat source (flame)
* water moved	* water cold in second
* bubbles from can/glass	
* temperature extremes	

- Does anyone think that they have an explanation for what happened? A hypothesis? (list student explanations)
- Does air have weight? How do you know? (balloon example)
- How much air is above us? (about 600 miles!)
- What impact does all of that air have on the earth's surface?

List Conclusions as They're Reached.
1. We live at the bottom of an ocean of air.
2. The air above us presses down on anything on the earth's surface (air pressure).

- What happens to air when it's heated? (it expands; flask/balloon demo)
- What happened to the air in the glass, and in the can, when it was heated?

- How do we know that some of the air escaped? (the bubbles)
3. Heated air expanded in can/glass; some air escaped.
- What happened to the air in the glass when the flame went out? How about when the can hit the ice water?
4. Cooling air contracted in can/glass.
  - WHY DID THE WATER MOVE INTO THE GLASS? THE CAN? (extend wait time; allow for multiple responses)
  - What role did air pressure play in these events? What did the air pressure do to the can?
5. Air pressure pushed water into the glass/can and crushed the sides of the can.

Three minutes

Culmination: Revisit the Structuring Device.
Wrap-Up: Knowing what we now know, how could we explain these two events? (encourage students to explain both events; account for similarities and differences)

Three minutes

Leap: Can you think of other ways that air pressure impacts us on the earth's surface? (encourage students to share examples)

We've seen that the weight of this ocean of air affects us in many different ways. I'm going to leave you with one more example: think about why this happens:

EGG/FLASK DEMO (light a match, quickly drop it into a flask, cover the flask with a hard boiled egg)

Assessment and Evaluation

For tomorrow, write a one- or two-page reaction paper explaining why you think the egg moved into the flask.

■ HANDS-ON PRACTICE ■

Plan a Directed Discussion by using the following template. Refer to Module 3 for a look at the Core Components of a lesson plan, and review Module 9 for detail on this type of discussion.

PRELUDE (for teacher reference)
- Rationale (with connection to national/state standards)
- Performance Objective (remember to be specific about what your students should be able to do to show you what they've learned)
- Materials and Lesson Aids

ENACTMENT *(student engagement; what might you say/do/ask at each stage of the lesson)*

- Hook
- Student Aim
  - Initial posing of the structuring device. How will you phrase this main question?
- Development
  - Student consideration of a sequence of trigger questions helps them understand a series of important points. What are the main points that they'll need to discuss?
  - How will you phrase each of these secondary questions?
- Culmination
  - Wrap-Up: What will you say/do/ask to help students answer the structuring device?
  - Leap: How will students use/apply these ideas in the future?

ASSESSMENT AND EVALUATION

- What will you ask students to produce during/after the lesson to show what they've learned?
- How will you evaluate this product?

ENDNOTES

1. Thanks to Joanna Kluever, Augustana College Class of 2000, for her contributions to this scenario.
2. Thanks to Creston Fenn, Augustana College Class of 2002, for his contributions to this scenario.

Module Ten:

The Exploratory Discussion Method

■ OVERVIEW: SCENARIO DEPICTING AN EXPLORATORY DISCUSSION

As a high school science teacher, John Rizzi believes, first and foremost, in challenging his students to "do" science. During their ecology unit, for example, his biology students undertook an authentic investigation of a nearby pond and stream, completing a detailed chemical analysis of the water and studying the organisms native to both habitats. Later in the unit, they have begun to apply ecological concepts they have learned to understand the interactions of living things in these and other ecosystems. Taking an interdisciplinary approach, Mr. Rizzi believes, makes these experiences more meaningful and impacting to his students. As they have investigated the influence of human activities on the biosphere, the teacher has integrated literature, songs, and poetry with their experiences, and he has challenged students to take a close look at (and possibly change) their own lifestyles in light of what they've learned.

On this Wednesday morning, Mr. Rizzi's third-period Biology I students enter the room to the strains of a song called *Out in the Country*, recorded by the rock group Three Dog Night in the early 1970s. The teacher invites his students to "listen for clues as to how the song's writer feels about the natural world." As the song ends, he invites students to share their thoughts on the lyrics. Many share environmental concerns that they have expressed during previous lessons, concerns that they felt were reflected in the song. Some of the comments are remorseful. In others, the teacher senses an admirable kind of let's take action spirit that he finds in many of today's students.

"We're almost finished with our ecology unit, and I'd like to give everyone a chance to apply some of what we've learned to our lives today," Mr. Rizzi tells the class. "I'm going to invite all of you to go back in time for a few minutes. The year is 1854. The U.S. government has made an offer to a Native American tribe in what is now Washington state to buy tribal land. The tribe's Chief Seattle has written a formal reply to the people of the United States, which I'd like to read to you now. As you listen, you might want to close your eyes and see what images come to mind as you hear his words."

With that, the teacher begins to read the haunting verses of the document that has come to be known as *Chief Seattle's Reply*. For the next three minutes, there is an unusual hush in the normally busy room as the students listen. They are seated in a large circle; some are looking at classmates, many have closed their eyes as the teacher invited them to do. Mr. Rizzi reaches the end of the text, and changes his tone slightly as he says, "Back to the present day. I'd like to invite you to share your ideas about what we just heard. We're going to have an open, Exploratory Discussion. Feel free to reply to each other; there's no need to raise your hands. I'd also encourage you to focus on specific comments made by Chief Seattle in his reply" (he passes copies of the text around the circle of students). "Our main question is this: *As American citizens living at the start of a new century, what can we learn from the words of Chief Seattle?*"

It doesn't take long for the exchange of ideas to begin; at the outset, a few of the more outspoken students offer comments, but then others join the conversation. Mr. Rizzi, who has taken a seat within the circle of chairs, is silent for the first few minutes as he inconspicuously records student comments on an overhead sheet. Many of the initial comments are fairly broad ("His people seem so much closer to nature." "Their pace of life is so much different!"). Students begin to build on each other's comments; when Luke mentions, "His people seem to have a whole different set of values," Michelle asks him what he means, and Kristin and Jeff jump in with examples. Amy mentions Chief Seattle's use of the word "savage." "I think he's mocking us when he says he's a savage," she says confidently.

"I've always wondered exactly what he means when he says that," relates Mr. Rizzi. "What do others feel about what he means when he uses the term 'savage'?" A number of students offer opinions. Some agree with Amy. Others offer the opinion that he has a completely different meaning for the word. "He's actually proud of the fact that he's a savage!" states Ken at one point.

Mr. Rizzi nudges the discussion in a related direction by asking "What view of the role of technology do people in the two cultures have?" Immediately, Nate says, "People in our culture have tended to rely on technology too much, and it gets us into trouble." A number of students share opinions on this and offer examples. "It makes you wonder what 'progress' really is!" states Laura at one point.

"The scary thing about this is that he's telling us what our future will be!" offers Diana in a somber tone.

"What predictions does he make, and are they accurate?" asks the teacher. Students mention a number of specific passages; as a final question, the teacher asks, "How do you think he might feel if he could see his land today?" The student replies seem heartfelt.

"Excellent discussion!" offers Mr. Rizzi. "I'd like to recap some of the ideas that you've shared" (he does this briefly as he turns on the projector and displays the notes he has taken on the overhead sheets). "*Chief Seattle's Reply* has had a big impact on my life. He urges us to teach our children that the earth is their mother. In the last ten minutes of class time today, I'd like you to meet in your regular lab groups to consider two questions: How can we teach future generations that the earth is their mother? And what would you be willing to change about your own way of life in the future as a result of hearing Chief Seattle's words?"

Focal Point 1: What Makes the Exploratory Discussion Method Distinctive?

A quick question as we begin our look at a second discussion method. How is the discussion that Mr. Rizzi conducted different in form from Ms. Jackson's discussion of satire?

Some of these differences will jump right out at you. The nature of the questions asked by the teacher is vastly different in the two discussions. The Exploratory Discussion is perhaps the most student centered of our discussion methods. When you think Exploratory Discussion, think brainstorming or freethinking, with a definite purpose. In Exploratories, students respond to an extremely open, broad Structuring Device (question); they have wide latitude in determining the direction of the discussion and in deciding just how the structuring question should be addressed. For these reasons, we have found Exploratory Discussions to be highly empowering for students who are used to being told what and how to think by teachers. The format allows students to use their imagination and creativity as they share and comment on one another's ideas.

Discussion 1: What Makes the Exploratory Discussion Method Distinctive?

The ultimate goal in most Exploratory Discussions is for students to identify alternatives in responding to the main, structuring question. An Exploratory Discussion might be used to identify alternate methods for solving a problem, explaining an event, or interpreting a piece of literature or artwork. Exploratory Discussions differ from the other two types in that no true resolution to the structuring question is necessary; the list of pros and cons, alternatives, implications, or ideas/suggestions is considered the resolution. These discussions are often used to begin a series of lessons or to challenge students to apply new ideas after a series of classroom experiences. As we will see, Exploratories provide teachers with a valuable tool for gaining insights into student experiences related to a new topic and for connecting elements within the topic to events relevant in students' lives.

Figure 10.1 displays a suggested template for planning Exploratory Discussions. This will provide you with a global feel for the stages in these discussions. As you look

---

PRELUDE

- Rationale (with connection to national standards)
- Performance Objective
- Materials and Lesson Aids

ENACTMENT

- HOOK—As an option, couple your attention grabber with the structuring device
- STUDENT AIM
  - Structuring device preface (i.e., set up/contextualize the main question)
  - Pose the structuring device as a question
- DEVELOPMENT
  - Students brainstorm in response to the structuring device
  - Teacher facilitates discussion with wait time, secondary questions
- CULMINATION
  - Wrap-up—Students/teacher recap ideas generated
  - Leap—How will they use/apply these ideas in the future?

ASSESSMENT AND EVALUATION PLAN

1. Assessment products (What will students produce in this/a later lesson?)
2. Evaluation (How will you evaluate this product, e.g., with a scoring rubric?)

FIGURE 10.1 Exploratory Discussion Lesson Planning Template

over the template, think about how Mr. Rizzi might have gone about planning each phase of his lesson.

Exploratory Discussion Method Markers

These method markers make Exploratory Discussions unique, and they will help provide you with an initial schema for planning and conducting them. Of the three discussion methods, you'll see that Exploratories are the most unstructured, but they do have a definite purpose and direction.

- The Student Aim conveys the general direction of the discussion. Once you establish a context for the discussion in your Hook, you'll convey the student aim by posing an extremely broad, open-ended structuring device as a question.
- As the Development unfolds, the teacher takes a step back in promoting a student–student interaction pattern. Students are given the widest possible freedom in determining how they will address the structuring question. As an interesting option, initial student brainstorming can take place in peer groups to promote maximum engagement of all students.
- As the Exploratory Discussion facilitator, you will occasionally ask additional questions to gently guide the exploration in new directions. In acting as facilitator, you'll ask these additional questions only as needed.
- During the Culmination, you should challenge students to return to the structuring device by reviewing the main ideas generated.

Already, you should have a sense that Exploratory Discussions are quite a refreshing departure from many of the methods used in classrooms today. Depending on your purposes, these open exchanges of ideas can be fairly brief (i.e., five minutes) to about one-half hour (after which time, we've discovered, students have usually done about all the brainstorming they can).

Up Close: Planning and Conducting an Exploratory Discussion

Prelude: Rationale

Let's return to the Exploratory Discussion conducted in John Rizzi's biology class as we provide you with our best advice for planning and conducting truly student-centered discussions. A discussion like Mr. Rizzi's, if effectively done, could challenge students intellectually and affectively on a number of levels. The discussion is a terrific example of what we call interdisciplinarity (a hallmark of constructivist classroom experiences). *Chief Seattle's Reply* could be analyzed as a historical primary source document, as a cultural artifact, or even as a piece of literature. It connects to the value systems held by people of two different cultures, and it would certainly cause most young people to take a closer look at their own actions and their environmental effects. There is also a powerful connection to ecological concepts and principles and to the impact of technology on society and the environment. Mr. Rizzi might have written a Rationale like this as part of his planning process: "During an open discussion focused on possible lessons learned through the reading of *Chief Seattle's Reply*, students will apply what they have learned regarding the environment and the impact of technology on the environment to the analysis of a historical and cultural text. This experience will enhance a wide range of critical-thinking abilities and verbal and small-group communications skills, and it connects to INTASC Standards 1 through 7." When using the Exploratory Discussion method, be sure to have a clear, compelling Rationale that describes a good reason for doing the discussion, and convey this to your students. You don't want them to come to believe that Exploratories are nothing more than informal chats with no real purpose.

Performance Objective

How could you, as a teacher, accurately assess what students had learned as a result of an experience like the biology Exploratory? Student comments made during the discussion would certainly indicate a great deal about the cognitive and affective connections that they made. Toward the end of this lesson, the biology teacher asked his students to respond to two thought-provoking, summative questions. A possible Performance Objective for this lesson: "Following a reading of *Chief Seattle's Reply*, students will brainstorm lessons that American citizens living today might learn from the text. In a peer-group setting, students will then respond in writing as a group to two questions designed to assess the impact of the discussion and will later share and defend these written responses in a full-class setting." We believe that it's essential to challenge students to apply ideas generated during Exploratory Discussions soon after the discussion takes place. Again, this is the best indicator of the true impact of the discussion. As you plan your first Exploratory Discussions, consider ways in which you might invite students to use ideas brainstormed by the group.

Materials

As educators, we firmly believe that you can't have a meaningful discussion in a vacuum. Your topic and structuring device, which flow from the subject matter that you invite students to investigate, must be compelling and (hopefully) relevant to your students. For example, in conducting the discussion described in the opening scenario in both high school and college classrooms, one of your authors can attest to the profound impact that *Chief Seattle's Reply* has on most students. As far as materials are concerned, pick something interesting as the focus for Exploratories. Ask yourself, "Will my students want to discuss this? How might they respond?" Once you've chosen your material, then ask yourself, "How will I use these materials before and during the discussion?" Mr. Rizzi made an important choice—he read the text for the students, believing that this might have the biggest impact, and he distributed copies of the text to refer to during the discussion. When thinking about your materials, remember your visual and auditory learners.

Because of their format, and the fact that students have a lot of control over the direction of Exploratories, consider a peer-group activity in the context of these discussions. Let students read, manipulate, or otherwise investigate your materials after you pose the structuring device, then share their ideas in a full-class setting, much as you might do in a concept lesson. More on this important option as we turn to the Enactment.

Enactment: Hook

Throughout this book, we have discussed the dozens of options that you have in trying to hook your students. As we mentioned in the Directed Discussion module, it's doubly important to involve your students early when conducting any discussion. This is especially true in Exploratories, the most open kind of discussion that you'll conduct.

John Rizzi's Hook (the song and accompanying questions) certainly established a theme for the discussion. In this case, the song featured a writer expressing some of the same feelings about nature as Chief Seattle conveyed in 1854. In essence, the reading of *Chief Seattle's Reply* served as a second Hook, since it came before the class launched into the true exploratory part of the lesson. The message here: try to make your Exploratory Hooks especially novel and inviting in an effort to create that thinker-friendly environment. Again, don't feel as though you have to rely on a gimmick to interest or entertain your students. Your goal isn't to entertain them, it's to open their minds for the discussion. Our experiences have shown us that even something relatively simple (e.g., music, a picture, a puzzling problem, a quote) can capture the imagination of your students, lend a bit of mystery and anticipation to the lesson, and pave the way for the honest sharing of ideas.

Student Aim

Again, the structuring device that you plan for any type of discussion conveys much about the Student Aim. In fact, the nature of the structuring device will dictate which discussion method you choose for a lesson. Remember that your planning for discussions will often begin with your articulation of this main structuring question, since it has such an impact on what will hopefully take place during the rest of the discussion.

Exploratory and Reflective Discussions are especially student centered. As a result, we have some special advice regarding the Student Aim for lessons that feature these methods. Think about how you might preface the structuring device. What might you say to set up this main question? Since you want to promote student–student interaction (you want students to listen to and respond to each other directly), our advice is to let them know this. Plan a statement that lets them know that the big question is on its way. For example, Mr. Rizzi told his class, "I'd like to invite you to share your ideas about what we just heard. We're going to have an open, Exploratory Discussion. Feel free to reply to each other; there's no need to raise your hands." He also reminded them to refer to passages in the text as they shared their ideas. With this straightforward statement, the teacher conveyed exactly what the students would have the freedom to do during the discussion. This will be vital in your first student-centered discussions, since many students aren't used to sharing ideas with each other regarding anything academic. Notice also that he told them directly that they'd be doing an Exploratory Discussion. Our advice is to teach your students the differences among the discussion methods that you'll use (many of the teachers with whom we've worked do this at the middle school and high school levels with great success). The advantage is that as soon as you say "Directed," "Exploratory," or "Reflective," you establish a set of expectations for everyone, and your student-centered discussions will take off with much less prodding from you as the teacher.

The Structuring Device

So you've thought carefully about how you'll set up your structuring device. Now it's time to consider how you might phrase that crucial question. Since your goal in conducting an Exploratory Discussion is to investigate alternatives, implications, advantages/disadvantages, and so on, the structuring device must be an inviting, open-ended question or statement. These broad questions or statements are designed to include peripheral topics and novel or creative explanations. As the examples below illustrate, Exploratory structuring devices are much less focused than those used in Directed or Reflective Discussions. You'll see that some of the examples are specific to certain unit topics, whereas others are more generic and adaptable to a range of topics. Our purpose is to encourage you to think about the possibilities.

1. (Science; following a teacher demonstration) "What are some possible explanations for what we've seen?" "What questions do you have regarding what we just experienced?"

2. "What are some alternatives to the Bush budget proposals in 2002?"

3. "How have women's roles in our society changed since World War II?"

4. "What are the environmental implications of locating an industry in a small, remote town such as _____?"

5. "Given ABC with segment AB = segment AC, how many ways can we show that S = C?"

6. "What are some possible interpretations of this text (e.g., poem/story/letter/speech)?"

7. "In what ways can the technology of a time period affect the literature of that era?"

8. (Given this situation within this novel/play/short story/historical context) "What possible actions could this person take?" "What would be the advantages or disadvantages to each course of action?"

9. "How would your life be different today if _____ had/hadn't happened (e.g., the Confederacy had won the Civil War; _____ had been elected president)?"

10. "How does building design reflect prevailing values during a period in time?"

11. "What are the advantages and disadvantages of continued research in genetic engineering on human stem cells?"

12. "What impacts did the events of September 11, 2001, have on life in the United States? How lasting might these impacts be?"

13. "What factors are important in passing controversial legislation/writing a good poem/preventing disease/designing a successful game plan?"

14. (In a unit on *Pygmalion*) "What would be some possible implications of Eliza Doolittle learning proper English?"[1]

15. "What song lyrics or/and dance steps could you use to convey to someone else how you went about solving this equation?"

16. "What are some possible ways to solve this problem? What are the advantages and disadvantages of each method?" (In a history or government class: "What are some possible ways to ensure the solvency of Social Security and other OASDI programs for the next fifty years?")

In brainstorming for possible Exploratory topics in your subject area, try variations on these questions. Note that these broad structuring devices emphasize generation of a set of alternatives rather than the stating and defense of value positions (i.e., you're asking students to brainstorm possibilities rather than to make and defend a best decision). Topics that challenge students to state and defend positions are better suited for Reflective Discussions, in which your students defend a point of view. These topics and issues can often be explored initially in this Exploratory format, as long as the teacher does not push for a true resolution to the issue or problem by requiring students to defend a particular point of view.

Development: Student Brainstorming in Response to the Structuring Device

You've carefully planned your structuring device, and you've posed it as you conduct your first Exploratory in class. As the discussion facilitator, what should you do next?

You want to encourage students to share their ideas, possibly taking certain intellectual risks as they do this. You want them to listen carefully to their classmates and to build on and at times challenge ideas put forth by peers. For these things to happen, you'll need extreme patience (especially in the first few Exploratories that you try). Extend your Wait Time I and II (see Module 4) until it "hurts." We have found that it frequently takes a few minutes for these discussions to get rolling. Wait for those initial responses. In an effective Exploratory, each teacher question should be followed by several responses, as students build on each other's ideas. Be careful not to interject immediately if students don't respond to each other right away; even if your students give you that deer-in-the-headlights look at first, be patient and encouraging. In many cases, restating or rephrasing the main question will promote interaction. Try this if the discussion begins slowly.

Certain other questioning techniques will enhance and improve the quality of the student–student interaction. In planning Exploratory Discussions, try to anticipate general categories of student response in question form. Ask yourself where the students should or might go as they explore the topic, and have questions ready to guide the interaction if necessary. You will sometimes find that students will exhaust one area of alternatives without addressing other possibilities. If the group fails to address an important point, simply ask a secondary question to jump-start the discussion in a new direction (e.g., "We've looked at _____ as one alternative. Have you considered _____ ?"). Be sure to give your students every opportunity to bring up these categories before interjecting, since they should determine the direction of the discussion (i.e., be careful not to turn your planned Exploratory into a Directed Discussion).

In our example biology discussion, the students began to respond to each other without much directing from their teacher. You'll find that this will most often be the case, especially when you set the discussion up effectively and students are used to this method. It seems as though Mr. Rizzi did ask at least a few of his secondary questions ("What view of the role of technology do the two cultures have?") to challenge students to explore new dimensions of the text. Again, we have found in planning Exploratories that it's useful to anticipate what students should/might explore and to have secondary questions planned in case the discussion bogs down (see the sample lesson plan at the end of this module for examples of this). Remember that in the case of Exploratories, these additional questions are things that you *might* ask, not things that you *have* to ask.

Promoting interaction and encouraging depth of thought among your students can be enhanced by asking a few probing and redirecting questions. We have found that the (limited) use of clarifying probes is very helpful in Exploratories ("Can you tell us what you mean by _____?"). These questions are designed in part to check the degree to which a statement has been understood by others. Reflective probes can help clarify student statements. To ask such probing questions, simply paraphrase all or part of the student's response, and he or she will often clarify or add something to the original answer, and other students may build on these ideas. Reflective clarifying questions can be preceded by a phrase such as "Did I hear you say . . . ?" Use clarifying questions yourself, and encourage students to use them as well if statements are unclear ("I'm not sure that I know what you mean. Could you say that in another way?").

As we have noted, it will be important for you to encourage students to compare and contrast statements made by members of the group. Asking redirecting questions can encourage this. Mr. Rizzi asked an effective redirect in responding to Amy's comment ("What do others feel about what he means when he uses the term 'savage'?"). Look for opportunities to do this when students make particularly insightful points. Try to keep as many students as possible engaged in the discussion; from time to time, you may want to direct questions toward individual students. Again, it will be important to strike a balance between necessary questioning and interfering with the flow of the discussion; too many teacher questions, even when open ended in nature, will inhibit student–student interaction, so be careful.

Another subtle but important planning consideration is the physical setting. We have found that seating students so that they can see and respond to each other makes a huge difference (see Module 15). If possible, seat students and yourself in a circle. This will help promote the student–student interaction that you're looking for. Sitting with the students sends the important message that they are responsible for leading the discussion with less direction from the teacher (Mr. Rizzi enhanced his Exploratory Discussion by doing this). If the initial part of the discussion will take place in a peer-group setting (consider this as an option), desks or seats can be arranged initially in pods or smaller circles.

Once students are used to Exploratories, another interesting option is to conduct two or even three discussions simultaneously, with students seated in smaller circles of eight to fifteen. The advantage of this approach is that more students have a chance to provide input; you as the teacher can spend time with each group, asking occasional questions. However you decide to seat or group your students, we highly recommend remaining at eye level with them; don't tower over the group, as this will send the message that you are going to direct the flow of the interaction.

Besides facilitating the discussion, we suggest that you write the main ideas generated by your students on paper or on an overhead sheet. The collection of ideas can later be shared with the class (the benefit of using overhead sheets) and saved and used in future lessons. Since the structuring devices are relatively unfocused, your students' contributions will not necessarily occur in a logical sequence. As a result, you may want to group random student contributions as you write them and later discuss possible emerging categories of alternatives. Especially toward the end of the discussion, make an effort to cluster student statements into categories of some kind. This can be accomplished by having you or your students summarize alternatives to the structuring question; this focusing is important when you do longer Exploratories ("Who can summarize the ideas that we've mentioned so far?").

Remember that Exploratory Discussions can succeed only if students feel free to express themselves, knowing full well that not everything they say will prove to be totally sensible. They must come to trust you as a teacher and as a facilitator of such open discussions. If students perceive the game to be one of finding correct answers, they are not likely to explore ideas no matter what you say, so take care to accept all student statements. When justifications are made, they should be done in a respectful and deliberate way, with patience and sympathy. It will be important for you to avoid the appearance of judging the value of contributions; remember that the value test of a contribution is logical, not personal. "Criticize ideas, not people" is an important critical-thinking rule to emphasize when conducting any discussion; model this kind of accepting, open-minded attitude for your students.

Culmination

Let's say that your first Exploratory Discussion has gone well. Your students found your main question interesting, and they responded to each other as they brainstormed a range of interesting ideas (some of these really surprised and impressed you. That's the beauty of doing Exploratories). How do you conclude a discussion like this?

First of all, it is sometime hard to tell when an Exploratory has run its course; this will be a judgment call on your part. Once you feel that students have generated enough useful ideas (or when you run out of time), we recommend returning to the structuring device and reviewing, or asking students to review, the main ideas generated. Remember that you're not pushing for a specific resolution or best answer to the structuring question. In a sense, the list of ideas generated actually serves as the Culmination. John Rizzi shared his overhead notes with his class as he recapped points made by the students; we have found that this practice is especially effective. In fact, students are often impressed with the variety of ideas that they can generate in a short time.

It's important to convey that your Exploratories have a definite purpose. In planning your leap, let students know how you'll be using these ideas in the future and why they're important. In meeting his Performance Objective, John Rizzi challenged his students to respond to two questions in writing that conveyed both the importance and the relevance of his chosen topic. Ask your students to do something to apply what they've learned in some concrete way, whether this happens during the same class period or in a future lesson. Get them to put those ideas to work!

Assessment and Evaluation

As with any of our three discussion methods, you might challenge students to produce something for you to evaluate during or immediately after the lesson. We have found that reflective or reaction-type papers are especially effective as a way to challenge students to think further about topics discussed (e.g., a response paper or journal entry would be ideal as an epilogue to Mr. Rizzi's lesson). As you plan your Exploratory Discussions, think carefully about what you might ask students to produce during or after the experience (see Module 14 for examples).

Focal Point 4: When Should You Use the Exploratory Discussion Method in Your Classroom?

Exploratory Discussions serve several purposes and can range in time from a few minutes (brief brainstorming sessions) to about one-half hour. These discussions can serve as excellent introductions to entire units or to lessons in which you use other methods. For example, you might begin a class period with a brief exploratory in which students generate alternatives, and then you might focus or expand on one of their ideas in a Directed or Reflective Discussion. This approach is very useful in math and science classrooms ("What do we need to know to solve this problem?" "What questions will we need to address before we begin this process?"). In these cases, the Exploratory can serve an ILPE-type purpose, with the teacher gaining valuable insights into initial student thinking on a new topic. As a science teacher, one of your authors has found Exploratory Discussions to be incredibly valuable for challenging students to articulate initial explanations for events/teacher demonstrations (i.e., science phenomena). Teachers in other subject areas can conduct brief Exploratories for the same purpose, asking students for initial responses to pieces of prose or for descriptions of historical events. Remember that in a constructivist classroom, investigating student-generated questions is a central focus, and the Exploratory format is ideal for accomplishing this (for one instance of this, think back to the Sitting Bull/Crazy Horse/Custer example in Module 1).

As we noted earlier, Exploratory Discussions can also serve to conclude a unit or a series of lessons by challenging students to connect new ideas to other concepts and principles; Mr. Rizzi's Chief Seattle discussion serves as an example. In a history class, a structuring device such as "What would your life be like today if _____ had/hadn't happened?" can cause students to think deeply about the significance of past events, making real-world connections between ideas discussed and their own experiences. In the same way, during a study of plays/novels/short stories, an English teacher might ask students to immerse themselves in a text to brainstorm possible actions that a character might take in a difficult situation.

As you will see, each of the three discussions will serve to empower your students. Student-centered discussions can play a huge part in creating that thinker-friendly classroom environment described in Module 1. By using these methods, a teacher is sending a clear signal to each student: your ideas are important, and the people in this classroom care about what you think. It is a message that is too often missing in classrooms at all educational levels. We have found that Exploratory Discussions are tremendously effective in promoting creative, outside-the-box thinking. For example, a student teacher working with one of the authors frequently invited his students to work in groups to complete different math problems that might be solved in various ways and then to design and perform skits or songs that conveyed to the rest of the class how the problem was approached.[2] Not only were these peer-group Exploratories fun for the entire class, but the teacher found that students remembered and could later use problem-solving approaches much more effectively.

A GLIMPSE INSIDE A CONSTRUCTIVIST CLASSROOM

As part of their probability and statistics unit in Ms. Claypool's Discrete Math course, students have been conducting and discussing a variety of probability experiments. They have flipped coins, rolled dice, even played card games as they have collected and analyzed data and discovered a number of important concepts. Ms. Claypool believes that the collection and analysis of real data is the most effective way to learn to apply the principles of probability and statistics, and she is about to challenge her students to embark on their most ambitious project yet. The class had discussed the process of polling to some extent. At the outset of today's class, she presents them with a new challenge. "As you know, Central High is considering a name change for the school mascot. Dr. Wigglefence (the principal) knows that this class has some expertise in probability and statistics, so he has chosen us to poll the student body to discover what kind of mascot might be preferred. We need to start this process today by doing some brainstorming. Here's our main question: *What questions or issues will we have to address to conduct the fairest and most complete student poll that we possibly can?*" For the next twenty minutes, the class brainstorms an impressive list of issues that must be resolved before the class can conduct its student poll (e.g., How many students should we question? How will they be chosen? What kinds of questions should we ask? How many? Should we ask open-ended questions? Or should we ask for the most popular choices and have a schoolwide vote?). In wrapping up the Exploratory, Ms. Claypool tells the class that they have anticipated many of the toughest issues facing pollsters and statisticians and that their next challenge will be to resolve each issue and to actually conduct the poll.

Tips for Technology Integration

- In the math classroom, a number of commercially available programs (e.g., Geometer's Sketchpad, Escher Interactive) can be used in conjunction with Exploratory Discussions. Our student teachers have frequently challenged students to experiment with various program functions (e.g., manipulating/discovering different types of tessallations) as they simultaneously share observations/results with classmates in response to exploratory questions.

- Internet connections between schools create the potential for conducting electronic Exploratories between students in classrooms miles apart (in a chatroom-type arrangement). Teachers or students can post open-ended, Exploratory-type structuring devices, which can be responded to by students in various classrooms. Students can then respond to each other's comments, creating an electronic forum for student–student interaction.

■ ROUNDUP ■

The purpose of Exploratory Discussions is to allow students to brainstorm alternatives, implications, pros/cons, or other ideas in response to an open-ended structuring device. Exploratory Discussions are exceptionally student centered; you should allow your students wide discretion in deciding how they'll respond to the structuring question. In these discussions, the teacher plays a facilitative role, asking occasional secondary, probing, and redirecting questions. Your main task as facilitator will be to ensure that the main question is "explored" in terms of both breadth and depth and that the discussion engages as many students as possible.

Remember our advice for conducting effective Exploratories. Plan a broad, inviting structuring device and possible secondary questions that you might ask at some point in the discussion. Be patient. It may take a few minutes for the discussion to get rolling, but the interaction will usually take off if you extend your wait time and encourage the group. The right seating arrangement can help. Arrange the

1 = structuring device: question as student aim

intention ⟶ examine two sides of an issue or controversy without making a value judgment

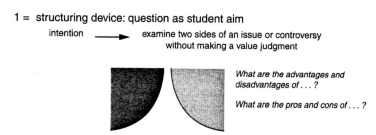

What are the advantages and disadvantages of . . . ?

What are the pros and cons of . . . ?

2 = elicit both sides of the issue or controversy

use questions or role-play based on instructional materials

S-S dialogue.
DO NOT LECTURE.
Steer discussion only
when necessary.

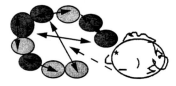

3 = organize points of view by headings

use board, overhead, etc.

PROs	CONs
1___	1___
2___	2___
3___	3___

4 = culmination: students answer structuring device

elicit implications without making value judgments

When . . . then . . . . If . . . then . . . . It appears that . . . when . . . .

©2001 Ina Claire Gabler

FIGURE 10.2 Exploratory Discussion Method Flow Chart

classroom so that students can see each other, and seat yourself at eye level with the group. Try to write ideas generated by the class (and possibly group these) so that they can be used or referred to later. Controversial or "hot" topics are most successful.

Exploratory Discussions can serve to empower your students, and they are very effective in allowing students to brainstorm ideas or questions that can be used later, all vital dimensions of the constructivist learning experience.

Take a look at the flow chart in Figure 10.2 and the sample lesson plan that follows; they will help you better understand what it takes to put together an effective exploratory. The Hands-On Practice sheet will guide you through the process of designing such discussions.

■ EXPLORATORY DISCUSSION SAMPLE LESSON PLAN

Unit Title: Biotechnology and Genetic Engineering (intended for a high school Biology course)

Prelude

Rationale

(Combines *What? Why? Justification*): Participation in an Exploratory Discussion focused on the value of research in biotechnology will help students understand that the scientific community and citizens will face a number of crucial ethical decisions in the future about how far such studies should go. Students will have an opportunity to consider the advantages and disadvantages as well as the implications connected with continued research. This experience will help students develop important critical-thinking and ethical decision-making abilities, and it connects to INTASC Standards 1, and 3 through 7.

Performance Objective

(Combines *preparation, product,* and *criteria*): Students will first review some of the major trends in biotechnology research. Then, following a student-centered discussion, students will summarize at least four advantages and disadvantages of continued research in the field and will support each statement by referring to evidence from the discussion and supporting reading materials.

Materials and Lesson Aids

1. A collection of previously assigned readings/handouts focused on trends in biotechnology research

2. A cartoon (featuring a dinosaur destroying a lab amid a group of shocked scientists)

Enactment

Time Estimate	Main Ideas/Concepts, Questions, and Teaching Methods Utilized
Five or six minutes	*Hook.* • What do you think of when you see this cartoon? (show cartoon on overhead) • What do the comments by the scientists show you? • Why would a cartoonist draw this? • What does this show you about the public's attitude toward scientific research? • Are there some legitimate concerns about this research? • Have you seen movies/TV shows or read articles that reflected some of these fears? (discuss examples from readings) You've actually had a chance to extract DNA, splice it with restriction enzymes, even to do some cloning of your own. Let's review for just a minute. • What is cloning? • What do you start with? End with? • In general, what did we do to the bacterial cells?
One or two minutes	*Student Aim.* For the past four weeks, we've been talking about biotechnology, about some of the research trends, and about what might happen in the future. Today, I'd like to spend some time talking about the future, about what scientists might do, and perhaps about what we should avoid doing. We're going to have an Exploratory Discussion, so feel free to respond to each other's comments without input from me. My question is this: *What do you see as potential advantages and disadvantages to continued research in biotechnology?*
Fifteen to twenty minutes	*Development.* Student-centered discussion with teacher moderation. Potential secondary questions: • How could we benefit in terms of agriculture/food production?

- Are fears within the public about eating genetically engineered products legitimate? Why/why not?
- What are the possibilities for treatment of human disease?
- For enabling more successful organ transplants?
- What benefits could come from stem cell research? What dangers do you see in this?
- Could research provide us with ways to save endangered species? Would this be a positive thing?
- What possible abuses do you see if research goes on at its current pace?
- Would you as a citizen favor any restrictions on research? If so, which ones?

Three or four minutes

Culmination.
Wrap-Up: You raised a range of important issues today! These are issues that will definitely impact us as citizens in the near future.
- Who can summarize some of the major point we addressed? (probe/redirect, based on responses)

Leap: Tomorrow, we're going to look at a specific situation and a set of issues connected to biotech research. Before then, I'd like you to consider an important question: Would you, as a future parent, ever want to be given the opportunity to decide in advance on the sex and the physical attributes of your children?

Assessment and Evaluation

What was the quality of the discussion in terms of cognitive level? (Cite criteria.)

How thoroughly did the students explore various issues? (Cite criteria.)

How well did they justify their assertions? (Cite criteria.)

Did students ask thoughtful questions? (Cite criteria.)

■ HANDS-ON PRACTICE ■

Plan an Exploratory Discussion by using the following template. Refer to Module 3 for a look at the Core Components of a lesson plan and to Module 10 for details on this type of discussion.

PRELUDE (for teacher reference)
- Rationale (with connection to national/state standards)
- Performance Objective (remember to be specific about what your students should be able to do to show you what they've learned)
- Materials and Lesson Aids

ENACTMENT (student engagement: what might you say/do/ask at each stage of the lesson?)
- Hook
- Student Aim
  - Structuring device preface (How will you set up/contextualize your main question?)
  - Posing the structuring device as a question. How will you phrase this main question?
- Development
  - Students brainstorm in response to the structuring device. What will you do to promote this? (e.g., through a special seating pattern; the use of reference materials)
  - Teacher facilitates interaction with secondary trigger questions. How will you phrase the secondary questions that you might ask?
- Culmination
  - Wrap-Up: What will you say/do/ask to help students summarize the main points discussed?
  - Leap: How will students use/apply these ideas in the future?

ASSESSMENT AND EVALUATION
What will you ask students to produce during/after the lesson to show what they've learned?

How will you evaluate this product?

ENDNOTES

1. Thanks to Rebecca Ayers, Augustana College Class of 1999, for this contribution.
2. Thanks to Nick Polyak, Augustana College Class of 1999, for this contribution.

Module Eleven:

The Reflective Discussion Method

■ OVERVIEW: SCENARIO DEPICTING A REFLECTIVE DISCUSSION

The students in Mrs. Garcia's first-period U.S. history class seem excited as they enter the classroom today. Over the course of the school year, they had come to expect the unexpected from their history teacher: interactive discussions, guest speakers, skits, group projects, even Mrs. Garcia, one of the other teachers, or a parent dressing up occasionally as a historic figure. Pocahontas, Thomas Jefferson, Henry David Thoreau, Susan B. Anthony, and the Marx Brothers had all made appearances this year. The desks are arranged in one big circle today, which is common for this history class. Before the bell rings, two students talk briefly about what they might do today.

"We've got to finish talking about World War II today," offers Shannon to Nikki. "I wonder what she'll have cooked up."

"I'm not sure, but we'll probably go out with a bang," Nikki replies. "That's one thing I really like about this class, she asks us interesting questions and listens to our ideas."

Mrs. Garcia doesn't waste a minute as she stands in front of the circle of desks. "Let's go back in time," she begins, her voice bright with anticipation. "It's July 1945. What's happening around the world in July 1945?" She pauses for a few seconds as hands shoot up. "Alexis?"

"The war's almost over. Germany already surrendered," answers Alexis confidently.

"Who can add something to what Alexis said?"

"President Truman just took over," notes Jack. "They want to set up the United Nations."

"Everyone's listening to swing music and dancing," adds Sue to a few chuckles.

"We're, I mean the U.S., is closing in on Japan, but they haven't given up!" says Nikki.

"You're all right. Today, we're going to focus on Nikki's point, and talk about what's happening in the Pacific," says Mrs. Garcia. "I'd like to welcome all of you to Washington, DC, for an important meeting of President Truman's closest advisors." She pulls on a string attached to the projector screen, which was lowered over the chalkboard, to reveal the words SECRET SESSION—PRESIDENT TRUMAN'S WARTIME ADVISORS.

"On these sheets I've got descriptions of the roles that you'll play in today's discussion. I've mixed them up randomly, so I'm not sure who will get what part." The students smile at each other—they had done lots of role-playing, and they found it interesting.

"When you receive your role, read it carefully. Each role will describe your character's initial point of view." Mrs. Garcia moves around the circle as she's speaking, handing each student a sheet of paper. When everyone has a role, she races through the attendance and waits for the students to finish reading. The room is unusually silent for about three minutes.

When everyone is finished reading, Mrs. Garcia continues. "Last night, you had a chance to read about a new and frightening weapon that's been developed, the atomic bomb. Your challenge today is to decide whether the United States should use the bomb to try to end the war in the Pacific. You're a group of the President's closest advisors, and he has entrusted you to make a decision today that could change history," she notes in a serious tone.

"Remember that this is an open discussion. Feel free to challenge each other's ideas, but remember that only one person speaks at a time. The President will be responsible for moderating. Who is President Truman?"

Nikki's hand shoots up to a mix of applause and chatter.

"All right. I'd like to call on the President to begin the meeting," Mrs. Garcia says. "The question before the council is this: *Should the United States drop an atomic bomb on Hiroshima, as suggested by the Joint Chiefs of Staff?*"

"Let's start the meeting. I'd like to start by asking for suggestions from the council," begins Nikki with an air of confidence. "Who has an opinion?"

For the next thirty minutes, the class of twenty-five debates the pros and cons of using the atomic bomb. Students speak as a range of characters—parents of servicemen in the Pacific, military officers, members of congress, arms manufacturers, religious leaders, and Eleanor Roosevelt—are all present at the meeting. The students rely on knowledge that they've gained during the World War II unit in stating their opinions and challenging each other with questions. Mrs. Garcia (who is the Secretary of State, she tells the group) challenges various students with occasional questions (What would happen if . . . ? Is there another alternative to . . . ? What else can you tell us about Mrs. Roosevelt's suggestion to . . . ?). But she relies on Nikki to moderate the discussion, and Nikki responds thoughtfully.

With fifteen minutes left in the class period, Mrs. Garcia reminds Nikki that the council needs to vote on whether to use the atomic bomb. The class has articulated three alternatives on which to vote, and Mrs. Garcia reminds the group that they can deviate from their character's original position if they believe they should do so. Nikki presents the alternatives and asks for a show of hands as the students make an individual decision. The students spend the last few minutes of class discussing their choice and reflecting on the discussion itself. Mrs. Garcia asks the group to write a brief essay for tomorrow in which they address three questions:

- What points did they consider as they made a decision? Why?
- What would they choose to do if they had served on such an advisory council, and why?
- Was the Truman administration justified in dropping an atomic bomb on Hiroshima? Explain and justify.

Focal Point 1. What Makes the Reflective Discussion Method Distinctive?

You've just witnessed what we call a Reflective Discussion. In conducting Reflective Discussions, your main goal will be to challenge your students to express and defend their thoughts regarding complex, value-oriented questions or issues. Perhaps more than any other constructivist teaching method, there is an emphasis in Reflectives on helping students develop their critical-thinking abilities. As we'll see, you'll be inviting students to consider an issue, search for and weigh evidence, listen and respond to the positions of others, consider multiple perspectives, and eventually make, share, and defend a final decision.

Discussion 1. **What Makes the Reflective Discussion Method Distinctive?**

These discussions occupy a place between Exploratory Discussions and Directed Discussions in terms of the degree of control that students have over the direction of the lessons. Reflectives share with Directed Discussions the characteristics of having a convergent, focused structuring question and a specific resolution to the question posed. They are similar to Exploratory Discussions in the degree of freedom that you'll afford your students over the flow of the interaction, even though the interaction is more focused. In Reflective Discussions, students are given opportunities to find ways to address academic problems and to make their own decisions rather than being guided by the teacher through the process step by step, as in Directed Discussions.

Figure 11.1 shows a suggested template for planning Reflective Discussions. As you take a look at the stages, think carefully about what Mrs. Garcia did in each phase of her Reflective Discussion.

PRELUDE

- Rationale (with connection to national standards)
- Performance Objective
- Materials and Lesson Aids

ENACTMENT

- HOOK—If possible, connect to structuring device to help contextualize the discussion
- STUDENT AIM
  - Structuring device preface (i.e., provide background information, provide students with ground rules for the discussion)
  - Pose the structuring device as a question
- DEVELOPMENT
  - Students debate/share and challenge opinions in response to the structuring device
  - Teacher facilitates interaction with secondary questions and extended wait time
- CULMINATION
  - Wrap-Up—Students/teacher recap arguments; students reach resolution on structuring question
  - Leap—How will they use these ideas? Wht will we do as a result of this decision?

ASSESSMENT AND EVALUATION PLAN

1. Assessment products (What will students produce in this/a later lesson?)
2. Evaluation (How will you evaluate this product, e.g., with a scoring rubric?)

FIGURE 11.1 Reflective Discussion Lesson Planning Template

The Nature of Values and Beliefs

We've noted that Reflective Discussions challenge students to use their values to make well-informed decisions on important questions/issues. Before continuing in our description of Reflective Discussions, we will pause to explain values in a bit more detail, to relate them to the constructivist learning perspective, and to suggest how teachers can best discuss values with their students.

As educational research has shown (see Module 1), regardless of what tasks students are engaged in, their past experiences and, consequently, associated frames of reference will have an immediate impact not only on how certain material is learned but also on how it will be used later. Each of our frames of reference is profoundly affected by the values system that we have constructed through interactions with family, friends, and others within our culture and the larger society. We define *values*, for the purpose of this discussion, as *the acts, customs, institutions, objects, and ways of behavior and thinking that members of a group of people view as desirable*. A *belief* is *a value that a person holds to be true*.

As soon as students decide that a particular solution to a problem is right or wrong, they are reflecting some value that they have learned in school or from family and friends. Clearly, some issues are more heavily value-laden than others. Values obviously have a profound effect on the way we see the world. Our system of values has an impact on how we perceive and interpret both past and current events. In an English class, students are making values choices when they state that the actions of a character in a story or play were justified. In geometry, a student selecting a method to complete a proof is making a values choice. Even the most mundane student tasks, such as listening and taking notes, are influenced by values and belief structures. In high school classrooms, for instance, taking notes to get a higher grade will be seen as crucial among students who plan to go to college. For students who see little value in school, taking notes may not be very important. Although it would be safe to say that most cultures have certain core values held by most members, individual values may differ significantly among people. The fact that people hold different values when it comes to certain issues is not necessarily bad, and discussion of these values should not be avoided in the classroom.

Dealing with values in the classroom can be a challenging task for teachers. In fact, there is a great deal of talk today about teaching values in the classroom, but those doing the talking can mean vastly different things when they say this. For some, teaching values means telling young people what to think, in essence what to value (a process that we and others might call *values inculcation*). It is our position that as teachers we have an obligation to deal with values directly as part of the learning experience but that we do not have the right to press or impose our own values on our students.

The approach that we recommend, which includes the use of methods such as Reflective Discussions, would be to challenge students to consider real, complex situations in which they and others will need to make difficult decisions that could be logically supported. As students work through these intellectually challenging classroom situations with the help of teachers and classmates, it is our belief that they will become better decision makers who are able to reason well at the highest intellectual levels (e.g., analysis, synthesis, and evaluation). Methods such as Reflective Discussions can cause learners to experience what we call *values disequilibrium*, a questioning of their own current value system and a possible change in this system based on experiences. In addition, by using procedures that achieve a thorough and balanced exploration when investigating value-laden issues, you can avoid conflicts with parents, peers, and school administrators. Like many of the constructivist teaching methods that we've introduced, Reflective Discussions can promote a valuable struggle in coming to understand complex situations and make well-reasoned decisions. That's what Reflective Discussions are all about.

In the previous module, we noted that Exploratory Discussions can be empowering to students. It has been our experience that Reflectives can have this very same impact. It is our belief that these discussions will help your students develop some of the most vital thinking abilities that they'll need in the future, both in school and beyond. For this reason, we urge you to make Reflective Discussions regular events in your classroom, regardless of which subject you teach. Remember that the main idea behind this method is to take students' current beliefs associated with a topic and to challenge these beliefs with new information and perspectives on that topic. Your overall goal will be for students to express their values or beliefs, to reconsider them in the light of new information, and to either reinforce or modify them in light of new experiences. To further this goal, you will present new information in a way that may create conflict or disequilibrium (cognitive dissonance) with current student value systems. The key is to spend the majority of the lesson in a discussion in which students take the leading role.

Focal Point 3: Reflective Discussion Method Markers

In the sections that follow, we'll see that Reflective Discussions are highly student centered but more highly structured than Exploratory Discussions. The method markers described in this section will provide you with an initial schema for planning Reflective Discussions.

- The Student Aim for Reflectives is more structured and specific than in Exploratories. You'll set up the discussion in the Hook, and then convey the Student Aim by posing a focused structuring device that calls for a value-based decision to a question. Although students may form initial opinions on this question, the structuring device won't be finally answered until the Culmination.

- As the Development proceeds, students will struggle with/debate the structuring device in a setting that features a high degree of student–student interaction.

- As the teacher, you'll moderate the discussion by asking secondary, probing, and redirecting questions (see Module 4) that will challenge students to carefully consider their position, its implications, and the implications of other possible positions.

- During the Culmination, you'll challenge each student to make and defend a final, individual decision regarding the structuring question.

Note the similarities and differences between the Reflective Discussion and the Directed and Exploratory methods. We'll focus on these characteristics as we discuss planning in the sections that follow.

Focal Point 4: Up Close: Planning and Conducting a Reflective Discussion

Like Exploratory Discussions, Reflectives are highly student centered, but they are more structured in that they challenge students to make and defend decisions. So, just what will you need to do to successfully plan and conduct these discussions? This will be our guiding question in the following sections.

Prelude: Rationale

We'll focus on Mrs. Garcia's history lesson as we analyze the Reflective Discussion method. Like all constructivist teachers, one of Mrs. Garcia's most important goals is to challenge her students to "live," or directly experience, her subject. For example, as her students "do" history (through research, analysis of primary source documents, interviewing people who lived through important events, and so on), she feels that it's vital to challenge them to struggle through some of the same complex issues and questions that people in various historical periods struggled through. This priority is certainly shown in this example Reflective Discussion. Her planning for the lesson might have started with writing a Rationale like this: "By participating in a role-play situation that challenges them to take and defend a position on an important historical issue, students will apply what they know about this historical context as they directly experience an authentic debate. This experience will help students develop and enhance a wide range of critical-thinking and verbal communications skills, and it connects to INTASC Standards 1 and 3 through 8." Again, as with Exploratory Discussions, convey your reason for doing Reflectives to yourself and to your students. Writing a clear, compelling Rationale can help you to do this. Your Performance Objectives will flow directly from the Rationale. (See Module 3, Part 1 for Core Components of a lesson.)

Performance Objective

We noted that writing Performance Objectives for discussions can be tricky. Listening to student comments can certainly provide some of the best indications as to what they're learning through the experience. Asking them to do or produce something in which they apply what they've learned is something that we'd recommend. Again, showing students that learning in your classroom is a generative process is vital (more on this when we discuss assessment in Module 14).

During or after Reflective Discussions, we also recommend challenging students to think (and talk or write) about how the experience influenced their thinking. Mrs. Garcia accomplished this with her writing assignment. In planning this lesson, her Performance Objective might have looked like this: "Following a brief review of the historical context, students will participate in a role-play in which they are challenged to take and defend a position regarding the dropping of the atomic bomb on Hiroshima. Individually, they will then address three questions in appropriate detail in a take-home essay, the contents of which will later be shared in class." Note that in the case of Reflective Discussions, student application of the lessons learned (and carrying out the Performance Objective) could take place during the discussion itself, later in the class period, or still later in an assignment or individual or peer-group research project. Any or all of these assessment options could be expressed in your Performance

Objective. As you plan lessons utilizing this method, think carefully about what you might do to challenge students to apply what they've learned and to reflect on how their thinking was influenced by the lesson.

Materials

The right materials and lesson aids can spice up any kind of discussion and can lead to a lively exchange of meaningful ideas. The materials that you use can vary as widely as discussion topics do. Text of all kinds, video clips, political cartoons, data sheets, maps, prints/sketches, computer programs, almost anything can help you provide students with the right context for intelligently considering your structuring question. For all three types of discussions, we have found that providing students with text to use during the discussion can make a tremendous difference. Immersing students into text of all kinds is vital, and using text during discussions can facilitate this.

When you conduct Reflective Discussions (and frequently Directed Discussions and Exploratories), you'll often want to create controversy. This can provide the kind of cognitive jolt that we described in Module 1. To accomplish this, you'll often want to utilize role-plays or debates (more on this in the following sections). If you choose to do this, some of your most important materials will include the role descriptions or debate guidelines that you'll need to distribute to students (again, further details to follow). In our history scenario, Mrs. Garcia had composed a wide range of roles for the class to play as they "became" President Truman's advisors. Each of these roles would need to be described on paper (thank goodness for word processing programs) and distributed to the students. Your role-plays and debates might include other textual materials for students to use. Science, art, and PE Reflectives might include a wide range of other materials. Again, think carefully about what your students will need to make their decisions.

Enactment: Hook

Now on to the actual conducting of the discussion. In planning your Reflective Discussion Hooks, think about what you might do to create controversy or to convey the feeling to your students that some kind of a problem exists. Mrs. Garcia asked some relatively open warm-up questions that began the process of taking students back to 1945. Then, she set the scene in a more definite way (and with a little flourish) by welcoming the class to a meeting of the president's advisors. In doing this, she was using the role-play as a Hook.

In planning the Hook for any of the three discussion methods, one key is to somehow connect to the problematic or challenging situation or question that will serve as the focus for the discussion. Doing this will let your students know that they'll be discussing something worthwhile; if you can convey a sense of urgency, drama, intrigue, or mystery in your Hook, it will be that much more effective. You can do this in any subject. For example, our glimpse into a math Exploratory in the previous module showed that a real application or situation can make just about any discussion topic feel more genuine.

Another overall goal for a Reflective hook is to convey to students that values do come into play in the consideration of the main question/issue. Try to make them aware, early in the lesson, that this will be a difficult decision because of the possibly conflicting values that the people involved might hold. For example, Mrs. Garcia's students quickly found that there would be a wide range of defensible opinions on the question that their teacher posed. The conflicting values perspective can be conveyed through your initial questions to the students or through the use of an article, a set of algebraic/geometric proofs, a film clip, a series of photographs, a poem, and so on.

Student Aim

We mentioned in the previous module that since Exploratory and Reflective Discussions are so student centered (and as so outside the norm for most students) that you should set up or preface the structuring device carefully. Let your students know that they will have the freedom (and responsibility) to decide how they will go about debating the central question. We suggest planning a statement to this effect, as Mrs. Garcia did for her discussion ("When you receive your role, read it carefully. . . . Remember that this is an open discussion. . . . I'd like to call on the president to begin the meeting."). Such a statement can, in a concise way, let your students know what the parameters for the discussion will be.

One of your biggest considerations in planning a Reflective Discussion will be how to phrase that main question. Structuring devices for Reflective Discussions usually take one of these general forms: Does X have value? Is/was X justified? What should we/he/she/they do in this situation? From these general examples, it follows that structuring questions/statements should have two necessary characteristics:

- They should provoke a defended stand on an issue, letting students know what kind of decision they need to make.
- They should identify one or more intellectual activities (Bloom's cognitive skills) associated with the Rationale and Performance Objective for the lesson.

When planning your structuring device, be careful that the range of possible student responses is not so broad that you cannot deal with them in depth during a class period (although Reflective Discussions can span several class sessions if necessary). For example, the structuring device planned and posed by Mrs. Garcia ("Should the United States drop an atomic bomb on Hiroshima, as suggested by the Joint Chiefs of Staff?") clearly conveys what decision her students are being challenged to make and also hints that other possibilities might be open for consideration (e.g., If not Hiroshima, would some other target be suitable?).

Consider the example structuring devices that follow. Note that some are written generically so that you might adapt them to a range of topics, whereas others are examples plucked from specific lessons. Again, our intent is to encourage you to consider the wide range of possibilities. Notice that although the structuring question is broader than in a Directed Discussion, it is important to provide some focus, as these examples illustrate:

1. Is the poem provided an example of Romantic poetry? Why or why not?
2. Given the alternatives available to this community, what is the best possible solution to the solid waste controversy?

3. T.S. George has argued that industrialized nations should not expect developing countries to control their birth rates because they themselves do not control their rates of consumption. Is he justified in making this argument? Explain.

4. Is it right for local school boards to decide what should or should not be read in public schools? Justify your viewpoint.

5. Should the children of illegal aliens enjoy the same educational opportunities enjoyed by the children of American citizens? Why/why not?

6. What is the best hypothesis available to explain this phenomenon?

7. Given the different methods of proof that we have introduced, what is the best way to solve this problem?

8. (After students read the beginning of a short story or historical vignette) What do you feel is the most likely ending for this story? Why?

9. Given the economic and environmental positions outlined in the article, was the Clinton administration's position on logging in old growth forests justified?

10. Given the information in this story problem, what is the best way to set up equations to find an answer?

11. Given the extent of the AIDS epidemic in large metropolitan areas, are school boards justified in distributing condoms in local high schools?

12. (While analyzing pictures associated with a current or historical event) What do you think the people in these pictures are thinking/feeling? Justify your viewpoint.

13. With the data/information that we have, what is the best decision that we can make regarding _____? Explain.

14. Given the evidence that we have, should we as a jury find Tom Joad guilty or innocent of murder?

15. Was the Bush Administration justified in calling for military tribunals to try suspects in the September 11, 2001, terrorist attacks?

16. (After reading/discussing a story, novel, or film) Was _____ justified in taking the action that he/she took?

17. (In a foreign language class) Given what you know about _____ culture, what would be the best response in this situation? (What might you say using the language?)

18. (In a PE class) Given this situation, what would be the best strategy for _____?

When planning Reflective Discussions, try using a variation on one of these questions as you articulate your own structuring device. Note that it is often possible and desirable to connect Reflective Discussion topics with earlier student experiences, both within and outside the classroom. For this reason, Reflectives are often very effective when concluding a series of lessons or to culminate a major research project. Notice also that topics for Reflective Discussions often involve making interdisciplinary connections, a highly worthwhile goal from the constructivist perspective. It follows that in planning these discussions, you may have to do some cognitive stretching of your own in anticipating potential student responses.

Development: Students Debate Options, Make and Defend Decisions

You have planned and posed an enticing structuring question. It's now up to the students to consider this question. How do you go about encouraging this? During a Reflective Discussion, your role is not to make your own value judgments or to push students toward given solutions but rather to act as mediator and facilitator as students think deeply about the question or problem. Whenever possible, you should help students to challenge each other respectfully and to look for flaws in reasoning. As you plan and conduct such a discussion, consider the following points.

First, think carefully about the present level of understanding and values of your students. Within your classroom, you should have a fair idea about how your students feel about certain issues. This serves as your starting point. Think back to previous lessons and determine where your students have demonstrated inconsistencies, disagreement, and confusion. For example, a math teacher may have noticed that some students always attempt to use a certain problem-solving method when confronted with a certain type of exercise. A social studies teacher might note that certain group members hold very biased views of some historical event or issue. An English teacher might have students who believe that a character in a book should have taken a different course of action. A science teacher might have learned that none of the group members recycle bottles and cans. Each of these examples shows ways in which you can gain insights into how your group members stand on certain issues.

Second, think carefully about some way to promote a degree of disagreement or controversy. You must begin the lesson by making students aware of the evidence that brings their values into question. As students face this evidence, you will help them clarify their present beliefs and explain why they feel the way that they do. This clarification will be developed by having students outline value positions as clearly as they can while discussing the topic or issue with others in the group. But remember that Reflective Discussions shouldn't stop with mere values clarification. Once the students have clearly defined the problem and clarified their own initial views, plan on exposing any contradictions in logic, and encourage others in the group to respectfully do the same. In doing so, students may gain a valuable sense of discomfort regarding their current viewpoints.

There are different ways to promote this feeling of values disequilibrium. If you are relatively sure that you have selected a topic on which students hold a range of opinions, you can structure the discussion in a straightforward way, posing the structuring device and allowing students to take the lead in expressing and defending their views. We have found two other techniques to be especially effective when it comes to creating values disequilibrium: you can set up a role-playing situation (as Mrs. Garcia did) or structure a formal or informal debate. We have found that both techniques can lead to a lively exchange of ideas and enhanced depth of understanding of the issues. Figure 11.2 takes a more detailed look at role-playing, which we have found to be particularly effective in the context of Reflective Discussions. This section includes a number of important considerations that come into play whenever you plan and conduct role-plays.

Actual debating during a Reflective Discussion is also an effective option. There are a number of possible variations that you might try. In less formal debates, you can

What is "Role Playing"?

The investigation of situations through placing students in another's position, challenging them to think about something, and then analyzing the process.

Keys to Effective Planning: What Do You Need to Do to "Set Up" a Role Play?

- Focus on a situation that is interesting, thought provoking, problematic. These situations can be *real* or *hypothetical*: create/recreate a scene from a novel, a historic event, a meeting designed to resolve an issue (any subject), a situation that your students could find themselves in (foreign language). If necessary, ask initial clarifying questions to make sure that students understand the situation (e.g., What are the issues here? Why are they important? How might _____ feel about this?). Controversy helps create a situation that will promote debate and disagreement. Real situations with community connections are especially relevant (What should our community do about _____?).

- You can ask your students to role-play real or imaginary people (e.g., historic figures, characters from novels/short stories). If you have time and opportunity, challenge your students to research the person that they'll play. It is often effective to spring roles on students when you introduce a situation (as Mrs. Garcia did in our scenario) to get a more spontaneous response. In either case, give students handouts that provide just enough background. Make suggestions about how the person could feel about the issue, but give students some space to inject their own thoughts. *It is often advisable to assign role-players to argue for a specific position.* Think about suggesting options within these role descriptions (should we do A, B, or C?), especially when role-playing is new to your students. Think carefully about whether you'll assign specific roles to students or hand out roles randomly. Try both approaches. An enticing role can draw out quiet students. It is also very effective to challenge students to argue from positions with which they disagree initially (create that cognitive dissonance). Do allow students to opt out of a role that makes them uncomfortable. (Never force students to take a value-based position.) Consider challenging a student to play a moderating role (once again, consider our history example, as one of Mrs. Garcia's students was chosen randomly to moderate the discussion as President Truman).

- Think carefully about the role that you will play as a teacher. It is usually advisable to take part in some way. If you feel that the situation will require extensive moderation (e.g., a high level of controversy; students who are inexperienced at role-playing), give yourself a role that will allow you to interject unobtrusively (e.g., the judge in a trial, or the mayor at a town council meeting; Mrs. Garcia became the Secretary of State). If you trust that students will be able to carry on a healthy debate without much guidance, give yourself a more peripheral role.

- Allow students enough time for the role-play. Don't rush things. Challenge them to make some kind of decision (i.e., reach a personal resolution on that structuring device) during the Culmination of the lesson. Class consensus on the question may be possible, but don't push this. Taking some type of vote or trying to reach a consensus is one option, but it is certainly not a requirement (consider a secret ballot if the issue is especially controversial).

- Spend time processing the role-play during the lesson wrap-up and in future lessons. Allow your students to step out of the roles and discuss the experience, especially if they've been asked to argue from a certain perspective. Plan processing questions (Was this a realistic situation? Why is this a difficult issue? How did it feel to play _____? What other solutions might have been considered? How do you feel about this issue? How did this experience change your thinking?). Challenge students to do a written response to the role-play, using guiding questions like those just listed.

FIGURE 11.2 Suggestions for Effective Role-Playing

simply assign half of your students to a pro position and half to a con, and open the discussion at that point. Another possibility is to formalize the debate a bit by splitting the class into teams, allowing team members to plan arguments and then present their case, with specific time limits and some allowance for counterarguments. Formal debates have some advantages and some drawbacks. There are some excellent opportunities for productive student–student interaction as the debate teams prepare arguments. During the presentation phase, be sure that students make some allowance for multiple spokespersons; we have observed many classroom debates in which more confident, verbally articulate students dominate the discussion. Set up team requirements that will ensure the involvement of each student. Other debate options include holding simultaneous debates in smaller peer groups and then convening the groups to discuss the results. This technique can work effectively in groups of four or six (e.g., three pro and three con).

Regardless of the format that you choose for the development, play a moderating role as the teacher. After asking your structuring question/statement, let silence reign as students complete the necessary thought processes. If your extended wait time (see Module 4) fails to promote discussion, ask a few comprehension questions to determine whether students understand the structuring question. A few preliminary questions can serve to break the ice and promote interaction.

If the responses to your comprehension questions suggest that students do understand the question and the topic, then restate your structuring device. If you conclude that student understanding is lacking, you may have to do some remedial teaching in the form of a mini presentation.

Above all, do not answer the structuring question yourself. If you become too heavily involved in the process of answering the question, little real student reflection will occur. If your students are still reluctant to address the question, you might consider soliciting individual reactions with secondary questions that toss a challenge to students, playing devil's advocate. Whether you choose to role-play or debate as part of the Development in a Reflective Discussion, remember that your role will be to moderate the interaction, to ask appropriate questions, and to make certain that as many students as possible stay involved. You want your students to interact with/debate each other to the greatest extent possible, so plan on intervening only to challenge students to think in more depth about certain points or to throw in a new twist that keeps the discussion moving.

To prepare for your moderating, try to anticipate possible student responses in advance. Note that in planning for Reflective Discussions, you must be prepared to react to many more lines of argument than in Directed Discussions. Plan for the most likely lines of inquiry, but, as when planning Exploratories, have secondary questions written and ready that will encourage students to investigate related ideas; if the discussion lags, or students do not take all facets of an issue into account, you can use these prepared questions. Consider these examples:

- If might is right in wartime, then wasn't dropping the first atomic bomb on Japan beyond moral scrutiny? Jose, what do you say to that?
- O.K., Penny, what if you were framed for a murder that you didn't commit? Would you still say the death penalty is a just practice?

- Let's say a hate group is sending false information over the Internet to stir up bigotry against people of your ethnic origin. Should that group be protected by free speech rights? Daryl, what's your view on that?

You can often jump-start the discussion by asking about a new area for consideration in this way: ("We've spent a lot of time discussing _____. Have you considered what effect _____ has on the issue?" Do everything in your power to establish a student–student pattern. The intellectual benefits to students will be great. Once you establish a teacher–student pattern, it's hard to break, since students will look to you for a response after every comment (remember that this will probably be their tendency, at first. Be patient in waiting for students to address each other). We will discuss this and similar issues in more depth as we discuss resocializing (Module 15).

If you need to ask secondary questions like these, your response to student comments at this point is crucial. Evaluating student replies, or asking probing questions, will probably result in a teacher–student–teacher interaction pattern developing. In this case, the lesson will look more like a Directed Discussion, which is highly undesirable given the nature of Reflective Discussion topics. The best thing to do is to respond with redirects and extended wait time ("What does the rest of the group think about Susanne's statement?").

We have found that student response to Reflective Discussions is usually highly positive; chances are that your Reflectives will take off as planned if you set them up effectively. As in Exploratory Discussions, one final consideration is your planned seating arrangement for the class. A setup that allows students to look directly at each other always seems to promote interaction. Consider circular seating patterns especially. As a moderator, place yourself within this circle, where you can capture student ideas in writing and ask occasional questions.

Culmination

Reflective Discussions are often lively and fast paced, and this makes them challenging to conclude. An effective Culmination, one in which you and your students reach some resolution to the main question, is essential. Students will quickly tire of discussions that seemingly never get anywhere. To the greatest extent possible, call on each student to formulate and express a *specific resolution* before the lesson ends. A consensus is often not achieved and not desirable, especially when you are discussing complex or emotionally charged issues.

For the Wrap-Up, you can provide a summary of main points or ask a student to do the same, but it is often effective to let each student express and justify his final point of view as a specific resolution with a brief statement. In the Leap, ask students to analyze their own thought processes ("Do you feel different about the issue now? Why?"). If you have asked students to play certain roles within the discussion format, it is a good idea to let them step out of these roles toward the end of the lesson to express their true views. Otherwise, the entire activity can become frustrating for the student, especially if he or she is asked to play a role with which he or she disagrees for the entire discussion.

In our history example, the teacher challenged her class to answer the main question in a couple of different ways. The presidential advisors stepped out of their roles to actually vote on the options that Mrs. Garcia had presented in setting up the role-play (Note: The teacher had no idea, in advance, what the classes decision would be. This is part of the excitement that Reflective Discussions can create, for both students and you). The class then had time to discuss the role-play itself and how it influenced their thinking, something else we highly recommend. The teacher also challenged each student to personally reflect on the decision they had made by responding to three challenging questions in a written theme. You can often use ideas expressed by students in these written responses as a springboard into future lessons, a great way to challenge students to see the connections between their classroom experiences.

One final suggestion on a possible Leap for your students. If students have strong feelings about the issue/problem involved, and it's a current issue, ask them to consider what action they might take to deal with the situation. Is there a person they might write to in order to express their opinion, as a concerned citizen or consumer? Could they invite a local elected official or company representative to visit the classroom to discuss the issue? Could you encourage the class to undertake further research as part of this process? Remember that one of your main goals as a constructivist teacher will be to help your students make connections beyond the walls of the classroom and apply what they've learned to real situations. Look for opportunities to do this when you conduct Reflective Discussions.

Assessment and Evaluation

As we noted in the Performance Objective section, asking students to reflect on what they have learned and to produce something that might extend their thinking can make Reflective Discussions even more meaningful. We have found that asking students to provide a written response to Reflective Discussions can serve to deepen their thinking not only about that particular issue but also about the thinking processes that were involved in the discussion.

Focal Point 5: When Should You Use the Reflective Discussion Method in Your Classroom?

Regardless of your subject area, we urge you to make frequent use of the Reflective Discussion method. These discussions promote complex thinking at the synthesis and evaluation levels, and they can make any topic more exciting and relevant to your students. Reflective Discussions can take place anywhere within a planned unit. They can serve as effective motivators toward the beginning of a unit, as you alert students to potentially new issues. These discussions are often effective when used following a Directed Discussion ("Now that you understand _____ in more detail, what decision would you make regarding _____?") or in conjunction with class research projects (see Module 14). Reflective Discussions are particularly effective near the end of a unit, or as a wrap-up to a series of lessons, since they challenge students to apply what they've learned to make sense of complex situations and to make well-reasoned decisions.

Once again, think back to the suggestions that we made about promoting critical thinking. The Reflective Discussion method is ideally suited for the context of justification, when you challenge your students to consider what they know to make well-informed decisions because they can help students pull the cognitive pieces together and use what they've learned in a meaningful context. The implication in doing this is that there is a purpose for learning about a topic and that learning in your classroom is generative (i.e., what your students learn in your classroom will be useful for understanding events in the real world).

Conducting Reflective Discussions, which focus on students' viewpoints and insist on intellectual rigor, sends the message that you actually care about what your students think. This implied confidence in your students will strengthen positive affect in your classroom (see Module 15) and help motivate the students to take on new challenges.

A GLIMPSE INSIDE A CONSTRUCTIVIST CLASSROOM

The students in Mr. Nemcek's Algebra I class have spent the past two weeks learning about matrices. In teaching each topic in each of his math courses, Mr. N tries to make as many real-world connections as possible, and that is his goal in today's lesson. After the bell rings, the teacher conducts a brief review of some of the topics covered, and then he asks an unusual question: "How fair would an election be if the person setting up the election knew in advance who the winner would be?" The students look at him quizzically; many reply that it would be unfair, that it shouldn't be allowed, and so on. Mr. Nemcek then tells the class that they are going to use what they know about matrices to determine the fairest way to elect a president for the school math club. The teacher then explains three different approaches that the 11 members of the math club could use to choose from among four candidates for club president. As one option, each person in the club could have one vote for their top choice. Option 2 would allow members two votes, which they could give to one candidate or split between two. The third option would allow voters to rank candidates 3, 2, 1, 0 based on their preferences. Mr. N challenges the class to "use what they know about matrices to determine what they think is the fairest way to elect a president." During the ensuing discussion, utilizing different matrix options provided by the teacher, the students discover that if someone knew in advance how each voter felt about the candidates in order of preference, it would be possible to have three different winners, depending on which voting method is selected! With the help of occasional questions from Mr. Nemcek, the class debates the pros and cons of each approach and finally chooses what they feel is the fairest method through, ironically, a class vote.[1]

Tip for Technology Integration

Taking a position, defending it, and reflecting on the process is a big part of the Reflective Discussion experience. We recommend the use of programs such as HyperStudio and PowerPoint as part of this process. Challenge students to share their position on an issue and their defense for it by developing and sharing a self-designed program with classmates. Projects like this can be done individually or in peer groups.

■ ROUNDUP ■

In your classroom, use Reflective Discussions to challenge your students to consider complex, challenging issues and problems, to consider and debate possible solutions, and to come to a final resolution that they can defend based on logical reasoning and an analysis of their own values. This method is perhaps the ultimate for helping students develop their critical-thinking abilities. They are challenged to search for and weigh evidence; to listen to and consider the positions of others, to consider biases, and, ultimately, to make, state, and defend a final decision, all of which are supremely important critical-thinking abilities. These discussions also challenge students to use what they have learned with regard to important topics, thus deepening and extending their understanding of central concepts and principles.

1 = structuring device: question as student aim

intention ⟶ examine two sides of an issue or controversy
and arrive at a value judgment with justification

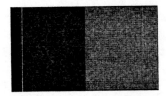

Which is the more effective. . . ?
Can we justify our point of view?

Do the detriments outweigh the
benefits of. . . ? Why?

2 = elicit both sides of the issue or controversy

use questions or role-play based on instructional materials

S-S dialogue.
DO NOT LECTURE.
Steer discussion only
when necessary.

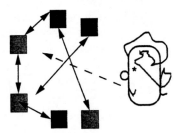

3 = organize points of view by headings

use board, overhead, etc.

PROs   CONs
1___   1___
2___   2___
3___   3___

4 = culmination: students answer structuring device

elicit value judgments with justifications   elicit implications
I think this is beneficial because. . . .   It's not moral because. . . .

FIGURE 11.3 Reflective Discussion Method Flow Chart

We believe that there are several important keys to conducting effective Reflectives. Obviously, a compelling topic, which students have some basic understanding of, helps. Your structuring device must invite some debate or consideration of options and must call on students to make some kind of a defensible choice. You must plan the discussion so that you promote a lively exchange of ideas and ideally some degree of controversy or disagreement among your students; using role-playing or debate techniques can help you do this. In addition, the Culmination to a discussion like this should call on students not only to make and defend a position but also to think carefully about the entire discussion process and how it impacted their thinking.

As you conduct your first Reflective Discussions, we urge you to be as patient as possible and to skillfully use the questioning techniques that we suggest. It might take some time for your students to become accustomed to this approach, but the benefits make the entire process worthwhile.

Take some time to explore the flow chart shown in Figure 11.3 and the complete Reflective Discussion lesson plan in the section that follows. We then invite you to use the Hands-On Practice sheet to plan your first Reflective Discussion.

■ REFLECTIVE DISCUSSION SAMPLE LESSON PLAN

Unit Title: Probability in Your Life (intended for a high school Algebra II or Probability and Statistics course)[2]

Prelude

Rationale

(Combines *What? Why? Justification*): By challenging students to first assess the validity of a set of statistics and then to use this information to make a real-life, value-based decision, I will provide multiple opportunities for students to apply mathematical concepts in authentic contexts. This experience will help students develop important mathematical reasoning and critical-thinking abilities, and it connects to INTASC Standards 1 and 3 through 7.

Performance Objective

(Combines *preparation, product,* and *criteria*): After analyzing a collection of statistical claims in a set of advertisements, the class as a group will brainstorm a list of concerns about the validity of any such claim. Then, in two large groups, students will prepare pro/con arguments and will debate positions for and against the legalization of gambling in Hawaii, with each student making a final decision on the question and supporting this decision with at least three pieces of evidence.

Materials and Lesson Aids

1. Set of advertisements scanned into a computer program

2. Equipment needed to project scanned advertisements
3. Handouts summarizing survey data related to legalized gambling in Hawaii

Enactment

Time Estimate	Main Ideas/Concepts, Questions, and Teaching Methods Utilized
Eight to ten minutes	*Hook.* Dozens of times every day we're exposed to ads like this (flash first example on screen) in which a company makes a statistical claim. • What do you notice about this ad? • What are they trying to tell us by making this claim? • Do you tend to believe these statistical statements? Why/why not? • Where would the advertisers get the data they're referring to? Flash other examples; ask similar questions, compare and contrast; note that many of the claims involve data from surveys, questionnaires, and opinion polls • What concerns would you have about the validity of any of these claims? Possible responses: sample size, nature of questions asked, bias of interviewers, selective use of data
Two or three minutes	*Student Aim.* An understanding of math can help you make sense of the things that people are trying to tell you, whether we're talking about ads or about other claims that someone might make. Today, we're going to apply our understanding of statistics to a real issue. For the next thirty minutes, you are all going to become citizens of Hawaii. We're here to debate an important issue that is soon to come before the legislature: Should the state of Hawaii pass a new law that would allow for legalized gambling?
Twenty-five to thirty minutes	*Development.* Explain the debate procedure: • Class will be split in half; pro and con positions chosen randomly • Sides will have ten minutes to prepare an argument, using data on handouts, which provides information on projected costs/revenues, public opinions on the issues, and gambling addiction figures Emphasize that each side should carefully analyze the sometimes conflicting, contradictory, outrageous claims made within the data!

- Each side will prepare a three-minute argument to be presented by four chosen spokespersons
- Each side will have a 90-second official rebuttal opportunity
- Debate will be followed by an open discussion and a vote
- Teacher's role: answer questions about the material, moderate the debate, then facilitate the discussion. Debate, with teacher moderation.

Open discussion; return to structuring device, allow students to step away from assigned debate positions. Potential questions:

- Which side seemed to have the stronger case? Why?
- Which claims seemed most believable? Why?
- How might pollsters/others gather data like these?
- What concerns do you have about the validity of the data?
- Did any of the statistics seem contradictory? How would you explain this?
- What else might citizens need to know to make a decision like this?
- Can a decision like this be made based on statistical information only? What other factors come into play?

Five minutes

Culmination.

- If you really were a member of the Hawaiian legislature, how would you vote on this issue? (show of hands)
- Why did you vote the way that you did? (sample opinions)

Wrap-Up: Today, we've seen that statistical data and the claims that people make based on them play a major role in all of our lives. Some of your major concerns regarding these issues were (provide summary).

Leap: During the next few days, I'd like you to look for examples of claims that people in the real world are making using statistics.

Look Ahead: On Friday, I'd like everyone to bring three examples made in print to class. Look especially for examples of claims that you're skeptical about based on what we did today (Assessment and Evaluation will come through this related assignment).

Assessment and Evaluation

Did the list of concerns directly relate to the claims of the advertisements?

Was each argument justified logically?

Was each argument justified with at least three pieces of concrete evidence?

■ HANDS-ON PRACTICE ■

Plan a Reflective Discussion by using the following template. Refer to Module 3 for a look at the Core Components of a lesson, and review Module 11 for detail on this type of discussion.

PRELUDE *(for teacher reference)*

- Rationale (with connection to national/state standards)
- Performance Objective (remember to be specific about what your students should be able to do to show you what they've learned)
- Materials and Lesson Aids

ENACTMENT *(student engagement; what might you say/do/ask at each stage of the lesson)*

- Hook
- Student Aim
  - Structuring device preface (How will you set up/contextualize your main question?)
  - Posing the structuring device as a question. How will you phrase this main question?
- Development
  - Students debate/share and challenge each other's opinions in response to the Structuring Device. What techniques (e.g., role-play, debate) will you use to promote this?
  - Teacher facilitates interaction with secondary trigger questions. How will you phrase secondary questions that you might ask?
- Culmination
  - Wrap-Up: What will you say/do/ask to help students reach a final resolution on the structuring device?
  - Leap: How could students use/apply these ideas in the future?

ASSESSMENT AND EVALUATION

What will you ask students to produce during/after the lesson to show what they've learned?

How will you evaluate this product?

ENDNOTES

1. Thanks to Carissa Rojanasumaphong, Augustana College Class of 2001, for her contributions to this scenario.
2. Thanks to Charles Haben, Augustana College Class of 1999, for his contributions to this lesson plan.

Module Twelve:

The Interactive Presentation Method

■ OVERVIEW: VIGNETTE DEPICTING AN INTERACTIVE PRESENTATION

Lights out, PowerPoint on. Nutrition is the topic, and a balanced diet is the theme. Mr. Singh projects slides of fish, chicken, beef, and soy. Vegetables. Fruits. Grains. Milk and cheese and smiling kids with terrific strong teeth. Double click and other slides portray overweight people, underweight people, advertisements of children gobbling down doughnuts and french fries and soda pop. Double click again and obese kids of every color fill the screen. Double click and there's a video of a grandmother hiking in some hills; she's svelte, strong, biting into an apple on the sound track.

Not a single student is falling asleep in the dark as Mr. Singh talks about each slide. Occasionally he asks a question, but he has his ten minutes and he's going full steam ahead, trying to impress on the teenagers in his classroom that their eating habits today will shape them tomorrow. Even in the dimmed room, even in the back, all of the candy-craving, potato chip-eating kids are alert, hanging on to every word. They're even scribbling.

Are these adolescents concerned with their old age? Is that the reason they're listening closely, jotting down notes, even drawing a thing or two—not doodles?

Mr. Singh's secret is the Interactive Presentation.

Before his first mini-talk and lights out, Mr. Singh gave instructions with Advance Organizer #1: During the mini-talk, pretend you've transformed into one of the people in the slides or video. Choose either a junk food eater or a healthful eater. Jot down three to five reasons that your new self would give for eating the way "you" do. Then pretend you're a nutritionist and analyze the diet of the new you. As a nutritionist, give at least three reasons the new you should or should not change "your" diet based on the mini-talk. Next, the nutritionist draws a concept map for the new you, interrelating at least three concepts about nutrition and health, which the nutritionist would inductively define (based on the facts in the mini-talk).

Then Mr. Singh gives his second mini-talk and Advance Organizer #2: Pairs of students will alternate roles as nutritionist and junk food addict. The nutritionist explains and analyzes his concept map to the wayward eater.

So you see, those junk food lovers are taking up the challenge about fish and kale, about teeth and bones, about health, yeah, and as Mr. Singh double clicks, he hopes that at lunch at least they'll eye soda pop warily and drink orange juice with their pizza.

■ DISCUSSION

The previous scenario partly demonstrates that the Interactive Presentation (IP) method combines all of our methods into one. Another advantage is that all techniques apply as well. You can see that the IP method meets various learning styles in one lesson. This method also helps you "catch up" with your teaching agenda should you fall behind. The IP helps give you an edge on time because it calls for small chunks of teacher presentations that we call *mini-talks*. In these ways, the IP method permits endless flexibility along with focus and rigor.

Focal Point 1: What Makes the Interactive Presentation Method Distinctive?

We begin with a global view or schema of the IP in Figure 12.1. Briefly, the IP features or method markers consist of what we call *parcels*. Each parcel contains 1) a mini teacher presentation (a mini-talk) and 2) a student product (a mini-task). An IP lesson may have as many or as few parcels as you prefer. Time and content guide that decision. Finally, a mini-discussion brings the key points into focus. In Focal Point 2, we describe each method marker in detail.

Focal Point 2: Interactive Presentation Method Markers

We know you love to talk about your subject. Well, here's your chance. But as a constructivist teacher, even as you're expounding full force, you need to remember this ancient Chinese proverb:

> I hear and I forget.
> I see and I remember.
> I do and I understand.

In keeping with this time-honored proverb, the IP method lets you talk about your subject while alternating with student input.

As we move through the IP method, we'll remind you of this Chinese proverb now and then as a preventive against turning the IP into a lecture, reducing your students to passive listeners.

Discussion 2: Interactive Presentation Method Markers

As you consider these method markers, imagine yourself in the classroom, incorporating various methods and techniques.

Teacher Mini-Talk

The mini-talk may take five or ten minutes. Longer presentations tend to lose students' attention. This method marker enables you to introduce or review concentrated

---

Parcel One
- *Mini-talk #1* with advance organizers
- *Mini-task #1* with method(s) and technique(s)

Parcel Two
- *Mini-talk #2* with advance organizers
- *Mini-task #2* with method(s) and technique(s)

Mini-discussion

FIGURE 12.1 Template for the Interactive Presentation Method

chunks of information along with concepts, principles, and themes with complementary textual, visual, and auditory materials. In the vignette, Mr. Singh used PowerPoint to display video as well as still images that functioned as focal points for comprehension, analysis, and synthesis. The mini-talk is most effective when it is clearly structured by a deductive or inductive framework. A clear and focused structure is especially important for effective impact within the brief amount of time allotted to you.

Student Mini-Task

The mini-task may take five to twenty minutes or longer in a block program. The mini-task segment consists of a well-structured and focused activity or activities. This task is carried out by a condensed method and techniques employed in longer segments in other lessons with a uniform method throughout. Students work on each task as they listen to the mini-talk, applying the information as directed. In this way, your students become active listeners, thinking as you present.

In Mr. Singh's class, the students role-played and took notes, interpreting and analyzing the information in the mini-talk in keeping with their roles. Through a role-play perspective, Mr. Singh's students also drew concept maps, which became a focal point in dyadic peer exchange. Finally, the students had to define the concepts themselves, briefly calling on the Inductive Concept method (Module 8, Part 2).

Altogether, Mr. Singh employed three techniques (role-playing, concept mapping, and peer-group learning) and one embedded method (Inductive Concept definition). Also, the teacher mini-talk itself is a complementary method.

Notice the integration of the Inductive Concept method with the concept mapping technique as well as the integration of role-playing with concept building. Mr. Singh could have decided on two methods with one technique each, or two or three techniques without a method in addition to the mini-talk. He planned according to his knowledge of how his students work within a given time frame.

Advance Organizers

The IP calls on the advance organizer, a technique described with examples in Module 3, Part 2. An advance organizer briefly describes or anticipates for the students what's just ahead and what they will be expected to do; it literally organizes your students' focus in advance of a task. In the IP, the teacher mini-talk contains one advance organizer for each task in the student mini-task segment. Review the following examples of advance organizers:

- During the mini-talk, try to identify all four concepts and jot them down for reference. Choose three of the four to interrelate in a concept map.

- As you listen, apply the heuristic (see Module 3, Part 2) "who, what, when, where, why, and how" to each of three principles that I will define and discuss.

- In the simulation you will see about the Mississippi River, pretend that you're the boat captain. In this role, jot down at least three cause-and-effect relationships affecting your ability to navigate the river and deliver goods.

- Before I begin, take a look at your activity sheet and notice the column headings for the table. After you fill in the table during the mini-talk, you'll apply the data to a controlled experiment that you design yourself.

- As you watch the video, jot down at least four ways in which the main character fools himself. Based on the dialogue in the video, jot down what you think his motives may be and why.

- (Written on board or handout) As you listen to Dr. Martin Luther King Jr.'s speech, jot down what you consider to be two or three of his most forceful arguments. Briefly describe your feelings about each. Phrases are O.K.

- As you listen to this folk song about the American Revolution, write at least two arguments each for the colonists and the loyalists. Compare and contrast these arguments to those of the French Revolution. Exchange your ideas with a partner after the mini-talk.

- (Written on board or activity sheet) During the mini-talk, identify at least three categories on the graph that demonstrate the concept of X. Write down at least one reason for each category. Be prepared to compare categories and to defend your interpretation with your neighbor.

- (Written on board or activity sheet) Fill in the first two main ideas with two supporting facts each as you listen to the second mini-talk. Anticipate in writing at least one other main idea in the third mini-talk that follows. Be able to justify your anticipated main idea. Relate to the theme of this lesson on your activity sheet.

- (Place an unhealthy plant on your desk) Write down three to five reasons for the plant's unhealthy state based on the mini-talk matched to the plant's appearance.

- (Written or oral) In any way you like, draw a representation of the relationship between the two events described in the upcoming mini-talk. Try to anticipate how this relationship connects to the theme.

- Choose a partner near you now. According to your birthdays, the older will take the role of R, described in the mini-talk. The younger will take the role of M. After the mini-talk, R and M will debate, citing at least four supporting reasons for their stand. Be ready to challenge each other respectfully. So take good notes!

Parcel

As seen in the template (Figure 12.1), a parcel consists of one mini-talk followed by one mini-task. Depending on the time frame, an IP may include one, two, or even three parcels.

If you're able to plan with two or more parcels, each parcel either develops ideas from the previous parcel(s) or adds related ideas, all governed by the lesson Rationale. Parcels must relate to one another.

Mini-Discussion

At the end of the last parcel, your students will need feedback on the quality of their completed tasks and insights. Feedback helps students process their ideas against those of their peers. They also need your input. Feedback can be accomplished in a mini-discussion in various forms, condensed versions of Directed, Exploratory, and Reflective Discussion methods (see Modules 9-11). The IP method may peak (e.g., express the overriding principles or theme) in the mini-discussion or in the Culmination, the final Core Component that directly follows the mini-discussion.

Cognitive Frameworks

Cohesion. Don't teach without it! An intentional deductive or inductive framework (see Module 2, Part 2) or a combination of both integrates the parcels—both internally and in concert with each other. These cognitive frameworks help you interrelate facts, concepts, and more, aided by Bloom's Taxonomy. Mini-task segments need such a well-stoked engine to take full advantage of the limited time frame, a constraint that helps your students focus quickly—if you plan well. Try to keep in mind that one parcel may be deductive and the other inductive or vice versa in the same lesson.

Focal Point 3: Integrating Core Components and Method Markers: A Template for the Interactive Presentation

Interactive Presentation method markers appear in the Development just as method markers in all the other methods do. Our suggested template for integrating the IP method with Core Components appears in Figure 12. 2. At your discretion, the mini-discussion can serve as the Culmination.

Focal Point 4: When Do You Use the Interactive Presentation Method in Your Classroom?

There are several situations that may call for the IP. One is when you might be tempted to lecture to "cover" a "lot of material." The mini-talk of the IP lets you "deliver"

PRELUDE (for teacher's reference)
- Rationale (*What* are you teaching? *Why* are you teaching this? *Justification*)
- Performance Objective (*preparation, product,* and *criteria*; unfolds in the Development)
- Materials
ENACTMENT (student engagement)
- Aim
- Hook
- Development (with method markers)
  Parcel One (may be deductive or inductive)
  - *Mini-talk #1* (with advance organizers)
  - *Mini-task #1* (includes Performance Objective)
  Parcel Two (may be inductive or deductive)
  - *Mini-talk #2* (with advance organizers)
  - *Mini-task #2* (includes Performance Objective)
  Mini-discussion
  - Culmination *(Wrap-Up* and *Leap)*
ASSESSMENT AND EVALUATION PLAN
- *Assessment Products*

FIGURE 12.2 Template for Integrating Core Components with Interactive Presentation Method Markers

information while your students are active learners, kept mentally alert by the various tasks you assign to them. In a constructivist approach, your students apply the small bundles of information from the mini-talk in ways that make them think—analyzing, synthesizing, and evaluating rather than parroting back what you've said. (Repeating what you've said is no indication of the depth of their understanding, if any.) Breaking up teacher talk into small bundles rather than in one long lecture enhances student absorption of the information.

Another situation for the IP is one in which you want to add variety, a mosaic of techniques and methods in a single lesson that keeps your students thinking every minute. All our methods have the potential to do this, but the IP moves from one technique and mini-method to another quickly. The assortment of tasks helps meet different learning styles in one lesson. The rapid pace helps to concentrate the mind.

Discussion 4: When Do You Use the Interactive Presentation Method in Your Classroom?

The IP—along with the other methods—carries out the wisdom of the Chinese proverb: They see and they remember. They do and they understand. This positive learning experience builds students' self-esteem, which in turn builds a positive attitude toward learning with you.

Pitfall

The trap for you, enthusiastic about your subject, is, yes, to talk too much during the mini-talk. The result? Your students are thrown back into the role of passive listeners. Most of your students will tune out in little time; you will wonder why they haven't learned what you so clearly explained. The fault lies not with the students. Remember the warning of the Chinese proverb: They hear and they forget (especially if they're not challenged to think). If you talk too much, your students will not have enough time to process the mini-tasks in a mini-discussion or even to complete their tasks.

Imagine yourself in this all too familiar situation. You're sinking into your seat, listening to a lecture in a subject that does not inspire you. How often do you watch the clock? How much do you retain after each lecture? How much enthusiasm do you feel during such a lecture? Most important, how much do you retain after each test for which you memorized what the teacher had said?

While you love your subject and just know that your students will catch the contagion by exposure to your enthusiasm, the truth is that, like yourself as a student in many other subject lessons, your typical student will be bored—yes, completely uninterested—in lengthy teacher talk, even in your subject. Most students are not inspired by the subject that any one of us teaches. Except for charismatic speakers, teacher talk alone will not light the torch. In case you should be one of those rarely gifted charismatic speakers, you may enthrall your students as an entertainer might, but what will they retain one week later as passive listeners, trying to repeat what you said?

The IP offers a motivating alternative to the traditional lecture as a time-efficient method. So rehearse your mini-talks to be sure they fit into the appropriate time frame. See Figure 12.3 for a comparison of the lecture and the IP.

Focal Point 5: **Up Close: Planning and Conducting an Interactive Presentation Lesson**

It's time to put flesh on the bones. What follows is a sample IP, an inductive framework that facilitates student expression of a theme based on the concept of bigotry. The lesson is designed for a block program of one-and-a-half hours. We describe this lesson one Core Component at a time.

Characteristics	Lecture	Interactive Presentation
1. Teacher role	1. Dispenser of information; primary thinker in the classroom	1. Facilitator of student thinking using small bundles of information.
2. Student role	2. Passive listeners; only occasional responders if at all.	2. Active thinkers; active responders.
3. Materials	3. Mostly orally delivered information; overhead transparencies; occasional graphics or other media are considered bonus attractions; mostly, materials are employed to emphasize the teacher's points, not to stimulate critical thinking.	3. Visual and auditory media are requisite materials designed to prompt student interpretation and critical thinking.
4. Method markers	4a. Mostly teacher talk.	4a. *Parcels* comprised of 1) teacher mini-talk(s), with visual and auditory materials used as prompts for critical thinking, and 2) active student input in the form of mini-tasks.
	4b. Teacher develops major concepts and themes.	4b. Students develop major concepts and themes in a mini-discussion based on mini-talk(s) and mini-task(s).

FIGURE 12.3 Comparison of the Lecture and the Interactive Presentation

■ SUBJECT: HISTORY
TOPIC: THE BENEFITS OF BIGOTRY

Prelude

Rationale

1. *What?:* To build on the concept of bigotry introduced yesterday, arriving at a unifying theme.
2. *Why?:* Students will interpret and analyze examples of bigotry to establish the psychological need of bigotry in some individuals. Learners will synthesize examples to establish a theme. This is a lead-in to the unit on Nazi Germany.
3. *Justification:* INTASC Standards 1, 2, 3, 5, and 6.

Performance Objective

1. *Preparation:* Two mini-talks and two mini-tasks will establish the psychological appeal of bigotry regardless of the targeted group. An activity sheet establishes a knowledge base and also prompts original interpretations.
2. *Product:* Students will be able to develop a theme in writing that synthesizes the two major concepts in their original words.
3. *Criteria:* Students will be able to answer at least ten questions on activity sheets following two mini-talks. See prompts on activity sheet. A standard five-paragraph essay will develop the theme.

Materials

Photograph of Ku Klux Klan (KKK)

Overhead transparencies as prompts for discussion

Activity sheets for mini-tasks

Video footage

Enactment

Hook

1. Display a picture of the KKK and a burning cross.
2. Say: "Let's brainstorm your ideas in response to this image."
3. Write the responses on the board: introduction to the concept of bigotry.
4. Project a transparency (Figure 12.4) with a quotation of an American Japanese during World War II: "The constitution is just a piece of paper." Review bigotry against obesity and homosexuality from yesterday's concept lesson.

Aim

(On transparency, Figure 12.4): What is bigotry's political value? What is bigotry's allure to the individual?

Big Questions:
1. What is bigotry's political value?
2. What is bigotry's allure to the individual?
****
A. Ku Klux Klan burning a cross: How does this act, using the ultimate Christian symbol, fit with Christian teachings?
B. Japanese Americans incarcerated in camps during World War II.
   1. Forced to sell homes and businesses in just one week.
   2. Distrusted because of their origins and the Pearl Harbor attack. Yet many were citizens. Older Japanese despondent. Suicides. Japanese regiment received the highest number of honors in the war.
   3. "The constitution is just a piece of paper."
C. Compare and contrast racial prejudice against the Japanese in World War II with rejection of obese and gay people discussed yesterday.

FIGURE 12.4 Overhead Transparency for Mini-Talk #1

Development (with Method Markers and Performance Objective)

PARCEL ONE (Inductive)

- *Mini-Talk #1* (Ten minutes)
  The Talk: The mini-talk relates the KKK in the Hook to the origins, rise, and present situation of the KKK. It also discusses the history of Japanese-American citizens' internment during WWII.
  Advance Organizer (a): Take notes on the elements of all seven key points during my talk about the KKK and Japanese internment during World War II (WWII). You'll be asked to relate these to your first mini-task.
  Advance Organizer (b): Now we're going to take a look at Colonial bigotry and figure out the benefits to the Pilgrims. As you watch this video, you'll answer some questions on the handout. Then you'll discuss other questions with a partner. Be prepared to relate the Colonial history to the KKK and Japanese internment in WWII. Let's quickly read the directions out loud beforehand in case you have any questions about them.
- *Mini-Task #1* (Twenty-five minutes): Students watch a five-minute video segment and respond to the activity sheet (Figure 12.5). Activity sheet includes culminating question to establish a principle.

PARCEL TWO (Deductive)

- *Mini-Talk #2* (Ten minutes): Project transparency with Sartre's quotation about anti-Semitism (Figure 12.6).
  The Talk: The mini-presentation first refers to the transparency. Then it outlines a summary of the main arguments in Sartre's book.
  Advance Organizer (a): Now I'm going to talk about Jean-Paul Sartre's book *Anti-Semite and Jew.* As you listen, I'd like you to make a list of the four major points and at least two examples of each major point.

Mini-Task #1

Question: Can you predict how Pilgrims in power would behave today?

Your Job:

A. As you watch the video, *The Shadow of Hate,*[2] answer questions 1–3 on your own.

B. After you watch the video, work with a partner and together discuss questions 4–6. Each of you write down the answers for 4–6. If you disagree, write down the answers you prefer. Support your reasons.

Questions:

1. Why did the first Europeans come to North America?
2. How would they describe freedom?
3. List the indicated number and type of persecutions they inflicted on the following groups.
   a. Native American Indians (1)
   b. Africans (1)
   c. Quakers (2–3)
   d. Baptists (2–3)

Discuss and answer with a partner:

4. How might the early Europeans (Pilgrims) have justified their cruelty toward the groups they persecuted?
5. How could the reasons the Pilgrims searched for religious freedom apply to their treatment of other racial and religious groups?
6. Compare and contrast the ideology of the Ku Klux Klan and Japanese-American internment during World War II with Pilgrim bigotry.
7. What limited judgments can you make about the psychological relationship between bigots and their victims? Support your viewpoint.
8. Predict how Pilgrims in political power might behave today. What groups might they join? What activities might they participate in? Would they hide their bigotry? Why?

Defend each viewpoint with at least three documented reasons.

FIGURE 12.5 Interactive Presentation Activity Sheet for Mini-Task #1

Later on, we'll discuss how or if Sartre's theory applies to an infamous trial.

Advance Organizer (b): Now we're going to watch a seven-minute video clip about a murder trial that took place in the South in the early twentieth century. As you watch, answer the questions on your second activity sheet (Figure 12.7). The last question asks you to consider Sartre's theory. Read the directions and ask any questions you may have before we begin.

- *Mini-Task #2* (Twenty-five minutes): Students watch a video about the trial of Leo Frank and answer the questions on the activity sheet. MINI-DISCUSSION: Directed Discussion brings together concepts and principles, establishing anti-Semitism as the "ultimate evidence" and as personal empowerment and a political weapon (ten minutes).

Culmination

Wrap-Up: Recap with the Big Questions on first transparency (Figure 12.4). Ask: "Who benefits from bigotry and how?"

> "If there were no Jews, the anti-Semite would make them."
> —*Anti-Semite and Jew*, Jean-Paul Sartre

FIGURE 12.6 Transparency for Mini-Talk #2

Mini-Task #2
Question: What was the ultimate piece of evidence against Leo Frank?
Your Job:
1. As you watch the video about Leo Frank, list one to three examples of anti-Semitism.
2. List as many pieces of concrete evidence as you can that supported Frank's guilt in the murder.
3. What was Tom Watson's motive in "convicting" Leo Frank in Watson's own publication?
4. Why was Watson elected to the U.S. Senate?
5. Compare and contrast the predominant gentile behavior in the Frank case with the Pilgrims' behavior in North America.
6. In this event, what role does anti-Semitism play for the public onlookers?
7. How does Sartre's theory about anti-Semitism apply to the Leo Frank trial? Be specific with at least four substantiated reasons.

FIGURE 12.7 Interactive Presentation Activity Sheet for Mini-Task #2

Leap: Students establish a theme, such as "bigotry as a means of power." Ask: "What is the underlying relationship between the two Big Questions?" "Tomorrow we'll begin to apply these ideas to the rise of the Nazis before WWII" (five to seven minutes).

Assessment and Evaluation Plan

Assessment Products: Evaluation Rubric and Point Scale

We invite you to outline the assessment products, including what you think are the key features for each product. Then design an evaluation rubric with 1) criteria for each task and 2) a point scale for this sample IP lesson. Remember to specify a minimum number of total points for acceptable achievement. Refer to Figures 12.4–12.7.

Tip for Technology Integration

Here's an idea for incorporating technology into the IP method. During an inductive mini-talk on photosynthesis, students watch a computer simulation of photosynthesis that parallels the talk. The coupling of a verbal description with animation addresses different learning styles, that is, linguistic, auditory, and visual. During the mini-task, students experiment with the simulation, for example, altering the variables or omitting steps in the process of photosynthesis, and observe the simulated outcomes. An original student analysis of the importance of each variable and step in photosynthesis follows, resulting in a student table, graphic representation, and so on, along with a student definition of photosynthesis.

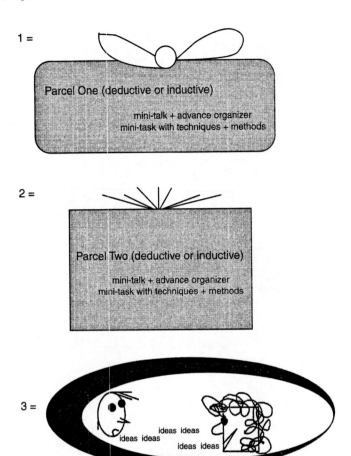

1 =

Parcel One (deductive or inductive)

mini-talk + advance organizer
mini-task with techniques + methods

2 =

Parcel Two (deductive or inductive)

mini-talk + advance organizer
mini-task with techniques + methods

3 =

ideas ideas
ideas ideas
ideas ideas

Mini-Discussion

directed, exploratory,
reflective discussions

©2001 Ina Claire Gabler

FIGURE 12.8 Interactive Presentation Method Flow Chart

■ ROUNDUP ■

The IP method is a medley of mini-talks and student products with various methods, techniques, and materials. The variety addresses a range of learning styles in a single lesson. Another advantage of the IP is that, like the lecture, it's time efficient, allowing your students to consider a substantial amount of information. Finally, if you follow the time constraints, the IP does not let teacher talk be excessive, and it guides your students to be critical thinkers, applying, analyzing, and synthesizing the information with a wide range of prompts. See the IP method flow chart in Figure 12.8 for a graphic representation.

■ HANDS-ON PRACTICE ■

With the template, the flow chart, and Bloom's Taxonomy in hand, try planning your own IP using the following template. You may want to continue to develop the same topic as in previous Hands-On Practices, or you may choose another topic altogether.

For two parcels, decide on two major, related concepts, principles, and/or themes that capture the heart of the Rationale. Assign one of those distinct ideas as the focus for each mini-talk. Also keep in mind that the overarching concept(s), principle(s), or theme may peak in either the mini-discussion or the Culmination.

Self-Instruct Planner for the Interactive Presentation Method

Subject _____ Topic _____

(Work on a separate piece of paper.)

PRELUDE (for teacher reference)
• Rationale (What two concepts, principles, and/or themes will capture the heart of this Rationale in the two mini-talks?)
  What are you teaching?
  Why are you teaching this?
  Justification
• Performance Objective
  Preparation
  Product
  Criteria
• Materials

ENACTMENT (student engagement)
• Aim
• Hook
• Development (with IP method markers)
  PARCEL ONE (may be deductive or inductive)
  • Mini-Talk #1 (with one or more advance organizers)
  • Mini-Task #1 (includes Performance Objective)
  PARCEL TWO (may be inductive or deductive)
  • Mini-Talk #2 (with one or more advance organizers)
  • Mini-Task #2 (includes Performance Objective)
  MINI-DISCUSSION (Include sample Trigger, Probe, and Redirected questions)
• Culmination
  Wrap-Up
  Leap

ASSESSMENT AND EVALUATION PLAN
  Assessment Products
  Evaluation Rubric Categories with Point Scale

ENDNOTES

1. Based on a lesson by Cyndie Morain when she was a preservice teacher at the University of Illinois in Urbana-Champaign.
2. *The Shadow of Hate* is a video available from the "Teaching Tolerance" program of the Southern Poverty Law Center, 400 Washington Avenue, Montgomery, AL 36104.

SUGGESTED READINGS

Atwell, N. (1987). *In the middle: Writing, reading and learning with adolescents.* Upper Montclair, NH: Boynton/Cook Publishers.

Eisner, E. (1985). *Educational imagination* (2nd ed.). Upper Saddle River, NJ: Merrill/Prentice Hall.

Middendorf, J., & Kalish, A. (1996). The "change-up" in lectures. *The National Teaching & Learning Forum*, 5(2), 1–5.

Shostar, R. (1990). Lesson presentation skills. In: J. M. Cooper (Ed.), *Classroom teaching skills* (4th ed.). Lexington, MA: Heath.

Methods Finale: Integrating Methods

Example #1/Sample
Combination for a Wide-
Ranging Unit

Example #2/Sample
Combination for a Unit of Three
Major Concepts

Here are two examples of combining methods with peer-group learning and other techniques of your choice for unit planning. Keep in mind that various techniques in addition to peer-group learning carry out every method.

EXAMPLE #1/SAMPLE COMBINATION FOR A WIDE-RANGING UNIT

1. Field-test your students' schema of a unit's Rationales with an ILPE.
2. Employ Directed Discussions and/or Inductive and Deductive Concept lessons to introduce each major concept, principle, and theme.
3. Develop further substance with an Interactive Presentation.
4. Explore concepts, principles, and/or themes further with an Exploratory Discussion.
5. Assign focused research on the concepts.
6. Enable students to evaluate and synthesize various aspects of major concepts, principles, and themes with a Reflective Discussion, applying their research findings and achieving high cognitive levels.
7. Incorporate peer-group learning techniques so that students can apply the concepts, principles, and themes introduced with the previously mentioned methods, discovering new facts and insights with guided independence using instructional materials.

EXAMPLE #2/SAMPLE COMBINATION FOR A UNIT OF THREE MAJOR CONCEPTS

PROCESS: FOR EACH OF THREE CONCEPTS:

A. Employ a Directed Discussion followed by an Inductive or Deductive Concept lesson.
B. Plan an Exploratory Discussion that examines two (or more) principles of the concept.
C. Design a peer-group learning activity that applies a given concept and/or derived principles.
D. Plan an Interactive Presentation to address any gaps you have identified in the students' level of understanding. Assign further focused research for more in-depth understanding. Different student clusters may research different aspects of the concept.
E. Plan a Reflective Discussion as a wrap-up of the concept. Students would apply their research findings in role-play, class debate, open forum, and so on, thereby learning from one another's research.
F. After the Reflective Discussion of the third concept, peer-group learning activities can create a product that interrelates all three major concepts of the unit.

NOTE: curricular constraints may require that you condense this model.

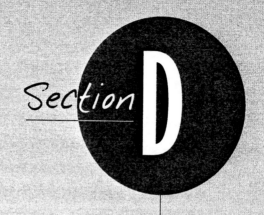

Section D

Putting It All Together

Modules 13, 14, and 15 in Section D provide a global view of planning and teaching. Although these modules appear at the end of the book, they may be read at the beginning of the course to provide an overview. If read last, they provide a synthesis of what has come before.

Module 13 addresses unit planning in two stages. Part 1 presents the basics, and Part 2 plunges into a more advanced level. Both parts take a step-by-step approach. Whereas Module 13 touches on assessment and evaluation, Module 14 takes an in-depth look at assessment and evaluation. This area often creates a disconnect between constructivist teaching methods and the instruments used to judge the quality of learning; the reason for this is that traditional instruments alone, such as tests, quizzes, and papers, are not wide ranging enough for you as a constructivist teacher to judge the quality of your students' learning. For this reason, Module 14 offers you a wide assortment of assessment and evaluation practices for constructivist student products.

Finally, your students and you as the teacher have likely been socialized in the traditional mode of learning and teaching. The unconscious assumptions from this past experience may impede the success of a constructivist learning process. We tackle this predicament directly in Module 15. Part 1 describes and demonstrates the elements of teaching and learning that must be refashioned for a vibrant constructivist classroom, from your students' affective needs to the teacher and student roles in an active learning environment. Part 2 discusses classroom management from a constructivist rather than a behavioristic perspective.

If you read Section D as a way to launch the methods course, we recommend that you look over these modules again after you have read the first three sections. In this way, the global view can give you a larger framework at the outset and then bring the parts together in the finale.

Module Thirteen:

Unit Planning

PART 1:
The Basics

■ OVERVIEW

Unit plans consist of three or more lessons related to the same instructional goal. A unit may span across one week or two or more months. When you teach with units, you help your students explore different aspects of a topic with in-depth understanding. This module introduces you to the components of unit planning. It can be read before Module 3 to provide a global view of planning first or after Module 3 as a way to organize individual lessons.

■ GOALS

Part 1 of this module contains the following features:

- A global view of unit planning
- A template of unit planning with Unit Components
- Related lesson Rationales
- Assessment and Evaluation
- The scope of a unit

Before we begin to address these goals, try to detect the elements of unit planning in the scenario that follows.

A Scenario

It's 1889. Prince Rilka of Svetlania recently visited his great uncle and great aunt, Count Peter and the Countess Teresa. One night, the Prince overheard their conversation. Both were ancient and nearly deaf, and they thought they were whispering, but Prince Rilka heard everything through the mahogany door. It seems that Princess Olga, grandmother of Prince Rilka, had fled the old country in the wake of an uprising and had buried the jewels she was unable to take with her, hoping to return for them in calmer times. Count Peter and Countess Teresa had spent years trying to find the buried treasure in vain, and, now that their days were few, they despaired of finding the jewels that they believed they had a right to as family heirlooms.

Prince Rilka was in his forties and still strong and willful. His family inheritance was dwindling, and he would soon be left with nothing. He lifted his ear from the door when he heard his aunt and uncle agree to retire for the night, and, before they rose from their chairs by the fire, our hero tip toed out of sight. As he hurried away, he vowed to analyze possible clues; if he could establish or just infer they existed, then he would seek out the buried jewels for himself, his wife, and his five children lest their titles be their only inheritance. This vow became his compelling goal.

Two questions plagued him. Was the rumor true? If there were buried jewels, what evidence could lead him to them?

The prince devised a plan. He would inquire among his relatives if they possessed Princess Olga's diary, which might reveal the location of the treasure. Or perhaps he could search for surviving letters in his relatives' attics. He might even find a hastily drawn map. He would also probe his older relatives for any untold stories about the flight of Princess Olga that might serve as clues. Of course, there was always the heart-breaking possibility that she had taken all her jewels with her and spent their worth.

And so, Prince Rilka set out to discover the truth.

—©2001 Ina Claire Gabler

Yes, this scenario does relate to unit planning. We will unfold the reasons step by step. But first, you need a global view before we relate unit planning to Prince Rilka's quest.

■ DISCUSSION

A significant difference between a solo lesson and a unit is that the latter can attain greater depth than a single lesson can. In a unit, each lesson builds on or complements the previous one, all organized around a shared topic.

Think of it this way. A unit has a kernel with offshoots. The kernel is the topic, and the offshoots are the individual lessons that develop the topic. So the first step in planning a unit is to select an appropriate kernel or centerpiece for your unit. Then determine how each lesson can develop the topic.

Focal Point 1: **A Global View**

For starters, take a look at Figures 13.1, 13.2, and 13.3 for graphic representations of unit plans in language arts, history, and science, respectively. These unit plans are all

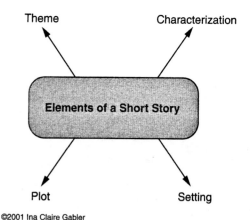

©2001 Ina Claire Gabler

FIGURE 13.1 Unit Planning: An Example in Language Arts

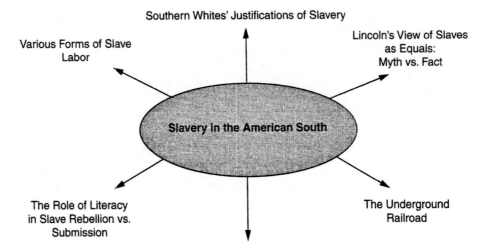

Southern Whites' Justifications of Slavery

Various Forms of Slave Labor

Lincoln's View of Slaves as Equals: Myth vs. Fact

Slavery in the American South

The Role of Literacy in Slave Rebellion vs. Submission

The Underground Railroad

Two Major Abolitionists: Their Expressed Motives and Fate

©2001 Ina Claire Gabler

FIGURE 13.2 Unit Planning: An Example in History

broad, without details. The intention is to give you a general schema of the kernel and its offshoots. Remember Prince Rilka's vow? Figure 13.4 is one way to represent his situation as a unit.

Discussion 1: A Global View

In the figures included here, the unit kernel is a broad topic that generates various strands. In a teacher-planned unit, you select the strands that you believe are most important for your students to know about the topic.

When you looked at Figures 13.1 through 13.4, you may have realized that each offshoot or strand can generate its own offshoots. In this way, each strand becomes an independent lesson. Consider Figure 13.5 as an example of this branching.

Focal Point 2: Unit Template with Unit Components

The concept maps in Figures 13.1 through 13.5 gave you a broad picture or schema of organizing a unit plan. Now we're taking the elements of a unit plan one step further with the unit template with the following four components: topic, goal, strat-

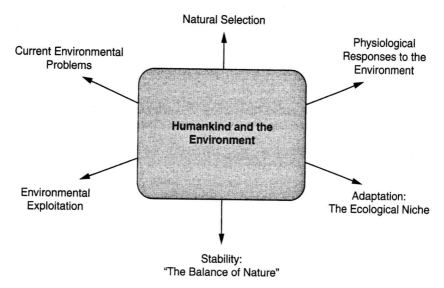

©2001 Michael Schroeder

FIGURE 13.3 Unit Planning: An Example in Science

egy, and driving questions. The outline below orders the four Unit Components into a template.

1. Topic
2. Goal
3. Strategy
4. Driving Questions

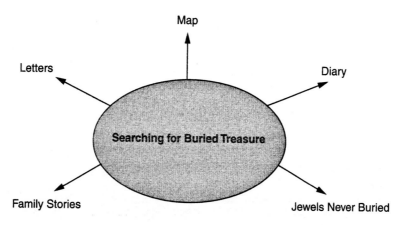

©2001 Ina Claire Gabler

FIGURE 13.4 Unit Planning: Prince Rilka's Quest

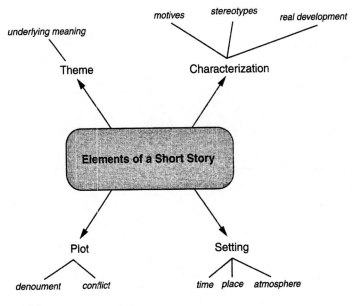

©2001 Ina Claire Gabler

FIGURE 13.5 Unit Planning: An Expanded Example in Language Arts

---

Unit Template with Unit Components

What follows is a description of each component for a unit plan. We'll show how each component relates to Prince Rilka's scenario. Later on, we provide subject area examples of unit components.

Topic

The *topic describes the focus of the unit.* The topic is not a single word or a noun with an adjective. The topic is expressed in a phrase with at least one key word that provides direction.

In the scenario with Prince Rilka, the topic could be expressed as "finding buried treasure." "Treasure" or "buried treasure" is too general for a topic. The key word "finding" gives direction.

Goal

The *goal* is the umbrella of the unit. *The goal states a broad instructional intention.* The intention includes both content and cognitive (thinking) skills that embrace several lessons, each one addressing a different aspect of the goal.

In Prince Rilka's scenario, the goal is Rilka's resolve to analyze possible clues; if he could establish or just infer that they existed, then he would seek out the buried jewels. The cognitive skills are "analyze" and "infer." The content or substance is to seek out the jewels.

Strategy

The *strategy describes a process*. The strategy describes *an instructional plan to carry out the goal*. The strategy also cites a course of action that carries out the goal and develops the topic.

For example, an instructional plan could be for your students to research a topic, interpret and analyze the information, and then create original products reflecting what they have learned—Websites, magazines, research papers, and so on. Another strategy could be for the students to solidify basic skills early in the unit and then apply those skills independently. All of the skills directly relate to the goal.

Prince Rilka's strategy is to inquire among his relatives to see if they possessed Princess Olga's diary . . . search for surviving letters in his relatives' attics . . . find a hastily drawn map . . . probe his older relatives for any untold stories about the flight of Princess Olga that might serve as clues. Notice how each step of the strategy (1) relates back to the goal of analyzing clues and seeking out the buried treasure and (2) describes a discrete action.

Since the strategy (sometimes called the "unit title") is often confused with the topic, we've drawn up a comparison of these Unit Components in Figure 13.6. As you review Figure 13.6, keep in mind that a topic is a concise focus whereas a strategy describes an instructional process.

Unit Topic	Unit Strategy
1. Language arts: *Interrelating the elements of short stories*	1. Explore how four elements of the short story—plot, theme, setting, and characterization—work together and build meaning.
2. History: *The worldwide effects of the Great Depression*	2. Examine the specific results of the Great Depression in the U.S. and Germany and trace the impact on the respective governments.
3. Math: *Probability in our lives*	3. Discover the importance of probability for decision making in crucial matters.
4. Art: *Drawing shapes*	4. Experiment with the proportions of line and form.
5. PE: *Applied basketball basics*	5. Apply dribbling, passing, and shooting skills to game situations.
6. Foreign language: *Idioms for socializing*	6. Learn ten conversational idioms and role-play their use.
7. Science: *The influence of genetic inheritance*	7. Analyze the findings of Gregor Mendel in his experiments with peas.

FIGURE 13.6 Topic versus Strategy

Driving Questions

The *driving questions* should make your students think about the point of the unit. *Driving questions point to the heart of the unit and whet curiosity.* These questions convey an exploratory approach.

Prince Rilka had two driving questions: Was the rumor true? If there were buried jewels, what evidence could lead him to them? Notice how these driving questions relate to the topic, goal, and strategy.

Examples of Unit Components

In the examples in Figure 13.7, notice how the components build on and complement one another. They set the stage for planning the individual unit lessons.

Focal Point 3 Writing Lesson Rationales

The Unit Components provide the scope for your unit lessons. Remember that each strand becomes an individual lesson that helps to develop the topic. The goal, strategy, and driving questions serve as signposts.

For example, you may remember that Prince Rilka's goal was to analyze possible clues; if he could establish or just infer they existed, then he would seek out the buried jewels. His strategy of searching in various ways for clues carries out the goal. Similarly, his driving questions provide a telescoped focus that relates to the topic, goal, and strategy.

In other words, the Unit Components must create cohesion for the unit's individual lessons. With cohesion in mind, examine the sample lesson Rationales that follow for each of three unit topics below. If you've not yet read Module 3, what you need to know here is that the Rationale has three parts that express the instructional intention of an individual lesson. Think of the Rationale as the instructional rudder for each lesson. At this point, you need to consider only the "What are you teaching?" part of the Rationale.

Examples of Rationales

EXAMPLE #1/FOREIGN LANGUAGE TOPIC: USING THREE VERBS IN IDIOMS

Rationale 1. What are you teaching? Students will learn to correctly use the verb *faire* in the present and past tense in five common French idioms.

Rationale 2. What are you teaching? Students will learn to correctly use the verb *aller* in the present and past tense in four common French idioms.

Rationale 3. What are you teaching? Students will learn to correctly use the verb *etre* in the present and past tense in four common French idioms.

Rationale 4. What are you teaching? Students will practice using the verbs *faire, aller,* and *etre* in the present and past tense in various French idioms during interactive role-play.

EXAMPLE #2/MATH TOPIC: GRAPHING EQUATIONS WITH MORE THAN ONE
UNKNOWN

Rationale 1. What are you teaching? Students will comprehend and solve three to five
algebraic equations with two unknowns for the first time. The algebraic problems
relate to real-life problem solving.

Rationale 2. What are you teaching? Students will learn to graph yesterday's (Rationale
1's) algebraic equations with two unknowns. They will analyze the graphs in their
own words and apply the graphs to the real-life problems.

Rationale 3. What are you teaching? In groups of three, learners will design their own
real-life problem with two unknowns. Peer groups will solve, graph, and analyze the
solutions of another group's problem for homework.

Topic (a phrase that narrows the area of learning	Overarching Goal (an instructional directive for content and cognitive skills)	Strategy (a plan to carry out the goal)	Driving Questions (point to the heart of the unit; pique student interest)
1. *Language arts:* Interrelating the elements of a short story	1. To develop students' ability to analyze the elements of a short story so that they develop critical reading skills and derive increased enjoyment and value from reading short stories for personal enrichment.	1. Explore how four elements of the short story—plot, theme, setting, and characterization—work together and build meaning.	1a. How can you decipher the riddle of a story? 1b. How can a story with an unfamiliar setting and characters you'll never meet be important to you?
2. *The Great Depression:* The Political effects of the Great Depression (GD)	2. To understand and evaluate the economic impact on U.S. and Nazi politics during the GD.	2. Examine the economic programs during the GD in the U.S. and Germany and trace the impact on the respective governments.	2a. What role did the GD in the '30s play in the rise and triumph of Nazism and in FDR's New Deal? 2b. Why did the GD have a different political impact on the American and German governments?

FIGURE 13.7 Examples of Unit Components

Now study Figure 13.8, which includes additional examples of Rationales with the Unit Components for English and history.

Focal Point 4: Assessment and Evaluation

How do you establish what your students have learned from the unit? Like lesson plans, a unit plan needs to include assessment and evaluation. First, you need to know the difference between assessment and evaluation. *Evaluation* is the process of making a judgment about the quality of student learning. *Assessment* is the act of identifying the relevant features of each student product you use to make these judgments: portfolios, presentations, questionnaires, tests, oral interviews, enactments, discussions, original Websites, and more. In a nutshell, assessment is data collection and evaluation is data analysis.

Discussion 4: Assessment and Evaluation

As a constructivist teacher, you need strategies other than multiple-choice or fill-in exams for judging what your students have learned. Students in a constructivist environment are active learners. They create original products, especially in units. They learn to question and think critically. In time, they become independent learners, selecting their own topics for projects and constructing their own insights justified with sources. You can see that as a constructivist teacher you will need strategies for judging your students' performance-based products instead of checking largely for rote memorization. We explore evaluation and assessment in depth in Module 14. For now, we're introducing it as an important part of the planning process. To assess and evaluate the quality of learning in a unit, ask yourself two questions:

- What products will my students generate?
- What are the criteria for acceptable achievement?

See Figure 13.9 for an overview of the difference between assessment products and evaluation.

Focal Point 5: Scope of Your Unit

New teachers are often challenged by unit planning. Don't be surprised or discouraged if your first topics and driving questions are too large, resulting in superficial lessons to address the many facets of your ambitious aspirations. Even experienced teachers sometimes underestimate how long a single lesson will take and are left with "spillover" from a lesson for a second day, unable to introduce the second lesson on time. So be prepared! As a new teacher, you will often underestimate how long a lesson will take. Another way of putting this common practice is to say that you will often overestimate how much you can teach in a single lesson.

Topic (a phrase that narrows the area of learning)	Goal (an instructional directive for content and cognitive skills)	Strategy (a plan to carry out the goal)	Driving Questions (point to the heart of the unit; pique student interest)	Three Lesson Rationales (instructional intentions for the unit)
1. *Language arts:* Relating the elements of a short story	1. To develop students' ability to analyze and interrelate the elements of a short story so that they develop critical reading skills and derive increased enjoyment and value from reading short stories for personal enrichment.	1. Explore how four elements of the short story—plot, theme, setting, and characterization—work together and build meaning.	1a. How can you decipher the riddle of a story? 1b. How can a story with an unfamiliar setting and characters you'll never meet be important to you?	• For *The Legend of Sleepy Hollow* (*LSH*) by Washington Irving, students will analyze how the setting and selected actions in the plot establish key characteristics for Brom Bones and Ichabod Crane. • Students will enlarge their understanding of *LSH* by analyzing the conflict between Brom Bones and Ichabod Crane. Learners will apply their analysis to metaphoric interpretations of the Headless Horseman. • Students will apply their analysis of *LSH* to evaluate how plot, setting, and characterization work together to build meaning. Students will then define one or more themes in *LSH* related to the students' own lives while the plot and setting may be unrelated to their lives.
2. *The Great Depression:* Political effects of the Great Depression (GD)	2. To understand and evaluate the economic impact on U.S. and Nazi politics during the GD.	2. Examine the economic programs during the GD in the U.S. and Germany and trace the impact on the respective governments.	2a. What role did the GD in the '30s play in the rise and triumph of Nazism and in FDR's New Deal? 2b. Why did the GD have a different political impact on the American and German governments?	• To comprehend and analyze the role of the New Deal solutions to unemployment. Why was the New Deal supported? Why was it opposed? • To comprehend and analyze the Nazi solutions to unemployment. What was the support base and why? • Students will compare and contrast the similarities and differences between the New Deal and Nazi economic solutions to the GD.

FIGURE 13.8 Examples of Unit components with Rationales/English

Sample Products for Assessment	Sample Criteria for Evaluation; Create Rubrics for the Following
1. Research paper or related products such as original magazines 2. Original Website 3. Original video 4. Enactment of a play 5. Role-play or debate based on research 6. Lab experiment 7. Original drawings or paintings 8. Demonstration of targeted motor skills 9. Role-play conversation in a foreign language employing targeted expressions, verbs, etc. 10. Portolios 11. Presentations 12. Interview skills 13. Student journals 14. Tests	1. Organization and structure 2. Written proficiency 3. Critical thinking: development of concepts, principles, and themes with documentation and clear logic 4. Satisfaction of the goal 5. Satisfaction of the Student Aims 6. Originality 7. Thoroughness 8. Growth from previous performance 9. Diction and enunciation 10. Drawing proficiency for targeted skills 11. Motor coordination 12. Production values 13. Test results in conjunction with other performance-based assessments

FIGURE 13.9 Sample Products and Criteria

Discussion 5: **Scope of Your Unit**

We call the inclination to overestimate how much you can teach within the time frame the *generosity factor*. The generosity factor refers to your desire to give all you can to your students, to shower them with learning. In a constructivist approach, learning is not measured predominantly by the number of facts your students temporarily remember. Of course, facts matter. They are the foundation of a higher order of thinking. But that's just it. A constructivist teacher takes the view that facts are the fuel for students' critical thinking—conceptualizing and generating principles and themes that demonstrate a high level of understanding.

So the danger in unit planning at first is that you will overreach, trying to incorporate too much information, and you may end up sacrificing in-depth thinking for a roster of facts and spoon-fed concepts and principles.

The Eye of a Flea

Consider the size of a flea relative to yourself. If one landed long enough on you, you could squash it with your finger. Yet, within that minute creature is a complicated life system. Respiration, digestion, elimination, reproduction. Imagine the brain, the heart, the circulatory system. If you wanted to plan a biology unit focused on the flea, you would have a great amount of information to teach. Would your students have the time to learn about all the internal systems of each organ and life function beyond a brush-stroke approach?

Now imagine just the eye of a flea. The insect's eye may be minuscule, but it is a complex organ with chemicals and interrelated parts and functions, an organ that "communicates" with the brain—which is another complex organ even in a flea. Now imagine planning a unit about just the eye of a flea. Your students would marvel at their in-depth learning about that ocular universe!

So, as a general practice, when you begin to plan a unit, strive for in-depth learning rather than a global sweep.

Examples of Unit Overreach

- History: World War II (What aspects of WWII)?
- Art: Drawing (What techniques? What materials?)
- Physical Education: Football (What type of play? What role for each player?)
- Science: Gases (What function or properties? In what context?)
- Language Arts: Reading novels (What elements? What type of novel?)
- Foreign language: Idioms (For which contexts? Slang or standard?)
- Math: Geometry (What aspects?)

You may have noticed that all the overreach examples are single-word topics rather than phrases with a directing key word or two or more key words. A single word is too general to provide useful focus. To start, however, you can begin the thinking process with a single word. Then decide on the specific direction you want to take. The questions after the single-word topics in the previous examples suggest a direction that each topic could take.

■ ROUNDUP ■

You can't plan a successful unit without cohesion among the Unit Components and the lesson Rationales. Every component must relate to the others. A well-focused goal and a specific strategy foster strong driving questions and focused lessons. Just as Prince Rilka needed to question many relatives and examine a variety of clues to find a possible buried treasure, a teacher needs a series of lessons, at least three, to facilitate the students' in-depth grasp of the topic. Finally we'd like to remind you not to overreach when you plan a unit.

■ HANDS-ON PRACTICE ■

Try your hand at outlining a unit plan with Unit Components and lesson Rationales instead of fleshed out lesson plans at this point. We provide the following unit template to guide your planning.

Self-Instruct Planner: Unit Outline

(Work on a separate piece of paper.)
We suggest that you practice with this exercise before you plan your unit outline.

Practice with Sizing a Unit Topic

> INSIDE TIP: Some of these units are too large for a three-lesson sequence. Others may work.
>
> YOUR GOAL: To help the hypothetical teacher who wrote the unit topic for your subject design an effective three-lesson unit. In this way, you help yourself develop an accurate schema for unit planning within time constraints.

> YOUR JOB:

1. Decide if a topic is too large or if it is workable in your subject area.

2. (A) List reasons why the topic is too large or workable. (B) List strands that occur to you about the topic.

3. If the idea shows potential, try to think of three segments for that unit, each of which could be taught as a separate lesson with its own Rationale. If the unit idea is too large, try to focus it better.

4. Pair up with someone in a different subject area for feedback. Same-subject peers may share your blind spots and assumptions.

REMEMBER THE EYE OF A FLEA!

Chemistry

Topic #1: The Experimental Method
Topic #2: Chemical versus Physical Change

Math

Topic #1: Probability in Medicine
Topic #2: The Algebraic Approach to Problem Solving

History

Topic #1: The Vietnam War versus the Peace Movement in the Sixties
Topic #2: The Role of Freed Slaves in the American Civil War

English

Topic #1: Stereotypes versus Well-Developed Characters
Topic #2: What Is the Meaning of Poetry?

Biology

Topic #1: Learning about the Cell
Topic #2: Darwin's Theory of Evolution

Art

> Topic #1: How to Draw
>
> Topic #2: The Range of Frank Stella

Physical Education

> Topic #1: To Learn Tennis
>
> Topic #2: Offensive versus Defensive Strategy

Music

> Topic #1: Reading Treble and Bass Clef Notes
>
> Topic #2: To Appreciate Classical Music

Write a Unit Outline

DIRECTIONS:

1. Decide on a unit topic in your subject area. Feel free to use one of the ideas in the practice above or select another one if you like.
2. Decide on at least three strands or lessons to develop the topic. Use the unit template with Rationales to guide your outline.
3. First draw a concept map of the unit. Then use the unit template that follows.

   Topic =

   Concept Map =

Unit Template + Rationales

1. *Topic:* The topic describes the focus of the unit in a phrase with at least one key word that provides direction.
2. *Goal:* The goal states a broad instructional intention. It includes both content and cognitive (thinking) skills that embrace several lessons.
3. *Strategy:* The strategy is an instructional plan to carry out the goal. The strategy cites a course of action or process that carries out the goal and develops the topic.
4. *Driving Questions:* Driving questions point to the heart of the unit and whet curiosity. These questions convey an exploratory approach.
5. *Rationales:* Each Rationale describes an instructional intention for one strand of the topic. The Rationale in part answers the question, "What are you teaching?" (Note: If you have read Module 3, try writing all three parts of each Rationale in this unit outline.)

Assessment and Evaluation

- *Assessment:* What are the products and materials your students will generate that embody the scope and quality of their learning? What are the relevant features you will look for?

- *Evaluation:* What are the criteria you will apply to determine an acceptable level of achievement for each product and material?

SUGGESTED READINGS

Black, P., & Wiliam, D. (1998, October). Inside the black box: Raising standards through classroom assessment. *Phi Delta Kappan, 80*(2), 139–148.

Mabry, L. (1999, May). Writing to the rubric: Lingering effects of traditional standardized testing on direct writing assessment. *Phi Delta Kappan, 80*(9), 673–679.

Newmann, F. N. & Associates (1996). *Authentic achievement: Restructuring schools for intellectual quality.* San Francisco: Jossey-Bass.

Perkins, D. (1991, October). Educating for insight. *Educational Leadership, 49*(2), 4–8.

Stiggins, R. J. (1995, November). Assessment literacy for the 21st century. *Phi Delta Kappan, 77*(3), 238–245.

PART 2:
Advanced Level

■ OVERVIEW

There are as many ways to plan a unit as there are teachers. Educators each have their own terms, approaches, and concepts of unit planning. For this reason, we've taken what we consider to be the most effective elements from several sources, many of them variant principles of one another, and adapted them to a constructivist approach. We've also added our own ideas and terms based on our combined teaching experience over the years.

In Part 1 of this module, we provided the basics of conceptualizing and organizing a unit. Part 2 of this module builds on Part 1 with a more extensive view. We therefore suggest that you familiarize yourself with Part 1 before proceeding with this more ambitious process.

■ GOALS

We intend to give you a solid base in planning professional unit plans by describing and/or demonstrating the following:

- Types of units
- A template for an extended unit
- A planning procedure with a timetable, assessment template, and evaluation rubric
- Selection and sequence of methods for a unit
- Selection of techniques, tools, and student products
- Teacher-directed or student-centered unit; contracts
- Example of an interdisciplinary unit

Focal Point 1: **Types of Units**

All units are characterized by a sequence of lessons radiating from the same focal point that we call the kernel. The individual lessons are offshoots of the kernel; they build on and complement one another. If the lessons are thorough and varied, the result becomes an in-depth development of the kernel. So, a well-planned unit creates cohesion, interrelating varied facts, concepts, principles, and themes.

Discussion 1: **Types of Units**

A unit can consist of three lessons, or it can span two months. In the process, your students create a range of products that meaningfully demonstrate what they are learning and how they are growing. You can see how planning units can greatly enhance the quality of your students' education compared with a dominant use of ad hoc lessons.

Flexibility matters. Whether in selecting methods, techniques, or the type of unit for a given instructional intention, you need to reflect on the content and cognitive skills you want your students to strengthen. Then decide what type of unit and methods will best serve that end.

Examples of Unit Types

Consider these unit types and their advantages. We call them the 3C's.

- *Core Unit.* A Core Unit *centers around one aspect of a topic or theme.* All the lessons in a Core Unit are devoted to that idea or kernel in one way or another. Examples of topics are "causes of the American Revolution," "Designing controlled experiments," and "The elements of drawing." Notice how a topic is expressed as a phrase, with one or more words that direct or characterize the focus ("causes," "designing," "elements") rather than a generalized single term that lacks direction ("American Revolution," "controlled experiments," "drawing"). Examples of unit themes are "religion and genocide," "war as resolution," and "football as strategy." (See Module 2, Part 1 for discussion of themes.) A Core Unit grounded in the Cognitive Ladder and Bloom's Taxonomy (see Modules 2 and 4) can progressively guide your students from lower to higher levels of learning within a cohesive framework. In this way, several Core Units can elevate your students' reading and/or performance levels. Similarly, two or more interrelated Core Units can establish the foundation for multifaceted projects.

- *Concept Unit.* A Concept Unit *explores various aspects of an abstract idea or general category.* Each aspect or offshoot of that category governs a separate lesson. Examples of Concept Unit ideas are ecology, nutrition, abolition, transportation, and stereotypes. Some aspects of nutrition, for example, might be components of good nutrition, related health risks, related birth defects, and quality of life. In this way, a Concept Unit enables your students to develop analytical skills around a broad focus. A Concept Unit is effective for developing a range of cognitive skills in diffident as well as confident learners, depending on the concept's complexity. As you can see, Core and Concept Units share similar advantages.

- *Combo Unit.* As the name implies, a Combo Unit *integrates two or more subjects focused on the same topic or theme into an interdisciplinary perspective.* For example, a Combo Unit on *Huckleberry Finn* by Mark Twain could integrate literary analysis with American history of slavery in the South along with the geography and characteristics of the Mississippi River. Whereas Core and Concept Units create cohesion within a single topic, theme, or idea, a Combo Unit goes further by creating interrelationships across various subject areas, demonstrating a cohesive richness in learning across a wide spectrum.

Focal Point 2: **Template and Timetable for Extended Unit Planning with an Assessment/Evaluation Schedule**

Figure 13.10 is a template or outline of a unit plan. This gives you a schematic view, the whole picture with its parts. Figure 13.11 presents an example of a timetable or calendar for the unit along with an assessment/evaluation schedule. Assessment is the act of collecting data from materials and products (including oral products such as enact-

---

Unit Components
1. Topic: the kernel or focal point.
2. Goal: states a broad instructional intention. It includes both content and cognitive skills that embrace several lessons.
3. Strategy: an instructional plan that carries out the goal.
4. Driving questions: at least two questions that point to the heart of the unit and whet curiosity. These questions convey an exploratory approach.

Related Rationales with Methods
Rationale #1/ILPE method: *What* will you teach? *Why* are you teaching this? *Justification:* INTASC Standards.
Rationale #2/Interactive Presentation method: *What? Why? Justification.*
Rationale #3/Exploratory Discussion method: *What? Why? Justification.*
Rationale #4/Inductive Concept method: *What? Why? Justification.*
Rationale #5/Directed Discussion method: *What? Why? Justification.*
Rationale #6/Interactive Presentation method: *What? Why? Justification.*
Rationale #7/Reflective Discussion method: *What? Why? Justification.*
Rationale #2/Student Presentations: *What? Why? Justification.*

Assessment and Evaluation Plan
Assessment Products
Diagnostic: ILPE method + questionnaires
Formative: role-play, concept maps, essays, dialogue (all discussions; Interactive Presentation), peer-group products, journals.
Summative: presentations + papers for presentations guided by rubric.

Evaluation
Rubric for each assessment product (content mastery, cognitive/motor/perceptual skills, growth)

FIGURE 13.10 Sample Template for an Extended Unit

Monday	Tuesday	Wednesday	Thursday	Friday
Rationale #1	Rationale #2	Rationale #2	Rationale #3	Rationale #4
Investigating Learner's Previous Experiences (ILPE) with questionnaires	Interactive Presentation (first of two days)	Interactive Presentation (continued)	Exploratory Discussion	Inductive Concept
Diagnostic Assessment	*Formative Assessment*	*Formative Assessment*	*Formative Assessment*	*Formative Assessment*
Rationale #5	Rationale #6	Rationale #7	Rationale #8	Rationale #9
Directed Discussion	Interactive Presentation	Reflective Discussion (role-play)	Reflective Discussion (debate)	Student Presentations
Formative Assessment	*Formative Assessment*	*Formative Assessment*	*Formative Assessment*	*Summative Assessment*
Rationale #9	Rationale #9	Possible spillover	Begin evaluations with rubric	
Student Presentation	Student Presentations			
Summative Assessment	*Summative Assessment*			

FIGURE 13.11 Sample Timetable for a Unit Plan with Methods and an Assessment/Evaluation Schedule

ments) and describing the included criteria. Evaluation is the act of judging that data according to the quantity and quality of the included criteria. (See Module 14 for an in-depth look at assessment and evaluation.)

Discussion 2: Template and Timetable for Extended Unit Planning with an Assessment/Evaluation Schedule

The unit template in Figure 13.10 contains the elements and flow of a thought-out unit plan. Coupled with the timetable in Figure 13.11, you can see how a unit might unfold. Thinking through the unit components (topic, goal, strategy, and driving questions) enables you to set the stage for more detailed planning with Rationales and constructivist methods. Each method facilitates a different perspective and way of building and integrating knowledge and critical-thinking skills.

You can match the individual characteristics of each method with a given lesson Rationale for optimum learning. Notice how Rationale #2 uses the Interactive Presentation to establish a foundation over two days. Similarly, Rationales #7 and #8 are both Reflective Discussions that build on each other. The first, #7, helps students explore one or more issues with role-playing, and #8 enables them to strengthen their judgment with a formal debate. These are examples of selecting methods to best serve the instructional intention or Rationale.

Focal Point 3: Assignment Template and Evaluation Rubric

Part of planning a dynamic unit includes an activity sheet that we call an assignment template. The following assignment template helps guide your students' learning in four ways. You may change the sequence of the steps according to a given lesson or class. This flexibility applies especially to the order of criteria and prompts.

1. *Student Aim:* The Student Aim expresses each unit lesson's Rationale in colloquial language for accessibility (see Module 3, Part 1).

2. *Product:* Your students need to know what the product is. Will they role-play? Will they interview people in the community and write neighborhood news articles? Will they carry out an original science experiment? Will they enact a play?

3. *Criteria:* Criteria refer to a specified number of items done correctly or a duration of time in which to practice a skill, etc. In this way, criteria set the standard for acceptable achievement. Each activity and product needs its own criteria.

4. *Prompts:* Prompts are questions and directions that guide independent learning in the Development section of each lesson. Stem words and questions derived from Bloom's Table in Figures 2.12, 2.13a, and 2.13b can serve as prompts embedded in your chosen method. However, these are just springboards. As a constructivist teacher, you'll create your own additional prompts tailored to each Rationale and method, enabling your students to carry out the necessary tasks as independent learners.

Examples for the Assignment Template

Some specific examples of the assignment template follow. Note the different sequence of criteria and prompts in these two examples. Would you use the same sequence of those two steps for these lessons? Why?

EXAMPLE #1/SCIENCE[1]

1. *Aim* (what students will learn): How many steps are in the process of purifying water? What are the different signs of each stage of purification?

2. *Product:* Your peer group will present its own plan for water purification.

3. *Criteria:* You and your peers need to establish three steps of water purification. Each of you must be able to identify at least two differences and two similarities among all the water samples.

4. *Prompts:*

   a. Order the bottles from least to most pure drinking water.

   b. Explain in writing why you put the bottles in that order.

   c. Tell what you think happens in each step of purification. How does the data support your view? What can you infer from the appearance of each bottle? Why?

   d. Present your results. Before you begin the presentation, write at least five guiding questions on the board for your classmates to answer at the end.

EXAMPLE #2/PHYSICAL EDUCATION

1. *Aim:* You, too, can successfully throw a football within twenty-five feet!

2. *Product:* You and your buddy will be able to successfully throw a football within twenty-five feet by the end of this class.

3. *Prompts:*

   a. Pay attention to the five attributes of throwing listed below based on the demonstration and discussion.
     Attributes
      i. Starting stance.
      ii. Eye focus.
      iii. Hand placement on the ball.
      iv. Arm motion during the throw.
      v. Proper release of ball.

   b. Give your buddy feedback on each of these items. Which are OK? Which need correction and why? Pay attention to eye, hand, and body coordination as described in the demonstration and discussion.

4. *Criteria:* Practice with a partner for at least twenty minutes. You should strive to throw a football as described and succeed with all five attributes of a successful throw by the end of class. Each of you must use a chart to analyze your throw for each attribute.

Just as the assignment template is necessary for your learners, an evaluation rubric is necessary for yourself. The categories and point system in your rubric help ensure that you will carry out thorough and thoughtful judgment of your students' work.

Below are sample categories of an evaluation rubric. See Module 14 for a detailed description of an evaluation rubric.

Sample Categories for an Evaluation Rubric

1. List the relevant features of the product. For example, the relevant features of a five-paragraph personal essay are the following:

  • *Structure:* Introduction, three body paragraphs, and a conclusion.

  • *Content:* The introduction must contain a thesis statement that expresses your point of view. Each paragraph in the body develops a main idea that supports your point of view in a different way. The conclusion repeats your point of view along with a summarizing interpretation, principle, or theme.

2. List the *criteria* that develop the relevant features.

- The introduction contains the three main ideas in the body as well as the thesis statement.
- Each body paragraph must contain at least three details to support the main idea.
- The conclusion must summarize the body paragraphs with an original interpretation.
- There must be at least two compound sentences and two complex sentences. In addition, there must be one question that introduces one of the paragraphs in an engaging way.
- To go beyond "7" on a 10-point scale (one example of scoring), the ideas should express earnestness that goes beyond perfunctory compliance with the criteria. In addition, the personal essay should contain at least two to three original examples of the main ideas.

3. How many of the criteria did the student include in the product?
4. On a point scale of your own making, evaluate the quantity and quality of each criterion in the student's product.

Focal Point 4: Planning Procedures

You may be asking yourself at this point how you begin planning a unit and making use of the unit template. The following suggested steps are a procedural guide for the planning process.

1. Select a focal point or kernel idea that relates to your curriculum at a given time. Most likely, a single word may hit you at first, such as "ecology." You then need to decide what you want your students to learn about ecology. You may want your students to examine a specific perspective. In that case, a Core Unit may best meet their learning needs at that time. If so, you need to express the topic as a phrase with a directing or characterizing word or words that channel the focus, such as "applying ecology to your neighborhood." Or, perhaps you want to have a more broad approach, with flexibility to examine various aspects of the kernel idea. If so, then you will want to plan a Concept Unit with individual aspects of ecology. Each aspect would govern one Rationale in the Concept Unit and would also be integrated with the other aspects of ecology as a unified issue. Examples of individual aspects include the food chain, acid rain, preserving tropical forests, and human survival. Finally, you may decide that a Combo Unit taught with a colleague would best achieve your instructional intention of integrating the concept of ecology with urban planning, for example. Remember, your choice of unit type begins with the focal point or kernel.

2. Decide on the offshoots of the focal point or kernel. Again, examine your curriculum. Which offshoots of the focal point or kernel need to be taught? Which offshoots can be subsumed under others? Jot down the related offshoots.

3. Organize your ideas into a concept map or outline. Brainstorm with the focal point and offshoots. Include ideas that branch from the offshoots (see Figure 13.5 in

Part 1 of this module). Then organize these ideas in a form best suited to your thinking process: a concept map, outline, or both.

4. Write related Rationales for individual lessons. Take your concept map and/or outline and identify the key issues. Write a lesson Rationale for each key issue. Then check to see that each Rationale relates logically and meaningfully to your unit's focal point. Adjust as necessary. Perhaps rethink your offshoots, concept map, outline, and so on. Persist with this step until you are satisfied with the Rationales.

5. Write the Unit Components. Using the lesson Rationales as rudders for each lesson, write out the Unit Components of topic, goal, strategy, and driving questions. Doing this is part of the thinking process. Each Unit Component should complement and build on the others. In this way, you'll grow into the unit as you plan the heart of it.

6. Fill in the unit template for "Unit Components" and "Related Rationales with Methods." Once you line up the key parts of the template, you can begin to reflect on which methods (and techniques) best develop the unit, one Rationale at a time. Which method can best provide the kind of foundation you want for your students? Do you want them to explore their own ideas first, then expose them to appropriate resources that enable them to reconsider their incomplete schemata? Do you want to introduce them to a knowledge base before they explore concepts? Do you want to guide their interpretation of a key principle, then branch out from there? How will you incorporate Bloom's Taxonomy and the Cognitive Ladder? (See Modules 2 and 4.) A different method facilitates each of these approaches. Once you select your first or second method, that will suggest the sequence of other methods matched to the remaining Rationales.

7. Plan each lesson completely. Once you've worked out the "map" of the unit, plan each individual lesson according to the lesson template in Module 3, Part 1. Again, make any necessary adjustments so the individual lessons build on and complement each other. Keep sight of the Unit Components. The lessons must carry out the topic, goal, and strategy and must address the driving questions. Always check for internal logic within the lessons and within the entire unit. A unit needs cohesion.

8. Fill in the template for the "Assessment and Evaluation Plan." Consider the tasks, discussions, products, and tests or quizzes throughout the unit. These will be your students' assessment materials. What will the diagnostic assessment(s) be? The formative and summative assessments? What categories and criteria will you use to evaluate your students' learning?

9. Plan a realistic timetable. Now that you have the details as well as the broad picture planned, decide how many days each Rationale or lesson will probably take with a given class. Which Rationales will need two or even three days? Which ones will fit into one day? Plan a timetable accordingly. We recommend that you allow at least one day for spillover.

10. Design the assignment template and the evaluation rubric.

Student Assignment Template

Decide on criteria and prompts for each student product, whether a discussion, a role-play, a concept map, an essay, or an original Website. In this way, the assignment template gives your students meta-awareness of the criteria you value in their learning process. In addition, you can invite your students to add their own criteria. What do they themselves want to achieve?

Teacher Evaluation Rubric

With student meta-awareness, the evaluation rubric that you use can also be used by the students as a checklist as they work. In this way, you encourage student self-evaluation as mature learners.

Discussion 4: Planning Procedures

There are other decisions you need to make in addition to those above. Will a given unit be completely organized by you as a teacher-directed unit? A constructivist teacher-directed unit facilitates an active student learning role throughout, but the teacher is responsible for the planning. Or are your students ready to plan and organize a meaningful unit themselves with your guidelines, based around a topic on the syllabus as a student-centered unit? Will they effectively design the assessment template and evaluation rubric with your guidance and final approval?

Another practice to consider is a contract agreement. In this approach, you write a contract that specifies standards for satisfactory achievement for grades A, B, C, and so on. Standards may include social behavior in peer groups, for example, as well as academic criteria. Those students who sign the contract must be held to it. It's a good idea for each student and you to sign two copies of the same contract, one for each student and one for you for ongoing reference. Contracts can motivate students to take a responsible and mature approach to learning.

Finally, be sure to include a wide range of techniques, materials, tasks, and products in addition to varied methods in the unit (see Module 3, Part 2). Each lesson should result in different kinds of outcomes: enactments, digital products, written products, original videos, peer-group products, and so on. This variety ensures that multiple intelligences and various learning styles are met.

Focal Point 5: Example of a Combo Unit Plan

The following example is based on a Combo Unit plan written by Jeremy Shubert and David Elder as the culminating project for their constructivist secondary methods course when they were preservice teachers at Millikin University in Decatur, Illinois. The unit combines ecology and history focused on a prototype rural community. For more sample unit plans, please see the Appendix.

The reason we chose a Combo Unit is that it demonstrates unit planning for individual subjects as well as two integrated subjects.

UNIT TITLE: A SUCCESSFUL RURAL COMMUNITY IN THE AMERICAN GILDED AGE

UNIT COMPONENTS

Topic: Factors or resources that constitute a successful and productive rural habitat environment.

Goal: American history and biology students will collaborate to gain better understanding of what a successful and effective rural environment consists of. Students will analyze, synthesize, and evaluate source materials from the perspective of both subjects. Students will apply that knowledge as authentic learning: they will create their own Website that portrays a possible rural productive community during the Gilded Age.

Strategy: Students from two different classes, one in ecology and the other in American history, will collaborate in pairs between the classes. Ecology students in each pair will first comprehend then compare and contrast the role of people, plants, and wildlife in both successful and endangered rural communities. History students in each pair will comprehend and then analyze various themes about prairie life in the Great Plains during the Gilded Age. Student pairs will teach each other via email since their classes meet at different times. They will integrate the information and analyses from both classes to carry out the goal of creating the specified Website.

Driving Questions:

1. What are the environmental dangers of human beings dominating rural landscapes and communities?

2. How can the history of the Great Plains help us design a successful rural community that would have existed during the Gilded Age?

RELATED RATIONALES WITH METHODS

Ecology

- *Rationale #1/Investigating Learner's Previous Experiences (ILPE) Method:* Students will be invited to share their conceptions about the causes of environmentally sound or imperiled rural communities. Students will also be encouraged to consider the impact of rural communities on urban communities (i.e., on themselves as city dwellers). Learners will compare and contrast their conceptions with those depicted in a video on thriving and threatened rural communities today.

- *Rationale #2/Interactive Presentation Method with Concept Maps, Original Charts, and Library Research:* Students will learn about the environmental effects of soybeans, corn, oak tree twigs, and pine tree twigs. Students will create concept maps and charts to interpret and apply the benefits and detriments of these plants for a rural habitat.

- *Rationale #3/Reflective Discussion Method:* In groups of four roles each, students will further discuss the impacts of various plants on farmers, local businesses, wildlife, and the community at large. Students will arrive at justified value judgments.

- *Rationale #4/Interactive Presentation with Directed Discussion:* Students will learn about various forms of wildlife: What are their needs? How do they satisfy their needs? How does wildlife affect rural human communities? How do human beings affect the wildlife?

- *Rationale #5/Inductive Concept/Principle Method:* Students will compare and contrast positive and negative aspects of the human influence on rural communities. (Principle: The human role decisively impacts rural habitats.)

- *Materials:* Websites with information about the role of people, plants, and wildlife in rural habitats along with definitions of key ecological terms; library sources in addition to the Internet; transparencies; electronic slides; white board; video; *On the Origin of Species* by Charles Darwin; *The Effects of Animal Behavior on Society* by Dick Lyell; and email collaborations.

American History

- *Rationale #1/Investigating Learner's Previous Experiences (ILPE) Method:* Students will share their notions about the physical characteristics of the Great Plains region during 1865–1900. What do they believe everyday life was like then, on the prairie? Compare and contrast these notions with a corresponding historical scenario.

- *Rationale #2/Directed Discussion Method (Deductive) and Library Research:* Students will comprehend the physical features of the Great Plains during the Gilded Age. Students will apply and analyze the effects of these features on Great Plains farmers at that time in original written scenarios.

- *Rationale #3/Interactive Presentation Method with Peer Dyads:* Learners will be introduced to two historical events: the national railroad network and the Homestead Act of 1862. In pairs, students will infer the impact of these events on farming in the Great Plains during the Gilded Age. They will convey these ideas with concept maps or outlines, as they prefer.

- *Rationale #4/Directed Discussion Method (Inductive):* Students will consider the various farming technologies developed during the Gilded Age. They will infer the advantages and any possible disadvantages for prairie farmers. Students will write daily journal entries describing the impact of technology as if they were farmers during that time.

- *Materials:* library sources, the Internet, original scenarios, transparencies, electronic slides, white board, email collaborations, still photos, barbed wire (prop as a Hook).

ASSESSMENT AND EVALUATION PLAN

Assessment Products

Diagnostic: ILPE Method + questionnaires

Formative: role-play enactments, role-play journal writings, concept maps, outlines, research findings related to key questions, brief reports, activity sheets, discussions, email correspondence (used for assessment with student permission).

Summative: An original Website that integrates learning from ecology and American history lessons.

Evaluation

Rubric for each assessment product (content and cognitive skills). Each category will be judged on a five-point scale. Peer work will be evaluated for both individual contributions and collective products.

Assignment Template for a Gilded Age Rural Community Website

1. *Aim:* What was it like to live in a thriving rural community in the American Gilded Age?

2a. *Global Product:* An original Website describing and depicting a successful rural community in the American Gilded Age.

2b. *Individual Products:* Each section of the Website governed by a criterion functions as an individual product. Collectively, the individual products create the global product.

3. *Prompts:*

   a. Collaborate with a peer in the (ecology/history) class. You may mutually choose each other or ask the teachers to select a partner for you. Share what you learn in ecology or history with your partner using daily email.

   b. Take detailed notes based on email correspondence.

   c. With your partner, create graphics such as charts, tables, and concept maps and/or written materials such as outlines throughout the unit as you and your partner prefer. These graphics/written materials should represent the integration of ecological and historical factors that would have contributed to a successful rural community in the Gilded Age.

   d. Be original. Interpret, analyze, integrate, and evaluate the information with your own ideas as much as possible, based on the source materials. Critical thinking counts.

4. *Criteria/Individual Products:* All criteria refer to a successful rural community in the Gilded Age as represented in your Website.

Ecology

   a. Describe at least three ways that each of the following impact the big picture of the rural environment: human beings, plants, and wildlife.

   b. In what ways do human beings, plants, and wildlife collectively affect the environment? Project the effect over a period of 10 years.

   c. Describe if any of the organisms experience greater success over any others. Are females more successful than males or vice versa? Are plants more adaptable than wildlife?

American History

d. Describe at least three effects of each of these physical prairie features in the Gilded Age: topography, climate, natural resources, animals in the region, crops that farmers produce, and environmental problems that troubled prairie farmers.

e. How did these physical features impact one another?

f. Include all the new farming technology in the Gilded Age. Identify each inventor, the function of the invention, and how it helped agricultural life in the Great Plains region.

g. Describe how the railroads and the Homestead Act were major contributions to the development of the Great Plains. Interrelate the physical features and farming technology with these two major contributions.

Integration

h. Demonstrate the interrelationships between all the ecological and historical factors. For example, how might have the physical features of the land and the railroads affected the regional wildlife, plants, and human behavior?

i. For each individual product, include at least three hypertext links for in-depth information. Hyperlinks may also include your own analysis or "what-if," "if-then," or similar scenarios.

j. Include at least one of your own original graphics with captions (tables, charts, concept maps, sketches, and so on) and, if possible, at least one story, poem, photo, etc., for each individual product.

Writing Skills

Professional literacy is a must. This is going up on the Web. Check grammar, punctuation, varied sentence structure, spelling, structure, and so on.

Sample Evaluation Rubric: Website of a Successful Rural Community in the Gilded Age

INDIVIDUAL PRODUCT: *Criteria* = Demonstrate the interrelationships between the ecological and historical factors.

GRADING: Point scale of 1–5. A score of 5 is outstanding. A score of 1 is poor.

RELEVANT FEATURES:

1. Integration. Are all three ecological factors (human beings, plants, and wildlife) related to all the historical factors (physical features, farming technology, railroads, and the Homestead Act)? Points: _____

2. Completeness. Are all the requirements met, including hyperlinks? Points: _____

3. Thoroughness. Is each item developed fully based on the unit information? Points: _____

4. Cognitive Skills. Is there a progression from the knowledge base to higher levels of analysis, synthesis, and evaluation? Points: _____

5. Originality. Do the examples merely repeat those in the sources? Are there examples that reflect valid, original analysis? Points: _____

6. Professionalism.
   a. Grammar and punctuation. Points: _____
   b. Varied sentence structure. Points: _____
   c. Structure and organization of information. Points: _____
   d. Accuracy of original graphics. Points: _____
   e. Appearance of original graphics. Points: _____

TOTAL NUMBER OF POINTS: _____
POINTS NEEDED FOR MINIMAL COMPETENCE: _____

SAMPLE LESSON PLAN OUTLINE: ECOLOGY

PRELUDE

Rationale #2/Two Days

What? Students will learn about the environmental effects of soybeans, corn, oak tree twigs, and pine tree twigs on a rural habitat.

Why? Students will deepen their understanding of the role of plants in a rural habitat. They will apply facts to original analysis and evaluation by comparing and contrasting positive and negative aspects of plant influence on rural communities.

Justification: INTASC Standards 1, 2, 4, 5, 6, 8, and 9.

Performance Objective

Preparation: Students will discuss, compare, and contrast the positive and negative aspects of plant involvement in rural communities. Students will begin to form justified opinions about their feelings of the role of plants in rural habitats with respect to the global product of the Website.

Product: Students will be able to create their own concept maps that represent the benefits and detriments of the targeted plants for a rural habitat.

Criteria: Concept maps must contain the following features.

1. At least three benefits of each plant on a rural environment.

2. At least three detriments of each plant on a rural environment.

3. At least one "what-if" or "if-then" cause-and-effect hypothesis for at least two plants in a rural community (e.g., "What would happen if corn crops failed for three consecutive years?").

Materials

Transparency pictures, excerpt from *Considering to Learn the Importance of Botany* by Michael Kent, excerpt from *The Origin of Species* by Charles Darwin, library sources with Internet, and white board.

ENACTMENT

Aim

How are plants powerful in rural communities?

Hook

Display four types of plants: soybean, corn, oak tree twigs, and pine tree twigs. What do you associate with this (soybean, corn, oak tree twig, pine tree twig) plant? How could a farmer's association with this plant be different from yours? How could it be similar to yours?

Development: Interactive Presentation (an outlined representation)

Day #1

Mini-Talk #1: Use picture transparency. Relate the picture to the knowledge base for the environmental impact of soybeans and corn.

Mini-Task #1: Students create a table with the benefits and detriments of soybeans and corn on a rural community. Students write one "what-if" question for each plant.

Mini-Talk #2: Read from book excerpts.

Mini-Task #2: Students will relate information in the excerpts to the oak tree and pine tree twigs. They will write key terms and concepts according to criteria in brainstorm fashion. Students will also write one "if-then" hypothesis according to prompts for one of the two plants. Students will exchange their brainstorm notes and hypothesis with a peer for comparison and to aid completeness.

Culmination

Wrap-Up: How are plants powerful for better or worse in rural communities?

Leap: Imagine that you are a (soybean, corn, oak tree twig, pine tree twig). What conditions would you need to survive in various seasons of the year? How could human beings benefit or harm your survival?

Day #2

Students will do library research about the targeted plants. An activity sheet contains prompts and criteria to ensure that the research significantly embellishes the students' information. Research may need to continue after school. Students will design their own concept maps according to the Performance Objective for homework.

ASSESSMENT AND EVALUATION PLAN

Assessment: List the criteria that each student included in her concept map.

Evaluation: Grade each of the following categories on a 5-point scale (1 point = poor, 5 points = outstanding):

- Completeness (How many requirements are included?)
- Thoroughness (Is the work shallow or in-depth? Are all the criteria met or exceeded?)
- Grasp of concepts and principles
- Originality

TOTAL POINTS _____ POINTS NEEDED FOR MINIMAL ACCEPTABILITY: 16

Monday	Tuesday	Wednesday	Thursday	Friday
Rationale #1 ILPE Method with video and questionnaire	Rationale #2 (first of two days) Interactive Presentation Method with tables and brainstorming	Rationale #2 (continued) Library research with activity sheet; original concept maps	Rationale #3 (first of two days) Reflective Discussion Method with role-play	Rationale #3 (continued) Reflective Discussion Method with oral reports written out for homework
Diagnostic Assessment	*Formative Assessment*	*Formative Assessment*	*Formative Assessment*	*Summative Assessment*
Rationale #4 (first of two days) Interactive Presentation with Directed Discussion	Rationale #4 (continued) Interactive Presentation with Directed Discussion	Rationale #5 Inductive Concept of Principle Method	Spillover	Website collaboration begins
Formative Assessment	*Formative Assessment*	*Formative Assessment*		*Summative Assessment*
Website collaboration continues	Website collaboration continues	Website collaboration continues	Website collaboration continues	Website collaboration continues
Summative Assessment	*Summative Assessment*	*Summative Assessment*	*Summative Assessment*	*Summative Assessment*
Website collaboration continues	Website collaboration continues	Website collaboration continues	Website collaboration continues	Website collaboration ends *Rubric Evaluation Begins*
Summative Assessment	*Summative Assessment*	*Summative Assessment*	*Summative Assessment*	

FIGURE 13.12 Timetable for Ecology

Figures 13.12 and 13.13 give you an overview of each subject's agenda for this combo unit.

Focal Point 6. Authentic Learning

When your students create products that go out into the world beyond the classroom, they have engaged in authentic learning. As the term implies, a student product

Monday	Tuesday	Wednesday	Thursday	Friday
			Rationale #1 ILPE Method with scenario and questionnaire	Rationale #2 (two days) Directed Discussion Method (Deductive)
			Diagnostic Assessment	*Formative Assessment*
Rationale #2 (continued) Library research; original written role-play scenarios	Rationale #3 Interactive Presentation Method with Peer Dyads	Rationale #4 Directed Discussion Method (Inductive)	Spillover	Website collaboration begins
Formative Assessment	*Formative Assessment*	*Formative Assessment*		*Summative Evaluation*
Website collaboration continues	Website collaboration continues	Website collaboration continues	Website collaboration continues	Website collaboration continues
Summative Evaluation	*Summative Evaluation*	*Summative Evaluation*	*Summative Evaluation*	*Summative Evaluation*
Website collaboration continues	Website collaboration continues	Website collaboration continues	Website collaboration continues	Website collaboration ends
Summative Evaluation	*Summative Evaluation*	*Summative Evaluation*	*Summative Evaluation*	*Rubric Evaluation Begins*

FIGURE 13.13 Timetable for History

created for an audience in the real world or created in a real-world context is an authenic product, as opposed to an "artificial" product intended primarily for the teacher. Authentic and artificial products both serve instructional intentions. But an artificial product may not have authentic value in the real world. Of course, some products intended for only the teacher can have educational value. In our view, such products are most meaningful when they serve as stepping stones, e.g., skill building, for an authentic product. Authentic learning can be very, very motivating for all your students—especially your at-risk students.

Examples of Authentic Learning

Authentic learning can result in products that have either a short or a long reach. They can be traditional products or cutting-edge digital products. Take a look at two examples.

EXAMPLE #1/COMBO UNIT OF ENGLISH AND HISTORY: TWO REPORTINGS OF THE CIVIL WAR

Students write two facsimile newspapers reporting on the military and social outcomes for the Union and Confederacy during the Civil War. Each peer group researches and writes journalistic articles from the North or South perspective on different topics. Audience: All students in the school, all faculty including the principal, the parents, the school and community libraries, and so on.

EXAMPLE #2/CORE UNIT IN MUSIC: THE EVOLUTION AND INFLUENCES OF THE AMERICAN MUSICAL

This unit explores the history of precursor musical forms leading up to the musical. Information about famous producers, composers, lyricists and performers as well as artistic and social influences, past and present, would be included. This research would result in an original Website with multimedia (photos, video, music) and hyperlinks. Audience: All computer users.

■ ROUNDUP ■

You can't plan a successful unit without cohesion among the Unit Components and the lesson Rationales. Every component must relate to and build on others. A well-focused goal and strategy foster an incisive driving question. An assignment template gives your students a compass and enables independent learning. Similarly, designing your own evaluation rubric forces you to reflect on what matters most in the learning process. The rubric also helps ensure thoughtful evaluation of your students' work. Giving your students your evaluation rubric in addition to their assignment template gives them meta-awareness of the instructional standards and helps them to become mature learners.

■ HANDS-ON PRACTICE ■

Try your hand at outlining an advanced unit plan. We provide the following templates to guide you. We suggest that you refer to planning procedures in Focal Point 4 first.

```
Unit Components
 1. Topic:
 2. Goal:
 3. Strategy:
 4. Driving Questions:

Related Rationales with Methods
Rationale #1/Method:

Rationale #2/Method:

Rationale #3/Method:

Rationale #4/Method:

Rationale #5/Method:

Rationale #6/Method:

Rationale #7/Method:

Rationale #8/Method:
```

FIGURE 13.14 Template for Advanced Unit Planning

Assessment Products	Evaluation Rubric
Diagnostic:	Product:
Formative:	Grading:
Summative:	Relevant Features with Criteria:

FIGURE 13.15 Assessment and Evaluation Plan Template

Self-Instruct Planner

(Work on a separate piece of paper.)

Subject:

Unit focal point or kernel:

Type of unit:

Reason for this unit type:

      Figure 13.14 provides a unit planning template. Figure 13.15 provides a template for your assessment and evaluation plan. Use Figure 13.16 for your unit timetable.

Monday	Tuesday	Wednesday	Thursday	Friday
Rationale #	Rationale #	Rationale #	Rationale #	Rationale #
Assessment Stage =	*Assessment Stage =*	*Assessment Stage =*	*Assessment Stage =*	*Assessment Stage =*
Rationale	Rationale	Rationale	Rationale	Rationale
Assessment Stage =	*Assessment Stage =*	*Assessment Stage =*	*Assessment Stage =*	*Assessment Stage =*
Rationale	Rationale	Possible spillover	Begin Evaluations with Rubric	
Assessment Stage =	*Assessment Stage =*			

FIGURE 13.16 Timetable for a Unit Plan with Methods and an Assessment/Evaluation Schedule

ENDNOTE

1. Based on a lesson by Sarah Holtschlag when she was a preservice teacher at Millikin University in Decatur, Illinois.

SUGGESTED READINGS

Angaran, J. (1999, March). Reflection in an age of assessment. *Educational Leadership, 56,* 71–72.

Kovalik, S. (1994). *ITI: The model: Integrated thematic instruction* (3rd ed.). Kent, WA: Books for Educators.

McDonald, J., & Czerniak, C. (1994, January). Developing interdisciplinary units: Strategies and examples. *School Science and Mathematics, 94*(1), 5–10.

McTighe, J. (1996, January). What happens between assessments? *Educational Leadership, 54,* 6–12.

Newmann, F. N. & Associates (1996). *Authentic achievement: Restructuring schools for intellectual quality.* San Francisco: Jossey-Bass.

Newmann, F. N., Secada, W., & Wehlage, G. (1995). *A guide to authentic instruction and assessment: Vision, standards and scoring.* Madison: Wisconsin Center for Education Research.

Panaritis, P. (1995, April). Beyond brainstorming: Planning a successful interdisciplinary program. *Phi Delta Kappan, 76*(8), 623–628.

Seely, A. E. (1995). *Integrated thematic units.* Westminster, CA: Teacher Created Materials.

Strong, R., Silver, H. F., & Robinson, A. (1995, September). What do students want and what really motivates them? *Educational Leadership, 53*(1), 8–12.

Wiggins, G., & McTighe, J. (1998). *Understanding by design.* Alexandria, VA: Association for Supervision and Curriculum Development.

D

Module Fourteen:

Assessment in a Constructivist Classroom

■ OVERVIEW

Bob Mota is a first-year history and social studies teacher at Eastridge High School. It's August, and Bob is planning carefully for the year ahead. He aspires to be the kind of teacher who actively engages his students on a daily basis: Bob has incorporated Eleanor Duckworth's (1987) advice on uncovering rather than covering subjects into his own teaching philosophy. He's confident that he has a working knowledge of his subject matter and the right teaching methods. In articulating the big ideas on which he intends to focus during the first quarter of the new school year, he is also thinking carefully about what activities, discussions, and other experiences might challenge his students to think deeply about the subject.

As a continuous part of his daily teaching, Bob has also taken seriously a piece of advice provided by one of his education professors: to get into your students' heads to the greatest extent possible to continually monitor the nature of their understanding. He has already learned firsthand that students sometimes create meanings from classroom experiences that are surprising, and his student teaching experience alerted him to the fact that students learn in incredibly different ways. Bob's dilemma: How can he gain the most useful insights into what students are learning? How can he ultimately translate what he's learned into some kind of course grade, as students, parents, and school officials will expect?

Bob has shared his concerns about assessment issues with his mentor in the department, Brad O'Brien. A colorful veteran teacher who has long emphasized what he calls a hands-on approach to instruction, O'Brien has shared valuable advice regarding the use of a wide range of assessment tools, including projects, in the classroom. "These students have such a wide range of interests, it's silly not to tap into them. That's how you can hook them on history," O'Brien noted. "I think that the best way to find out what they've learned is to actually get them to do something and to share what they've learned with me and with their classmates. Every student has something to offer. You'd be amazed at what some of these students can do if you just give them a chance."

Taking Brad's advice into account, Bob is beginning to develop his own assessment plan and to carefully couple his assessment to his teaching. Looking back, he recalls that as a student, he frequently objected to the use of tests and worksheets that didn't allow him to truly express what he had learned; the tests especially seemed to be add-on's that weren't always related to what had happened in the classroom. He always resented the fact that when you finished a test, the information seemed to be forgotten as the class moved on to new material. Bob is determined to integrate a variety of assessment approaches into classroom events. The big question is how to do this.

■ GOALS

As a student who will soon be challenged to operate a classroom, perhaps for the first time, you probably share many of Bob Mota's concerns about assessment. We hear a great deal about assessment today, especially in light of today's movement toward state and national standards. Placing great emphasis on the unique ways in which learners make sense of classroom experiences, a constructivist approach to teaching would imply that you use a variety of assessment approaches and that these techniques strongly complement your teaching methods. Translating all of this into the daily operation of a classroom must sound complicated at this point.

In this module, we will address these concerns and others as we share our advice on assessment and evaluation. Specifically, we'll focus on the following questions:

- What is assessment, and why should we be concerned about assessing the nature of student learning?
- How can you implement an authentic, performance-based assessment approach in your classroom?
- What role should tests play in your assessment approach? What form should these tests take?
- What special role should student projects and research play in a constructivist classroom?
- How can you use a range of assessment techniques to assign grades in your classroom?

While investigating each of these questions, we'll provide you with as much practical advice as possible, with the hope that you'll be able to construct your own assessment philosophy.

Focal Point 1: **What Is Assessment?**

At the outset, we feel it is important to make a distinction between two terms that are frequently used when considering what students have learned: *evaluation* and *assessment*. Based on your understanding of Bloom's Taxonomy, you'll recall that to *evaluate* something is *to establish a set of standards and to then judge to what degree something meets those standards*. When we talk about evaluating student performance or the nature of student understanding, this means that we're making a judgment about the quality of student learning. *Assessment is the means by which we gather the information that we'll use to make these judgments*. As you'll see later in this module, it will be important for teachers to use a wide variety of techniques (what Brad O'Brien called tools) throughout the teaching process to make accurate judgments.

Discussion 1: **What Is Assessment?**

We believe that it will be useful for you to consider three types of assessment, all integral parts of the teaching process. *Diagnostic assessment* is *the process of gaining insights into students' existing knowledge of and attitudes toward a topic*. Diagnostic assessment is an ongoing, integral part of constructivist teaching and is one of the processes central to ILPE lessons (see Module 7). It is especially important to conduct diagnostic assessment early in a series of lessons, since we need to gain necessary early insights regarding students' knowledge and interest. As we have seen, this knowledge is essential if we are to relate lessons to students' previous experiences. Remember that diagnostic assessment gathered in ILPE lessons can be collected formally (via questionnaires, for example) or informally (by asking students to respond to open-ended verbal questions).

Formative assessment is *the process of gathering information regarding student learning during classroom learning experiences.* As you conduct lessons as part of a unit, we will suggest that you emphasize formative assessment to a great extent. As Bob Mota noted, students make unique sense of any experience, so you'll need to check continually on the nature of their understanding. The good news is that constructivist teaching methods naturally include formative assessment: as you question and interact with students and listen to students interact with each other, you'll have multiple opportunities to gain useful perspectives on their understanding. In this module, we suggest more formal ways to make formative assessments, through the use of quizzes and other written assignments, student presentations, interviews, and the collections of student work that might be included in portfolios.

The third type of assessment is *summative,* which is *the process of gathering information at the conclusion of a unit or series of lessons.* Summative assessment will allow you to evaluate how much students have learned, what they can do now that they couldn't do before, and how their attitudes toward the topic/subject have changed. For better or worse, written tests have been the traditional means for conducting summative assessment, but tests have severe limitations, depending on how they are used, as Bob Mota recalled in reflecting on his own experiences as a student. We suggest that written tests still be used as part of the mix of techniques to make final judgments about what students have learned but that a wide range of techniques be used to truly understand student learning. We also suggest that all assessment should be formative; what we learn about student learning should continually inform our approach for future lessons.

Focal Point 2: Why Should We Assess Student Learning?

So, why should we assess student learning? There are a number of vitally important reasons. In a constructivist classroom, we advocate using a range of assessment approaches that are intimately connected to learning events. Our observation of hundreds of classrooms over the years leads us to believe that there has been far too much emphasis placed on summative assessment and that assessment is often largely disconnected from teaching events. We recommend a heavy emphasis on formative assessment approaches, to the extent that assessment is at times indistinguishable from teaching.

Discussion 2: Why Should We Assess Student Learning?

One of the main reasons for emphasizing formative assessment is that information gained from assessment should impact your planning. Being in touch to the greatest extent possible with the nature of your students' understanding will allow you to make adjustments in planning future lessons. As Bob Mota recalled from his own experiences as a student, teachers too often are unaware of their students' struggles with understanding certain ideas until an end-of-the-unit test, when it is too late to try something different. Emphasizing formative assessment approaches in your classroom will allow you to effectively do the following:

- Continually monitor student learning.
- Make yourself aware of misconceptions.
- Allow you to make planning decisions based on what you have learned.

A second compelling reason to assess student performance is that assessment events can provide engaging learning experiences for all students involved. Later in this module, we'll discuss the value of student presentations, shared projects, and other assessment techniques that have tremendous instructional value. We have found that by challenging students in some way to convey what they know and what they have learned about a topic can have incredible meaning for peers. There is value in involving the full range of classroom voices in both learning and assessment events, and the right kinds of assessment approaches will allow this to happen.

A third reason to assess student learning is that assessment can provide students, parents, and others with direct feedback on the nature and quality of what the student has learned. Young people are curious to know how they're doing in the classroom; frequent, purposeful feedback will allow you to send these messages to students. It has been our experience that the right assessment approaches can encourage students to think about their own thinking and to make adjustments in their ways of thinking, a point that we'll expand on later in this module. Assessment techniques can be highly motivating for students when teachers provide feedback that is honest and authentic but phrased in an encouraging way. We have found a world of difference between focusing on the negative in providing comments ("you didn't do this") and pointing out the possibilities ("next time try this"). A teacher can nearly always find something positive and encouraging to say when a student has made a genuine effort to show what she has learned.

This brings us to an important point, something that we will emphasize throughout this module: avoid associating assessment with rewards and punishments. Our experience has shown us that far too often, getting the right grade becomes more important than learning for too many students. We strongly suggest that you make very minimal use of tangible rewards (e.g., gold stars, stickers, and candy) in your classroom. Under no circumstances should you bargain away class time ("Do this and we'll have a free period on Friday.") or use an assignment as a reward or punishment ("Don't do this and you'll get a worksheet to take home."). We have seen the negative impacts of such practices in classrooms at every level. Essentially, these teachers send the unmistakable message that precious class time and assignments are trivial bargaining chips. To the greatest extent possible, make learning something interesting the ultimate reward in your classroom.

Focal Point 3: How Can You Implement an Authentic, Performance-Based Assessment Approach?

We define *performance-based assessment techniques* as those that *allow teachers to observe and evaluate what students are able to do as they are engaged in a learning experience that involves thinking at higher cognitive levels.* This may seem like a broad definition; note that our major emphasis here is on thinking at higher cognitive levels.

Given this definition for performance assessment, what assessment techniques might be included in the mix in your classroom? Given the right function or role, a wide range of techniques might be considered performance based: student presentations, research projects, investigative lab activities (especially in science and PE classrooms), student-produced skits, journals, written assignments (completed alone or in a peer-group setting), and interviews could fall under this umbrella. It is our position that tests and quizzes could also be considered performance based, again, given the right design. We will discuss the design of these assessment instruments in detail in the sections that follow.

Discussion 3: How Can You Implement an Authentic, Performance-Based Assessment Approach?

The problems associated with the misuse of and overreliance on written assessment, particularly with standardized, multiple-choice tests, could certainly fill a whole separate text. As a result, we think it is important to briefly review some of these problems, partly to sell you, as a future teacher, on a different approach. It has been our experience, and the experience of other educators, that the overuse of paper-and-pencil assessment instruments, especially tests, tends to do the following:

- Pushes teachers and students to focus on lower cognitive-level thinking and the regurgitation of disconnected facts (Kohn, 1996). We have witnessed far too many teachers over the years who sincerely believed that they were challenging students to think deeply about subjects fooled into believing they had succeeded while students were filling their papers with teacher-provided words that had little real meaning to the students involved.

- Offers little real insight into the way that students think about the topic. We have found that this is especially true of tests that feature an overemphasis on multiple-choice, true-false, and matching-type questions. Given a constructivist perspective, we would expect each student to interpret each question in a unique way, given his or her current frame of reference. As a result, each student might have myriad reasons for answering a question in a certain way. We have seen countless students reason through test questions in incredibly creative ways, only to arrive at a response that was wrong on an answer key.

- Favors students for whom that learning style is most powerful. Remember that students with certain learning-style preferences (e.g., abstract-sequential) tend to perform well on tests; other learners struggle to a much greater extent. Quite frankly, we have worked with large numbers of students at all levels over the years who were considered to be high achievers but who, in fact, were most proficient at reproducing information on tests. As we stated in Module 1, we believe that a rich mix of assessment techniques is the fairest way to assess the learning and thinking abilities of a wide range of learners and the best way to challenge each student to develop new skills and abilities.

- Narrows, even dictates, the curriculum in unacceptable ways (Kohn, 1996). Our advice is to avoid letting the tail wag the dog when it comes to assessment and teaching. If you wish to place emphasis on learning experiences that challenge students to think deeply about topics, then provide them with a range of ways to demonstrate to you (and to themselves) what they have learned.

- Fails to challenge students to apply new understandings in authentic, real-world contexts. Written assessment instruments offer us very limited snapshots of what students know on a given day. Again, written instruments can tell us whether students have acquired information but less about whether they can use knowledge. We believe that this is an important distinction to keep in mind in your classroom.

Despite these concerns, we feel that tests and quizzes should have an important place in your mix of assessment approaches for several reasons. First, as we will see in the sections that follow, tests that are well designed can provide educators with valuable insights into what students have learned and into their ways of reasoning through problematic situations. Second, your students will certainly be required to take tests later in their high school careers and in college classrooms. We believe that it is your responsibility to help them become better thinkers and, as a result, more thoughtful test takers.

Which Assessment Tools Should You Utilize?

To a great extent, this will depend on the grade level at which you teach and on the nature of your subject matter. The assessment approach taken by a math teacher in a senior calculus course will be much different from the approach used by a middle school PE teacher, for example. Our experience has shown us that weaving a variety of approaches into your repertoire will provide you with the fullest possible picture showing what students have learned and will help ensure that each unique learner has a fair chance to succeed.

The questions now become: Which techniques should I use? And how should I use them? Keep in mind that the methods that we have suggested will allow you to informally assess student learning on a continuing basis. In the sections that follow, we describe a range of options for assessing student learning more formally and provide you with some good practical advice for implementing each technique in your constructivist classroom.

Examples of Performance-Based Assessment Techniques

Now consider the following assessment techniques and think about how you might use them in your subject area.

EXAMPLE #1/STUDENT PRESENTATIONS

We recommend that all teachers make frequent use of student presentations for a number of reasons. Our experience has shown us that presentations can enhance the confidence of students, help them develop important oral communications skills, and significantly enhance their understanding of subject matter. There seems to be a lot of wisdom in the old saying that you learn something best when you try to teach it to someone else. In addition, presentations can provide you with wonderful teachable moments, opportunities to generate discussion and consider new ideas. We have also found that such presentations can help you create a thinker-friendly community in your classroom by challenging students to step into the teacher's role; there is tremendous value in incorporating multiple voices within daily classroom discourse.

Student presentations can take a number of different forms. They can range in length from a few minutes to extended periods of time, and they can be conducted by one student or by small groups. Presentations can be very informal and ungraded (e.g., a pair of students explaining a process for finding an answer to a math problem) or extended and graded (e.g., a group of four students explaining their research findings after an extended project). In the following sections we describe some possible ways to weave student presentations into your classroom routine.

Brief, informal presentations can provide students with opportunities to share ideas and to describe their thinking to you and their classmates. For example, math teachers at any grade level might start class by asking pairs of students to go to the board to record their solutions for solving a complex problem. We have found that inviting several pairs of students to discuss problem solutions and write them on the board simultaneously allows each pair to check their thinking with a classmate first. Asking each pair of students to then take the lead in describing their approach can provide the teacher with valuable perspectives on the thinking of each student. Teachers in any subject can challenge small groups of students to discuss questions and then report on their responses. As students are doing this, we recommend addressing probing questions to the presenters and redirecting questions to the rest of the class to pull them into the discussion.

Formal student presentations can be done by individual students or by pairs or peer groups as large as four or five. Presentations like this are especially useful in conjunction with student projects; they can provide students with extended opportunities to share what they have learned with classmates. Presentations can take countless forms: speeches in which students respond to specific questions or issues; more improvisational experiences in which you ask individuals or groups to plan and present something on the spot; and carefully planned group performances. A longtime colleague, for example, takes an interesting approach that encourages ninth graders to utilize props as they become more comfortable with presentations. At various points in the school year, he'll ask his students to prepare a presentation that includes the use of at least three props that will fit inside a paper grocery bag (e.g., "The 1920s in a Bag"). As part of this process, the teacher presents students with broad topic suggestions (e.g., Social Issues of the 1920s; Science and Technology; Architecture; Leisure Activities). Students are free to choose just about any props (from baseball gloves to campaign buttons) to share with the class as they plan their five-minute presentations.[1] In teaching chemistry, one of your authors periodically challenged groups of students to conduct interactive class demonstrations of chemical reactions. This turned into an effective learning experience because students were challenged to choose and research a specific reaction in enough depth to explain it in detail to classmates.

To make such presentations effective learning opportunities for the entire class, we make the following suggestions:

- Prepare students by giving them specific guidelines for the presentations. These guidelines should include guiding questions focused on the content of the presentation (e.g., "How did this Supreme Court decision impact later interpretations of Freedom of Speech?") and advice on presentation length, use of visuals, and involvement of group members (e.g., each member must take an active part). Another possibility is to challenge presenters to ask their classmates questions during presentations, making presentations as interactive as possible. We have found that this practice helps presenting students focus on the content of the presentation at a deeper level and helps keep listeners engaged.

- Design a scoring rubric that will allow you to evaluate the presentation and to provide feedback to individuals or groups of students. A *rubric* is an instrument that specifies criteria and a rating scale for evaluating a student's performance. As we'll see in the sections that follow, rubrics are usually one- or two-page paper-and-pencil instruments. We also suggest sharing scoring rubrics with your students in advance so that they become aware of your expectations. Another option is to involve students in the construction of such rubrics; ask the class to think about what would make for an effective presentation and how each of these dimensions should be evaluated.

- As always, your first priority should be to engage each student in your classroom during student presentations. We recommend that you give students listening to the presentations questions to consider as advance organizers as they hear the presentations. You can write these on the board or include them in a handout. Another effective option is to ask students to complete a peer evaluation on which they provide presenting groups with feedback. We have found such peer evaluations to be very effective in keeping students engaged and focused during presentations. Another possibility to enhance engagement involves spreading presentations over several class sessions (e.g., two ten-minute presentations followed by a related teacher-conducted lesson) to avoid listener burnout.

- As the teacher, be ready to ask presenters at least a question or two after each presentation. As noted earlier, we also recommend asking redirecting questions to challenge class members to consider ideas presented at a deeper level.

Again, we have found student presentations to be very effective in engaging students and in offering insights into the thinking of both the presenters and the students listening. For formal presentations, design an assessment instrument that will allow you to provide presenters with direct feedback on their performance.

EXAMPLE #2/STUDENT JOURNALS

We have also found the use of student journals to be effective in challenging students to think about their experiences (and their own thinking processes) in more depth. Our advice for teachers of all subjects is to ask students to maintain class journals and to make regular (i.e., at least once a week) entries in response to guiding questions. For example, a math teacher might ask students to write about their thought processes as they solved a particularly challenging problem. Teachers in any subject might ask students to take and defend a position following a Reflective Discussion and to write about how their thinking about the issue changed as a result of the experience. More open-ended journal entries can allow students to respond to experiences in any way they choose. For example, you might ask students to journal in response to remarks made by a guest speaker. What comments they respond to, and the position taken in agreeing or disagreeing with the remarks, is left to the student.

Actually evaluating journal entries is tricky and certainly subjective, but we suggest that you collect journals and provide written comments periodically. We recommend assessing students specifically in terms of how they address questions or issues, the depth in which they discuss these matters, and their use of evidence in taking and defending a position. You can design a scoring rubric that will convey to the student something about the quality of their journal entries.

You will probably find that some students will respond exceptionally well to journaling, whereas others will react negatively at first. Regardless of their initial reactions, we recommend sticking with journals as a course requirement. We practice an option that many students have found useful in both high school and college classrooms: allow students to tape record verbal journal entries and turn in a cassette. This option is especially appealing to students who struggle with written work, including those that have disabilities associated with reading or the processing of written material.

EXAMPLE #3/STUDENT INTERVIEWS

We have found that asking students to interview a person outside the classroom can provide for exciting learning experiences. Consider including an interview option when assigning class projects, or assign interviews and a written or verbal response to them as separate assignments. We have found that writing questions for and then actually conducting an interview has several benefits for students. Writing interview questions can help immerse students in a topic; remember our advice to actually teach your students the levels of Bloom's Taxonomy to help them become effective question writers and develop meta-awareness of their own thinking processes. Actually conducting the interviews can be an incredible learning experience for students. For example, we have found that asking students to interview parents or other adults with regard to science-related issues adds significantly to their perspective on the importance of these issues.

We suggest that you carefully explain and describe important steps in conducting effective interviews. Regardless of your subject, this is well worth the time invested.

Explain some of the principles of effective questioning in terms your students can understand (e.g., be sure to pause after you ask a question to give the other person some thinking time). Note that there is an important but subtle dual purpose in doing this: you can help your students understand why you do what you do as you question them in the classroom. This is another example of the importance of teacher modeling in the classroom. Give your students an opportunity to practice conducting interviews with a partner in class, and provide them with feedback.

Assessing and providing feedback on interview assignments can come through your evaluation of your students' response to the interview experience. Ask students to write some sort of reaction paper, or to do a brief presentation in which they reflect on what the interviewee had to say (you could even give students a written or presentation option). It helps to provide students with guiding questions that will help them reflect on the interview (e.g., What was the most interesting/surprising comment made by the person that you interviewed? Do you agree/disagree with the person's positions on this issue? Why/why not? Did his/her comments impact your thinking on this issue? How?). Be sure the student thinks at least briefly about the interview process itself (e.g., I could have conducted a better interview by doing _____.).

EXAMPLE #4/THEMES/PAPERS/LABORATORY REPORTS

Other written assignments should also play an important part in your assessment approach. These written assignments can take many forms and may be directly linked to performance assessment experiences. Examples include a lab report in which students reflect on a science investigation conducted in or outside of class; a response paper addressing questions related to a novel or short story discussed in class; and a written explanation of the processes that a group of students used to solve a complex, real-world math problem outside of class.

EXAMPLE #5/ORIGINAL WEBSITES, VIDEO, AUDIO MATERIAL, AND OTHER MEDIA PRODUCTS

Your students can create various media with the content of any of the products described above and create authentic-learning products for audiences beyond the classroom. In addition to the content, your students would learn the features of the media and how to manipulate them to full educational advantage, following your guidelines and criteria.

Our experience has shown us that developing scoring rubrics for assessing student work of any kind is helpful for both students and teachers. Rubrics can help teachers, students, and parents understand the expectations that are a part of any assignment (remember our advice on sharing the scoring rubric in advance, and occasionally giving students a voice in helping you to develop rubrics). Equally important, rubrics can make the assessment and actual grading of assignments much more manageable. For advice on developing a scoring rubric, see Focal Point 5.

What Role Should Tests Play in a Constructivist Classroom?

For reasons discussed earlier, we believe that tests and quizzes should be one of your main assessment techniques, part of the mix of assessment approaches used in any constructivist classroom. Even though tests would not generally be considered to be performance based, they can allow you to receive detailed insights into the current level of your students' understanding. It's also worth noting that it is possible to build performance tasks into a test. For example, science teachers can incorporate lab practical elements into a testing situation: during a test, students could be challenged to do brief hands-on investigations and to discuss procedures and data analysis in a test essay. In a similar way, a math exam could include a complex problem that students could work through in pairs, reflecting on the process and the results in a test essay.

The questions become: What qualities do well-designed tests share? And how do teachers go about designing such tests? Much has been written in recent years about the testing process, and educators and researchers have provided advice for teachers related to test design (Airasian, 1994; Alleman & Brophy, 1998; Wiggins & McTighe, 1998). Based on educational research, and on our own classroom experiences, we begin by noting that effective tests are characterized by the following:

- A sense of relevance, validity, and balance. To say that a test is valid is to say that the test measures what it intends to measure: test questions connect to important facts, concepts, and principles that were emphasized as part of classroom learning experiences. In addition, questions fairly represent the cross section of subject matter within an instructional unit (i.e., nothing is either completely left out or grossly overemphasized).

- A range in terms of the degree of challenge offered in the questions. You'll be seeking to gauge students' understanding of a wide range of facts, concepts, and principles, so ask questions that range from accessible to highly challenging.

- Variety in the types of questions asked, with different types of questions (e.g., essay and multiple choice) grouped together to avoid confusion on the part of students. We'll discuss this dimension of test construction in more detail in the sections below.

- Clarity in the way that questions are phrased. To the greatest extent possible, write questions that will be completely understandable to each of your students; avoid excessive jargon or vocabulary that is inappropriate for your students. Regretfully, we have seen a number of teachers over the years alienate students who perceived test questions to be needlessly tricky and jargon filled.

- A high degree of reliability. To say that a test is reliable is to say that it is consistent; the test could be given to different groups of students and different times and would yield similar results.

- Appropriate length. At the middle school and high school levels, we suggest planning tests that most students could complete within forty to forty-five minutes. Allow enough time for the test; don't penalize students who are especially careful or thorough or those who might have physical or cognitive disabilities that might slow their reading or writing processes. Have something else ready for fast finishers to do, whether this might be a head start on a future assignment, an interesting extra credit opportunity, or even an educational activity or game.

- A structure that allows for fair evaluation and timely return to students. Once again, the use of scoring rubrics for essay questions can make your grading process much more manageable.

Implicit within all of these points is another important suggestion: construct your own tests rather than rely on ready-made tests that often accompany textbooks. Hopefully, textbooks will serve as a reference in your classroom rather than as the driving force behind your curriculum, and the experiences you will provide for your students will go well beyond textbook material. At the very least, supplement textbook-provided tests with questions of your own design.

Keeping in mind this general advice, what kinds of questions might be part of a well-designed test, and how should you go about writing these questions?

Essay Questions

Based on our experiences, essay questions should be included in each and every test at the middle school and high school levels. Among different question types, we have found that well-written essay questions promote the highest degree of divergent thought and creative responses among students and almost certainly the greatest degree of thought at the analysis, synthesis, and evaluation levels. Essay questions provide students of all ages with the opportunity to show that they can think critically: to integrate facts, concepts, and principles as they use what they have learned to put together logical arguments. Asking students to answer essay questions can also challenge them to further develop abilities associated with written expression.

We suggest using Bloom's Taxonomy as a tool to help you write essay questions. Although possibilities for essay questions are just about unlimited, including phrases like these in your essay questions will challenge students to think at a range of cognitive levels:

- Compare and contrast _____.
- Explain the relationship between _____.
- What do you feel is the best explanation for _____?
- What evidence can you give that would support _____?
- Do you agree or disagree with this statement: _____. Why?
- How could we improve _____?
- Is _____ justified in saying _____? Why/why not?
- How would _____ respond to _____?
- How could you prove that _____?
- Evaluate the following: _____.

We suggest that you remind students to utilize their critical-thinking abilities as they think about and write responses (e.g., state your reasons clearly; support what you say with reasons/evidence). This can and should be done with both middle school and high school students. Include enough of this sort of context with the question so that students know what you're looking for in a response, but make sure that the main question doesn't get lost; you may want to embolden the main question to be certain that it stands out sufficiently. We have also found it helpful to request some minimum number of reasons or required pieces of evidence within an essay question (e.g., "Provide at least three reasons why . . ." "Support your position with at least five pieces of evidence . . ."). You might consider placing such statements in a set of directions at the start of the essay section so that students won't lose track of the main questions.

One of your most crucial decisions will be how many essay questions to include on your tests. Obviously, one consideration will be how long and involved the questions are. In general, we recommend at least two essay questions per test. Asking for only one extended essay will limit the scope of ideas addressed in the essay format and can inadvertently penalize students who may have a deep understanding of the material as a whole but not that particular part of the subject matter. An option is to allow some student choice in responding to essay questions (e.g., answer two of three or three of the following four questions). We favor options of this sort because they seem to allow students to take greater ownership of the responses, reduce anxiety over the testing process, and give all students a chance to show that they can express themselves.

Here's some advice on grading essay questions. Again, using a scoring rubric, even a simple one, can make the process much more manageable and can clearly convey to students the strengths and weaknesses in each response. Take the time to provide written comments on each essay; note the strengths, and make suggestions about how the essay might have been improved (e.g., "Next time, try to . . ."). Try to provide students with written comments specifying two or three specific strengths and suggestions; providing these comments on a separate grading sheet seems to help. As you grade essays, be as consistent as humanly possible. When it's feasible, grade the essays without looking at the names of the students to protect from inadvertent biases.

Short-Answer Questions

We highly recommend the use of short-answer questions, which are items that students can respond to in one or a few sentences. Questions like this can allow students to express thoughts and opinions in a variety of ways, and they greatly increase the range of material that you test on any given exam. Once again, Bloom's (see Figures 2.12, 2.13 a and b) is an incredibly useful tool as an aid to writing short-answer questions. Thinking in these terms, questions can range from the knowledge and comprehension levels (e.g., Please list ____; Explain ____; Compare and contrast____; How would you define ____ in your own words?) through evaluation (e.g., Evaluate ____'s position on ____. Is he/she justified?).

We have found it useful to limit the length of the answers to short-answer questions and to clearly convey this to students (e.g., "Support your position in no more than three sentences."). Although this might at times limit the scope of responses, forcing students to be a bit more concise with some responses has advantages in challenging students to choose their most important reasons, most compelling pieces of evidence, and so on.

Other possible questions in this category include those that can be answered with a single word or phrase, most often falling at Bloom's knowledge and comprehension levels. These can be fill-in-the-blank items (e.g., "The union general at the Battle of Gettysburg who initially decided to defend the high ground at all costs was _____.") or completely stated questions (e.g., "Which novel includes the line "It is a far, far better thing that I do than I have ever done"?").

Multiple-Choice Questions

We're sure that your school experiences have shown you that multiple-choice questions are a staple as part of most tests at the secondary level. We have already discussed some of the limitations of multiple-choice questions. Our two most serious objections to their overuse is that such questions can be interpreted in legitimately different ways by different learners and that multiple-choice responses show teachers little about the thinking processes students used (Was the response based on true higher-order thinking? Or was it an outright guess?). With these limitations in mind, we would also note that there are some advantages to including multiple-choice questions on your exams. They can provide you with a quick sketch of the subject matter knowledge of your students, and they can be graded quickly (a consideration even in a constructivist classroom).

Multiple-choice questions can take several forms. One option is to provide a modified fill-in-the-blank question; you provide students with a sentence that omits a word, and it is up to them to choose the best word or phrase possible.

A specialized connective tissue called _____ is composed mostly of plasma, dissolved substances, and some cellular components.

  A. Bone
  B. Cartilage
  C. Muscle
  D. Ligament

Note that the blank could come at the beginning, middle, or end of what is called the stem sentence. Also note that we provided four choices in this question; experience has shown us that four parallel items (i.e., answers that are similar in length and form and that all fit grammatically) are most effective for multiple-choice questions. Variations on this type of question include questions in which students are challenged to complete a partial sentence with the most appropriate concluding phrase.

Other options for multiple-choice items include questions in which students are challenged to consider a stem question or statement and to select the most appropriate complete statement or question in response.

In Spanish, what would be the most appropriate response if one were asked, "Si le presto el libro, cuando me lo devuelve?"

  A. No. Lo siento mucho.
  B. La semana proxima, sin falta.
  C. Me parece muy bien.
  D. Si, claro.

In this case, the question would challenge students to translate both the initial question and the responses and then to decide which reply is best, given the context.

Among the choices, B addresses the question most appropriately, and A and D provide responses that address the question much less completely.

When it comes to using multiple-choice questions, we have two final pieces of advice. First, avoid, or at least greatly minimize, the use of "none of the above" as a response. In talking to students, we have found that this tends to lead to increased student guessing and disregarding of other choices, possibly because this response is often used in what students tend to perceive as trick questions. Second, consider allowing students to justify or explain their answers to such questions in a sentence or two if they feel that this is necessary (e.g., think about how useful this would be in the case of the Spanish question that we just discussed). Although this complicates test grading, we have found that this option can provide some fascinating insights into the student's thinking and can alert teachers to poorly written questions (e.g., when large numbers of students misread your intent with the question).

Matching and True-False Questions

Two additional possibilities for test questions are matching and true-false items. Based on our experiences, both have severe limitations, but they can provide useful information in some cases.

Matching questions can challenge students to place people, places, terms, or other ideas in some kind of context. The implicit challenge is to compare and contrast a list of ideas. When writing matching questions, place a list of informational items on the left side of a page; these items are designed to start the thinking process within your students. List responses in a column on the right. Two important pieces of advice: list about twice as many responses as informational items (this tends to cut down on guessing and makes the questions more challenging) and be careful about listing too many (i.e., more than eight to ten) items to be matched, as this can be needlessly confusing.

Based on our experiences, we do not recommend the use of true-false questions. First of all, it is difficult to write statements that are always and absolutely true or false (stop for a moment and try this). Students can frequently, and justifiably, find gray area in most of these statements. Second, students frequently view true-false questions as trick questions that don't truly allow them to show that they have learned something about your subject matter (again, a justifiable argument, given some of the tests that we have seen over the years). Finally, what we would call the guessing factor comes into play most significantly in true-false questions. Was the student's answer truly the result of deep thinking, or merely a mental coin flip? Given these limitations, we suggest that such questions be avoided as a regular part of your tests or quizzes. If you choose to ask these questions, we suggest that you allow students to justify/explain their responses.

In summary, tests can and should be one of many (not the one and only or even preeminent) assessment techniques that you employ in your classroom. They can provide useful information about what students have learned and how they think, but be wary of their limitations.

Quizzes

We support the frequent (e.g., weekly or biweekly) use of quizzes. Even a five-minute quiz can provide you with a brief, relatively informal snapshot of what students have learned.

Quizzes can take a wide range of forms. Our advice is to use a variety of question types when quizzing students, both within and between quizzes. For example, at times you'll find it appropriate to ask students to answer a single broad question to assess their understanding of important concepts and principles. Using a quiz that consists of a single question has its limitations; students are put in an all-or-nothing position, they can either address the question or not. But if the question is significant enough, and addresses ideas that have been the focus for several class periods, the effect of this is minimized.

We have found that brief quizzes consisting of four or five short-answer questions can be particularly effective. Asking students to respond to such questions in one to three sentences can allow you to assess understanding of a range of ideas in a relatively short amount of class time. In addition, such quizzes can be graded fairly quickly and returned to students, thus providing them with useful feedback regarding their understanding of important facts and concepts. For a number of reasons, we do not recommend use of a limited number of multiple-choice, true-false, or matching items as the sole items on quizzes. Quizzes consisting of a few such questions have limited reliability and validity because they challenge students to consider a very narrow range of ideas and do not provide much opportunity for students to explain *or* justify their responses. Experience has shown us that student guessing can play far too large a role in such quizzes.

Again, five- to ten-minute quizzes can provide useful snapshots into student understanding. On occasion, you may find it useful to give slightly more involved quizzes lasting fifteen to twenty minutes. Such quizzes can allow you to build in more questioning variety (e.g., such a quiz might consist of five short-answer questions and an essay or five multiple-choice and five short-answer questions). It has been our experience that students perceive such quizzes to be especially fair, as they allow assessment of a wider range of ideas and multiple means for expression.

We have also found occasional use of oral quizzes to be an effective change of pace in any subject area. Oral quizzes have the advantage of allowing students who are especially effective verbal communicators to express themselves effectively. We guarantee that you will encounter students who seem to flourish in classroom discussions and who display a deep and flexible understanding of important ideas but who struggle to express themselves in writing; oral quizzes can give such students an opportunity to demonstrate what they know. Try conducting oral quizzes consisting of three to five short-answer questions, that is, questions that could be answered in a sentence or two. The biggest challenge to giving such quizzes is that they are difficult to evaluate and tough to administer logistically. To get around these difficulties, we suggest constructing simple quiz rubrics, which allow you to provide students with immediate feedback on the quality of their answers. We have found that the most effective way to administer such quizzes is to call individual students to a quiet part of the room while other students are engaged in independent work of some kind (e.g., a written assignment). Teachers who have larger classrooms and longer (e.g., block) class periods will obviously have greater opportunity to use the oral quiz approach.

Consider the use of a variety of quiz formats within your mix of assessment instruments. The advantages to frequent quizzes are many. They provide both you and your students with frequent feedback on the nature of student understanding. In Focal Point 6, we suggest possible weighting of quizzes compared with other assessment techniques.

Focal Point 5: What Special Role Should Student Projects and Research Play in a Constructivist Classroom?

Among the most promising performance assessment techniques are student projects. We recommend frequent use of projects in all subjects and at all grade levels. Depending on the context, projects can take a number of forms. Extended projects, particularly those involving in-depth research of subject matter and student choice in expression, are especially suited to constructivist classrooms. Such projects can promote the kind of deep thinking that is often missing from classrooms.

The questions become, "What kinds of projects are possible?" "Which will promote the greatest degree of student understanding?" These questions are particularly important given the investment in class time that many projects entail. In the sections that follow, we provide you with advice on how to put together meaningful project assignments and examples of project assignments that might work in various subject areas.

Why Emphasize Projects?

Projects, when well designed, involve what has been termed an authentic assessment approach (Wiggins, 1998). As we use the term here, *authentic assessment* refers to the use of assessment techniques that emphasize the in-depth investigation of relevant, real-world questions, problems, and issues. Again, we urge you in the strongest possible terms to include projects that reflect an authentic assessment emphasis within your mix of assessment techniques, regardless of subject and grade level. We have found that such projects can help students do the following:

- Develop critical-thinking abilities as they investigate complex issues, events, problems, and so on.
- Develop their creativity, as they consider new ways to convey ideas to you and their classmates.
- Feel enhanced ownership of subject matter as they connect to their own learning style and personal interests in choosing what they will investigate, how they will investigate it, and how they will convey what they have found to others.
- Stretch and flex beyond their personal intellectual and affective comfort zones as they are challenged to try new or different ways to express their ideas.

In addition, we have found that the frequent use of projects can be personally and professionally reinvigorating for the teachers involved, as students generate new insights and endless new ways of expressing their ideas.

■ WHAT CHARACTERIZES ENGAGING RESEARCH PROJECTS?

Having conducted, and having helped preservice teachers conduct, a wide range of projects over the years has provided us with the opportunity to consider elements of engaging student projects. Based on our own experiences, and on a review of relevant research, we have found that engaging projects are characterized by the following:

- They are driven by challenging, intriguing guiding questions. Such questions capture the imagination and attention of students and serve the useful function of structuring the project (i.e., the question can help students determine what needs to be researched and how the project will eventually be evaluated). In considering guiding questions for projects in your classroom, remember that any of the questions that we posed in the discussion modules could serve as useful guiding questions for projects. Their use could provide any project with a Directed, Exploratory, or Reflective tone (see Modules 9, 10, and 11 for examples).

- They allow for a degree of student choice. As you will see in the sections that follow, student choice can come in several places. You might allow students to work alone, with a partner, or within a peer group; to choose from among guiding questions to investigate, or to articulate their own guiding question; or to choose from among options for expressing what they have learned (e.g., through a presentation, a research report, a skit, a mural, a computer program, an exhibit, a position paper).

- They build in opportunities for students to share what they have learned with classmates (i.e., there is a strong emphasis on performance). This element of projects maximizes opportunities for peer teaching and promotes student pride and ownership of a finished product. We have also found that this sharing element promotes a feeling of community and mutual support within classes, and this seems to reinforce the belief that learning is a complex process that can take many forms.

- They feature use of an evaluation instrument that provides students with qualitative feedback on their effort. Such an assessment instrument usually takes the form of a project assessment rubric that is flexible enough to provide fair evaluation regardless of the final form the project takes.

What Forms Can Projects Take?

When it comes to class projects, the possibilities are just about unlimited. In the sections that follow, we discuss some of these possibilities, present suggestions for effectively integrating and evaluating the projects, and provide final logistical advice.

As we have emphasized throughout this book, one of the hallmarks of constructivist teaching is that students are consistently challenged to "become" historians, mathematicians, linguists, scientists, and more. The use of research projects promotes this worthwhile goal, as students are challenged to "do" the subjects. It is our view that immersing students, even young students, in the complexities of each discipline, and challenging them to struggle with questions and new ideas, will have far greater impact than telling them about the subject. Well-designed research projects can introduce this "doing" dimension into your classroom.

History/Social Science

One of the most noticeable and exciting trends that we have seen in history education has been the increased use of artifacts that include primary source documents, or pieces of text written by the people involved in (or perhaps witnesses to) historical events. Such texts can include excerpts from diaries, letters, speeches, court decisions, passages from books, plays, magazine or newspaper articles, movie scripts, and books written at the time. Asking students to analyze such text can certainly challenge them to think historically, as they question motives and interpretations of others and actually walk in the shoes of people who lived events. We urge all teachers to take care to select source materials that are age appropriate (i.e., understandable and accessible), asking students to analyze text in peer groups of two to three with necessary help from the teacher and to communicate your purposes in using the documents.

Using primary source documents can provide an exciting dimension to class projects in just about any subject. Other useful elements can include film analysis and investigation of posters, political cartoons, and other artifacts. Asking students to complete historical film reviews can be a very effective way to hook students on your subject. We recommend providing students with guiding questions to help them focus on particular elements of the film (e.g., Do students feel that events are accurately portrayed? How did they feel about the portrayal of characters within the film? What biases did they sense on the part of the people who made or performed in the film?).

We have found that challenging students to write and conduct personal interviews can be especially effective in a range of subjects, particularly in the social sciences. For example, students might interview a war veteran, a local office holder (past or present), or a business owner or professional who might have particular expertise on a subject. Asking students to interview friends and relatives can be especially meaningful for students. For example, in a unit on immigration, a history or foreign language teacher might ask students to find an acquaintance who has experienced settling in a new country and becoming a citizen firsthand.

Science

Research projects in science seem to be a natural fit. When well designed, such projects can truly challenge students to "become" scientists. The *Fishy Mystery* scenario portrayed in Module 6 is a terrific example, as students are challenged to solve a complex, real-world problem with tremendous local relevance.

We have found that science projects can take on an inquiry orientation and/or an issue orientation. The *Fishy Mystery* is an example that encompasses both orientations, as students are challenged to choose (even devise) ways to test the water involved and to test for and consider the impact of local sources of water pollution. Frequently, science projects will reflect what has been termed a science/technology/society approach (Bybee, 1985; Hurd, 1980), in which students are challenged to investigate (and even take action on) real-world science problems that are embedded within political, cultural, and economic issues. Consider the possibilities if students were challenged to investigate the following guiding questions:

- How does human energy consumption impact the environment? How can homes/businesses/our school become more energy efficient?

- What hope does research on human stem cells hold for the treatment of disease? Should the federal government fund such research? On what basis?

- What genetically engineered products are on the market today? Which are likely to be produced in the future? What guidelines should be established to regulate such products?

- How can we construct the model rocket/mousetrap-powered vehicle/paper airplane that travels fastest/furthest/in a desired direction? What principles of energy and motion are connected to this process?

- Using data collected both in and out of class, what explanations can we generate to account for the phases of the moon/the apparent motion of the sun, planets, and stars in the daytime/night sky?

Obviously, the list of possible guiding questions for science research projects is endless. The choice of such questions will depend on your school (and possibly district or even state) curriculum, on your own interests as a teacher, and hopefully on the interests of your students. Actually challenging students to articulate such questions can and should be a component of your research procedure.

Note that each of the research questions listed previously is rich with interdisciplinary possibilities. To varying degrees, each question connects to math, literature, political science, economics, and both cultural history and the history of science. We urge you to make the most of these kinds of connections in your classroom; they have a unifying effect on the curriculum in general, and they certainly send the message that all subject areas are connected to each other and that the knowledge within them is relevant.

Math

We feel that research in math classrooms is essential for a number of reasons. As is true in other subjects, projects can challenge students to "become" mathematicians as they use what they've learned to investigate complex, real-world situations. Our own experiences and research evidence (e.g., Peak et al., 1996) shows that these kinds of authentic experiences are lacking in most math classrooms.

Projects in math can challenge students to apply what they've learned to solve complex problems. We have found that projects that require students to choose (and possibly devise) their methods are especially effective. For example, as part of a probability and statistics unit within an Algebra II course, a teacher might ask students to design a computer program that could be used to analyze results when students conduct polls using preference, approval, and weighted voting procedures. As part of this process, students might actually conduct a poll and analyze the data collected. In a geometry course, students might study possible apportionment patterns for elections to the U.S. or their own state house of representatives. In investigating possible apportionment patterns, students might be asked to evaluate the fairness of various patterns in terms of the representation of voting constituencies. Note that both of these examples involve real, complex situations that are rich with mathematical context.

We highly recommend projects that challenge students to investigate the history of mathematical thought. Just as in science, challenging students to view mathematics as a human endeavor, and mathematical concepts and principles as human constructs, is essential. Math and science can then be seen as efforts of human beings to make sense of and explain the world in which they live. Frankly, our experience has shown us that students frequently feel that math and science are so complex (and unchanging) and therefore inaccessible that they are not worth investigating. The investigation of people who struggled to understand mathematics-rich, problematic situations, we have found, can have a liberating effect on students. Such projects could include research on the contributions of mathematicians from various cultures. For example, students at a range of grade levels could be challenged to investigate, report on, write about the origins of various numeration systems, and even to devise lessons in which they might challenge classmates with activities involving alternative systems. Another option would be to ask students to search for and report on the origins of mathematical concepts (e.g., pi, Fibonacci sequences, Markov Chains, and matrices).

English/Language Arts

As is the case in other subjects, there is an enhanced focus on student projects and research in the language arts classroom. The most recently adopted standards established by the National Council of Teachers of English (NCTE), for example, suggest that students should have frequent opportunities to raise questions and pose problems; to gather, evaluate, and synthesize data; and later to develop ways to share what they've learned as they investigate these questions (NCTE, 1996).

We feel that the galaxy of possibilities for student research is certainly as broad in the language arts as in other subject areas. Interdisciplinary possibilities are especially interesting here. For example, the literature of any time period can serve as a window into important historical events. This same literature can reveal much about the influence of scientific and technological trends on people living through that same time period. Connections to mathematical concepts are possible as well.

For example, let's suppose that a high school English teacher planned a unit on the literature of Cold War America. She might ask students to read novels, short stories, biographies, and/or poems written by authors of the time and to articulate thought-provoking research questions (e.g., How did the threat of nuclear conflict impact the writing of Ray Bradbury?). With help from the teacher, individual students (or even small groups of peers researching similar questions) might investigate multiple data sources (e.g., newspaper/magazine articles, diaries, films, and interviews with people who lived through events) as they seek to address the question that they have articulated. As a culminating event, the teacher might challenge students to prepare exhibits for a class museum, to plan presentations that could take on a variety of forms (e.g., skits and imaginary newscasts), or to complete written assignments. In a research project such as this, the teacher might present students with a range of options in terms of possible questions, research methods, and final product form or might constrain choice so that each student experiences some similar experience (e.g., each group will do a presentation or prepare a museum exhibit).

In the previous pages, we have shared a number of possible suggestions for research projects in the four major subject matter areas. Projects in other disciplines (e.g., the fine arts and foreign languages) might draw on similar themes. For teachers of any subject, the question now becomes: How do I go about evaluating the final products of student research efforts?

Evaluating Student Projects

Whatever your subject area, we suggest that you develop project evaluation rubrics as part of your planning process. As noted earlier, the use of such evaluation instruments has several advantages. First, sharing a rubric with students as they begin planning a project will help convey your expectations. Second, a rubric can communicate feedback to students in a straightforward way. Third, we have found that using a well-designed rubric can enhance the fairness (i.e., reliability and validity) of your evaluation; each project is subject to the same set of evaluation criteria. Finally, using a rubric will make the evaluation of projects manageable for you as the teacher (let's face it, this is a major consideration, especially when you are faced with large class sizes and a huge number of projects).

Rubrics can take many forms. In fact, suggestions on designing rubrics could fill an entire book. In the following pages, we'd like to present you with some general advice for designing such instruments, presented in a step-by-step format. As we work through rubric design, note that this advice applies not only to rubrics designed to evaluate a range of project types but also to written works such as papers and test essays.

Decision #1: What Are Your Evaluation Criteria?

Your rubric will be structured around a set of criteria. Your first, and perhaps most important, decision will be to decide exactly what you'll wish to evaluate and to translate this into understandable language for your students.

Whatever your subject area, we suggest that your statements of evaluation criteria must share the following characteristics:

- Connection to important content, thinking processes, and presentation requirements. You must satisfy yourself that these are the essential criteria that you want evaluated.
- Clarity and accessibility. Students (and others) must be able to understand the points being evaluated.
- Sufficient (but not too much) detail. You'll need to spell out what's expected without making your statements of criteria so wordy that your rubric becomes cumbersome.
- Observability. To evaluate something, you have to be able to see it in a way that will allow you to make judgments on it.
- Flexibility. This is especially important when it comes to evaluating projects in which students have options (e.g., could your rubric be used to evaluate a skit or a computer program if both of these options are available to students?).

To illustrate the importance of each of these points, let's suppose that our social studies teacher, Bob Mota, is designing a rubric to evaluate a project in which students investigate the experiences of ethnic groups that have immigrated to the United States during the past two hundred years. Let's also suppose that Bob has given his students a range of options regarding their final product, with some type of class presentation, in which individuals or small groups of students share what they have learned, as part of the assignment. Students must also provide written material of some kind to provide background and context for their presentations. Now, Bob is faced with the challenge of designing a rubric that will allow him to evaluate many different kinds of finished products. In general, he wishes to evaluate students' understanding of important concepts and principles; their selection and analysis of reference materials in addressing a central, guiding question; and the quality of their presentations.

After much consideration, Bob decides on several evaluation criteria related to each of these three general areas. He will tell his students that a strong final product, including written and presentation components, will be one in which students do each of the following:

- Articulate a thought-provoking guiding question that can be investigated.
- Choose and appropriately list enough primary and secondary source documents for use in their investigations.
- Thoroughly analyze each of these chosen reference materials, as evidenced through both the presentation and the final written product.
- Display a deep, flexible, and historically accurate understanding of important concepts and principles, as evidenced through both the presentation and the final written product.
- Complete a presentation that is engaging and displays a high degree of innovation and creativity on the part of the students involved.
- Take an active part in the presentation.
- Complete a final written product accompanying the presentation that is clear, sufficiently detailed, and well organized and that reflects what was said and done during the presentation.

At this point, Bob is relatively certain that these seven criteria convey the most important dimensions of the research project. He feels that each criterion is significant and observable; nothing seems to be missing. In addition, he feels strongly that the items are about equally important and that weighing each item equally is fair, and he will provide students complete and accurate feedback on their performance. There is also a high degree of flexibility within the criteria; Bob feels that he can fairly evaluate the presentation and written products, however the students choose to complete them. In addition, Bob has considered one more important point: with a bit of tweaking, the criteria that he has established could be included in other project rubrics, saving him valuable time in the future.

So, the first major step is complete. Bob has articulated his evaluation criteria. Now comes his next major decision: How can he use these criteria to construct a complete rubric that is understandable and reliable?

Decision #2: How Do You Construct a Scale to Measure Each Criterion?

The second major component of any rubric is an evaluation scale. In most cases, this is a set of numbers that conveys to students how well they completed some portion of the assignment involved.

Bob has a number of options to consider when it comes to a scale. One approach would be to simply list a scale of numbers next to each of his criterion. He might choose a scale anywhere from 3 to 10, with the numbers reflecting judgments ranging from completely unsatisfactory to highly effective. But Bob feels he needs to get a bit more specific. His students should know what a score of 1, 3, or 5 really means, for example. If the rubric is to be used as a learning tool, and not just as a way to score an assignment, Bob believes that he needs to build in a bit more detail. He is conscious of providing feedback that is helpful and a final score that is fair. As he confides to his teaching mentor Mr. O'Brien, "I'd like to come up with a rubric that two different teachers could use and arrive at about the same score."

So Bob decides to base his scoring scale on a 5-point system and to provide a quality indicator for points 1, 3, and 5 on each of the seven criteria. He feels that a scale of 5 will allow him to effectively distinguish degrees of quality of performance without becoming too confusing for students or too complex to be practical. As a side note, we recommend using a scale of 4, 5, or 6 points for most rubrics. Fewer than 4 points doesn't seem to allow a teacher enough room to differentiate, especially for complex, extended kinds of assignments; more than 6 points tends to get too confusing for those involved. This range is supported by research on classroom assessment (Arter & McTighe, 2001). It has been our experience that a 5-point scale tends to offer enough flexibility and a balance between the strengths and weaknesses within each criterion.

Figure 14.1 shows Bob Mota's complete evaluation rubric for the immigration project. In designing your own rubrics in the future, we urge you to follow the same path and to ask yourself the same kinds of questions that the social studies teacher has. Note that Bob has provided himself with enough space to provide written comments for each point, something we highly recommend within any rubric. When developing rubrics of any kind, remember that evaluation of student work, especially when students are provided with a range of options in a complex task, is always an inexact process. But by keeping in mind our advice, it is possible to generate rubrics that will enable you to evaluate student products in the fairest way possible and to provide students with the formative feedback that will allow you to make the entire process a valuable learning experience.

At this point, we have provided you with a smorgasbord of assessment techniques that you might utilize in your constructivist classroom. Returning to our advice in Module 1, we remind you of some important advice: rely on a wide range of assessment techniques in your classroom. This is essential if you are to get the fullest possible picture of what your students are able to do and to provide each student the fullest possible chance to show you what he or she is able to do. One final question remains: How do you as a teacher put these pieces together for a complete assessment package?

Evaluation Rubric: Immigration Project

1. Your group articulated a thoughtful, focused guiding question that can be investigated.

1	2	3	4	5
The question needs greater focus and depth.		Question is thought provoking and sufficiently focused.		Outstanding question; challenging, focused, would require thorough investigation.

COMMENTS:

2. Your group chose and appropriately listed enough primary and secondary sources for use in this investigation.

1	2	3	4	5
More sources needed. Should utilize more primary sources, greater diversity of material.		Sources are adequate. A range of materials, including primary and secondary sources, is utilized.		Excellent reference list, with a wide variety of printed and electronic sources, primary and secondary.

COMMENTS:

3. Your group thoroughly analyzed each of your references, as evidenced through the presentation and the final written assignment.

1	2	3	4	5
Greater depth in analysis is needed, with more emphasis on multiple viewpoints and alternative explanations.		Adequate analysis of materials, with consideration and explanation of multiple viewpoints.		Outstanding, in depth analysis of references, with multiple viewpoints and explanations investigated.

COMMENTS:

4. Your group displayed a deep, flexible, and accurate understanding of historical concepts and principles, as evidenced through the presentation and the final written assignment.

1	2	3	4	5
Explanations conveyed a basic understanding of important ideas.		Explanations reflected a clear, accurate, detailed understanding of concepts and principles.		Explanations reflected a deep, well-contextualized understanding.

COMMENTS:

FIGURE 14.1 Bob Mota's Project Evaluation Rubric

(Continues)

5. Your presentation was engaging and interactive and displayed a high degree of creativity on the part of group members.

1	2	3	4	5
Presentation needed a greater degree of interaction, use of visuals and other techniques to engage classmates.		Presentation was sufficiently engaging. The group took steps to actively engage and challenge the class.		Presentation was highly engaging. The group used a variety of creative techniques to engage, challenge thinking of class.

COMMENTS:

6. Each group member took an active part in the presentation.

1	2	3	4	5
Greater involvement of group members was needed. One/two members dominated the presentation.		Most group members were adequately involved at various points in the presentation.		Each group member was actively involved at every point in the presentation.

COMMENTS:

7. Your final written product is clearly written, well organized, and sufficiently detailed and reflects what was said and done during the presentation.

1	2	3	4	5
More detailed description of events, support for positions needed. Some errors in organization and writing mechanics.		Written product is organized, clearly written, with sufficient detail and a few mechanical problems (e.g., misspellings, grammatical mistakes).		Outstanding written product; organized, featuring vivid detail, clearly stated and well-supported positions.

COMMENTS:

FIGURE 14.1 Continued

Focal Point 6: How Can You Utilize a Range of Assessment Techniques to Assign Grades in Your Classroom?

Which assessment techniques you use, and to what extent, will be one of your most important decisions. Again, using a variety of techniques, emphasizing formative assessment and an authentic, performance-based approach, will be important in a constructivist classroom. Our final advice is to put together a system that includes a point system that will allow you to somehow convert all of this to grades for your students.

Why Institute a Point System?

At first consideration, utilizing a point system might seem a bit unconstructivist. Admittedly, it's challenging to translate any student performance into some number of points. We have encountered many teachers over the years who fool themselves into thinking that a point system can be completely objective and that such a system can take important decision-making discretion out of the hands of teachers. It's important to realize that regardless of your system, evaluation and grading is always a tremendously subjective process; what is evaluated and how it is evaluated is always based on a series of value-based decisions on the part of the teacher. The last message that you want to send to your students is that accumulating points is the ultimate goal in your classroom.

So, considering all of these potential flaws, why use a point system in your classroom? First of all, regardless of where you teach, almost every middle school and high school teacher will be asked to provide grades for students. This is simply a fact of life for secondary teachers. Second, you will need to clearly convey to students, parents, and colleagues how you plan to go about providing grades. Based on our experiences, a system that allows you to communicate in advance what approximate percentage of points will be awarded in which areas provides a valuable road map for everybody involved. These beginning percentages can then be used to determine how many points might be awarded for various assignments and can allow you to weigh each assignment more easily (i.e., this in-class peer-group assignment will be worth _X_ points). Finally, a point system will make your final grade determinations at the completion of each quarter much more manageable. And this is a major consideration: in a traditional school setting, you'll be asked to fairly assign one hundred twenty to one hundred fifty grades each quarter. Even in schools featuring so-called A-block scheduling, your grade load will be at least sixty to ninety students per quarter.

In short, a point system will allow you as a teacher to communicate much about how you will evaluate student performance to all of the important players connected to your constructivist classroom. The question becomes: How do you design such a system?

Step #1: Decide Which Assessment Techniques You'll Rely on and in What Proportion

We have advised using a wide range of assessment techniques. Closely coupled to this is another piece of advice: make sure that each assessment technique is allowed a significant piece of the total grade. In addition, your means of evaluating students must complement the learning experiences that students have in your classroom. What you assess, and to what extent, communicates much about your teaching philosophy.

Our advice is to write a syllabus for each of your courses at the start of the school year in which you state approximate percentages that each assessment product will contribute to each student's quarter, semester, and final grades. In doing this, you'll be challenged to make a number of important decisions. Some of these decisions will no doubt depend on your subject, grade level, and students. But our own classroom experiences, and an extensive review of assessment-related research, leads us to recommend an assessment package that includes the following characteristics:

- A significant emphasis on research projects and related assignments and presentations. Depending on your subject, we recommend that 15 percent to 30 percent of possible points be awarded for projects, presentations/performances, and associated assignments (this might mean using one to two such projects per quarter). These projects could include individual and peer-group projects.

- Thoughtful written assignments (which might include papers/themes, journals, lab reports, and poems/short stories/skits) should play a major role in all subjects at all levels. Even in math and science classrooms, students should be challenged to write about their own thinking. We recommend that 10 percent to 30 percent of your course grades be based on such written work.

- For the many reasons that we stated earlier in this module, tests deserve to play a prominent role in your assessment package. In our view, one of the principal problems with traditional classrooms has been a gross overemphasis on written exams. Again, depending on your subject and grade level, we recommend that 15 percent to 25 percent of your course grades be based on tests (remember that this could include tests that are more performance based, such as lab practicals and oral exams).

- Quizzes can provide quick, relatively informal snapshots on the nature of student learning for both you and your students. We recommend that 5 percent to 15 percent of your points be based on quizzes.

- Other kinds of in-class and homework assignments should compose part of your assessment package. Depending on your subject, you may want to include such assignments in one category (e.g., in math classrooms, students will frequently complete problem-solving assignments in and out of class). Again, we recommend that this category include assignments completed by individual students and peer groups (written work and brief presentations). Try to devote 10 percent to 20 percent of your course grades to such assignments.

- Finally, we recommend that you devote 5 percent to 10 percent of your point total to an evaluation of attendance and class participation. This sends the unmistakable message that learning is not a so-called spectator sport in your classroom. Such an evaluation might seem extremely subjective, but we believe that it is essential. Your options here include keeping track of student contributions during full-class and peer-group discussions and activities. Reassure students that in awarding some number of participation points, how much they say is not as important as the quality of their shared ideas and that you will note their contributions in a range of class settings.

Use these suggested percentages as guidelines in setting up your assessment system. Again, we recognize that much will depend on your subject, grade level, and students.

Step #2: Base Possible Points Awarded on These Established Percentages

Now that you have established a sort of road map for weighing your evaluations, we suggest assigning a certain number of possible points for each assignment based on these decisions. If you are fairly certain at the start of a term about how many projects, tests, papers, and so on, you might assign in a term, you can base your point system on a set number (e.g., we have found it useful to build a system around 1000 possible points each quarter, based on the percentages chosen in advance).

Again, such an approach sends messages to students and others regarding the relative importance of any assignment. For example, if Bob Mota based his grading system on 1000 possible points, he might tell his students when assigning his immigration project that it would be worth a total of 200 possible points, if this extended research project were the main project planned for the quarter. In such a system, four unit tests that he had planned for a quarter might be evaluated at 50 possible points each.

During any given term, you will be challenged to evaluate assignments completed by your students and to record and track points accumulated by students. (Computer-based grading programs can make such record keeping much more manageable. We recommend using these systems if possible.) Your final challenge will be to total the points at the conclusion of a term and to make grading decisions accordingly.

Step #3: Assign Term Grades Based on Points

Issues related to grading have been debated for decades, but most secondary teachers will be asked to assign grades of some kind. In the previous sections, we provided advice about how to evaluate student performance and why we should do this. A final, important piece of advice is when figuring both assignment and term grades, assure students that in making your decisions, you'll be evaluating their performance against some preset standards, not that you'll be comparing students and awarding limited numbers of high grades. A system based on such preset standards is termed *criterion referenced*. You'll find that in using such a system, there will be times when large numbers of students achieve at a high level, and the grades that you award will reflect this (at times, sad to say, the opposite may be true). Sending the message that you have not decided in advance how many grade "winners and losers" there might be on any assignment is vital. Our classroom experiences, and a body of research (Kohn, 1996), indicate that an overly competitive environment can have a profoundly negative impact on the community feeling within a classroom. Students can pick up the message that they're working against classmates for rewards.

On individual assignments and at the end of each term, you'll probably be expected to convert point totals to letter grades based on some set standards. Traditionally, grades have frequently been based on a scale such as the following:

90 to 100 percent = A

80 to 89 percent = B

70 to 79 percent = C

60 to 69 percent = D

Below 60 percent = F

Our advice is not to set such grade expectations in stone. There will be occasions when you'll expect students to score higher than 90% to achieve a grade that indicates true excellence. At other times (e.g., on exams featuring exceptionally challenging, inquiry-oriented problems), your expectations might be different. We do suggest letting students (and parents) know in advance what potential scores might mean in terms of the grades you give.

■ ROUNDUP ■

In this module, we have shared our best advice on assessing student performance in your constructivist classroom. Remember that assessment techniques are the means by which a teacher gathers information that reveals something about the nature of student learning and that evaluation is the process of making judgments about the quality of student learning based on information gathered.

For a number of reasons, we have suggested using a wide range of assessment techniques. Each of your students will be truly unique in many respects, with a wide range of talents and abilities. As a result, giving them multiple and varied opportunities to show you what they have learned makes sense. Not only will you receive a much clearer picture of what they have learned, but you'll provide each student with some opportunity to succeed. Using a range of techniques, we have found, also has the effect of challenging all students to stretch beyond their current cognitive and affective comfort zones, which is vital in today's changing world.

We have also emphasized a more formative approach to assessment than is seen in many traditional classrooms. Assessment should be a continuous, on-going process. Give yourself frequent opportunities to informally assess student learning. Use each assessment technique as a learning tool; share what you've learned with students, and change your approach based on what you've learned.

Our final piece of advice is to establish a classroom community in which it is possible for everyone to succeed, if only in the most modest way. We've noted that the right approach can capture the attention of, and even inspire, the most discouraged, disinterested student. By following the advice shared here, you will at least provide each student with some chance to show you that he or she has learned something.

ENDNOTE

1. Thanks to Arnie Shilheny, history teacher at Pleasant Valley High School in Bettnedorf, Iowa, for this example.

REFERENCES

Airasian, P. (1994). *Classroom assessment.* New York: McGraw-Hill.

Alleman, J., & Brophy, J. (1998). Assessment in a social constructivist classroom. *Social Education, 62*(1), 32.

Arter, J., & McTighe, J. (2001). *Scoring rubrics in the classroom.* Thousand Oaks, CA: Corwin Press.

Bybee, R. (1985). What should the scientifically and technologically literate person know, value, and do as a citizen? *NSTA Yearbook,* 79–94.

Duckworth, E. (1987). *The having of wonderful ideas and other essays on teaching and learning.* New York: Teacher's College Press.

Hurd, P. (1980). Science, technology, and society: New goals for interdisciplinary science teaching. *The Science Teacher, 42*(2), 27–47.

Kohn, A. (1996). *Beyond discipline: From compliance to community.* Alexandria, VA: Association for Supervision and Curriculum Development.

NCTE. (1996). *Standards for the English language arts.* Urbana, IL: National Council of Teachers of English.

Peak, L. (1996). Pursuing excellence: A study of eighth grade mathematics and science teaching, learning, curriculum, and achievement in an international context. Washington, DC: U.S. Department of Education.

Wiggins, G. (1998). *Educative assessment: Designing assessments to inform and improve performance.* San Francisco: Jossey-Bass.

Wiggins, G., & McTighe, J. (1998). *Understanding by design.* Alexandria, VA: Association for Supervision and Curriculum Development.

Module Fifteen:

Resocializing

PART 1:
The Importance of Change

■ OVERVIEW

change Change changE cHange **chAnge** chaNge **chanGe** Change **changE**

Ain't nothin'
like puffin'
on a pipe,
settlin' in,
feelin' that the world's just right.
Hmm mmm!
comfy & cozy &
keepin' out nosy
pokes
trying to stoke
up trouble, double
talkin', fast walkin'
through my mind,
sayin',
"Times a' changin',
Sam.
Just listen
to that man."
Invasion
of a kind.
But I'm stayin'
just the way
I
am.
Yes, siree.
I'm fine with me.
Ain't no hurry
to rise up out of my nice
stuffed chair
and hit cold air
to cross the street
just to meet
a stranger.
    —©2001 Ina Claire Gabler

    Change. We fight it. We find all kinds of reasons that it's not necessary. We justify things as they are merely because they always have been so. Why do we resist change?

We can offer many reasons. Take the verse *Change,* for example. We all like to feel comfortable. After all, staying with the familiar gives us the sense that we fit into the world in a defined place. New ideas may challenge our perceptions of things, and, because of that, new ideas may make us feel insecure, wobbly on our legs, just plain strange. We're not sure how to proceed when once we felt certain of the rules. The longer we stick with the familiar without challenging ourselves to discover new pathways, the more likely that we will become rigid and stale. This is when we risk blaming our students when they lack zest for learning.

This module is devoted to the importance of change. We invite you now to reflect on the role you will play as a teacher and the part you will encourage your students to take in their learning.

■ GOALS

We hope to encourage you to reflect on your assumptions about teaching. This reflection includes comparing traditional practices with constructivist ones in the following areas:

- Awareness of a wide range of your students' needs
- The importance of the classroom setting
- The nature of the teacher's response to students
- Teacher and student roles
- Materials versus methods
- Meta-awareness
- Modeling the peer-group setting

■ DISCUSSION

If you are willing to weather uncertainty in the process of changing, if you embrace the spirit of discovery and growth at whatever age you may be, then the more likely you will be the type of teacher who is ever youthful, ready to try new things all through your teaching career.

This aspiration is a rough road at times. Many students have a negative attitude toward school. Often they have not succeeded in the traditional-style classroom. Some students lack a home environment that fosters study. Low self-esteem, anger, and boredom are frequent consequences of the broken contract between our schools and the students they are meant to enrich.

With self-initiated and motivated students, almost any teaching mode will harvest bounty. Of course, this statement raises the question of standards, which are the goals and criteria by which we work toward success in school. But for now, let's assume that success means doing well on exams and maintaining a stake in being an engaged student.

With at-risk or bored students who do not excel, however, the challenge to be an innovative teacher is a trumpet call. But even motivated students are entitled to take joy in learning through creative teaching. We believe that every human being wants to learn.

If our students seem flat, uninterested; if they don't seem to care about grades; or if they don't seem motivated to challenge themselves or able to think critically, we as teachers have not found the way to reach those particular students. Shoveling on more of the same teaching approach—teacher talk and question-answer dialogue that seeks "right" answers, much like an oral quiz—may not be the way to stir your students' interest. We need to discover what their frames of reference are and relate our subject to that; and we need to find methods of actively engaging our students with what we know is valuable in our subject area so that the students experience the value for themselves rather than listen to our claims and take our word for it. In other words, we need to use our intelligence and imagination in fresh ways.

Which brings us back to the importance of change. Change in the student role. Change in the teacher role. Change in the very concept of what constitutes learning and teaching. If your students have been socialized over the years to take a passive role, they need to be resocialized into taking an active role. That means that you may want to reflect on your concept of the teacher's role. If you assume that the teacher takes the limelight as the dispenser of knowledge (Cuban, 1996; Freedman,1992; Johnson & Johnson, 1989; Kyle et al., 1996; Putnam, 1997; Slavin, 1995), that role dovetails into a passive student role. To be on the cutting edge as a constructivist, hands-on teacher who facilitates active learning—critical thinking and problem solving—you may need to reconsider your assumption about the teacher's role as it applies to yourself.

With these points in mind, let's turn to the elements that change a traditional classroom into a constructivist one.

Focal Point 1: **Maslow's Needs Hierarchy**

Teacher and student roles interact to shape the classroom environment. These roles, in turn, are bound up with your students' and your own needs.

Needs and change are interrelated. In his book *Motivation and Personality,* Abraham Maslow (1987) describes a hierarchy of human needs that now bears his name. If you sincerely want to help your students change their self-perceptions from passive listeners to active learners, then Maslow's Needs Hierarchy is an important guide. The hierarchy is summarized in Discussion 1. As you consider each need, think of how it could apply to resocializing your students as constructivist learners—and to resocializing yourself as a constructivist teacher.

Discussion 1: **Maslow's Needs Hierarchy**

Wisdom Is Always News
[T]he individual is an integrated, organized whole . . . it
means the whole individual is motivated rather than just a part . . .
[S]atisfaction comes to the whole individual and not

just to part of him. Food satisfies John Smith's hunger
and not his stomach's hunger.

—Abraham H. Maslow (1987, p. 3)

A Foundation of Needs

How do we as educators motivate the "whole" person within the four walls of a class-room? What triggers a teacher's motivation to be the focal point or to be a facilitator? What triggers a student's motivation to persist with a task through the wax and wane of interest in pursuit of excellence? If Maslow is right, then the answer lies in the grat-ification of values and needs for both teachers and students as human beings. Accord-ing to Maslow, these needs occur in the following hierarchy:

1. *Basic physiological needs:* These range from physical hunger, shelter, sex, and sleep to the need for activity. There is an endless range of physical survival needs, which could include the need for sensory stimulation.

2. *Safety needs:* Like physiological needs, safety needs have a wide range according to the individual. Examples of safety needs are security; stability; protection; freedom from fear, anxiety, and chaos; structure; law; and so on (p. 18).

3. *Belonging and love needs:* This needs center involves mutual affection with friends, spouse, extended family, and community members. If an individual is not able to establish such affection relationships, the results can be destructive: disorientation, isolation, and the like. Gangs satisfy the need to belong, as do various training and self-help groups.

4. *Self-esteem needs:* Self-respect and esteem for others fall into this needs center. The first tier includes desire for competence, strength, achievement, and mastery as well as independence and freedom. The second tier includes the desire for high repu-tation, recognition, appreciation and dignity, and so on. Satisfaction of these needs re-sults in self-confidence, worth, capability, and the sense of being useful in the world.

5. *Self-actualization need:* In Maslow's words, "What humans can be, they must be" (p. 22). Self-actualization is the need for fulfillment in one's own terms, according to one's gifts and abilities. It is the desire to increasingly become what we have the po-tential to be. On this level, one achieves by choice as singer, writer, carpenter, athlete, teacher, hotrod racer, or any pursuit that manifests one's individual talents.

Although he describes these basic needs as emerging in a hierarchy, that is, the gratification of a lower need (e.g., physiological needs) permits the expression of a higher need (e.g., safety needs), Maslow emphasizes that these needs are not linear. For example, a student's act of persisting in a writing task for school may express safety and esteem needs (maintaining a high average and staying in an advanced class), love needs (earning parental and teacher approval), and self-actualization needs (desiring to be-come a professional writer one day).

The Importance of Affect

The common denominator of the needs in Maslow's hierarchy is affect. "Affect," the noun, *refers to feelings, a state of mind, state of being, and so on.* The affect of your stu-dents in your classroom significantly influences the quality of learning. Chances are that as a student, you yourself were turned on to learning for its own sake in those classes in which you experienced positive affect.

Examples of Maslow's Needs in the Classroom

Let's explore Maslow's hierarchy in terms of your students' attitude or affect in your classroom.

1. *Basic physiological needs:* Applied to classroom learning, this need level ranges from your students' being well fed and well slept to being physically comfortable in the seating arrangement, room temperature, lighting, and so on, so that they can concentrate. If you notice students who frequently sleep in your class or who are chronically irritable, some of their physiological needs may be deprived. This shortfall may result from a student working too much at a job, neglect at home, substance abuse, and more. Referring such students to a guidance counselor or a school breakfast program or calling parents may help.

2. *Safety needs:* The feeling of safety is absolutely crucial in a constructivist classroom! In this instance, safety translates into a nonjudgmental atmosphere that welcomes all responses. No boom or disapproval should fall on students who give "wrong" answers in earnest. Instead, the constructivist teacher seeks to guide insight into appropriate schemata (examples follow later). As for those students who clown and toss out silly answers to win laughs, let them know that you expect them to take the lesson seriously—even, if appropriate, while acknowledging the humor. It is important to remember that at times there *are* right or wrong answers. Or valid versus facile interpretations. So not everything goes. But a constructivist teacher emphasizes the thought process as an exploration that leads students to an appropriate schema with documented justifications. This matters. Many times, students give the "right" answer without meaningful understanding (Fosnot, 1989).

3. *Belonging and love needs:* Is it painful to remember your prepubescent and teenage years? For many of us, it was a time of self-doubt, and with that feeling came the strong need for acceptance and belonging. This is the time of life when peer pressure reigns supreme. It makes sense that feeling safe to express ideas in your classroom ties in with a teenager's belonging and love needs. Nobody likes to feel diminished in a group, but especially young people with tender egos. Love in this instance has a broad application, from your approval and peer approval to parental approval. The practice of affirming students' ideas and efforts to participate along with sending home even form letters of earned praise (e.g., for classwork, preparation, and so on, as well as for quality work) can help build positive affect in your classroom. This supportive approach is especially helpful for at-risk students (Lowan, 1990; Morris, 1991; Romano, 1987) and for those insecure about their learning ability. These students need to build a new self-image that's compatible with school success. (It's important to be consistent but not overly zealous or patronizing with this type of positive reinforcement.) So we're talking about the interrelationship among social needs, self-esteem, and learning in your classroom.

4. *Self-esteem needs:* Self-esteem ties in with self-expectations. If a student has developed the self-concept of being an inadequate student over the years, then she will obviously not take the risks important for learning or exert much effort to engage in

school. Helping this young person to change her self-image as a competent learner will slowly improve her positive self-esteem in your classroom. This positive affect will build on itself if your setting is safe, affirming, and challenging without intimidation. The willingness to take risks and reach out for learning relates to the student's perception of self-empowerment (Weiner, 1972). For example, if a 14-year-old boy with a low reading level believes it is "too late" for him to learn how to read and write according to his age, that student believes that self-empowerment is beyond his will, that his undeveloped literacy skills reflect his inborn inability to read and write well. In this case, you might try to find motivating reading materials (perhaps outside your subject area, depending on his interests) that ensure success for him at first, then increase the difficulty of the materials. In this way, the 14-year-old begins to see that he can learn with motivation and that his perseverance will eventually lead to success. We know this is harder than it sounds, and that some students need far more than occasional encouragement. As always, you as the teacher will need patience, persistence, and imagination. Most of all, you will need faith in a student's ability to transcend disappointments in learning how to learn—his disappointments and yours. As more of your students develop positive self-esteem and increasingly take risks in the stimulation of a constructivist setting, they will grow in self-confidence as learners. Your own self-confidence as a teacher will also strengthen.

5. *Self-actualization need:* You and your students both need this: the fulfillment of the goals that personally matter to each of you. For yourself, this may mean being an effective constructivist teacher whose approach integrates the social and learning needs of your students. Your self-actualization may include watching your students blossom, or an at-risk student raising her hand for the first time.

As for the students themselves, many of them may not yet know what they want to strive for. After years of boredom and failure to excel in a traditional school setting, many of them will be deadened to the joy of learning—for shouldn't learning be exciting? stimulating? gratifying? deepening?

So we'll repeat ourselves here: everybody wants to learn. If you make efforts to relate your subject to your students' world, if you create a safe environment in which positive affect and self-esteem can thrive, many of your students will rediscover the joy in learning that they once knew in kindergarten and first grade. That rediscovery is the beginning of their self-actualization. As these students awaken from slumber, both you and they will be amazed at how capable they are.

Of course, some, if not many, of your students will have a clear sense of what they want; they will be confident because they have enjoyed success in school. In this instance, your task will be to challenge them in new ways so that their imaginations and critical-thinking skills reach higher levels. They may also come to value learning more for its intrinsic value than for kudos and high GPAs.

Focal Point 2: The Setting

The *classroom setting*, otherwise called *setting*, refers to the overall learning environment. The environment, in turn, is comprised of two aspects. One is the instructional mode that fosters different teacher and student roles, from teacher centered to student centered. The other environmental aspect of the setting refers to the physical configuration of the room. The distinguishing feature of the setting is the nature of teacher-student interaction. Underlying all these elements is the teacher role as dispenser of knowledge versus facilitator.

Discussion 2. The Setting

In a teacher-centered setting, you would be at the center of the lesson, dispensing information, interpreting, analyzing, evaluating as if filling up your students' brains. In this setting, you might ask occasional questions, but they would be mostly on a low cognitive level, stressing right versus wrong with little if any expectation of your students to engage in a thinking process of their own. In the teacher-centered setting, your students assume a passive role as listeners, memorizers, and repeaters of information. The interaction pattern in the teacher-centered setting is mostly teacher-student (t-s), with some s-t on a mostly low cognitive level.

At the opposite end of the pole is the student-centered setting. In this learning environment, you expect your students to be independent learners, self-initiators. The student role in a student-centered setting is one of active learner, a problem solver, a seek-and-finder, a learner-learning-how-to-learn who knows that mistakes are an essential part of the learning process. In the student-centered classroom, your teacher role is that of a well-prepared facilitator, mentor, catalyst, someone who learns along with your students, especially in exploratory lessons in which the outcomes are not yet known. The interaction pattern in a student-centered setting is largely s-s, with some s-t-s in the form of mentoring.

In the middle of this continuum is the teacher-directed/student-focused setting. As the setting name suggests, in this context you as the teacher steer your students, but at the same time, your students take an active role, engaging in critical thinking and even, for example, selecting topics and formulating questions for a unit that you design. In addition, you relate the lessons to your students' frames of reference. In this setting, the interaction pattern is a combination of t-s, t-s-s-t, and s-s.

Conscious awareness of the differences among learning environments enables you to resocialize your students—along with yourself—from this kind of setting with this t-s interaction to that kind of setting and that kind of s-s interaction. Figure 15.1 encapsulates the features of these three settings.

Examples of Elements in the Setting

Several elements contribute to, but do not ensure, a student-centered or student-focused setting. Here's a list of the major elements:

EXAMPLE #1/PHYSICAL CONFIGURATIONS: HOW ARE THE DESKS ARRANGED?

(a) *Open Seating.* We suggest that on the first day of the school year your students sit in the conventional row configuration to which they're most accustomed. On

Teacher-Centered	Teacher-Directed and Student-Focused	Student-Centered
• The teacher is the focal point. • The teacher controls all content, ideas, projects, and performance criteria. • Students must think mostly in the teacher's terms.	• The teacher selects the focal points but tries to relate information to the students' frames of reference. Teacher mostly facilitates. • Students' interpretations are encouraged and compared to an appropriate schema. • Students choose their topics within the teacher's prescription. • Some teachers permit students to envision their own topics with justification and teacher approval. • The teacher usually decides on standards of performance but may also encourage students to design their own with the teacher's approval.	• Students take initiative governed by the teacher's instructional Rationales. • Students conceive of appropriate topics and projects and work together in small groups as peer mentors, collaborators, or as individuals. • Students assign roles to themselves and one another. • The teacher is essentially a co-learner and resource person who makes clear what the Rationales are. • Performance criteria are usually determined by the teacher, but sophisticated students may determine even the criteria, with teacher approval, by which the teacher evaluates their work.

FIGURE 15.1 Teacher-Centered......Student-Centered Settings

that first day you can inform your students that on the next day the seats will be arranged in a circle or in a U shape with one or two staggered rims. The configuration of the seats can be the impetus to begin meta-awareness and resocializing in the following ways.

The first time they are seated in an open configuration in your classroom, you might ask why they think you want them to sit this way and what is the difference in how they feel in this arrangement. Try arranging the desks in a circle. Or in a double horseshoe with seats in the second rim staggered in between spaces of the seats in the first rim so that every student has an unobstructed view. (See Figure 15.2 for a graphic representation of this seating arrangement.) In both of these open configurations, you're free to stand and facilitate discussions as well as to sit among the students as you choose—on the side, in the back, or in front. The open-seating configurations give every student an up-close feeling, right there in the midst of what's happening. There is no back of the room, only up-front seats.

(b) *Peer-Group Seating.* Other times the desks can be arranged in small-group clusters. We suggest three to five members to a group, with four being the optimal number for most activities. Dyads or pairs are also effective depending on your instructional intentions. Activity sheets with social roles are key for productive, independent peer-group learning (see Module 5).

(c) *Rows.* This traditional configuration arranges students so that they all face you in the front of the room. Students in the back often feel removed from you up there at the podium. Some students, especially those who are not successful or engaged with your subject matter, intentionally sit in the back to hide out, a situation that only increases their alienation.

EXAMPLE #2/TEACHER AND STUDENT ROLES: ACTIVE VERSUS PASSIVE LEARNING

(a) Awareness of the physical arrangement in the room and its influence on the learning atmosphere can lead into a discussion of teacher and student roles. Such discussions may be brief, a prelude to a lesson, and repeated for emphasis and a more in-depth meta-awareness in following lessons.

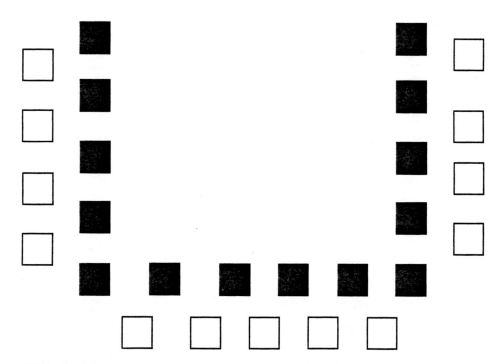

FIGURE 15.2 Staggered Horseshoe Seating

(b) Some student responses may be silly and immature, others serious. The immature responses may be evidence that those students have been socialized to be passive listeners with little sense of responsibility for their own learning. They may feel threatened at first rather than positively challenged by the notion of an active student role. Immature responses mark the challenge of your resocializing.

EXAMPLE #3/ASKING QUESTIONS: PROMPTING CRITICAL THINKING

As a global advance organizer (see Module 3, Part 2, and Module 12), inform your students that you will be asking questions more than lecturing or explaining. Otherwise, students may react in the following ways:

(a) They may feel uneasy about the necessary mind shift as quickly as you would like, since they are accustomed to being passive and feel safe in that familiar role with prescribed behavior.

(b) They may feel threatened by frequent questions, thinking that you are poking them for "right" answers. So it's a good idea to assure them that you're after the process of sharing ideas, that so-called mistakes are a necessary part of the thinking process and learning, that if they participate thoughtfully, it doesn't matter if they're right or wrong as individuals. At the end, they will arrive at justified conclusions as a team.

Now consider this. You might want to open a brief discussion about the value of asking and formulating questions. You might ask them "Why?" a lot (e.g., "Why do questions help you learn?" "Why is it important to think on your own?"). You could also ask them how they feel at first about the technique of questioning. Some students may feel nervous about the new role you're asking them to take, and a discussion may help ease doubts about your motivation.

EXAMPLE #4/ESTABLISHING RULES: CREATING A SAFE ENVIRONMENT

Take a look at these examples.

(a) Don't interrupt.

(b) Never laugh at someone else's response. All smart people make mistakes when they're learning.

(c) Don't mock or name-call.

(d) Always be respectful, especially when you don't agree with someone else's viewpoint. Treat your classmates the way you want them to treat you.

You can also invite the students to codify their own rules for a safe learning setting.

Now study Figure 15.3, which describes the continuum from a teacher-centered to a student-centered context, and reflect on the following six questions. Use these questions as prompts to discuss your assumptions about teaching and learning with a peer or with the entire class.

	Teacher-Centered	Teacher-Directed and Student-Focused	Student-Centered
Source of Initiation Content	Teacher-dispensed ideas Subject focused = right vs. wrong answers	Teacher's and students' ideas Student focused = material related to students' frames of reference; thought process emphasized	Students' ideas with teacher guidance Student focused = material related to students' frames of reference; thought process emphasized
Social Interaction	None or limited t-s	t-s as facilitation; t-s-s-t; s-s	s-s; t-s as facilitation
Teacher's Role	Dispenser of knowledge	Informed facilitator, resource, and dispenser; prepares and guides students to think logically and critically; provides learning stucture; encourages students' original insights with documented justifications	Informed facilitator, resource, and co-learner; prepares and guides students to think logically and critically; encourages students' original learning structures and insights with documented justifications

©2001 Ina Claire Gabler

FIGURE 15.3 Classroom Settings

1. Which setting is what you and your students are accustomed to?
2. Which setting is conducive for a constructivist approach? In what ways?
3. Which setting would be most comfortable to you at this moment? Why?
4. What are the advantages and disadvantages of each setting?
5. What beliefs about teaching and learning might you want to reconsider based on the features of the three classroom settings described? How do these beliefs relate to the teacher's role? The students' role?
6. When would you employ each setting and why?

● Pause here to discuss these questions with peers before you continue.

Continuum

The teacher-directed/student-focused setting and the student-centered setting are not rigidly distinct. Instead, they can permeate each other on a continuum. The defining difference between these two settings is that in the teacher-directed setting, you as the teacher provide the learning structure(s), that is, a plan for learning or carrying out an activity, lesson or project, prompts and directions, Rationales, and so on. In the student-centered setting, you would define what the broad goals are, but the students would create their own learning structures best suited for carrying out those goals.

Both settings overlap in significant ways. For example, your students in both settings must formulate their own questions and tasks to direct the thinking process. Similarly, students in both settings obtain source materials in addition to the ones you provide, building the knowledge base itself and formulating concepts, principles, and unifying themes, adding materials as necessary. So the teacher-directed/student-focused setting is a precursor to the student-centered setting in which you as the teacher become a co-learner for projects of new inquiry while also facilitating and guiding that inquiry.

Looks Can Deceive

A classroom setting may appear to be student-centered. Students are arranged in small groups working together. The teacher meets with individual students in quiet conferences. Yet, even you as the teacher may be deceived. If the lesson is designed so that you dictate what the students write and you emphasize right versus wrong answers rather than the thought process to arrive at understanding, then in fact such a setting is teacher-centered, not student-centered.

Conversely, students may sit in rows, and you may stand in front of the classroom. But the teacher-led discussion invites students to think independently and arrive at their understanding of facts and concepts, generate original principles with documented justification, or decide on their own unit topics and driving questions. Such a setting is in fact student-focused or student-centered with you as facilitator.

Postdiscussion

Both the teacher-directed/student-focused and student-centered settings are fertile ground for a constructivist approach. Use of these two settings may be alternated as your social and academic objectives would indicate.

Is there a place for the teacher-centered approach? How could it be modified and integrated into a constructivist approach in a traditional school system? After you have mulled this over, see Module 12 for one idea.

Keeping the ideas of your discussion about the various settings in mind, let's turn to a crucial component in the process of change in your classroom.

Focal Point 3: **Response**

Teacher response or *response* is *the nature of teacher and student interaction.* We believe that teacher response is the single, most important factor that characterizes the classroom setting as teacher-centered, teacher-directed/student-focused, or student-centered (Atwell, 1987; Calkins, 1983; Meier, 1995; Michaels, 1987; Morris, 1991; Sperling & Freedman, 1987).

DISCUSSION 3: Response

As the teacher, your teacher response is more significant for the encouragement of your students' active involvement in learning than whether the students sit in rows, a circle, or peer groups; whether they experience a fifty-minute lesson or an extended problem-solving project; or whether they use books or computer technology. Seemingly student-centered physical configurations and materials may camouflage a teacher-centered environment in which students must echo the teacher's viewpoints (Freedman, 1992; Sperling & Freedman, 1987). Consider these pointers:

- *Questions.* Do you ask real questions that invite the students' ideas and viewpoints with justifications? Or do you ask leading questions with embedded answers, the answers you want to hear? (See Module 4.)

- *Catalyst.* Do you encourage students to come up with their own justified solutions based on adequate preparation, materials, and guidelines? In other words, do you facilitate? Or do you dictate what students "should" be thinking?

- *Process.* Do you emphasize the right answers as the end point? Or do you emphasize the thinking process, strewn with mistaken concepts, that ultimately leads students to appropriate schemata with in-depth understanding? Do you, in fact, spotlight the necessity of misconceptions as part of the learning process? Do you also insist on student justifications in their own words? Or are you satisfied with the rote repetition of standard definitions, thereby sacrificing intellectual rigor for the sound of fixed and "right" responses?

- *Affect.* As you pose questions and facilitate invention in the learning process, do you acknowledge the value of the students' contributions to building a logical development of a concept, of the answer to an inquiry question, and so on? Are mistakes received as a welcomed part of the learning process rather than as wrong answers? Do you sincerely appreciate your students' potential to learn and to strengthen their critical-thinking skills, and do you let them know that? Is your classroom a safe environment, practicing a team approach to learning whereby no one feels stupid and everyone feels valued?

To briefly sum up, teacher response is the key to a Maslowian classroom setting where positive affect nurtures the whole student toward independent, critical thinking (Boone & Hill, 1980). Your response, in turn, is influenced by your assumptions of the teacher role and student role.

Examples of Response

Here are some samples of teacher responses in a constructivist approach that help create positive affect by making each respondent feel valued:

1. This is an exploration. Don't worry about right or wrong answers. Every thoughtful response helps move things along.

2. (Collective praise after a series of responses) These have all been thoughtful comments that show you're getting at the heart of the matter.

3. (In response to students disagreeing with each other) You're both helping us get a deeper understanding by challenging each other respectfully, in a thoughtful way.

This is just what we want! Now, based on what Sandy and John have been saying, let's list the pros and cons and see where they lead us.

4. (In response to a mistaken fact or concept) (a) A lot of people would agree with you about that, Jenny. Would you like to take a look at more of the basic issues and see if you still take the same view? (b) What makes you say that? (c) (And after listening to the reason) Okay. Your answer makes sense based on what you've just quoted from the journal. Now take a look at the fifth paragraph on page three. How does that compare or contrast with the information you just referred to?

This type of respectful teacher response gives students a chance to arrive at more developed conclusions while inviting them to think things through more—not necessarily asking someone else to supply the desired answer and deprive the first respondent of the satisfaction of completing his thought process. As the teacher, you affirm rather than discount misconceptions as valued efforts while guiding students to more thought-out conclusions based on more information. Note how the last response asks the student to compare or contrast information, coaxing Jenny into critical thinking. Now consider the teacher's intention with these responses.

5. (a) Why do you say that the Mexicans were treated badly in the war, Jose? (b) (After Jose cites one or two documented reasons) Okay, Jose, those are justified reasons. Now who else would like to give your view on those reasons, with evidence? (c) Who can add to what Jose and Lucretia have said? (d) Who thinks the Americans were justified and why? (e) Who agrees and why? (f) Who thinks the Americans were not justified and why?

6. Who can sum up what Stan, Jesus, and Emily have said?

7. Who disagrees? Why? What's your evidence?

8. Why would a lot of people agree with Ruth even though most of you disagree with that view?

In examples 5 through 8, the teacher is bringing more students into the discussion with Redirected questions (see Module 4). This type of teacher response, inviting varied student responses on the same issue, enables the class to arrive at an appropriate schema with justifications, building on early, insufficient student answers while also affirming the students' participation. In this way, all responses are welcomed without your passing a value judgment. At the same time, you're facilitating a more comprehensive examination of an issue.

Focal Point 4: The Teacher Role

By *roles* we mean *the teacher's and students' behaviors, practices, and responsibilities in the learning process as complements and parallels one another.* The *teacher role* refers to the nature of interaction between you and your students. Do you tell them the facts, concepts, principles, and themes with only occasional opportunity for your students' critical thinking? Are you the focal point of the lesson? Or do you plan the activity sheets and other materials so that you facilitate your students' thinking process up

Bloom's cognitive ladder? In these ways, the teacher role shapes the setting and is bound up with the nature of teacher response.

Examples of the Teacher Role

Below are two scenarios depicting two types of teacher roles. A discussion follows each scenario. Try to list the characteristics of each teacher role depicted.

EXAMPLE #1/THE PERFORMER

SCENARIO #1

The curtain goes up and the spotlight shines. You're on. The star of the show. Giving your heart and soul to the part. The audience listens and watches, enveloped in the dark, enraptured by your sterling performance. They laugh with you, cry with you. They applaud wildly and bring the house down. In short, you become the talk of the town.

You've earned it. After all, it isn't easy to learn all those lines, interpret the character's conflicting motivations, decide to emphasize this quality over that one so that the portrait does not succumb to stereotyping. You want to make sure that the audience comes away with a clear understanding of the character, one which you have honed to perfection and to critical acclaim. Your heartfelt desire is to touch hundreds more, maybe thousands of people with your in-depth characterization so that audiences go home ruminating on the brilliant insights you have given them. And even though you thrive on applause, your motives are sincere, for how could all those people grasp the character's complexity without you to show the way?

Discussion 4a: **The Performer**

In Scenario #1, you have been posited in the role of a star performer. All eyes are on you. And in fact, you have a lot to offer. You've studied the part as it relates to the play's theme; you've mapped out the relationship of your character to all the other characters; and you've cultivated the fine art of acting so that your depiction is natural, earnest, even compelling. The audience is duly impressed by your mastery and bursts with applause. Yes, their admiration is your just desert. And you have the satisfaction of knowing that you have given them your best, fashioned their understanding of an enigmatic character and a profound play, down to every word and subtle allusion.

So what's the problem?

Nothing, as long as you're an actor on the stage. But let's briefly look at this performer model from the perspective of the teacher role.

Teacher as the Star

If you're the kind of teacher who performs in the spotlight of the classroom stage with your students as a captive and perhaps appreciative audience, beware. You may fall prey to the well-intended but misapplied generosity factor. Well intended because after all, by preparing thoroughly, by bringing in a variety of creative materials, and by explaining so clearly what and why and how, by expounding on the if-thens with articulated insights over which you so lovingly labored, you are giving generously from your mind and heart to your students. And their applause resounds in the form of all those right answers on the exam. Or, as is often the case, the students crash on the exam, and leave you bewildered. Didn't you cover the material thoroughly? Didn't you explain so clearly to them? Wasn't your Hook a gem, in full regalia of period costume?

You give and give and they just don't get it. That's when the misapplied generosity factor insidiously turns into student blaming: it's the students' fault, they just can't learn, they just don't care, don't listen, and so on. As for students who got it, their right answers gleaming on the exam, they're confirmation of your sterling performance and of the value, for some students at least, of giving all you've got as the consummate teacher.

Such is a frequent outcome of the teacher-centered role. In the teacher-centered setting, the teacher is the dispenser of information, the repository of knowledge and knowing, the mental mover in the classroom. The signs are lecturing, the teacher's voice being the dominant sound in the classroom. The students are encouraged to concur with and repeat back what the teacher and text have said. Even if your students are captivated, what will they retain a week later? How have they developed critical-thinking skills as you entertain them? Now let's take a look at another scenario that depicts a different teacher role.

EXAMPLE #2/THE DIRECTOR

SCENARIO #2

You assemble the performers for a discussion of each part in the play. Ostensibly, it's a comedy. But you perceive some darker threads in the writing, the potential for poignancy, even subtle satire. A delicious prospect, to direct such an unsuspectingly rich work! Eagerly, you open the discussion to the actors you will direct.

Now, you're bursting at the seams to tell them your interpretation of this theatrical gem. But you've learned from experience that when you force your interpretation on the actors, their inspiration, the stuff of a magical performance, is often missing. Yes, they will do a competent job because they're talented and you know your craft as a director. But you want more from them. You want them to shine.

So you don't spill the beans. You're all assembled, bleary-eyed, in the early morning, with Styrofoam cups of coffee, seated at a wooden table on the stage of the empty theater. Everyone has a copy of the play with the notes you had asked them to write about their views on the characters, theme, implications, and so on. You sip your first taste of schlock coffee and begin.

Not with assertions. Not with your opinions or goals about the play. All that's tucked in your mind and put aside. No, instead of spouting your own brilliant ideas, you open with an invitation: "Okay. Let's explore this work a bit, swap ideas. We'll go around the table. So, Vanessa, how do you feel about your character Sarah?"

And you don't let Vanessa off with a word or two. You probe her a bit. Ask her to point to dialogue and action and author's directions to justify her interpretation, perhaps modify it a bit. And you ask others how they viewed Vanessa's character and why. Compare and contrast, stir up the mental stew. "Do you agree, Dustin, that Sarah's a tough gal, a broad, so to speak?" "Why? What does she say or do that makes you see things that way?" "Okay, Dustin. Then why does your character Stan ignore her at first? Wouldn't he want to grab her attention?" "What are some possible implications about Stan's motives in this scene? What's in the dialogue and situation that make you say that?"

In not much time, everyone's forgotten about the coffee because they're getting into it, big time. Sinking their teeth in, chewing the script. Making it theirs.

And a funny thing happens—as you've finally learned it inevitably happens in such forums. Not only do the actors hit on ideas that you did, arriving at interpretations based on their own spontaneous insights along with your questions that direct their observations, not only that, but they've hit on insights that you, the brilliant director, did not see. So now you're getting excited, too, because the dialogue and probing have opened up the play for everyone. Everyone has a stake in its interpretation. Sometimes you thrash it out as a group as to what to emphasize. And that's the most delicious morsel.

All this leads up to rehearsals, the process of bringing the characters to life. Now you all know what to aim for, and guess what. As the rehearsals take on a life of their own, more ideas—new character motives—come to light. So as you direct the performers, coaxing out subtleties, humor, irony, shaping unexpected satire, you all work together in the joy of creating an original and deep performance.

At curtain call the audience goes wild. They give a standing ovation. The performers take repeated bows. As you watch in the wings, you know you had an important part in a fine production that helped to bring out the best talent in the actors and that touched a lot of people—yourself included.

Discussion 4b: **The Director**

In Scenario #2, you take on a different role, that of the director who elicits ideas and talents from the actors. Before the curtain rises on the first performance, you prompted, coaxed, challenged, asked for support of their interpretations, and invited comparisons and contrasts, guiding and also clarifying. In this way, your actors felt confident of their perceptions and conclusions and made the characters and the entire play theirs. No one in the audience sees you or knows what your role has been in the outstanding production. Your influence has been invisible to the onlooker, invisible perhaps even to the actors you have skillfully opened to their finest measure because you have served as the unobtrusive guide for their own thinking, affirming their own spontaneous viewpoints. The spotlight is on them, and yet, without your reflective facilitation, without your skilled and subtle control that fostered their critical analyses, the performances would not have attained such heights.

Teacher as the Catalyst

The director's role in Scenario #2 is analogous to the teacher's role in the teacher-directed/student-focused or student-centered settings. For most of us teachers, this student-centered approach is a potentially threatening role at first. It seems to turn the classroom upside down. Students, who may lack the maturity of professional actors, appear to be in control, and the teacher appears to lack authority—every teacher's nightmare of chaos. An irretrievable loss of order. Organization shattered as the students take over. No real learning. An unappealing prospect indeed.

But in fact, just the opposite is true in an effective student-centered or student-focused constructivist setting. Like the director, you must exercise control in a student-centered environment or the students simply will not follow the steps and procedures necessary for rigorous learning. With actors, the director simply lays out procedures and makes clear what is expected at a given time. With preteens and teens in a traditional school setting, you will need to establish rules and procedures and carry them out in a consistent manner.

At the beginning of the school year, it is often advisable to begin teaching in a way to which the students have been previously socialized, that is, in a conventional up-front-in-the-classroom practice. Little by little, as you win the students' respect and confidence, you resocialize the students—and at first yourself as well—to the teacher and student roles appropriate to a constructivist learning environment. (This stage should make full use of meta-awareness, discussed in Focal Point 7.)

As the guide, facilitator, or catalyst, you must be exceedingly prepared and exquisitely organized as well as flexible. Invisible teaching is proactive teaching and cannot succeed without well–thought-out planning. Thorough planning includes how to sequence the prompts (questions and tasks that guide a thought process) and materials, how to couple questions to content, and how to define individual student roles in peer groups so that the students know how to proceed on their own (see Module 5).

Expressway versus Back Roads

You will plan for them to reach a given destination via the expressway, and they will most likely take the back streets, enticed by scenic distractions.

Only if you have planned well will you have a compass in your mind that will guide them to the desired town on those back roads. You can employ various techniques. Effective questioning refers them back to the substantive materials you've provided or to which they have access, directing them to forgotten prompts, providing support as they wade through frustration; providing confidence in their ability to arrive at the destination.

As you facilitate in this way, the students see that you clearly value their efforts to learn. In other words, as an invisible teacher you imbue your students with faith in their ability to learn by providing scaffolding or assistance in the thinking process. Guided in this way, your students will feel a personal victory as they employ facts to substantiate their insights, interpretations, comparisons, and contrasts as critical thinkers. In short, invisible teaching is rigorous teaching.

Invisible Teaching

As the invisible teacher, you contradict the traditional norm: like the director, you remain in the wings during the performance. Your students take the spotlight. That shift from a traditional teacher-centered experience is not only your students' victory, but yours as well. More and more, your students need you less and less as the year progresses. In this way, you give them a priceless gift: in a constructivist classroom, students learn how to learn; and they learn how to teach one another. The methods in this guide book give procedures and practices to help you achieve this outcome.

We do not mean to suggest that lecture does not have its place. Mini-lectures are useful to launch a unit or project, to summarize midpoint in a lesson or in the Culmination. In fact, one of the methods we promote is the Interactive Presentation, which includes segments of mini-lectures or mini-talks. Mini-talks with student input help provide clarity and cohesion. But as a dominant pedagogy, lecturing, for the most part, does not generate your students' original thinking and it does not foster initiative in the challenge and joy, the sense of personal accomplishment, that accompany active learning with positive affect.

Focal Point 5: The Student Role

You can see from our description that the teacher role governs the student role. A teacher-centered setting results in a passive student role. This passivity translates into the students being listeners and imitators, with little if any sense of responsibility for and active engagement with their own learning. By contrast, in a student-focused or student-centered setting in which you as the teacher facilitate and guide, your students are active learners, increasing their responsibility for their own learning, planning the steps of learning, formulating questions, and so on, stimulated and eventually empowered as independent thinkers. Because our description of the teacher role included the complementary student roles, we now move on to the next focal point.

Focal Point 6: Materials and Methods

Materials and Methods refers to the relationship between instructional tools, that is, devices and materials such as activity sheets, books, videos, overhead projector, and computer technology (see Module 3, Part 2), and active student learning. Materials in and of themselves—including dazzling software—do not govern active versus passive learning. Rather, instructional methods help implement your instructional intention in a teacher- or student-centered environment.

Discussion 6: Materials and Methods

Materials and methods is the heart of the matter. The most dazzling materials in technology are only as effective as the instructional method, employing the materials to full advantage (see Section C, *Introduction to Methods*). Otherwise, focus, cohesion, and intellectual rigor are at risk. The newest technology can be used merely to carry out teacher-centered response.

Relying on the materials to give direction is like relying on an airplane alone to get you where you want to go. An airplane needs not only a compass but a map, not to mention a pilot.

On the other side of the coin, effective methods are compromised by inappropriate and shallow materials. As much thought must be given to selecting the content and level of substantive materials as to the method of instruction. A superficial text without in-depth supplementary materials or a software program that is more entertaining than instructional undermines an inductive method that seeks to strengthen critical-thinking skills.

Examples of Materials and Methods

We provide a range of examples of materials in Figure 3.5 in Module 3, Part 2. In addition, you can find a summary of our methods in *Introduction to Methods* in Section C.

Focal Point 7: Meta-awareness

Meta-awareness is *a concept that refers to knowledge of the thing itself*. Learning about the learning process, thinking about the steps of thinking, and so on. For example, your students' meta-awareness about the process of learning could involve awareness of the thinking process, moving from a knowledge base of facts to the higher levels of analysis, synthesis, and evaluation. As the teacher, you would introduce these concepts to your students, complete with the correct terms, and encourage them to consciously apply Bloom's Taxonomy (see Module 4) as a tool to develop and strengthen their learning skills.

Discussion 7: Meta-awareness

In other words, meta-awareness is a bird's-eye view that gives students conscious awareness. It lifts the veil between the practice and the underlying intention.

Active versus Passive Learning

Meta-awareness is a useful key to resocializing your students—and yourself—about the virtues of active versus passive learning. Lifting the veil in this case involves awareness of various teacher and student roles, the classroom setting the roles create, along with the corresponding advantages and disadvantages. It also includes the importance of questions (1) as prompts to guide thinking as students respond and (2) as tools to cultivate critical thinking as students themselves learn to formulate and sequence questions according to Bloom's Taxonomy, related to instructional materials, just as you are in this course.

Giving your students meta-awareness is a bold step. It is the ultimate in invisible teaching: giving the spotlight away. But if you have your students' best interest at heart, the rewards are tremendous. Meta-awareness can heighten your students' motivation over time and turn bored students into active participants as they increasingly grow accustomed to and appreciate their empowerment as learners.

Remember Maslow

Above all, remember the importance of affect as the gateway to learning in a constructivist classroom. Without a safe, nonjudgmental environment in which everyone feels valued as a thinking person, only students arriving at your door already confident will succeed. Try to incorporate Maslow's Needs Hierarchy (described at the beginning of this module), remembering that every student is a whole person with an array of needs, not merely a cerebral repository of information. But don't go overboard! Beware of condescension or praising every response.

Examples of Meta-awareness

EXAMPLE #1/READING SKILLS

Yes, you want your students to understand the plot of *Huckleberry Finn* and to discuss the controversial issues it raises. You also want them to realize that they're striving to develop their ability to interpret on a higher cognitive level. That means the students strive to analyze Mark Twain's characterizations and themes replete with various implications for today. In this way, your students are consciously aware that they are carrying out a thinking process that leads to evaluation and critical thinking, the higher cognitive levels beyond the mere knowledge base of details and events literally applied to a fixed historical context and not much more. This approach to reading can be applied to any subject.

EXAMPLE #2/THE LEARNING PROCESS

You might devote some time to an Exploratory or Reflective Discussion about teacher and student roles and about different methods of learning, both teacher and student centered. Similarly, you can introduce Bloom's Taxonomy and invite a discussion based on examples of each cognitive level. Consider these suggestions for follow-up:

(a) Let students practice writing questions based on the taxonomy related to instructional material and posing those questions to their classmates.

(b) The next level is to teach them how to evaluate their own questions based on the responses of peers. Did the questioners succeed in guiding their classmates to a high cognitive level of interpretation and evaluation?

(c) Of course, students' evaluation of other students' responses depends on their own grasp of the given material. Again, an Exploratory or Reflective Discussion would help clarify the issues. In this way, students increasingly cultivate critical-thinking skills with growing awareness of the cognitive and academic intentions of the Rationale.

Focal Point 8: Modeling Peer-Group Learning

Modeling (see Module 3, Part 2) is the act of demonstrating an individual behavior or procedure. It can mirror a cognitive process or social patterns back to the students. Modeling can therefore be used to socialize students as fruitful peer-group learners, focused thinkers, and persevering individual learners. As you model for your students—or set up modeling situations with students who model procedures for their peers—you are also teaching yourself what is required of you as a facilitator along with what is required of your students as active participants in learning.

Modeling Peer-Group Learning

Take a look at the following example of modeling peer-group learning (see Module 5). Notice that the students need to consider their social responsibilities as well as the learning activity.

EXAMPLE #1/SOCIALIZE YOUR STUDENTS TO WORK IN GROUPS

When you first establish peer-group work in your class, be sure to take one class period to introduce students to appropriate peer interaction. Do this whether or not students have had group work in other classes. Your students may need to unlearn bad habits or to examine, perhaps for the first time, the learning benefits of a student-centered setting. This is all part of building meta-awareness of being active learners.

(a) Enlist one or two peer groups to model how you want your students to interact.

- Design a peer-group activity especially for modeling student-student (s-s) interactions, both social and academic. This modeling activity may double-dip as meaningful instruction. The activity sheet is crucial. It must specify social roles as well as directions for the task. (See Module 5, Part 2.)

- The student demonstration that models desired behavior must include following the directions on the activity sheet, from assigning roles to attempting the task. You may coach the demonstration groups in advance to intentionally act out conflicts with rude behavior and then with respectful behavior so that the class sees the difference in action. Invite recipients of aggressive and then kinder behavior to share their feelings. Discuss how feelings affect how they learn.

- Encourage reactions from the entire class at different points in the modeling enactments. Establish from the students why respectful interaction is important, for example, improved group spirit, better learning, and so on.

- Based on the modeling, guide the class to codify their own procedures for group interaction.

(b) Establish the spirit in which peer-group work takes place: cooperative, not competitive. This emphasis requires more than one or two sentences.

- Try an Exploratory or Reflective Discussion (see Modules 10 and 11, respectively) that identifies the advantages and disadvantages of competition and cooperation. Avoid giving points or grade credit for cooperating. This external motivation undermines the effort to encourage students to work as teammates for positive affective reasons (Michaels, 1987).

(c) If you want students to critique each other's work, train them in what to look for and how to comment. Use modeling. This should take one or two class periods.

- Provide sample phrases on a handout: "That's a good idea because . . . . Maybe we can also say that . . . ," "Let's try to follow the instructions to keep on target . . . ," "I like your idea about X. But I think the teacher wants us to develop it more. Maybe we can do that together," "Let's pay attention to each other more. We need to work as a team. Luvenia, say your idea again and this time we'll listen better."

- Use modeling to practice these sample phrases so that the class sees how they can be effective. Again, you might want to briefly coach the demonstration groups in advance. Invite comments from onlookers. Make the point that they will quickly figure out their own comments in different situations so that they maintain team spirit while they learn. The sample phrases are like training wheels to launch them. The rehearsal is an investment with high returns on more fruitful and efficient group work in the future. Different types of group learning may require their own modeling for future lessons or projects. You may want to tell your students this.

(d) Discuss roles in peer-group learning. Include a discussion on the teacher's and students' roles in peer-group learning. Some pointers could be the following:

- What are the students' responsibilities for their own learning?
- What is the teacher's responsibility in a peer-group learning activity?
- What are the advantages for the students?
- How is an active student role different from a passive student role?
- What are the implications about the students in an active or passive role?

In this way, you are facilitating your students' increasing meta-awareness of their part in quality learning. You're also expressing faith in their ability to learn.

Focal Point 9: Thinking Process: Designing Heuristics

As you can see in the example of modeling peer-group learning, an outcome of modeling and meta-awareness is often the codification of procedures that guides the students' critical-thinking skills up the ladder of Bloom's Taxonomy. *A codified, step-by-step approach to digging up the deeper meanings or carrying out a process is called a heuristic* (see Module 3, Part 2).

Discussion 9: Thinking Process: Designing Heuristics

Really useful heuristics employ meta-awareness of the thinking process—whether for analyzing literature, historical events, a work of art, a science experiment, solutions for a math problem or sports strategies, or musical techniques. In a constructivist classroom, students can create their own heuristics if you do some or all of the following.

1. Model the thinking process for your students and ask them to spot the important elements.

2. Require one group of students to write down their observations of another group's discussion, suggesting the behaviors to be noticed: defining, making connections, noticing repeating details, social behaviors that impede or further the group's discussion, and so on. Then have the groups swap places and give each other feedback at the end of a completed cycle. This practice helps develop meta-awareness and thereby helps students to compile a heuristic for a given procedure or cognitive effort (Metzger, 1998).

3. Encourage Exploratory or Reflective Discussions. Inject only with broad questions or comments to suggest that students reexamine a metaphor, or identify repeating words, reconsider from a different angle (without saying what that is), and so on. This approach can also help students create codified steps in a thinking process appropriate to a given subject area. Obviously, there will be overlap in thinking processes for various subjects, and such double-dipping will strengthen your students' skills in learning how to learn independently.

4. Provide pertinent information that your students don't know yet so the students can justify their approach with a documented knowledge base (Beware of just air between you and your students!).

5. Similarly, provide a particular example (e.g., require that students analyze a specific short story, experiment, math problem, painting, football play, idioms in a foreign language, musical techniques, and so on) from which the students extrapolate the generic elements of analysis. Then require that they generalize a heuristic for that thinking strategy, procedure, and so on.

Example of a Heuristic

Students' learning how to learn is a process in which you do the following:

- *Reflect* with analysis of what worked, what didn't work, and why.
- *Replan* accordingly.
- *Retry* patiently.

This three-bullet strategy is an example of a procedural heuristic.

Focal Point 10: Affect as the Gateway to Learning

Call us sentimental, but we believe that students' feelings count. We're not saying there's a feel-good magic wand. There's not. Your students—and you—will definitely not change in a day or a week or a month. Resocializing takes time, patience, and imagination.

Discussion 10: Affect as the Gateway to Learning

When a lesson flops, try to resist blaming the students. Instead, reflect on how you might replan so that the lesson incorporates your students' world and engages them in a stimulating activity that carries out your instructional intention. Remember to reconsider the setting and the nature of your response. Have you been trying to stuff their minds with information? Or have you prepared materials and sequenced questions so that your students are guided to explore information, interrelate facts, think through concepts, and arrive at justified evaluations? Did you plan in a way that hooks into the students' interests or context?

Now consider this: Did the progression of the lesson enable the students to feel confident as they traveled from one cognitive level to another? Without student confidence, the most well-structured lesson falls flat. Again and again, we return to the importance of imagination. You can't pique your students' imagination unless you stretch your own. It takes imagination to effectively plan a motivating lesson or inquiry project.

This is where you can use this book as you cross the threshold from being a college student to being a preservice teacher. Our constructivist methods, anchored in Bloom's Taxonomy, and awareness of setting help you enliven any content in any subject—whether you teach in a school with a traditional time frame or in a block program. These methods and your eventual adaptations of them suited to your needs will serve you as you progress from novice to seasoned teacher.

Focal Point II: **Resocializing Yourself**

It's time to have a fireside chat with yourself or with a peer. You might benefit by examining your assumptions of effective teaching and the teacher's role after 16 years of apprenticeship of observation. Why do you want to teach? If the reason is to be the entertainer in the spotlight, you might want to reconsider the value of that for your students in terms of their—and your own—self-actualization, based on Maslow's Needs Hierarchy.

Discussion II: **Resocializing Yourself**

As you take your students step by step into the domain of constructivist learning, you are also training yourself along with them. For this reason, go slowly at first. Reflect on the outcomes. If you find yourself blaming the students, reflect a bit. Remember that everybody wants to learn. Instead of faulting the students, replan the same lesson or project so that the students will be able to engage with the knowledge base, concepts, and themes next time. Ask yourself, "Is my approach dry? The same old routine? Have I used my imagination?" Have you brainstormed with an innovative colleague?

Find a Mentor

Brainstorming with another teacher brings us to the next important practice. Try to find an experienced teacher in your school who is innovative—regardless of the subject matter. The elements of the classroom setting matter more than the subject. There are a lot of creative, student-centered teachers who would be delighted to help you. Not only will you learn from their experience, but they also will pick up fresh ideas from you as well as the methods you are learning in this constructivist program: a professional swap.

■ ROUNDUP ■

Resocializing is the key to creating a vital, constructivist classroom. The elements of resocializing revolve around two major concepts. First, Maslow's Needs Hierarchy reminds us that our students are not just brains to be jammed with facts but young people with a host of needs that must be respected for them to develop the courage of independent and active learners. Students need to feel valued, just like you do. Second, meta-awareness is crucial for your students to jump on board with you. Meta-awareness incorporates appreciation of the teacher and student roles in a constructivist learning experience, the importance of questioning along with the setting. To aid the process of building meta-awareness, modeling social and learning behaviors—demonstrating how they are bound up with each other—gives the students a clear picture of what you expect from them.

Along with your students, you need to resocialize yourself. You yourself may be a product of teacher-dominated instruction, and you may be holding on to that schema with the best of intentions. If that worked for you as an AP student or a student with a high stake in school achievement, remember that many if not most of your students will not fall into that category for various reasons: they may be poor test takers, they may have low self-esteem as a result of being low tracked, or they may not have adequate support at home. But they have the ability to excel, whatever they have achieved—or have not achieved—in a setting that reawakens their natural curiosity and love of learning. The nature of your response can either discourage your students from taking necessary risks in learning or encourage your students to reach beyond their grasp. Will you be the innovative teacher who makes a difference? It's not easy, but you can do it. Your classroom can be vibrant with discovery—if you persevere with efforts to resocialize.

■ HANDS-ON PRACTICE ■

Acid Test: Analyze Two Classroom Scenarios

A Bit of Nitty Gritty. We invite you to explore your grasp of settings and teacher–student roles by analyzing these two classroom scenes.

Directions:

(1) Jot down three to five significant details in each scenario below. Describe each setting in terms of the following, with justification:

    a. teacher-centered

    b. teacher-directed/student-focused

    c. student-centered

(2) Refer to Maslow's Needs Hierarchy. In each scenario, what needs are being met? Whose needs are being met? Justify your interpretations.

Scenario #1

Ms. Santos: Ms. Santos, a history teacher, organizes her thirty middle school students into heterogeneous peer groups of four or five. Students are assigned textbook exercises about World War II as the behavioral objective/mastery task and do the assignment together. As they work, a hum of student interaction fills the room. Ms. Santos circulates from group to group. When she stops by each group, she enthusiastically praises students one-on-one for their right answers; then she refers the individual students who write wrong—or no—answers to the pages in the textbook where the right answers can be found. Ten minutes before the period ends, Ms. Santos convenes the class collectively. She reads each exercise question aloud and calls on individual students for the right answers; she motivates the students by entering an "A" in the grade book for each right answer. Proudly, she demonstrates to the class a string of "As" in her grade book, praising them for learning the material so well.

Scenario #2

Mr. Washington: Mr. Washington, a history teacher, organizes his thirty middle school students into topic groups of four or five. The students chose their topics from a list of 20 topics about World War II drawn up by Mr. Washington. In addition, the students generate their own subtopics by consulting school library sources and Web sources that Mr. Washington has alerted them to. Each topic group creates questions that they think are important for each subtopic based on their research. Mr. Washington consults with and advises each group or individual student who may need guidance. The Performance Objective is for each student to write an article on the subtopic of choice. The teacher also distributes a list of criteria for content and writing skills that each article and magazine must satisfy. The articles on subtopics are collected into topic magazines. This means that each group publishes a magazine. Collectively, these magazines cover World War II in significant scope and some depth.

Guidelines

If you are in a classroom, we encourage you to analyze these two scenarios according to the following activity sheet in a peer-group setting. If you are reading this outside a classroom, use the activity sheet on your own or with someone else in the program. In either case, note the design of the activity sheet for social roles and the academic task as a peer-group learning experience (see Module 5).

ACTIVITY SHEET FOR SANTOS AND WASHINGTON SCENARIOS

Directions:

ROLES FOR TASK ONE.

1. Time keeper: announces when five minutes are left.
2. Recorder: jots down the group's ideas on paper or on a transparency.
3. Moderator: ensures that each person participates.
4. Each group member will be a friendly prober of other group members' comments.

ROLES FOR TASK TWO.

1. Same roles as those for Task One.
2. Presenter: introduces the group's ideas in the class discussion.

YOUR JOB:

A. TASK ONE (fifteen minutes): For each scenario, infer the following. Justify your views in terms of details from the scenarios.

1. the teacher's belief about effective teaching

2. the teacher's belief about the students' role as learners

3. the resulting beliefs the students may have of themselves as learners

B. TASK TWO (20 minutes): Apply your analysis from Task One here.

1. Discuss among yourselves how Maslow might analyze the teacher–student relationship in Ms. Santos's and Mr. Washington's classes. Explore from teacher and student angles. Suggested guidelines follow:
   (a) Emotional and psychological safety needs: whose?
   (b) Self-esteem and self confidence needs: whose?
   (c) Self-actualization: whose?

2. Reflection: Offer two or more suggestions to one or both of these teachers so that their materials and methods better meet the Maslowian needs of some or all of their students while also striving for intellectual rigor. You may hypothesize different learning styles and confidence levels. Justify your suggestion in terms of intellectual rigor as well as affect. Always ask yourself, "Why am I doing this?"

C. (If appropriate) Class convenes for discussion of your ideas and to process this as a peer-group learning experience.

REFERENCES

Atwell, N. (1987). *In the middle: Writing, reading and learning with adolescents.* Upper Montclair, NJ: Boynton/Cook Publishers.

Boone, B., & Hill, A. (1980). If Maslow created a composition course: A new look at motivation in the classroom. ERIC ED 191 053.

Calkins, L. (1983). *Lessons from a child: On the teaching and learning of writing.* Portsmouth, New Hampshire: Heinemann Educational Books.

Cuban, L. (1996, October 9). Techno-Reformers and classroom teachers. *Education Week on the Web.* Available at: http://www.edweek.org/ew/vol-16/06Cuban.h16.

Fosnot, C. T. (1989). *Enquiring teachers enquiring learners: A constructivist approach for teaching.* New York: Teachers College Press.

Freedman, S. W. (1992). Outside-in and inside-out: Peer response groups in two ninth-grade classes. *Research in the Teaching of English, 26*(1), 71–107.

Johnson, D., & Johnson, R. (1989). *Cooperation and competition: Theory and research.* Edina, MN: Interaction Books.

Kyle, W. Jr., Schmitz, C., & Schmitz, E. (1996). Possible lives or shattered dreams? *Electronic Journal of Science Education, 1*(2). Available at: http://unr.edu/homepage/jcannon/ejse/kyle.html.

Maslow, A. (1987). *Motivation and personality.* New York: Harper & Row, Publishers, Inc.

Meier, D. (1995). *The power of their ideas: Lessons for America from a small school in Harlem.* Boston: Beacon Press.

Metzger, M. (1998, November). Teaching reading: Beyond the plot. *Phi Delta Kappan,* 240–246, 256.

Michaels, S. (1987). Text and context: A new approach to the study of classroom writing. *Discourse Processes, 10,* 321–346.

Morris, C. (1991, March). Giving at-risk juniors intellectual independence: An experiment. *English Journal,* 37–41.

Putnam, J. (1997). *Cooperative learning in diverse classrooms.* Upper Saddle River, NJ: Merrill.

Slavin, R. (1995). *Cooperative learning: Theory, research, and practice.* Boston: Allyn & Bacon.

Sperling, M., & Freedman, S. W. (1987). A good girl writes like a good girl: Written response to student writing. *Written Communication, 4,* 343–369.

Weiner, B. (1972). Attribution theory, achievement motivation, and the educational process. *Review of Educational Process, 42*(2), 203–215.

SUGGESTED READINGS

Bunce-Crim, M. (1991, September). What is a writing classroom? *Instructor,* 36–38.

Cleary, L. M. (1991). Affect and cognition in the writing processes of eleventh graders. *Written Communication, 8*(4), 473–507.

DiPardo, A., & Freedman, S. (1988). Peer response groups in the writing classroom: Theoretic foundations and new directions. *Review of Educational Research, 58*(2), 119–149.

Duckworth, K., & Lind, K. (1989). Curricular goals and motivating strategies with non-college-bound students in science and social studies. ERIC ED 307 112.

Lowan, J. (1990). Promoting motivation and learning. *College Teaching, 38*(4), 136–139.

Pokay, P., & Blumenfeld, P. C. (1990). Predicting achievement early and late in the semester: The role of motivation and use of learning strategies. *J Educational Psychology, 82*(1), 41–50.

Romano, T. (1987). *Clearing the way: Working with teenage writers.* Portsmouth, NH: Heinemann Educational Books.

Siu-Runyan, Y. (1991). Learning from students: An important aspect of classroom organization. *Language Arts, 68,* 100–107.

PART 2:
Constructivist Classroom Management

■ OVERVIEW

In Part 1 of this final module, we discuss the process of resocializing, which really amounts to challenging your students to buy into the creation of a constructivist learning community. In this final section, we will pull together a set of suggestions and answer some final questions on how to establish and maintain such a community.

We hear a great deal about issues related to classroom management and discipline. In fact, classroom management has become a whole separate field within education in the minds of some. As you read through and perhaps experience our methods and techniques, it should be apparent that effective teaching must go far beyond managing students. Our approach to *classroom management*, which we would define as *the system that you establish to operate your classroom on a daily basis*, is different, based on a number of primary beliefs. These foundational beliefs include the following:

1. Classroom management, like assessment and evaluation, should be seamlessly connected to teaching. This implies that your approach to dealing with problems and disagreements should reflect that same spirit that you bring to your teaching.

2. The vast majority of students of all ages sincerely want to learn and can learn and do not need to be bribed, bullied, or threatened into learning.

3. Effective teaching will prevent most discipline problems, and the right approach in the classroom will allow teachers to reach virtually any student.

4. In establishing a management system, teachers should give students a high degree of genuine responsibility. This implies that you treat students as responsible young adults who are capable of making important decisions rather than as children who need to be told what to do and how to act.

Our suggested methods and techniques flowed from these beliefs. At this point, we hope that you agree with each of these statements. We believe that these beliefs are profoundly important and should form the central core of beliefs for constructivist teachers. In fact, if you push these statements hard enough, they should influence everything that you do in your classroom, and certainly your approach to management. In this section of the book, we present some final suggestions on how to establish a system that reflects such core beliefs.

■ GOALS

In presenting a final set of suggestions for establishing a classroom management system, we address the following questions:

- How can effective teaching prevent most discipline problems?
- How can you involve your students in establishing a management system?
- How can classroom meetings help to address management concerns?
- How can you involve parents as collaborators in the learning process?

In offering the best practical advice that we can regarding these questions, we rely most heavily on our own classroom experiences, and we draw on the advice of a number of educators and theorists, including Lawrence Kohlberg (1981) and his focus on helping students become responsible, moral citizens; William Glasser (1986) and his reality therapy approach; Jacob Kounin (1970) and his suggested desist strategies; and Alfie Kohn (1996) and his emphasis on involving students in making important decisions. Of course, Abraham Maslow (1968) and his focus on meeting the needs of students in the classroom, as discussed in Module 15, Part 1, has had a major influence on our beliefs.

Focal Point 1: How Can Effective Teaching Help Prevent Discipline Problems?

In essence, our textbook has been about classroom management from the first module onward. Our experiences in dozens of schools during the past 20 years have shown us that most students act up in class because they are bored, frustrated, alienated, in short, disengaged. The key to avoiding discipline problems in the classroom, then, is to engage students in truly meaningful learning experiences to the greatest extent possible each and every day.

In making our claim about effective teaching preventing problems, we have two additional statements. First, there are students in every school who, sometimes because of factors outside the control of teachers and schools, are extremely difficult if not impossible to reach. Even the most idealistic of educators would have to admit this reality; and if these students won't meet you half way, there's not much you can do about it. Second, our intent is not to blame dedicated teachers for discipline problems. As we have noted throughout this book, a range of factors sometimes force teachers to take approaches that they wouldn't necessarily take, in essence, making the compromises that Sizer (1984; 1996) so eloquently described. A system that emphasizes didactic approaches, coverage of vast amounts of material, and order and enforced silence in classrooms actually makes it more difficult to manage things.

With this said, we believe that there is a great deal that teachers can do, even within fairly traditional school settings, to change this situation. The next section will offer some practical suggestions for doing just this.

Discussion 1: How Can Effective Teaching Help Prevent Discipline Problems?

An interactive, constructivist approach is good preventive medicine against discipline problems because students are likely to be engaged in relevant, meaningful experiences on a daily basis. We can make this claim based on a wealth of experience in classrooms from the middle school through the college/university level. Consider once again that our suggested teaching approach places emphasis on meeting the needs of students at Maslow's three highest levels. If you effectively use the methods and techniques that we have described, you'll help your students build personal connections to you as the teacher and to their peers and develop their self-esteem and a sense of personal fulfillment. You'll do this by showing them that they can learn something relevant and meaningful that will help them understand the world around them in new ways.

We've seen this approach encourage and empower the most disheartened individuals and groups of students. In recalling one telling example, one of your authors remembers working with a particularly discouraged group of high school students in a basic biology class. Initially, these students seemed to have little interest in biology and school in general; they were taking this class simply because they needed to pass one science course to graduate. Some had failed the course once or twice already. We started with a focus on the human body and how it works, and what people need to do to stay healthy. We organized the curriculum around guiding questions that the students generated as a group, and we took an inquiry-oriented, hands-on approach. Slowly, student interest grew to the point where the extra chatter was subsiding, attendance improved dramatically, and several of the students were coming in regularly after school to continue their investigations. In one true breakthrough moment, the class was about to investigate a set of sheep lungs as part of our research on the effects of smoking on the body. One student, a vocal leader in the class who had initially shown little interest in science, was disturbed by some classmates talking as directions for the activity were being explained. He passionately told the class that he and others wanted to focus on the activity, that it was important, and that "anyone who didn't want to be there could get the hell out." At that moment, the extra chatter stopped as the offending students realized that they had stepped outside of the expectations that the students had set for themselves. The entire class then focused on listening to the directions, and the transition from a group of discouraged individuals to a true community was complete. This is the impact that a student-centered approach can have.

We have shared a number of suggestions for implementing each of our methods and techniques. As you prepare to step into your own classroom, here's some final overall advice related to effective teaching and the prevention of problems.

Never Underestimate the Importance of Planning Thoroughly

We talk about planning in some depth. Our sincere hope is that you carry this advice into your own classroom; this isn't something you do only as part of a class assignment, or when you're student teaching. We have met a handful of preservice teachers over the years who felt that they could get by without in-depth planning. Don't expect to step into the classroom and wing it and be successful, especially as a beginning teacher. If you don't plan thoroughly and thoughtfully, you're headed for major problems! Of course, your plans won't always work, but if you think through potential problems in advance, chances are that you'll have the ability (and the confidence) to make adjustments and to take advantage of the teachable moments that we discuss.

As you plan, consider and use the teaching methods introduced herein. Plan on utilizing multiple methods within each classroom period. For the most part, don't stick to any one format for more than twenty-five to thirty minutes; this seems to be an upper limit of engagement for most students. This will mean shifting from one method to another at least once in a fifty-minute period. You might, for example, begin a session with a brief Interactive Presentation (Module 12), move into a twenty-minute peer-group activity (Module 5, Part 1), and then allow students to share ideas generated in a full-class Exploratory Discussion (Module 10). Using a variety of methods and techniques, even in a single class period, will be a key to your success (remember the preferred learning styles research we mention). And use all of your time. Teachers frequently run into trouble when providing free time at the end of any class period.

Whichever method you're using, question your students continuously to help them remain engaged in the learning experience. If you're presenting new ideas, question students to check on their understanding. Even if you have a number of new ideas to convey, don't present information for more than four or five minutes without questioning students; we all know that it's too easy for students to drift off, even if your presentation is interesting.

Find a Way to Relate to Each of Your Students

As a constructivist teacher, you'll have multiple opportunities to interact with your students one-on-one and to really get to know them as individuals. Find out as much as you can about the experiences/interests of each of your students, and try to connect to these whenever possible as you plan future lessons. Students who are turned off to school often have special interests and talents that you can tap into (in fact, it's often not the rowdy students that will worry you most, but those who are so discouraged that they don't want to do anything). Providing students with options frequently is a good way to reach them (e.g., as we suggest in Module 14, let students decide whether they'd rather do a presentation, write a paper, make a film, write a song, or paint a picture to show you and their classmates what they've learned).

Reflect Carefully on Your Own Progress as a Teacher

Don't forget that reflecting realistically on classroom events is an essential dimension to effective, constructivist teaching. You'll be trying many of these methods and techniques for the first time when you step into your classroom. As with anything that we try for the first time, there will *be* some bumps, maybe even some outright flops, along the way. Don't be discouraged when something doesn't work as well as you had hoped; this is all part of the learning process. Make adjustments and try again. Don't fall into the student-blaming, complaining-in-the-teacher's-lounge trap when things don't go quite right.

As part of the process of reflecting on your teaching, make it a habit to audio-tape/videotape yourself to monitor your progress. The things that you notice yourself doing (or not doing) on tape are often incredibly revealing. Pay close attention especially to the way that you question your students. Another related suggestion: find yourself a colleague to serve as an unofficial mentor, and invite this person to watch you teach occasionally.

Effective Teaching and Stopping Minor Problems

Thorough planning and engaging methods prevent most problems, but not all of them. A constructivist classroom will often be a loud, active place; students will get excited as they participate in activities/discussions (as noted, it's a sad truth that some of the quietest classrooms are actually the least productive in terms of meaningful learning). One of the things that you absolutely need to do to be a successful teacher is to be aware of everything that's going on in the room. This sounds like a tall order, but continually scanning the room with your eyes, moving around the room and standing in spots where you can see each student will help you develop this sort of awareness.

Even though you want your classroom to be an active, lively place, it's vital that you react to inappropriate behavior immediately (most often, this behavior will include activities such as excessive talking). Think of a progression of actions that you can take as the teacher to deal with minor problems, actions that are seamlessly connected to your teaching. For example, let's say you're conducting a Directed Discussion (Module 9), with students seated in a U-shaped arrangement. Three students in the most distant part of the room are talking, and you're relatively sure they've drifted out of the discussion. Try the following progression of actions:

1. Make eye contact/deliver a disapproving look (I bet we can all remember teachers who could deliver a stern message without saying a word).

2. Ask one of the disengaged students a question to pull them into the discussion.

3. Move toward the students, as the lesson continues. Stand right next to the student if necessary (your proximity will be enough to stop many problem behaviors). If you can't move toward the student for some reason, say his or her name in a non-threatening way.

4. If the problem continues or reoccurs, move casually toward the student and bend down and say something to him or her ("Can you please contribute something to the discussion? We'd like to hear your thoughts on this.").

5. If the problem continues or reoccurs, ask the student to move to a different part of the room (an unoccupied desk some distance away).

6. If the problem is serious enough, ask the student to talk to you in the hallway. Tell the student that you'd like to have him participate, and ask if there is a problem (it may have nothing to do with your class). If this is something that has happened before, you can get a bit more assertive in the hall, without starting a confrontation in front of the rest of the class. This is a real danger if you challenge a student directly in front of his peers.

It has been our experience that a progression of responses like this, all of which would seem indistinguishable from the actual teaching of the lesson, will take care of the vast majority of your minor problems, especially social talking at the wrong times.

If the problem that you're facing is more serious (e.g., a heated argument develops between two students), our advice would be to jump to the higher steps in this progression right away (e.g., talk to both of these students in the hall to defuse the situation). In the case of serious problems that continue over time, try as hard as you can to talk to the student involved before or after class, some time when you can communicate with her one-on-one without interruption. Communicating with colleagues and parents should be an important part of this process as well (more on this later in the module). Try to deal with these situations yourself, without sending students to the office; you don't want to send the message to students or administrators that you can't deal with problems. Rely on administrators for advice and support but not to solve your problems for you.

Focal Point 2: How Can You Involve Students in Establishing a Management System?

The first few days that you spend with any class are vitally important. Our advice is to set the stage for the coming year by conducting interactive activities that introduce your students to you, to each other, and to your subject. Conduct your initial ILPE lesson on your first day of class, and make this first lesson especially memorable. We have found that doing this will establish some positive expectations among your students.

On the second or third day of class, discuss classroom rules and procedures with your students in an open way (we prefer the term "guidelines" over "rules"). There are a variety of approaches that you can take in doing this. We believe that it's useful to think of these approaches as falling on a kind of continuum. At one end of the spectrum is a very direct approach. Tell your students what your expectations are. If you choose this approach, make these expectations high, and at least explain your rationale for every guideline that you establish (e.g., "Our number one rule in this class will be mutual respect for others. This is vital because . . .").

A Directed Discussion Approach to Establishing Guidelines

The degree to which you allow student input in forming class guidelines is up to you. We can tell you from experience that students are much more likely to take ownership of (and then live by) rules or guidelines that they have helped to establish. Let's return for a moment to our continuum of approaches for establishing class policies and guidelines. In the center of this continuum is what we might consider to be a Directed Discussion approach. We have found that such an approach is far superior to simply telling students what the rules will be. You begin the discussion by talking to students about what you envision the class doing in the coming weeks and months. You then pose the question, "What guidelines will we need to establish to allow us to do all of these things?" Then, you ask a series of focused questions aimed at helping students articulate a set of guidelines and procedures for the class ("We're going to have open discussions and activities in this class almost every day. What guidelines regarding talking will help us do this?"). By the end of the discussion, the class will have articulated a set of policies and procedures for the rest of the year.

A Reflective Discussion Approach

The most open, student-centered way to establish class guidelines involves taking a more Reflective Discussion (Module 11) approach. With this third approach, you begin the discussion by sharing the same kind of vision that you have for what the class will be doing. At this point, you open the discussion for greater class input. What are some of the things that they would most like to do and to learn about? Then, you let students know that every class needs a set of operating guidelines, and you open the floor for their suggestions on what these guidelines should be. As the teacher, you then moderate a discussion in which the students choose, perhaps by consensus or by vote, what the final guidelines will be. As the moderator, you can offer your own input as part of this process.

Why Allow Student Involvement in This Process?

As we've noted, our experience has been that students are far more likely to abide by a set of rules and procedures that they have had some voice in creating. Many teachers might view this process as risky, fearing that it will open the classroom to utter chaos, but this has not been our experience. Students of any age will want to establish consistent procedures so that they know what to expect. We have seen a consistent, if not universal, student desire for the creation of a supportive environment in which everyone feels safe enough to share ideas. In fact, students will often be far tougher on themselves than any teacher might be when it comes to establishing rules.

Our advice is to try either the Directed or Reflective Discussion approach for establishing classroom guidelines. You'll find that students will agree with many/most of your suggestions and that there is a definite empowering feeling for students that comes through these approaches. Starting the schoolyear with such an empowering, democratic approach will send some important messages about what students will experience in your class. If you don't feel secure in allowing this much student input, especially as a beginning teacher, at least enter the term with a fair set of rules/procedures, and share these with students in an open way. Let students know what your rules are and why you've established them. Remember that Rule #1 for teachers should be to treat students like young adults and not like children. Establish an atmosphere of trust early on, and be fair and consistent when it comes to classroom management.

What Classroom Guidelines Might You Consider Adopting?

Make your guidelines and policies simple and straightforward; don't burden students with too many rules, or you'll risk creating an oppressive classroom atmosphere. Possible classroom guidelines might include any or all of the following:

- Respect one another's right to speak. Listen carefully to others; one person talks at a time.
- No obscene or abusive language in the classroom.

- Everyone should be in his seat when the bell rings (check on the tardy policy in your school). Challenge students to consider this possibility because you'll want to use every possible minute of your class time.

- Late assignments will lose 10 percent of their total possible point value for each day they are late. Those turned in more than five days late may be turned in for a maximum of 50 percent of their original point value.

- Assignments that include plagiarized material will receive a failing grade.

Our experiences have shown us that these particular guidelines can be very effective in helping you establish a thinker-friendly community in your classroom. It might help to clarify the last two on the list. We have found that establishing a system for make-up work whereby students are penalized to a degree for late assignments works most effectively; this might make more sense when considering the alternatives. One option is to accept assignments anytime, which seemingly penalizes those students who work hard and complete assignments on time. At the other end of the scale is a turn-it-in-when-it's-due-or-not-at-all approach. Our problem with this policy is that it could mean that a student, for example, who has serious problems outside of school for a time and misses a series of assignments, will fall so far behind that she has no chance to pass your course. We suggest giving such students some chance to complete assignments and to turn them in for at least partial (e.g., 50% percent) credit.

We highly recommend a very strict plagiarism guideline, especially in an era when abundant references and cut-and-paste options make this kind of cheating relatively easy. We suggest that teachers of all subjects clearly communicate to students what plagiarism is (don't assume they know this) and why it can't be tolerated in your classroom community.

A list of guidelines similar to these should be all most teachers need when it comes to classroom rules, with a couple of notable exceptions. Science and PE teachers will certainly want to communicate special safety rules from time to time, and PE teachers may want to establish rules related to dressing for activities.

Using the procedures that we have discussed can help you establish a feeling of community in the classroom. Putting constructivist methods and techniques into practice can enhance and further develop this feeling. We believe that periodic classroom meetings are essential in taking your community to higher levels yet.

Focal Point 3. How Can Classroom Meetings Help Solve Problems?

Within any community, problems are solved (or at least addressed) by committed people who have some stake in the welfare of the community as a whole. This should be the case with your classroom community. At both the middle school and high school levels, we have found that periodic classroom meetings can provide students with a forum for discussing important issues and can further enhance the feeling of empowerment of students in your classroom.

We suggest that you conduct monthly or quarterly meetings in each of your classes, or more frequent meetings if problems arise. In experimenting with this approach in the high school classroom, one of your writers found that the Exploratory

Discussion format worked very effectively. Seat yourself in a circle of chairs with your students. Begin by communicating the purpose for the meeting, which is to assess the recent progress of the class as a community and to address issues of concern. Then ask a broad, inviting question to begin the discussion (e.g., "What have we done as a class recently that helped you to learn something useful?"). Ask other open-ended questions to encourage students to expand on their initial ideas. Then, ask a question aimed at generating suggestions for further improvement (e.g., "What can we do to further improve the learning atmosphere in our classroom?"). If students are reluctant to contribute ideas at first, start with some of your own suggestions to prime the pump (e.g., "One thing that I'd like to see us try would be _____"). As with any effective Exploratory, try to generate as many ideas as possible; be sure to record these ideas and to discuss class progress on them periodically.

Meetings are also effective in solving specific problems that arise. Again, set the context for such a meeting, then share your concern (e.g., "I have a problem that I need your help to solve"). In meetings of this type, allow students to share their concerns as well, and try to develop a consensus as to how to solve the problems discussed ("We agree that all of these concerns need to be addressed. What suggestions do you have for doing that?"). Meetings such as this can be tremendously effective for solving recurring problems in any classroom. We believe that the reason for their effectiveness goes back to issues of trust and responsibility; if you as the teacher show that you have enough respect for your students to challenge them to address problems facing the class, students will generally respond in a positive way.

Focal Point 4: How Can You Engage Parents as Learning Collaborators?

We believe that parents are the great, untapped resource for middle schools and high schools. Although some schools have developed exemplary programs for promoting parental involvement, we believe that, for the most part, American secondary schools do a woeful job at reaching out to parents (unless, of course, there is a specific problem).

One of your first tasks should be to write the guidelines that you establish as a class into a syllabus. Include within this document some contextual information about the course (e.g., What are your major goals? What kinds of experiences will students share in this course?). Each student should have a copy of your syllabus. Drop by the principal's office and leave a copy (show administrators early on that you're a competent professional).

Make sure that parents get a copy of the syllabus as well. One of your primary early-year goals should be to get parents involved as essential collaborators, and the beginning of the year provides you with an opportunity to begin this process. Write a cover letter introducing yourself, include a copy of your syllabus, and mail this to every parent (the office should be able to provide you with addresses, possibly with address labels). Here's the next step in the process of connecting to parents: Call each parent some time during the first month of school as a follow-up to your letter. Introduce yourself, ask them if they've looked at the syllabus and have any questions, and tell them about what you hope to achieve as a teacher. This sounds like a lot of work, but it pays dividends. You'll establish an early, positive rapport with parents, and if you ever have concerns about a student, a call home will likely get a positive response. We've found that most parents (90 percent+) appreciate this initiative. It's especially important these days, when there is a tendency among some to blame teachers when problems arise.

Make it a point to contact parents periodically during the schoolyear. Call home with good news about a student; this can provide an incredible boost at times for both the parent and the student involved. Another possibility is to publish a monthly or quarterly class newsletter that can be mailed home. This is relatively easy to do, especially with some of the slick computer programs available today. You can give students the responsibility to write and collect articles for the newsletter and even to produce it on class computers. We have found that this is a great way to keep parents involved and informed and that it can create a wonderful level of excitement for students as well.

■ ROUNDUP ■

In Part 2 of this module, we addressed just some of the many issues related to classroom management, which we have defined as the daily operation of your classroom.

We noted that the best way to approach management is to consider it as an integral part of your teaching. We provided numerous, additional examples to support our belief that effective, engaging teaching will prevent most discipline problems in any classroom.

We also presented advice on how to involve your students in establishing a set of guidelines for their classroom, and why it is important to do this. We feel that some level of student involvement is essential in creating a thinker-friendly community. In this same section, we suggested possible guidelines that you might consider adopting in some form for your own classroom.

Finally, we discussed the usefulness of classroom meetings as forums for addressing issues of concern for teachers and students and the value of engaging parents as essential collaborators. Both of these initiatives can dramatically enhance the feeling of community in classrooms and can create an additional level of commitment and excitement for everyone involved.

REFERENCES

Glasser, W. (1986). *Control theory in the classroom.* New York: Harper & Row.

Kohlberg, L. (1981). *Essays on moral development.* New York: Harper & Row.

Kohn, A. (1996). *Beyond discipline: From compliance to community.* Alexandria, VA: Association for Supervision and Curriculum Development.

Kounin, J. (1970). *Discipline and group management in the classroom.* New York: Holt, Rinehart, & Winston.

Maslow, A. (1968). *Motivation and personality.* New York: D. Van Nostrand.

Sizer, T. (1984). *Horace's compromise: The dilemma of the American high school.* Boston: Houghton-Mifflin.

Sizer, T. (1996). *Horace's hope: What works for the American high school.* Boston: Houghton-Mifflin.

EPILOGUE: ON TO YOUR CLASSROOM

It's your first year teaching, and you're anxious to create an active-learning constructivist classroom. You've reconfigured the seating to suit various lessons and methods. Little by little, you're developing your questioning skills. You bring in various instructional materials that provide your students with stimulating sources. You notice that more students are participating, getting involved—even asking questions, a sure sign that they're engaged. Two of your classes have even reached the point where they're assigning themselves tasks in groups, deciding on the topics that they need to learn to explore the unit goal. All in all, despite a few setbacks and disappointments with which you're still grappling, you feel that you're on your way as an invisible teacher, with the students more and more taking the stage.

A few colleagues, however, think that you are somewhat too "invisible" in the classroom. Some of them are skeptical about giving students the freedom—and responsibility—to make so many important decisions. Your classroom is sometimes noisy with the sound of students discussing and debating ideas, something that is not often seen in some of the other classrooms. Your first formal evaluation is around the corner. How will you respond to some of the skepticism among your colleagues?

Before we address that question, another one needs to be asked: Why do so many teachers and educational administrators mistrust a student-centered, constructivist approach? You know from ongoing assessment and evaluation that your students are learning in depth. They tell you that for the first time, they enjoy your subject. There are even lessons that end with your students still talking about the ideas as they leave the classroom. Many of your students stop by before and after school to ask you questions related to these ideas, even to do additional activities or to finish something that they've started in class. Obviously, there is a disparity between your constructivist practice and the perception that many other (but definitely not all) educators may have of it. What causes this disconnect?

We believe that a primary reason is the classroom setting. The teacher is not always at the front of the room talking at students sitting quietly in neat rows. (Perhaps too quietly.) A constructivist classroom may appear to lack structure. When students are exchanging their ideas in a lively hum, it seems as if they're socializing, not learning what they "need to know."

Such appearances may raise some on your colleagues' eyebrows. They may sincerely question the value of such "permissive" methods, or they may even be threatened if they've heard your students talking enthusiastically; perhaps those colleagues have not been able to engage their own students in the same way. Or they may earnestly believe that you are not keeping up with the curriculum and not imposing disciplined standards on your students.

So to get back to the original question, How do you meet professional criticism of a constructivist approach? We believe that it is important to address the misconceptions. First, you can allay their concerns by informing the professional skeptics that a constructivist lesson is even more structured and thoroughly planned than a typical traditional lesson. For the most part, traditional lessons structure only the content. Constructivist lessons structure both the content and the process, providing prompts (questions and tasks) that guide active student engagement. Substance is related to students' frames of reference and motivates learners. Students not only learn content and develop high cognitive skills, they also learn how to learn.

Behind the scenes in this process, a constructivist educator must be well informed to facilitate effectively; she must apply knowledge of her students' various learning styles for maximum advantage; he must constantly be assessing and evaluating throughout the learning to catch gaps of learning or loss of interest. In short, a constructivist teacher is a well-prepared, intellectually rigorous teacher who challenges his students to think about significant ideas at the highest levels (Brooks & Brooks, 1999; Newmann, 1997; Wiggins & McTighe, 1998).

Motivated students working conceptually retain more of the curriculum, which is the compass of your syllabus. In fact, the students may examine that syllabus and in time design a learning plan. They retain more because their learning matters to them.

As for the bottom line: Research has shown that "diverse, active, and intellectually provocative forms of instruction" result in the best test scores (Wiggins & McTighe, 1998, p. 132). Not only that, but "constructivist students" develop a greater ability than traditionally taught counterparts to think deeply as they use knowledge outside the classroom: these students experience learning as part of their lives and personal enrichment.

At this point, we'd like to remind you to revisit the *Fishy Mystery* scenario in Module 6. You may recall that this scenario depicts ideal constructivist teaching and learning, integrating student-centered methods in a way that is instructively rigorous and also motivating. As ideal as this picture may seem, it demonstrates authentic learning that motivates students, and not only the already successful students. Authentic learning can motivate those students who are bored, disinterested, or lacking the necessary skills, the very students you might think could "never do this." From our experience, such students are often the ones to become the most engaged in authentic learning, seeing relevance in school for the first time. This motivation prompts them to learn the necessary skills in a meaningful context.

Chances are that there may be one or more teachers in your school quietly employing student-centered methods also. We suggest that you work with them. Exchange ideas, plan interdisciplinary units and projects. In this way, the more teachers in your school who are committed to engaging students and challenging them with in-depth learning, the more the numbers of those teachers will grow.

Remember that constructivist teachers care deeply about their students, about their interests, about the development of their thinking abilities, about their joy in learning. Constructivist teachers continuously try to create classroom experiences that will prepare their students for a brighter future. Show your students that you care, in everything you do.

Be among those who have "the courage to be constructivist" (Brooks & Brooks, 1999).

REFERENCES

Brooks, M. G., & Brooks, J. G. (1999, November). The courage to be constructivist. *Educational Leadership*, 18–24.

Newmann, F. N. & Associates (1996). *Authentic achievement: Restructuring schools for intellectual quality*. San Francisco: Jossey-Bass.

Wiggins, G., & McTighe, J. (1998). *Understanding by design*. Alexandria, VA: Association for Supervision and Curriculum Development.

■ GLOSSARY ■

affect (noun): State of mind or being; emotions associated with mind or being.

Aim or Student Aim: A Core Component in a lesson that expresses the instructional intention in colloquial or catchy language to interest the students or in a way that relates to students' frames of reference.

analysis: The process of breaking down an idea, product, or event into its elements; examining and characterizing these elements.

a priori: Knowledge or understanding that exists independent of experience.

artifact: A human-made product for future use.

asynchronous: Not in parallel time; taking place at different times.

authentic learning: Classroom instruction and related products that have real use beyond the classroom; instruction and related products within a real-world context outside of the classroom.

bidirectional: Characterized by positive or negative mutual influence; a cause-and-effect dynamic whereby a cause of the first party produces an outcome in the second party, which in turn reflects back as another cause to the first party. Examples: A teacher encourages a slow learner to respond. The student's brief response in turn prompts the teacher's further encouragement, which results in even more student response. Or a teacher shows impatience with a slow learner. The student withdraws and the teacher grows even more impatient, losing interest in that student. The student then cuts that teacher's class.

Bloom's Taxonomy: A hierarchy of cognitive levels that provides a framework for teaching and learning.

chip: A small electronic component that performs processing, control, or memory functions in computers and other electronic devices.

cognitive: Referring to the rational mind, thought, and/or the thinking process.

cognitive dissonance: A clash of accepted beliefs with new information that contradicts those beliefs; the mental discomfort caused by a clash of perceptions and/or beliefs.

Cognitive Ladder: A hierarchy of mental constructs increasing in complexity from facts and concepts to principles and themes.

cognitive taxonomy: A ranking or hierarchy of increasingly complex thought processes.

compare and contrast: Analyzing an idea, product, or event by establishing the similarities and differences between and among the various elements.

concept: An abstract idea or notion, such as *liberty, stereotypes, feminism, genocide, brotherhood, morality,* and so on, containing specific characteristics, examples, and, sometimes, nonexamples; a component of the Cognitive Ladder.

convergence (of media): The integration of various media, such as TV, audio, video, printed matter, telecommunications and computers, into one medium.

Core Components: Seven structuring elements of a lesson plan (Rationale, Performance Objective, Materials, Aim, Hook, Development, and Culmination).

critical attributes: Characteristics always present in and essential to a concept, object, and so on. For example, some critical attributes of a chair are the seat, seat support, and back support.

critical thinking: The mental process of reasoning with logic using the higher cognitive levels.

Culmination: A Core Component that concludes a lesson; consists of a Wrap-Up that summarizes and a Leap that points to new principles and insights related to the given lesson.

data: Facts; bits of information obtained by observation.

database: A computer-based archive of information indexed by categories so that it can be searched.

data set: A coherent collection of data that in turn consists of discrete pieces of information or evidence.

Development: A Core Component of a lesson that unfolds the substance of the topic with a method; also called the body of a lesson plan.

didacticism: A pedagogy comprised of lecturing; the tendency to overuse lecturing.

digital: The representation of any kind of information (e.g., text, images, video, and so on) in binary form, that is, in ones and zeros, so that it can be processed, stored, or transmitted by computers.

digital products: Human artifacts created with computer technology.

digital divide: The gap between people or communities that are able to access and effectively use information technologies, including the Internet, and those that cannot.

disconnect: Two or more ideas or practices being out of concert with and opposing each other.

double-dip: The same object, product, or process serving two uses.

driving questions: At least two questions that complement each other and address the key issues of a unit.

dyad: A group consisting of two individuals.

extrinsic motivation: An external prompt such as a teacher's grade, money, or praise for doing something.

fact: An item of information; a component of the Cognitive Ladder.

facilitation: The act or process of guiding, enabling, fostering, or mentoring.

Geographic Information System (GIS): A computer-based system for entering, searching, and displaying spatial data in which digital maps can be "overlaid" on top of each other to reveal how different types of features are related in space.

Global Positioning System (GPS): A computer-based communications system in which radio signals beamed from satellites in stationary orbit above the earth permit any location and its elevation to be pinpointed with great precision.

goal: A broad instructional intention carried out by discrete lessons, projects, and units that address various aspects of that intention.

handouts: Instructional, nonbook materials distributed to students in class, especially activity sheets.

Hook: A Core Component in a lesson; may include a prop, role-play, anecdote, engaging question, visual aid, and more, designed to capture the students' interest, especially but not only at the beginning of a lesson.

hyperlink: A term within computer text that provides the user with more detailed information in one or more media about that term.

hypertext: Computer text that contains hyperlinks that may consist of multimedia.

information technology (IT): Integration of computing and high-speed transmissions relaying multimedia forms of data: visual, audio, print.

inquiry learning: A pedagogy characterized by overarching questions governing learners' open-ended exploration of data and problem solving.

inservice teacher: A practicing teacher.

INTASC Standards: The Interstate New Teacher Assessment and Support Consortium's ten standards for training new or preservice teachers; they emphasize social, affective, and cognitive goals in a student-centered approach to teaching.

Internet: A global network linking millions of computers in more than 170 countries.

intrinsic motivation: Desire or interest to do or learn something for its own sake rather than for external rewards.

invisible teaching: A teaching role that facilitates and mentors students in the learning process, with the well-prepared teacher functioning as a catalyst rather than as the focal point.

learning styles: Various individual modes and postures of learning, ranging from different cognitive processing of information (abstract versus concrete) to sensory preferences (visual, audio, print).

metacognition: A kind of meta-awareness, specifically, mental awareness of mental processes.

meta-awareness: Conscious perception of the thing itself, for example, learning about the learning process, thinking about how you think, and so on.

microchip: Same as *chip*.

microprocessor: Same as *chip*.

multimedia: The combination of different media, such as text, graphics, sound, video, and animation, into a single document or software program.

multiple intelligences: Theory of the cognitive scientist Howard Garner; describes various types of equally valuable intelligences, such as linguistic, mathematical, kinesthetic, and personal, that impact learning.

noncritical attributes: Variable characteristics of a concept, object, and so on. For example, some variable characteristics of a chair are its height, material, and types of back support.

objective: Discrete instructional intention that carries out a larger instructional goal.

open ended: Having no predetermined outcome; permitting exploration of ideas and the generation of original concepts, principles, and so on.

pedagogy: A teacher's instructional practice.

peer-group learning: An instructional practice in which two or more student peers learn together in small groups; an umbrella term for the various forms of student interaction in the learning process, such as response groups, cooperative learning, group learning, and so on, each having its own characteristics.

Performance Objective: A Core Component that results in a student product or products; concretely demonstrates learning; contains three parts: preparation, product, and criteria.

preservice teacher: A student teacher or teacher in training not yet in the service of teaching.

principle: A rule or insight derived from one or more concepts; a rule or insight that may generate one or more concepts; a component of the Cognitive Ladder.

problem solving: An open-ended instructional practice of organized inquiry. Students use established procedures to investigate data and solve one or more overarching questions.

project: A long-term instructional process in which students conduct research and generate products related to an overarching goal and/or question(s); may be a problem-solving enterprise, an inquiry learning experience, a skills-building effort, and so on. Students have specific tasks and instructions. Differs from a unit in that discrete lessons are not a dominating structure of a project.

prompts: Questions and directions that guide students' activities as independent learners.

Rationale: A Core Component that articulates the teacher's instructional intention; it contains three parts: What are you teaching? Why are you teaching this? Justification.

real time: Describes computer process of entered data; the latest entry of updated computer data.

resocialize: The process of reorganizing or shifting values, perceptions, and behaviors within a familiar context.

rubric: A template of categories and criteria for evaluating student work.

scaffolding: A concept of learning theorist Jerome Bruner; refers to various external supports in the learning process; may include reference materials, guiding questions, peer assistance, and more.

schema; schemata (pl.): A global view that includes salient elements of a concept or situation. Individuals may possess incomplete or incorrect notions of a schema.

scientific visualization: A combination of computer-based tools and methods that employ computer-based graphics technology to process, create, and analyze images of scientific data to facilitate recognition of patterns and trends in the data.

setting: The practices and physical configurations of a learning environment.

stakeholder: Any person or group with a vested interest in formulating and deciding on a policy or action that affects the community of which it is a part. For example, in a community that is deciding how land within its jurisdiction is to be used, stakeholders would likely include residents, business owners and groups, farmers, environmental organizations, and government officials. Each has a separate interest in the decision that may or may not coincide with the interests of the other stakeholders.

strategy (for a unit): An instructional plan for carrying out the goal of a unit.

student-centered: A learning environment in which students interact with one another and take an active role in their own learning; students often select topics and assign themselves and peers learning tasks, with the teacher as an informed facilitator.

student-focused: A learning environment in which the students' frames of reference are integral to the learning experience; students interact with one another and take an active role in their own learning, with the teacher organizing and directing the lesson.

student role: The student's stance or posture toward learning, especially whether passive or active.

taxonomy: A hierarchical organization of elements within the same context.

teachable moment: A timely opportunity to teach something.

teacher-centered: A pedagogy characterized by the teacher being the authority of knowledge and the dispenser of information in the classroom; students are viewed as receptacles of learning.

teacher-directed: A learning environment in which the teacher organizes the structure and content of a lesson or unit, and the students take an active role in exploring the resources and generating their own justified concepts, principles, and themes.

teacher role: The teacher's stance or posture toward teaching and learning, especially whether a dispenser of information or a facilitator of students' learning.

teleapprenticeships: A teacher education model that complements the traditional face-to-face apprenticeships by using electronic networks to link university coordinators, student teacher supervisors, school district master teachers, instructors, student teachers, and the students being taught by them.

theme: A general abstract idea that embraces interrelated facts, concepts, and principles; a component of the Cognitive Ladder.

topic: An organizing idea of a lesson, unit, or project.

unit: An interrelated series of lessons that develop and explore a larger instructional goal.

values disequilibrium: A mental state in which previously held beliefs and values are threatened by the introduction of contrasting beliefs and values; part of the process of adjusting one's schema.

virtual reality: An interactive, computer-generated, multimedia environment in which the viewer no longer just looks in from the outside but participates from inside the scene, which changes in response to the person's movements and other activities.

visualization: The process of representing ideas or evidence visually, whether as a drawing, concept map, graph, image, or movie.

Web: See *World Wide Web*.

wireless: Wireless digital communications networks connecting people and computers or devices such as digital cellular phones and portable digital assistants (Palm Pilots, for instance) free of any cable links.

World Wide Web: A vast, rapidly growing collection of hyperlinked multimedia documents that can be accessed anywhere on the Internet via a browser software program. Also known as WWW or the Web.

zone of proximal development: A social learning theory espoused by Lev Vygotsky, an early twentieth-century Russian educational researcher, that postulates that a person on the verge of readiness will learn a given concept, procedure, and so on by interacting with one or more people already familiar with the content.

■ APPENDIXES ■

■ INTERSTATE NEW TEACHER ASSESSMENT AND SUPPORT CONSORTIUM (INTASC) STANDARDS

Standard One—Knowledge of Subject Matter

The teacher understands the central concepts, tools of inquiry, and structure of the disciplines(s) he or she teaches and can create learning experiences that make these aspects of subject matter meaningful for students.

Standard Two—Knowledge of Human Development and Learning

The teacher understands how children learn and develop and can provide learning opportunities that support their intellectual, social, and personal development.

Standard Three—Adapting Instruction for Individual Needs

The teacher understands how students differ in their approaches to learning and creates instructional opportunities that are adapted to diverse learners.

Standard Four—Multiple Instructional Strategies

The teacher understands and uses a variety of instructional strategies to encourage students' development of critical-thinking, problem-solving, and performance skills.

Standard Five—Classroom Motivation and Management Skills

The teacher uses an understanding of individual and group motivation and behavior to create a learning environment that encourages positive social interaction, active engagement in learning, and self-motivation.

Standard Six—Communication Skills

The teacher uses knowledge of effective verbal, nonverbal, and media communication techniques to foster active inquiry, collaboration, and supportive interaction in the classroom.

Standard Seven—Instructional Planning Skills

The teacher plans instruction based on knowledge of subject matter, students, the community, and curriculum goals.

Standard Eight—Assessment of Student Learning

The teacher understands and uses formal and informal assessment strategies to ensure the continuous intellectual, social, and physical development of the learner.

Standard Nine—Professional Commitment and Responsibility

The teacher is a reflective practitioner who continually evaluates the effects of his or her choices and actions on others (students, parents, and other professionals in the learning community) and who actively seeks out opportunities to grow professionally.

Standard Ten—Partnerships

The teacher fosters relationships with school colleagues, parents, and agencies in the larger community to support students' learning and well-being.

REFERENCE

Darling-Hammond, L., ed. (1992). *Model standards for beginning teacher licensing and development: A resource for state dialogue.* Washington, DC: Interstate New Teacher Assessment and Support Consortium, Council of Chief State School Officers.

■ SAMPLE UNIT PLAN 1: A MIDDLE SCHOOL CORE UNIT OUTLINE FOR SPANISH

Media Representation of Cultural Stereotypes

(Note: The authors wish to thank Becky Listowski-Szuba for her permission to base the following outline on her foreign-language unit plan, written as the culminating project for her methods course when she was a preservice teacher at Millikin University in Decatur, Illinois. Ms. Listowski-Szuba's and other preservice unit plans were published in-house as a handbook intended for other teachers' use. The unit has been adapted here in outline form so that you can provide your own details and creativity.)

Topic
Media representation of cultural stereotypes.

Goal
The unit will focus on the role of media in creating cultural stereotypes and to what extent the media has validity in its representation of cultures. Students will interpret, analyze, synthesize, and evaluate examples of media representation. A desired outcome would be that students gain respect for Spanish culture while understanding the importance of studying other cultures.

Strategy
The unit takes an overall inductive approach, with some parts being deductive. Students will examine Spanish culture through peer-group learning. Learners will enhance critical-thinking skills by analyzing data and making their own value judgments based on accumulated research. Students will examine the role of the media in shaping our beliefs and attitudes, explore the Internet as a research source, and enhance their abilities to differentiate facts from deceptive material.

The unit would ideally be team-taught with an English teacher who conducted a unit on journalism and the role of the media. This topic could even be used as a schoolwide unit. A history class could focus on the role of media in whatever event it might be discussing, for example, propaganda for war. A math class could deal with statistics and their distortion in the media. Gym/health classes could discuss the image of fitness in the media.

Driving Question

How do we as readers know how to sort out the good, the bad, and the ugly from the media to find the most accurate representation of the facts?

Culminating Product

A bias-free newspaper with original articles about Spanish culture.

Unit Materials

- The Internet (for example, "Spain Online")
- Email with students at Francisco Salinas High School in Salamanca, Spain, because this school has a combined Spanish-English curriculum
- American headlines with cultural bias
- Spanish newspapers and magazines
- Interview data
- Original teacher handouts (activity sheets, scenarios, and simulated headlines)

Lesson Rationales

The unit lessons are collectively justified by all INTASC Standards.

1. ILPE Lesson

   What? Why?: To explore students' schemata of stereotypes and where they come from. Cognitive skills include comprehension of the relationship between stereotypes and the media and analysis of the reasons that misconceptions about a group can be dangerous.

2. Inductive Concept/Principle Lesson, Part One

   What? Why?: To develop the principle that media as tools can inform citizens about current events but can also distort reality and give people an unrealistic representation of a culture. Students will compare and contrast biased media images of the United States in Spain's media, infer through induction, and analyze excerpts from the media in terms of their valid representation of the culture.

3. Inductive Concept/Principle Lesson, Part Two

   What? Why?: To build on the principle that media as tools can inform citizens about current events but can also distort reality and give people an unrealistic representation of a culture. Students will compare and contrast biased media images of Spain and Spanish people in the United States, infer through induction, and analyze excerpts from the media in terms of their valid representation of the culture.

4. and 5. Deductive and Inductive Lesson: Two Days

What? Why?: To build on the previous lesson in more depth. I will define the principle that people learn about other places and cultures through the media (watching the news and reading the newspaper). On the first day, pairs of students will examine Spanish newspaper headlines from which they will infer impressions. On the second day, pairs of students will explore Spanish newspapers on the Internet and learn about Spanish culture. Cognitive skills range across Bloom's Taxonomy from comprehension and application to analysis and evaluation.

6., 7., and 8. Preparation for a Reflective Discussion Lesson: Three Days

What? Why?: To acquire further knowledge about Spanish culture through interviews with students in Spain and research (the Internet and outside resources/books) in preparation for a Reflective Discussion.

9. Reflective Discussion Lesson

What? Why?: Students will discuss their impressions of Spanish culture and Spaniards before and after this unit. They will arrive at validated judgments about Spanish culture and about the reliability of media in portraying cultures other than their own. Discuss signs of bias in headlines and news stories.

10. Culminating Product

What? Why?: To apply the knowledge from this unit to writing a newspaper, as a class, that reflects their findings, analyses, and evaluations of Spanish culture.

Assessment and Evaluation Plan

To the preservice teacher using *Engaged Minds*: We invite you to revisit this Core Unit plan and to list the various assessment products for diagnostic, formative, and summative assessments. Remember that assessment products can be elements in a discussion as well as physical products such as written assignments. For an evaluation rubric, list the criteria for each assessment product that you think would indicate acceptable achievement. Then devise a point scale. See Modules 13 and 14 for more details on assessment and evaluation.

■ SAMPLE UNIT PLAN 2: A COMBO UNIT OUTLINE FOR HIGH SCHOOL ENGLISH AND HISTORY

The Vietnam Conflict: Why Does It Matter to You?

(Note: The authors wish to thank Melissa Schrey and Tina Gross for their permission to base the following outline on their interdisciplinary unit plan written as the culminating project for their methods course when they were preservice teachers at Millikin University in Decatur, Illinois. Ms. Schrey's and Ms. Gross's and other preservice unit plans were published in-house as a handbook intended for other teachers' use. The unit has been adapted here in outline form so that you can provide your own details and creativity.)

Topic

Relating the Vietnam Conflict to the present.

Goal

Teaching this unit would allow us as teachers to use new methods, materials, and resources in connection with a topic that is relevant to students. The Vietnam Conflict was a major defining event of the 1960s, and it continues to define our lives today. Awareness of this period would lead the students to a better understanding of their own generation and of how social and political forces are shaping their generation. Students will take an academic approach to the topic, moving through Bloom's Taxonomy in a cyclical cognitive sequence. There will be cognitive dissonance as the knowledge learned in the classroom conflicts with the popular cultural views of the Vietnam Conflict that inform the students' schemata. Students will be encouraged to resolve this cognitive dissonance by evaluating their previous perceptions and the information in this unit.

Strategy

The overall unit will carry out the inductive cognitive model. In the different lessons within the unit, both inductive and deductive approaches will be used. We will begin by focusing specifically on the political and social controversy associated with the Vietnam Conflict. We will guide the students as they analyze and evaluate key issues of the Vietnam Conflict and apply the outcomes of that war to their own lives.

We believe that there is a mutual influence of literature and political and social events within a given period. Therefore, our two disciplines work together to create an in-depth view of the topic. The historical information will be complemented in English class with readings of personal narratives, newspaper articles, books, songs, and so on, about the Vietnam Conflict. As the segments progress, the thinking will enter higher cognitive levels because the students will be synthesizing material learned from the previous lessons.

Driving Questions

1. What were the controversies of the Vietnam Conflict?
2. How do these controversies apply to you?

Culminating Product

Students will integrate concepts, principles and themes from both subject classes and will create their own magazine for peers, parents, school faculty, and the school's Website.

Our suggested topics for the magazine are the following:

- Political controversies
- Social controversies
- Why does the Vietnam Conflict matter to me? (combine social, political, and personal consequences)

Our suggested magazine sections are the following:

- Editorials
- News articles
- Factual essays
- Interviews (with Vietnam veterans, parents and other relatives who lived through the era, history teachers, and so on)
- Fictional stories
- Poems
- Political cartoons

Students may decide on different or additional topics and segments with teacher approval.

Unit Materials

1. The Internet as a research tool and model for electronic magazines
2. Personal narratives in printed articles
3. Email contact with Vietnam vets
4. Email contact with Vietnamese people who survived the war (if a translator is available)
5. Historical print sources from class and the library
6. Contemporary newspaper and magazine articles; contemporary news footage, if possible
7. Contemporary nonfiction accounts, for example, of the then Secretary of Defense Robert McNamara
8. Protest songs of the era
9. Videoclips
10. Activity sheets

Lesson Rationales

A. HISTORY

All lessons are justified by all the INTASC Standards.

1. ILPE Lesson

   What? Why?: Students will free-write about their impressions of the U.S. political conflicts of the Vietnam war so that I can learn what they know, what their misconceptions are, and so on, and can plan accordingly. Confer with the English teacher about this information.

2. Interactive Presentation Lesson, Part One

   What? Why?: Based on the ILPE inquiry, students will deductively learn about two key U.S. political conflicts during the Vietnam Conflict to begin a knowledge base for later analysis. Student tasks will include role-playing and creating concept maps.

3. Interactive Presentation Lesson, Part Two

   What? Why?: Based on the ILPE inquiry, students will deductively learn about two more key U.S. political conflicts during the Vietnam Conflict to build a knowledge base for later analysis. Student tasks will include synthesizing the facts by writing a simulated news report and creating a political cartoon (completed for homework if necessary).

4. Inductive Concept Lesson, Part One

   What? Why?: Students will analyze two examples of social conflicts during the Vietnam Conflict and will characterize and define the various areas of these social conflicts.

5. Inductive Concept Lesson, Part Two

   What? Why?: Students will analyze two additional examples of social conflicts during the Vietnam Conflict and will characterize and define the various areas of these social conflicts.

6. Reflective Discussion Lesson

   What? Why?: In peer groups, students will simultaneously role-play investigations into one political and one social conflict of the Vietnam Conflict as a way to compare and contrast various points of view. Roles include Secretary of State, a Vietnam veteran, a Vietnamese villager, and an inner-city drafted soldier. They will apply the information from previous lessons and the various source materials. Students will break role and evaluate their present views on the discussed issues and compare these views with their beliefs at the beginning of the unit.

7. Directed Discussion Lesson, Part One

   What? Why?: Students will analyze two political outcomes of the Vietnam Conflict that influence political policies today.

8. Directed Discussion Lesson, Part Two

   What? Why?: Students will analyze two social outcomes of the Vietnam Conflict that influence people's lives and governmental policies today.

9. Reflective Discussion Lesson

   What? Why?: In a whole-class discussion, students will examine some present-day political and social consequences of the Vietnam Conflict. How could various political and social policies have been less detrimental during the Vietnam Conflict? Are moral principles pertinent during war? If so, whose moral principles and in what situations? This Reflective Discussion involves synthesis and evaluation.

B. ENGLISH

1. Exploratory Discussion Lesson

   What? Why?: Based on homework readings, students will explore the differences between the newspaper accounts and the personal accounts of a particular event of the war; students will establish that each style of writing has distinct advantages and disadvantages in presenting information. Cognitive skills include comprehension, interpretation, and analysis.

2. Inductive Concept/Principle Lesson, Part One

   What? Why?: After comparing and contrasting the concepts and themes in three protest songs of the Vietnam era, students will define at least four principles of Vietnam Conflict social protest. They will compare and contrast the social issues in the songs with the social issues discussed in history class.

3. Inductive Concept/Principle Lesson, Part Two

   What? Why?: Continuation of yesterday's lesson (#2 above).

4. Interactive Presentation Lesson

   What? Why?: Students will be introduced to the themes and controversy in a non-fiction memoir of the Vietnam Conflict as a way to motivate them for reading excerpts from the book. Student mini-tasks will include role-playing the Secretary of Defense writing memos to the President of the United States and the House Chief of Staff writing a strategy for dealing with the press.

5. Exploratory Discussion Lesson

   What? Why?: Students will discuss two key issues in the book excerpt that they read for homework. They will analyze the validity of the content based on their Vietnam Conflict history lessons. They will also discuss whether the writer is a reliable source of information based on what they've learned so far.

6. Preparation for Reflective Discussion Lesson, Part One

   What? Why?: During the next two days, students will prepare for a peer debate. The issue is whether money should fund a full report of the political and social issues of the Vietnam Conflict.

   Preparation includes library and Internet research (email correspondence with Vietnam veterans or interviews with people involved in the Vietnam war as well as sources used to date in both history and English classes).

7. Preparation for Reflective Discussion Lesson, Part Two

   Continue yesterday's activity (#6 above).

8. Reflective Discussion: Debate (possibly two days)

   What? Why?: Students will role-play members of the present-day Congress. They will look back at the conflict rather than being directly involved with it. One side will be in favor of increased funding for a full investigative report, whereas the other wants to kill the bill. Students will justify their break-role positions based on the research they have prepared in class and completed for homework. This Reflective Discussion will synthesize and evaluate much of what they have learned in the unit. The Culmination will ask students whether their views on the Vietnam Conflict have changed as a result of this unit. If so, how and why?

Assessment and Evaluation Plan

To the preservice teacher using this book: We invite you to revisit this Combo Unit plan and to list the various assessment products for diagnostic, formative, and summative assessments. Remember that assessment products can be elements in a discussion as well as physical products such as written assignments. For an evaluation rubric, list the criteria for each assessment product that you think would indicate acceptable achievement. Then devise a point scale. See Modules 13 and 14 for more details on assessment and evaluation.

■ INDEX ■